Conflict between Equals

OXFORD PRIVATE LAW THEORY

Oxford Private Law Theory publishes leading work in private law theory. It commissions and solicits monographs and edited collections in general private law theory as well as specific fields, including the theoretical analysis of tort law, property law, contract law, fiduciary law, trust law, remedies and restitution, and the law of equity. The series is open to diverse theoretical approaches, including those informed by philosophy, economics, history, and political theory. Oxford Private Law Theory sets the standard for rigorous and original work in private law theory.

ALSO PUBLISHED IN THIS SERIES

Oxford Studies in Private Law Theory
Volume III
Edited by Paul B. Miller and John Oberdiek

Responsibility for Negligence in Ethics and Law
Aspiration, Perspective, and Civic Maturity
Verónica Rodríguez-Blanco

Conflict between Equals

Tort Law beyond Wrong, Harm, and Cost

Avihay Dorfman
"The Friends of Joe Jamail" Regents Chair in Law
University of Texas at Austin School of Law and Tel Aviv University

OXFORD
UNIVERSITY PRESS

OXFORD
UNIVERSITY PRESS

Great Clarendon Street, Oxford, OX2 6DP,
United Kingdom

Oxford University Press is a department of the University of Oxford.
It furthers the University's objective of excellence in research, scholarship,
and education by publishing worldwide. Oxford is a registered trade mark of
Oxford University Press in the UK and in certain other countries.

Published in the United States of America by Oxford University Press
198 Madison Avenue, New York, NY 10016, United States of America.

British Library Cataloguing in Publication Data

Data available

Library of Congress Control Number: 2025950517

ISBN 978-0-19-897987-6

DOI: 10.1093/9780198979869.001.0001

Printed and bound by
CPI Group (UK) Ltd., Croydon, CR0 4YY

The manufacturer's authorized representative in the EU for product safety is
Oxford University Press España S.A. of Parque Empresarial San Fernando de Henares,
Avenida de Castilla, 2 – 28830 Madrid (www.oup.es/en or product.safety@oup.com).
OUP España S.A. also acts as importer into Spain of products made by the manufacturer.

MIX
Paper | Supporting responsible forestry
FSC® C013604
FSC
www.fsc.org

To Gili, Rani, Dana, and Ben—my dearest justice seekers

Acknowledgments

This book has benefited from comments by many colleagues as well as by workshop and conference participants in Berkeley, Harvard, Hebrew U., NYU, Northeastern, Tel Aviv, Texas, Toronto, University of South California, Wharton, and Yale.

For very helpful comments on this manuscript or parts of it, I am deeply grateful to Haim Abraham, Scott Altman, Ronen Avraham, Oren Bar-Gill, Jane Baron, Sam Baswick, Yitzhak Benbaji, Leora Bilski, Michael Birnhack, Yishai Blank, Andrew Botterell, Oren Bracha, Alan Brudner, Martha Chamallas, Vincent Chiao, Tom Christiano, Kevin Clermont, Chiara Cordelli, Nico Cornell, Yaron Covo, Hanoch Dagan, Natalie Davidson, Erik Encarnacion, David Enoch, Chris Essert, Cindy Estlund, Willi Forbath, Ward Fransworth, Mark Geistfeld, Mark Gergen, John Goldberg, Adi Goldiner, David Grewal, Tara Grove, Ehud Guttel, Alon Harel, Filipe Jimenez, Julian Jonker, Larissa Katz, Greg Keating, Sari Kisilevsky, Alon Klement, Tom Kohavi, Lee Kovarsky, Roy Kreitner, Doug Kysar, Alexy Lahav, Joanna Langille, Jennifer Laurin, Tim Liau, Eliav Lieblich, Assaf Likhovski, Daniel Markovits, Richard Markovits, Erin Miller, Gilad Mills, Crescente Molina, Jennifer Nadler, Yifat Naftali Ben Zion, Anthony Niblett, Eric Orts, Stephen Petal, Ariel Porat, Haggai Porat, Amit Pundik, Jonathan Quong, Veronica Rodriguez-Blanco, Brishen Rogers, Issi Rosen-Zvi, Larry Sager, Irit Samet, Anthony Sangiuliano, David Schorr, Amy Sepinwall, Liz Sepper, Assaf Sharon, Zoë Sinel, Adam Slavny, Henry Smith, Jordan Steiker, Nomi Stolzenberg, Jean Thomas, Christina Tilley, Yofi Tirosh, Julia Tomassetti, Kim Treiger, Sabine Tsuruda, Gary Watson, Arnold Weinrib, Leif Wenar, Sean Williams, Katrina Wyman, Ben Zipursky, and two OUP anonymous reviewers. Thanks also to my torts students at Tel Aviv, Cornell, and Harvard for their illuminating questions and insights—and to the outstanding casebook I have used throughout, and whose influence on my thinking is evident in this book: John Goldberg et al., Tort Law: Responsibilities and Redress (1st through 5th editions).

I am deeply grateful to Leora Bilski, Hanoch Dagan, Mark Gergen, John Goldberg, Greg Keating, Roy Kreitner, Daniel Markovits, Ariel Porat, Arthur Ripstein, Cathy Sharkey, Ernie Weinrib, and Ben Zipursky for their enriching and thought-provoking discussions over the years on the fundamental questions that underpin this book.

I wish to note the financial support of ISF grant no. 3400/24.

Contents

PART III. THE EQUALITY THEORY OF TORT LAW

PART IV. CONCLUDING REMARKS

PART I

TORT LAW'S CHALLENGES

Introduction

I. The Main Themes: Conflict and Equality

This book argues that tort law—viz., the law governing interactions between private persons by way of determining and imposing directed duties of other-regard—has to be understood and ultimately vindicated as the actualization of two theories: the conflict theory and the equality theory of tort law. The former takes up the function of tort law, whereas the latter takes up the form of tort law. The conflict theory suggests that *the* moral function of tort law is to address human conflict and, in particular, conflicts of interest between private persons, such as free speech versus good name or liberty of action versus bodily integrity. Tort law addresses conflicts of interest by engaging with the values underlying human conflict. It does so by determining legal rights and duties that constitute the appropriate response to the value of the conflict at hand. Conflicts admit of different kinds of value, and tort law can engage with values in the right way only insofar as it, first, identifies the kind of value at hand and, second, administers a fitting response. Thus, some conflicts are inherently valuable and, for this reason, tort law engages with them in the right way by constructing (and, at times, facilitating) them. Other conflicts are tolerably valuable, in which case tort law engages with them by containing their negative side effects. Finally, some conflicts are valueless and, so, tort law's task is preventing them in advance or eliminating their impact ex post facto.

The equality theory takes up the form of tort law. The human conflict to which tort law responds takes the form of one-to-one interaction, and this (by no means trivial) way of organizing the world reflects a commitment to treating parties to a conflict as equals. The equality theory suggests that tort-law structures conflicts according to a certain egalitarian ideal, namely, that of relating as equals. On this ideal, equality is relational rather than distributional—it concerns pairwise or transactional equality, rather than equality in the overall distribution of resources and opportunities in society. The relational equality at the center of my argument is also one of substantive, rather than formal equality: It takes seriously differences in both the interest and the condition of the interacting parties. Thus, instead of setting aside the normative differences between interests, such as the difference between bodily integrity and property, substantive equality incorporates the priority of the former over the latter into the terms of the interaction. So too with respect to the difference of condition such as the vulnerability of a potential victim due to

Conflict between Equals. Avihay Dorfman, Oxford University Press. © Oxford University Press 2026.
DOI: 10.1093/9780198979869.003.0002

their disability, lack of information, or insufficient experience, can call for greater care and respect from a potential injurer. By incorporating interest and condition differentials into the terms of the interaction, tort law secures the ability of the parties in a conflict to relate as substantive equals.

The conflict and equality theories are not independent normative accounts that merely happen to converge in the context of tort law. Instead, they form a hierarchical relationship in which the equality theory complements the conflict theory, as will become clear in Section V of this Introduction.

My ambition in developing and defending the conflict and equality theories of tort law is not only to understand tort law as the positive law of this or that jurisdiction. Nor do I limit the study to understanding tort law more abstractly, that is, as a universe of normative ideas quite apart from its positive-law incarnation. Nor, lastly, do I seek to justify tort law, by asking whether the normative ideas embodied in current or traditional tort law are defensible. Instead, I wish to offer a *normative vindication* of tort law: The question I seek to answer is not what tort law is, or whether that "is" is justified or permissible, but rather why tort law at all. The latter question asks whether we need to worry, or might we even wish, that tort law cease to be. The answer I defend in the book is that we should worry and, so, not wish this much. I argue that both the conflict and the equality theories are necessary to making this showing, namely, that we have to have tort law, properly conceived. Once again, by tort law I do not mean the backward-looking law of responding to wrongdoing, solving disputes, and allocating resources back, but rather the forward-looking law (common law or otherwise) that *constructs*, and then enforces, terms of interpersonal interactions by determining and imposing legal rights and duties.

Before pursuing all of that, however, I wish to identify three shortfalls in the contemporary understanding of tort law.

The *first* shortfall concerns a major theoretical deadlock in the study of tort law. In particular, tort theory is divided into two competing understandings of its practice—that is, as the law of individual wrongs against discrete victims and as the law of accidental, widespread harms. Tort theories often address this clash by emphasizing one understanding at the expense of the other. I argue that this way of coping with the complexity of legal practice cannot succeed and, moreover, that tort law is far more intricate than what dominant tort theories acknowledge.

The *second* shortfall goes to the conception of tort law—what "law" is tort law. I argue that identifying tort law with the law of wrongs, recourse, or cost-internalization fails doubly: It does not account for both the actual and the ideal workings of tort law.

The *third* shortfall focuses on an immensely influential view that there are only, or mainly, two competing conceptions of equality against which to understand and evaluate tort law: one is formal equality and the other pertains to equality in the overall distribution of resources in society. These two views correspond to two different forms of justice, namely, corrective and distributive justice, respectively. This dichotomous picture, influential as it is, is conceptually and normatively false. It leaves out the substantive conception of relational equality that underlies the equality theory of tort law that I defend in this book. Moreover, the dichotomy at issue is at odds with the actual working of the principle of equality in contemporary liberal society.

Discussing these three shortfalls, I argue, reveals why a fresh start is called for. Hence, the overarching questions for the remainder of the Introduction is this: Why tort *theory*, and why *now*? As will become clear, whereas conventional accounts of tort law identify the basic concern to which tort law responds with some notion of wrong, harm, or cost, I argue that the true concern is, and should be, human conflict. Wrong, harm, and cost are derivative concerns and thus occupy a downstream position in the tort-law universe.

II. Beyond the Traditional versus Modern Divide

Two prominent pictures of tort law figure in contemporary discussions. The first picture features a deliberate punch in the face, or any other intentional interference with the person or property of a single individual. It is often called the traditionalist view and is primarily held by noninstrumental accounts of the value of tort law. The second picture replaces the intentional-wrongdoing-against-an-individual picture with one featuring an accidental infliction of widespread harm to society. It tells the unfortunate story, for example, of a defective product (consider an asbestos-laden part in an industrial pump) potentially causing terminal illness to a multitude of users and bystanders, including mere strangers who happen to suffer from first- and second-hand exposure to the dangerous product. The type of tort-law claims that this latter scenario brings about is often called modern tort law, and it is primarily defended on either welfarist or distributive justice grounds.

The two pictures pull in profoundly different directions, captured by two sets of distinction: First, wrongdoing versus accidental harm-causing as the key ground for imposing liability; and second, a concern with a discrete victim versus mass torts.[1] Moreover, each pursues its own way of addressing the problems that tort law is set to solve; in fact, they provide different ways of understanding what the problems are in the first place. As a result, tort theory is

[1] Both distinctions are nicely captured by the title of one of the most important books in the history of tort theory, Guido Calabresi, The Costs of Accidents (1970). The title highlights three transformational pillars of modern tort law (according to Calabresi): Costs, rather than injuries, are the key concern; accidents, rather than intentional wrongs, are at the heart of tort law; and, finally, tort law pursues a fundamentally social problem (as indicated by using costs and accidents in the plural). Needless to say, Calabresi is a prominent member, more accurately, key painter, of the accidental-infliction-of-widespread-harm picture.

split into two approaches.[2] One approach, associated with corrective justice and civil recourse theories, primarily illuminates the punch-in-the-face picture of tort law whereas the other approach, associated with economic analysis of law as well as the writings of Gregory Keating, takes the second picture to stand at the heart of the tort law of modern, industrialized societies.[3] It is not surprising that the former approach identifies tort law with the common law of torts and, further, contrasts tort law with regulation,[4] whereas the latter finds robust continuity between tort law and the regulatory apparatus of the modern administrative state.[5] There are many moral, institutional, and economic implications for taking sides in this debate. Most importantly, what grounds should inform courts and other tort-law architects in making decisions and formulating new rules. Indeed, core doctrinal questions, such as the role of the duty element, the standard of reasonable care, the place of strict liability, the causation inquiry in the face of uncertainty, the right measure of compensatory damages, the nature and legitimacy of awards of punitive damages, and the choice of the right plaintiff—for example, the victim, a class action, or a state agent in the case of public nuisance—receive substantially different answers based, in large part, on whether one identifies tort law with this or that picture. Furthermore, the role of liability insurance in tort law is largely dictated by which picture one subscribes to: the punch-in-the-face picture (which denies a role for insurance against liability for deliberate wrongdoing, as it is viewed as both legally or economically unjustified) or the accidental-infliction-of-widespread-harm (which calls for a substantial role).[6]

[2] One might wonder what explains this trend. It might be the different interpretive and normative challenges that tort law presents relative to both contract and property law. Unlike the general principles of contract or property, there is no one tort that is considered *the* generic tort; nor is there a unified skeletal core that all, or most, torts share. Rather, there are many of them and they protect different interests, some more fundamental than others, over highly diverse contexts. Accordingly, tort theory is in part a sustained attempt to reject the thought that tort law is just a purely contingent political fact.

[3] Gregory C. Keating, Reasonableness and Risk: Right and Responsibility in the Law of Torts 305 (2022). To be sure, the division between the two approaches is not always crystal clear. Nor do I claim that every tort theory there is can be characterized in terms of either one of these approaches. *See, e.g.*, Kenneth S. Abraham & G. Edward White, *Conceptualizing Tort Law: The Continuous (and Continuing) Struggle*, 80 Md. L. Rev. 293 (2021).

[4] *See, e.g.*, Arthur Ripstein, Private Wrongs ix, 28 (2016); John C. P. Goldberg & Benjamin C. Zipursky, Recognizing Wrongs 50, 153 n.7, 171 (2020).

[5] *See, e.g.*, Gregory C. Keating, *Is Tort Law "Private"?*, *in* Civil Wrongs and Justice in Private Law 351, 357, 359, 371 (Paul B. Miller and John Oberdiek eds., 2020); Catherine M. Sharkey, *Modern Tort Law: Preventing Harms, Not Recognizing Wrongs*, 134 Harv. L. Rev. 1423 (2021) (book review).

[6] The latter approach to insurance liability is defended in Kenneth S. Abraham & Catherine M. Sharkey, *The Glaring Gap in Tort Theory*, 133 Yale L.J. 2165 (2024). Contrary to the view expressed by Abraham and Sharkey, the idea that liability insurance plays a defining role in the development of modern tort law seems overstated. Many of the important cases I will discuss in this book—cases that have, to some extent, shaped what tort law is and the ideals it implicitly or explicitly embodies—do not reflect the allegedly defining influence of liability insurance on tort liability. There is, however, a very different dimension of insurance that ought to play a substantial role in how we think about *substantive* equality in tort law. I return to this dimension in Chapter 13, text accompanying note 26.

Against this backdrop, proponents of both approaches take any number of steps to cope with the tension between the two pictures. Often, they do so by inflating the importance of the picture to which they subscribe and downplaying the importance of the rival picture. One such step appeals to historical and social facts about the world. On this front, advocates of the accidental-infliction-of-widespread-harm picture observe that the punch-in-the-face picture has long taken the back seat (in fact, ever since the dawn of the twentieth century).[7] They further propound their case by identifying judicial decisions that make explicit statements about modern tort law.[8] However, their opponents can also find ample evidence in the case law to substantiate their case against the withering away of the more traditional tort law that the punch-in-the-face picture illuminates.[9] Another strategy is one of explaining away core features of the competing picture—for instance, some advocates of the punch-in-the-face picture seek to marginalize the doctrine of strict tort liability as its broad acceptance and importance might threaten the integrity of their appeal to the centrality of wrongdoing. Hence, they may say that torts of strict liability should better be characterized as a licensing device which means that strict liability is in reality an activity-fee and the defendant is essentially a licensee, rather than a wrongdoer.[10] Alternatively they might seek to discover latent elements of fault in what is perceived as strict liability.[11] Or, they can also concede that strict liability figures in the lived-experience of tort law but that it is "on the wane"[12] and, so, that there exist only "pockets of strict liability."[13]

Finally, another strategy is to dismiss the two-picture understanding of tort law and instead, embrace a unifying picture. Some corrective justice theorists, on the one hand, and lawyer economists, on the other, have taken precisely this route. For instance, they argue that a single substantive principle, independence in the case of corrective justice and efficiency in the case of economic analysis, can explain much of tort law, and that its theoretical power cuts across the distinction between the punch-in-the-face and the accidental-infliction-of-widespread-harm picture. I take stock of the merits of some of these attempts throughout this book.[14] For

[7] Samuel Issacharoff & John Fabian Witt, *The Inevitability of Aggregate Settlement: An Institutional Account of American Tort Law*, 57 VAND. L. REV. 1571 (2004); Keating, *supra* note 5.

[8] Sharkey, *supra* note 5, at 1423, 1438, 1446. For instance, in *Loomis v. Amazon.com LLC*, 63 Cal. App.5th 466, 490 (Cal. C.A. 2021), Justice John Wiley (in his concurrence) identifies "the deep structure of modern tort law" with "a judicial quest to minimize the social costs of accidents."

[9] *See, e.g.*, Scott Hershovitz, *Treating Wrongs as Wrongs: An Expressive Argument for Tort Law*, 10(2) J. TORT L. 1, 17, 33, 39 (2018).

[10] GOLDBERG & ZIPURSKY, *supra* note 4, at 191.

[11] RIPSTEIN, *supra* note 4, at 136–40.

[12] Gregory C. Keating, *Strict Liability Wrongs*, *in* PHILOSOPHICAL FOUNDATIONS OF THE LAW OF TORTS 292, 295 (John Oberdiek ed., 2014). Keating, of course, rejects this observation.

[13] ERNEST J. WEINRIB, THE IDEA OF PRIVATE LAW 171 (1995).

[14] Another important reductionist account, offered by Mark Geistfeld, suggests that tort law often operates on normative commitments that resonate with other bodies of law (such as criminal law, on the one hand, and contract law, on the other). On this view, "Tort law becomes normatively distinct only when it applies to behavior within the paradigm of compensatory reciprocity." Mark A. Geistfeld,

now, it is enough to assert that these reductionist tendencies may yield theoretical coherence (though not necessarily normative appeal) at the high cost of rendering their prescriptions too thin and abstract. Tort theory, and legal theory more generally, must maintain a sufficiently concrete level of engagement with the legal practice it purports to theorize.[15]

These and other arguments to the contrary notwithstanding, the two pictures at issue do capture something fundamentally true about tort law. By fundamentally true I mean transcending both the historical debate about the rise of modern tort law and the disagreement among academic lawyers about "where the action is."[16] The punch-in-the-face picture captures value*less* conflicts, ones that we, thereby, ought to prevent or seriously curb. By contrast, accidental-infliction-of-widespread-harm features what I will call in subsequent chapters tolerably valuable conflicts. Such conflicts endanger the life and limb of people, to be sure. However, contrary to violent attacks and other forms of flagrant misbehavior, these conflicts arise out of otherwise valuable practices and activities, which are often subject to, and regulated by, the liability insurance industry. For instance, defective products (or medical malpractice, for this purpose) represent negative byproducts of things (or services) that are generally desirable for us all. As I argue in Chapter 2, and further demonstrate in Chapters 3–9, eliding the difference between these two kinds of conflict is normatively indefensible. As it should, tort law addresses these two on different terms, reflecting the qualitative distinction between valueless and tolerably valuable conflicts.[17]

That said, I deny that the equal importance of the two pictures is a source of concern for either theory or practice. In fact, I challenge the terms of the debate surrounding the two pictures of tort law. The real difficulty is that two pictures are *too few*, rather than too many. That is, there are in fact three pictures, not two, and none is reducible to one of the other two. The missing picture features what I will call inherently valuable conflicts, consisting of clashes of interest that we have compelling reasons to facilitate and even bring into existence, as opposed to contain, let alone prevent.

Moving beyond the divide between traditional versus modern tort law does not stop at identifying and elaborating the novel, third picture of tort law (although it surely is this also). Instead, the inclusion of that picture changes the way we

Hidden in Plain Sight: The Normative Source of Modern Tort Law, 91 N.Y.U. L. Rev. 1517, 1544–45, 1569 (2016). According to Geistfeld, the paradigmatic cases concern accidental, noncriminal infliction of injury. *See* Mark A. Geistfeld, Torts, Contracts, and Categorical Reasoning in the Common Law (unpublished manuscript) at 6.

[15] *See further* Hanoch Dagan & Avihay Dorfman, Relational Justice: A Theory of Private Law ch.1 (2024); Daniel Markovits & Alan Schwartz, *Plural Values in Contract Law: Theory and Implementation*, 20 Theoretical Inq. L. 571, 576–77 (2019).

[16] Keating, *supra* note 5, at 351.

[17] There is an additional difficulty with marginalizing one of the two pictures: It may also be self-defeating in that it distorts the one picture of tort law that the tort theorist does address given the reciprocal influence that each picture exerts on the other.

approach—that is, explain, justify, and vindicate—tort law. The question should not be which one of the two pictures dominates, or should dominate, the other but rather this: Is there a framework that can organize the multifaceted practice called tort law into a normatively appealing body of law? Such a framework would have to explain in a nonreductive fashion both the place of all three pictures of tort law and the principle that holds them together. Moreover, for such a framework to count as successful, it must be able to go beyond coherence and provide, as any good legal theory does, normative resources to understand in theory and determine in practice the rules that make up the law of torts. The conflict theory of tort law, I argue in Chapters 2–10, is this framework.

III. Beyond the Law of Wrongs, Recourse, and Cost-Internalization

What law is tort law? For the most part, the answers on offer cast tort law in terms of negative values: Tort law is the law that responds to certain forms of human failing by either preventing or redressing them.[18] On this view, tort law is often identified with the law of wrongs, harms, recourse, and cost-internalization. Its basic task is to correct injustices, redress wrongs, and deter antisocial behavior. I argue that emphasizing the preventative, redressive, and deterrence aspects of tort law is theoretically and practically problematic. From a theoretical point of view, placing these aspects at the center of tort law amounts to tracing the shadows on the wall rather than the thing casting these shadows. Or, to change metaphors, wrongs, harms, redress, and cost-internalization are dependent variables of a more fundamental task of tort law, which is that of determining substantive rights and duties. As I argue in Chapter 2, these rights and duties are determined by reference to the value of the conflict between the pertinent interests. Accordingly, the ongoing debate in tort law theory over whether tort law's wrongs are genuine moral wrongs[19] cannot be fully resolved without taking up the more basic question of what substantive rights we have and whether, and under what conditions, their violation should be deemed wrongful.[20] With respect to practice, the view that tort law is the

[18] *Cf.* F. H. Lawson, *The Creative Use of Legal Concepts*, 32 N.Y.U. L. Rev. 909, 909 (1957) (criticizing the tendency to reduce legal analysis to topics, such as "negligence ... trespass," which emphasize the "pathology of law").

[19] *Compare* Steven Schaus, *A Simple Model of Torts and Moral Wrongs*, 97 Notre Dame L. Rev. 1029 (2022) *with* Rebecca Stone, *Private Liability without Wrongdoing*, 73 U. Toronto L.J. 53 (2023); Liam Murphy, *The Artificial Morality of Private Law: The Persistence of an Illusion*, 70 U. Toronto L.J. 453 (2020); Larry Alexander & Kimberly Kessler Ferzan, *Confused Culpability, Contrived Causation, and the Collapse of Tort Theory*, *in* The Philosophical Foundations of the Law of Torts 406 (John Oberdiek ed., 2014).

[20] The argument in the main text may (arguably) also have implications for assessing recent influential philosophical accounts of interpersonal morality that invoke such principles as "what we owe to each other," "the second-person standpoint," "the moral nexus," and more. They focus on questions of moral wrongs and duties, rather than basic interests and rights. One way to approach these accounts

law of wrongs, harms, redress, and cost-internalization does not reflect the actual working of tort law, at least as represented by the canonical cases that make up the law of tort as we know it (in treatises, restatements, and scholarly discussions).

Exploring these two difficulties will further motivate the conflict theory of tort law: A theory that highlights, among other things, the distinctive capacity of tort law to construct (or facilitate) valuable conflicts, rather than merely prevent valueless ones. This theory will occupy the first half of the book.

Consider the celebrated case of *Vosburg v. Putney*, a prominent member in the torts canon for at least two propositions: What counts as a battery and what should be the scope of the batterer's liability?[21] The case features a twelve-year-old schoolboy who playfully kicked his classmate in the shin. Arguably, the kick was a friendly gesture akin to a tap on a friend's shoulder. The victim ultimately suffered a permanent substantial disability due not merely to the kick, which was slight but also to an underlying condition he had. The Wisconsin Supreme Court held that the kick counts as a battery even as the batterer did not intend to harm the victim. The court further decided that liability should extend to cover the entire harm to the victim even though his underlying condition—his thin shin, as it were—was unbeknownst to the batterer.[22]

Torts as wrongs. If tort law is the law of wrongs or, more precisely, private wrongs, it is only natural to read *Vosburg* as addressing the question of what might constitute battery in such a case. On the torts-as-wrongs conception, the point of the decision is to answer whether can there be wrongfulness in touching a person in the absence of any intent to harm him or her. *Vosburg* answers in the affirmative. The court seems to suggest that the kicking was wrongful because it violated the school's internal rules of proper conduct. Some tort scholars might provide a different grounding: A kicking is wrong because it lacks the consent of the victim. Whatever the answer is, if tort law is the law of wrongs, it follows that the basic task of the court is to determine which actions constitute substandard behavior of a certain kind.[23]

is to take them to be offering structural (metaethical) theories of interpersonal morality, in which case they may not be able to generate the substantive principles on the basis of which we could determine what, in this or that case, counts as wrong. Alternatively, these accounts can be viewed as making substantive (ethical) claims about the content of moral duties and what constitutes their violation. This latter understanding, I think, invites the difficulty raised above, namely, that asking what we owe to each other (et alia) without first establishing what interests and rights we have is akin to tracing the shadows on the wall rather than the thing casting these shadows.

[21] For discussion and elaboration of this reason and others, see James A. Henderson, Jr., *Why* Vosburg *Comes First*, 1992 Wis. L. Rev. 853, 853. For a comprehensive study of *Vosburg* in its context, see Zigurds L. Zile, *Vosburg v. Putney: A Centennial Story*, 1992 Wis. L. Rev. 877, 979–89.

[22] Vosburg v. Putney, 50 N.W. 403 (Wis. 1891).

[23] I say *of a certain kind* because some theories of tort law (including the one I defend in this book) understand the wrongs in question as violation of norms that link the tortfeasor and the victim to each other.

Torts as recourse. If it is also, or even primarily, the law of recourse and, in particular, the law of victim's recourse, *Vosburg* becomes a definitive expression of what tort law is about. There, a victim is afforded a right to pursue his batterer so as to react against his wrongdoing. Corrective justice theorists explain the meaning of victim reaction by reference to rectification, namely, the setting right of a wrong,[24] while civil recourse theorists cast victim reaction in terms of redressing the wrong done to him and in this way obtaining satisfaction.[25] Either way, *Vosburg* is a powerful champion of tort law as the law of victim recourse. It holds the wrongdoer liable not merely for the predictable injury caused by lightly kicking the victim but rather for the full extent of the injury even though it is largely an upshot of an idiosyncratic underlying condition (a.k.a. a thin skull).[26]

Torts as cost-internalization. If tort law is primarily tasked with the optimal internalization of the social costs of human action, the tort of battery sets out to induce potential batterers to act in a socially efficient way when contemplating whether to make physical contact with other persons. *Vosburg* is an occasion to show how to integrate intentionality into cost/benefit analysis.[27] An intentional kick should attract liability not only when the actor seeks—that is, deliberately—to harm the victim but rather also when this actor is merely aware, or can be aware, of the harmful consequences that kicking another person might cause (though I doubt whether this explanation can make sense of *Vosburg*).[28] A (rational) kicker can decide whether or not to impose the probable costs of the kick on the victim by assessing these costs against the benefits he expects to reap from so acting. On the cost-internalization conception, imposing liability for battery is not about deterring wrongful behavior but rather about seeing to it that the decision to create that contact takes into account the social costs of the encounter. *Vosburg* is also an excellent proving ground for the economic defense of the thin-skull doctrine: Instead of awarding damages according to the suffering of the average victim, tort law invokes the more efficient scheme of individualized computation of damages so that both the thin and the "rock-hard" skull victims receive compensatory damages that fit their respective actual sufferings.[29]

24 *See, e.g.*, Ernest J. Weinrib, *Civil Recourse and Corrective Justice*, 39 FLA. ST. U. L. REV. 273 (2011).

25 *Compare* GOLDBERG & ZIPURSKY, *supra* note 4, at 118–19, 156.

26 RIPSTEIN, *supra* note 4, at 267; John C. P. Goldberg & Benjamin C. Zipursky, *Vosburg v. Baxendale: Recourse in Tort and Contract*, *in* CIVIL WRONGS AND JUSTICE IN PRIVATE LAW 463, 471–72 (Paul B. Miller & John Oberdiek eds., 2020).

27 Keyth N. Hylton, *Intent in Tort Law*, 44 VALP. L. REV. 1217, 1231 (2010).

28 *Id.* Hylton, who provides a careful and elegant economic analysis of intentionality in torts, argues that there were good reasons for the *Vosburg* court to suppose that Putney was, or could have been, aware of the potentially harmful consequences of kicking Vosburg. He contrasts this analysis with a case involving three- and four-year-old defendants. *See id.* at 1231.

29 WILLIAM M. LANDES & RICHARD A. POSNER, THE ECONOMIC STRUCTURE OF TORT LAW 250 (1987). For a nonrelational defense of the thin-skull rule, based on considerations of fairness across the entire victim class, see Mark A. Geistfeld, *Proximate Cause Untangled*, 80 MD. L. REV. 420, 453–54 (2021).

Certainly, tort law is to some extent the law of wrongs and of recourse, and also sometimes induces actors to internalize the costs of their intentional (and unintentional) behavior. That said, saddling tort law with any of these conceptions fails to describe the actual practice of tort law, namely, what is the real place of wrongs, recourse, and cost-internalization in the grand scheme of tort law. It also fails to capture the normativity of tort law, namely, why it matters. The source of both problems is that there is a *preliminary* question that determines the questions of wrongfulness, recourse, and cost. It is the question of what substantive rights do parties to a physical encounter have in the first place, which, in turn, depends on a prior account of the value of the underlying conflict of interests at issue. That inquiry renders important aspects of the practice and normativity of wrongs, recourse, and cost-internalization.

Begin with actual practice. *Vosburg* reaches the points of wrongfulness, recourse, and cost-internalization only after, and because, it takes up the prior question of what rights and duties attach to parties engaged in an encounter such as the one at issue. To do so, the court considers the conflict between bodily integrity and sociability in the context of children-at-play. The basic interest not to be contacted could give way to competing interests. Indeed, the court contrasts the actual case with a playful kick delivered on the playground of the school. It also, perhaps more implicitly, contrasts the actual case with a kick in class occurring *before* class has been called into order. A third contrast is with respect to the absence of school rules concerning pupils tapping each other on the leg as a way to get each other's attention. Finally, the court could (arguably) consider the difference between middle school children and law school (i.e., adult) students engaging in a similar physical contact. These contrasts provide a richer sense of what is at stake: The court is acutely aware that certain forms of touching, including nonconsensual touching, can be *valuable* and, therefore, permissible. Hence, the questions the court asks are not merely what constitutes a violation of the right to bodily integrity and what recourse should be afforded in reaction to this violation. Rather, it considers how sociability, properly conceived, implicates the interest in bodily integrity in order to decide the scope of the legal right to bodily integrity: When does the victim hold such a right against the kicking classmate? Only then can the court decide whether such kicking constitutes a wrong—a violation of a right—or counts as a social cost, and whether victim recourse includes getting compensation for the full extent of the injury.

The conditional character of deciding the wrong, the recourse, and the cost questions is not only conceptual but rather also normative. The question of substantive right, and its underlying interest, partially dictates how stringent the standard of other-regard should be. For instance, strict liability with respect to undermining our bodily integrity in the case of battery does not imply a similarly stringent standard when making defamatory statements in the tort of defamation or causing emotional harm in the tort of intentional infliction of emotional distress.

Indeed, the competing interests at issue and the value of the conflict between them inform many legal decisions made by appellate courts.[30] Similarly, the doctrine of the thin-skull plaintiff that is at full display in *Vosburg* turns, almost completely, on the value of the plaintiff's interest and the value of the conflict between this interest and the competing one.[31] This is why tort law extends that doctrine to the case of thin emotional skull but denies similar extension to thin proprietary skull.[32] Hence, the case for victim recourse varies with normative considerations, namely, the value of the victim's interest and of the conflict between this and the competing interest; it is *not* a self-standing principle of rectification or of setting right a wrong.[33]

Objection: Much Ado About Nothing? Perhaps, however, tort law has very little to do with substantive rights, let alone with the conflicting interests that underlie such rights. The claim is that determining substantive rights and duties in tort law is not an issue. People have basic rights to bodily integrity, property, reputation, and so on. Others have the correlative duties not to batter, steal, and defame them. Calling these rights and duties into tort law is a straightforward exercise of reproduction akin to the computer function of copy and paste. The pasted rights and duties reflect immemorial customs or some other extralegal norms. Alternatively, they can reflect judgments made elsewhere in the law—say, the law of property—before being reproduced in the law of torts. Either way, tort law is a transmission belt for implementing *fully specified* or *easily specifiable* rights and duties. Or so the objection might go.

This objection, however, rests on two mistaken assumptions. Criticizing them reinforces the crucial role of tort law in determining substantive rights and duties. Further, doing so makes it more appealing to consider the value of the conflicts that underlie the determination of these rights and duties, which is what the conflict theory of tort law sets out to do.

The first assumption is that substantive rights and duties are fully specified or easily specifiable extralegal norms of reciprocal respect. This observation is false. It is one thing to specify basic rights at a highly abstract level, quite another to say that their content can be discerned apart from legal analysis. Tort law often fills out

[30] See, for example, the discussion of facilitating uncompromising journalism (among others) in Chapter 4 as an illustration of the ways courts integrate questions of value into the legal analysis of rights, liabilities, and remedies in the law of torts.

[31] *See further* Hanoch Dagan & Avihay Dorfman, *Substantive Remedies*, 96 Notre Dame L. Rev. 513, 558 (2020).

[32] The need to decide whether unusually fragile property entitles its owner to recover the entire property damage arises when the unusual magnitude of the damage could not have been reasonably anticipated.

[33] The argument in the main text shows why corrective justice's adherence to a measure of make-whole compensation may not account for the distinction between physical and proprietary thin skulls. By contrast, civil recourse theory—and especially its commitment to fair and reasonable compensation as opposed to make-whole compensation—may have the normative resources to explain the variance between the different parts of the doctrine.

the content of rights. Consider the right to privacy. Even given that we have such a right, precisely what does it mean to have it, that is, what "it" is? And what duties arise as a result? I doubt whether answers to these normative questions can be gleaned from extralegal norms or expectations. At other times, tort law delineates the scope of substantive rights, as when in *Vosburg* the court considered under what circumstances bodily integrity gives way to sociability. Thus, even when the content of the right to bodily integrity is, let's assume, a priori fixed, it is still necessary to determine the outer limits of its claim. Certainly, the right to bodily integrity comes to an end, as it were, in the face of certain forms of consensual and even nonconsensual contact, as I argue in some detail in Chapters 3 and 4. Here, too, I doubt whether any satisfying answer to this normative and contextual inquiry can be found in our extralegal norms (assuming, for the sake of the argument that these are appealing norms at all).

The second assumption may concede the previous point but insist that the task of filling out the content and determining the scope of abstract rights is performed somewhere else in the law. Tort law merely operates on preexisting legal determinations made, say, by property, contract, fiduciary law, and restitution law (et alia). This assumption is mistaken, too. Consider three familiar instances from the lived experience of tort law—establishing rights, rendering them determinate, and defining their scope. To begin with, tort law engages in the business of establishing substantive rights. For instance, the torts of privacy, inducement of breach of contract, and intentional infliction of emotional distress are three tort frameworks whose most fundamental normative contribution to the legal order lies in *establishing* substantive rights, namely, to privacy, contractual security, and emotional tranquility, respectively. Questions concerning wrongdoing and victim recourse can have a point at all *only because* these rights have been established by tort law.

Next, tort law is especially important not only to establishing legal rights but rather also to rendering determinate established legal rights. For instance, even if the right to bodily integrity is (for the sake of the argument!) given by some other body of law, tort law engages in the crucial task of filling out its content—thus, what aspects of the body's integrity should be protected and how rigorous it should be are two key missions extensively pursued by appellate opinions, Restatements of torts, and tort scholars (among others).

Finally, establishing rights and rendering them determinate may often leave open the further task of defining their scope in the face of competing rights and countervailing considerations (as in the *Vosburg* decision). Consider the tort of assault. After establishing that there is a legal right not to be caused to apprehend an imminent attack on one's own person, and upon rendering this right determinate by subjecting "apprehension" to a standard of reasonable apprehension, tort law must also settle the scope of this entitlement. The tort of assault limits the right in several ways, including by excluding conditional and future-looking threats, however debilitating, from the scope of the right's protection.[34]

Against this backdrop, identifying tort law with the law of wrongs, recourse, and cost-internalization does not begin to capture where the action is, namely, the conflicting interests of the parties which, in turn, help to determine what substantive legal rights they have. Determining the latter makes possible, and informs (without necessarily dictating) our answers to the questions of what counts as wrong, what burden should be deemed social cost, what victim recourse requires, and when and how it can be invoked. *Vosburg* is, indeed, a canonical case, but the propositions that render it canonical cannot be specified, and defended, apart from the question of substantive rights. The conflict theory of tort law will address precisely this question.

IV. Beyond Formal Equality

What conception of equality underlies tort law? The prevailing theoretical orthodoxy is that the justice that tort law is morally responsible to achieve can be either corrective or distributive. Some advocate the former, others the latter, and even those who are critical of the either/or picture of tort law's justice argue for a certain combination of both.[35] A key aspect of the corrective/distributive division of justice is equality. Corrective justice is said to manifest a principle of transactional equality that is most accurately characterized as formal equality. The terms of interaction fixed by tort law are said to treat the interacting parties as equals, irrespective of differentiating factors such as powers, vulnerabilities, needs, and virtues.[36] To say that these parties are formally equal is to suppose that all that matters, for the sake of doing justice in the law of torts, is to conceive of them as equally constituting no more and no less than a capacity for choice.

Distributive justice, by contrast, embodies a commitment to equality in the overall allocation of resources in society. It denies the freestanding (though not necessarily the instrumental) significance of transactional equality, that is, as between the interacting parties.[37] For reasons I develop elsewhere, however, the distributional conception of equality fails to make an appealing case for the

[34] Brooker v. Silverthorne, 99 S.E. 530 (S.C. 1919).

[35] *See* John Gardner, Torts and Other Wrongs ch. 3 (2019); Hanoch Sheinman, *Tort Law and Distributive Justice*, *in* Philosophical Foundations of the Law of Torts 354 (John Oberdiek ed., 2014); *see also* Adam Slavny, Wrongs, Harms, and Compensation: Paying for Our Mistakes ch. 7 (2024).

[36] Weinrib, *supra* note 13, at 77–83; Arthur Ripstein, *Civil Recourse and Separation of Wrongs and Remedies*, 39 Fla. St. U. L. Rev. 163, 181 (2011).

[37] *See* Samuel Scheffler, *Distributive Justice, the Basic Structure and the Place of Private Law*, 35 Oxford J. Legal Stud. 226, 231–33 (2015).

explanation and vindication of tort law.[38] The withering away of the distributional conception seems to further reinforce the case for tort law's formal equality. This is so because, as just explained, it is generally assumed among tort theorists that the justice of tort law can be either corrective or distributive or a combination of both.

Is there a compelling case to be made for formal equality? Two leading contributions to the study of tort law have made the case for formal equality highly influential. The first is Holmes who, in his lectures on the common law, popularized the contrast between the legal and moral standards of evaluating human conduct. In his discussion of negligence law, Holmes employs the standard of reasonable care to show that this standard declines to take "personal equation into account,"[39] which means that "personal characteristics,"[40] "varieties of temperament, intellect, and education,"[41] and "powers and limitations"[42] do not form a legitimate set of considerations for imposing tort liability. Holmes defends this position on the grounds of "general welfare,"[43] but what he means is a basic commitment to transactional equality—the injuries caused by a person with a diminished capacity for exercising care are "no less troublesome to his neighbors than if they sprang from guilty neglect."[44] Holmes makes it clear that the tort duty of due care is not about the moral question of how the defendant behaves but rather about the legal question of fair terms of interaction between him and his victim. Save for some exceptions, Holmes believes that bracketing off difference is entailed by the latter concern.

The second is Ernest Weinrib's pathbreaking defense of tort law (and private law) in terms of corrective justice with a particular emphasis on formal, transactional equality. He intimates that "we cannot understand the normative character of corrective justice until we elucidate the normative significance of its equality."[45] His elucidation suggests that equality "consists in abstracting from the parties' particularities."[46] Interestingly, like Holmes, Weinrib employs the standard of reasonable care to bring home formal equality's commitment to abstracting from particularities.[47] Weinrib argues that this standard's indifference to what Holmes

[38] Avihay Dorfman, *Private Law Exceptionalism? Part II: The Basic Difficulty with the Argument from Formal Equality*, 31 Can. J. L. & Juris. 5, 11–13 (2018). Notice, however, that I have also argued that considerations of relational justice can give rise to private responsibility for ameliorating poverty and to reducing compensatory damages in the face of crushing liability. *See* Dagan & Dorfman, *supra* note 15, at chs. 14 & 7, respectively.

[39] Oliver Wendell Holmes, Jr., The Common Law 108 (1991) [1881].

[40] *Id.*, at 107.

[41] *Id.*, at 108.

[42] *Id.*

[43] *Id.*

[44] *Id.*

[45] Weinrib, *supra* note 13, at 77.

[46] *Id.* at 81.

[47] Weinrib acknowledges the continuity between Holmes and his account, saying that Holmes's "arguments against strict liability and the subjective standard fit readily within Kantian right." *Id.*, at 172. *See also id.*, at 177.

has called the "personal equation" of the one who owes a duty is entailed by the demands of formal equality.[48]

It is hard to exaggerate the immense influence of both Holmes and Weinrib on the role of formal equality in tort *theory*. That said, tort law, understood as a universe of ideas about equality among other things, defies the formal conception of transactional equality. It regularly draws on considerations that resonate with a competing understanding of what it means for parties to a tort interaction to relate as equals. Hence, rather than overlooking them, tort law often determines rights and duties and imposes liabilities based, in part and within limits, on the particularities or the personal equation of the parties. But courts, for obvious reasons, do not go beyond asserting sentiments and making ad hoc observations that do not give us an idea of what is the underlying conception of equality to which they appeal.

To this date, no comprehensive conception of equality for tort law other than the formal conception has been developed in its stead.[49] The problem is not only or even mainly theoretical—it's practical and doctrinal and, no less important, *political*. Bluntly put: If you want to appeal to equality in making legal and policy arguments in the law of torts, formal equality is the only, or almost the only, game in town. So it's either this or appeal to other principles.

The discussion that follows is meant to motivate the demand for a substantive conception of equality. Indeed, the *equality theory of tort law* that I develop in the second half of the book aspires to both articulate and defend a substantive conception of transactional equality. The equality theory turns some of the arguments I have made before regarding the existence and appeal of substantive equality in tort law and in private law, more generally, into a sustained account of equality in tort-law interactions.[50] It constructs a genuine alternative to the more dominant views about tort law's egalitarian commitments.

The standard of reasonable care, on which both Holmes and Weinrib draw, provides a shaky foundation for the proposition that tort law embodies a commitment to formal equality. To begin with, it is shaky because this standard is far from being fully or even consistently committed to excluding personal equation—it does so in some category of cases but not in many others. In fact, tort law regularly takes into account the respective conditions of the parties as well as the interests underlying their respective rights.[51] Doing so may further suggest that the real reason why the standard of reasonable care sometimes abstracts from the personal equation of the ower of duties in some cases, but not in others, has nothing to do

48 *Id.*, at 178.

49 This is not to say that tort theorists have not challenged the formal conception or even argued for the importance of distributive justice considerations to tort law's corrective justice. *See supra* note 35.

50 *See* Avihay Dorfman, *Negligence and Accommodation*, 22 Legal Theory 77 (2016); Dorfman, *supra* note 38; Dagan & Dorfman, *supra* 15, ch. 5.

51 *See id.*, *See further* Chapters 13–15.

with formal equality. I argue in Chapter 15 that the reason is substantive equality. The priority of the interest of the risk-bearer in bodily integrity over the liberty interest of the risk-creator explains why the latter, though not the former, should get no solace from the law. This form of explanation defies formal equality precisely because it turns on, rather than abstracts from, some particularities of the parties.

Furthermore, even if both Holmes and Weinrib are right about some category of cases in negligence law (and, recall, I argue that they aren't), there exists an awesome gap between an account of the standard of reasonable care and an account of the law of torts in its entirety. Tort law makes ample reference to personal equation along two basic dimensions, which together form the *egalitarian calculus* underlying the equality theory being proposed. First, the condition or situation of the person often partially determines the terms of the interaction. To fix ideas, courts would consider "the relative size, age, experience, sex and physical demeanor of the participants" in order to decide whether threatening the plaintiff not to leave a secluded area amounts to false imprisonment or, alternatively, it is better seen as a mere request.[52]

Second, the normative interest of the person—say, in bodily integrity—matters, too. Ordinarily, protecting life and limb places a more pressing demand than protecting economic interests. And even within the confines of one such interest, courts pierce the formal category of legal entitlements to create hierarchies between different instances of the same entitlement so as to reflect more accurately, and so less formally, the underlying interest. For instance, courts may treat a person's right to being protected against trespassing on her unoccupied farmhouse less favorably than if the trespass occurs on her dwelling house.[53] Although both are instances of having a property right, the underlying purpose of the right—viz., the human interest capable of justifying private control of resources—implicates the scope of the right, the intensity with which it is protected, and the remedies to which violation of the right might give rise.

To conclude, this book discusses a variety of torts, including false imprisonment, battery, trespass to land, private and public nuisance, defamation, products liability, negligence, inducement of breach of contract, and other run-of-the-mill cases, showing that contrary to what the formal conception of equality implies, considerations of condition and of interest do, and indeed must, influence tort law in deep and profound ways.

That said, a substantive conception of transactional equality is not hidden in plain sight. The doctrinal resources that make up this conception would require an elaborate work of reconstruction. Articulating such a conception would further require a sustained theoretical account of what equality demands and why transactional equality matters in general. Indeed, the philosophical literature on

[52] Black v. Kroger, 527 S.W.2d 794, 800 (Tex. App. 1975).
[53] *Cf.* Katko v. Briney, 183 N.W.2d 657 (Iowa 1971).

relational equality, as I show in Chapter 11, has not enough to contribute to the theory of equality in and around tort law, the law governing terms of involuntary interactions between private persons. I take up these challenges in the second part of this book.

V. The Nature of the Connection between the Conflict and the Equality Theory

The conflict theory provides an account of the moral function of tort law while the equality theory vindicates tort law's pairwise structure. The latter vindication addresses the very existence of the pairwise structure of tort duties. More specifically, it establishes, first, why have duties at all and, second, why these duties must be *tort* duties.

However, the connection between the conflict and equality theories runs deeper: They form a hierarchy in which the equality theory complements the conflict theory. Specifically, the equality theory enables the conflict theory to address *tolerably valuable conflicts*. To see this, recall that the equality theory introduces an egalitarian calculus based on interest and condition differentials. On this theory, terms of pairwise interaction are substantively equal if, and only if, they properly account for differences in interests and conditions. However, when it comes to inherently valuable or valueless conflicts, the conflict theory already possesses the normative resources needed to address these conflicts—from identifying the value of the conflict to determining the terms of interaction. In this context, the equality theory has nothing to add to the task of determining the terms.

To fix ideas, if a conflict of interests is inherently valuable, conflict theory suggests that tort law must determine rights and duties in a way that creates the conditions necessary for the conflict to arise (i.e., to exist and flourish). This requirement entails assessing how to address the competing interests and whether the conditions of either party should be accommodated. Conversely, if the conflict is valueless, conflict theory calls for preventing it, thereby presupposing a prior judgment about the relative importance of the competing interests. After all, a conflict is considered valueless precisely because of how one party's interest (say, the life of a drowning infant) stands in opposition to the interest of another party (such as saving time and freedom by not [effortlessly] rescuing the infant). Therefore, in both cases, the normative framework of conflict theory is not only necessary but also sufficient to address the conflicts at issue in the right way, leaving equality theory in a dormant state.

By contrast, the equality theory plays a crucial role in addressing tolerably valuable conflicts. In these cases, conflict theory calls for managing the conflict by containing its adverse effects on the interests and conditions of the parties involved. The task of containment depends on assessing the relative importance of the competing claims. The equality theory provides an egalitarian calculus (involving both interest and condition) to guide the containment analysis. In this way, equality theory complements the conflict theory by articulating the normative standard necessary to address tolerably valuable conflicts in the right way. Chapters 13–15 further elaborate on and illustrate this complementarity relationship.

VI. The Book's Structure and the Road Ahead

The argument of this book rests on five main pillars. What follows is a very brief outline of each, along with a road map of the chapters to come:

1. *The crux of the matter: Conflicts of fundamental interests.* It is not harm, wrongdoing, or social cost that gives us reason to have tort law in the first place but rather human conflict—specifically, conflict between our fundamental interests. How we respond to these conflicts then determines which harms, wrongs, or costs should be addressed by tort law, and in what ways. In arguing that conflict of interests lies at the moral center of tort law, as it should, I do not reduce tort law to dealing solely with the disvalue, as it is commonly done by those who view it only in terms of harm, wrongdoing, or cost. Instead, I argue that conflict between fundamental interests can also be a source of positive value, in which case tort law, understood as the law of conflict, is not primarily about preventing and ameliorating injustice but about creating the necessary conditions for certain valuable goods to emerge.
2. *The solution: The conflict theory.* Properly addressing conflicts of fundamental interests requires a theory of conflict. This book develops such a theory by elaborating on the nature and normative significance of three types of conflicts: inherently valuable, tolerably valuable, and valueless conflicts. While preventing or curing some conflicts is certainly one important implication of the theory, it is not the only implication. Furthermore, preventing or curing is not the most significant entailment of this theory, normatively speaking. The theory emphasizes the importance of containing conflict and, most importantly, constructing the necessary conditions for certain type of conflict to arise. This transforms how we should understand, assess, and vindicate the moral function of tort law.
3. *Enter, tort law.* The first virtue of tort law is its ability to engage with conflicts in accordance with the prescriptions of the conflict theory. This theory provides a normative framework for determining legal rights and duties by reference to the underlying interests at stake—particularly, the value of the conflict between them. These rights and duties ultimately decide what to make of the conflict at hand. At times, tort-law rights and duties construct the very conditions necessary for a conflict of interests to arise and, to some

extent, thrive. For example, by recognizing an exemption for a halfway house or a church from the general tort duty not to interfere with the reasonable use and enjoyment of neighboring property, tort law ensures that our communal environment can realize what I shall call the good of liberal toleration. At other times, by contrast, tort law resolves or at least minimizes conflict by defining rights and duties accordingly. For instance, imposing a tort duty on polluting factory not to interfere with the reasonable use and enjoyment of land can eliminate the conflict between the factory's interests (those of its owners and workers) and those of its residential neighbors—as a result, the factory would have to relocate, adopt cleaner production technologies, or cease operations altogether. More broadly, tort law undertakes the constructive task of determining legal rights and duties, thereby setting the terms of interaction based on the value of the conflict between the underlying interests.

My emphasis on the constructive function of tort law is particularly important within tort theory. The conflict theory challenges accounts that view tort law primarily as a response to preexisting disputes, such as reallocating resources to victims, redressing wrongs, or internalizing antisocial behavior. According to conflict theory, tort law uses legal rights, duties, and doctrinal rules to *construct* the foundational "rules of the game" that govern interaction in various social contexts, including roads, the neighborhoods, hospitals, workplaces, markets, parks, school, and the discursive sphere (where we both engage in expressive activities and consume information and ideas about our world). These rules are primarily prospective: They establish the preconditions for engaging with human conflict in a principled and structured way.

4. *Conflict and equality, integrated.* The equality theory of tort law initially arises as an account of the value of tort duties, that is, legal, directed, and choice-independent obligations. These duties make possible a distinctive form of egalitarian interaction between agents. Beyond this foundational value, the equality theory complements the conflict theory by supplying the normative resources needed to address tolerably valuable conflicts. These resources constitute what I shall call the egalitarian calculus, which serves to articulate the content of tort duties. In this way, the equality theory constructs terms of interaction—rights, duties, and other doctrinal rules—reflecting a commitment to a *substantive* conception of relational equality.

Many cases of negligence, products liability, and nuisance, as well as certain categories of defamation, fall in the class of tolerably valuable conflicts. Returning to the examples of nuisance mentioned above, some land-use conflicts are neither inherently valuable nor necessarily valueless. They often result from flawed land-use regulation and inadequate technology that inadvertently place two perfectly legitimate activities in conflict—to illustrate, consider flat owners whose glass walls allow visitors at a nearby art gallery to view the interiors of the homes. The conflict theory guides the inquiry about whether this conflict should be contained, and if so in what ways. In order to engage in containing, tort law establishes rights and duties that reflect the egalitarian maxim of "live and let live." The equality theory of tort law provides an interpretation of this norm as it subjects the task of containing the conflict to the demands of substantive equality. According to these demands, tort rights and duties must take into account both the relative importance of the parties' competing interests and their respective conditions or circumstances.

5. *Normative ambitions and their consequences*. The core ambition of the conflict and equality theories is to vindicate tort law, to explain why have tort law in the first place. The argument I present has implications for current tort doctrine. In some instances, I offer new justifications for existing legal rules. In others, I propose revisions to current doctrine—some modest, others more substantial. In still other cases, I defend the creation of new, currently nonexistent torts and doctrinal rules.

   Such variance reflects the normative ambition of this book, as just noted. It also reflects the view that tort law—as it currently exists—need not get it right in every instance and, just as importantly, does not work itself pure. This book defends an evaluative framework—based on the conflict and equality theory—for bringing greater, and more robust, correspondence between the demands of tort law and the demands of reason.

6. *Roadmap*. The opening chapter of this book, Chapter 1, introduces the challenges that any normative tort theory must ultimately face. The rest of the book provides a sustained attempt to vindicate tort law in three principal stages. The first stage, Chapters 2–10, defends the conflict theory of tort law in general and in particular areas of tort law. Chapter 2 establishes the key concepts and the basic argument for the conflict theory of tort law. It explores the idea of conflict and the interests that lie at its center. This chapter also elaborates the distinction between inherently valuable, tolerably valuable, and valueless conflicts and argues that the most basic moral task of tort law's judges, lawmakers, and practitioners is that of engaging with value in the right way. They ought to do so not directly by making ad hoc judgments in specific cases but rather indirectly by constructing doctrinal rules and determining rights and duties that embody the kind of value underlying the conflicts at issue. Chapter 3 takes up inherently valuable conflicts, Chapter 4 (a special segment of) tolerably valuable conflicts, and Chapters 5 and 6 valueless conflicts. Chapter 7 shows how tort law can give effect to the prescriptions of the conflict theory. I argue that the conflict theory is a *legal* theory and, consequently, that tort law is the *practice* of the conflict theory.

Chapters 8 and 9 provide a detailed analysis of proprietary torts (private and public nuisance and trespass to land, respectively), demonstrating how the conflict theory provides a normative framework to both understand and determine substantive rights and duties concerning the use and control of land. Chapter 10 defends the case for recognizing a novel tort of discrimination, using conflict theory to help delineate the scope of the general duty of nondiscrimination.

The second stage, Chapters 11–16, defends the equality theory of tort law as a general, philosophical account of relational equality and in respect to particular doctrinal questions in and around tort law. Chapter 11 explains why equality, rather than independence, must occupy the moral center of tort law. Chapter 12 argues for a special connection between tort duties and an ideal of relating as agents. It defends a principled delineation of the normative boundaries between involuntary and voluntary obligations and, moreover, rejects the Coasean picture of tort law as a residual or derivative branch of contractual ordering. Chapter 13 extends the analysis of relating as agents to relating as substantively equals, introducing the role of tort duties in fixing terms of interactions that meet this (substantive) standard of relational equality. Chapters 14 and 15 demonstrate how the equality theory determines the question of what counts as reasonable care in the law of negligence and beyond. Chapter 16 extends the reach of the equality theory to the domain of civil procedure and evidence law, arguing for a substantial revision of the legal standard for allocating the burden of persuasion in tort litigation. Although the seeds of the third stage can be traced to Chapters 13–15, it culminates in Chapter 17. Its ambition is to show that the conflict and the equality theories can form an articulated unity, as opposed to a collection of separately appealing accounts about the value of tort law. In particular, I explain how each theory bears on the other and demonstrate the important extent to which they are mutually reinforcing. Chapter 17 pursues this task in the course of defending the case for a novel tort: Private censorship.

1

Why Tort Law? Two Challenges

Introduction

This book's overarching claim is that the answer to the question of why have tort law in the first place is twofold. The first comes down to the conflict theory—tort law is necessary in order to engage in the right way with the value of certain conflicts. The second is the equality theory—tort law is necessary in order to determine terms of interactions that treat the interacting parties as equals. But before I take up these answers, I begin with defending the question itself, namely, why care about tort law?

Tort theory, like private law and legal theory more generally, is traditionally organized around a distinction between explanation and justification. Explanatory theories vary in their ambition, scope, and methodology but they share a commitment to engage with the "is," namely, with identifying and analyzing the actual reasons, principles, and values underlying the law of torts.[1] This endeavor can focus on tort law current in a specific jurisdiction, cover a longstanding tradition such as the common law of tort law, or even attempt the analytically more ambitious goal of understanding the very nature, or the idea, of the thing we identify as tort law, and uncovering its necessary implications.

Normative theories, by contrast, focus on "should" questions, such as should we let tort law stand, should tort liability be based upon fault, should tort law respond to formal or substantive equality, and so forth. They do not merely seek to understand the moral ideal underlying current tort law but rather to see if that ideal is justified in the sense that there is some value in it so that it is permissible and even desirable to go for it. This mode of assessment, moreover, does not turn on making a comparative argument to the effect that tort law is superior to its alternatives. I take the judgment that tort law is "entirely defensible"[2] to be an instance of justification in both senses just described. Fundamentally, normative theories engage

[1] Explanatory approaches to tort law differ in many respects, including in particular in their methodologies of hermeneutics (*see, e.g.*, Benjamin C. Zipursky, *Pragmatic Conceptualism*, 6 Legal Theory 457 (2000); Andrew S. Gold, The Right of Redress 18–20 (2020)) and in their substantive commitments within the realm of political philosophy (see, in the case of contract theory, Peter Benson, Justice in Transactions (2019)). On the role of explanation within a justificatory framework, see Nicholas McBride, The Humanity of Private Law 32 (2018).

[2] John C. P. Goldberg & Benjamin C. Zipursky, Recognizing Wrongs 270 (2020). *See also id.*, at 120 ("eminently justifiable").

Conflict between Equals. Avihay Dorfman, Oxford University Press. © Oxford University Press 2026.
DOI: 10.1093/9780198979869.003.0003

with tort law seeking to assess it according to some moral criteria. Like their explanatory counterparts, normative theories also vary in a number of ways, but only one of them is my concern here and will be at the center of these pages.

The explanatory/normative distinction has been extensively considered in tort theory.[3] Some have defended not only its coherence but also the value of keeping these theoretical ambitions strictly divorced.[4] Others have argued for mixing (and to this extent blurring the distinction between) the "is" and the "should" of tort and private-law theory,[5] while others have questioned the distinction's centrality, including by casting doubt on its very possibility.[6]

The disagreement between supporters and opponents of the explanatory/justificatory distinction is illuminating. Focusing on how to draw the battle lines, however, tends to emphasize the boundaries of each category, thereby deflecting attention from a concern with their content. In particular, the "justificatory" category obscures an important difference between two ways of engaging in normative tort theory. I argue for a distinction between mere justification and vindication, which captures a *third* standard of theory construction (above the "is" and "should" standards) that is based on must—*must* we have tort law?[7] Whereas justification concerns itself with whether we should let tort law stand, say, because it is permissible, desirable, or even warranted, vindication asks whether it is obligatory to have tort law. Further, I argue that this third standard is particularly consequential to the theoretical study of tort law. For instance, justifying tort law merely by answering the question "what is tort law for?,"[8] or by seeking tort law's "idea"[9] or "point,"[10]

[3] Tort theory is not distinctive in this respect. *See, e.g.*, SCOTT J. SHAPIRO, LEGALITY 2–3 (2011). Ronald Dworkin has challenged the distinction when it comes to law. His challenge, however, presupposes a conception of law as constitutive of what he calls political morality. *See* RONALD DWORKIN, JUSTICE FOR HEDGEHOGS 405–15 (2011).

[4] JULES L. COLEMAN, THE PRACTICE OF PRINCIPLE: IN DEFENCE OF A PRAGMATIST APPROACH TO LEGAL THEORY 4–5 (2001); *see also* Paul B. Miller, *The New Formalism in Private Law*, 66 AM. J. JURIS. 175, 218–19 (2021).

[5] *E.g.*, ARTHUR RIPSTEIN, PRIVATE WRONGS 20–21, 295 (2016); ERNEST J. WEINRIB, CORRECTIVE JUSTICE 35 (2012). *See also* GOLDBERG & ZIPURSKY, *supra* note 2, at 113–14.

[6] *See* JOHN GARDNER, TORTS AND OTHER WRONGS 28 (2019).

[7] Vindication has been used in different ways before. Sometimes it has been used to designate something weaker than justification. *See, e.g.*, Herbert Feigl, *On the Vindication of Induction*, 28 PHIL. STUD. 212 (1961). By contrast, I use it to denote a stronger standard than justification. I argue that a liberal state has an *obligation* to provide a certain law of torts. In other words, it is impermissible not to have such law.

Adam Slavny offers another (not inconsistent) standard that he calls foundationalism. His standard does not consider whether, and why, we must have something like tort law, but rather what might justify the non-juridical notion of "corrective duties." ADAM SLAVNY, WRONGS, HARMS, AND COMPENSATION: PAYING FOR OUR MISTAKES 1 (2024). These duties are akin to duties of repair or redress in response to wronging or harming another person. The morality of these duties can then inform our assessment of the actual (or ideal) tort law. *Id.*, at 2, 5. Notice that Slavny's approach places *corrective* duties, rather than primary duties, substantive rights, interests, and conflicts of interest, at the center of the moral universe he explores.

[8] GARDNER, *supra* note 6, at 27.

[9] Or even of private law, more generally. ERNEST J. WEINRIB, THE IDEA OF PRIVATE LAW (1995).

[10] RIPSTEIN, *supra* note 5, at 295.

might not satisfy the demands of good normative tort theory. Instead, I argue that tort law calls for vindication, and that vindicating tort law faces two foundational challenges.[11] Subsequent chapters defend an answer to both.

I. The Limits of Justification: When, and Why, "Should" Is Not Enough

I begin by exploring whether, and why, a justification of a practice or an institution might satisfy the demands of good theory. Justificatory theory, recall, relies on the "should" standard. Its ambition is to defend a practice or render it legitimate by subjecting it to relevant normative criteria. I argue that justification of a practice may be apt only insofar as the stakes of having it are sufficiently low (in a sense explained below).

Consider the game of chess. A theoretical engagement with it can ask the question "is" in order to render the game more intelligible, possibly in response to an outsider wondering about it. It can then proceed to the justification question: Should this game, properly explained, be played? I do not mean that as a question about a particular instance of playing chess—perhaps you must play chess with me (or I must play it by myself in my head) if it is the only available game we have and we are in a desperate situation and playing chess is the only way to kill time without losing ourselves. Rather, the question concerns the game of chess itself. The "should" question will likely focus on the game's valuable contributions to the players—fostering sociability, strategizing, competitiveness, improving cognitive and mental faculties, and so forth.

However, justifying the game of chess falls short of offering us a normative vindication of it, in that it does not ask why we must have it—including why invent or support the game of chess. Accordingly, the reasons for action generated by the "should" question cannot answer the "must" question, for it is one thing to justify chess and quite another to say that we must have it.

One way of bridging the gap between "should" and "must" would be to say that no good case can be made for the "must," meaning that there is no reason for insisting specifically on chess. We should have it, but we do not have to have it.

[11] Sandy Steel has recently explored the question of whether tort law is morally necessary, reaching somewhat skeptical conclusions. *See* Sandy Steel, *On the Moral Necessity of Tort Law: The Fairness Argument*, 41 Oxford J. Legal Stud. 192 (2021). Although we both discuss some notion of what I call vindication, our accounts differ about three substantive questions. First, Steel focuses on the vindication of victims' rights of action (which he calls "Tort Plus"), whereas I focus mainly on primary or substantive rights and duties (which he calls "Tort Minus"). Second, the challenges to vindicating tort law that I identify in this chapter are entirely different from the ones Steel emphasizes. Third, Steel does not address the question of whether the justification of tort law (what I call the "should" question) can satisfy the demands of good normative tort theory. His exploration of the moral necessity of victims' rights of action is compatible with an affirmative answer to this question. By contrast, I defend the opposite conclusion, namely, that ultimately answering the "should" question is not enough.

But this attempt to consider the difference between justification and vindication is unmotivated because we could simply say that we should not care about the vindication of chess to begin with. A justification, on its own, provides much of what we need in terms of reasons to engage (or to refrain from engaging) with chess. This chess detour is meant to emphasize that when the stakes are low, vindication does not pose an interesting question. By contrast, when the stakes are sufficiently high, normative vindication might be called for and, at some point, even required.

By low and high stakes, I mean the interests that are implicated when dealing with the practice at issue (recall, it is not about a particular instance of contemplating whether to play chess but rather about the game itself). These interests may be implicated in both negative and positive ways, and they may be "tethered" to the participants themselves or to third parties. Concerning chess, the stakes are typically low in the sense that the lack of it (i.e., not inventing, playing, or supporting the game) does not harm the interests of third parties—bystanders and others, including future generations—who are not involved in the game itself. Nor does it lead supporters to incur substantial setbacks given the availability of other (present or future) attractive strategy games.

Now consider the opposite case, namely, practices whose implications demand vindication, rather than merely justification. I begin with the paradigm case—war—and then move to an example closer to torts—private property. Normative theories of war often employ the language of justification. Just war theory is perhaps the most celebrated example. However, language can be misleading here. Justifications of war, ranging from pacifism to just war theories, are all about normative vindication. On the pacifist account, the only live question is whether war can ever be permissible. The answer is negative and, therefore, we have to not-have wars, full stop. On the just war account, we can have wars only when we have to have them. In other words, only those wars that meet highly stringent conditions, especially the "necessity" and the "cause" ones, could be justified: A war must be an option of last resort so that there is no other, less harmful way of averting certain evils. Talk of permission to wage a war or kill in a war might obscure the sense in which the space between the permissible and the obligatory diminishes significantly or even entirely: If it is permissible to wage a deadly war, it must be so because there is a requirement to do so.[12]

Hence, just war theories transform justification into vindication by narrowing the reasons for resorting to war to the bare minimum. We should wage war only because, and only insofar as, we *must* (grudgingly) do so. The reason that justification is not enough and vindication becomes the only game in town returns the argument to the high stakes involved in wars as well as the existence of viable alternatives. Unlike chess, a standard of "must," instead of "should," is a prerequisite

[12] *See* Kieran Oberman, *The Myth of the Optional War: Why States Are Required to Wage the Wars They Are Permitted to Wage*, 43 Phil. & Pub. Aff. 255 (2015).

to any good normative theory of war given the adverse consequences to the lives (et alia) of civilians and participants as well as the wide range of non- and less violent alternatives to war potentially able to avert this evil (such as diplomacy, economic incentives, sanctions, boycotting, and so forth).

War is not just a paradigm case but also an extreme one, and we can say that in wars the stakes are not just high but unusually high. Nothing in the argument turns on the example of war, however, and a case much closer to torts is the institution of private property. Beyond the explanatory ambition of property theory, normative theories widely agree that the task is not merely to ask whether private property is legitimate or its actual values and virtues justified. Rather, the task is vindication—why do we have to have private property rather than other ways of organizing the control over and use of scarce resources in a society?[13] Indeed, anything short of arguing that *this* particular arrangement is necessary, as opposed to *usufruct* or some other watered-down use-based rights, will not do.[14] Again, vindication is called for because the stakes are high: First, private property is a source of inequality and non-freedom on a grand scale; and second, the availability of circumscribed forms of property rights presents alternatives that could alleviate at least some of these adverse consequences.[15] It is time to turn to normative tort theory to understand why vindicating tort law matters.

II. Why Is Vindicating Tort Law Especially Challenging?

Many students and scholars of tort law are interested in rendering it more intelligible. Thus they may engage in explaining, interpreting, and justifying tort law, including by uncovering its underlying values and rationales. Doing so may help us assess our current practices but cannot provide a *normative vindication* of tort law. For some of them, tort law or the idea of tort law is a given, that is, it is something that should be taken at face value. They ask the "is" and "should" questions without claiming that the answers to these questions are also an answer to the "must" question, namely, why have tort law in the first place. Existing tort law, even the ideal prototype version, can be good or bad, but the normative vindication of tort law aims deeper. The stakes are high as the interests that tort law gives effect or responds to are among the most fundamental ones—life and limb, emotional well-being, privacy, reputation, and property. Moreover, a number of suitable ways

[13] For instance, Marx and Engel's Communist Manifesto calls for the abolition of private property. That said, Marx accepts rights to what he calls *personal* property (note that he did *not* mean personal as the inverse of real property). *See* Avihay Dorfman, *Private Ownership*, 16 Legal Theory 1, 12–15 (2010).

[14] *See further id.*, at 3–10.

[15] For more on the moral requirement of circumscribing private property in the face of its adverse consequences (in terms of distributive and relational injustices), see Hanoch Dagan, A Liberal Theory of Property 4, 5, 49, 69, 199 (2021).

for protecting these interests is available, consistent with the liberal commitment to freedom and equality, as discernable both in actual practice and abstract speculation. Tort law, that "cumbrous and expensive machinery,"[16] is anything but sui generis. It is closer to war or to private property than to chess in this respect. A justificatory project, I argue, cannot answer the basic question: Why have tort law? By contrast, vindication is required.

What makes the normative vindication of tort law especially challenging and interesting? In particular, there are two questions that, separately, require us to address the vindication question of whether we must have tort law. The first asks whether tort law represents the most rational way to do whatever it is supposed to be doing (say, correcting injustice, providing satisfaction to victims, or instilling optimal deterrence). The second concerns the nature of the value that tort law is identified with: Is tort law in the business of preventing certain forms of human failing, or is it a legal institution whose fundamental function is to construct (and, at times, facilitate) valuable forms of interaction? Roughly, the former takes stock of the form peculiar to tort law, what I will call the *tort-law way* of solving problems (whatever they are), whereas the latter asks a functional question, namely, what *kind* of problems is tort law expected to address? The two are mutually reinforcing: Not only is the tort-law way of doing things questionable, but its emphasis on preventing and addressing human failings further frustrates the vindication of tort law. I take each in turn.

III. The Tort-Law Way of Solving Problems: Skepticism concerning Form

The challenge underlying the vindication of tort law cannot begin without first appreciating how tort law presents itself, and how it operates in the world. We may be so used to it that we find tort law almost natural, but there is nothing natural or obvious in a human-created institution with a complex set of rules such as tort law. The worry is twofold: Why tort *law* and why *tort* law. The first pertains to the legal as opposed to ethical, social, political, and other extralegal rules and institutions. Why should *law* be deemed indispensable to the task of preventing or addressing certain forms of human interaction? The second concern touches on the specific legal form—the *tort* form. Even if we assume that law must be part of the solution to the problems we face, why look for it in *tort* law? In particular, why is it necessary to protect our interest in bodily integrity (et alia) by imposing *directed* or *relational*

[16] Oliver Wendell Holmes, Jr., The Common Law 96 (1991) [1881]. Administering tort law is, indeed, expensive in part because it requires a set of public institutions. This fact about tort law suggests that its vindication must respond (in the right sense) not only to participants but also to those who are required to support it (such as taxpayers). *See* Filipe Jimenez, *Justifying Private Law*, *in* 2 Oxford Studies in Private Law Theory 1 (Paul B. Miller & John Oberdiek eds., 2023).

legal duties that link a duty-ower to a right-holder? For instance, the tort of negligence connects the duty to drive safely and the right of a passerby to safety. Thus, not only is the driver under a legal obligation to conduct herself reasonably but also *owes it to* the passerby, who is thereby viewed as the duty-owner, as opposed to the mere beneficiary of the obligation.[17]

The following examples will serve to illustrate both aspects of the suspicion about tort law—as a form of law in general and in its specific tort version. Suppose that physicians, moved by sincere ethical commitment and reputational concerns, were able to provide better and safer professional help to their patients than the most successful version of tort law could ever ensure. Perhaps in combination with a competitive market for liability insurance, this scheme would also furnish adequate (extralegal) avenues for redressing injuries caused by substandard medical treatment. Famously, lawyer economists argue that in a world with trivial transaction costs, contracting will be the new, and better, tort law. Historically speaking, the contractarian approach has been on display (though in a world with high transaction costs) until the early twentieth-century landmark decisions of *MacPherson v. Buick* and *Donohue v. Stevenson*.[18]

Alternatively, the law could resort to administrative and criminal-law duties that, unlike tort duties, are not owed to specific others but to society as a whole (much like the duties against running a red light and committing treason). Victims of violations of these duties would be entitled to adequate compensation for their injuries from the state. The state would also be in charge of disciplining violators in a perfectly fitting way. Once again, let's suppose that this or any other legal alternative to tort law *could* outperform tort law in protecting these rights and addressing their violations. Certainly, there is no necessary—that is, non-contingent—reason to presume that these or other available or yet-to-be-created substitutes would do worse than tort law in attaining whatever any current tort law is designed to achieve.[19]

Is there a reason for *insisting* on the tort-law way of linking risk-creator and risk-bearer through a legal duty of care and a legal duty of repair? Can friends of freedom—as independence or as autonomy—or friends of efficiency raise serious

[17] In tort law, being a duty owner is reflected in at least two ways. One way is the foreseeability requirement as articulated by Cardozo in *Palsgraf v. Long Island R.R. Co.*, 162 N.E. 99 (N.Y. 1928). A duty of care exists only if the existence of the victim (or victim class) within the zone of danger is reasonably foreseeable. A second way is the doctrine of assumption of risk. Properly conceived, this doctrine grants the right-holder the option to waive the duty owed to her even as the same duty (i.e., with the same content) remains intact with respect to all other foreseeable risk-bearers.

[18] MacPherson v. Buick Motor Co., 111 N.E. 1050 (N.Y. 1916); Donoghue v. Stevenson [1932] A.C. 562 (H.L.) (appeal taken from Scotland).

[19] Some tort-law skeptics may even be willing to go with less than my hypotheticals. *See, e.g.*, David Enoch, *Tort Liability and Taking Responsibility*, *in* Philosophical Foundations of the Law of Torts 250, 250–51 (John Oberdiek ed., 2014); Alon Harel, *Theories of Rights*, *in* Blackwell's Guide to the Philosophy of Law and Legal Theory 191 (Martin P. Golding & William Edmundson eds., 2005).

objections to any of the ideal situations described?[20] One might protest that this may (arguably) be a fair question to ask about negligence law but less appropriate to intentional torts such as battery (dealing with instances such as punching an innocent person in the face). Yet, it is possible to imagine a society where a combination of ethical commitment, reputation, and social (nonlegal) pressure would parallel the most successful version ever of the tort law of battery (or, for that matter, any other tort). Should we then care that there is no relational legal duty to respect bodily integrity, that is, a legal duty owed to and owned by potentially every single member of society?

One possible answer would be that some kind of value is involved in the tort "relation" and tort duties are necessary to uphold it. But is there? The suspicion only grows stronger when you pause to reflect on the typical connection between a tort duty-ower and a right-holder. The relational cast of tort-law duties puts additional normative pressure on the "why tort law" question precisely because the merely *juridical* relations established by these duties are, in some sense, too coincidental and inconsequential to bear the weight of vindication.[21]

Two properties of juridical relations created by tort duties make tort law an appealing proving ground for the skeptic, both concerning why tort *law* and why *tort* law. The first is that, paradigmatically, tort relations are *fleeting*. Relations of driver/passenger in negligence, assailant/victim in assault and battery, factory/nearby resident in nuisance, and many other interpersonal clashes lack substantive quality or value. Contrary to duties that arise in connection with a valuable relationship, one that we might want to be part of and maintain, typical tort duties are only "loosely relational," as the reasons for their existence do not turn on the value of preexisting relationships between duty-owers and their beneficiaries.[22] The fleeting and loosely relational relationships pave the way for a second property: These are relationships of *forbearance*.[23] Thus, the subject matter of the juridical match between my duty to drive safely and your right to safety is to avoid one another. It is thus not surprising (but indefensible, as I argue in Chapter 6 and

[20] As I argue in Chapter 11, modern Kantians' resort to freedom as independence may not account for core segments of tort law, namely, instances of inadvertent wrongdoing governed by the law of negligence and the rule of no-liability for nonfeasance. *See also* Avihay Dorfman, *The Independence of Tort Law*, 44 L. & PHIL. 653 (2025). Hence, I will argue that there are reasons to be skeptical about the ability of Kantian independence to vindicate tort law and, in particular, its peculiar way of establishing juridical relationships of forbearance (and the grounds for tort law's reluctance to impose affirmative duties).

[21] *See* John Gardner, *Dagan and Dorfman on the Value of Private Law*, 117 COLUM. L. REV. ONLINE 179, 192–93 (2017); Gregory C. Keating, *The Priority of Respect over Repair*, 18 LEGAL THEORY 293, 321 (2012); Dilan A. Esper & Gregory C. Keating, *Putting "Duty" in Its Place: A Reply to Professors Goldberg and Zipursky*, 41 LOY. L.A. L. REV. 1225, 1250 (2008) ("treating duty as strongly relational tends to corrode the generality of duty doctrine"). Even defenders of the relational significance of tort law are acutely aware of this challenge. *See, e.g.*, RIPSTEIN, *supra* note 5, at 81; John Oberdiek, *It's Something Personal: On the Relationality of Duty and Civil Wrongs*, *in* CIVIL WRONGS AND JUSTICE IN PRIVATE LAW 301 (Paul B. Miller & John Oberdiek eds., 2020).

[22] JOHN GARDNER, FROM PERSONAL LIFE TO PRIVATE LAW 50 (2018).

[23] Gardner, *supra* note 21, at 192.

elsewhere[24]) that leading corrective justice theorists go a step further and argue that *affirmative* tort duties, including duties of rescue that are anything but forbearance, are flatly inconsistent with the demands of (corrective) justice.[25]

This characterization of tort duties as governing fleeting relationships of forbearance can be contrasted with contractual relations.[26] Contracting may surely revolve around trivial matters (say, buying a soda can from a superstore) but does require both parties to form intentions and, in particular, *interlocking intentions* in favor of engaging in a reciprocal exchange.[27] To this extent, contractual relations differ from the fleeting relations prevalent in tort law. Contractual relations are chosen, self-imposed obligations and their very point is a form of engagement with, rather than forbearance of, others.

Saying that tort duties involve fleeting relations of forbearance does not mean that these relations are not valuable.[28] They are.[29] However, it does invite the suspicion that their value is purely *instrumental.* It could be argued that all that is required is to ensure protection from risks such as those generated by irresponsible driving. Hence, it is not surprising that the relational structuring of tort duties, and especially the duty of care in the tort of negligence, has been a subject of constant debate, including "Duty Wars."[30] With the arrival of the Third Restatement of Torts,[31] these debates reflect the suspicion that the tort-law way of linking duties and rights is simply a legal technology whose merits should *ultimately* be assessed vis-à-vis other possible technologies of safety.[32] Some such technologies may be legal, others may draw on extralegal practices, while yet others may combine both.

[24] *See also* Hanoch Dagan & Avihay Dorfman, Relational Justice: A Theory of Private Law ch. 6 (2024).

[25] Weinrib, *supra* note 9, at 10; Peter Benson, *Misfeasance as an Organizing Normative Idea in Private Law*, 60 U. Toronto L.J. 731 (2010); Ripstein, *supra* note 5, at 54.

[26] On the relational dimension of property rights, see Avihay Dorfman, *The Society of Property*, 62 U. Toronto L.J. 563 (2012).

[27] *See* Daniel Markovits, *Contract and Collaboration*, 113 Yale L.J. 1417, 1461–62 (2004). Certainly, there are several ways of explaining what such an exchange requires and nothing in my argument turns on siding with one of them.

[28] *Contra* Percy H. Winfield, *Duty in Tortious Negligence*, 34 Colum. L. Rev. 41, 48–51, 65–66 (1934) (arguing that duty in the law of torts is the upshot of historical accident); Tony Weir, *Suicide in Custody*, 57 Cambridge L.J. 241, 242–43 (1998) ("The function of duty concept at common law is to conduce to an apparent rationalization of a decision, reached on other grounds, that a defendant must—or need not—pay for harm suffered by the plaintiff").

[29] *See* Hanoch Dagan & Avihay Dorfman, *Postscript to Just Relationships: Reply to Gardner, West, and Zipursky*, 117 Colum. L. Rev. Online 261, 263 (2017).

[30] *Compare* W. Jonathan Cardi & Michael D. Green, *Duty Wars*, 81 S. Cal. L. Rev. 671, 714–19 (2008) *with* Ernest J. Weinrib, *The Disintegration of Duty*, *in* Exploring Tort Law 143 (M. Stuart Madden ed., 2005); Ripstein, *supra* note 5, at 81; Benjamin C. Zipursky, *Foreseeability in Breach, Duty, and Proximate Cause*, 44 Wake Forest L. Rev. 1247, 1258–60 (2009); John C. P. Goldberg & Benjamin C. Zipursky, *The Moral of MacPherson*, 146 U. Pa. L. Rev. 1733 (1998).

[31] Restatement (Third) of Torts: Liab. for Physical Harm §§6–7 (2010). The Restatement notes that "Except in unusual categories of cases in which courts have developed no-duty rules, an actor's duty to exercise reasonable care does not require attention from the court." *Id.*, at § cmt. *b*.

[32] *See, e.g.*, Edwards v. Honeywell, Inc., 50 F.3d 484, 487 (7th Cir. 1995) (Posner, C. J.) (wondering "[w]hy duty should be an issue in a negligence case is not altogether clear, however").

One way out for the noninstrumentalist is to emphasize cases in which tort duties are associated with *special* relationships, including voluntary undertakings and role-based relations (e.g., teacher/pupil).[33] This strategy, however, seeks to beef up the juridical relationship by drawing on preexisting or supervening relationships. It thereby sidesteps the worry that, *generally*, tort duties are fleeting relations of forbearance. Justifying the tort-law way of solving problems, therefore, is not enough. The challenge for normative tort theory is to explain why we must have directed or relational tort-law duties.

A promising way of meeting this challenge, as I argue in Chapter 12, is to argue that tort duties construct egalitarian frameworks of interaction between private persons. These frameworks matter because they make possible a certain form of human interaction that I call relating as agents. I argue that doing so depends on having legal duties with the following dual nature: On the one hand, these duties must be *publicly* mandated and fixed, which means that these duties arise independently of an actual or hypothetical contract; on the other hand, these duties must be *privately* owed and owned. Simply put, tort duties must be imposed and their content determined by operation of law, rather than choice, and the responsibility for discharging them must fall to private persons, rather than public officials (or to the community). The argument is that a tort-law duty is constitutive of the ability of parties to relate in subsequent voluntary transactions as agents. Tort duties, those which protect our fundamental interests (say, in bodily integrity), are not the residue or leftovers of contract but rather contract's foundation; without tort duties, there is no contract.[34] The next stage of the argument adds another, no less important challenge to the vindication of tort law.

IV. Tackling Negative Value: Skepticism concerning Function

What *kind* of value underlies tort law? This is a preliminary or metaethical question. Rather than seeking to identify a specific substantive value, it seeks to characterize it as negative or positive. To be sure, a value is a good, be it negative or positive one. That said, a negative value concerns the realization of good (say,

[33] *See* Goldberg & Zipursky, *supra* note 30, at 1829 (emphasizing the "relationship-sensitivity" of the duty while defending the relational foundations of the duty across different categories of negligence law). Courts often emphasize this, too. *See, e.g.*, Marshall v. Burger King Corp., 856 N.E.2d 1048, 1057 (Ill. 2006) (the "touchstone" of a duty analysis is "to ask whether a plaintiff and a defendant stood in such a relationship to one another that the law imposed upon the defendant an obligation of reasonable conduct for the benefit of the plaintiff"); Coates v. Southern Md. Electric, 731 A.2d 931, 936 (Md. 1999) (noting that a relationship between the parties is "inherent … in the concept of duty."); Huston v. Konieczny, 556 N.E.2d 505, 508 (Oh. 1990) ("In tort law, whether a defendant owes a duty to a plaintiff depends upon the relationship between them").

[34] The contrary argument, that tort duties are the residue or leftovers of contract, is most famously defended by the economic analysis of tort law. It is also endorsed in Ronald Dworkin, Law's Empire 295 (1986).

protecting freedom) by avoiding evil, which in the case of tort law means certain forms of human failing.[35] For instance, vaccines may make the world a better place in the negative sense of preventing certain infectious diseases. Positive value, by contrast, concerns the realization of good by creating (or helping to bring about) good, as in forming friendships. To get at the heart of this distinction, consider the following question: Need we worry about tort law ceasing to be, or might we actually wish that? I wish to show that we should wish that tort law ceases to exist if, and only if, tort law deals solely with the realization of negative value.

To begin with, there are two ways to understand this question. Instrumentalists answer that we need not worry because tort law is merely one technology among others.[36] If an all-things-considered better system becomes available for attaining whatever tort law purportedly seeks to achieve—justice, compensation, recourse, optimal deterrence, et alia—then its loss is no reason for concern. It is as simple as that.

Yet, there is a subtler and more demanding way of understanding this question. At first glance, the answer of those who reject instrumentalism regarding tort law, meaning those who (rightly) believe that tort law is a "repository of moral reasoning"[37] about principles and values, can simply be expected to be contrary to the answer given by instrumentalists. For them, tort law is constitutive of certain valuable things. Kantian theories of corrective justice, for example, take tort law to be constitutive of a rightful condition in which persons can interact on terms of equal independence. More generally, as Gardner observes, corrective justice theorists believe that tort law is constitutive of a certain moral principle of corrective justice.[38] Moreover, civil recourse theory identifies a different constitutive relationship, namely, between tort law's right of action and freedom, saying: "A free person—the opposite of a slave—is . . . one who is not left powerless to respond to violations of rights granted to her by law."[39]

Noninstrumentalists, however, confront a challenge here. If tort law addresses negative value—that is, if its moral aim is that of tackling certain forms of human failure—then the reason for having it is *necessarily dependent, and to this extent contingent, on the absence of other, more effective ways of realizing this negative value*. To render this point vivid, consider two paradigm cases: private nuisance and battery.

Begin with nuisance and, in particular, live-and-let-live disputes between neighbors. Familiar examples might be a cement plant causing substantial dust

[35] For more on negative value, see Joseph Raz, *The Rule of Law and Its Virtue*, *in* The Authority of Law: Essays on Law and Morality 210, 224 (1979).
[36] This is well captured in the title of Leon Green's famous article, *Tort Law Public Law in Disguise*, 38 Tex. L. Rev. 1 (1959).
[37] Weinrib, *supra* note 9, at 10.
[38] Gardner, *supra* note 6, at 28, 44, 52.
[39] Goldberg & Zipursky, *supra* note 2, at 129–30.

and noise to nearby neighbors or a physician complaining that his neighbor, a confectioner, uses large mortars, the noise and vibration of which pass through a common wall right to the physician's consulting room.[40] Noninstrumentalists have to acknowledge that both are the outgrowth of either ill-conceived zoning laws or deficient technologies of noise- and vibration-cancelling. No such disputes would have occurred had proper land-use regulation been in place. Essentially, we can engineer our way out of conflicting land uses. So, yes, nuisance law is (arguably) constitutive of the ability of neighbors to interact as free and equal persons; and (let's assume) having a right of action against a nuisance creator is constitutive of the victim's freedom.[41] That said, we have no reason to constitute or even secure all these valuable things if a better way—on all conceivable fronts—of addressing the imperfections that make nuisance disputes possible in the first place becomes available. For instance, the shift from tents to buildings as places of dwelling instantly preempted many instances of private nuisance among neighbors. More generally, no one would, and certainly no one should, insist on keeping alive these nuisance disputes if proper zoning regulations and/or adequate technology could easily dissolve them. The mere fact that tort law possesses its own internal moral logic or the possibility that it is noninstrumentally valuable, perhaps because it is constitutive of corrective justice or civil recourse, does not matter in a nuisance-free world. This conclusion is a straightforward implication of saying that tort law is tasked with realizing negative value.

Now consider battery. H. L. A. Hart invites us to imagine a world where we would be invulnerable due to some technological improvement in the armory industry. Will the law of battery or of murder survive this improvement?[42] Consider Arthur Ripstein's response to this thought experiment. Ripstein, who argues that "[t]ort law is a system that not only protects but *constitutes* each person's entitlement to use their bodies and property,"[43] resists the redundancy charge by arguing that "Hart's [invulnerable creatures] might have little temptation to trespass on each other, but if they did so, they would do wrong, because they would use one another for ends they did not share."[44]

[40] *See* Boomer v. Atlantic Cement Co., 257 N.E.2d 870 (N.Y. 1970); Sturges v. Bridgman 11 Ch. D. 852 (C.A. 1879), respectively.

[41] I grant these views for the sake of the argument. I take stock of the categorical importance of the *victim*'s right of action in Chapter 5. *See also* Hanoch Dagan, Avihay Dorfman, & Issi Rosen-Zvi, *It's (Not All) Personal: Civil Litigation and the Values of Rights of Action*, 75 Am. U. L. Rev. (forthcoming 2026); Hanoch Dagan & Avihay Dorfman, *From Civil Recourse to Class Action: A Comment on John Goldberg & Benjamin Zipursky's Recognizing Wrongs*, 27 Jerusalem Rev. Legal Stud. 57, 60 (2023).

[42] H. L. A. Hart, *Positivism and the Separation of Law and Morals*, 71 Harv. L. Rev. 593, 623 (1958)

[43] *See* Ripstein, *supra* note 5, at 7–8.

[44] Arthur Ripstein, Force and Freedom: Kant's Legal and Political Philosophy 68 (2009). Ripstein's discussion of the Hartian thought experiment is meant to highlight Kant's approach to theory construction—beginning with the metaphysics of the thing (say, property) and only then consider the context in which it is applied (say, scarcity, vulnerability). That said, I take the significance of Ripstein's

This response is unpersuasive in two ways. In the first place, the emphasis on "but if they did [trespass on each other]" merely explains *away* Hart's thought experiment. More dramatically, instead of refuting the redundancy charge, Ripstein capitulates to the Hartian suspicion that there is no *positive* value in the law of battery except for dealing with various forms of human failing (i.e., preventing the negative). A better way of refuting the redundancy charge is to show that the law of battery still stands for a value *apart from* addressing pathologies or failures. I take up battery law in more detail in Chapters 3 and 5 and show that the right response to Hart's redundancy charge should have been that this body of law could be a source of positive and not merely negative value. Battery law can facilitate (and even bring about) inherently valuable conflicts. On this account, the underlying value of battery law is positive in that it makes possible valuable forms of human interaction (such as those involving contact sports and empathetic gestures among friends and intimates). But there is no way out of the Hartian challenge if, instead, tort law is saddled with a negative value. This is because the value of tort law is necessarily dependent on having a prior reason, which Hart's thought experiment preempts, to care about instantiating it. As Hart's thought experiment preempts this reason, tort law becomes redundant.

Indeed, signing up for the preventative task means that the answer to the question of need we worry, or might we even wish, that tort law cease to be is that we might, or even should, wish that tort law cease to be. This is precisely what the logic of engaging with negative value implies. Indeed, a smallpox immunization was immensely valuable back in the day (to be sure, it was not constitutive of freedom or even of life itself but it was surely a matter of life and death for all too many people). The complete extinction of the disease pathogen, however, suggests that we now have a reason *against* getting vaccinated for smallpox. Its value, in other words, is wholly dependent on having a prior reason to appreciate its deployment.

I now wish to emphasize two points that return the argument to the distinction between justification and vindication of tort law. Contemporary tort theory identifies the law of torts with negative value. Moreover, the pursuit of such value may not be enough to meet the demands of normative vindication.

Tort theory tends to understand the law of torts in terms of addressing certain forms of human failing and their fallout. This view is so natural in the common law tradition that the subject matter—*tort* law—bears this understanding. Note that the label "tort law" stands between two other legal traditions. On the one hand, civil law tradition sometimes views tort law as the law of involuntary obligations, potentially allowing its extension beyond human failings to capture the primacy of the obligation rather than merely its breach. On the other hand, the Jewish law tradition saddles tort law—"Dinay Nezikin" or law of harms—with damages law and so reduces it to bare remedialism.

engagement with Hart to be broader so that it might reveal a deeper idea about Ripstein's conception about the reason for tort law.

Moving beyond semantics, leading scholars often identify tort law with the law of private wrongs, relational injurious wrongs, or simply wrongs.[45] Tort law, it is suggested, instantiates a moral norm of correcting injustices,[46] provides civil recourse for victims against their injurers,[47] tackles serious accidental harms to bodily integrity,[48] communicates the injustice done by the defendant to the plaintiff,[49] and economizes on the social cost of accidents and other risky activities.[50] Even the modern-Kantian view that tort law is constitutive of a rightful condition comes down to the negative value of preventing situations in which persons—say, neighbors caught in a nuisance scenario or potential victims of battery—are unilaterally subordinated to the determining choices of other private persons.

Contrast these ways of approaching the value of tort law with the kind of value underpinning contract. A contract constructs a certain interpersonal framework of mutual engagement that would likely not have occurred otherwise, including collaborations that are either intrinsically or instrumentally valuable to the interacting parties and often to society as a whole.[51] Contract law does that by empowering persons to bring into being new legal rights and obligations to govern their practical affairs going forward. Thereby, contract law sometimes contribute to a *positive* value in the sense that it aims at creating good, rather than tackling human failings.[52] This is not to say that contract law does not deal with human failings, such as breach of contract, bad faith, and unconscionability. Contracting (or promising) itself may even sometimes serve as a way to remedy the promisee's preexisting vulnerability to exploitation by a powerful promisor.[53]

[45] *See* ROBERT STEVENS, TORTS AND RIGHTS 2 (2007); RIPSTEIN, *supra* note 5, at 104; GARDNER, *supra* note 6, at 333, 334; GOLDBERG & ZIPURSKY, *supra* note 2, at 207, 263.

[46] GARDNER, *supra* note 6, at 44. Gardner further embeds his account of the law of torts in the value of protecting people's existing life track by way of granting them "security rights." GARDNER, *supra* note 22, at 183.

[47] John C. P. Goldberg & Benjamin C. Zipursky, *Civil Recourse Defended: A Reply to Posner, Calabresi, Rustad, Chamallas, and Robinette*, 88 IND. L.J. 569, 573 (2013).

[48] Gregory C. Keating, *Is Tort Law "Private"? in* CIVIL WRONGS AND JUSTICE IN PRIVATE LAW 351, 357, 359, 371 (Paul B. Miller & John Oberdiek eds., 2020).

[49] Scott Hershovitz, *Treating Wrongs as Wrongs: An Expressive Argument for Tort Law*, 10(2) J. TORT L. 1, 3, 33, 39 (2018).

[50] R. H. Coase, *The Problem of Social Cost*, 3 J.L. & ECON. 1 (1960); GUIDO CALABRESI, THE COSTS OF ACCIDENTS (1970).

[51] There are, of course, a number of ways to characterize the nature of the contractual framework, say, as a form of coordination between equal persons, as an autonomy-enhancing mechanism of reciprocal assurance, and as a joint welfare maximization framework (et alia). *See* Markovits, *supra* note 27; HANOCH DAGAN & MICHAEL HELLER, THE CHOICE THEORY OF CONTRACT (2017); Robert E. Scott, *A Joint Maximization Theory of Contract and Regulation*, *in* RESEARCH HANDBOOK ON PRIVATE LAW THEORY 22 (Hanoch Dagan & Benjamin Zipursky eds., 2021), respectively. The point I am making, concerning contracting and its positive value, is a general one and does not single out a particular characterization.

[52] I say *sometimes* because even if some contracting is necessary to establishing instrumentally and non-instrumentally valuable relations, it is not clear what the precise scope of the claim is.

[53] See Seana Valentine Shiffrin, *Promising, Intimate Relationships, and Conventionalism*, 117 PHIL. REV. 481, 504 (2008), who is focusing on the significance of promise-making to tackle the ills of power imbalance between the parties (including, in particular, intimate friends).

Of course contract engages with negative value. However, as just explained, it does much more than that. In particular, the moral achievement of contracting is not in addressing breach of contract but rather in facilitating or even empowering parties jointly to create their practical arrangements. We thus need to worry about contract law ceasing to be due to the loss of the activities and human interactions it makes possible. Consequentially, we should not wish for this to happen.[54]

Now consider the connection between engaging with negative value and the distinction I introduced between justification and vindication. Recall that justifying tort law, by which I mean answering the "should" question, only establishes that it belongs in the class of defensible and indeed respectable candidates to carry out the preventative chore. But as I have argued above, tort law is closer to war and private property than to chess so that the *ultimate* normative question it raises is the "must" rather than the "should" question. The stakes that are involved in making and keeping such a legal institution are high. They include our basic and often conflicting interests in freedom, equality, bodily integrity, privacy, reputation, property (et alia). They also involve allocating substantial amount of scarce resources to get the institution of tort law up and running. And precisely because justification (properly conceived) is not enough, tort law calls for its normative vindication, which is an answer to the "must" question of *why* have tort law in the first place.

Identifying tort law with negative value undermines the prospects of its vindication. Tort law's value—in terms of constituting independence, corrective justice, and so on—depends on having a prior reason to tackle certain forms of human failing. Hence, we do not have to have tort law and, certainly, we need not worry, and even wish, that tort law cease to exist. The examples mentioned above (and others) reinforce the view that there is *no* loss in terms of justice or freedom if the problems of human failing to which tort law is a response have fortunately subsided. Indeed, no one has a reason to complain if incredibly "smart cars" would displace entirely the duty of care owed by drivers to their fellow motorists and pedestrians. To be sure, a technological transformation of this sort may surely give rise to some meritorious complaints. But the point is that the elimination of tort law from the practical affairs of motorists is not one of them, *if* tort law is a guardian of negative value only. As I will argue below, however, the condition at issue ('if tort

[54] Can artificial intelligence or some other technological improvement change the analysis? Consider the difference between inventing an armory in the tort-law case and creating a machine-learning/AI program that could displace contracting entirely. The former presents a technological improvement over tort law if, and only if, tort law is identified with negative value. By contrast, the latter is *not* an improvement relative to contracting because a contract is not merely a technology of preference satisfaction. Rather—and here is one way to specify its positive value—contract is a framework of mutual understanding between free and equal agents for which a computer algorithm is not a substitute at all. *See further* Przemyslaw Palka, *Algorithmic Central Planning: Between Efficiency and Freedom*, 83 L. & Cont. Prob. 125 (2020); Hanoch Dagan, *Why Markets? Welfare, Autonomy, and the Just Society*, 117 Mich. L. Rev. 1289 (2019).

law is a guardian of negative value') does not obtain, as tort law may engage with positive value. Accordingly, it *might* meet the challenge of normative vindication.

Indeed, attending to its positive value will mark the first step toward tort law's vindication. It will require an argument to the effect that tort law, contrary to its plain meaning (tort stands for the Latin word 'to twist'), is not reducible to the law of *wrongs (or harms or costs)*, including the law of preventing, rectifying, and redressing wrongs. Hence, a better approach to vindicating tort law would be to argue that there are conflicts that are valuable and that we thereby have to facilitate and, if necessary, even create the conditions for their existence. Tort law on this approach, is the law of conflicts (of a certain kind).

For instance, as I argue in Chapter 8, there are conflicts that nuisance law is required to embrace (within limits). Two familiar instances illustrate this observation. The first involves practicing religious faith in and around suburban residential communities—for instance, church bells and muezzins summoning Christians and Muslims to prayer. The second features protected homes and caring facilities for persons with mental disabilities located in residential districts. Both cases can give rise to allegations of private nuisance. For instance, claims may arise that the exercise of religious faith and the living presence of mentally disabled persons in a residential neighborhood unreasonably interfere (say, noise-wise) with neighbors' ability to use and enjoy their own dwellings. The complaint combines the gravity of the interference with the availability of more suitable locations on which to house the said activities, namely, *non*residential or mixed districts.

It might be tempting to treat such instances as unfortunate accidents (recall the cement plant located near a residential district in *Boomer* and the confectioner living in close proximity to the physician in *Sturges*) brought about by either ill-conceived zoning laws or inadequate technologies of nuisance-abating. However, I will argue that integrating religious ways of life, or welcoming the living presence of people with mental disabilities into everyday society, calls for a very different reaction, normatively speaking, than a conflict whereby your neighbor decides to house her pig in the parlor instead of the barnyard.[55]

Note that the proposed approach does not imply that identifying tort law with positive value necessarily secures vindication. Perhaps there are different ways to respond to, and indeed realize positive values, and tort law is just one of them. My response is that tort law is best viewed as *constitutive* of the positive value with which it is associated. Thus, tort law is not merely one instrument out of many for bringing about a positive value. Instead, it plays the noncontingent role of bringing about and sustaining interactions, whose merit is partially *dependent on* the (primary and secondary) rights and duties established in particular by tort law.

[55] *See* Village of Euclid v. Amber Realty Co., 272 U.S. 365, 388 (1926).

Note, moreover, that the vindication of tort law does not entail an argument that the state (or the relevant political authority, more generally) has an obligation to provide us with every aspect of existing tort law, be it the tort law of this or that jurisdiction. In fact, vindicating tort law does not entail an obligation to provide us with *any* such aspect of our (or others') existing law of torts. Instead, the argument from vindication treats actual tort law as a universe of ideas concerning what to make of conflicting interests between free and equal persons. Therefore, the argument from vindication establishes that the state meets its obligation only insofar as it provides us with rules for the governing of some of these conflicts. The grounds for selecting the appropriate class of conflicts have to do with the moral importance of the *interests* in question—as I argue in the next chapter, these will have to be interests that are crucial to our ability to interact as free and equal agents. They also have to do with the value of the *conflicts* between these morally important interests—conflicts that are of positive value. It means that the vindication of tort law does not rule out the resort to other legal and extralegal arrangements in order to supplement tort law, or even supplant parts of it, as long as these other arrangements do not undermine the tort law that we must have.

Concluding Remarks

A successful vindication of tort law establishes why tort law must matter. It can also both illuminate desirable currents in contemporary law, on the one hand, and identifies, and corrects for, doctrinal shortcomings, on the other. As argued in these pages, the vindication of tort law faces two basic challenges: The peculiar, tort-law way of doing things and the negative value with which it is often saddled.

The rest of the book provides a sustained attempt to address these challenges. Concerning the latter, functional challenge, an appealing way forward will be that of identifying the positive value that is, and should be, at the moral center of tort law. Thus, the task will be to demonstrate that valuable conflicts, properly conceived, could exist and that tort law is required to create the conditions necessary for them to arise. Concerning the former, formal challenge, I will defend a conception of relational equality that bears the burden of explaining both why tort *law* and why *tort* law, that is, why have the peculiar tort duty instead of other legal ways of protecting interests and why insist on legal, as opposed to equally effective extralegal, ordering. Tort duties, on this approach, construct egalitarian frameworks of interaction between private persons. They make possible a certain form of interpersonal standing that is a prerequisite to the ability of persons to participate in subsequent voluntary (e.g., contractual) transactions as free and equal agents.[56] I argue, with an eye to the public/private distinction that animates important parts of legal and political theory, that tort duties are fundamentally public in that their existence and content must, rather than may, be provided by operation of law; that said, they are at the same time fundamentally private in that the responsibility to discharge them must, rather than may, fall to private persons. Only thus can the egalitarian ideal of relating as agents (and, ultimately, as substantively equals) be actualized. In that, the equality theory is a beginning of a theoretical synthesis of my two earlier studies of the value of "the public" and the value of "the private."[57]

[56] The two ways just sketched must also be shown to hang together in a coherent fashion, as already explained in the Introduction. I take up this challenge in Chapters 12–15.
[57] *See* Avihay Dorfman & Alon Harel, Reclaiming the Public (2024) and Dagan & Dorfman, *supra* note 24, respectively.

PART II

THE CONFLICT THEORY OF TORT LAW

2

The Conflict Theory

Foundations

Introduction

The answer to the question of "why tort law" begins with identifying the substantive and structural problems that give us reason to have tort law in the first place. It is only after establishing this much that the argument can proceed to exploring whether or not solving these problems requires tort law in particular and, moreover, what substantive rules and doctrines are required. The ambition of the present chapter is to identify, and develop a characterization of, the problems to which tort law is a response.

By thinking about tort law in terms of a "response," I mean that the legal rights, duties, liabilities, and remedies that tort law recognizes and imposes are normative answers to the question of how to cope with conflicts of interests. I argue that giving effect to these rights (et alia) depends on a certain theory of conflict. Coping with conflicts is not reducible to curing them. Indeed, a key insight underlying the conflict theory is that the near-universal consensus among tort theorists that tort law is the law of wrongs, harms, or cost-internalization should be rejected precisely because it identifies tort law with one or another curing mechanism. While curing conflicts is certainly an important mission, it is not the only one. Furthermore, curing is not the most significant one, normatively speaking. Along with offering a cure for conflicts, tort law engages in containing conflicts and, most importantly for the vindication of tort law to succeed, constructing the conditions for some conflicts to arise.

I argue that *the most fundamental distinction* underlying tort law—viz., the law governing interactions between private persons by way of determining and imposing directed duties—is given by three different ways of approaching human conflict. Some interpersonal conflicts are inherently valuable, others are only tolerably valuable, and yet others are valueless. Accordingly, the *first virtue* of tort law is that of responding to conflicts in the right way. As I show in Chapters 3–10, doing so turns on determining the rights, duties, liabilities, and remedies that best fit the kind of value (or disvalue) that underlies the conflict at issue. Before I take up this lead, I wish to introduce the conflict theory by presenting its basic pillars: Interests, conflicts, values, and legal rights. I then illustrate how these four pillars interact by reference to the interest in our own good name.

Conflict between Equals. Avihay Dorfman, Oxford University Press. © Oxford University Press 2026.
DOI: 10.1093/9780198979869.003.0005

I. Fundamental Interests: Prepolitical and Extrajuridical

A *theory* of conflict among primarily private (and natural[1]) persons underlies the acts and consequences falling under the purview of tort law.[2] Conflict, to be sure, need not mean a Hobbesian condition of war of all against all (although it could involve small-scale versions such as a brutal attack on an innocent patron in a bar[3]). Rather, it affects the less extravagant, everyday encounters among private persons. My plan to cross the street and your plan to drive your car might come into conflict. So too your plan to offer a job to a talented risk-analyst who happens to provide me, in a contract, exclusive consulting services may conflict with my interests. My desire to enjoy peaceful weekends on my porch conflicts with the practice of muezzins summoning Muslims to prayer or the ringing of Church bells. Likewise, my writing of a newspaper article containing some controversial allegations against an aspiring labor-union leader may conflict with this person's interest (and the interests of the workers).

Precisely what is meant by conflict, among whom, and over what? The conflict theory concerns conflicts of interests and, in particular, what can be called *fundamental* interests. They are fundamental in two senses. First, they are brute interests, that is, prepolitical and extrajuridical, at least at their core. We all have an interest in our own physical and emotional integrity, self-expression, self-determination, voluntary valuable human interaction (ranging from friendship to collaboration, association, and community), good name, privacy, material well-being, using the outdoors, and knowledge, to name few straightforward interests.[4]

[1] Throughout, I focus on tort law as it applies to individuals acting in their capacity as private persons, rather than citizens or public officials. Moreover, I consider natural, rather than incorporated, artificial persons (such as corporations). The exclusion of business torts involving only corporations follows from the conflict theory's concern with fundamental interests and the value of the conflicts between them. *Cf.* Hanoch Dagan, Avihay Dorfman, & Katharina Pistor, The Liberal Firm (unpublished manuscript).

[2] I say *primarily private persons* in recognition of the fact that tort law may also take up conflicts involving public officials and state institutions (as risk-creators and, less frequently, as victims, on which see Ehud Guttel & Ariel Porat, *Tort Liability and the Risk of Discriminatory Government*, 87 U. Chi. L. Rev. 1, 7–13 (2020)). Some tort theorists believe that this possibility makes it implausible to develop a successful theory of tort law as the law of involuntary obligations among *private* persons. *See* Paul B. Miller & Jeff Pojanowski, *Torts Against the State*, *in* Civil Wrongs and Justice in Private Law 323 (Paul B. Miller & John Oberdiek, eds., 2020). This claim, however, turns on the assumption that the best way to account for tort law is by invoking the *common denominator* methodology.

[3] In fact, one of the most penetrating observations made by Hobbes is that the state of nature exhibits a continuum, ranging from the core case of a state of nature all the way to our modern statist condition. As Hobbes observes, "when taking a journey he [i.e., we included] arms himself and seeks to go well accompanied, when going to sleep he locks his doors, when even in his house he locks his chests, and this when he knows there be laws and public officers." Thomas Hobbes, Leviathan ch. 13 (Richard Tuck ed., 1996). The idea, that I emphatically reject, that tort law sublimates a Hobbesian state of war into civil-law disputes is developed in Joel Levine, Tort Wars (2018).

[4] This framework is rooted in the liberal ideal of substantive freedom (or individual autonomy). It does not take the further step of grounding the interests at issue in human flourishing. Autonomous persons must have these interests secured (in some, nontrivial measure), but they do not have to utilize them according to the dictates of human flourishing or in some other virtuous way.

We also have somewhat inchoate fundamental interests in getting our fair share of the benefits and burdens of cooperation with other persons and, more abstractly, in being treated with some care and respect by our fellow creatures, including *independently* of political or even social associations. Indeed, I take it that all else being equal, we cannot harm or subordinate other persons even in a stateless condition. Unlike our good name or physical integrity, inchoate interests may need further elaboration and, most importantly, what can be called institutional instantiation. For instance, sometimes our fundamental interest in relating to others as equals cannot be specified apart from the particular social practice that governs our interactions with these others. Some of these social practices are not prepolitical in any interesting way. Instead, law may be formative of some practices. For instance, private property, incorporation, and employment are legal and social institutions that construct (in the sense of bringing into existence) the normative landscape with which to determine what counts as relating as equals and, further, facilitate the pursuit of the self-determining life.

The second sense of "fundamental" is that the interests at issue are truly basic, normatively speaking. Indeed, what unites these interests is that they are constitutive elements of being in the world as free and equal persons.[5] They reflect what we need qua private individuals, and they are derivable from the conception of the human being as a free and equal person. Thus, these interests are essential for both leading an autonomous life and relating to others as equals.

Furthermore, talk of interests should be contrasted with legal rights, on the one hand, and with preferences or tastes, on the other. Fundamental interests preexist legal rights in the simple, prepolitical sense just mentioned. In fact, as I argue below, they provide the normative grounds for such rights. And because they are fundamentally important to our being free and equal persons, they not only preexist legal rights but rather also *survive* them. The case for survival arises when the law assigns rights that knowingly or inadvertently undermine fundamental interests. For instance, rights of free speech often conflict with the interests we all have in our emotional well-being and good name. For instance, tort law often recognizes (and, as I argue presently, should recognize) a right to make certain defamatory statements even when, and sometimes precisely because, they undermine the interest of their targets in maintaining their good names. The fact that other people are legally entitled to harm one's good name or feelings does not annihilate one's interests. Rather, it *limits* what one is entitled to do by way of restraining these other people, ex ante, and reacting against them, ex post. Thus, although one does not and should not engage in silencing people who are exercising their rights

[5] This conclusion seems to resonate with any number of liberal theories of value. It further informs liberal political theories of justice (e.g., John Rawls's early account of justice) because any attempt to decide what justice requires depends, to some extent, on earlier views concerning what *might* make people's lives go well. In Rawlsian terms, these views add up to a thin theory of the good.

of free speech, the interests in maintaining one's good name and emotional integrity may still give one a perfectly valid *reason* to feel offended, to want to clear one's name, and to resent the speaker for the harm done. An interest survives not only in the obvious sense that one is not under any legal duty at all to abstain from doing and feeling all of these feelings. Rather, having a legitimate reason to resent others and to feel deeply offended (et alia) means that there is no *moral* duty to refrain from so doing or feeling.

Interests should also be contrasted with preferences. The latter are deeply subjective depending on our tastes and whims. Interests, by contrast, are objectively given. Our bodily integrity, sociability, good name (et alia) are, in some measure, preference-resilient. Moreover, unlike preferences, which may be illicit, interests are necessarily of (some) value. For example, a preference for lying does not align with the fundamental interest in self-expression, even though it could align with other interests, such as that of saving the life of your loved one in the famous murderer-at-the-door dilemma.

I do not argue that interests are necessarily inalienable. Rather, the argument is that interests stand apart from preferences in the sense that their value is not determined by the sheer willingness of their holders to trade them for material gains. Interests represent "features" of being a person that should not be treated as commodities whose fate is determined at the bargaining table. Tort law precedes contracts in the order of justification. These features must figure as constraints on, rather than the upshots of, choice because they are necessary *pre*conditions for human agency. Although life and limb is a paradigm case, tort law also deals with other fundamental interests, such as reputation, free speech, privacy, and certain aspects of liberty of action, including the liberty to use and enjoy the outdoors. They make human agency possible and, so, may not be left to the contractual parties' choosing, at least not in the same way we treat market commodities. Their alienability is, therefore, limited, depending on the satisfaction of certain demanding conditions I discuss in Chapter 12.

Finally, it is important to note that some of the fundamental interests, as understood in conflict theory, are structurally relational—that is, their value makes essential reference to another person (or persons). For example, the interests mentioned above such as privacy, good name, freedom of expression, property, the ability to relate to others as equals, and human interaction are relational in nature: privacy makes essential reference to what others must do or refrain from doing; freedom of expression similarly involves others not interfering with our expressive acts. By contrast, other fundamental interests are not structurally relational, as their value does not depend on what others do or refrain from doing. Interests such as physical and emotional integrity, as well as self-determination, have self-standing value. Analytically speaking, these interests are not relational in form.

That said, synthetically speaking, these interests take on a relational dimension in light of our human condition, specifically the fact of *interdependence*.[6]

[6] *See* Hanoch Dagan & Avihay Dorfman, *Just Relationships*, 116 Colum. L. Rev. 1395, 1415–16 (2016).

Our practical affairs are shaped by interactions with other private persons. This applies not only to deep, ongoing relationships, but also to more superficial, and episodic, encounters with strangers whose conflicting plans may intersect in ways that significantly affect the life, limb, and other fundamental interests of those involved. Moreover, the prevalence of interdependence, it is important to note, is not limited to ongoing relations but also to episodic ones. Against *this* backdrop, even interests such as physical and emotional integrity, and self-determination, acquire a relational character. Section II further explores the human condition and the circumstances that give rise to it.

II. Conflict: A Tripartite Classification

I began with the existence of fundamental interests, which are the object of the conflicts that figure in the conflict theory. What are we to make of the subject of this theory, namely, conflicts? Do they exist, and what explains their existence? My answer is twofold.

One kind of conflict—what I call inherently valuable conflict—is something that we have reason to embrace and want. Talk of embracing and wanting is not meant to convey a psychological description of how we feel about things. Nor is it meant to make a sociological observation of how conflicts are viewed through the lens of this or that culture. After all, people react very differently to conflicts on both personal and communal levels, ranging from conflict aversion to conflict seeking. Instead, the argument is normative: We have *reason* to embrace and want inherently valuable conflict. This reason suggests that tort law must see to it that inherently valuable conflicts exist and indeed thrive, at least to a certain point. Its task does not focus on discrete instances of such conflict but rather on the conditions necessary for such instances to arise in the first place. I shall argue in subsequent chapters that the torts of defamation, intentional infliction of emotional distress, inducement of breach of contract, battery, nuisance, and trespass can do precisely this (among other things). Thus, tort law is required to determine rights and duties so as to construct the conditions necessary for such conflicts to pervade our practical lives. For instance, as I argue in Chapter 8, placing a church, a protected house for the mentally and cognitively disabled, or a halfway house in a residential district ought not to count as nuisance even if (let's assume) the interference at issue can be easily muted by relocating the activities at issue to other areas. Nuisance law (and its regulatory cognates such as zoning law) constructs the conditions necessary for an inherently valuable conflict to arise.

But what about all the other conflicts, that is, those that are not inherently valuable? We have no freestanding reason to construct (or facilitate) them. Instead, our task is to cope with their existence—by containing them, if they are tolerably valuable, and by eliminating them, if valueless. How pervasive are they in our world?

I take it that properly conceived, conflict is a *given* feature of practical life.[7] In particular, it is the outgrowth of the combination of *human nature* given the *human condition*. Human nature may mean different things, but my focus is on the fact that we are creatures who are both reasoning and fallible. As a result, free and equal people hold divergent conceptions of the good life that leads them to pursue divergent ends, including adopting divergent means to bring about these ends. At the same time, however, our fallibility means that people occasionally fail to live up to the demands of right reason, including the demands to respect others, in some ways and to some extent.

The reason why human nature as just described gives rise to conflicts has to do with the human condition, especially the following two: That we live in a *free* society and that our lives are *interdependent* (as opposed to self-sufficient, socially and economically speaking). Thus, the combination of human nature with our human condition generates interpersonal conflicts at different levels and dimensions to be explored below.[8]

A key implication of the preceding observation is that conflicts may occur between persons not only when they occupy the position of the proverbial Holmesian "bad man." Rather, the conflicts that figure most prominently in the conflict theory of torts implicate the "puzzled man"[9] and ultimately even decent law-abiding persons, namely, the ones who recognize the potential tension between their respective interests and *want* to conduct themselves in light of this recognition. The morality of tort law makes its first step by responding to *these* conflicts. Once again, I argue that there are (only) three kinds of them: inherently valuable, tolerably valuable, and valueless conflicts.[10] I take each in turn.

A. Inherently Valuable Conflicts

When basic interests come into conflict, the lawyerly instinct is to view the conflict as a *bad* thing to which the fitting reaction is one of resolving it, or at least seeking to resolve it.[11] In the case of tort law, this instinct has received sophisticated elaborations by different theoretical accounts, such as corrective justice, civil recourse, economic analysis, and Rawlsian theories. The notions that tort law is the

[7] *Cf.* H. L. A. Hart, *Rawls on Liberty and Its Priority*, 40 U. Chi. L. Rev. 534 (1973).

[8] On my account, therefore, interpersonal conflict is one of the circumstances of justice (along with moderate scarcity and certain others). The concept of circumstances of justice has been made familiar by David Hume and, more recently, by John Rawls, A Theory of Justice 109–12 (1971); John Rawls, *Kantian Constructivism in Moral Theory*, 77 J. Phil. 515, 536 (1980); John Rawls, Political Liberalism xvii (1993).

[9] H. L. A. Hart, The Concept of Law 40 (2d ed. 1994).

[10] Valueless conflicts, on this definition, include conflicts that are net disvalue as well.

[11] Lawyers are not alone on this front, to be sure. It seems prevalent among philosophers as well. *See, e.g.*, Seema Eftekhari, *Should All Freedom Be Basic?*, 29 J. Ethics & Soc. Phil. 107, 133 (2024).

law of wrongs, cost-internalization, or of accidental infliction of widespread harm to society compete over the best elaboration of this instinct. That said, I argue that some conflicts are inherently valuable and, so, should not be viewed as constituting a problem that warrants a cure. Indeed, in order for them to realize their value, these conflicts must be engendered, rather than resolved. This is not to say that "engendering" must be limitless; as I argue below, one of the conflicting interests should have only some, rather than lexical priority over the other.[12]

An inherently valuable conflict features a competition between interests that pull in opposite directions, where that "pulling" is integral to viewing the conflict as valuable. More specifically, the conflict is inherently valuable because it is uniquely related to the value at issue. Its unique relation is given by a combination of *implication* and *distinctiveness*: The value is an implication of the conflict and its realization cannot be possible in the absence of the conflict. To this extent, the value is a property that the relevant conflict distinctively possesses.

To illustrate, consider artistic expression that in deep and profound ways challenges long-standing ethical, religious, or political firmly held convictions. Let's assume that in some such instances, the interest in self-expression deals a genuine blow to the emotional well-being and even the dignity of those who hold these convictions. This conflict, I shall argue, is inherently valuable and, so, should not be mitigated, let alone sanitized. It is *valuable* in the sense that it facilitates a certain liberal culture among free and equal agents that I defend in Chapter 3. And it is *inherently* valuable in the sense that the value—liberal culture—is, first, an implication of the conflict and, second, its realization cannot be made possible by creating nonconflictual settings where *both* of the conflicting interests receive the fullest protection possible.

On this understanding of what makes it valuable, I argue that inherently valuable conflicts are ones that, within limits, we all have a reason to want to exist and to some extent thrive. This reason may carry negative implications, such as to avoid eliminating it. It also has affirmative ones, such as to embrace such a conflict at least to some, nontrivial extent by constructing its possibility or facilitating it. Tort law, as I argue presently, does the construction and facilitation by way of determining rights, duties, liabilities, and so on. These rights (et alia) represent normative answers to the question of how to cope with conflicts of interests; to wit, the character and the scope of a tort-law *right* to X (say, emotional well-being) is determined by reference to the value of the conflict between an *interest* in X and its competing interest (say, free expression). Further, what counts as legal wrongdoing is determined against the baseline set by the right to X.

To unpack this characterization—viz., to provide a deeper sense of what the *value* at issue might be and the sense in which a conflict is *inherently*

[12] Lexical priority captures the impermissibility of sacrificing the prime interest for the conflicting one. I reject the lexical priority interpretation in the main text below.

valuable—Chapter 3 will explore three illustrations deliberately drawn from different walks of our practical lives: conflicts of self-expression versus reputation and/or emotional well-being; sociability versus bodily sovereignty; and market competition versus promissory commitment. Chapters 8–9 add other instances of inherently valuable conflicts, analyzed in terms of the legal framework of nuisance, both private and public, and trespass to land. Chapter 10 demonstrates how the category of inherently valuable conflicts helps to illuminate the scope of the (proposed) duty of nondiscrimination. These are illustrations of a broader claim, namely, that some conflicts between the fundamental interests of private persons are inherently valuable.

Integral to the analysis of such conflicts is the delineation of their scope. This is because not every instance of conflict, for example, between free speech and reputation, is necessarily inherently valuable. Further, recall that the priority of one interest over the conflicting one is not one of lexical priority, meaning that the priority of the prime interest does not justify the total negation of the other. As I emphasize in Chapter 7, scope delineation is not an exercise in ad hoc assessment of one instance at a time. Instead, tort law does the delineation in a systematic fashion, constructing legal rules, doctrines, and categories so as to replace resort to ad hoc method with principled determinations.

B. Tolerably Valuable Conflicts

If inherently valuable conflicts give us a reason to embrace or to want them, the category of interpersonal conflicts picks out ones that we have reason to *tolerate*. This is because such conflicts of fundamental interests are the adverse byproducts of otherwise desirable human activities. These conflicts are not inherently valuable. We would have gotten rid of them if only we could, say, by engineering our way out of such conflicts. Therefore the conflict should be left to stand only because, and only insofar as, it is a negative side effect of valuable activities. Tort law's task is to contain this side effect. To get a better sense of the category of tolerably valuable conflicts, consider the following illustrations.

We constantly use products to help us solve problems or advance our ends, anything from using a car to using a chemical compound to clear a clogged drain. Using these and other products is helpful, and at times even consequential to leading a good life. At the same time, however, it can also generate substantial risks to users as well as to bystanders. Using a car puts the liberty of action of the driver in a potential conflict with the safety of other motorists and pedestrians; and manufacturing an effective drain cleaner exerts pressure toward conflict with the physical safety of the user and bystanders. These conflicts can be avoided simply by renouncing driving or refraining from manufacturing drain cleaners. A better way to eliminate them is to introduce technological innovations that would make driving or drain clearing risk-free. However, the former is undesirable whereas the latter is, at this point, infeasible. Therefore, these conflicts should be allowed in one way or another, assuming, as I do, that driving and manufacturing drain cleaners is desirable (in different ways and for different reasons, of course). Notice that there is nothing inherently valuable in conflicts arising out of using cars and drain cleaners. We can say that they are tolerable side effects of desirable activities. Further, their tolerability is purely *contingent* on the absence of alternative means to engage in these activities without producing such conflicts.

The history of tort law dealing with tolerable interpersonal conflicts renders vivid the contingency dimension. In particular, conflicts that seemed at a certain point inevitable have either disappeared or eroded significantly. For instance, the question of railroad liability for fires had figured prominently in real-life cases and in the first generation of economic analysis of tort law. Such liability concerns a conflict generated by steam trains emitting sparks in the vicinity of crops and buildings. The interests underlying both activities (railroading and agriculture) were sufficiently important to justify some mechanism of containing—rendering tolerable—the conflict they produced. One such mechanism was the legal standard of reasonable care, focusing the law's attention on the precautions that either party ought to have taken. Implementing spark arresters and reducing speed in the face of dry weather and high wind were often required; farmers, on their end, were deemed contributory negligent, say, for spreading loose cotton to dry within a striking distance from a railroad track.[13] The interpersonal conflict at issue was tolerable but only contingently so.

Now that steam engines are no longer in use, the conflict's adverse consequences can no longer be deemed tolerable unless, of course, when used for educational purposes—say, as part of an interactive exhibition at a railroad museum. Sometimes, however, technological innovation does not make the conflict disappear. Instead, it erodes the conflict dramatically by transforming its nature. Thus, the use of explosives can be desirable if done for civilian tunneling purposes. But at the same time it creates serious risks, including risks that are beyond the control of professionals exercising reasonable care. Such was the case with transporting nitroglycerine, an easily detonated explosive liquid used for tunneling and mining during the nineteenth century. Alfred Nobel's innovation reduced, although it did not eliminate, precisely this risk by mixing the nitroglycerine liquid with dynamite powder. Contemporary explosive materials, such as RDX and C-4, virtually eliminate this (i.e., transporting-generated) risk. But the improvement is not just quantitative, namely reduction in risk *levels*; rather, it is also qualitative, as it makes it possible to subject the risk triggered by transporting explosives to *systematic* human control. Indeed, transporting modern explosives becomes as

[13] Haas v. Hines, 91 So. 58 (1922).

dangerous as transporting bags of flour.[14] In tort-law terms, the nature of the risk of transporting modern explosives has changed so that it no longer merits strict tort liability. Instead, a standard of reasonable care is sufficient to make the transport of explosives a relatively safe activity.[15]

The preceding characterization of tolerable conflicts extends beyond the domain of products to capture many conflicts familiar from the law of negligence law (for instance, medical malpractice). It also covers some parts of nuisance law, as I explain in Chapter 8. And it also illuminates intentional torts, as I explain in Chapter 9. For instance, some property-related conflicts fall into this category. Land encroachments would be one such conflict. Consider a bone fide construction of a fence that, as it happens, partly intrudes into a neighbor's backyard.[16] An act of conversion in which I (mistakenly) wear a coat of another patron as I leave the restaurant would be another example of such a conflict. Although we would prefer not to have such conflicts in the first place, we allow them to stand and deploy tort law (among other things) to contain them so as to make them tolerable, as I demonstrate in Chapters 8–9, 14–15. It is important to note that the negative side effects that warrant containment are measured in terms of the fundamental interests that make up the conflict in question. They do not open a back door to all-things-considered assessment of all possible side effects (such as social costs that do not implicate fundamental interests).

C. Valueless Conflicts

The third and final category of interpersonal conflicts pertains to tensions we have no reason to tolerate, let alone embrace. These are cases of *valueless* conflict, for which the warranted reaction should be prevention, alleviation, and so on. There are in fact two different kinds of valueless conflicts, one straightforward and one more intricate.

Begin with the straightforward kind. Punching a person in the face, using explosives to advance a criminal plot, making an offensive touching, locking a person in a barn, and maliciously spreading lies and falsities about another person are all instances of valueless conflicts. For instance, the assailant's desire to do harm and the bodily safety of the person standing within a punching distance are in conflict so that the satisfaction of one's liberty entails the frustration

14 *See* Restatement (Third) of Torts: Physical & Emotional Harm §20(b)(1) & cmt. *h* (2010); Walker Drug Co. v. La Sal Oil Co., 902 P.2d 1229, 1233 (Utah 1995).

15 *See further* Indiana Harbor Belt R. Co. v. American Cyanamid Co., 916 F.2d 1174 (7th Cir. 1990).

16 On the general tendency among modern courts to deny injunctive relief in circumstances of good faith encroachment if the injunction would amount to inflicting hardship on the encroacher, see Lee Anne Fennell, *Efficient Trespass: The Case for "Bad Faith" Adverse Possession*, 100 Nw. U. L. Rev. 1037, 1042 n.21 (2006).

of the other's well-being. However, there is no reason—because there is no value—in having such a conflict in the first place. It is an instance of human failing and *nothing* more.

One may wonder whether valueless conflicts are truly valueless. To mention some of their contributions, suing the wrongdoer is certainly a form of asserting one's self-determining agency and equal standing against the injurer in public and the imposition of liability can be a fitting response to an instance of injustice.[17] On a more communitarian note, valueless conflicts are opportunities for reaffirming publicly held convictions and, as Nils Christie famously argued, norm clarification.[18] Even wars, or at least some wars, might have some positive contributions to societies and to individuals.[19] However, this way of identifying value in valueless conflicts conflates two different levels of normative analysis. In particular, it runs together ex ante and ex post assessments of value. To fix ideas, consider the case of heinous crimes, such as child abuse or rape. From an ex ante perspective, we have reason to take significant measures to prevent them and we certainly do not wish them to occur, as they are utterly valueless. Unfortunately, some such crimes do come to pass, and when they do the most we can make is to address them. Addressing such crimes is valuable, therefore, but only ex post facto. It cannot give us reason to facilitate, or even allow, them ex ante. Another way to put this point is that valueless conflicts are truly valueless; this much is true even as responding to valueless conflicts in the right way is valuable.

The other kind of valueless conflicts picks out failed easy-rescue cases. These cases are different from the previous cases—the "punch-in-the-face" cases—in the way that valuelessness is identified. There is no difficulty in determining that punching another in the face is just wrong (unless justified under special circumstances of necessity or self-defense). However, this is not true for cases of easy rescue. I shall argue that what makes the conflict in these cases valueless cannot be determined *apart* from the parameters of the conflict itself. (Notice, also, that the category of easy rescue is not limited to paradigmatic life-and-death situations as they can also capture other, very different instances of aiding others, such as finding lost or mislaid objects.)

To see this, consider the case of a small child drowning in a shallow puddle right before your eyes. You can pull her out (or alert her parent who is busy talking on the phone); or, you can stick to your plan of sitting idly by on a bench and doing nothing. Unlike punching another in the face, merely spending some quality time on a park bench is valuable, other things being equal. However, when this activity clashes with the predicament of a drowning child, an otherwise valuable end can lose its momentum. And the reason turns on the extreme disparity between the

[17] I take up these claims in Chapter 5.
[18] Nils Christie, *Conflicts as Property*, 17 Brit. J. Crim. 1 (1977).
[19] Margaret MacMillan, War: How Conflict Shaped Us (2020).

conflicting interests. Thus, the severe predicament of the child and its effortless amelioration transforms a person's interest in sitting idly by into something that we should neither embrace nor tolerate. The conflict, therefore, should count as valueless, as I explain in more detail in Chapter 6.[20]

By characterizing this conflict as valueless, I do not mean to suggest that all valueless conflicts are equally valueless, or that the fault on the part of an assailant and a failing rescuer is morally or legally similar. After all, there are many different condemnable behaviors out there, and there is no need to suppose that they exhibit similar shortcomings. Accordingly, a fitting legal response to valueless conflicts should give effect to such variance, such as in deciding what remedial rights should be afforded to victims of valueless conflicts. Chapter 5, for that matter, argues that the fitting response to two subsets of valueless conflicts, deliberate and relational wrongdoings, require personal rights of action, rather than merely rights to material redress.

III. Legal Rights as Building Blocks for Addressing Conflicts

The legal rights that ground tort duties and liabilities stand in a special relationship to the fundamental interests at the center of the conflict theory. In particular, these rights are devices that enable the interests: Fundamental interests call for legal rights in order to turn purely abstract commitments into appealing principles of action. I defend this claim in three principal stages. First, I mention familiar reasons for understanding the enabling relationship between interests and rights. Second, I argue that conflicts add another, major reason to viewing legal rights as interests' enabling devices. In that, I argue that the conflict theory partially *determines* what legal right an interest-holder should have. Finally, I illustrate the significance of the latter stage by reference to the interest in good name. I argue that the legal right to one's own good name is the upshot of subjecting the fundamental interest in good name to the demands of the conflict theory, in which case this right *already incorporates* the value of the conflict between the interest that underlies this right and the competing one (say, self-expression).

At a very abstract level, our fundamental interests are easily discernable and specifiable apart from law and other social practices. Consider, for instance, our interest in bodily or emotional integrity. Further, this interest can have practical bite even given the high level of generality in which it is framed. It should be clear, for instance, that a deliberate punch in the face of an innocent person undermines this interest. That said, an answer to the question what bodily integrity requires

[20] *See also* Avihay Dorfman, *Relational Justice and Torts*, *in* Research Handbook on Private Law Theory 321, 328–33 (Hanoch Dagan & Benjamin Zipursky eds., 2021); Hanoch Dagan & Avihay Dorfman, Relational Justice: A Theory of Private Law ch. 6 (2024).

beyond straightforward cases is far more challenging. Consider, for example, questions such as how to draw a principled boundary between causal and offensive touching, or do threats—and precisely what kind of threats—undermine bodily integrity. More generally, fundamental interests suffer from indeterminacy the moment we set our foot beyond the straightforward cases. A key moral function of legal rights and of law more generally is to render these interests more determinate.[21] In doing so, legal rights succeed where interests may not: a right entails a duty that protects the underlying interest(s), whereas an interest, by contrast, lacks this "vital link" to a duty.[22]

Legal rights are enabling devices of fundamental interests in another, more basic way as well. Even if fundamental interests are rendered sufficiently determinate, or already are so, *legal* rights are necessary in order to turn them into duty-imposing rules. Unlike the difficulty of indeterminacy, the challenge of imposing duties to respect, in some ways, the interest-holders is a substantive rather than epistemic one. It is not about filling out the details of this or that interest but rather about who has the standing to create law and, in particular, dictate conduct by way of imposing and enforcing duties. Legal rights, because they take the form of law, can provide this standing mechanism, as I argue elsewhere[23] and, closer to our discussion, as the equality theory of tort law that I present in Chapter 12 seeks to establish.

Legal rights can also solve another substantive difficulty integral to fundamental interests: The realization of some interests turns on vesting their holders with normative powers to create complex arrangements of housing, working, and worshiping (among other things). Thus, unlike interests that ground legal rights akin to Hohfeldian claim-rights, such as the right to bodily integrity, some autonomy interests may not get off the ground without the ability to own things and enter voluntary arrangements such as contracts, trusts, and corporations. Hence a certain type of legal right—viz., normative power—provides interest-holders a facility for manifesting their autonomous agency in the world.[24]

So far the analysis has drawn on standard arguments for understanding the nexus between fundamental interest and legal right in terms of a functional relationship of enablement of various kinds. The next one supervenes upon all the others, and it is this one that is key to the conflict theory: A legal right reflects a conclusion about what to make of the conflict between its underlying interest and another interest (or interests). For instance, the right to privacy determines how much protection the fundamental interest in privacy should receive *in light of* a conflicting fundamental interest (or interests). Legal rights, therefore, are not merely institutional expressions of their respective underlying fundamental interests. Rather, they are

[21] *Cf.* John Gardner, *Dagan and Dorfman on the Value of Private Law*, 117 COLUM. L. REV. ONLINE 179, 197 (2017); JOSEPH RAZ, BETWEEN AUTHORITY AND INTERPRETATION 178 (2009).
[22] John Tasioulas, *The Inflation of Concepts*, AEON (Jan. 29, 2021).
[23] AVIHAY DORFMAN & ALON HAREL, RECLAIMING THE PUBLIC ch. 2 (2024).
[24] *Cf.* HART, *supra* note 9, at 27–28.

also responses to the tensions arising among different interests. Hence, even if a legal right could render its underlying interest more determinate, ground the imposition of duties to respect interest-holders, and create legitimate empowerment mechanisms, the legal right remains substantively defective insofar as it leaves unaddressed the all-pervading existence of conflicting interests. To make good on the latter requirement, determining legal rights requires a theory of conflict.

Notice that it does not matter whether the conflict theory enters the analysis at the preliminary stage of rendering the interest more determinate, or at a later stage. Instead, the point is that a theory of conflict is both a reason for using legal rights as enabling devices for fundamental interests *and* a normative framework for determining such rights.

Recall that conflicts of fundamental interests are pervasive in two ways. Some—tolerably valuable and valueless conflicts—are pervasive as a matter of fact as they are the outgrowth of the combination of human nature with the human condition. Others, namely, inherently valuable conflicts, should be made pervasive in the sense that we have reason to construct the conditions necessary for such conflicts to pervade our practical lives. Against this backdrop, legal rights must do more than providing an institutional expression of their underlying interests, taken separately. Instead, they should attend to the ways "their" interests conflict with other interests (e.g., the right to privacy should attend, in the appropriate way, to the conflict between the interest in privacy and the interest to use and enjoy the outdoors). Thus, a gap between a fundamental interest in X to the legal right to X reflects, among other things, the pressure exerted on the former by conflicting interests. Hence, a right to X protects those aspects of the interest in X that warrant protection in light of the value of the conflict between interest X and a competing interest. Therefore, the conflict theory is called for to determine whether an interest/right gap is warranted in the first instance and, if so, what aspects of the interest should be included in the legal right.

Notice that courts and lawmakers may adopt a different methodology. They may define legal rights without considering the impact of conflicting interests. In that, they postpone the analysis of conflict to the stage of adjusting and balancing conflicting legal rights, rather than fundamental interests.

However, doing so represents a distinction without a difference: The considerations that make up the conflict theory can be invoked at either stage of the analysis. We can let the conflict theory guide the shift from fundamental interests to legal rights, and we can use the same to address the conflict at the level of legal rights. Indeed, the latter method is not really a wholly different way of engaging with the conflict theory.[25] Talk of fundamental interests and their corresponding

[25] There are differences, to be sure, but they are institutional, not substantive. Thus, addressing the conflict at the level of rights, rather than interests, might require substantial judicial discretion, perhaps even ad hoc decision-making authority. As I argue in Chapter 7, there are compelling reasons to resist this method.

legal rights would be replaced with talk of *prima facie* or *provisional* legal rights and corresponding *definitive* or *ultimate* legal rights.[26] Thus, what matters is that the conflict theory is in the business of determining legal rights (or definitive rights) by addressing the values of the underlying conflicts of fundamental interests (or *prima facie* rights). The rest of this book elaborates and illustrates this theory. At this stage of the argument, I seek to do two things. First, I explain in general terms how the conflict theory guides the progression from interest to legal right. Second, I illustrate this sequence by reference to the interest in one's own good name and its corresponding legal right.

According to the conflict theory, the tripartite distinction between inherently valuable, tolerably valuable, and valueless conflicts is the independent variable, whereas the scope of the protection given to fundamental interests is the dependent variable. In identifying the kind of value to which a conflict gives rise, the conflict theory delineates the scope of the protection that the conflicting interests ought to receive as a matter of (legal) right. In the case of an inherently valuable conflict, the scope of the protection of one of the conflicting interests must be specified in a sufficiently generous fashion, whereas the scope of the protection of the competing interest must be defined in a sufficiently narrow way. Doing so constructs the conditions necessary for the conflict at issue to thrive, up to a point. The question of what interest gets priority over the other depends, of course, on the value or good we seek to realize (as will be discussed below). If, however, the conflict is tolerably valuable, the scope of the protection that the conflicting interests should receive must be determined so as to contain the adverse side effects (in terms of a setback to the clashing interests). Finally, if the conflict is valueless, then one of the conflicting interests (the morally inferior one) should receive little or no legal protection at all in order to prevent the conflict from ever arising or, after the fact, mitigate to the fullest extent possible the damage done.

Notice that the conflict theory does not allow for legal rights to take the form of general or uniform rights whose actual strength remains constant irrespective of the relevant considerations. For instance, the right to privacy protects some elements of our fundamental interest in privacy. We may refer to this right in general or in uniform terms by calling it "*the* right to privacy" as some bill of rights and statutes often do; further, there are even good reasons to depict some such rights in these broad terms.[27] However, it is important to understand that the legal protection of privacy, like most other rights, is far more circumscribed as it responds to the considerations that determine when, and with respect to whom, an

[26] Accordingly, whereas provisional rights may conflict, ultimate ones cannot. This is also how I read Waldron's analysis of conflicting rights. Jeremy Waldron, *Rights in Conflict*, 99 ETHICS 503, 506 (1989).

[27] *See further* Chapter 10; Hanoch Dagan & Avihay Dorfman, *The Tort of Discrimination*, 16 J. TORT L. 393 (2023). The line of reasoning in the main text above is further reinforced by President Franklin D. Roosevlent's claim, made during his 1937 Address on Constitution Day, that the U.S. Constitution is a "layman's document" rather than "a lawyer's contract."

interest-holder should have a legal right to privacy. We do not have a similar right to privacy in our dwelling house and in the public park; nor do we hold a similar right to privacy against the state's tax authority and against our next-door neighbor. The right to privacy is a shorthand for a commitment to a *set of rights to privacy*.[28]

The transition from the right to X to a set of rights to X is, in fact, the lived-experience of the liberal legal order. It would be wrong to suppose that the bold assertions made in a typical bill of rights reflect, with sufficient precision, the rights we actually hold. For instance, the First Amendment entrenches *the right* to free speech. To begin with, the right does not exist with respect to many expressive activities (such as securities advertisement).[29] And even when it does, legal protection varies dramatically depending, among other things, on the type of speech (say, political versus commercial speech), the context (the town square versus court of law), and the addressees of the speech (government versus landlord). This way of approaching legal rights is not limited to constitutional rights. The rights that figure in tort law—the topic of this book—exhibit this property as well.

The conflict theory provides the normative framework with which to identify and assess the considerations that guide the determination of legal rights. It is not an exhaustive framework, to be sure. However, as I argued above, it is a necessary one—to wit, the pervasiveness of conflicts of fundamental interests requires a theory concerning the right way of addressing them.[30] In its absence, as the next section illustrates, there is no nonarbitrary way to determine what aspects of a fundamental interest should give rise to a claim of legal right.

IV. Illustration: From an Interest into a Right to One's Own Good Name

An interest in good name, as mentioned above, is fundamental in the sense that one's own good name is a necessary condition of one's ability to be with others in the world as a free and equal agent.[31] The basic threat to good name stems

[28] *Cf.* Christopher Heath Wellman, *On Conflicts Between Rights*, 14 L. & Phil. 271, 277–78 (1995); Russ Shafer-Landau, *Specifying Absolute Rights*, 37 Ariz. L. Rev. 209, 213 (1995); Joel Feinberg, *Voluntary Euthanasia and the Inalienable Right to Life*, 7 Phil. & Pub. Aff. 102 (1978).

[29] Frederick Schauer, *The Boundaries of the First Amendment: A Preliminary Exploration of Constitutional Salience*, 117 Harv. L. Rev. 1765, 1770 (2004).

[30] To preempt an objection motivated by the economic approach reflected in the Coasean theorem, Chapter 12 establishes that contracting is not an alternative to the conflict theory: The fundamental interests protected in tort law are preconditions for practice of voluntary interactions between free and equal persons.

[31] John Rawls has emphasized the significance of the social bases of self-respect, which are, roughly put, the recognition by social and political institutions that provides persons with a sense of self-worth. Rawls, *supra* note 8, at 62, 178–79. Good name is related to but nonetheless stands apart from Rawls's social bases of self-respect in at least one way: Good name is not limited to what Rawls calls the basic structure of society and, in particular, to institutions. It purports to ground inter*personal* duties.

from statements that lower one in the estimation of the relevant group or community, and thus undermine one's ability to interact with others on equal footing. Lowering statements consist of communications that expose a person to hatred, ridicule, contempt, obloquy, or distrust. Notice that there are several key elements that go into the questions of what good name is and what might constitute setbacks to good name. Focusing on the latter, we need to know more about what "lowering" means, whose estimation counts, what is the nature of the injury, what statements or communications are likely to inflict such an injury, do the intentions or attitudes of the perpetrator matter, and more.

Given the moral significance of the interest in good name, the combination of these (and other) open questions calls for a legal right to one's own good name. This right, as explained above, can render the interest more determinate. Further, it can lend legitimacy to the existence and enforcement of a duty against smearing another person's good name. There are, however, any number of ways, ranging from maximalist to minimalist articulations, to define the legal right to a good name that can be made compatible with the requirements of determinacy and legitimacy. The conflict theory, I argue, is necessary for a successful transition from the interest in to the legal right to a good name. Further, it is not only necessary but also highly consequential: The thresholds of determinacy and legitimacy are rather low, and so it is the conflict theory that does the heavy lifting.

The history of defamation law reinforces this point. For instance, the working theory of the early modern tort of defamation (consisting in libel and slander) was probably that of protecting "the existing social hierarchy from verbal attack, no matter how justified or grounded in truth."[32] As I explain in Chapter 16, this theory has deep roots in a certain religious conception of the good life and, by implication, of the sanctity of people's interest in their good name. On this view, the legal right's protection of the fundamental interest in a good name should take a maximalist approach. Having such a right can certainly render the interest at issue more determinate and, in some measure, secure the legitimacy of imposing legal duties of respect for the good name of others. That said, there can be other, less expansive but no less determinate, ways to define the legal right to a good name.

Once again, the history of defamation law suggests itself. Where upholding a person's good name is thought to guard against lowering this person's estimation in the eyes of a certain community, the legal right to the same has undergone dramatic transformations since early modernity. A few illustrations are apt. Consider the question of what forms of potentially defamatory statements are protected against by the legal right to a good name. In criminal libel law, the right used to protect against defamatory statements was irrespective of their truth or

[32] David Howarth, *Libel: Its Purpose and Reform*, 74 M.L.R. 845, 848 (2011). For illuminating discussion, see Leslie Kim Treiger-Bar-Am, *Defamation Law in a Changing Society: The Case of Youssoupoff v. Metro-Goldwyn Mayer*, 20 Legal Studies 291, 296–97 (2000).

falsity: "the greater the truth, the greater the libel," as it was then believed.[33] This is no longer the case. Another bone of contention was what to make of nonverifiable or nonfalsifiable statements. Certainly, statements of nonfactual opinion, rhetorical hyperboles, caricature, ridicule, and satirical critique (to mention some such) can cause substantial injury to a person's good name. It depends, of course, on the circumstances, the stature of the statement-maker, and the content of the statement. Here, too, the legal right to a good name at one time provided protection against such statements; for instance, ridicule, as the Restatement observes, has been a "common form of defamation."[34] This is no longer the case in many, though not all, liberal democratic legal orders, where the legal right protects only against false defamatory *factual* or *fact*-based statements.[35]

Another key question that has seen a major historical shift concerns the question of fault. Certainly, the interest in good name does not specify the nature of the (moral) wrong involved in besmirching one's reputation. This is the case irrespective of whether reputational losses are associated with either the dignity or the welfare of the victim. The legal right to a good name necessarily decides this question of fault in one way or another. Early common law of defamation took the position that fault of any sort is not required, extending legal protection of the interest in a good name to truly innocent publications that might have resulted, as a matter of sheer happenstance, in potential reputational loss as well as to statements containing fairly trivial inaccuracies.[36] Such an expansive scope is still good law in some jurisdictions and under some circumstances but, as I show in Chapter 4, modern defamation law has adopted various elements of fault so as to reduce the scope of the right to a good name. Thus, violating this right often turns on the existence of actual malice, negligence, irresponsible communication or journalism, or other fault-based requirements that, in effect, further circumscribe the legal protection that the interest in good name receives.

I offer two final observations to further reinforce the argument that like other fundamental interests, good name does not entail any specific legal right to the same. They concern, first, the content and the target of the statement and, second, the standard against which to assess what counts as defamatory. I take each in turn.

The first point regards the statement. It is possible to define the right to a good name broadly, to capture defamatory statements, irrespective of their value to the public or some segments thereof. Likewise, it is possible to disregard the identity

[33] This maxim is attributed to Lord Mansfield. *See The Greater the Truth, the Greater the Libel*, 26 Can. L. Times 394 (1906). *See further* Amy Gajda, Seek and Hide: The Tangled History of the Right to Privacy 15 (2022).

[34] Restatement (Second) of Torts § 566 cmt. *d* (1977).

[35] Defamation law in Israel, for instance, can cast its liability net on nonfactual statements as well. CA 4534/02 Schocken v. Herzikovich, PD 58(3) 558 (2004). This was (though no longer) true in other common law jurisdictions. Judge Learned Hand's decision in Burton v. Crowell Pub., Co., 82 F.2d 154, 156 (2d Cir. 1936) is a case in point.

[36] *See* E. Hulton & Co. v. Jones [1909] A.C. 20; Sharpe v. Stevenson, 34 N.C. 348 (1851), respectively.

of the object of a reputational attack, granting similar legal rights to good name to all potential victims, irrespective of their role in the economy, academy, civic society, church, or politics. A different approach takes such distinctions seriously in the sense that the legal protection of the interest in one's own good name may vary accordingly. It is even possible to single out the value of the statement—whether it is about a matter of public concern—as the crucial differentiating factor in delineating the scope of the right to a good name, as it is the case in Canada[37] and perhaps also in the United States.[38]

Finally, consider the different definitions of the "community" whose estimation of the victim sets the standard of defamatory-ness. Once again, the fundamental interest in good name only tells us that lowering a person's standing in the eyes of *some others* might be inimical to this person's ability to function as a free and equal agent. It does not entail, as a matter of conceptual necessity, whose eyes must count. On one extreme, the relevant community may be a moral construct, depicting the point of view of morality itself. The standard of "right-thinking people" can be viewed along these lines, identifying defamation with *moral* desert. However, our interest in good name can also be on the line in the sense that people's reputation can be seriously besmirched even if their true character does not, morally speaking, warrant any such reaction.[39] Familiar examples are imputations of sexual permissiveness, disease, or political ideology, none of which should necessarily adversely affect a person's estimation in the eyes of *right*-thinking people. As Judge Learned Hand observed, "A man may value his reputation even among those who do not embrace the prevailing moral standards."[40]

Hence, the opposite extreme to the moralistic standard for the legal right to a good name incorporates a sociological standard. The standard of defamation would be based upon the estimation of any subgroup of the population that would *actually* find the statement defamatory. For instance, suppose that a statement "X is

[37] Grant v. Torstar Corp. [2009] 3 SCR 640, at para. 106.

[38] *Cf.* Snyder v. Phelps, 562 U.S. 443 (2011) where on free speech grounds the US Supreme Court blocked the imposition of tort liability on a church leader for intentionally inflicting emotional distress on the plaintiff by picketing and displaying highly insulting signs—for example, "You're going to hell," "God hates you"—near the location of the plaintiff's son's funeral (who was killed in Iraq in the line of duty). Interestingly for defamation law (which was not at the center of this case), the Court set to one side the distinction between private and public figures, focusing on the significance of the public concern of the insulting signs for the purpose of extending constitutional protection of free speech even where the victim is a private person (at a stage of profound grief). This approach resonates with the plurality opinion in *Rosenbloom v. Metromedia, Inc.*, 403 U.S. 29, 43–44 (1971) (repudiated by *Gertz v. Robert Welch, Inc.*, 418 U.S. 323 (1974)), saying that "[i]f a matter is a subject of public or general interest, it cannot suddenly become less so merely because a private individual is involved."

[39] For very helpful discussions, see Adam Slavny, *The Normative Foundations of Defamatory Meaning*, 37 L. & PHIL. 523, 540 (2018); Eric Descheemaeker, *Mapping Defamation Defences*, 78 M.L.R. 641, 651 (2015); Lyrissa Barnett Lidsky, *Defamation, Reputation, and the Myth of Community*, 71 WASH. L. REV. 1 (1996); Roy Robert Ray, *Truth: A Defense to Libel*, 16 MINN. L. REV. 43, 56 (1931). A contrastive view, which identifies reputation with morally deserved reputation, is defended in ARTHUR RIPSTEIN, PRIVATE WRONGS 214–17 (2016); LAWRENCE MCNAMARA, REPUTATION AND DEFAMATION (2007).

[40] Grant v. Reader's Digest Ass'n, 151 F.2d 733, 734 (2d Cir. 1945).

a law-abiding citizen" is likely to cause some people in the community—say, Mafia members—to shun X.[41]

In between the two extremes—the purely moral and the purely sociological—there are any number of ways to specify a standard of which statements are to be considered defamatory that allows for both moral and/or some sociological facts to decide the question.[42] For instance, a statement that "X is a Communist" does not nowadays amount to defamation unless, however, X's community is highly sensitive to such allegations and so may likely lead them to seriously lower their estimation of X.[43] More generally, the standard can incorporate the views of "a substantial and respectable *minority*" of members of the community, to the exclusion of those "with views sufficiently peculiar to regard as derogatory what the vast majority of persons regard as innocent."[44]

There are, of course, other variations on the moral-and/or-sociological theme. The point of these illustrations is not to settle the question but rather to show that the move from an interest in good name to a right to the same must draw on considerations that go far beyond those of determinacy. There are, after all, many plausible articulations of the legal right and at least some of them can be made sufficiently determinate. Hence, what is missing is a normative framework that determines, or guides the determination of, what aspects of the interest in good name warrant legal protection, in what way, and to what extent.

This is where the conflict theory enters the picture. A nonarbitrary way to turn a fundamental interest's abstract commitment to good name into a legal right must consider the conflicting demands arising from the existence of other fundamental interests (along with other nonfundamental considerations such as institutional ones). Only then can the choice between the various different—and sufficiently determinate—articulations of the right to a good name be grounded in value.

The conflict theory is, therefore, a *legal* theory. It provides a framework to both understand and determine basic legal rights and their corresponding duties. It is a legal theory in another, related sense: It employs legal rules, doctrines, and categories in order to specify what aspects of the interest in good name receive legal protection. In that, the conflict theory does not engage in ad hoc, free-floating analysis to decide whether it is desirable to grant legal protection, one case at a time (nor does it intervene in "a particularized fashion," invoking a second-order system of equitable doctrines to "solve problems of high uncertainty and complexity"[45]). The legal right at issue, like most other rights, is not tailor-made. One implication of invoking legal rules, doctrines, and categories as conflict theory's raw materials is that the legal right to a good name might provide over- and underprotection in

[41] *Contra* Byrne v. Deane [1937] 1 KB 818.
[42] *See* Slavny, *supra* note 39.
[43] *See* Nguyen-Lam v. Cao, 171 Cal. App. 4th 858 (2009).
[44] RESTATEMENT (SECOND) OF TORTS § 559 cmt. *e* (1977).
[45] Henry E. Smith, *Equity as Meta-Law*, 130 YALE L.J. 1050, 1059 (2021).

some cases and to some interest-holders. A successful implementation of the conflict theory should, therefore, reduce the likelihood of this implication to a bare minimum.

Notice that by saying that the conflict theory is a legal theory I do not argue that it can determine the outcome of cases. Nor can it *fully* determine the specific details of any legal doctrine or the precise scope of each and every category in this or that jurisdiction. In fact, it should not even aspire to do either. Maintaining a gap between theory and doctrine—avoiding excessive granularity—is warranted for several reasons, two of which are worth noting here.[46]

The first is that the conflict theory does not displace democratic institutions and their commitment to the particular society's aspirations, traditions, and constraints. As a result, the choice between several plausible doctrinal rules may be partially informed by such "local" considerations on top of the prescriptions derived from the conflict theory. For instance, the choice between actual malice and negligence as alternative standards of fault in the tort of defamation may often turn on local traditions and commitments, rather than on the conflict theory. Another reason for maintaining a theory/doctrine gap is that any one piece of doctrine is imbricated over other doctrines. As a result, it is often undesirable to assess a particular doctrinal rule on its own without also assessing neighboring doctrines that exert some influence on the former. For instance, the difference between actual malice and negligence cannot be fully understood without taking into account civil procedure's rules of pretrial discovery. Arguably, in the absence of a rigorous discovery process, victims of defamation may not be able to prove actual malice, in which case a standard of negligence might be a better fit. By contrast, actual malice makes better sense in a jurisdiction with generous pretrial discovery procedures.[47] Against the backdrop of these and other reasons, the conflict theory identifies the considerations and raises the questions that along with other considerations guide the determination of legal rights out of fundamental interests.

How does the conflict theory work, then? This section sketches the structural features of this theory and subsequent chapters, especially Chapters 3, 4, and 17, defend the substantive aspects of this question. Determining the legal right to a good name, for instance, turns on responding to the conflict between the fundamental interests in good name and free speech in the right way. It requires us to engage with the kind of value underlying the conflict. The three-place distinction between inherently valuable, tolerably valuable, and valueless conflicts implies, as already argued, that the legal right to a good name is not unidimensional.

When the conflict is valueless, good name should receive robust protection against reputational attacks. This is why, to give an example, the right to a good

[46] *See also* Dagan & Dorfman, *supra* note 20, at ch. 1.
[47] Arguably, English law's choice of a standard of reasonable journalism and US law's choice of actual malice correspond to this line of thinking.

name should protect us against defamatory statements of fact that are known, or can easily be known, in advance to be false. By contrast, when the conflict is inherently valuable, the interest in good name should take the back seat in order to facilitate fearless exchange of ideas, as I argue in the next chapter. Thus, to illustrate, although a speaker who shares his or her unusually critical views about another can certainly deal a blow to the latter's interest in good name, there should be virtually no legal protection against such an attack, hence no legal right to prevent speakers from, say, employing satire to besmirch a person's reputation in the eyes of some others. Likewise, I shall argue that there should not be a right against the assertion of true statements *even if* such statements can undermine a person's good name in the eyes of the relevant community.

One might protest that the only person to blame for reputational harm caused by true statements is the victim themselves, charging them with something like contributory negligence or even assumption of risk. Yet there are cases in which the victim is not to blame for their reputational loss even when a defamatory statement is true. Consider imputations of religious, sexual, political (et alia) heterodoxy that concern morally permissible, perhaps even morally courageous, behavior that, nonetheless, is likely to cause reputational harm to this person given the social group or the business community with whom this person interacts. While this person's reputation might be damaged, there is no real reason to hold them morally responsible for engaging in these kinds of heterodoxy. But because the conflict between free speech and good name is inherently valuable, the victim should not have a claim of right, in which case it is an instance of *damnum absque injuria*. Or so I shall argue in the next chapter.

Finally, some conflicts fall between the inherently valuable and the valueless ones. These occasions feature uncertainty as to whether the clash between free speech and good name is either valuable or valueless. The typical source of uncertainty lies in the difficulty of ascertaining the accuracy of a statement at the time of its publication or utterance. If true, no legal protection against the reputational harm is warranted. If false, however, the clash between free speech and good name turns valueless, as just explained. That said, we are currently lacking a truth machine able to generate right answers reliably and instantly.

The major challenge, therefore, is what to make of statements whose accuracy may not be readily ascertained in real time. The determination of the right to a good name (and, correspondingly, the right to free speech) addresses this challenge. On one extreme, granting maximal legal protection to good name implies that the speaker would have to act at their peril; on the other, minimal or no right to the same implies that speakers can deliver their reputational attacks with impunity. The category of tolerably valuable conflicts tackles the shortcomings that plague both extremes by setting out to contain the negative side effects—measured in terms of setbacks to reputation—of facilitating a liberal culture of free and fearless speech (as I argue in the next two chapters). The notion that some "breathing space" must be kept to minimize self-censorship is a surface manifestation of containment.

One way to do the "containing" is by incorporating a condition of fault. Thus, the right to a good name protects against defamatory statements that are tainted by the insinuation of some substandard behavior. As mentioned above, there can be different doctrinal manifestations of fault, and they can take the form of rules or of standards. Actual malice represents the former whereas irresponsible communication or negligence the latter. There are other doctrinal levers, as it were, that can be employed in the service of containing the conflict—for instance, the allocation of the burden of proving falsehoods as I show in Chapter 16, a requirement to prove serious harm as opposed to mere harm,[48] and treating statements on matters of public concern more leniently than other statements represent some such levers. As mentioned above, the ambition of the conflict theory is not to settle things down to their last detail; jurisdictions may, and should, go their own way in this respect. Rather, it seeks to provide the normative framework to guide the determination of rights whose underlying interests are in conflict.

The preceding gloss on the conflict theory illustrates an approach to determining legal rights by attending to the conflict between fundamental interests. Subsequent chapters defend the substantive arguments concerning both the value of the conflict and the legal rights to which it gives effect. But even before the argument proceeds to substantiate these claims, one observation is worth repeating: There are legal rights, rather than a right, to a good name, reflecting the different kinds of value of protecting the interest in a good name vis-à-vis the interest with which it conflicts. This is true, I shall argue, in the case of the other rights that figure in the law of torts. And these rights are not merely determinate renditions of extrajuridical interests but rather also expressions of how we ought to assess the conflict between such interests.

[48] *See* Section 1(1) of England's Defamation Act 2013.

3
Inherently Valuable Conflicts
Elaboration and Illustrations

On the conflict theory, tort law is tasked with facilitating valuable conflicts, including by constructing the conditions necessary for them to arise. It makes good on this task by way of determining rights and duties. This way of proceeding suggests that rather than correcting, recognizing, or internalizing the costs of wrongs (or harms), realizing *positive* value is, and should be, at the moral center of tort law. Questions such as what constitutes wrongdoing (or harming) or what costs should be internalized focus on the dependent variables; by contrast, the conflict theory addresses the independent variable. Inherently valuable conflicts, therefore, come first in the order of vindication.

This chapter argues that a conflict of fundamental interests counts as inherently valuable if the value in question is an implication of the conflict in the sense that the realization of this value is not possible in the absence of the conflict, such as by creating nonconflictual mechanisms to bring it about.

To provide a deeper sense of what the *value* in inherently valuable conflict might be, and the sense in which a conflict is *inherently* valuable, I consider three cases deliberately drawn from different walks of our practical lives: Conflicts of self-expression versus reputation and emotional well-being, sociability versus bodily sovereignty, and market competition versus promissory commitment. All three are illustrations of a broader claim, namely, that some conflicts between fundamental interests are inherently valuable. Other chapters in this book will provide additional cases of inherently valuable conflicts.

I. The Construction of a Liberal Culture: Good Name and Emotional Well-Being Meet Free and Fearless Speech

A. The Good of Liberal Culture

The practice of "free and fearless reasoning and communication of ideas"[1] may often be unsettling and inconvenient. It can also go further by exerting pressure toward conflict with people's fundamental interests in their good name and

[1] Thornhill v. Alabama, 310 U.S. 88, 95 (1940).

Conflict between Equals. Avihay Dorfman, Oxford University Press. © Oxford University Press 2026.
DOI: 10.1093/9780198979869.003.0006

emotional well-being. More broadly, it is a platitude of a liberal society that the conflict between the interests in free speech, on the one hand, and good name or emotional well-being, on the other, is not merely a theoretical possibility but rather a *lived-experience* (notice again the talk of interests, not legal rights). I argue that this reality is not something to be lamented but rather embraced and even to some extent encouraged.

I do not argue that the fundamental interest in free speech is, all else equal, stronger than the interest in good name or emotional well-being. Rather, the argument is that putting the two in conflict can sometimes be valuable and, moreover, that the value in question can be realized only if the former interest gets some measure of priority over the latter. To see why this conflict is, within limits discussed below, inherently valuable, consider the following hypothetical case.

The conflict-sanitizer. James Madison, quoting and adopting a statement by John Marshall, observes that free speech

> is often carried to excess ... but the remedy has not yet been discovered ... perhaps it is a shoot which cannot be stripped from the stalk without wounding vitally the plant from which it is torn. However desirable those measures might be which might correct without enslaving the press, they have never yet been devised in America.[2]

Enter, conflict sanitizer. The conflict sanitizer I (hypothetically) devise is a sophisticated technology because it does it all and does it well: It allows us to eat the cake and have it too. More specifically, it eliminates the conflict between free speech and good name or emotional well-being, while providing no less than maximal protection to both interests. In the law, this protection manifests itself in the form of recognizing maximalist legal rights to both free speech and good name or emotional well-being. The sanitizer allows a person to speak out as he or she sees fit while insulating the people targeted by the speech from any adverse consequences. Regarding reputation-undermining speech, the conflict sanitizer deflects the defamatory part of the speech from those who might have judged the person in question negatively. Regarding emotionally offensive speech, the conflict sanitizer prevents the hurtful aspects of the speech from taking their toll on the victim.

There are any number of ways to achieve these outcomes. One way is by instantaneously and meticulously substituting defamatory and offensive speech with noninjurious speech. Another is to administer a pill that defuses the cognitive and noncognitive effects of experiencing the speech of others. For instance, those who take the pill will not be able, cognitively speaking, to factor the

[2] Quoted in *Rosenbloom v. Metromedia, Inc.*, 403 U.S. 29, 51 (1971).

reputation-undermining statements into their estimation of the statements' target; and, similarly, the pill will take away the emotional pain and suffering that would have been caused by offensive speech to the victim. Hence, the question is: Might we wish that some such conflict sanitizer be invented? And until then, should we understand the setback caused by free and fearless communication to our good name and emotional well-being as regrettable (perhaps even tragic)?

The answer is "no." Conflict sanitizers, including the most sophisticated version ever, are necessarily defective and the source of the defect does not lie in their ability to play tricks on people's thoughts and deliberations. That is, such a technology is defective even when it could avoid all forms of manipulation, for instance, by securing our consent to taking the pill. Instead, the basic problem lies in doing away with the conflict itself. Merely providing maximal protection to free speech, good name, and emotional well-being falls short of what the *conflict between these contending interests* can distinctively engender: The construction of the conditions necessary for a certain public culture, a liberal culture, to arise.

By culture I mean a set of values, attitudes, and practices in light of which people live.[3] In that, a culture defines a distinct way of making sense of the world on the basis of certain assumptions and convictions that are shared by those who practice the culture at issue. A liberal culture aims, negatively, at identifying, confronting, and resisting (when necessary) all forms of unfreedom and inequality that beset contemporary institutions, customs, and ways of thinking.[4] Positively, a liberal culture guides the construction of new forms of human and social relation (in work, commerce, education, family, church, etc.) consistently with treating the parties as free and equal.[5] This latter task can proceed indefinitely as the quest for new forms evolves (ideally, progresses) in response to social, economic, and political change.

Notice, moreover, that talk of a *public*, liberal culture might tempt one to conceive its underlying value as ultimately collective and political, and its organizing legal framework as public law. However, my point is that the significance of the individual's interest and its positive collective consequences are deeply connected. The realization of the latter—the value of free speech to society as a whole coming into conflict with an individual's good name or emotional well-being—cannot count as valuable apart from protecting the individual's interest. (This is why the good of liberal culture is not reducible to the economic problem of positive externalities and the related challenge of producing public goods). This is specifically the case for the *liberal* culture whose basic commitment is to respect all its members, taken severally, as free and equal agents.

[3] Allen Patten, Equal Recognition: The Moral Foundations of Minority Rights 51 (2014).

[4] Another sense in which a culture is liberal is insofar as it contrasts with a culture whose regulative ideal is the pursuit of virtue and human flourishing. A liberal culture eradicates social and political barriers to the pursuit of the virtuous life but does not require it.

[5] An additional effect is the deepening of our appreciation of existing norms and relations insofar as they meet the demands of justice.

Hence, the good of liberal culture cannot be specified apart from its commitment to the free and equal status of the private individual, and its organizing legal framework is irreducibly private law (the law that constructs, rather than merely protects, terms of interactions between people qua private persons) and, in particular, tort law. More abstractly, this culture-wide good must presuppose a relational normative universe where people interact, including at the pairwise level, on terms that reflect their status as free and equal agents. The private dimension of liberal culture further manifests itself in the spheres of action impacted by this culture: The workplace, the market, the place of worship, the school, the family, and the community of neighbors (to mention a few). There, confronting forms of unfreedom and inequality, on the one hand, and constructing new forms of human and social relation, on the other, need not, and should not, make an essential reference to the national or political identities of the participants.

Why does a liberal culture depend on the conflict between free speech and good name or emotional well-being? Why isn't it enough to extend free speech protections to all forms of valuable speech, except when it is hurtful or harmful? The answer lies in the indispensable role of rebuking, reproaching, ridiculing, and challenging the powerful, hegemony, orthodoxy, social mores, conventions, and any other micro and macro aspect of reality worth questioning and reforming.[6] As the US Supreme Court observed, it is the "function" of free speech to "invite dispute" so that free speech "may indeed best serve its high purpose when it induces a condition of unrest, creates dissatisfaction with conditions as they are, or even stirs people to anger."[7] Providing maximalist protection for both free speech *and* good name or emotional well-being will not do. Rather, putting them on a collision course and, further, ensuring that the former takes *some* measure of priority over the latter, are necessary conditions for a liberal culture to arise.

B. Illustrations and Elaboration

Consider the case of Henry Ford suing, on a libel theory, the jingoistic *Chicago Tribune* for calling him an "ignorant idealist" and an "anarchist" for his alleged view that workers of his company should lose their jobs if they respond to the duty to serve the National Guard to defend the border with Mexico.[8] (The outcome of the decision is rather ambivalent, with the court finding for Ford and awarding

[6] Contrast with the public culture associated with what Joseph Raz calls the validation of forms of life. Joseph Raz, *Free Expression and Personal Identification*, 11 Oxford J. Legal Stud. 303 (1991).

[7] Terminiello v. Chicago, 337 U.S. 1, 4 (1949).

[8] The full editorial and important details about the legal proceedings can be found in Weymouth Kirkland, *Some American Causes Celebres: Henry Ford v. The Tribune Co.*, 9 Am. Bar Ass'n J. 90, 91 (1923). *See also* Samantha Barbas, Actual Malice: Civil Rights and Freedom of the Press in New York Times v. Sullivan 23 (2023).

him nominal damages in the amount of 6 cents; a case like this is bound to lose under today's law of defamation). It will be important to distinguish between an abstract characterization of what this case is about—the resort to speech to resist power and orthodoxy—and its concrete instantiation in the facts of this case. Thus, in asserting that Ford is an "idealistic ignorant" and "anarchist," the author of the *Tribune*'s editorial is not merely making a factual claim that can be readily assessed as true or false.[9] Nor does the assertion apply narrowly to the convictions (or follies) of an unusually influential figure. Instead, the author of the editorial exercises his or her fundamental, extrajuridical interest in self-expression by slitting open the underbelly of the powerful, be they public or genuinely private persons in a position of relative power, be they employers, landlords, religious leaders, husbands in patriarchal family relationships, and so on. The author rebukes, rather than merely reproves, a person in a position of power. Doing so can certainly inflict grave emotional pain on this person and, indeed, on any person in his shoes. Further, it in effect lowers, or at the very least could lower, this person's standing in the eyes of some others and, moreover, deter these others from associating with him in commercial, social, or political settings. That said, I argue that the author's free speech interest should be respected *because* of, rather than merely despite, its potentially harmful consequences.

Indeed, the conflict sanitizer can render this point vividly. Suppose that we could eliminate the insult and reproach in question by employing the sanitizer. The editorial author may then be able to convey his or her message without causing any pain or setback to Ford's (extrajuridical) interest in reputation, perhaps by sugar-coating talk of idealistic ignorance and anarchism. Yet, something of a value is necessarily missing, namely, the conflict between free speech and good name or emotional well-being. Not being entitled openly and vigorously to subject others to some measure of contempt, ridicule, reproach, and so forth, undermines the good of liberal culture. It precludes our ability to stand up to existing conditions and beliefs by challenging and castigating them, rather than merely by doubting and airing them. Doing so, as is readily available to us from the practice of investigative and muckraking journalists, social activists, satirists, artists, internet pundits, dissenters, heretics, and so forth, sometimes requires undermining, to some extent, the interests of others in their good name and/or emotional well-being.

The case of Henry Ford is a rather quaint illustration of the value of conflict. It suffers from two shortcomings. First, it focuses on *factual* assertions of defamatory (and offensive) statements, and so fails to demonstrate whether conflicts that arise in connection with assertions of opinions are germane to the good of liberal

[9] However, the trial court did subject these assertions to factual assessment, including considering whether Ford had adequate knowledge of American history. *See* Robert & Marilyn Aitken, *Pride and Prejudice: The Dark Side of Henry Ford*, 32 LITIGATION 53, 54 (2005).

culture. Second, it might not provide the most powerful illustration of speech harming the victim's good name and emotional well-being. This is because, one might argue, Ford essentially waived his interest in good name and emotional well-being in choosing to go public with his controversial views both in favor of pacifism and against employees' rights. I do not think this latter concern is right as it conflates two different notions of assuming risk: Inviting a rejoinder and inviting a rejoinder that also harms one's fundamental interests in good name and emotional well-being. Assuming the former risk does not entail the latter. Be that as it may, I seek to preempt the two worries anyway by moving the discussion closer to our world to show that such worries are orthogonal to, and so lie beside, my point: The conflict between free speech and good name or emotional well-being can be inherently valuable.

Consider the following two cases. The first is *Hustler Magazine, Inc. v. Falwell.* There, a newspaper published an ad parody, featuring a fake interview in which a "nationally known minister" and a political commentator, Reverend Jerry Falwell, allegedly described himself as losing his virginity to his mother, acting immorally, and preaching only when he is drunk. The publication "of an ad parody offensive to him, and doubtless gross and repugnant in the eyes of most" set out to attack Falwell's hypocrisy and, more generally, hypocrisy surrounding political and religious conservatism.[10] The second is *Fisher v. Washington Post Co.*, where an art critic published a column containing harsh criticism of a new exhibit of paintings at a local art gallery.[11] The critique targeted Fisher, the owner of the art gallery and its curator, asserting that the paintings are "badly hung among many commercial paintings" and as a result the value of the exhibition "is completely destroyed," turning a "fine arts gallery" into a "commercial outlet."[12]

Both Falwell and Fisher may well experience a reduction in their estimation by members of their respective communities—the former must maintain integrity that people believe in, in order to pursue his religious calling and his livelihood; the latter depends for his success on how members of the artistic community and gallery-goers view his work.[13] Their interest in good name, that is, can be damaged by their critics. The setback to good name is an upshot of *non*verifiable statements of opinion (including rhetorical hyperbole). Moreover, this setback is not *morally* deserved—clearly, Falwell and Fisher did not act in ways that amount to waiving or assuming away their interest in their own good names. Indeed, their conduct or decision, it is possible to say, was clearly legal and morally legitimate.

The *Fisher* court notes that "[t]he social values inherent in a free interchange of opinion far outweigh the injury which such discussion might cause to a person

[10] Hustler Magazine, Inc. v. Falwell, 485 U.S. 46, 50 (1988).
[11] 212 A.2d 335 (D.C. Ct. App. 1965).
[12] *Id.*, at 336.
[13] *Id.* at 337.

in the public eye."[14] But the conflict between free speech and good name (and, arguably, emotional well-being) goes deeper. The injury to the latter interest is not merely a regrettable side effect of having the former. In fact, the two interests interact in an entirely different way—the setback caused by free speech to good name (and/or emotional well-being) is valuable because it creates the conditions necessary for the good of liberal culture to arise. The *Hustler* court hints at this direction when it states that a society devoid of a certain use of the parodical form—as a "weapon of attack, of scorn and ridicule and satire"[15]—is "poorer."[16]

The conflict sanitizer helps to illustrate this point, once again. The art critic will then be able to pen the exact same column but the gallery owner will suffer no reduction in his relevant community's estimation of him; he will also experience no emotional pain as a result. A special pill or some other sanitizing mechanism will do the trick of providing maximal protection to all the interests concerned. However, as I argued above, constructing this nonconflictual sphere necessarily undermines the good of liberal culture. That is, it erodes our ability as individuals and as a community of free and equal individuals to challenge existing conditions and, as in the *Falwell* and *Fisher* cases, engage in unapologetic, scathing critique of conservatism and aesthetic choice, respectively. This is why, as I argue presently, the interests of Falwell and Fisher in their good name (and also emotional well-being in Falwell's case) should not receive legal protection in the form of legal rights. Accordingly, the critical publications in question should not count as defamation in law *even if* they harm, or likely to harm, their reputation. The critical distinction is not between harmful and harmless statements but rather between harmful statements that give rise to a valuable conflict and harmful statements that do not. Legal rules such as fair comment and the distinction between facts and (nonprovable) opinion are doctrinal manifestations of this way of approaching the conflicts at issue, which is further explored below.

C. Four Expansions

I wish to expand on these claims in four different directions. First, I argue that the interest in free speech or self-expression is not reducible to its political or democratic significance. Second, I elaborate on the previous chapter's claim that the conflict theory is a legal theory that sets out to provide a normative framework for determining the legal rights at issue and, ultimately, what counts as wrongful

[14] *Id.*
[15] *Hustler*, 485 U.S. at 54 (internal quotation omitted).
[16] *Id.* at 55.

defamation, or infliction of emotional harm, in law. Third, I argue that viewing the conflict between free speech and good name or emotional well-being as inherently valuable does not entail an absolutist protection of the interest in free speech, to the exclusion of its conflicting interests. Nor do I argue for the lexical priority of free speech over good name or emotional well-being. Instead, the conflict warrants no more, and no less, than some measure of priority (on which more below). In the course of making this point, I also offer preliminary observations on how tort law can address the question of scope of the duty and consequent liability for its violation. Fourth, and finally, I argue that the moral necessity of addressing inherently valuable conflicts by way of determining and imposing legal rights and duties is explained by reference to the equality theory of tort law that I develop in the latter half of this book.

1. Speech beyond Democracy and Politics

Talk of liberal culture is not meant to suggest that the conflict between speech and good name or emotional well-being is only or even mainly of political or democratic significance. To begin with, the value of free and fearless communication is not limited to political speech and its contribution to collective self-governance and public discourse. It extends, as it should, to other domains of expressive engagements, such as art, academia and science,[17] adversarial litigation,[18] health care,[19] employment,[20] landlord–tenant relationships,[21]

[17] Robert Post has argued that freedom of speech (and especially the traditional First Amendment principle of free speech) and academic freedom are wholly distinct ideals. *See* Robert Post, *The Classic First Amendment Tradition Under Stress: Freedom of Speech and the University*, *in* The Free Speech Century 106 (Lee Bollinger & Geoffrey Stone eds., 2019); *cf.* Robert C. Post, Democracy, Expertise, Academic Freedom: A First Amendment Jurisprudence for the Modern State 85, 95–96 (2012). Although there are no doubt important differences—moral, legal, and contextual—between them, it seems to me that they are ultimately grounded in individual autonomy (of the speaker, listener, and thinker) and that the context, and the value associated with a particular context, may certainly affect the contours and the quality of free speech. But even then, different contexts do not break free speech in two distinct subcategories—after all, you cannot have, say, a truly Yale University in an illiberal and nondemocratic state. More generally, although Post is surely right to deny that a generic principle of free speech can determine what the legal right to free speech requires in a particular context (say, in higher education, work, public discourse, etc.), there is reason to believe that such a principle can and should inform the contextual analysis, as I show in Chapter 17.

[18] Consider the broad freedom of lawyers in an adversarial system to make assertions and draw implications in the course of representing their clients (say, when questioning a witness or in making open arguments to the jury). For more on the legal privileges of lawyerly speech in adversarial systems, see Daniel Markovits, A Modern Legal Ethics: Adversary Advocacy in a Democratic Age ch. 2 (2008).

[19] Robert Post, *Informed Consent to Abortion: A First Amendment Analysis of Compelled Physician Speech*, 2007 U. Ill. L. Rev. 939.

[20] The question of employees' speech concerns protestations and other expressive forms of distancing themselves from their employer's policy or particular decision. I take up this matter in Chapter 17. *See also* Sabine Tsuruda, *Working as Equal Moral Agents*, 26 Legal Theory 305 (2020); Cynthia Estlund, *Freedom of Expression in the Workplace*, The Oxford Handbook of Freedom of Speech 410 (Adrienne Stone & Frederick Schauer eds., 2021).

[21] *See* Chapter 17.

commerce,[22] religious life,[23] and the family.[24] Accordingly, it is a mistake to identify the interest in self-expression with democracy and the legal right to free speech with a constitutional entitlement held primarily against the government and other state actors. Instead, this extrajuridical and prepolitical interest is ultimately grounded in individual freedom and equality and, therefore, its legal expression—a right to free speech—should also protect us against private persons, including in particular private persons who wield either normative or de facto power over us (in such settings as employment, landlord/tenant, and spousal relationships), which point I develop in detail in Chapter 17.

2. From Conflicting Interests to Tort Law: Determining Legal Rights and Wrongs

The conflict theory provides a normative framework for determining legal rights by reference to their underlying interests and, in particular, the value of the conflict between them. The starting point of the analysis is the identification of the prepolitical interests in question. Focusing on the conflict between free speech, on the one hand, and good name or emotional well-being, on the other, the former interest concerns the ability of persons to manifest their expressive agency in the world as speakers, thinkers, and listeners[25]; whereas the latter concerns, first, reputation defined (for social or economic purposes) in terms of the actual estimation of some others as to one's character and, second, emotional well-being.[26]

The conflict theory addresses the conflict between our prepolitical and extrajuridical interests in free speech and good name or emotional well-being by engaging with its underlying value. It is a *legal* theory, as argued above, as it does the "engaging" by drawing on doctrinal rules to distill legal rights, corresponding duties, and standards with which to assess what constitutes violation of these duties. Two illustrations will be offered. They concern core doctrinal rules and principles in the tort of defamation and intentional infliction of emotional distress, respectively.

[22] The distinction between political and other forms of speech partially tracks distinctions between the various values underlying the ideal of free and open communication. Political speech is more closely associated with the value of democratic legitimation (see Post, *supra* note 17, at 15). Other forms of speech may be valuable not only because they serve democratic legitimation but rather because of their importance to individual autonomy, truth-seeking, and community-formation (et alia).

[23] The question of a minority within a religious minority raises the broader question of the permissible limits of pluralism, and it includes the intra-community free speech rights of the former minority.

[24] Bell Hooks, *Talking Back*, 8 Discourse 123 (1986–87).

[25] *See further* Chapter 17.

[26] As mentioned in the previous chapter with respect to reputation, I use the phrase "some others" to exclude those who hold irrational views (such as flat Earthers) or profess intolerable ideologies (such as Nazism). By contrast, the class of some others is *not* limited to the traditional common-law standard of "right-thinking people," if what is meant by this is people whose estimation of others is based solely on *moral* desert. People's reputation can be damaged even if their true character does not warrant, *morally* speaking, negative reactions. For a classical study of reputation's ends, see Robert C. Post, *The Social Foundations of Defamation Law: Reputation and the Constitution*, 74 Calif. L. Rev. 691 (1986).

Defamation. Consider, first, the distinction between factual statements and statements of opinion that make no reference to factual claims, that is, claims whose contents are not readily verifiable or falsifiable. As I argued in the previous chapter, both types of statement can, depending on the circumstances, undermine the interest in good name of those whom the statements concern. Courts recognize this much.[27] Hence, the legal significance of the fact/opinion distinction is not predicated upon the distinction between harmful and nonharmful speech. Instead, it concerns the different values (or disvalues) associated with the harm caused by *both* factual and opinion-based statements to a person's good name.[28]

Factual statements that can seriously harm a person's interest in good name can be divided into two kinds. Some reputation-damaging factual statements are also false, and other such statements can be true. It is important to note that although both can be harmful, only false statements warrant legal protection in the form of a legal right to good name (and even then the right should be further circumscribed so as to allow for some breathing space to reduce chilling effect on free speech). This is because the conflict between free expression of falsehoods and good name is valueless. Factual statements that contain true allegations should be left to stand, and the legal right to good name should not guard against them *not* because they cannot undermine good name but rather because the conflict between free expression of the truth and good name is inherently valuable.

Now consider statements of opinion (which are not readily verifiable or falsifiable). Allegations that amount to rhetorical hyperbole, ridicule, parody, satire, and the like can certainly damage a person's reputation; a recent empirical study further suggests that the reputational effects of satire (and, by extension, other forms of criticism coupled with humor) tend to be greater than nonsatirical criticism.[29] That said, the conflict between a typical act of making such expressions and good name can be inherently valuable because of, rather than in spite of, the potential harm to reputation. Notice that the value at issue is not necessarily an attribute of a particular instance of conflict (say, the conflict in *Ford*, *Falwell*, or *Fisher*). After all, not every instance of rhetorical hyperbole, ridicule, satire (et alia) can in fact contribute to a better understanding of a predicament or to challenging existing social, economic, or political conditions. It is also very difficult (perhaps even absurd) to quantify contribution of this or that statement. Instead, carving out rhetorical

[27] *See, e.g.*, Wilkow v. Forbes, Inc., 241 F.3d 552, 557 (7th Cir. 2001) where Judge Easterbrook noted that "uncharitable opinion" and other allegations of "greed," "sharp dealing," and resort to "name-calling" are not defamatory under Illinois law *even when* they lower a person's "standing" in the eyes of the relevant community (here, lenders).

[28] *See* Burton v. Crowell Pub. Co., 82 F.2d 154, 156 (2d Cir. 1936), where Judge Learned Hand observed that "[t]he only reason why the law makes truth a defense is not because a libel must be false, but because the utterance of truth is in all circumstances an interest paramount to reputation[.]"

[29] Hooria Jazaieri & Derek D. Rucker, *Softening the Blow or Sharpening the Blade: Examining the Reputational Effects of Satire*, 154(5) J. EXPERIMENTAL PSYCHOLOGY 1201 (2025).

hyperbole and other critical statements of opinion from the purview of defamation liability creates the *conditions* necessary for the good of liberal culture to arise.[30]

Intentional infliction of emotional distress. The second illustration focuses on the conflict between free speech and emotional well-being. As a legal theory, the conflict theory guides the determination of legal rights to free speech and to emotional well-being by considering the conflict's value. It does so, once again, by employing legal doctrine. A key doctrinal standard concerns the character of a statement—does it raise "a matter of public concern"[31] or, somewhat differently, is there "a public interest in others being able to listen" to such a statement?[32] A matter of public concern should not be limited to political matters. Nor does it have to be of interest to everyone.[33] Instead, it can concern social, economic, religious, and all other matters that bear on existing conditions or challenge deeply held convictions. The class of people who should take an interest in a statement of public concern can include the entire community, though it can also be pertinent to a subset, including a small subset, thereof.

Rendering determinate such a standard is, no doubt, a difficult task. However, its initial ambiguity—viz., its propensity for multiple interpretations—does not mean that it is empty, meaningless, or conclusory. For the present purpose, however, we can set this worry to one side by considering cases in which distinguishing between public from nonpublic concern is straightforward, that is, without the benefit of a theory of what counts as a public concern.

I argue that a conflict between free speech and emotional well-being that raises a matter of public concern should fall into the category of inherently valuable conflicts. It should, therefore, give rise to a robust legal right to free speech at the expense of the legal right to emotional well-being. By contrast, conflicts between the same interests that cannot generate public concern should have the inverse order of rights, elevating the right to emotional well-being at the expense of free speech. Between these two opposite prescriptions, there exist conflicts in which the question of public concern defies a clear answer at the time of uttering the offensive statement, owing to uncertainties about the relevance of a statement to the public (as when a statement hinges on factual assertions that are not easily verifiable in real time).[34]

Consider *Snyder v. Phelps.* There, on free speech grounds, the US Supreme Court blocked the imposition of tort liability on a church leader (and his family

[30] In US defamation law, for example, actionable defamatory statements must include (or imply) assertions of fact. Milkovich v. Lorain J. Co., 497 U.S. 1 (1990).

[31] Snyder v. Phelps, 562 U.S. 443, 458 (2011).

[32] Rhodes v. OPO, [2015] UKSC 32, para. 76.

[33] *See* Cynthia L. Estlund, *Speech on Matters of Public Concern: The Perils of an Emerging First Amendment Category*, 59 Geo. Wash. L. Rev. 1, 55 (1990). *See also Snyder*, 562 U.S. at 453–54.

[34] I leave the category of tolerably valuable conflicts in and around the tort of intentional infliction of emotional distress to another occasion.

members) for intentionally inflicting emotional distress on the plaintiff by picketing and displaying highly insulting signs next to the plaintiff's son's funeral.[35] The key factor in making this decision was that these statements involved matters of public concern—to wit, protesting the widespread acceptance of a certain—arguably, liberal—conception of sexual choice in society and in government.

According to the conflict theory, the ability to challenge how things stand resonates with the good of liberal culture. To realize this good, speech must be allowed to have real bite, including by picking on, even skewering deeply held convictions, habits, and norms. Moreover, speech must be respected as an authentic expression with regard to the speaker's choice of words, style, and so on. Sugar-coating speech, therefore, may not do even if the content of the speech would point in the same direction: A diplomatic disapproval is not the same as the hurtful condemnation of homosexuality as sinful.

Further, protecting both speaker's authenticity and the real bite of free speech at the expense of emotional well-being is not some unfortunate upshot of our failure to insulate the latter from the excesses of the former. Rather, it reflects our first-best solution, namely, what we ought to do even if some such insulation would have been available. The conflict sanitizer illustrates this point: Suppose that the Phelps family members could engage in the exact same expressive activity, but that none of it will ever penetrate the emotional makeup of Snyder (for instance, thanks to a fantastic new pill called anti-IIED). In this nonconflictual situation, both parties will enjoy maximal legal rights against interference with their respective prepolitical interests. That said, the value of such legal rights diminishes dramatically precisely because creating a nonconflictual setting is inimical to the good of liberal culture. To avoid this normative loss, the tort of intentional infliction of emotional distress must determine legal rights so as to construct the conditions necessary for the good at issue to thrive.

Viewing a certain statement as raising a matter of public concern is a doctrinal resource on which tort law draws in determining the legal rights of the interacting parties. If the statements made by the members of the Phelps family are of this type—for example, expressing social, moral, or political critique—then their fundamental interest in free speech should also be recognized as a legal right as against Snyder whereas Snyder's interest in emotional well-being should not be protected by law. Notice that my argument does *not* suggest that there is value, not to mention inherent value, in the specific statements made by the Phelpses. If anything, there are good reasons to condemn their choice of words, the location of speaking out, and especially the timing of doing so.[36]

[35] *Snyder*, 562 U.S. at 448.

[36] *See* Ernest J. Weinrib, Reciprocal Freedom: Private Law and Public Right 167–73 (2022); Benjamin C. Zipursky, Snyder v. Phelps, *Outrageousness, and the Open Texture of Tort Law*, 60 DePaul L. Rev. 473 (2011).

Once again, in saying that the conflict between free speech—when this speech raises a matter of public concern—and emotional well-being is inherently valuable, the conflict theory seeks to construct the *conditions* necessary for the good of liberal culture to thrive. Hence, it does not concern itself with the content of a particular statement; nor does it assess the prospects of social change linked to a particular statement. Instead, for the purpose of determining legal rights, the conflict theory calls for the priority of the interest in free speech over the interest in emotional well-being if exercising the former raises a matter of public concern. Ultimately, it comes down to a rule of no liability for emotional harms caused by those making statements on matters of public concern.

By contrast, expressive activities on matters that raise no public concern should receive the opposite treatment. Thus, the interest in free speech should take the back seat and the interest in emotional well-being should receive robust protection in the form of a legal right against wrongful infliction of emotional harm.[37] This is so for a combination of reasons. Whereas the freedom to engage in expressive activities might severely harm the emotional well-being of another person, facilitating the former at the expense of the latter *cannot* contribute to the good of liberal culture unless the speech is of a matter of public concern. Indeed, intending to cause one emotional discomfort by using racial slurs or resorting to intimidating language does not take an issue with how things in society stand.[38] It is far removed from expressive acts of challenging orthodoxy, sanctimony, power, and so forth.

The doctrinal home for such an assessment lies in the standard of public concern. On the conflict theory, the failure to meet this standard results in recognizing a legal right to emotional well-being and its correlative duty against wrongfully inflicting emotional harm on the right-holder. This way of determining legal rights and duties, it is important to note, is not reducible to ex post facto judgments of liability. Rather, the conflict theory—which is, recall, a legal theory—operates constructively and prospectively by determining terms of interactions between people pursuing conflicting interests. When the interaction revolves around matters that raise no public concern, tort law should fix its terms by first preventing (if possible) and only then ameliorating the emotional harm.

To conclude this discussion, let me address the following objection: The conflict theory is not a tort-law theory but rather one of constitutional theory.[39] The case of *Snyder v. Phelps* self-consciously draws on the constitutional right to free speech to change the traditional, common-law rights and duties created by the tort of

[37] I use *wrongful* in recognition of a range of ways to characterize improper behavior: Intentional, reckless, and negligent infliction of emotional harm. In principle, there is no reason to rule out liability for negligence.

[38] *See, e.g.*, Littlefield v. McGuffey, 954 F.2d 1337 (7th Cir. 1992); Hunt v. state, 69 A.3d 360 (Del. 2013), respectively.

[39] *See* Rachel Bayefsky, Dignity and Judicial Authority 103–04, 107 (2024); *see generally* Cristina Carmody Tilley, *Rescuing Dignitary Torts from the Constitution*, 78 Brook. L. Rev. 65 (2012).

intentional infliction of emotional distress. My response is that the conflict theory is a tort law theory that means that the preceding analysis is not one of constitutional law theory. To see that I wish to introduce a distinction between the substantive and the institutional; I then reinforce this distinction by offering a comparison between the American and the English ways of determining rights and duties in connection with the tort in question.

To begin with, the constitutional path marshaled by the *Snyder* court provides the institutional outlet for legal change. The First Amendment is invoked by this Court as what H. L. A. Hart would call a secondary rule of change, which is a legal mechanism for introducing changes in existing primary rules (along with other mechanisms such as statutory change, adopting new precedents, and more).[40] Deploying the First Amendment as an agent of legal change does not determine the nature of this change. In the case of the tort of intentional infliction of emotional distress, the change concerns what one private person owes another which is, in turn, an answer to the prior question of what interpersonal rights we—private persons—have. This question takes up the substance of a legal change whose institutional engine, to change metaphors, is the constitution. Thus, the First Amendment functions as a Hartian secondary rule used to change the primary rule, the substantive right and its correlative duty, of the tort of intentional infliction of emotional distress.

The analytical distinction between the institutional and the substantive aspects of the *Snyder* decision can be further substantiated by reference to English tort law. There, a somewhat similar tort has substantively evolved without the benefit of the First Amendment's institutional outlet, but as integral to the common law itself. Hence both the secondary rule of change and the primary rule subject to the change are part and parcel of English tort law. In *Rhodes v. OPO*,[41] the UK Supreme Court refined the tort of intentional infliction of emotional harm, first created in *Wilkinson v. Downton*[42] in light of the conflict between free speech and emotional well-being. Among other things, the *Rhodes* court recognized that, save for some exceptions, an author is entitled to publish a book even if doing so inflicts psychiatric illness. The court recognized the priority of freedom of speech over emotional well-being, saying that "It is difficult to envisage any circumstances in which speech which is not deceptive, threatening or possibly abusive, could give rise to liability in tort for willful infringement of another's right to personal safety."[43] The court grounds this right in two considerations: One's right to tell the world the truth about one's struggle and suffering, on the one hand, and the "corresponding public interest in others being able to listen to [one's] life story in all its searing

[40] *See* H. L. A. Hart, The Concept of Law 95–96 (2d ed. 1994).
[41] [2015] UKSC 32.
[42] [1897] 2 Q.B. 57.
[43] *Rhodes*, [2015] UKSC at para 77.

detail," on the other hand.[44] This characterization can plausibly be made more general by emphasizing the interest in free "speech which is not deceptive, threatening or possibly abusive," on the one hand, and the "general interest" in such speech, one the other.[45] Thus, placing free speech on matters of public concern before emotional well-being, as the conflict theory dictates, makes no institutional reference to the constitutional right to free speech. Instead, the common law of tort law finds the institutional engine of change within its own set of commitments.

3. The Relative Priority of Free Speech over Reputation and Emotional Well-being

The preceding analysis implies that the conflict theory rejects the view that only free speech matters and our interest in good name or emotional well-being does not count. This theory suggests that some measure of conflict is required if the conflict is inherently valuable. I now wish to argue that *only* some measure of such conflict is required. It means that free speech should enjoy relative, rather than lexical priority. Here is why.

Two reasons call for limiting the priority of the interest in free speech over that in good name or emotional well-being. The first reason is that giving lexical priority to free speech over the other interest is inconsistent with deeming the latter a *fundamental* interest. Negating it entirely necessarily impairs our ability to interact with others as free and equal persons, as I argued above.

A second, reinforcing reason concerns the good of liberal culture. This is the point at which the conflict theory assumes the task of determining legal rights to free speech and to good name or emotional well-being. A conflict between interests is inherently valuable *only because and only insofar as* it distinctively constructs the conditions necessary for the realization of that good. However, not all instances in which free speech clashes with the good name or emotional well-being of another meets this standard. To give an example, as mentioned above, making false statements about a person's criminal record is an obvious case in point. If anything, this example shows that some conflicts between free speech and good name or emotional well-being are better viewed as inimical to the idea of liberal culture. Accordingly, they cannot be treated as inherently valuable; instead, they are valueless. This is precisely why the US Supreme Court rightly rejected Justice Black's view that the press should have unconditional immunity from liability for defamation—the flaw in his position lies in assuming that the priority of free speech over good name should be absolute.[46]

[44] *Id.*, at para. 76.
[45] *Id.*, at paras. 77 & 76, respectively.
[46] *See* New York Times Co. v. Sullivan, 376 U.S. 254, 293 (1964); Curtis Publishing Co. v. Butts, 388 U.S. 130, 172 (1967).

Against this backdrop, the conflict theory insists that the basic normative task of defamation law and the tort of intentional infliction of emotional distress is to assess whether the conflict in question is inherently valuable, tolerably valuable, or valueless. It is on the basis of this analysis that legal rights—to free expression and to reputation or emotional well-being—are determined. By implication, the standard of "defamation" employed by the law in order to decide what counts as violating the *legal right* to a good name reflects this prior determination. Likewise, imposing liability for intentional infliction of emotional distress turns on a parallel prior determination.

4. Why Law? From Conflict to Equality Theory

Notice that nothing I have said so far shows why *law*, and in particular *tort* law, is necessary to construct the conditions for a liberal culture to arise. Perhaps denying legal rights to free speech would be more conducive to robust public engagement in critical thinking and truth seeking. The suggestion (to which I oppose) is that repression and starvation might make people more, rather than less, active in ways that support the liberal cause of securing freedom and equality for all. Suppose (for the sake of the argument) that this empirical prediction turns out to be correct. Should we roll back modern defamation law and reintroduce a near maximalist protection of good name? My answer is in the negative.

Indeed, establishing legal rights to free speech is required to secure the equal standing of interest-holders. It is the fact of being *entitled* to realize one's interest in self-expression that enables one to relate to others, including powerful private persons, as equal. This is so because having an entitlement of this kind creates the special standing of the speaker to engage in expressive acts without first having to secure permission. This claim, along with one concerning substantive equality, figures prominently in the equality theory of tort law that I defend in the latter half of the book, including in connection with horizontal rights to free speech. More broadly, the equality theory establishes that in a liberal society, relationality, and specifically just terms of pairwise interactions, forms a fundamental pillar of the legal order.

II. The Good of Sociability and Battery Law: Bodily Sovereignty Meets Liberty of *Inter*-action

It is certainly true that bodily sovereignty is essential to leading an autonomous life. All else equal, a physical attack is just wrong. According to tort law, it may sometimes be wrong even when consented to.[47] Even a mere touching can be wrongful

[47] Consent does not count as a defense to battery in instances of valueless conflicts featuring criminal acts. Dueling is perhaps the paradigm example. *See also* Francis C. Bohlen, *Consent as Affecting Civil Liability for Breaches of the Peace*, 24 Colum. L. Rev. 819 (1924).

when done under certain circumstances and for offensive purposes—for instance, when it amounts to sexual harassment or other forms of unauthorized touching that take advantage of a person's vulnerability. But does it follow, and is it true for Ronald Dworkin to say, that "touching someone without his permission, however gently, violates a taboo?"[48] Or for Cardozo to assert that "Every human being of adult years and sound mind has a right to determine what shall be done with his own body?"[49] I think not.

To begin with, it is not clear why innocently tapping me on my shoulder to ask for the time is different than just making a similar request save for the touching. The tapping is unauthorized in the sense that no permission has been asked or (let's suppose) even assumed, but the more important point is that such permission need not be secured in order to render the touching permissible. Do we have any good reason to live in a world in which this contact is impermissible unless consented to? I suppose that Dworkin would have responded by taking back the "however gently" from the assertion just cited. Accordingly, it can be permissible—and at times even valuable—for a stranger to be in charge of our body if, and only if, it is nothing but an innocent and trifle touching.[50] The fact that we occupy what Prosser called "a crowded world," lacking the possibility of "erect[ing] a glass cage around [our]self," only reinforces this judgment.[51]

However, a conflict between bodily sovereignty and our interest in human interaction can be valuable beyond the triviality of the tap-on-the-shoulder type of encounter. I argue that this conflict can sometimes count as inherently valuable precisely because the realization of the good of sociability must, to some extent, come at the expense of preserving bodily sovereignty. Notice that bodily sovereignty is a subset of bodily integrity or safety: It concerns one's ability to control who may touch one's person, rather than the ability to prevent others from inflicting harm by carrying out a violent or offensive attack, a point to which I return below.

The good of sociability is an implication of the conflict and, for many people, its realization is not possible in the absence of the conflict, such as by creating nonconflictual mechanisms to bring it about. I take sociability first and then explain why, sometimes, the realization of this good calls for a conflict between our interests in human interaction and bodily sovereignty.

[48] Ronald Dworkin, Justice for Hedgehogs 288 (2011). Dworkin grounds this assertion in a certain principle of dignity which, in turn, calls for a nondelegable, personal responsibility for our lives. On this view, we should be "in sole charge of what happens to or in our bodies." *Id.*

[49] Schloendorff v. Society of New York Hospital, 105 N.E. 92, 93 (N.Y. 1914).

[50] *See, e.g.*, Collins v. Wilcock [1984] 1 W.L.R. 1172. My analysis conflicts with the idea of freedom as independence only if independence is characterized in absolutist terms. However, a conflict need not arise if independence "admit[s] of degree," as Joseph Raz has argued. Joseph Raz, The Morality of Freedom 373 (1986). *See also* Anna Stilz, Territorial Sovereignty: Philosophical Exploration 112, 116 (2019).

[51] William L. Prosser, Handbook of the Law of Torts 37 (4th ed. 1971).

Sociability can mean many things, but I shall use it in the formal sense most famously associated with the work of Georg Simmel: An idea of interacting with others *purely for the sake* of being with them in the world.[52] The basic thought is that our fundamental interest in human interaction, which is a subset of our interest in liberty of action, consists of interpersonal engagements of instrumental and/or noninstrumental value. The good of sociability concerns the latter. To illustrate, whereas people often converse for the purpose of exchanging information and ideas, we may also find ourselves engaging in conversion simply out of an authentic desire to experience one another as connected persons. As Simmel puts it, "talking is an end in itself . . . the content is merely the indispensable carrier of the stimulation, which the lively exchange of talk as such unfolds."[53]

Sociability can manifest itself in the world in any number of ways (such as in a game of hide and seek or in sharing a meal). One of them includes physical contact as an expressive act of what Simmel calls "togetherness."[54] Empirical research even suggests that physical contact (of the right kind) may even be the most significant vehicle of sociability.[55] Under the appropriate circumstances, grabbing your hand, picking up a neighbor's child who is wailing, placing an arm around your shoulder, hugging, chafing you playfully on the arm, wiping your tears, slapping lightly on your back, and some nonviolent forms of horseplay among friends and relatives *could* be conceived as instantiations of sociability without, and irrespective of, securing or assuming consent. I say could, rather than would, because some people are strongly reluctant to display empathy in a physical way. It might be their natural instincts, the culture in which they live, or any other factor that leads them to shun the physical manifestations of sociability.[56] My argument, however, focuses only on those who do find it valuable, perhaps even irresistible, to make certain physical contact part of what it means for them to practice sociability.[57]

Is the conflict between our interests in human interaction and bodily sovereignty inevitable? Analytically speaking, it is not. Normatively, however, its existence is

[52] Georg Simmel & Everett C. Hughes (trans.), *The Sociology of Sociability*, 55 AM. J. SOC'Y 254 (1949). Simmel adds to his conception of sociability a liberal commitment to freedom and equality between the interacting parties. *Id.*, at 256, 257.

[53] *Id.*, at 259.

[54] *Id.*, at 255.

[55] Alberto Gallace & Charles Spence, *The Science of Interpersonal Touch: An Overview*, 34 NEUROSCIENCE & BIOBEHAV. REV. 246 (2010).

[56] Moshe Ludlow, the protagonist of McBride's novel *Heaven & Earth Grocery Store*, even notes that "[t]hose things [i.e., social touchings] were almost forbidden in [the U.S.]." JAMES MCBRIDE, HEAVEN & EARTH GROCERY STORE 275 (2023).

[57] More broadly, the question of what sociability requires or commends is partially influenced by our culture. For instance, the different attitudes toward sociable physical contact between people living in different places might be vast (and important differences may obtain even among members of either one of these societies). As a result, sociability would be practiced differently in these two settings, which means that the law of battery would have to draw, *not* uncritically though, on conventional understandings of sociability in order adequately to give effect to sociability's value.

necessary in order to create the conditions for practicing sociability among those who deem certain (i.e., nonviolent and nonoffensive) physical contacts integral to sociability. Consider the conflict sanitizer once again.

The simplest and most effective sanitizer is that of consent. Insistence on implied or express consent as a prerequisite to sociable touching might lead one to believe in eating the cake and having it too: Bodily sovereignty gets its maximalist protection without thereby annihilating our interest in human interaction.

That said, consent can undermine sociability because it destroys the authenticity and spontaneity necessary for experiencing a sense of togetherness.[58] Indeed, it is not about the material burden of seeking consent or otherwise figuring out whether apparent consent is imputable; after all, this burden can sometimes be easily met. Rather, a consent requirement obligates us to *filter* authentic and spontaneous expressions of true friendship, rendering them conditional ones. Further, it makes such expressions wholly dependent on whether our friend approves of them. It, therefore, fundamentally alters the interaction.[59]

To see why conditionality may be problematic, imagine seeing your friend in a state of deep sorrow and desperation. Suppose your emphatic instincts compel you to hug them as an expression of solidarity and comfort. You can act in other ways, to be sure, but this course of action makes most sense to you. There is a loss, in terms of sociability, in having to take into consideration the consent requirement *before* you launch your show of empathy. In short, considering consent on such occasions is one consideration too many.[60]

However, perhaps we can devise a better conflict sanitizer than that of consent. It is better in the sense that it does away with the need to filter empathetic engagement by subjecting it to the implicit or explicit consent of the other party. Consider again Hart's hypothetical case of perfectly invulnerable people, for instance, due to some technological improvement in armory technology.[61] Although Hart wants us to imagine a world free of brute, physical violence, I wish to refocus attention on another sort of invulnerability to sociable touching. Thus, instead of military armory, the conflict sanitizer will feature a social-distancing armory, according to which people will be able to numb their feelings, senses, as well as any other cognitive and

[58] I suppose that pretending to be a friend is not the same as being a friend. *See further* Simmel, *supra* note 52, at 258.

[59] The forthcoming *Restatement (Third) of Torts: Intentional Torts to Persons* §1 TD No 4 (2019) draws a sharp distinction between implied consent, on the one hand, and actual, apparent, or presumed consent, on the other. Actual, apparent, or presumed consent all require the actor to pause and ask for consent, which (as I argue) changes the interaction. Presumed consent is valid only if the actor believes their friend would consent if asked, and if the circumstances warrant not asking for seeking actual consent. The argument from sociability explains why, in some cases, the mere possibility of pausing to ask for consent should *not* prevent an actor from engaging in genuinely sociable contact without first obtaining consent.

[60] Borrowed (very loosely) from Bernard Williams, Moral Luck 18 (1981).

[61] H. L. A. Hart, *Positivism and the Separation of Law and Morals*, 71 Harv. L. Rev. 593, 623 (1958).

noncognitive faculty that would have been affected by social touching. As a result, to give an example, hugging will be felt by huggees as if they were hand-waved for hello from a distance. This way, the interest in human interaction could be fully satisfied on the side of the hugger without thereby infringing the bodily integrity of the huggee. For instance, consider a high school teacher rushing to hug their tearful student who is devastated by ongoing academic failure. Thanks to the sanitizer, the latter will not be able to experience the hug as a physical contact; instead, the teacher's hug will be felt by the student on a par with a genuine, though contactless gesture (say, showing the heart-hands symbol).

However, something is missing, normatively speaking. The conflict sanitizer at issue erodes sociability and its consequent notion of togetherness along two dimensions. The first concerns the intensity of sociability. Indeed, it is one thing for the devastated student to experience a contactless gesture; quite another to be embraced by the teacher's empathetic hug. The second dimension runs deeper. Hugging the student without first securing authorization, and doing so even if there is no good reason to assume implicit or hypothetical consent, reflects a demand for the *involuntary surrender* of the student's absolute bodily sovereignty. It is only a momentary surrender, to be sure, and it does not involve violence, deception, or abuse. Making such a demand allows the teacher to share in the student's condition in a special way: The hug is a physical act of emotional "taking" in which the hugger assumes, without the leave of the huggee, some of the student's dire feelings of devastation. This way of coming at togetherness is not reducible to what the hugger feels for the huggee. Nor is it reducible to what the hugger wants the huggee to feel. Rather, it is also about the hugger wanting the huggee to feel that the hugger shares in—"takes" some of—the student's feelings. The hug is, therefore, a physical conduit for the emotional connection between the two. Notice that a structurally similar argument can be made in the perfectly inverse case where the student spontaneously hugs the teacher in celebration of recent academic success. Here, instead of taking, the hugging student shares in—positive feelings.

Against this backdrop, I argue that the conflict between human interaction and bodily sovereignty can be inherently valuable, and that this characterization requires that the realization of the former must, in some measure, come at the expense of the latter. A cold, sanitized form of social relations, especially among friends and family, cannot substitute for an authentic hug (et alia). While touching without first securing permission may require the involuntary surrender of bodily sovereignty, doing so may not only be permissible but sometimes also valuable.

***

As in the previous discussion of free speech versus good name or emotional well-being, and for similar reasons, the priority of the interest in human interaction over bodily sovereignty is relative, not lexical. To begin with, the priority is necessarily circumscribed in the sense that it is limited to constructing the conditions for inherently valuable conflicts only. Many instances of touching others without securing their consent are valueless and so cannot ground the priority in question. Punching a person in the face and making offensive advances are cases at point.

But does it mean that sociable touching—physical contacts that can sustain the good of sociability—should gain priority over bodily integrity? Certainly not. The priority of the former is relative, rather than lexical, reflecting the idea that the interest in bodily sovereignty is fundamental, too. A clear boundary lies when a sociable touching turns violent, offensive, or otherwise improper.[62] Further, even a sociable touching that is not designed to harm another may be deemed wrongful on account of its ability to cause harm. This is why, to give an example, nonconsensual horseplay involving a playful kick that unexpectedly results in injury is treated as an ordinary instance of battery (with the exception, to be discussed in Chapter 4, of contact sports).[63] More generally, a liberal society cannot turn persons into mere means to sociability, in which case tort law should not recognize a legal right to engage in sociable touching that undermines, or is likely to undermine, the safety of persons without prior authorization.

III. The Good of Egalitarian Market Relations: Stability Meets Competition

Free, open, and competitive markets, I take it, constitute a basic pillar of the liberal-egalitarian society.[64] Some measure of conflictual market relations, I argue, is inherently valuable. Tort law, in turn, should determine rights and duties so as to construct the conditions necessary for such a conflictual state of affairs to arise. I wish to show that the tort of inducement of breach of contract is a normative framework for doing that. My focus is on relations of production, broadly conceived to include working relations including those that go beyond traditional employment relationships. An obvious extension is a contractor recruited to provide some service. But the category of production relations also covers interactions between different actors along the supply chain, such as the relationship between the manufacturer and the distributor of the same good. (Notice that the argument going forward does not suggest that contract law must remain passive, say, by enforcing noncompete covenants or reinforcing power imbalances.)

[62] The shift from the principled argument for sociability's value to its implementation in law can be very challenging. The challenge on this front is one of line drawing, and it is further exacerbated by obvious evidential hurdles. The major worry is that authorizing sociable forms of physical contact might open the door to unauthorized sexual contact, which is flatly impermissible.

[63] *See, e.g.*, Cole v. Hibberd, No. CA94-01-015, 1994 WL 424103, at *2 (Ohio App. 1994).

[64] *See, e.g.*, Elizabeth Anderson, *Ethical Assumptions in Economic Theory: Some Lesson from the History of Credit and Bankruptcy*, 7 Econ. Theory & Moral Practice 347 (2004).

I argue that the conflict theory is deployed in the service of addressing one way of engaging in market competition, namely, interfering with contractual relations. It features a business opportunity, the acceptance of which would necessarily frustrate an outstanding contractual obligation.[65] A celebrated example is competition between two opera houses for the service of an opera singer.[66] In offering the singer to perform at the owner's theater, the owner of one opera house interferes with the singer's contractual obligation to perform at the other house. The latter house complains that the interference by the former house should be deemed impermissible or wrongful. Any nonarbitrary way to decide the matter depends on a prior question: What rights do the two parties have? And this question, in turn, depends on the prior question of what to make of the interests underlying their respective rights and, in particular, the value of the conflict between these interests.

The conflict I wish to take up is *not* the contract-law concern with the interaction between the promisor, who is the singer, and the promisee, who is the owner of the latter opera house. Rather, it is about the one that arises between the promisee and a third party making a lucrative business offer to the promisor, which is to say between the owners of the opera houses. This conflict pits "contract stability" against "free competition."[67] In terms of the conflict theory, contract stability is a subset of our fundamental interest in being self-determining agents who are, thereby, able to determine ends, in part by inducing others' assurances about the future—for instance, the singer's promise to perform at the owner's opera house functions in this way. A promised performance, that is, allows the owner to consolidate and stabilize a plan of action. Free competition, too, is a subset of a fundamental interest in self-determination, as the ability to compete is often integral to determining what ends to pursue and how. Both subsets of self-determination matter in general, though their significance grows further still in light of our human condition, namely, the prominence of markets in our life (as workers, consumers, investors, house dwellers, and so forth).

The two interests exert pressure toward conflict, especially when broadly construed. Analytically speaking, there are a number of ways to address this conflict, ranging from assigning maximal legal protection to one interest at the expense of the other, and vice versa. There are, of course, many other in-between ways to cope with it. Hence, the real question is normative, not analytical. The conflict theory commences its normative inquiry by identifying the kind of value underlying the conflict. I argue that within limits this conflict can be inherently

[65] Inducing breach of at-will (or other voidable) contracts is typically considered as the subject matter of a different tort—intentional interference with prospective economic advantage. Although my argument in the main text focuses solely on the inducement, not interference, tort, my analysis and its conclusion can be extended, with some modifications, to capture the latter tort as well.

[66] Lumely v. Gye (1853) 2 E & B 216.

[67] Harry Kalven, Jr., *Torts: A Quest for Appropriate Standards*, 53 CAL. L. REV. 189, 193 (1965). Kalven's presentation of the distinction is fully consistent with the common law's self-understanding. A leading decision is *Imperial Ice Co. v. Rossier*, 112 P.2d 631, 632 (Cal. 1941).

valuable and, therefore, that the tort of inducement of breach of contract should determine legal rights and duties so as to construct the conditions for the interests in question to come into conflict.

But the "coming into conflict" is inherently valuable only insofar as these rights and duties give the interest in free competition some measure of priority over the interest in contract stability. Within limits, the interfering opera house should have the right to compete with the other opera house, including by luring away the singer. I argue that this way of constructing the conflict between free competition and contract stability is valuable because it brings about what I shall call the good of egalitarian market relations. This value is inherent to the conflict in the sense that its realization would not be possible in the absence of the conflict, say, by creating nonconflictual mechanisms to bring it about.

A. The Good of Egalitarian Market Relations

Securing the prominence of the interest in free competition may—sometimes, depending on the circumstances—turn out to promote optimal allocation of scarce "human resources," foster greater innovation, and improve overall growth.[68] However, the reason why the conflict between free competition and contract stability is inherently, rather than contingently, valuable rests on its connection with self-determination and equality.[69] The basic idea is that a contractual promise to perform a task (including work) should not prevent market actors from competing over the promisor's service. It means that a robust freedom to compete, including by luring away a promisor, at the expense of the promisee's stability interest, gives rise to an important *emancipatory* implication: Markets without the vulnerability of workers, contractors, and providers to relations of control and of dependency.[70] I shall call it the good of egalitarian market relations. The immediate beneficiaries of the good at issue are the workers, contractors, service providers, and other

[68] *See, e.g.*, Orly Lobel, Talent Wants to be Free: Why We Should Learn to Love Leaks, Raids, and Free Riding (2013).

[69] *Cf.* David Howarth, *Against* Lumley v. Gye, 68 M.L.R. 195, 224 (2005) who supports abolishing, or substantially restricting, the inducement tort on "economic efficiency" grounds. The argument he makes suggests that while "morality" may not support his view, efficiency does. By contrast, I argue on *moral* grounds that the tort in question should be restricted to cases of targeting and other independently repugnant acts of inducement.

[70] Vulnerability to relations of control and dependency admits of degree, but the more important point to emphasize is that it exists even when the worker (et alia) is high-skilled and talented one. On the structural asymmetry between capital and labor (broadly conceived), see Claus Offe, Disorganized Capitalism: Contemporary Transformations of Work and Politics 177–78 (1985); *see also* Samuel Issacharoff, *Contracting for Employment: The Limited Return of the Common Law*, 74 Tex. L. Rev. 1783, 1787–89 (1996). Empirical studies reinforce this point. *See, e.g.*, Matt Marx, *The Firm Strikes Back: Non-Compete Agreements and the Mobility of Technical Professionals*, 76 Am. Soc. Rev. 695 (2011).

promisors participating in the supply side of the market as genuinely—in contrast to formally—free and equal agents.[71]

The emancipatory implication of markets is extensively discussed in connection with the more basic, get-go question of why have markets in the first place.[72] At the get-go stage, markets are liberating in the sense that they displace economic orderings structured around relations of fixed hierarchy or bondage (as in feudalism). But the basic insight underlying emancipation or liberation also applies beyond the get-go question to inform the design of the market's rules of the game. Hence, paraphrasing on the *jus ad bello* versus *jus in bello* distinction, the liberating appeal of markets should operate not only at the "ad market" stage but also at the "in market" stage. A robust freedom to compete is particularly important in order to sustain non- or less-hierarchical forms of market relations by lowering the obstacles on *intra*-market mobility. As I argued in the case of free speech, the connection between the right to compete and its consequent emancipatory value is not a contingent one. Rather, realizing the latter and protecting the former are two aspects of the same good of egalitarian market relations (and as mentioned above, this conclusion implicates contract law as well).

This way of justifying the priority of competing-by-luring over contract stability suggests that the inevitable harms it inflicts on employers, promisees, and other market actors—in terms of undermining a subset of their fundamental interest in self-determination—is not something to be lamented. This is because the conflict between the interests on the inducer's side and on the promisee's side is not only valuable but rather inherently valuable (on which more below). Accordingly, we should not defuse this conflict *even if* doing so will not undermine the economic function of markets, which is that of allocating goods in the service of efficient investment, production, and consumption. As I shall argue below, a core task of the tort of inducement of breach of contract, properly conceived, is to determine rights and duties in ways that *give effect* to the conflict of interests in question by constructing the conditions necessary for such conflict to arise.

B. Why Conflict?

Perhaps, however, my argument moves too quickly from the observation that egalitarian market relations are good to the conclusion that this good is inherently valuable. Must an ideal of egalitarian market relations call for both robust freedom

[71] I take up the special case of employment relations in Chapters 9 and 17. I also discuss market relations in and around the demand side (especially consumers of goods) in Chapter 9.

[72] Elizabeth Anderson, Private Government: How Employers Rule Our Lives (and Why We Don't Talk about It) 2–4, 17–22 (2017).

to compete and the harm it entails? In other words, is the conflict at issue contingently, rather than inherently, valuable?

My answer is in the negative. Resort to the conflict sanitizer can show why. Suppose that the state provides generous universal income and training support to those who seek to walk away from their promised performance (as workers, providers, contractors, etc.). The program will apply universally and indefinitely, that is, to any and all promisors who decide to quit their jobs for as long as they wish. Such an engagement can substantially weaken the control and dependency to which promisors, such as workers, are typically subject. In addition to this arrangement, sanitizing the conflict will further require granting promisees a right against third parties seeking to lure away their (the promisees') promisors. Third parties, in turn, will be entitled to compete in the market, including for talented workers and providers, save for the right to do so by interfering with existing contractual relations. The generous training programs provided by the state may serve as a potentially vast repository of quality candidates on which competitors could draw. All in all, the conflict sanitizer can manufacture a nonconflictual state of affairs wherein contractual stability receives maximal protection against third-party competitors and the setback to the freedom to compete may be partially offset by the state's educational programs. Most importantly, the conflict between contract stability and free competition is muted without thereby giving up on the good of egalitarian market relations. Or so one might object.

That said, the conflict is *inherently* valuable, which means that deconflictualization is bound to fail, normatively speaking. Indeed, the most generous safety net ever may adequately guarantee the *financial* interest of those who quit their work in the market, but work (ideally) is not reducible to its financial returns. Instead, it is (ideally) a ground project, part of what might make life meaningful.[73] Another way to put it is to say that the conflict sanitizer changes the *quality* of the good of egalitarian market relations. The conflict between free competition and contract stability extends the realization of this good beyond the current contractual relation between the promisee and its promisor to capture all other contractual relations between this promisor and his or her future promisees. By contrast, the conflict sanitizer limits the egalitarian ideal to a subsisting contractual relation. As just noted, however, the value of work entails more than a choice between the current contract and state programs. It follows that the conflict between contract stability and free competition is valuable and that its valuableness, in terms of the good of egalitarian market relations, cannot be realized in the absence of this conflict.

[73] *See* John Gardner, *Liberals and Unlawful Discrimination*, 9 Oxford J. L. Stud. 1, 11 (1989). For more on the role of ground projects in the life of free and equal people, see Hanoch Dagan & Avihay Dorfman, Relational Justice: A Theory of Private Law 48–49 (2024).

C. From Conflicting Interests to the Tort of Inducement: Determining Legal Rights and Wrongs

The conflict theory seeks to determine legal rights and duties that would reflect the underlying interests in conflict and, in particular, the value of the conflict between them. As a legal theory, it draws on doctrinal rules, as opposed to ad hoc judgments, to get at the right determinations. The tort of inducement of breach of contract possesses some such rules, and it is by analyzing them that the conflict theory can demonstrate its practical bite with respect to the conflict under consideration.

The elements that make up the prima facie case of the tort of inducement consist in knowledge of a contract between a promisor and a promisee-third party, intentional interference with the promisor's performance of this contract, loss to promisee, and a causal connection between the interference and the loss.[74] The rights to contract stability and to free competition are called into law through the back door opened by these elements. In particular, the element of "intentional interference" is a doctrinal hook with which courts not only decide whether the defendant has wronged the plaintiff-promisor and, consequently, whether the defendant is liable for so doing, but also what legal rights the respective parties have in the first place.

Thus, the question of what counts as intentional interference, sometimes also cast as what counts as inducement or procurement, is essentially about how to address the conflict between the respective interests of the plaintiff-promisee and the defendant-inducer. Intentional interference can be construed very broadly to capture any instance of knowingly causing a breach of the contract between the promisor and the plaintiff-promisee. On this approach (to which I object), the interest in contract stability receives maximal legal protection, granting the promisee a *quasi* in rem right against interference by *any* competitor with actual knowledge of the existence of a contractual relation between the promisee and the promisor.[75] Thus,

[74] Another element or privilege is called justification, and it concerns weighty considerations that relieve one of liability for the inducement tort. *See generally* RESTATEMENT (THIRD) OF TORTS §20 (2020).

[75] Peter Benson has recently offered a property-based theory of the tort of inducement. On his account, the promised performance should be treated as an asset and, therefore, as putting the rest of the world under an (*in rem*) obligation. PETER BENSON, JUSTICE IN TRANSACTIONS 94 (2019). If this is right (and in my view it is not), then it should follow that *any* business offer that happens to cause a breach of contract and, hence, deprive the promisee of an asset—the promised performance—should count as wrongful. Knowledge of the existence of the promisee's right should not matter on the property-based view. After all, in the torts of trespass and conversion, the property right of the owner is just as invisible as the contractual right held by the promisee, but the law of tort does not condition liability for trespass and conversion on obtaining knowledge about the right's existence and/or the right-holder's identity. Secondly, Benson's characterization of the promisee's right to performance in terms of an *in rem* right renders mysterious his insistence on a requirement of some malice on the part of the inducer. *Id.*, at 93. After all, why should we care whether the inducer made a business offer *for the purpose* of depriving the promisee of the promised performance? Normally when protecting property rights, the law does not condition liability for trespass and conversion on whether the trespass or conversion was made for the purpose of depriving the owner of a possession. Indeed, the fact of entering, using, and so on, can be sufficient to render the act wrongful.

making a business offer to the opera singer amounts to "intentional interference" just in the case where its maker knows that the singer has committed to perform at another opera house. Some past and present courts take a somewhat similar approach.[76]

However, the conflict theory rejects this way of addressing the human conflict at issue. The better view follows the preceding analysis: As the conflict between free competition and contract stability can be inherently valuable, the element of intentional interference must be construed so as to construct the conditions necessary for this conflict to arise. Further, the construction of these conditions must also see to it that free competition enjoys only some, rather than absolute or lexical, priority over contract stability. These two prescriptions are further reinforced in the approach taken by some leading American and English authorities.[77]

What constitutes (wrongful) inducement? One way of securing the relative priority of the interest in free competition over contract stability is by incorporating a requirement of targeting into the element of intentional interference. Thus, the interference must not only be intentional but also purposeful in a certain way. For instance, a business offer knowingly causing a breach of contract can constitute wrongful interference if its purpose, or one of its primary purposes, is to deprive the promisee of the promised performance. That is, depriving the promisee of the promised performance must be either the *end* of the business offer or a *means* to achieving some other end.[78] By contrast, a business offer whose *foreseeable consequence* is causing the promisor's breach of contract does not count as wrongful.[79] Notice that what matters in distinguishing between being an end and a means to an end, on the one hand, and being a foreseeable consequence, on the other, is not merely the motive behind the business offer but the purpose or goal it is designed to achieve.

[76] *See, e.g.*, CA 123/50 Bauernfreund v. Drezden, P.D.5 1559 (1951) [Israel]; Millar v. Bassey [1994] EMLR 44 [England]; G.W.K. Ltd v. Dunlop Rubber Co. Ltd. [1926] 42 T.L.R 376 [England]. The Restatement (Second) of Torts 766 cmt. *j* (1979) suggests that intentional interference occurs when the defendant "knows that the interference is certain or substantially certain to occur as a result of his action." Hence, it includes "interference that is incidental to the actor's independent purpose." *Id.* The Restatement further notes, however, that such instances of interference may not ground liability insofar as the interference they involve may not be "improper." *Id.*

[77] *See* Imperial Ice Co. v. Rossier, 112 P.2d 631 (Cal. 1941); OBG Ltd v. Allan [2007] UKHL 21, 30 para. 43.

[78] It seems that this formulation is not inconsistent with the analysis that Weinrib provides for the "intention" element of the inducement tort. Unlike Benson (*supra* note 75), Weinrib defends the inducement tort on the private persons' duty to support a fair system of *public right*, which includes the legal institution of contracts. *See* Weinrib, *supra* note 36, at 80–82. My account, by contrast, defends the targeting requirement on the normative basis of the conflict theory.

[79] See *Imperial Ice Co.*, 112 P.2d at 633, 634. The House of Lords has adopted a somewhat different articulation of a similar approach. In announcing that *Millar v. Bassey* [1994] EMLR 44 was wrongly decided, Lord Hoffman (followed by Lords Walker and Nicholls) has noted that there cannot be liability for inducing breach of contract if the breach is "merely a foreseeable consequence" of the causal event, namely, the business offer. *See* OBG Ltd v. Allan [2007] UKHL 21, 30 para. 43. *Contra* Robert Stevens, Torts and Rights 279, 281 (2007).

To illustrate the targeting requirement, consider a leading case, *Imperial Ice Co. v. Rossier*, featuring a business opportunity, the acceptance of which would necessarily frustrate an outstanding contractual obligation. There, A, an ice distributor, accepted an offer from B, an ice manufacturer, to distribute ice in a certain geographical area. Doing so would necessarily cause A to breach a contractual promise made to C, another distributor, namely, not to compete in the sale of ice in that same area.[80] The court addressed the question of whether making the offer while being aware of its possible consequence—breach of a subsisting contract—is not only necessary but also sufficient to render B liable in tort to C. This way of putting the question only points toward the bottom line of a broader inquiry, namely, determining the rights to free competition and to contract stability of B and C, respectively. Speaking for the court, Justice Traynor rejects the possibility of identifying intentional interference with knowingly causing a breach of contract, emphasizing that "[i]t is necessary to prove that [B] intentionally and actively induced the breach."[81] According to the conflict theory, intentional and active inducement should reflect the targeting requirement just mentioned. On this view, the right to compete with the likes of B does not license luring-by-targeting. Accordingly, inducement is wrongful if its primary purpose—reflected in the outward behavior, rather than their internal motive, of the wrongdoer—is to break the contractual relationship between the promisee and promisor. Returning to the opera case, the right to free competition should not include an entitlement to lure away the singer when doing so is part of a plan to harm the other opera house.[82]

Relative, rather than either absolute or lexical, priority. The conflict theory guides the legal determination of rights by engaging with the value of the conflict between underlying interests. The preceding discussion suggests that free competition, including by luring, should come at the expense of contract stability, and the task of the inducement tort is to determine rights and duties accordingly. Ultimately, doing so seeks to construct the conditions necessary for conflicts to arise. To be sure, this way of proceeding is warranted only insofar as the conflict between the two interests is inherently valuable. This is not the case, however, when extending free competition to luring will likely—even systematically—produce valueless conflicts. One such instance has been mentioned a moment ago: When the purpose of the interference is that of harming the promisee.

Another, larger class of cases in which the interest in free competition does not give rise to a legal right to compete by luring concerns resort to unlawful means, such as fraud, violence, and other repugnant attempts to cause a promisor to

80 *See* Imperial Ice Co., 112 P.2d at 632.
81 *Id.*, at 633.
82 It is not entirely clear what to make of the requirement of "malice" as laid down in Lumely v. Gye (1853) 2 E & B 216. On my account, this requirement expresses the idea that the inducer acts *for the purpose of* depriving the promisee of a promised performance, as opposed to causing such harm as a foreseeable consequence of seeking to enrich their own artistic repertoire.

breach a contract with a third party.[83] Resort to such means may or may not be part of a purposeful strategy of destroying a competitor. The reason why they make the conflict between free competition and contract stability valueless is that they undermine the basic rules of the game—spreading lies or engaging in violent acts, to give an example, is inimical to the legitimacy of market ordering. Accordingly, the good of egalitarian market relations becomes pointless if the very possibility of market relations loses its appeal.

***

To vindicate tort law, recall, we have to face the question: Need we worry, or might we even wish, that tort law cease to be? If tort law's moral aim is to address negative value—viz., preventing and ameliorating certain forms of human failure—then vindication cannot get off the ground. Indeed, it will be absolutely better to live in a world free of nuisance disputes thanks to adequate zoning laws, improved insulation technologies, and so forth. That said, the preceding discussion shows that tort law is not reducible to addressing negative value. More specifically, rather than merely preventing or ameliorating wrongdoing, harm, or social cost, tort law has a constructive moral function. It determines rights and imposes duties in order to create the conditions necessary for inherently valuable conflicts to arise. Its value is freestanding in the sense that no other technology—in particular, no conflict sanitizer—can replace the moral function of tort law in connection with inherently valuable conflicts. Subsequent chapters, particularly 8–10 and 17, further elaborate and illustrate the central place of inherently valuable conflicts in the lived-experience of liberal societies and, consequently, the role tort law plays in securing their existence. I now wish to move the argument from inherently to tolerably valuable conflicts.

[83] *See, e.g.*, Imperial Ice Co., 112 P.2d at 632.

4

Tolerably Valuable Conflicts

Duties Liberate

If inherently valuable conflicts give us a reason to embrace them or to want them, the following category of interpersonal conflicts picks out ones that we have reason to *tolerate*. This is because such conflicts are the adverse by-products of otherwise desirable human activities. Toleration's practical manifestation is containment—to wit, tort law engages with this category of conflicts by containing the adverse by-products. It does that by invoking both the *restricting* and the *enabling* aspects of tort duties. For instance, a duty of ordinary care both restricts certain acts and enables others, such as unreasonably and reasonably risky driving, respectively. But unlike the case of inherently valuable conflicts, the enabling (and restricting) that goes into governing tolerable conflicts is ultimately contingent. In particular, tort law should enable (and at times restrict) certain behaviors for lack of better alternatives of eliminating or reducing the negative side effects of the underlying activities. I discuss paradigm areas of tolerably valuable conflicts, including in particular the case of negligence, in Chapters 14 and 15.

This chapter focuses almost exclusively on the enabling part of tort law's engagement with tolerably valuable conflicts. Doing so is important for two different reasons. The first reason is integral to the conflict theory. The ambition of conflict theory is in part to transcend the tendency to identify tort law, and tort duties in particular, with the task of addressing negative value. The second reason is to connect the case for the conflict theory to our broader understanding of legal duties. I wish to challenge a highly influential distinction in general jurisprudence between two kinds of legal rules, namely, power-conferring and duty-imposing rules. I seek to show that at times tort duties engage in the active facilitation of valuable pursuits and, perhaps surprisingly, such duties function in some respects more like power-conferring rules than as duty-imposing rules.[1]

[1] One respect in which tort duties and legal powers necessarily diverge concerns the standing to change the normative situation of others (and of the power-holder as well). Only legal powers can produce this standing.

Conflict between Equals. Avihay Dorfman, Oxford University Press. © Oxford University Press 2026.
DOI: 10.1093/9780198979869.003.0007

I. Two Legal Rules: Duties and Powers

The distinction between power-conferring and duty-imposing rules has been very influential since its introduction by H. L. A. Hart. The distinction breathes new life into the idea that coercive orders do not exhaust the modern legal system, as "one of the great contributions of law to social life"[2] comes in the form of vesting private persons and public officials with legal powers (such as the power to form a contractual arrangement). Rather than instructing people to "Do this whether you wish to or not," power-conferring rules provide facility of the sort: "If you wish to do this, this is the way to do it."[3] On Hart's view, therefore, the contrast between restraining and enabling human action maps onto the distinction between legal duty and legal power.

In this chapter I argue against this view. Tort duties are also, and irreducibly so, enabling devices. In particular, they enable valuable conflicts, including tolerably valuable ones. This is good news for the conflict theory of tort law, as it reinforces the possibility of deploying a basic pillar of tort law—duty—in the service of addressing valuable conflicts. Chapter 3 focused on the connection between tort duties (and their correlative rights) and constructing the conditions for inherently valuable conflicts to arise. This chapter takes up the connection between tort duties and the enabling of tolerably valuable conflicts.

My argument contrasts with the conventional view that primary tort duties are primarily restricting measures designed to "deter [people] from improprieties."[4] In providing mandatory reasons for action, these duties are most prominently viewed in tort law and theory as requiring their holders to moderate their conduct, say, by taking precautions, changing courses of action, or refraining from engaging in potentially injurious acts. The *value* of these measures is of a negative kind: They are desirable *because* they aim at preventing or reducing injuries caused by human failure.

However, I argue that this view suffers from an important shortcoming as it rests on the narrow conception of tort law as the law of wrongs (or harms), according to which primary duties set the baseline against which to determine what behavior counts as wrongful (or harmful). By contrast, the conflict theory of tort law is not reducible to the law of wrongs, harms, or costs and, so, to the prevention of wrongs, harms, or unjustified costs. Hence it can elaborate the positive value of primary tort duties. This chapter shows that sometimes the facilitation of valuable practices captures a morally significant role of primary tort duties. Rather than merely restricting certain forms of risk-creating behavior, these duties *enable*

[2] H. L. A. Hart, The Concept of Law 28 (2d ed. 1994).
[3] *Id.*
[4] *Id.*, at 29.

them. Accordingly, I argue that the facilitation of a potentially injurious action may sometimes be required in spite of the risk involved.

II. Two Modes of Enabling: Allowing and Facilitating

To set the scene, it is important to distinguish between two senses of a duty's enabling function: allowing and facilitating valuable forms of human action. The conflict theory emphasizes the latter and, so, it will be apt to distinguish this sense from the former sense of allowing, which is the more familiar function of primary tort duties. On the allowing sense, a duty enables risk creators to do whatever it is they are not duty-bound to refrain from. For instance, a typical duty of care prohibits risk-creators from running unreasonable risks only. By implication, it relieves them of the responsibility to eliminate reasonable risks. Hence a person owing a duty can pursue her ends *even when* doing so puts others' lives in danger.[5] This way of characterizing the enabling side of the duty has been invoked by many different tort theories in the course of explaining why a regime of strict tort liability is, all else equal, morally deficient: It undermines the freedom of risk-creators and as such fails to treat risk-creators and risk-bearers as equals.[6] By contrast, a duty of reasonable care and a fault-based regime more generally do better because they ensure against the excessive subordination of risk-creators to the safety of their potential victims.[7] For these risk-creators are allowed the freedom to act insofar as doing so subjects others to no more than a reasonable risk of harm.

So understood, its enabling aspect functions as no more than a moral constraint—a ceiling—on the duty's *principal task*, which is to say preventing wrongdoings and their resulting injuries. Tort duties are prohibitions *with a limit*. Enabling as allowing, therefore, is a description of the positive flip side of such limitation, and nothing more. It is the functional equivalent of what property lawyers would call the reverter.

However, the enabling side of tort duties can do and often does more than simply constraining duties' imposition on the freedom of their bearers. I argue that it can sometimes also give effect—indeed, be *designed* to give effect—to forms of valuable action that may not have been able to arise without tort law's support. In other words, the argument is that tort duties can function as enablers not merely in the weak sense of (passively) allowing action but rather in the strong sense of actively

[5] *See, e.g.*, Adams v. Bullock, 125 N.E. 93 (N.Y. 1919) (the duty of reasonable care does not demand utmost care).

[6] I say *all else equal* in recognition of category of cases (e.g., ultrahazardous activities) in which strict liability might be morally superior to fault-based regimes. *See* Chapter 14 below.

[7] *See* Oliver Wendell Holmes, Jr., The Common Law 108–09 (1991) [1881]; Ernest J. Weinrib, The Idea of Private Law 182–83 (1995); Mark A. Geistfeld, Tort Law: The Essentials 86 (2008); Alan Brudner, The Unity of the Common Law 274, 294 (2d ed. 2013).

facilitating it. On this view, facilitating is sometimes a function of rather than a by-product of tort duties, so that sustaining a certain valuable practice becomes an integral part of what these duties should be doing.

I develop this claim in connection with four examples: The tort duties owed by investigative journalists, corporate directors, participants in contact sports, and professionals. They feature tolerably valuable conflicts of interests that, unlike inherently valuable ones, should ideally be defused—invoking one or another conflict sanitizer—if only we could. Lacking an effective sanitizer, the conflict theory addresses such conflicts by containing them. Hence tort duties set out both to restrict certain types of risky behavior and to facilitate other forms of risk creation. Focusing on the enabling dimension of the duty, I demonstrate that the values underlying the conflicts of interest in and around uncompromising journalism, corporate entrepreneurship, vigorous sports competitions, and professionalism inform the determination of the tort duties in these cases.

III. Facilitating Uncompromising Journalism

Viewed from the bottom line, the tort of defamation answers the question of when a particular publication entitles its victim to redress his or her reputational injury. Therefore, it is tempting to suppose that this tort primarily deals with wrongdoing and redress—more specifically, that its task is either to articulate the wrongdoing involved in defaming another person and/or to provide a cause of action for exacting some remedy from the defamer. Not quite.

On the conflict theory of tort law, the tort of defamation is tort law's framework for dealing with conflicts between our interests in speech and in reputation. It does so by determining rights, rather than merely recognizing their violation and redressing them, by reference to the kind of value underlying the conflict at issue.

At times, these conflicts feature uncertainty as to whether the clash between free speech and good name is either valuable or valueless. The typical source of uncertainty lies in the difficulty of ascertaining the accuracy of a factual statement at the time of its publication or utterance. If true, no legal protection against the reputational harm is warranted—the conflict is actually inherently valuable. If false, however, the clash between free speech and good name turns valueless. Since we are currently lacking a reliable, instant truth machine, the tort law of defamation is called for to address the conflict by way of containing its negative side effects (measured in terms of the conflicting interests). Given the fundamental interests at stake, the task of containment counsels against granting maximal legal protection to either free speech or good name, each at the expense of the other interest. Ruling out both extremes, however, does not mean that the conflicting interests must be treated as equally important in the law of defamation. In particular, the good of liberal culture defended in Chapter 3 maintains its appeal as we move from inherently to tolerably valuable conflicts. This is because and insofar as the exercise of free speech is about, or purports to be about, matters of public concern. Hence, I argue that the duty in the tort of defamation has an irreducibly enabling dimension, namely, it facilitates what may be called a practice of *uncompromising journalism*. The facilitation in question is grounded in the construction of a liberal culture, rather than merely or solely in a democracy.

The conventional description of the tort of defamation tells a story of two torts: a traditional common-law tort and a constitutional one.[8] The traditional common-law tort of defamation imposes a duty of strict liability on publishing defamatory falsehoods of, and concerning, another person. It is strict in the sense that the risk of making a factual mistake rests solely on the defendant, irrespective of how much precaution he or she has taken to avoid the falsehood.[9] It is, to an important extent, plaintiff-friendly.

The second tort departs from the former in deep and profound ways. Most importantly, the risk of making a factual mistake rests almost solely on the plaintiff. It is, therefore, defendant-friendly. The legal explanation for this is that this tort stands for the application of the constitutional right to free speech—the First Amendment in the case of the United States—to the case of defamatory falsehoods. Such a *con*-tort, so to speak, governs the interactions between two pillars of democracy: the press viewed as the fourth branch of the government, on the one hand, and accountable public officials viewed as the backbone of political authority, on the other. Further, it does the governing with respect primarily to *political* speech, which resonates with and is influenced by Alexander Meiklejohn's democratic theory of free speech.[10]

Indeed, the constitutionalization of the tort is designed to sustain a vibrant democracy by enlisting the media in the service of holding public officials accountable to the electorate and, hence, rendering available all pertinent political ideas and information to the electorate.[11] To do so, the con-tort of defamation turns the traditional common law's terms of interaction between the defendant and plaintiff on their head. Instead of imposing a duty of strict liability, US law holds the defamer free to publish defamatory falsehoods as long as doing so does not exhibit "actual malice," namely, knowledge of falsity or reckless disregard of whether the defamatory statement is false.[12] (Other jurisdictions apply different standards, such as that

[8] Accordingly, treatises and casebooks on tort law often divide the subject matter of defamation into common-law and constitutional aspects of the tort. Scholarly treatment of defamation (and other torts such as privacy and IIED) often follow this path. *See, e.g.*, RACHEL BAYEFSKY, DIGNITY AND JUDICIAL AUTHORITY 103–04 (2024).

[9] A famous illustration is *E. Hulton & Co. v. Jones* [1910] A.C. 20. *See also* Peck v. Tribune Co., 214 U.S. 185, 189 (1909).

[10] ALEXANDER MEIKLEJOHN, POLITICAL FREEDOM: THE CONSTITUTIONAL POWER OF THE PEOPLE (1948). *See also* William J. Brennan, Jr., *The Supreme Court and the Meiklejohn Interpretation of the First Amendment*, 79 HARV. L. REV. 1 (1965).

[11] Frederick Schauer, *Public Figures*, 25 WM. & MARY L. REV. 905, 918 (1984); Robert C. Post, *Defaming Public Officials: On Doctrine and Legal History*, 1987 AM. B. FOUND. RES. J. 539, 555.

[12] New York Times Co. v. Sullivan, 376 U.S. 254, 280 (1964).

of responsible communication or reasonable journalism.) Moreover, the burden of proving actual malice, with no less than "convincing clarity," is placed on the victim, rather than on the defamer.[13] The scope of the con-tort of defamation has been further extended beyond public officials to capture defamatory statements against a public figure, defined in terms of achieving "general fame or notoriety in the community and pervasive involvement in ordering the affairs of society."[14]

The picture of a world divided into the traditional tort and the con-tort of defamation is widely accepted, including among critics of the latter law.[15] That said, it is not an accurate presentation of the traditional tort and, moreover, it fails to distinguish between substantive and institutional aspects of the tort of defamation, a point I have discussed in more detail in connection with the *Snyder* decision and the tort of intentional infliction of emotional distress in the previous chapter. I shall not repeat the latter point, which applies to the current study as well, focusing instead only on the former criticism.

The traditional common-law tort of defamation has already made important progress toward recognizing the importance of free speech. Although partially influenced by the constitutional status of free speech,[16] its evolution—towards free speech progressivism—first and foremost reflects a better understanding of the normative underpinnings of the tort of defamation and of tort law, more generally.[17] It boils down to the duty's role in facilitating risk-taking among professional and nonprofessional journalists.

To begin with, the traditional tort duty against making false and defamatory factual statements in matters of public concern is no longer a strict liability duty, in which case the defamer is no longer acting at his or her own peril. Moreover, the parties on the opposite ends of this tort duty are *private* persons, and the subject matter of the defamatory statement does not involve, including not indirectly, the exercise of political authority or the accountability of public officials. It is not even considered political speech, that is, the type of speech whose value is to "check tyranny and foster self-government."[18] Rather, it is free speech in the context of our *social* life as private persons, one that is "intrinsic to liberty and dignity and

[13] *Id.*, at 285–86.

[14] In addition, a private person can count as a "limited purpose public figure" by being drawn into or voluntarily injecting herself into a specific public controversy. Gertz v. Robert Welch, Inc., 418 U.S. 323, 351 (1974).

[15] *See* Schauer, *supra* note 11, at 918; Richard A. Epstein, *Was New York Times v. Sullivan Wrong?*, 53 U. Chic. L. Rev. 782 (1986). *See also* Nathan B. Oman & Jason M. Solomon, *The Supreme Court's Theory of Private Law*, 62 Duke L.J. 1109 (2013).

[16] *See Gertz*, 418 U.S. at 347.

[17] In *Curtis Publishing Co. v. Butts*, 388 U.S. 130, 155 (1967), Justice Harlan invokes "ordinary tort rules"—meaning the common law of defamation—to support the proposition that "the publisher's interest in circulating [publications on matters of public interest]" should be considered when determining whether a defamatory falsehood warrants liability.

[18] Dun & Bradstreet, Inc. v. Greenmoss Builders, Inc., 472 U.S. 749, 787 (1985) (Brennan J., dissenting).

instrumental in society's search for truth."[19] It concerns the ability of private persons to interact as free and equal and to experience the liberal culture of free and fearless speech, as discussed in Chapter 3. The traditional tort has checked its traditionalist shackles at the door of the modern, liberal society.

Consider *Sisler v. Gannet Co., Inc.*[20] The case concerns a journalist in a local newspaper with a circulation of 58,000 readers in a New Jersey area who published a series of articles on a credit transaction between a local bank, Franklin State Bank, and Sisler, who was its former president and cofounder. Sisler received a large loan from this bank shortly after his retirement. Its purpose was to finance a horse-farm business he had established. The journalist suggested that the terms of the loan reflected serious inadequacy of security, so as to paint the transaction in insider-dealing colors. In fact, however, the borrower had adequately secured his loan; it turned out that the journalist made a mistake—he had "misinterpreted" the relevant records.[21] That mistake eventually harmed Sisler's commercial reputation and, in particular, undermined a possible business transaction he was about to make with a third party.

The conflict between the journalist's drive to inform the public about insider-dealing and the commercial reputation of Sisler has nothing specifically to do with democracy or collective self-governance. Sisler was not a public official, nor was he a public figure.[22] The lender, moreover, was an "area bank,"[23] meaning a relatively small banking institution and so (arguably) highly unlikely to wield substantial clout over national or state politics.[24] Nevertheless, the court deemed the information conveyed by the articles a matter of legitimate public concern.[25] The reason it provided is right on point. Negatively, the court asserted that the value of free speech is not limited to "reporting government activity respecting banking."[26] Affirmatively, the court found that the "public" to whom information on insider-dealing should flow is a certain class of persons acting in their capacity as *private* individuals: "Private actors at all levels, including shareholders, financial analysts, depositors, and potential customers have a legitimate interest in a bank's dealings."[27] On this account, the value of free speech underlying uncompromising journalism is not to be identified with democracy and the political sphere into which it falls, but rather primarily with our autonomy and equal standing as

[19] *Id.*, at 787.
[20] 516 A.2d 1083 (N.J. 1986).
[21] *Id.*, at 1085.
[22] *Id.*, at 1090.
[23] *Id.*, at 1089.
[24] A concise history of the FSB is available at https://www.usbanklocations.com/united-jersey-bank-franklin-state-18805.shtml.
[25] *Sisler*, 516 A.2d, at 1090. Its view—that matters of economic or commercial concern are of public concern—is by no means idiosyncratic. *See* Dun & Bradstreet, Inc. v. Greenmoss Builders, Inc., 472 U.S. 749, 762 n.8 (1985).
[26] *Id.*
[27] *Id.*

private persons (such as depositors, potential customers, and shareholders) in the economic sphere.

From a doctrinal perspective, the con-tort of defamation does not apply to the publications at issue. If anything, First Amendment considerations set a floor of fault-based duty below which the New Jersey common law cannot go.[28] However, these considerations do not specify a particular standard of appropriate journalistic behavior beyond such floor. Against this backdrop, the New Jersey's highest court, using language that comes very close to the conflict theory, says that "the press's investigation into such a matter is not wholly unexpected or aberrational, and indeed, is to be encouraged."[29] By correctly identifying the conflict between free speech and reputation as warranting facilitation, or in its own words "encourage[ment]"[30] rather than sanitation or restriction, the court moved to determine the content of the journalist's duty. The crucial point here is that it is the *duty's role* to secure the facilitation of uncompromising journalism.

Thus, the court refused to settle for a standard (familiar in some non-US common-law jurisdictions) of reasonableness as this standard—owing to its open-endedness—might invite self-censorship. Instead, the court suggested that uncompromising journalism is made secure by lowering the bar to *actual malice*—the journalist's duty is to avoid publishing statements she either knows to be false or recklessly disregards their potential falsity.[31] In this way the tort duty at issue is no mere conduct-restricting rule as it is primarily a powerful facilitator of the valuable practice of uncompromising journalism. In that, the duty is tasked with creating the conditions for a liberal culture of free and fearless speech. Moreover, the court makes it clear that its holding should not be identified with federal or state constitutional law. Instead, this decision rests on "principles of common-law."[32] In other words, it is not a variation on the con-tort of defamation, but rather an evolution of the traditional common-law tort of defamation in light of tort law's responsibility to engage with value in the right way.

The *Sisler* decision is not an outlier, to be sure. It represents a growing trend among courts, namely, of coming to terms with the idea of tort duties as facilitating valuable conflicts, rather than merely restricting certain forms of human failure.[33] For instance, New York's highest court decided that the journalist's duty is to avoid acting in "grossly irresponsible manner."[34] Importantly, it means that, unlike

[28] A fault floor governs defamatory statements made against private persons if such statements raise a legitimate public concern. *See* Gertz v. Robert Welch, Inc., 418 U.S. 323, 347 (1974).

[29] *Sisler*, 516 A.2d at 1093.

[30] *Id.*

[31] *Id.* Moreover, the burden to prove this much is the victim-plaintiff's. *Id. Compare* Philadelphia Newspapers v. Hepps, 475 U.S. 767, 776 (1986).

[32] *Sisler*, 516 A.2d at 1095.

[33] *See, e.g.*, Diversified Mgmt., Inc. v. Denver Post, 653 P.2d 1103 (Colo. 1982); Aafco Heating & Air Conditioning Co. v. Northwest Publications, 321 N.E.2d 580, 585–86 (Ind. App. 1974), certiorari denied, 424 U.S. 913 (1976); Dienes v. Associated Newspapers, 358 N.W.2d 562 (Mich. App. 1984).

[34] Chapadeau v. Utica Observer-Dispatch, 341 N.E.2d 569, 571 (N.Y. 1975).

most other professionals governed by tort law, mere negligence in gathering, processing, and disseminating information on matters of public concern is not wrongful.[35] As with the *Sisler* decision, the context of the New York conflict has nothing essentially to do with democracy and the political sphere. It does not implicate the political speech of the press and its readers, nor does it involve the conduct of public officials who hold political authority or of public figures. Instead, it concerns the publication of certain false statements by a local newspaper in connection with the arrest of a school teacher for possessing street drugs.[36] The court deems this sort of information a "legitimate public concern"[37] because of its impact on the relationships formed in and around the school community to which the teacher belongs, involving parents, pupils, teachers, and school management.[38] Information such as this influences the deliberations and judgments of all of these parties as they write and rewrite their relationships, set and assess expectations about appropriate behavior, and come to terms with their surrounding environment, more generally. On this account, vigorously protecting free speech extends beyond democratic politics to capture our interests as free and equal persons engaging in everyday interactions as *private* persons.

Thus, the answer to the question of why "the press should be accorded any greater protection than a doctor, a lawyer, the driver of a motor vehicle, and anyone else whom society holds accountable for the consequences of negligent behavior" finds its grounds in the value of facilitating uncompromising journalism.[39] Part of what it means for the conflict between free speech and harm to reputation to count as tolerably valuable under the right circumstances is the need to reconstruct the underlying duty of defamation law in a way that provides generous "breathing space"[40] to investigative journalism. The duty at issue is a facility for, rather than merely a constraint on, a truly committed practice of journalism.

IV. Facilitating Entrepreneurship Corporate Management

That tort duties are enablers of valuable human actions not merely in the weak sense of allowing them but rather in the strong sense of *facilitating* such actions is on vivid display in the duty of care owed by directors and other high ranking officers of for-profit corporations and, especially, publicly traded corporations.

[35] *Contra* Lansdowne v. Beach Journal Pub. Co., 512 N.E.2d 979, 992 (Oh. 1987) (Brown J., dissenting) (wondering why the press "should be accorded any greater protection than a doctor, a lawyer, the driver of a motor vehicle, and anyone else whom society holds accountable for the consequences of negligent behavior.").

[36] *Chapadeau*, 341 N.E.2d at 570.

[37] *Id.*, at 571.

[38] *Id.*

[39] *Lansdowne*, 512 N.E.2d at 992.

[40] New York Times Co. v. Sullivan, 376 U.S. 254, 272 (1964) (quoting NA.A.C.P v. Button, 371 U.S. 415 (1963)).

I argue that this duty plays a crucial role in sustaining valuable forms of creating and taking business-related risks over and above what a standard of fiduciary's or trustee's reasonable care would normally allow.

The tort duty of care owed by corporate directors (et alia) arises out of their status as fiduciaries. Fiduciaries in general owe duties of loyalty such as the obligation to act in the best (or even sole) interest of their beneficiaries. They also owe due care. The fiduciary's duty is, in essence, a tort duty of reasonable care, purporting to restrict imprudent fulfillment of the role of a fiduciary, such as the case of a trustee failing to act cautiously in the administration of a property trust.[41]

However, when it comes to corporate directors and managers, the restrictive dimension cannot even begin to scratch the surface of what this tort duty does. On a canonical articulation, the business judgment rule—viz., the content of the duty of care at issue—sets out to "protect and promote the full and free exercise of the managerial power" of directors (et alia).[42] Thus, the business judgment rule introduces robust relaxation of the duty of due care. Setting to one side doctrinal intricacies and variance across jurisdictions, the rule in question means, at bottom, that absent gross misconduct on the part of directors and top managers, making business decisions in the face of risk and, more importantly, uncertainty is fully compatible with the level of care required of them. Indeed, as one court has observed, "it is only in a most unusual and extraordinary case that directors are held liable for negligence in the absence of fraud, or improper motive, or personal interest."[43]

There are two common explanations for this rule, neither of which gets at the heart of the matter. The first one has to do with epistemic concerns. It suggests that judges may lack the requisite knowledge and experience to assess business decisions.[44] However, lack of expertise and inadequate information plague judicial intervention in a number of tort-law contexts, including cases of product liability and breach of fiduciary duties (outside of business corporations). None of these other areas commands the unusually lax approach underlying the business judgment rule. The second explanation hones in on a particular implication of insufficient expertise and information on the part of judges: The hindsight bias.[45] The worry is that judges, who are humans too, might not be able to resist judging business decisions with the benefit of hindsight. As a result, the worry goes, courts will turn the fiduciary duty of reasonable care into a de facto regime of strict tort liability. This, in turn, might force directors to shun risky business decisions.[46]

41 *See* Andrew Gold & Paul Miller, *Fiduciary Governance*, 57 Wm. & Mary L. Rev. 513, 547 (2015).

42 Smith v. Van Gorkon, 488 A.2d 858, 872 (Del. 1985).

43 Bayer v. Beran, 49 N.Y.S.2d 2, 6 (Sup. Ct. 1944).

44 Dodge v. Ford Motor Co., 170 N.W. 668, 684 (Mich. 1919).

45 Jeffery R. Rachlinsky, *A Positive Psychological Theory of Judging in Hindsight*, 65 U. Chic. L. Rev. 571, 620–22 (1998); Frank H. Easterbrook & Daniel R. Fischel, The Economic Structure of Corporate Law 98–100 (1991).

46 For an argument combining the two common explanations, see Holger Spamann, *Monetary Liability for the Breach of Duty of Care?*, 8 J. Legal Analysis 337, 339 (2016).

Although this explanation seems more appealing than the former, it is ultimately unconvincing. This is so because it wraps a contingent supposition—viz., that judges are highly likely, or even more likely than not, to fall prey to the hindsight bias—in a deterministic cloak. Like all humans, surely judges are prone to any number of biases, including the hindsight bias. However, engaging in high stakes cases does not predetermine their ability to moderate, and even overcome, their biases, especially when they become acutely aware of such proneness.[47] Hence, it is not clear that a remedy in the form of the business judgment rule is required at all. Even if some such remedy is required, it is not clear why the peculiar relaxation brought about by the business judgment rule is called for. After all, there exist other familiar ways in which tort law makes the standard of ordinary care less demanding *short of* targeting only "egregious cases in which deliberate violations are evident." The business judgment rule takes the relaxation of the standard of care a step further: It does not merely aim at dialing down the standard of care to correct for the hindsight bias. Rather, it aims at a more radical impact, namely, "promot[ing] the full and free exercise of the managerial power."[48]

Thus, I argue that the fiduciary duty of care of business corporations is best viewed as sustaining a *corporate culture of entrepreneurship*, according to which managers are expected to function as entrepreneurs rather than merely custodians of wealth. The culture in question is the outgrowth of the conflict between two approaches to promoting the welfare interests of stakeholders in the face of market uncertainty, namely, a risky or a conservative one.[49] Indeed, the business judgment rule facilitates business decisions not only in the face of substantial risk, namely, observable causalities whose probability and intensity are more or less assessable, but rather also of *uncertainty*, namely, where there is no intelligible way of forming rational expectations of future events.[50] To be sure, although the doctrine that reflects this spirit of entrepreneurship is most famously known, in its American version, as the business judgment rule, there are parallel doctrinal manifestations in other liberal legal orders.[51]

[47] Scholarly works on the hindsight bias (such as the ones mentioned in *supra* note 45) make the demand of judicial *awareness* relatively easy to meet.

[48] Smith v. Van Gorkon, 488 A.2d 858, 872 (Del. 1985).

[49] I use *stakeholders* so not to prejudge the scope of the class whose conflicting interests count for the purpose of determining tort duties by engaging with conflicts in the right way.

[50] The *locus classicus* is FRANK H. KNIGHT, RISK, UNCERTAINTY, AND PROFIT (1921). The connection between the business judgment rule and Knight's distinction between risk and uncertainty has been explored in Amir N. Licht, *The Entrepreneurial Spirit and What the Law Can Do About It*, 28 COMP. LABOR L. & POL'Y J. 817 (2007); *see also* Christopher M. Bruner, *Is the Corporate Director's Duty of Care a "Fiduciary" Duty? Does It Matter?*, 48 WAKE FOREST L. REV. 1027, 1045–46 (2013).

[51] *See, e.g.*, Peoples Department Stores v. Wise, 2004 SCC 68, paras. 64–65 (Canada); F & C Alternative Investments (Holdings) Ltd. v. Barthelemy [2011] EWHC 1731 (ch.) (England). *See also* Brian R. Cheffins & Bernard S. Black, *Outside Directors Liability Across Countries*, 84 TEX. L. REV. 1385 (2006).

The underlying point behind such a culture of "aversion to risk-aversion" has to do with the thought that the volatility associated with market uncertainty is no mere unfortunate side effect of the business setting within which for-profit corporations operate. Instead, it is a key leverage in creating value for the corporation (et alia) by pursuing risky business strategies. Indeed, unlike a trustee of a property trust whose role is primarily one of custodianship, by which I mean the preservation of value of the entrusted property, the ethos of fiduciaries of for-profit corporations is to convert risk and especially uncertainty into opportunities for creativity, innovation, and growth. Hence, the business judgment rule "promote[s] the full and free exercise of the managerial power" not so much because cognitively biased judges might demand too much prudence. Rather, it is because too much prudence, including in the form of the standard of reasonable care applicable to fiduciaries in most other settings, is inimical to the fiduciary role of directors and top officers of for-profit corporations.

V. The Sporting Life, with Fervor: Facilitating Vigorous Competition

The duty to use ordinary care so as to avoid inflicting bodily injury on others reflects a core tenet of modern tort law, as it should. Indeed, protecting life and limb has always figured prominently in the law of torts, and for the last century or so, guarding against accidental infliction of injury to life and limb has come to dominate the study and the practice of tort law.[52] Hence the tort of negligence restricts the creation of unreasonable risk of harm by imposing a duty of ordinary care. The flip side is that of allowing risky activities whose risk levels remain reasonable or ordinary. So doing, as I observed above, is the residue of what is left permissible for a risk-creator to do after taking all the precautions deemed necessary by the standard of reasonable care.

By contrast, interactions in contact sports—for example, soccer, basketball, water polo, and baseball, to name a few[53]—goes beyond allowing. I argue that the duty of care in the context of contact sports transforms itself into a *facilitator of vigorous engagement* in social interactions. It creates the condition necessary for such engagement by facilitating, in some measure, the conflict between the freedom to compete and the competitors' physical safety. The turn to facilitation is not coincidental, nor is it the by-product of some other institutional consideration affecting the duty of care. Instead, facilitating certain forms of risky behavior is a signature

[52] *See* the Introduction to this book.

[53] American football and rugby are no mere contact sports as they are better cast in terms of collision sports. For this reason, I set them—as well as boxing and certain other combat sports—to one side as they raise difficult questions given the systemically excessive risk of severe, long-term harm that they involve.

feature of the duty of care in question. Further, this duty introduces robust relaxation of the standard of due care expected from participants in the sporting activities at issue. Absent deliberately injuring another player or engaging in outright reckless conduct, aggressive play is fully compatible with the level of care required of participants.[54] By implication, bodily injury caused by negligence may often count as "foul play" according to the internal rules of a game, but it does not give rise to tort liability because it does not constitute breach of the duty of care.

There are two common explanations for this duty rule that should be dismissed before I can get to the heart of the matter. The first is presented in terms of assumption of risk (or consent, more generally). In particular, the thought is that participants in contact sports explicitly or implicitly assume the risk of injurious contacts.[55] As a result, participants are relieved of their duty of reasonable care (or, alternatively, cannot be deemed liable to other participants for breaching the duty).

This explanation fails, however. It rests on shaky empirical grounds and, moreover, misses the important point about the duty rule in question, namely, that its relaxation does not turn on the willingness of participants to encounter risks of bodily injury. Certainly, participants in contact sports assume some risks of being harmed by their peers. But the crucial question is precisely *what* risks are being assumed. I suspect that participants do not normally assume the risk of being injured by carelessly aggressive conduct of another participant.[56] My suspicion obviously applies to professional athletes whose livelihood literally depends on staying out of harm's way. But it is also true with respect to mere amateurs engaged in contact sports, including people spontaneously starting an informal game (as in pick-up basketball). After all, the human interest in bodily integrity is so important as to undermine the empirical plausibility of imputing to rational participants the choice to encounter *careless* behavior potentially causing serious impairment. Moving beyond these shaky empirical grounds, there is a deeper difficulty with the assumption-of-risk explanation: The reason underlying the relaxation of the duty does not concern the choice of the participant. Thus, a participant in contact sports is entitled carelessly to inflict bodily injury on another participant *even when* the latter is not willing to assume any such risk and *even when* the former is fully aware of this fact. I shall argue below that a better way to understand the relaxation of the duty has to do with the conflict theory of tort law—in particular,

[54] *E.g.*, Knight v. Jewett, 834 P.2d 696, 711 (Cal. 1992); Karas v. Strevell, 884 N.E.2d 122, 130 (Ill. 2008); Feld v. Borkowski, 790 N.W.2d 72, 76–77 (Iowa 2010). English tort law adopts a similar position in *Condon v. Basi* [1985] 1 W.L.R. 866.

[55] *See* Mark P. Gergen, *Consent across Private Law*, *in* Interstitial Private Law 89, 108–09 (Samuel L. Bray et al. eds., 2024). Gergen's explanation, which is vulnerable to my critique in main text below, focuses on recreational sport. My account, by contrast, appeals to the good of (competitive) sporting life which necessarily cuts across the recreational/professional sports divide.

[56] *See also* Blake v. Galloway, [2004] 1 W.L.R. 2844, 2852 (C.A.), observing that "[i]t is difficult to envisage circumstances in which a participant in a contact sport or game would be taken to have impliedly consented to an act which would otherwise amount to a battery … a breach of the duty of care … will only be established where there has been recklessness or a very high degree of carelessness."

this duty is tort law's response to the tolerably valuable conflict underlying contact sports.

The second inadequate explanation is that a limited duty of care is grounded in the recreational nature of the activity, rather than a contact-sports nature. It fails because recreational activities that pose unreasonable risks to life and limb should not, and as a matter of law do not, receive favorable treatment in tort law.[57] If anything, participants in dangerous recreational activities should be required to face stringent demands of care than those who have to engage in risky activities in the course of making a living (say, driving to work) or pursuing other ground projects. The argument from recreational activities, therefore, loses momentum.

I argue that contact sports should be accommodated but not because they are a subset of recreational activities. In fact, professional contact sports are not recreational in an important sense. Rather, contact sports should be accommodated due to their intrinsic qualities as social practices whose value depends on facilitating the conflict between competition and bodily safety. Unlike the demands of a duty to exercise due care, the freedom to compete in the context of contact sports requires the liberty to act on the basis of an *instinctual* mode of decision-making, as I explain below.

On many occasions, the conflict between bodily integrity and the freedom to compete, including in ways that could pose substantial risk to others, is valueless. Consider friends car-racing each other on a busy highway. As such, the task of tort duties is to prevent the conflict. Contact sports also feature a conflict between the freedom to compete (including in certain risky ways) and bodily safety. However, the special context of sports makes this conflict a tolerably valuable one. To see this, I wish to distinguish between two questions. First, what makes sports (including contact sports) valuable? Second, what might make the conflict between freedom to compete and safety in contact sports (tolerably) valuable? The answer to the former question is rather straightforward: Engaging in sports (and games, more generally) is good for a set of reinforcing values related to sociability, agency (as games crystalize the experience of purposive acting),[58] well-being, and the pursuit of physical, intellectual, and aesthetic excellence in the face of difficulty.[59] Contact sports present various instantiations of this set of values.

The second question lies at the moral center of the relaxation of the duty of care. The conflict at issue is tolerably valuable because, while vigorous and powerful play is integral to the competition that animates contact sports, there is currently no way to do away with its harmful effects. Thus, eliminating vigorous and

[57] In the famous case of *Summers v. Tice*, 199 P.2d 1 (Cal. 1948), the court found the standard duty of reasonable care to be applicable to recreational contexts (specifically, hunting, which as least nowadays may raise serious doubts concerning tort law's understanding of what is recreation).

[58] *See* C. Thi Nyugen, *Games and the Art of Agency*, 128 Phil. Rev. 423, 432 (2019).

[59] *See* Thomas Hurka, *Games and the Good*, 40 Proc. Aris. Soc'y 217, 221–24 (2006).

powerful play undermines both the *competitive* character and the *challenge* that are integral to participating in these sports.[60]

Relaxing the duty, by contrast, facilitates competition and challenge, and vigorously at that. To see this, begin with the role of competition in sports (including contact sports). Unlike competition in the market for the consumption goods whose value is instrumental, that is, as a means to improve the quality and lower the cost of products, competition between participants in a sport is itself valuable. Participants compete (at least in part) for the sake of the competition. The conflict between the freedom to compete and bodily safety captures a crucial dimension in the competitive spirit characteristic of contact sports. Consider baseball without tagging out, soccer without tackling, or basketball without defense, pick-n-roll, and boxing out. More generally, consider such sports played by participants who do not engage each other in a significantly physical way. They are therefore left with a gentleman's version of the sport, say, basketball without contact, featuring players who can score points without facing any meaningful pushback from the opponent team (consider the NBA All-Star game as of late[61]). To this extent, the elimination of the conflict between freedom to compete and bodily safety changes the character of the game in a certain way: It virtually destroys its competitive edge. Indeed, as the California Supreme Court correctly observes, "it may well alter fundamentally the nature of the sport."[62]

Doing away with the conflict would also undermine another definitive element of contact sports, namely, the pursuit of sporting excellence. The pursuit in question manifests itself by obliging every participant to overcome the physical and intellectual challenges artificially created by the rules of the game. For instance, the game of basketball manufactures a basic challenge by rendering it impossible to advance the ball without either dribbling or passing. Now imagine what would be the case if basketball leaves no room for physical contact and, so, drastically erodes the conflict between the freedom to compete and bodily safety. We would then see basketball's radical transformation into a shooting practice in which participants' main challenge is accurately to slip the ball into the basket.[63]

[60] The philosophical literature on contact sports is vast. My discussion has benefited from the analyses made in Diana Abad, *Sportsmanship*, 4 Sport, Ethics & Phil. 27 (2010); R. Scott Kretchmar, *Simon on Realism, Fallibilism, and the Power of Reason*, 43 J. Phil. Sport 41 (2016).

[61] *See* Dan Woike, *NBA Has a Problem: The All-Star Game Is Not Much of a Game*, L.A. Times (Feb. 20, 2023) ("a woefully boring All-Star Game devoid of defense in any real shape or form"). https://www.latimes.com/sports/story/2023-02-20/nba-all-star-game-problem-lack-of-competitiveness.

[62] Knight v. Jewett, 834 P.2d 696, 710 (Cal. 1992). The case concerns touch (American) football, but the court explicitly suggests that its ruling and reasoning apply to baseball (and, by implication, other contact sports) as well.

[63] By emphasizing competition and excellence I do not mean to deny another prominent virtue of sports (and games, more generally): sociability. That is, eliminating the conflict at issue will likely also undermine both social cooperation between teammates and coordination across competing teams (i.e., a publicly shared commitment to comply with the rules of the particular sport). Thus, although a shooting practice sustains some aspects of sociability among the participants, it falls far short of the social relations that a competitive basketball game opens up. More importantly, whereas the former does not turn on the society of others, the latter is inconceivable without it.

Thus, because it is valuable (though not inherently valuable), tort law's response must be one of containing the conflict between the freedom to compete and players' safety, and doing so requires facilitating some measure of vigorous and powerful play. Engaging with the kind of value of the conflict involves easing off the built-in contrast between the duty of reasonable care, which demands *introspection*, and authentic participation in a contact sport, which demands acting *instinctually*. In doctrinal terms, this means that the tort duty of care must take a facilitating role, necessarily at the expense of some extent of protecting the right to bodily integrity. Hence, unlike many other instances of creating risk of bodily injury to others, participants must be afforded ample discretion as to how much risk they can impose on other participants. To be sure, I do not mean that participants would face no restrictions on how aggressive and irresponsible their game could go; the task of containing tolerably valuable conflicts, recall, calls for some restrictive measures as well. Instead, it means that save for deliberately or recklessly injuring other participants, players must be largely free, legally speaking, to choose the level of physicality and playfulness they see fit. The limited duty of care in the context of contact sports—sometimes also referred to as the contact sports exception—reflects this conclusion.[64]

VI. Facilitating a Community of Professional Practice

The doctrine of professional custom, governing the conduct of professionals such as physicians, lawyers, and accountants, that I now wish to discuss does not concern inherently valuable conflicts. Instead, it arises in connection with tolerably valuable conflicts. For instance, medical malpractice reflects the negative side effects of an otherwise valuable practice. Nevertheless, the duty of care associated with professional custom provides an important facility for professionalism. It, too, demonstrates why the Hartian distinction between duty-imposing and power-conferring rules does not map onto the distinction between restricting and enabling human action. Tort duties, as I argue throughout this chapter, can have an irreducibly facilitative mission. More generally, tort law is in the business of pursuing positive, not merely negative, value.

I begin with a brief characterization of the doctrine of professional custom. I argue that it does *not* address the "what" question—viz., what counts as professional due care. Rather, it focuses on the "who" question—viz., who gets to fix the content of the duty of professional due care. What might explain this unusually deferential stance toward professionals? I shall argue that the most familiar answers,

[64] Although the contact sports exception has been widely adopted in the United States, a minority of jurisdictions remain loyal to the ordinary duty of care, sometimes for institutional and extra-torts considerations. *See, e.g.*, Estes v. Tripson, 932 P.2d 1364, 1365 (Ariz. Ct. App. 1997).

especially the epistemic advantage of professional knowledge, fail because they understand the doctrine at issue in terms of the restrictive role of tort law. By contrast, I argue that this doctrine reflects tort law's facilitative role, namely, the facilitation of a certain community of professional practice.[65]

Begin with legal doctrine. When it comes to professionals such as physicians, lawyers, and accountants, courts are unusually deferential. The legal standard of due care is set by those subject to it, namely, the practicing professionals. This does not mean that courts would never intervene. But the deference is highly unusual when compared to the duties owed by laypersons, such as people using their cars or inviting others into their premises. Indeed, these laypersons do not get such a privileged role in determining the degree of care they owe to others. Instead, courts determine it for them, and in the course of doing so courts also set aside disabilities and other sources of undercompetence on the part of these persons.[66] Moreover, the level of deference to practicing professionals is even unusual when compared with organized activities, such as mass production and transportation, whose practitioners abide by sector-wide standards of safety. Their industry custom is, at best, probative of what care counts as due care: It merely provides an epistemic shorthand with which courts identify the *independently* existing legal standard of care.[67]

Holmes famously observed that "what usually is done may be evidence of what ought to be done, but what ought to be done is fixed by the standard of reasonable prudence."[68] This is not only a point about the nature of morality, as Holmes's observation concerns law and, in particular, tort law. However, when it comes to determining professionals' due care, the contrast between the "is" and the "ought" is turned on its head. What should be done is given by what is done. Hence, the content of the duty of care is fixed by operation of professional practice, rather than law.

This point does not merely reflect the process of proving, ex post facto, whether or not the defendant-professional breached a duty of due care. Rather, it reflects the ex ante guidance stage of determining what, and how much, care is owed by the likes of the defendant-professional to their patients or other clients. To begin with, establishing the standard of professional due care turns on experts' say, rather than on what juries or judges believe it should be.[69] Further, these experts are called in

[65] The concept of professionalism—what it means to be a professional and why professionalism matters—has seen important transformations in response to changing circumstances and revised convictions. *See, e.g.*, Rebecca Roiphe, *The Decline of Professionalism*, 29 GEORGETOWN J. LEGAL ETHICS 649 (2016). Except for the outright denial of professionalism (which is often advocated by some populists), my discussion is compatible with a number of them ranging from the strictly meritocratic to the more democratic-egalitarian conception of professionalism.

[66] *See further* Chapter 15.

[67] RESTATEMENT (THIRD) OF TORTS: PHYS. & EMOT. HARM § 13 (2010). A classical formulation is *T.J. Hooper*, 60 F.2d 737 (2d Cir. 1932).

[68] Texas & P. Ry. Co. v. Behymer, 189 U.S. 468, 470 (1903).

[69] There are exceptions to this rule, to be sure. One exception concerns plain and simple matters, and other exceptions, instances of extreme mistakes.

order to *report* on prevailing practice, rather than assess what in their view professional care should entail. As one court has explained, "professional prudence is defined by actual or accepted practice within a profession, rather than theories about what 'should' have been done."[70]

One immediate implication of the unusual deference just described is that the doctrine of professional due care need not bear on the *level* of care. Indeed, vesting practicing professionals with the authority to fix the content of their duty reflects tort law's hands-off approach as to how demanding this duty should be. At times, the prevailing practice among professionals sustains a standard of care that falls below the legal threshold that would have been invoked by courts, namely, ordinary care. For instance, the nursing standard of care in the use of a lift to transfer a patient from a wheelchair to a bed falls below the standard of ordinary care in so using.[71] At other times, however, professional care may exceed ordinary care. It has been often observed that physicians can be overly cautious and, so, exercise more care than they should ideally have exercised, a custom that (when taken to an unwarranted extreme) is pejoratively called defensive medicine.[72] Once again, the doctrine of professional due care does not concern the question of *what*, and so how much, care counts as due. Instead, it picks out a question of standing, namely, *who* gets to determine what counts as due care.

What might explain the doctrine of professional care? The conventional wisdom centers on the epistemic advantages of expertise. The animating idea is that courts are not sufficiently competent to make substantive decisions on matters of professional knowledge and expertise. However, this explanation fails. To begin with, as noted above, it is incoherent because courts do not hesitate to tackle epistemic hurdles in all other cases involving intricate knowledge and expertise. For instance, courts routinely evaluate the safety of products' design in order to decide—independently of industry custom—whether they are reasonably safe for users. The evaluation does not end with exposing manufacturing defects as it involves assessment of the very design of the product, including the trade-off between the risk and the utility of the design. Doing so turns on a detailed understanding of applied scientific knowledge concerning the design of complex mechanical, electrical, and computational systems. To meet this intellectual challenge, courts resort to experts to educate them on these intricate matters. However, unlike the doctrine of professional care, courts get to set the legal standard of products safety and, additionally, whether the design of a particular product is defective, safety wise.

[70] Osborn v. Irwin Memorial Blood Bank, 5 Cal.App.4th 234, 282 (1992).

[71] Myers v. Heritage Enters., Inc., 820 N.E.2d 604, 611 (Ill. App. 2004) ("If the jury had been instructed that it could determine how a reasonably careful person would have acted under the circumstances, it may have determined that [certified nurse's aides] were, in fact, negligent, despite [expert testimony] that these professionals met the [professional standard].") Eventually, however, the court decided that certified nurses' aides did not constitute a profession for negligence law's purposes.

[72] *See, e.g.*, GEISTFELD, *supra* note 7, at 213; Robert Cooter & Ariel Porat, *Disgorgement Damages for Accidents*, 44 J. LEGAL STUD. 249, 273 (2015).

Moreover, the argument from the epistemic advantage of expertise loses momentum when considering the *scope* of the doctrine of professional care. Contrary to certain professional medical practices, the doctrine applies more broadly to capture professionals such as lawyers, architects, and accountants.[73] For instance, attorneys' practice appears far less complicated, say, than cardiology[74] and at any rate not more difficult to comprehend by jurors, not only by judges, who are also lawyers, than the design of complex mechanical systems in products liability law.

A better way to make sense of the doctrine of professional care is to focus on its role in facilitating professionalism and, in particular, a *community of practice* among professionals. I seek to explain its value by contrasting this community with the cases of artisans, craft-persons, and market competitors. Although professionals sometimes resort to artisanship and craftsmanship and often compete in markets, their service draws on a community of practitioners in ways that artisans, craft-persons, and market competitors do not.[75]

To see this, consider the ways we assess the quality of products and services produced by artisans and then by manufacturers. A tailor-made product made by an artisan of a particular craft can be assessed independently of any practice—say, the quality of a home-made bakery's bread does not turn on what other bakers, or fans of baked goods, happen to judge it to be. Its taste for the individual to whom it is tailored is all that matters for the purpose of guiding the baker's deliberation as to what kind of bread to bake and how to bake it. By contrast, a manufacturer engaging in mass production of a generic good, or the provision of a generic service, draws on market demand in order to determine the desired quality of the good or service. In that, the overall assessment of the good or service is given by catering for the preferences of potential buyers of the good or service. A guild of manufacturers and other forms of strategic cooperation among providers is not only unnecessary but also (often) detrimental to the market mechanism of assessing quality by way of competition.

By contrast, there is an important sense in which work-related deliberations by professionals are different. Unlike artisans, professionals *cannot* decide what to do and how to do it without drawing on a preexisting set of norms that serves as the baseline against which to determine what counts as quality service. For instance, accountants cannot perform their task of assessing the financial condition of a corporation merely by appealing to theirs—or their clients' best judgments of what counts as professional performance. Their success (or failure) cannot be assessed independently of standards whose underlying idea is set by the basic

[73] *See, e.g.*, Olson v. North, 276 Ill. App. 457, 475 (1934); Lentino v. Fringe Emp. Plans., Inc., 611 F.2d 474, 480 (3d Cir. 1979) (Penn. Law).

[74] *See further* Benjamin C. Zipursky, *Legal Malpractice and the Structure of Negligence Law*, 67 Fordham L. Rev. 649, 677–78 (1998).

[75] *Cf.* Jonny Thakkar, *Moneymakers and Craftsmen: A Platonic Approach to Privatization*, 24 Eur. J. Phil. 735, 740–45 (2016).

objectives of the accounting profession, namely, producing accurate financial information (which, in turn, requires collecting, analyzing, and interpreting data). Unlike market actors, professionals should not guide themselves solely by the logic of profitmaking and the norm of preference-satisfaction to which it calls. For instance, physicians are trained healers and, so, ought to deliberate as to what to do and how to do it by reference to the objectives intrinsic to their calling; lawyers, who are officers of the justice system and upholders of the rule of law more generally, should make their decisions and preform their professional tasks with an eye to these market-independent commitments.

Hence the question for these professionals becomes what set of norms and expectations (other than the ones invoked by artisans and market competitors) can inform and guide their workplace deliberations. More generally, how could they systematically turn the abstract objectives of their respective professions into practical wisdom? A certain community of practice is the answer. Such a community is not merely a living version of a service manual designed to guide its users by spelling out directives that address any conceivable situation. Rather than being a mere stockpile of technical knowledge, the community of practice (ideally) provides its members a distinctive way to approach the world, say, to think like a lawyer or to attend to others as a doctor. It does so by constituting its own specific language as is recognized to be typical for (and in some cases even exclusive to) its domain of application and far less typical outside of this domain. This language has its own set of categories of understanding the world (consider the legal category "rights" or "rights of action"). It also gives rise to its own ways of determining what actions to take in response to various states of affair. Moreover, a community of practice provides professionals with a certain ethos, say, of physicians as healers or lawyers as upholders of the rule of law,[76] which in turn informs their deliberations in connection with particular cases and with setting policies, more generally.

Against this backdrop, the tort-law doctrine of professional due care plays a substantial role in facilitating a community of professional practitioners. It does that in two ways. Negatively, it insulates practitioners from external imposition by regulators, courts, and market pressures (that might come in the form of patients' or clients' demands). The insulation at issue is not all-encompassing, to be sure. In particular, it does not cover the managerial and administrative aspects of practicing the profession in question, as these are not distinctive of professional practice. Nor does it capture the responsibilities of professionals in their more general capacities as citizens or private persons. Nor, finally, does it include the power to fix standards of admission to the relevant profession. Rather, the doctrine of professional care

[76] For more on the dual loyalties of lawyers, as zealous advocates to their clients and as officers of the court and of the legal system, see W. Bradley Wendel, *Understanding the Complex Loyalty of Lawyers: Dual-Commission, Governance Mandate, and Intrinsic-Limit Analyses*, *in* 2 Oxford Studies in Private Law Theory 159 (Paul B. Miller & John Oberdiek eds., 2023).

insulates the practice from external regulation of the discretionary powers of professionals to decide questions that lie at the core of their calling—say, what medical treatment to administer to a patient who suffers from certain symptoms or in the case of accountants, how to prepare financial statements during inflation-rocketing times. It therefore frees professionals from having to subject their workplace deliberations to objectives set by the market, government, or some other forces. Instead, it makes it the case that the decisions made by practitioners can, and should, be governed by professional objectives.

Affirmatively, the doctrine of professional care helps to sustain a community among practicing professionals by treating the community's own standards as dispositive (i.e., decisive) of due care. In doing so, tort law empowers the professional community as a whole to decide for its participants what counts as professional and what professionalism requires in everyday practice. This way of empowerment, in turn, facilitates community-building. This is because getting at the right decisions and identifying the right objectives do not arise in a vacuum. A community of practice is valuable precisely because it fills out this vacuum.

* * *

The conflict theory establishes a normative framework with which to understand, assess, and ultimately vindicate tort law. On this framework, the near-automatic identification of tort duties with conduct-restricting rules must be rejected. More generally, the jurisprudential divide between duty-imposing and power-conferring rules ought to give way to a better understanding of why duties matter and what practical difference they can make. Indeed, the four duty rules explored above suggest that tort duties can, and should, engage not merely in allowing but rather in facilitating tolerably valuable conflicts. The conflict theory further provides the normative resources to determine under what circumstances facilitation is warranted or even required. The answer comes down to the first virtue of tort law, namely, responding to conflicts in the right way by engaging with their underlying value.

Engaging with value, as this chapter demonstrates, does not end with identifying a conflict as inherently valuable, tolerably valuable, or valueless. This chapter's focus on tolerably valuable conflicts suggests that the next stage in the analysis is to contain these conflicts' negative side effects by determining duties (and rights) that restrict certain acts, on the one hand, and enable others, on the other. The preceding discussion has addressed the enabling dimension of tort duties to show that the *right measure* of facilitation—the types and the extent of permissible risk creation—is itself a question of value. For instance, the value of contact sports informs the legal determination of the tort duty to which participants are subject. The same is true with respect to the respective values underlying investigative journalism, corporate entrepreneurship, and professionalism. More broadly, it can extend to many other social practices that generate tolerably valuable conflicts.

5

Valueless Conflicts

Why and When Suing in Tort Law Matters

The elaboration of the conflict theory has so far mainly focused on the constructive and enabling aspirations of tort law as manifested in connection with inherently and tolerably valuable conflicts, respectively. Chapters 8–10, 14–15, and 17 return to these matters. I now wish to shift attention to tort law's engagement with *negative* value and, in particular, valueless conflicts. I do this by applying the conflict theory's normative framework to a rather basic question in tort theory: Why does the right of action of tort victims matter? Addressing this question is important for different reasons, but I wish to flag the two that are closely related to the conflict theory. Most generally, this question is a subset of the larger challenge of vindicating tort law, namely: Why have tort law in the first place? So far my answer has focused on constructing the conditions necessary for certain (inherently and tolerably) valuable conflicts of interests to arise. It will be apt to consider whether rights of action should be part of the answer, too. Indeed, I argue that the case for rights of action against deliberate wrongdoers and for what I call relational wrongdoers should form part of the answer to the vindication question.

The second reason the question at issue is important to the conflict theory is that it provides an occasion for exploring the value in engaging with valueless conflicts. That is, although valueless conflicts are truly valueless, responding to them in the *right* way can be valuable. Hence, because the first virtue of tort law is to respond to conflicts in the right way by engaging with their values, the question of why rights of action matter is integral to what the conflict theory sets out to do. I wish to show that with respect to instances of deliberate wrongdoing as well as relational wrongdoing, victims' rights of action (noninstrumentally) matter.

I argue that vesting the victim with a right of action is the right way to respond to valueless conflicts that take the form of either deliberate or relational wrongdoing.[1] Doing so is not merely instrumentally valuable, for instance, in bringing about the desirable outcome of recovering from the wrongdoer. It is also noninstrumentally valuable in that it allows victims of deliberate and relational wrongdoings to reassert publicly their status as free and equal agents vis-à-vis their respective

[1] The argument draws, in part, on Hanoch Dagan, Avihay Dorfman, & Issi Rosen-Zvi, *It's (Not All) Personal: Civil Litigation and the Values of Rights of Action*, 75 Am. U. L. Rev. (forthcoming 2026).

Conflict between Equals. Avihay Dorfman, Oxford University Press. © Oxford University Press 2026.
DOI: 10.1093/9780198979869.003.0008

wrongdoers. The right to pursue the wrongdoer is, therefore, no less crucial for the victim's ability to restore this status than to secure a damages award.

I. Victims' Rights of Action: Are They Mere Means or Also Valuable in Themselves?

To set the scene, it is important to note that the question concerning the value of rights of action does *not* address the other two types of right that figure in tort law: primary rights and secondary rights of repair. Thus, the question I seek to explore presupposes primary rights, such as to bodily integrity. It also presupposes secondary rights of redress or repair against injurers. The question I pursue in this chapter concerns the institutional arrangement responsible for enforcing (or vindicating) the former two rights.[2] In particular, the question is a normative one, focusing on whether there are *non*instrumental reasons to single out the victim as the agent of enforcement (or vindication). By noninstrumental reasons I mean that tort law should treat victims' rights of action as valuable in themselves, rather than as more or less effective means to be deployed in the service of enforcing or vindicating primary and secondary rights.

Hence, I wish to explore *why*, and then *when*, personal rights of action are integral to vindicating the victim's substantive rights. I believe that contemporary tort theory does not answer this question in a satisfactory fashion. Furthermore, for the most part, it does not have the normative resources to answer the *when* question. My answer to the question is that rights of action can sometimes be noninstrumentally valuable. But unlike influential tort theories, I emphasize the qualified language in which it is framed: "Sometimes" rather than "always" or even "typically." I do not believe it is plausible to hold that *all* personal rights of action are noninstrumentally valuable. To render more vividly this intuition, compare a case of a manufacturer of a defective product causing property damage to the product's user with a case of deliberate sexual harassment. Is the right to sue the injurer for material redress in this case of products liability and the right to sue a perpetrator in a sexual harassment case different applications of the same moral commitment? I think not. Once again, I argue that deliberate wrongdoing represents one category of cases and relational wrongdoing another, for which the right of action is noninstrumentally valuable.

Before I lay out my argument, it will be apt to make two critical observations about some influential approaches to the question of why tort-victims' rights of

[2] The tripartite distinction between primary, secondary, and tertiary rights is further explored in JOHN GARDNER, FROM PERSONAL LIFE TO PRIVATE LAW 213–14 (2018). The conceptual foundations underlying this distinction have been laid out in Coleman's annulment thesis. *See* Jules L. Coleman, *Tort Law and the Demands of Corrective Justice*, 67 IND. L.J. 349 (1992).

action matter. These observations are called for in order to clarify precisely what is at stake when we assess the case for rights of action in the law of torts.

II. What's *Not* at Stake: Accountability and Material Redress

Accountability. There are several different articulations of an intuitively powerful idea, namely, that tort law is an institution of interpersonal accountability.[3] A major aspect of this institution is the victim's right of action, characterized as the right to "hold [the injurer] accountable"[4] or at the very least to see to it that the injurer "is subject to being held to account or deemed responsible to [the victim]."[5] I wish to cast some doubts over the relationship between having the right to bring a tort action against one's injurer and the intuitive idea of holding this person accountable. The critique goes to the issue of what rights of action do, rather than whether holding an injurer accountable is morally required or otherwise appealing. While these rights may do different things, I argue that they do *not* give their holders an entitlement, including power, to *hold* another person accountable. Simply put, a right to sue a person is not a right to hold this person accountable, responsible, et alia.

Some aspects of the civil litigation system instantiate a certain idea of interpersonal accountability. However, the right of action is not one of them.[6] To begin with, a right of action can certainly empower the victim to sue the defendant, but it does *not* generate a duty on the part of the defendant to appear in court to respond to the victim's allegations, as the injurer, qua defendant, is not strictly speaking under an obligation to do this much. Having to respond to the victim is, in fact, akin to a burden: The injurer is free to choose between debunking the victim-plaintiff's complaint, acceding to the allegations, and simply paying damages (without conceding wrongdoing). Rational people may elect the latter option without necessarily taking themselves—or being taken by the victim and society, more generally—to be accountable or responsible for what happened. For instance, an all-things-considered decision to pay the required sum may be motivated by a well-to-do defendant seeking to economize on time, energy, and other scarce

[3] *See, e.g.*, Matthew A. Shapiro, *The Indignities of Civil Litigation*, 100 B. U. L. Rev. 501, 516–17 (2020); Stephen Darwall & Julian Darwall, *Civil Recourse as Mutual Accountability*, 39 Fla. St. L. Rev. 17 (2011); Jason M. Solomon, *Equal Accountability Through Tort Law*, 103 Nw. L. Rev. 1765 (2009). A somewhat related idea that I set to one side is to conceive of tort law as a system of interpersonal responsibility. *See* Scott Hershovitz, *Harry Potter and the Trouble with Tort Theory*, 63 Stan. L. Rev. 67, 79 (2010). An important variation on the responsibility theme is the identification of tort law, or parts thereof, with the notion of outcome responsibility. *See* Tony Honoré, Responsibility and Fault 23–39 (1999); Stephen Perry, *The Moral Foundations of Tort Law*, 77 Iowa L. Rev. 449, 496–514 (1992).

[4] John C. P. Goldberg & Benjamin C. Zipursky, Recognizing Wrongs 10, 73 (2020).

[5] *Id.*, at 177.

[6] For a different critique of the notion that rights of action practically empower victims, see Ori Herstein, *How Tort Law Empowers*, 65 U. Toronto L.J. 99 (2015).

resources. An accountability-based right of action would surely have to prohibit, or at the very least restrict, the defendant's right to do that. Thus, it is one thing to say that a right to sue is crucial to initiate legal proceedings against an injurer,[7] yet quite another to say that it is about holding that person accountable. Indeed, there may be something about these legal proceedings that can contribute to, or even bring about, interpersonal accountability, but it is not the right to initiate them. It is also not clear, as I argue presently, why this right is a necessary prerequisite to legal proceedings oriented, in part, toward interpersonal accountability.

What other elements of civil litigation can sustain interpersonal accountability? Perhaps the most important accountability element lies in the court itself. Thus, the court holds the special authority to hold litigants accountable.[8] The court's authority is not merely epistemic, but rather practical and, in particular, political authority. Indeed, they hold the power to find for or against litigants by assessing their respective conduct on the basis of the relevant legal standards. They further possess the power to impose liability, award damages, and grant injunctions in accordance with the law. Another element of accountability arises when the court finds for the plaintiff, as it is only then that victims get some power in the direction of holding their injurers accountable by exercising their entitlement to seek the damages awarded to them. Hence, the answer to the question of why a tort-victim's right of action matters, that is, is noninstrumentally valuable rather than merely as a means, is better not cast in terms of the power to hold the injurer accountable.

Material Redress. Talk of making the victim whole or obtaining civil recourse against them suggests that the victim is entitled to have their injury repaired or redressed by the injurer. The ultimate object of this entitlement is described by corrective justice theorists as "rectification" and, by civil recourse theorists, as obtaining "satisfaction" from the wrongdoer.[9] The crucial question, then, is precisely what is meant by rectification or satisfaction? Most immediately, this entitlement calls for *material* redress as a means to enforce (in corrective justice's case) or vindicate (in civil recourse's case) the substantive rights of the victim. Typically, it involves awarding compensatory and, if necessary, super-compensatory damages for the pecuniary and nonpecuniary losses suffered at the hand of the wrongdoer.

An entitlement to material redress, however, leaves open the issue of how—in what ways and to what extent—it should be brought about. Indeed, it is one thing to insist on the victim's entitlement to benefit from material redress, and quite another to say that the victim must be the agent of such redress. The traditional

[7] *See id.*, at 112.

[8] *See id.*, at 109. *But see* ANDREW S. GOLD, THE RIGHT OF REDRESS 71–73 (2020).

[9] On rectification, see Ernest Weinrib, *Corrective Justice in a Nutshell*, 52 U. TORONTO L.J. 349, 350 (2002); Jules Coleman & Arthur Ripstein, *Mischief and Misfortune*, 41 MCGILL L.J. 91, 93 (1995) ("Corrective justice concerns the rectification of losses owing to private wrongs"); *see generally* ERNEST J. WEINRIB, RECIPROCAL FREEDOM: PRIVATE LAW AND PUBLIC RIGHTS 26 (2023). On satisfaction, see GOLDBERG & ZIPURSKY, *supra* note 4, at 117–19; John C. P. Goldberg, *Two Conceptions of Tort Damages: Fair v. Full Compensation*, 55 DEPAUL L. REV. 435 (2006).

common law model of tort-victims' rights of action is certainly a means—a legal technology—to bring about material redress, but it is not the only one. It is not clear why a right to material redress is insufficient to enforce or vindicate the victim's substantive right if, let's assume, the right to material redress is fully and adequately satisfied by some other legal mechanism.[10] In other words, it is not clear why, and when, victims' rights of action as such are integral to enforcing or vindicating their substantive rights. The example mentioned above, concerning a simple products liability case resulting in damage to the user's property, vividly renders this point.

I argue, negatively, that rights of action are often of instrumental value only. Affirmatively, I defend the claim that vesting the tort-victim with a right of action is a noninstrumentally valuable way to respond to valueless conflicts that take the form of either deliberate or relational wrongdoing.

III. Deliberate Wrongdoing

A. Characterization

Among the many different types of wrongs that make up the law of torts, some types feature an additional or parasitic dimension of wrongfulness triggered by the illicit behavior of the wrongdoer. For instance, the one who deliberately attacks an innocent victim is not only harming the person of the victim but rather also intends, in the sense of *means*, as such. Unlike the case of inadvertently causing serious bodily harm, the deliberate wrongdoer also executes a plan to inflict such harm. Jean-Jacques Rousseau observed that from an early stage in the natural development of social life, "any intentional wrong became an affront because, together with the harm resulting from the injury, the offended party saw in it contempt for his person, often more unbearable than the harm itself."[11]

I wish to offer a somewhat different interpretation of the dual nature of deliberate wrongdoing. Rather than the talk by Rousseau (and more recent theorists) of contempt and, implicitly, humiliation and distrust on top of the material injury,[12]

[10] *Contra* Larissa Katz & Matthew A. Shapiro, *The Role of Plaintiffs in Private Law Institutions*, *in* PRIVATE LAW AND PRACTICAL REASON: ESSAYS ON JOHN GARDNER'S PRIVATE LAW THEORY 239, 255 (Haris Psarras & Sandy Steel eds., 2023) ("personal considerations ... support a presumption that rights holders themselves should hold [the power to sue] by default"); TIMOTHY LIAU, STANDING IN PRIVATE LAW: POWERS OF ENFORCEMENT IN THE LAW OF OBLIGATIONS AND TRUSTS 246–51 (2023); GOLD, *supra* note 8, at 41, 66, 75.

[11] Jean-Jacques Rousseau, *Discourse on the Origin and Foundations of Inequality Among Men*, *in* THE DISCOURSES AND OTHER EARLY POLITICAL WRITINGS 166 (Victor Gourevitch ed. & trans. 1997) [1754].

[12] *See, e.g.*, Linda Radzik, *Tort Processes and Relational Repair*, *in* PHIL. FOUNDATIONS L. TORTS 231, 235–37 (John Oberdiek ed., 2014). *See also* Nathan B. Oman, *The Honor of Private Law*, 80 FORDHAM L. REV. 31 (2011).

a wrong done deliberately can constitute a second, parasitic wrong to our fundamental interest in self-determination. The argument can be further extended, as I explain presently, to capture acting with either knowledge to a substantial certainty of the resultant injury or reckless disregard thereof. Material redress, I argue, does not provide an adequate response to either. By contrast, victims' rights of action, provide a fitting response.

To flesh out the dual nature of deliberate wrongdoing, consider the contrast between deliberate and accidental wrongdoing.[13] Imagine a case in which both forms of wrongdoing result in the exact same serious physical injury. On the deliberate end, a person intentionally strikes another in the eye; and a similar injury occurs when a person seeking to separate two fighting dogs raises a stick over his shoulder, accidently striking a person standing closely behind him in the eye.[14] I argue that despite the identical bottom line of serious injury, the two instances represent substantively different forms of interpersonal mistreatment. Deliberately infliction of a similar injury sets them apart.[15]

Indeed, the deliberate manner in which the harm is perpetrated gives rise to another wrong, which is to say subordinating the victim to the pursuit of one's own ends. Subordination, the underlying immoral conduct, should not be understood externally or ex post, namely, as a state of affairs. Instead, the subordination relevant to deliberately disregarding the bodily integrity of another expresses the intentional singling out of a person for mistreatment. It involves the identification of a particular person—the would-be victim—as the object of the misconduct, and thus represents the total reduction of a person into a mere instrument at the hands of the injurer.

Carelessness, by contrast, does not entertain the special subordinating character just mentioned.[16] Its resultant harm can be reasonably foreseeable. Indeed, the injurer may even be subjectively aware of the risks of harm to passersby associated with raising a stick over his shoulder. That said, the outcome is just accidental—a failure of inattention, imperfect control over one's bodily movement, or want of consideration of the safety of others. It might ground liability for the resulting

[13] The proposed distinction aligns (to a limited extent) with Jean Hampton, *Correcting Harms Versus Righting Wrongs: The Goal of Retribution*, 39 UCLA 1659 (1992). That said, my account parts way with Hampton along several key dimensions. Hampton defends a distinction between wrongful actions that require retribution and compensation and those that merit compensation only. My account does not defend Hampton's argument that retributive justice or some other punitive-like measures are the fitting response. Moreover, Hampton identifies the underlying value of retribution with a *non*relational theory of human value (which can extend beyond my focus on relational autonomy and equality).

[14] The latter incident very loosely follows the facts of the celebrated case of *Brown v. Kendall*, 60 Mass. 292 (1850).

[15] The following analysis draws, in part, on Avihay Dorfman, *Can Tort Law be Moral?*, 23 Ratio Juris 205, 209–10 (2010).

[16] *Contra* Weinrib, *supra* note 9, at 100; Arthur Ripstein, Force and Freedom: Kant's Legal and Political Philosophy 171 (2009); Scott Hershovits, *Treating Wrongs as Wrongs: An Expressive Argument for Tort Law*, 10(2) J. Tort L. 405, 426 (2017).

injury, to be sure.[17] However, it involves nothing by way of acquiring intentions—and making a choice—in favor of singling out the victim of the careless act. Taking one's attention off the road for a very short time may surely amount to substandard behavior; but it is hardly an act of intentionally turning any person in particular into an object of mistreatment.

Thus, in deliberately striking another in the eye, the injurer is not only wronging the victim by unjustifiably harming her but rather also wronging the victim in a different way, namely, by undermining her being a self-determining agent.[18] To understand the nature of this setback, it will be apt to emphasize its two basic aspects. First, the setback to the victim is substantive, as opposed to superficial. It does not merely threaten to thwart this or that plan of the victim (say, to safely cross the street) but rather seeks to deny the victim the very status of being a self-determining agent who is entitled to decide what (if any) plans to make in the first place.[19] Second, the setback to the victim as a self-determining being also has an irreducibly relational dimension. This is because the interest in self-determination picks out not only the relationship between a person and the choices (or actions) they make but also the relationship between that person and others.[20] In particular, the significance of self-determination is in part given by an interpersonal element—that being self-determining requires that *others* treat us in a certain way, namely, as free and equal agents who are, thereby, entitled to write their life stories. Deliberately striking an innocent person in the eye brings out the relational dimension of self-determination as it reflects the active rejection on the part of one person—the injurer—of the very idea that another one—the victim—is a self-determining being. (Another instructive illustration is the tort of deceit, which involves the deliberate interference with a person's decision-making process.)

Although the discussion has so far emphasized the distinction between deliberate and accidental wrongdoing, the normative space between the two encompasses other forms of wrongdoing as well. Two such forms are worth noting at this point. The first is acting with knowledge to a substantial certainty that the conduct of the injurer would harm another person, say, by practicing boxing skills

[17] For more on the immorality of negligence, see Seana Valentine Shiffrin, *The Moral Neglect of Negligence*, *in* OXFORD STUD. POL. PHIL. 197 (David Sobel et al. eds., 2017).

[18] For an account that focuses on impaired relationships and "relational harms," see Radzik, *supra* note 12, at 237, 240, 244.

[19] The distinction between a particular choice and the status of a person as an autonomous agent differs from another familiar distinction in private law theory, namely, between a particular choice and the capacity for choice. A deliberate wrong (such as assault and battery) may undermine a person's status as an autonomous agent without necessarily impairing the person's capacity for choice.

[20] *See* Catriona Mackenzie & Natalie Stoljar, *Introduction: Autonomy Refigured*, *in* RELATIONAL AUTONOMY: FEMINIST PERSPECTIVES ON AUTONOMY, AGENCY, AND THE SOCIAL SELF 3 (Catriona Mackenzie & Natalie Stoljar eds., 2000). *See also* Joel Anderson & Axel Honneth, *Autonomy, Vulnerability, Recognition, and Justice*, *in* AUTONOMY AND CHALLENGES TO LIBERALISM: NEW ESSAYS 127 (John Christman & Joel Anderson eds., 2005).

on a crowded beach.[21] The second is acting with reckless disregard, by which I mean refraining from attending to an obvious and substantial, though readily preventable, risk of injury created by the injurer, say, by driving aimlessly while being heavily (and voluntarily) intoxicated.[22]

While not exhibiting a deliberate plan to inflict an injury, both forms of wrongdoing should be regarded as undermining the victim's autonomous being on top of their person. One reason for this is epistemic: Proof of acting with knowledge to a substantial certainty of harming the victim or of displaying reckless disregard toward them can allow courts to infer what presumably is the case, namely, deliberate wrongdoing on the part of the injurer.[23] The more important reason, however, is substantive, as it suggests that both forms do in fact undermine the autonomous being of the victim and to this extent should not be treated as a variation on accidental wrongdoing. Instead, they warrant a similar response to the one arising from deliberate wrongdoing (on which more below).

Thus, although the injurer does not acquire intentions in favor of singling out another person for some serious mistreatment, wrongdoings associated with either knowledge in lieu of intent or reckless disregard implicate the injurer in *making a choice* that has reference to the vulnerability of the victim. In particular, the injurers acquire intentions to act in ways that are obviously very likely to place the victim in harm's way and, nonetheless, decide to proceed anyway, especially including when preventing the harm is relatively easy. Hence, unlike deliberate wrongdoing in which the injurer acts *because* so acting is detrimental to the safety of the victim, the injurer with near-certain knowledge or reckless disregard acts *despite* the obvious and very serious, though readily mitigatable, threat to the safety of the victim.

The shift from doing-so-because to doing-the-same-in-spite of the outcome is certainly important for a number of reasons and for different legal and extralegal purposes. That said, the latter shares (at least) one property with the former, which is that of denying the victim the status of an autonomous being. In the case of the injurer acting with the near-certain knowledge of causing the prerequisite injury,

[21] The doctrine of knowledge in lieu of intent figures in the law of intentional torts. *See* Garrett v. Dailey, 279 P.2d 1091 (Wash. 1955). *See generally* Restatement (Third) of Torts: Phys. & Emot. Harm § 1 (2010).

[22] *See* Thompson v. Bohlken, 312 N.W.2d 501, 505 (Iowa 1981) (noting that "the difference [between deliberate and recklessness] is illustrated by comparing the throwing of an object with intent to strike another and throwing it without such intent, but believing that it will, in fact, strike another, and proceeding with indifference as to whether it does not." *See further* Restatement (Third) of Torts: Phys. & Emot. Harm § 3 (2010). My definition of recklessness can account for instances of date- and acquaintance-rape involving the perpetrator "unreasonably creating circumstances that undermined [the victim's] ability to consent freely." W. Jonathan Cardi & Martha Chamallas, *A Negligence Claim for Rape*, 101 Texas L. Rev. 587, 596 (2023).

[23] One way this logic can be implemented in civil litigation is by placing the burden of proving consent on the defendant. This way of allocating the burden of persuasion in the tort of offensive battery is anyway warranted by other compelling considerations. *See* Chapter 16.

the parasitic wrong to autonomy manifests itself in knowingly treating the victim as a mere recipient of a tortious conduct (as when the boxer knows that beachgoers will likely become his punching bags). Whereas in the case of failing to attend to a very obvious and substantial, though readily mitigatable, risk of harm, the injurer inflicts the parasitic setback on the victim's autonomy by displaying conscious indifference to generating a serious risk of injuring the former.

B. Responding to Deliberate Wrongdoing: The Case for Victims' Rights of Action

Why might having the right to sue the deliberate wrongdoer, quite apart from the right to material redress, matter to the victim? The answer is that although material redress could be a fitting response to the physical injury from which the victim suffers, it does not fully address the setback to his or her interest in self-determination. Simply put, material redress absent a personal right of action may leave intact the relational aspect of the setback to the victim's self-determination.

Indeed, adequate material redress purports to repair all the adverse physical and emotional, pecuniary, and nonpecuniary, consequences visited upon the victim by the injurer. It can include compensatory and super-compensatory damages, including punitive damages. Ultimately, the victim has a right to receive a check that reflects the full monetary value of the injury's adverse consequences. However, securing this right to material redress by compelling the injurer to pay damages ex post facto may not compensate for, not to mention take back, the deliberate rejection of the status of the victim as a self-determining being. What is also required is a framework that provides the victim with the facility to reassert his or her autonomous status not necessarily in general, against the world at large, but rather *against the injurer*, in particular. An extralegal, voluntary framework may be appropriate but, as the equality theory I defend in Chapter 12 suggests, what is specifically required is an *institutional* framework, which is to say personal rights of action.[24]

To see this, consider why punitive damages may fall short of furnishing a fitting response to the deliberate wrongdoing at issue. An award of punitive damages can

[24] An informal mechanism by which the victim can reassert his or her autonomous status will likely also include the payment of (some measure of) compensatory damages. One might invoke the repayment rule to counter this suggestion, arguing that fully compensating the victim of a wrong prior to her bringing a legal suit might not count as a defense, so that the wrongdoer would be compelled to compensate the victim once again. *See* Stephen A. Smith, *Duties, Liabilities, and Damages*, 125 Harv. L. Rev. 1727, 1744–49 (2012); *see also* Stephen A. Smith, Rights, Wrongs, and Injustices: The Structure of Remedial Law 196 (2019). I disagree, however. To begin with, the repayment rule is better viewed as standing for purely instrumental reasons, as it precludes real-life disagreements and violence that will likely occur when the enforcement of substantive rights can be made independently of court rulings. Moreover, the argument from the repayment rule need not fail the informal mechanism after all. This is because the defendant could invoke basic principles of restitution law to estop the plaintiff from suing for what turns out to be double recovery.

sometimes function as an injunctive relief granted ex post.[25] Whereas injunctive relief can be used to prevent certain gross violations of rights, an award of punitive damages may aim to convey a similar message—that such violations should not have occurred in the first place. To achieve this much, a punitive damages award should be quantified to turn the injurer's deliberate scheme into a losing proposition.

That said, the functional similarities between punitive damages and injunctive relief do not make the former a perfect substitute for the latter. Unlike an order restraining a would-be assailant from launching his or her malicious attack on the victim, an ex post facto payment of super-compensatory damages can never prevent the injurer from running his or her deliberate plan of rejecting the status of the victim as an autonomous being. Nor, most importantly, can it force the injurer to *treat* the victim as an autonomous agent at the remedial stage. At most, it forces the injurer to deal with the victim as a beneficiary of the right to material redress. In other words, the injurer is duty-bound to respect the victim as a patient in the form of a payee who is entitled to no more than receiving the injurer's money. It turns out, therefore, that the deliberate disregard of the victim's self-determination remains an ongoing concern for the terms of interaction between the two even as the victim receives a hefty award of punitive damages.

Can there be a way for the victim of deliberate wrongdoing, of the strike-in-the-eye line of cases, to reassert his or her status as an autonomous person? Looking from the other side, can there be a way to compel the injurer to interact with the victim at the post-wrong stage on terms that secure the status of the latter as a self-determining person? The answer to both lies in granting victims' rights of action on top of rights to material redress. Such rights construct terms of interaction under which victims are entitled to *reassert their self-determination* vis-à-vis their injurers. In that, tort-victims' rights of action are not only a means to the end of material redress but rather also valuable as such, that is, quite apart from whether they are the best legal technology to secure adequate material redress.

Reasserting one's self-determining agency against the injurer consists in two elements. The first is waivability: The victim alone gets to decide whether or not to pursue the injurer. The victim manifests his or her autonomous agency against the injurer by determining how a past wrong should reflect on his or her life going forward. At times, "leaving it behind" may be the right thing to do for purely instrumental reasons concerning time, energy, and reluctance to invoke the adversarial torts system or for noninstrumental reasons stemming from the victim's deep commitments, say, to forgiveness or mercifulness. At other times, as Goldberg and Zipursky rightly observe, refusing to "lump it"[26] may better resonate with

[25] *See further* Chapter 12; Hanoch Dagan & Avihay Dorfman, *Substantive Remedies*, 96 Notre Dame L. Rev. 513, 537 (2020).
[26] Goldberg & Zipursky, *supra* note 4, at 175.

the victim's effort to rewrite his or her life story in response to being deliberately wronged by another. A right to sue the injurer is a legal instantiation of this course of action.

Suing the injurer constructs an interpersonal engagement wherein the victim reasserts his or her self-determining agency as against the injurer. The engagement is structured around two key layers—an epistemic and an evaluative one. On the epistemic front, the two parties make (often competing) claims concerning the facts of the matter, ultimately allowing the fact-finder to establish who did what. Notice that the allocation of the burden of proving these claims may vary according to a number of considerations.[27] This variance means that the responsibility to substantiate factual claims, explain what happened, and counter the claims of the other party need not rest on one party in particular.

A personal right of action against the injurer gives rise to an interpersonal engagement between the two parties over the pertinent factual questions. To be sure, this engagement is not one of joint commitment to produce the facts of the matter. Nevertheless, it can counter the wrongful denial of the victim's status as a self-determining being. This is because both parties in the lawsuit are implicated in a process of responding to the factual claims made by the other in the sense that each party's factual claim is a *response to* what the other party has claimed. It is precisely in this respect that the two can come to deal with each other's point of view and, ultimately, with each as an autonomous being.

A second layer of the victim/injurer engagement concerns evaluative claims. Determining who did what only sets the stage for the legal question of what both parties should have done or refrained from doing. The inquiry on this front addresses standards of behavior and assesses the actual conduct of either party in light of these standards. Here, too, the lawsuit implicates the parties in a process of making claims in response to those made by the other. Responsiveness gets the parties closer to vindicating the setback to the victim's self-determination. This is the post-wrong stage in which the parties confront head-on the difference between, among other things, mistreating the victim by inadvertently causing harm and by deliberately rejecting his or her status as an autonomous being. The parties can agree or disagree on how either party should have acted (such as whether the victim is also to blame for what happened). That said, there can be no denying that the injurer, now acting as a defendant, is required to recognize, and make evaluative claims based on the recognition, that the plaintiff is a self-determining person.

* * *

As I observed above, the defendant is to face a burden, rather than an obligation, to appear in court to confront the victim's complaints. Can the former undermine the

[27] *See* Chapter 16.

noninstrumental value of the victim's right of action simply by paying the material redress stub outright? The answer, as it is currently the case, is "yes." The conflict theory and its emphasis on engaging with the valueless conflict associated with deliberate wrongdoing in the right way suggests that the law should be reformed so as to make good on the victim's loss of opportunity to reassert her agency vis-à-vis the defendant (in case the defendant chooses to avoid all interaction with the plaintiff, say, by sending her a check). There are a number of ways to accomplish that, ranging from awarding damages to reflect the victim's loss at issue all the way to compelling the defendant to at least confront his victim in a court proceeding. Choosing between these and other alternatives depends on substantive and institutional considerations that might vary substantially between jurisdictions. Discussion of this sort is beyond the scope of this chapter.

IV. Relational Wrongdoing

A. Characterization

Another form of wrongdoing that calls for personal rights of action concerns itself with the impairment of a special relationship of a certain character. It is true, as I argue in Part II of this book, that tort duties are relationally structured so that every wrongdoing is relational. However, my present discussion takes up instances of what can be called *thick* relationality. It features, first, a relation of dependency that, second, plays a substantial role in the life of the victim (consider typical employment, landlord/tenant, parent/child, and romantic relationships). It therefore captures only a subset of the relational universe that tort duties construct. Accordingly, the category of relational wrongdoing that stands at the center of this chapter is not reducible to all the other instances of wrongdoing in tort law. In particular, relational wrongdoing, properly conceived, has a distinctive property: The wrongdoer not only harms the person or property of the victim but also impairs the relationally just terms of the interaction between the two. The latter setback reflects the additional or parasitical wrong that makes up what I call relational wrongdoing. Suing enables the victim not only to obtain material redress but also to reassert her equal standing with respect to the defendant with whom she *already* stands in a special relationship. Reasserting can, thereby, repair the deficient—viz., inegalitarian—way in which the employer, landlord, and the like relates to her.

At first glance, it might look suspicious to identify the injustice of relational wrongdoing with subjection of a special relationship to inegalitarian terms of interaction. A relation of dependency often presents itself as inherently inegalitarian. After all, an employer is the employee's boss, and the lessor is the lessee's landlord. On closer inspection, however, relations of dependency can still be subject to a standard of equality. The difference this standard purports to make concern those aspects of relational dependence that are rightly deemed unjustified.

To begin with, the standard at issue is one of substantive, rather than formal, equality (and it is further defended in Part II of this book). Parties relate to each other as equals if their terms of interaction reflect, rather than disregard, the relevant differences between them. For instance, the division of responsibility for the safety of the workplace between an employer and their employee should incorporate the power imbalance between them, including the vulnerability of the employee to the employer's control over both the design and the enforcement of safety policies. By contrast, disregarding their difference, that is, treating the parties as perfectly equally responsible for ensuring the safety of the workplace as formal equality commands, runs afoul of what a commitment to liberal-egalitarian terms of employment interaction might mean.[28]

Thus, the fact that a particular relationship is asymmetrically structured, as in employment relations, does not mean that its justness should not be assessed by reference to a standard of transactional equality. Indeed, a commitment to substantive equality explains why dependency should give rise to elevated responsibility and duties on the part of the party depended upon. An employment relationship may count as egalitarian, in the sense that its terms of interaction take the power imbalance between the parties seriously, only if employers bear responsibility for the safety of their employees and, moreover, if the amount of such responsibility is commensurate with the level of dependency of the latter on the former. Relational wrongdoing concerns the subjection of the victim of a wrong to inegalitarian terms of interactions between those who already stand in a certain relationship of dependency. It undermines victims' interest in an egalitarian relationship *on top of* setting back their interest in physical safety.

A case of sexual harassment in the workplace can illustrate what relational wrongdoing might mean. Consider an employee who is subject to a series of offensive touchings by a coworker. Among other things, and setting to one side the wrong directly inflicted by the harasser, the victim can complain that the employer committed a wrong by failing to provide a safe workplace. Further, suppose that, unlike the injurer who deliberately strikes another in the eye, the employer's failure is one of negligence, reflecting want of due care. The victim may be entitled to recover for the resulting dignitary, physical, and emotional harms suffered under, among other things, common-law theories of negligence and/or statutory schemes of workers' compensation. To this extent, material redress might be a fitting response to all of the adverse consequences brought about by the wrongful actions of the employer.

That said, the employer wrongs the victim in another way as well, rendering insufficient the right to material redress. The tortious conduct at issue also impairs the

[28] *See* Avihay Dorfman, *Assumption of Risk, After All*, 15 Theoretical Inq. L. 293 (2014).

parties' ongoing interaction by placing the employee under inegalitarian terms of the employment relationship. More specifically, the employee becomes vulnerable due to the employer's deficient responsibility for the employee's safety. By giving effect to terms of interaction between coworkers that place the would-be harasser in a position of de facto power with respect to the bodily integrity of the employer's victim, the employer fails to deal with the employee as a free and equal person.

What makes a work-related instance different from a one-off harassment is the thick, relational context in which it occurs. Simply put, tort law need not care about impaired relationships if they lack value for the victim. A fleeting relationship, not to mention no relationship at all, does not call for repair. Instances of harassment in the workplace are different. The harasser and the victim are not mere strangers, as their ongoing interaction as coworkers matters to both; this relationship, in turn, is facilitated, and often even constructed, by the employment relationship they each have with the employer. To this extent, their interaction is part of a larger web of interactions, relations, and expectations that make up, for either one, an important sphere of human activity called work. Hence, unlike the fleeting relationship between parties in a one-off incident of harassment, an employment relationship should figure in the normative analysis as a source of value that thereby warrants protection. Repairing the latter, therefore, may add another remedial dimension to the one concerned with responding to one-off incidents. The injury, that is, is not only to the victim's person but also to the victim's relationship with the employer. As the torts doctrine of superseding cause confirms, a careless misconduct of employers is not defeated by the deliberate wrongdoing of the immediate tortfeasor-harasser.[29] This is because the affirmative duty to provide employees with a reasonably safe workplace amounts to a core employer's responsibility for employees' core interest.

The work context (like the other contexts I mentioned, such as that of landlords and their tenants) features the two significant elements that are jointly necessary for the impairment of a relationship to constitute relational wrongdoing: structural dependency and intrinsic importance. Dependency refers to the normative and economic manifestations of the power imbalance associated with typical employment relationships: The (limited) authority of employers over their employees and their relatively better access to capital, resources, and means of production, respectively.[30] Importance signals that work captures a significant role in the life of free and equal persons; for these, work can be a ground project that thereby gives meaning to their life.[31]

[29] *See* Restatement (Third) of Torts: Phys. & Emot. Harm § 19, 34 cmt. *d* (2010).

[30] On employers' authority within the larger universe of authority relations, see Avihay Dorfman & Alon Harel, Reclaiming the Public ch. 1 (2024).

[31] *See* Dagan & Dorfman, Relational Justice: A Theory of Private Law 48–49 (2024); Hugh Collins, *Relational Justice in Work*, 24 Theoretical Inq. L. 26, 44 (2023); Sabine Tsuruda, *Good Faith in Employment*, 24 Theoretical Inq. L. 206, 211–12 (2023).

This is not to say that sexual harassment between strangers is less (or more) offensive or devastating, nor does it mean that an act of sexual harassment that occurs out of an important context for the victim is less (or more) culpable. Rather, the relational context in question—consisting in dependency and importance—opens another dimension of injury from which the victim can suffer, namely, an impairment of an ongoing relationship of the relevant kind.

B. Rights of Action as a Facility for Reclaiming Victims' Equal Standing

Why, then, should the victim of relational wrongdoing of the sexual-harassment-at-the-workplace type be entitled to a right of action against the employer, rather than merely a right to receive material redress from that employer? The answer is that material redress (including super-compensatory damages) falls short of repairing the setback to the relationship between the victim and the employer. Material redress could make it more likely that, going forward, just terms of the employment relationship will be better enforced. In that case, employers will live up to their responsibility for the safety of the workers. That said, material redress cannot set right the already impaired relationship between the two. Indeed, receiving a payment may be a fitting response for the dignitary, physical, and emotional bruises from which the victim suffers, but it leaves intact past subjection to inegalitarian, perhaps even oppressive, terms of interaction with both other coworkers and the employer.

To properly address the relational predicament, the victim should be able to reassert her equal standing, that is, entitlement to have been treated as an equal by the employer. Treating the employee as an equal means that the employer should have exercised the quality and quantity of care reflecting the employee's vulnerability to workplace harassment (among other safety concerns).[32] As in the case of reasserting one's agency in relation to a deliberate wrongdoer, reclaiming equal standing begins with granting the victim-employee the right to decide whether to sue the employer for failing to provide a reasonably safe workplace environment. It further means that, if the victim so decides, the victim should have a right to confront the employer under terms that reflect their equal standing.[33]

A personal right of action can give rise to such terms by entitling the victim to make epistemic and evaluative claims against the employer and, in this way, to reassert the status of an equal person not merely vis-à-vis society as a whole, but also in relation to the employer, in particular. In turn, the employer-defendant bears

[32] Notice that a parallel argument can be made with respect to the noninstrumental value of a right to pursue the *harasser* in response to deliberate wrongdoing.

[33] *See also* Hershovitz, *supra* note 3, at 101.

the burden of responding to these claims by making counterclaims about what happened and what legal implications should follow therefrom. In that, the employer deals with the employee on terms that reaffirm the responsibility of the employer qua employer to provide the employee with a safe workplace environment befitting the status of a free and equal person.

As in the case of deliberate wrongdoing, engaging wrongdoers in the form of pursuing them in a civil action is of freestanding significance, rather than a mere means for bringing about material redress. Notice, moreover, that as in the case of deliberate wrongdoing, the defendant is not duty-bound to engage the plaintiff. The burden to do so allows the defendant to send the employee a check instead, as it were, to which my response (recall) is that the defendant may have to make good on this choice, say, by being compelled to pay additional compensation to repair the plaintiff's lost opportunity of reasserting equal standing.

V. The Scope of the Claim: A First Approximation

The argument so far has focused on what might explain the freestanding value of personal rights of action. Rather than saying that all, or even most, instances of wrongdoing warrant such rights, I identified two categories of wrongdoing for which rights of material redress alone fail to provide a fitting response. I now seek to move from characterization to scope, addressing the question of what cases should fall in either category. This question of scope in part concerns the right way (or ways) to implement normative considerations in the law and the challenges that it might pose to existing legal doctrine. It is beyond the ambition of this study to provide for every jurisdiction an exhaustive list of causes of action that fall in the category at issue. Instead, the task is to articulate the basic guidelines with which to determine the scope question.

Notice that for the implementation task to be successful, two requirements must be met. The first concerns the more general commitment to the rule of law (which is further discussed in Chapter 7). The tort law of personal rights of action should minimize unconstrained power so as to reduce reliance on individualized knowledge and radically ad hoc judgments. The second requirement concerns the viability of a system of civil litigation that cares about distinguishing between the instrumental and the noninstrumental value of a personal right of action. Courts and litigants must have a relatively straightforward method of identifying whether the complaint made by the plaintiff should trigger a personal right of action. In the absence of such a method, personal rights of action may (absurdly) require an entire legal process of its own.

Note, moreover, that giving effect to the noninstrumental value of personal rights of action does not exhaust the protection of victims' rights. In particular, their secondary right to material redress remains an ongoing concern. In many cases, secondary rights are best protected by granting personal rights of action, in which case the latter are instrumentally valuable to vindicating the former. But in other cases, personal rights of action and rights of repair might pull in opposite directions, such as when the former are noninstrumentally valuable and at the same time provide an inferior mechanism for bringing about material redress. Addressing the trade-off between personal rights of action and rights of repair goes beyond the question I consider, which is the value of personal rights of action, and should, therefore, be left for another occasion.

A. Deliberate Wrongdoing

The category of deliberate wrongdoing consists of two key properties: A certain behavior and its resulting injury. The behavioral component of deliberate wrongdoing picks out instances of especially culpable mistreatment, consisting of acting with either the intent to cause harm, near-certain knowledge that such harm will be caused to a person's basic rights, or reckless disregard for such rights. The resulting harm that warrants a personal right of action concerns the rejection of the status of the victim as a self-determining being. In principle, all tortious incidents that meet these requirements should entitle the victim personally to sue the injurer to reassert his or her self-determination.

The significance of the distinction between deliberate (et alia) and accidental wrongdoing to the question of why, and when, rights of action should be made personal finds its expression in modern tort law. Most importantly, some of the most comprehensive statutory tort reforms of the twentieth century—workers' compensation schemes in the United States and the New Zealand comprehensive tort reform—have abolished or significantly weakened personal rights of action of tort victims.[34] For the most part, however, these reforms entitle victims of deliberate wrongdoing to pursue their injurers directly. In the US case of workers' compensation schemes, workers can sue their employers for deliberately inflicted work-related injuries (including also acting with near-certain knowledge of the resulting injuries).[35] In New Zealand, victims can personally sue to recover punitive damages (or to secure injunctive relief) for instances of wrongdoing that meet my definition of deliberate wrongdoing as well as reckless disregard.[36] To this extent, those who claim that workers' compensation schemes and the New Zealand

[34] For more, see Avihay Dorfman, *Relational Justice and Torts, in* Research Handbook on Private Law Theory 321, 326–28 (Hanoch Dagan & Benjamin Zipursky eds., 2020).

[35] *See, e.g.*, Johns-Manville Prod. Corp. v. Contra Costa Superior Court, 612 P.2d 948 (Cal. 1980).

[36] The majority in *Couch v. Attorney-General* [2010] NZSC 27 decided that punitive damages can be awarded if the injurer had intended harm to the plaintiff or had been reckless in that regard.

reform had both abolished vast areas of tort law[37] are not only mistaken to identify the law of torts with rights of action and material repair but also fail to distinguish between rights of action whose value is purely instrumental and rights of action that are integral to responding to conflicts in the right way.

Apart from these reforms, however, the law of torts does not make a consistent effort to distinguish between accidental and deliberate wrongdoing. On one hand, some torts do turn on the deliberate nature of the wrong or on there being recklessness. Intentional infliction of emotional distress, fraud, and the post-*Sullivan* tort of defamation (which requires actual malice) are familiar cases in point. On the other hand, however, some veteran torts make no special reference to deliberate wrongdoing. Thus, intentional torts such as battery and trespass to land give rise to causes of action that cut across the distinction between deliberate and nondeliberate wrongdoing. For example, intentional battery only requires an intention to create physical contact with the victim, irrespective of whether the batterer also intends to harm or offend this victim.[38] Further, most tort causes of action do not single out the additional injury to the victim's autonomy for special remedial treatment. At most, courts may hold injurers accountable for their deliberate wrongdoing in the domain of material redress, that is, by increasing the recovery of the victim by way of awarding punitive damages.

Thus, the argument from deliberate wrongdoing challenges the traditional distinction among common law torts between intentional activity accidentally producing wrongful spillovers and accidental wrongdoing.[39] Dating back to the separation between two major forms of action, trespass and trespass on the case, traditional common law fails to identify a qualitative *moral* difference between the two.[40] Trespass to land, like the tort of battery mentioned above, counts as an intentional tort, but the notion of intentionally lacks moral content.[41] Thus, an intention to place one's foot on a tract of land could count as wrongful, irrespective of whether doing so was meant to impinge on the right of the landowner. Neither ill- nor good-will on the part of the potential trespasser has any bearing on whether this entry amounts to a wrong.

Against this backdrop, the noninstrumental value of the right to pursue deliberate wrongdoers serves as a form of constructive critique of intentional torts. In the face of pressing demands for reform, and in light of the increasing costs of litigating cases, tort law should recognize the independent significance of

[37] *See* Weinrib, *supra* note 9, at 110–11; Alan Brudner with Jennifer M. Nadler, The Unity of the Common Law 315 (2d ed. 2013); Goldberg & Zipursky, *supra* note 4, at 267, 394–95. *See also* John Fabian Witt, The Accidental Republic 202, 206 (2004).

[38] *See* Vosburg v. Putney, 50 N.W. 403 (Wis. 1891).

[39] *See* Avihay Dorfman & Assaf Jacob, *The Fault of Trespass*, 65 U. Toronto L.J. 48, 75 (2015). *See also* Richard A. Epstein, *Nuisance Law: Corrective Justice and Its Utilitarian Constraints*, 8 J. Legal Stud. 49, 65–66 (1979).

[40] *See further* Dagan & Dorfman, *supra* note 25, at 524 n.54.

[41] *See further* Chapter 16.

deliberate wrongdoing, at least for the purpose of deciding whether to grant personal rights of action (in addition to rights to material redress). Thus, instead of defending all rights of action as essential aspects of tort law, the preceding argument sets a much higher threshold for cutting back on victims' right to pursue deliberate wrongdoers than for all other, instrumentally valuable rights of action. On this argument, it is impermissible to replace the former rights with other means of securing material redress if the basis for replacement hinges on considerations purely of efficiency (such as reducing administrative costs). Curtailing such rights for other, weightier reasons may be deemed permissible if victims are sufficiently compensated for "taking" their personal right to sue. The affirmative side of this same point is the case for greater government support of a victim's right to sue in cases falling in the category of deliberate wrongdoing.

Another dimension of recognizing the distinctive value of rights of action in connection with deliberate wrongdoing is to add an element of deliberateness to the prima facie case of traditional intentional torts. In particular, the plaintiff would have to make a threshold showing that the defendant acted with an intent to injure them or with knowledge to a substantial certainty that their conduct would cause such an injury, or with reckless disregard for the victim's safety. In reality, such an element already figures in the law of tort remedies. Indeed, courts often require the showing of deliberate misconduct in order to trigger their authority to award punitive damages.[42]

B. Relational Wrongdoing

The second category emphasizes tortious behavior that, moreover, impairs a special relationship (along the two dimensions of structural dependency and intrinsic importance). Existing causes of action, however, do not make explicit reference to the distinctive injury involved in relational wrongdoing, properly conceived. This is not to say that the value of an ongoing relationship between the plaintiff and the defendant plays no role in considering what tort duties are owed, what constitutes their breach, whether the defendant should be held liable, and what would be the proper remedy (such as awarding damages for loss of companionship).[43] For instance, the fact that the defendant and the plaintiff relate as friends can affect the question of liability for injuries caused in the course of engaging in horseplay or as a result of running a practical joke.[44] Further, negligence law imposes affirmative duties to warn or aid those who stand in a "special

[42] *See, e.g.*, Taylor v. Browning, 927 P.2d 873, 884 (Idaho 1996).
[43] *See, e.g.*, Courtney G. Joslin & Lawrence C. Levine, *The Restatement of Gay(?)*, 79 Brooklyn L. Rev. 621, 653–54 (2014).
[44] *See* Zgraggen v. Wilsey, 200 A.D.2d 818, 819 (NY Sup. Ct. App. Div. 1994); Wartman v Swindell, 25 A 356 (N.J. 1892), respectively.

relationship" to the plaintiff-victim. Likewise, the existence of a special relationship can justify imposing tort liability for purely economic loss.[45] Finally, some causes of action—including, most famously, loss of consortium (and its corollary alienation of affection)—address the loss associated with setting back the interest of a third party in an ongoing relationship with the direct victim of a tort.[46]

But these references to plaintiff-defendant relationships are different. The point there is not to repair the setback to the previous terms of the interaction between the victim and his or her injurer.[47] Rather, it is fully directed at the question of material redress—whether the injurer owed a duty to the plaintiff, what was its content (such as how much care is owed), and so forth. Left unaddressed is the freestanding concern for the additional injury, namely, the impairment of a relationship of a special kind.

There exists a relatively easy fix, though. As argued above, the category of relational wrongdoing hinges on a combination of dependency and importance. Cases that fall in this category figure prominently in the private law of work, housing, family, and love life,[48] among other familiar contexts that are imbued with dependency relations of importance. Such contexts can then be used as proxies for those complaining about being relationally wronged. In practical terms, plaintiffs may be required to draw on established contexts (such as work) to make their case for a personal right of action against the wrongdoer, rather than merely for material redress. It may also be required to make room for a residual context, as it were, for special relationships that meet the dependency and importance requirements even as they arise independently of an established context. The role of a residual category is to address the fact that special relationships evolve in response to changing social, economic, and political circumstances. Civil procedure law would have to find a sensible way to construct a category of residual context that could fit.

Conclusion: Rights of Action and Valueless Conflicts

On the conflict theory, tort law's moral function is to address (certain aspects of) human conflict, and it does so by engaging with the kind of value underlying the conflict. In the case of valueless conflicts, tort law is called for to prevent the conflict in advance and, if doing so fails, relieve its impact ex post facto. Focusing on the latter, I have argued that there is nothing mechanical or straightforward in the

[45] *See* Restatement (Third) of Torts: Phys. & Emot. Harm §§ 40–41 (2012); Restatement (Third) of Torts: Liab. for Econ. Harm § 4 (2020), respectively.

[46] *See, e.g.*, Whittlesey v. Miller, 572 S.W.2d 665, 666 (Tex. 1978).

[47] *See also* Jay M. Feinman, *The Jurisprudence of Classification*, 41 Stan. L. Rev. 661, 702 (1989). *Cf.* Benjamin Shmueli, *Relational Torts: Tort Litigation in Cases of the Will for Rehabilitation of Close Relations*, 39 Ohio St. J. Disp. Resol. 561 (2024).

[48] *Cf.* Cardi & Chamallas, *supra* note 22.

way elimination is administered. Indeed, this chapter suggests that on closer, normative analysis, victims' rights of action might be integral to what a successful response to a certain valueless conflict requires.

The conflict at issue involves either deliberate or relational wrongdoing. I have argued that two forms of wrongdoings—deliberate and relational—can constitute a second, parasitic harm to our fundamental interests in self-determination and equal standing. To address this harm, an adequate response must go beyond a right to material redress. More specifically, victims' rights of action provide a fitting response as they instantiate a valuable way to reassert their self-determining nature and equal standing as against the injurer. Chapter 12 further reinforces this argument by establishing that the case for victims' rights of action, including in particular rights to pursue the injurer, find additional grounding in the equality theory of tort law.

6
Valueless Omissions
Easy Rescue Redux

Introduction

Staying within the category of valueless conflicts, this chapter addresses the tort doctrine governing omissions. The specific question I explore is whether we should have legal rights requiring others to come to our rescue, particularly when doing so is relatively easy. I apply the normative framework of conflict theory to the no-liability rule in cases of easy rescue—"the rule against tort liability for failing to rescue," even when, for example, "two persons [] stand aside and watch a third jump to his death: there is no legal duty to rescue."[1] The stakes are high because leading tort theorists argue that this rule—and the larger category of nonfeasance liability to which it belongs—lies at the *moral* center of tort law, meaning one cannot even begin to plausibly understand and justify tort law without defending the no-liability rule.

Another and more important reason for focusing on this rule is to call attention to the institutional complexities of integrating morality and legality. This chapter suggests that the *real* difficulty with easy rescue cases is not moral or substantive since the conflict between the freedom of a would-be rescuer and the life of the rescued person is typically valueless. Instead, the difficulty is primarily institutional: Tort law, being a legal institution, must meet certain rule-of-law constraints on how far it can reflect and give effect to value considerations. This recharacterization of the easy rescue case can better explain (core aspects of) the traditional no-liability approach, but, more significantly, it can show why this approach must be substantively revised regarding the responsibility of social hosts for their guests' wrongdoings. Hence, this chapter demonstrates how institutional considerations can be integrated into the (substantive) conflict theory of tort law.

[1] Alan Brudner, The Unity of the Common Law 278 (2d ed. 2013); Vellino v. Chief Constable of Greater Manchester [2002] 1 W.L.R. 218 at [13] (*per* Schiemann L. J.), respectively.

Conflict between Equals. Avihay Dorfman, Oxford University Press. © Oxford University Press 2026.
DOI: 10.1093/9780198979869.003.0009

I. Nonfeasance: A Characterization

The nonfeasance/misfeasance distinction is used in tort law (of the common law tradition) to characterize the nature of the connection between a defendant and the risk that has materialized into the plaintiff's injury. Misfeasance covers all instances in which the defendant created or contributed to the creation of this risk. By contrast, nonfeasance takes up all instances in which the risk at issue exists entirely apart from any action (or inaction) by the defendant.[2] As one court has recently observed, "[c]lassically, a case of nonfeasance involves a situation when a bystander comes across someone suffering harm from causes not of the bystander's making."[3]

The doctrine of nonfeasance liability consists of a rule and a line of exceptions. The rule is that there is no liability for nonfeasance, including even in cases of easy rescue.[4] Tort law extends this rule to extremely easy rescue cases as when courts note that "an ordinary bystander is under no duty to rescue a child drowning in what he knows to be shallow water, or to prevent a neighbor's child from hammering on a dangerous explosive"[5] or that "two persons [] stand aside and watch a third jump to his death: there is no legal duty to rescue."[6] This rule gives way to several exceptions, according to which a duty of easy rescue may lie. These exceptions fall in three categories: undertaking, special relationship, and imperilment.[7]

This characterization of the rule of no liability for nonfeasance contrasts with the account offered by the Toronto School of corrective justice. According to this school, nonfeasance refers to cases where the defendant would be called upon to confer a *benefit* on the plaintiff. Misfeasance, in contrast, describes situations where the defendant actually injures the person or property of the plaintiff through a breach of *duty*.[8]

This approach, however, is wholly conclusory and merely restates the crucial questions: *What* rights do we have, and, ultimately, *why* do we have them?

[2] Restatement (Third) of Torts: Phys & Emot. Harm §37 (2012) (nonfeasance concerns "[a]n actor whose conduct has not created a risk of physical or emotional harm to another."). *Compare* Sandy Steel, Omissions in Tort Law 18 (2024).

[3] Ramsey v. Georgia S. Univ. Advanced Dev. Ctr., 189 A.3d 1255, 1284 (Del. 2018).

[4] Steel, *supra* note 2, at 2, 27.

[5] Estates of Morgan v. Fairfield Family Counseling Ctr., 673 N.E.2d 1311, 1319 n.2 (Oh. 1997).

[6] Vellino v. Chief Constable of Greater Manchester [2002] 1 W.L.R. 218 at [13] (*per* Schiemann L. J.), respectively.

[7] *See* Restatement (Third) of Torts: Phys. & Emot. Harm §§39–44 (2012) (listing the three basic exceptions, imperilment (§39), special relationships (§§40–41), and undertakings (§§42–44)). A fourth exception, statutory imposition of an affirmative duty, is just another form of special relationship. *Id.*, §38. *See further* Avihay Dorfman, *Relational Justice and Torts*, *in* Research Handbook on Private Law Theory 321, 328–33 (Hanoch Dagan & Benjamin Zipursky eds., 2021).

[8] *See* Arthur Ripstein, Private Wrongs 54 (2016). *See also* Peter Benson, *Misfeasance as an Organizing Normative Idea in Private Law*, 60 U. Toronto L.J. 731 (2010); Ernest J. Weinrib, The Idea of Private Law 10 (1995); Martin Jay Stone, *Gregory Keating's Framework for Understanding Tort Law*, 45 L. & Phil. 95, 101–03 (2026).

Put differently, the claim that the misfeasance/nonfeasance distinction merely reflects an antecedent system of rights implies that the distinction between the two depends entirely on the applicable system of rights. But then the concept of nonfeasance adds nothing to the analysis: It all boils down to whether the plaintiff holds a right against the defendant. If so, then by definition, this is a case of misfeasance. If not, then by definition, it is a case of nonfeasance.

II. The Right Response to Conflicts: The Case of Easy Rescue

As I argued in Chapter 2, the case of easy rescue features a valueless conflict given the extreme disparity between the conflicting interests: The imminent vulnerability of the drowning infant as opposed to the freedom of a bystander to narrowly attend to their own business. The rescue operation required of them is genuinely easy, which means that the strain on their freedom is wholly trivial. In this picture, tort law should not tolerate, let alone embrace, the conflict in question. Instead, it should prevent it by imposing a duty of easy rescue and, if necessary, holding the failing rescuer liable.

And yet, existing law upholds the no-liability rule for cases of easy rescue.[9] What might explain this awesome gap between the prescriptions of the conflict theory of tort law and the tort law posited by common-law courts?[10] By "explain," I mean only normatively compelling explanations rather than historical or sociological ones that fail to come to terms with the valueless nature of the conflict at hand. (In Chapter 11, I criticize the Kantian explanation, showing that the imposition of a duty of easy rescue need not implicate the duty-ower's independence.) My explanation focuses on certain institutional constraints on the imposition of easy-rescue duties. I argue that nonfeasance liability is treated differently from misfeasance liability because its implementation in law raises the specter of what I shall call *illegality*. To further substantiate this explanation, I show that *all* the exceptions to the no-liability rule pick out factual circumstances that raise no such concerns.

Two concerns of illegality figure most prominently. One is the challenge of singling out duty-owers without implicating the legal system in arbitrary enforcement. Since situations calling for rescue may involve any number of potential rescuers (consider a crowded beach on a hot summer day), singling out the defendant as the bystander whose failure to rescue warrants the imposition of liability may be difficult. The worry is *not* merely epistemic—how can we be sure that the defendant was at the forefront in the shoreline? Rather, the worry is

[9] *See* sources cited in *supra* notes 1, 4–6.

[10] As Robert Stevens puts this point, "If I watch a baby drown in an inch of water, few would doubt that I am in some sense responsible for the death, and yet no damages are payable." He concludes that from a legal point of view "I can walk away." ROBERT STEVENS, TORTS AND RIGHTS 10 (2007).

substantive—why pick the defendant when many others *could* have competently met the task of saving the drowning plaintiff's life?

The "why only me?" is directed at the law as a legitimate institution rather than specifically at the plaintiff. That is, the defendant did wrong the plaintiff morally by failing to assist her and thus cannot complain about being sued. His complaint addresses the *legal system* for exempting all other wrongdoers. Typically, though not necessarily, arbitrariness is far less acute in cases of misfeasance: The fault line separating the wrongdoer from all other bystanders precludes the arbitrariness charge.[11] Accordingly, the compelling institutional consideration is to treat nonfeasance cases differently because (and insofar as) they fail to meet the challenge of singling out the duty-ower. In this explanation, the rule of no liability for nonfeasance answers an institutional, rule-of-law prescription against arbitrary legal enforcement. As I argue presently, *all* the exceptions to this rule pick out factual situations that face no such concern.

Another challenge is that nonfeasance liability must be limited to easy rescues, a constraint that implicates tort law in the intricate task of line drawing. A doctrine of nonfeasance liability cannot coherently require duty-owers to respect right-holders at the expense of their *own* safety and freedom. After all, the conflict between the drowning infant's and the bystander's interests is valueless precisely because saving one does not undermine the safety or freedom of the other. Easy rescue, therefore, is all that conflict theory can demand.

However, line drawing poses a serious challenge because a tort duty, like most legal duties, must transcend ad hockery. It should give would-be rescuers relatively clear reasons for action——to wit, is this a case calling for rescue, and, if so, is there a duty to rescue, and what kind of action might it require? Typical cases of misfeasance, by contrast, do not introduce these difficulties since they involve tortfeasors creating the very risk for which they owe others a duty of care—for them, it should be reasonably clear (given that the duty element requires reasonable foreseeability) that their activities may put certain others in imminent danger.

What makes the line-drawing exercise especially challenging for both rescuers and courts? Expertise, broadly defined as including a person's abilities and knowledge, is crucial in determining whether rescue is needed in the first place and, if so, what rescue efforts count as sufficiently easy. Indeed, both determinations depend on the ability of the would-be rescuer to identify the situation as calling for rescue and assist the person caught in an imminently dangerous situation. To avoid case-by-case appeal to individualized knowledge about a particular person's expertise,

[11] The identification difficulty in the nonfeasance context differs from the typical difficulty of tortfeasor identification in connection with misfeasance cases: Whereas the latter asks who caused the injury, the former asks why only me. Imposing a joint-and-several-liability regime may only replicate the why-only-me problem if the class of potential nonfeasorers is large enough (so now the question would be why only *us*).

courts need a category-based analysis concerning the *kind* of persons whose special training, knowledge, and position render them appropriate duty-owers.

The celebrated case of *Tarasoff v. The Regents of the Univ. of Cal*[12] illustrates the institutional limitations associated with line drawing when a psychologist failed to warn or otherwise protect the intended victim even though his patient had told him that he planned to kill her. This example is a straightforward instance of nonfeasance since the psychologist had neither created nor contributed to the risk to the victim's life, and, moreover, there was no special preexisting relationship between them. The *Tarasoff* court acknowledges the "general rule"[13] of no-liability for nonfeasance but carves out an "exception"[14] a patient posing a "serious danger of violence"[15] to another person.

What explains the court's decision to carve out a nonfeasance duty to warn is that the two noted institutional limitations are muted. Concerning arbitrary enforcement, this worry can be set aside because only the psychologist, his supervisor, and two of his colleagues were privy to the patient's murderous plan. Concerning line drawing, the psychologist here is not a mere stranger who happens to be aware of the killer's plan but a professional therapist treating a patient. Most importantly, the patient had informed him of the plan during the treatment. The psychologist thus occupies a unique position vis-à-vis the *victim*—he can assess, reasonably accurately, the gravity of the threat that his patient poses to her life and act on his assessment—in what would count as an easy-rescue effort—simply by warning the victim.

Hence, the real difference between the *Tarasoff* exception and the general rule of no liability for nonfeasance comes down to institutional considerations rather than foundational moral commitments. *Tarasoff* is not the only exception that fits this explanation, and all the traditional, common-law exceptions to the no-duty rule are best seen in this light. These exceptions fall into three categories: undertaking, special relationship, and imperilment.[16] I set the first two aside since, to some extent, they can be explained by an appeal to the Kantian commitment to independence and formal equality.[17] My focus is on the third category, imperilment, which rejects the teachings of corrective justice and illustrates my institutional explanation of the nonfeasance liability doctrine, holding that cases in the imperilment category are *not* marred by the two institutional limitations mentioned above.

[12] 551 P.2d 334 (Cal. 1976).
[13] *Id.*, at 343.
[14] *Id.*
[15] *Id.*, at 345.
[16] *See* Restatement (Third) of Torts: Phys. & Emot. Harm §§39–44 (2012) (listing the three basic exceptions, imperilment (§39), special relationships (§§40–41), and undertakings (§§42–44)). A fourth exception, statutory imposition of an affirmative duty, is just another form of special relationship. *Id.*, §38.
[17] I say *to some extent* because some types of special relationship cannot possibly be redescribed in terms of undertaking or some other voluntary assumption of responsibility.

The imperilment rule deals with situations where a person innocently causes physical harm or innocently creates a continuing risk of physical harm to another person. In such circumstances, that person may owe a duty of due care "to prevent or minimize the harm" or (in English tort law's parlance) "to avert or lessen the risk" to the other person, which is basically a form of a duty to rescue.[18] Consider someone who innocently struck someone hiding behind the bushes with a baseball. The injurer had carefully looked around before striking the ball. His conduct is absolutely faultless. Moreover, the injurer could not have owed the victim a duty of care because (recall *Palsgraf*[19]) there is no duty absent reasonable foreseeability concerning the victim (or victim class). According to the imperilment rule, the incident can nonetheless trigger a duty to mitigate the extent of the harm incurred by the victim.[20] This duty does not depend on the victim's fault or innocence and exists even when the victim has acted irresponsibly or even assumed the risk (say, hiding in the bushes hoping to be hit by the ball).[21] Moreover, the duty does not turn on the victim being rendered helpless by the injury. In short, the harm is not wrongful.[22]

In these circumstances, imposing a duty to assist does not implicate the law in arbitrariness precisely because the imperilment rule works out a *principled* delineation of the category of duty-owers, viz., rather than recruiting all passersby, the rule singles out the (innocent) injurer. In terms of the second institutional limitation, the imperilment rule assumes that all else being equal, the injurer is properly positioned, epistemically speaking, to appreciate the emergency. Since "all else is not always equal," the imperilment rule only gives rise to a duty to rescue if the harm innocently caused to the victim is reasonably foreseeable.[23] Moreover, the content of the duty can further ameliorate the second worry associated with line drawing: A duty of rescue under the imperilment rule is one of reasonable mitigation, rather than elimination, of the innocently caused harm (or risk).

The imperilment rule, as one court has observed, "reflects the type of basic decency and human thoughtfulness which is generally characteristic of our people."[24] It adequately responds to the valueless nature of the conflict between the parties involved. Indeed, the disparity between the existential interest of a person caught in some imminent threat and the liberty interest of his or her innocent injurer is just the inverse of "basic decency and human thoughtfulness." The imperilment rule removes one item from the universe of easy rescue cases and makes it a tort duty

[18] RESTATEMENT (THIRD) OF TORTS: PHYS. & EMOT. HARM §39 (2012); Mitchell v. Glasgow CC [2009] 1 A.C. 874 at [40], respectively.

[19] Palsgraf v. Long Island R.R. Co., 162 N.E. 99, 99 (N.Y. 1928). On the duty-based explanation of *Palsgraf*, see Avihay Dorfman, *Foreseeability as Re-Cognition*, 59 AM. J. JURIS. 163 (2014).

[20] *See* RESTATEMENT (THIRD) OF TORTS: PHYS. & EMOT. HARM §39 (2012).

[21] *Id.*, cmt. *g*.

[22] *Id.*, cmt. *e*.

[23] DAN B. DOBBS ET AL., THE LAW OF TORTS 619 (2d ed. 2016).

[24] South v. Nat'l R. R. Passenger Corp. (AMTRAK), 290 N.W.2d 819, 837 (N.D. 1980).

to attend to the vulnerability of a person imperiled by the innocent conduct of the duty-ower. This removal, I argue, concerns *institutional* limitations on the right engagement of tort law with value.

III. From Valueless to Tolerably Valuable Conflicts: Social Hosts

The preceding analysis identified institutional, rather than moral, considerations standing in the way of a general duty of easy rescue. I will now deploy the conflict theory in an attempt to extend legal analysis to easy rescue cases that arise in connection with *tolerably valuable conflicts*. The focus of the discussion is on the possible responsibility of hosts for potential injuries inflicted by their intoxicated guests whom the hosts had served alcohol. I criticize tort law's traditional rule of no duty.[25] Furthermore, I argue that imposing a duty is consequential in preventing the conflict between sociability and safety in social gatherings from becoming value*less*. Imposing such a duty is part of what it means for courts to engage with conflicts in the right way, that is, by containing the excesses of their negative side effects so as to keep them tolerably valuable.

A paradigmatic case is a gathering of adult friends at which the host—viz., a noncommercial agent—serves alcoholic beverages. The host maintains the supply of drinks even though some of the guests are clearly intoxicated. Soon after the gathering ends, one visibly intoxicated guest drives home and accidentally crashes into another car. Why should the social host owe the injured driver a duty of care? Note that the question is not about the content of the duty. Perhaps the content of the duty should be that the host must refrain from serving alcohol to visibly intoxicated guests, warn them before heading home, call a taxi to take them, and so forth. As long as the duty remains one of easy rescue, the more urgent question I seek to address pertains to the very existence of such a duty—why is there a duty in the first place?

Contrary to the preceding analysis of cases of easy rescue arising from valueless conflicts, the case at issue features a conflict of a different kind of value. To begin with, social gatherings are generally valuable for many obvious reasons (such as, but not limited to, sociability). Drinking alcoholic beverages may (arguably) also contribute to the value of social gatherings by helping some participants overcome barriers and anxieties hindering openness, accessibility, and other prosocial attitudes. Providing drinks, however, could also prove dangerous not only to those who consume them but also to third parties whose lives are placed at risk as a result.

[25] *See* Childs v. Desormeaux, [2006] 1 S.C.R 643 (Can.). *See generally* DAN B. DOBBS ET AL., THE LAW OF TORTS §424 (2d ed. 2021) available at https://1.next.westlaw.com/Document/I4022deaddb4c11e18cd29897efb1f23a/View/FullText.html?ppcid=910dbd4560a94d45a819149c77dafe74&originationContext=documenttoc&transitionType=CategoryPageItem&contextData=%28sc.Category%29.

Thus, this conflict pits the interest of the host (and his or her friends) in sociability against the interest of third parties in bodily integrity. To see why the conflict should count as tolerably valuable and what is the role of the host's duty of care in that being the case, I begin by discussing the two other kinds of value that often underlie conflicts. The conflict at issue can never amount to an inherently valuable one. There is no reason for wanting or embracing such a conflict unconditionally. It would be better if we could sustain sociability without generating any risk to third parties, such as drivers and pedestrians. On the other hand, the conflict at issue may certainly be valueless, as would be the case had the host provided his or her guests with ultra-toxic beverages, let alone psychedelic drugs, before they headed home.

Against this backdrop, the task of tort law in this case is to contain the excesses of intoxication so as to make the conflict between sociability and the safety of third parties tolerably valuable. By containing the excesses of intoxication, I mean reducing the negative side effects of drinking affecting third parties to a tolerable level. The argument for a duty to exercise reasonable care can now be viewed in this light, that is, as an implication of tort law's proper engagement with conflicts.

The argument has so far focused on the foundational or substantive level of analysis. As argued above, however, the basic reasons behind tort law's possible and justifiable reluctance to impose duties of easy rescue are institutional rather than foundational. It would thus be apt to show that the two institutional constraints discussed above—singling out the duty-ower and line drawing—can be adequately addressed in the social host context.

Singling out the duty-ower is an answer to the arbitrary enforcement of easy rescue. Unlike the case of a crowded beach, however, a social gathering poses no such problem since singling out the host is predicated on their very role as host of the party.

Concerning line drawing, the institutional case for imposing a duty of care on the social host turns on this person's ability to identify the situation as calling for "rescue" and respond accordingly. Distinguishing commercial sellers of alcoholic beverages (say, pubs and bars) from social hosts will help to clarify this issue.[26] Typically, social hosts lack the expertise, experience, and resources characteristic of commercial sellers, and a duty of easy rescue should thus not require from them more than a prohibition on serving visibly intoxicated guests.

Hence, the major institutional constraints on the imposition of affirmative duties of easy rescue do not prevent deeming social hosts responsible in some reasonable measure for the safety of third parties, drivers or pedestrians. Their responsibility (meaning the content of the duty, a.k.a. the breach element) may amount to a duty

[26] Commercial sellers are often subject to dram shop laws. These laws (at least in their modern instantiation) are designed to protect third-party victims of drunk drivers, intoxicated by alcoholic beverages they acquired from commercial sellers.

to refrain from knowingly dispensing alcoholic beverages to guests who are visibly intoxicated and need to drive. Alternatively, it can require other measures, more or less demanding, but I set this question aside. My goal here was to defend the existence of a duty: Bringing it into existence is part of what it takes to contain the excesses of sociability.

IV. The Bigger Picture: Bridging the Gap

Conflict theory helps to trace back the source of tort law's reluctance to impose duties of easy rescue to some institutional limitations on the ability of tort law to respond to the valueless nature of the conflict at issue. Moreover, by casting into sharp relief the interaction between substantive and institutional considerations, conflict theory provides a critical lens for assessing the preference of the current law for the rule of no liability for nonfeasance. The discussion mentioned several doctrinal contexts wherein conflict theory makes a theoretical and practical difference, but covering all the possible options exceeds the scope and the ambition of this chapter. Instead, conflict theory provides the normative framework for constructing further interventions into the doctrine of nonfeasance liability.

Thus, the future development of the doctrine must seek the eradication of unjustified gaps between the substantive and institutional levels. Whereas the substantive commitment is to prevent valueless conflicts or contain tolerably valuable ones by imposing a duty of easy rescue, the institutional level takes up the implementation of this duty in law. Indeed, to comply with conflict theory, the doctrine of nonfeasance must not exceed the appropriate understanding of how the "substantive" and the "institutional" should interact with one another as, respectively, a *ground for* and a *limitation on* this duty.

7

The Legal Practice of Conflict

Tort Law in Action

Introduction

Chapters 2–6 provided the raw materials with which to explain how tort law can give effect to the prescriptions of the conflict theory, which is the main ambition of this chapter. At the most abstract level, tort law is tasked with responding to conflicts of interests in the right way. Doing so is the first virtue of the law of torts. The three categories of conflict determine what way counts as right. This is because each category dictates a certain way of engaging with value. Tort law should construct the conditions necessary for inherently valuable conflicts to arise, contain tolerable conflicts, and prevent valueless conflicts. This means that the law-making apparatus of tort law must follow the sequence of identification and determination: It must first identify the relevant category of the conflict in question and, on this basis, determine legal rights and duties. Constructing, containing, and preventing conflicts of fundamental interests are abstract organizing principles on which tort law draws in order to determine rights, duties, liabilities, and doctrinal rules, more generally.

Notice that legal practice, broadly defined to include law-making and law-changing, law-applying, law-advising, and law-learning, engages with value quite routinely. The principle and policy considerations that figure in this practice are variously anchored to liberal, utilitarian, and conventionalist value systems. It is not a question of whether law can be understood and assessed apart from value but rather what values are the right ones. To this extent, the conflict theory does not break new ground, as legal practice is not, and must not be, value-free or value-neutral. Its more distinctive claim in the domain of value is, to repeat, that tort law's first virtue is to respond to conflicts of interests in the right way by engaging with these conflicts' respective values.

It will also be apt to note that nothing in the conflict theory prevents legal change and dynamism in response to changed circumstances and revised convictions. Rules of change, as H. L. A. Hart called them, are necessary meta-rules in every modern legal system and for every constantly evolving society.[1]

[1] H. L. A. Hart, The Concept of Law 92–93 (2d ed. 1994).

Conflict between Equals. Avihay Dorfman, Oxford University Press. © Oxford University Press 2026.
DOI: 10.1093/9780198979869.003.0010

Moreover, lawmakers, including courts, may often make mistakes concerning the kind of value underlying a certain conflict (in the same way that they could make mistakes when implementing, say, efficiency, Kantian right, or any other substantive theory). In the case of defamation law, the conflict between free speech and good name was for many centuries, including well into the twentieth century, understood as primarily valueless due to the fact that free speech was not worthy of robust protection vis-à-vis good name. Sexual harassment in the workplace often, and regrettably, fell into the category of tolerably valuable conflicts, viewed as a negative by-product of an otherwise valuable activity of productive work. But law has gradually (and imperfectly) moved away from this mistaken conception of value to the point of casting sexual harassment in the workplace (and elsewhere) as corresponding to a valueless conflict that ought to be prevented, rather than merely contained. Against this backdrop, I argue that the conflict theory is not merely consistent with a system of rules of change. Rather, it requires such a system in order to improve its prospects of getting it right.[2]

The discussion that follows seeks to give a sense of tort law as the *practice* of the conflict theory. To do so, I take each category of conflict in turn. This chapter also ends with a discussion of the implications of the rule of law to the conflict theory, explaining (as I already did, to a lesser extent, in previous chapters) that the connection between morality and legality entails a commitment to doctrinal rules, as opposed to what I shall call free-floating normative analysis. Indeed, there are many ways for prescriptive theories, such as applied ethics, to go normative. But when it comes to legal theory, "going normative" has its own rule—to wit, the rule of law.

I. Responding to Inherently Valuable Conflicts: Construction

To respond to conflicts in the right way, tort law must first identify a conflict as inherently valuable, and then determine the rights and the duties that best construct the conditions for it to exist. The conflicts at issue concern fundamental interests, which are (recall Chapter 2) constitutive elements of being in the world as free and equal persons, by which I mean as substantively free and equal persons.[3] Any liberal legal order has a compelling reason to recognize them (and most, though not

[2] I do not, however, discuss in detail what legal form must it take (say, a common-law system of lawmaking or a legislative lawmaking process). I take up this question in Chapter 17 and elsewhere. *See* Avihay Dorfman & Alon Harel, Constitutionalism and Majoritarianism Reconciled (unpublished manuscript); Avihay Dorfman & Alon Harel, Reclaiming the Public ch. 3 (2024); Avihay Dorfman & Alon Harel, *The Necessity of Institutional Pluralism*, 43 Oxford J. L. Stud. 753 (2023).

[3] I defend the latter point (concerning the importance of substantive freedom and equality) in Hanoch Dagan & Avihay Dorfman, Relational Justice: A Theory of Private Law (2024).

all, of them are recognized in the modern tort law of liberal societies).[4] And, in the case of inherently valuable conflicts, any liberal legal order has a compelling reason to construct the conditions necessary for these interests to come into conflict, in some measure. The first stage in the analysis, therefore, is identifying conflicts as inherently valuable.

Identification. The basic task here is to figure out whether a conflict between two or more interests can be valuable and, if so, whether the value in question turns on engendering, rather than resolving, the conflict. The three cases discussed in Chapter 3 (defamation and/or intentional infliction of emotional distress, battery, and inducement of breach of contract) provide illustrations of what might count as inherently valuable conflicts. There are other inherently valuable conflicts that can be identified in this way, which I take up in Chapters 8–10 and 17.

The method with which to conduct identification begins with the hypothetical conflict sanitizer mentioned in Chapter 3. The sanitizer helps investigate what might be lost by eliminating the conflict between competing interests while providing maximalist protection to either interest. As demonstrated in Chapter 3, a conflict counts as inherently valuable if even a flawless sanitizer cannot but fail, systematically and regularly, to realize the value associated with this conflict. I now wish to explore the next stage of responding to inherently valuable conflicts, which is that of determining what rights and duties we have.

Determination. By determining rights and duties, I mean either recognizing the very existence of the primary right and duty or filling out the content of existing ones. At times, tort law does not need to recognize a right as it already exists. For instance, freedom of speech and property rights already receive recognition in constitutional and property law, respectively. There, tort law would have to fill out the content of such rights. At other times, however, recognizing the very existence of the conflict is of the essence of responding to the value underlying it in the right way. The right to compete in the market, including by luring workers and contractors, is (arguably) a creature of tort law as much as other rights, such as bodily integrity, emotional well-being, and privacy. Part of what it means for tort law to engage with the value of market competition in the right way is to call the right at issue into being (if, indeed, it has not been acknowledged elsewhere in the law).

But calling it into being is not enough, for tort law must also determine its content—precisely what it means to have such a freedom. As is often typical in

[4] One fundamental interest that has so far not received sufficient recognition is free expression as between private persons. *See* Chapter 16. Another is our interest, as private persons, to use and enjoy the outdoors, which is currently protected, to a limited extent only, by the tort of public nuisance. *See* Hanoch Dagan & Avihay Dorfman, *Public Nuisance for Private Persons*, 74 U. Toronto L.J. 198 (2024). Lastly, our interest in being treated as an equal is also only partially protected by antidiscrimination statutes. *See* Chapter 10; Hanoch Dagan & Avihay Dorfman, *The Tort of Discrimination*, 16 J. Tort L. 393 (2023).

the law of torts in the common-law tradition, the determination is made by a process of backward induction: The existence and content of the right are implicitly given by deciding the duty question, that is, does a competitor-lurer owe a duty of noninterference to a contractual promisee. By focusing on the doctrinal hook of "duty," tort law is in a position to engage with the conflict between competition and contract stability. To fix ideas, without repeating myself too much, tort law fails its task when it determines the duty's content by reference to the priority of contract stability over free competition (say, by supposing that the contractual promises must get a quasi in rem protection from any third party who is fully aware of these promises). It also fails by assigning *too* little weight to contract stability, say, by deciding that a lurer who deploys repugnant means—say, fraud—does not violate the duty of noninterference. Instead, tort law *begins* to respond to the conflict in question in the right way when it imposes, at minimum, a requirement of targeting and/or unlawful means (such as deception). This way of proceeding does not stop at the right/duty level, as there are other doctrinal hooks through which tort law can further reflect the hierarchy between competition and contract stability—for instance, who bears the burden of proving the element of "justification," what remedies can be granted, and so on.[5]

In these and other means, tort law engages with value by way of *constructing*, rather than preventing or even containing, conflicts. Of course, tort law cannot literally bring this lived experience into being. Rather, its responsibility is to create the conditions for free and equal persons to shape the market (in the case of the inducement tort) in the appropriate way. In that, tort law enters the domain of *positive* value. Tort law does not address human failings at this point. Competing-by-luring, properly conceived, is not a pathology calling for a cure. Instead, tort law becomes a facility for liberating self-determining agents—employees, contractors, and promisors on the supply-side of the labor market, more generally—from relations of dependency and, ultimately, market inequality.

The most straightforward way in which tort law constructs the conditions necessary for inherently valuable conflicts to arise is by not imposing duties on actors, which is an implication of recognizing these actors as holding legal rights to engage in conduct in furtherance of their fundamental interests (say, in free expression, competition, or sociability). Further downstream is the recognition that acting in these (rightful) ways cannot count as wrongful, harmful, or costly. Concrete instances have been discussed in Chapter 3, and others are provided in Chapters 8–10, and 17.

[5] Justification is an element (or defense) that considers whether an otherwise impermissible act of inducement is justified. For instance, convincing a patient to quit a highly stressful job in a lucrative law firm might amount to inducing a breach of contract by the physician. But doing so can be justified in light of the imminent risk to the patient's life.

There are, however, other legal mechanisms in and around the law of torts that can further advance tort law's engagement with inherently valuable conflicts. Consider the following three. The First mechanism is Anti-SLAPP statutes,[6] whose purpose is to sustain free and fearless speech against meritless, retaliatory defamation lawsuits. These statutes enlist various procedural hurdles in the service of reducing the chilling effect of tort liability to free speech. The second mechanism is substantive, rather than procedural, and it concerns preemptive rules such as those rendering noncompete agreements impermissible. The impermissibility can be strict but it can also take a rather circumscribed form (in recognition of the different circumstances and considerations underlying competition in the labor market).[7] Such a rule could sometimes preempt the resort of employers and contractors to the tort of inducement of breach of contract as a means to erode inherently valuable conflicts in connection with work relations. The third mechanism to the same effect goes to restricting rights of action, rather than substantive rights. The tort of public nuisance is a case in point, as it restricts the right to sue for public nuisance. A holder of a primary right to use and enjoy the public sphere does not have an exclusive right, and at times simply does not have a tertiary right, to sue the tortfeasor.[8] As a result, suits by attorneys general, cities, and states figure prominently in public nuisance litigation. As I show in Chapter 8, public nuisance governs inherently valuable conflicts involving, among other things, public demonstrations. Restricting the right of victims to sue might indirectly reinforce demonstrators' ability to pursue their valuable activity. These and other mechanisms are warranted insofar as they support tort law's first virtue of responding to conflicts—here, inherently valuable ones—in the right way by engaging with their kind of value in the right way, including by creating some such doctrinal mechanisms.

II. Responding to Tolerable Conflicts: Containment

The conflict sanitizer can often yield the opposite conclusion, namely, that sanitizing the conflict while providing maximal protections to the ex-conflicting interests provides a more desirable way of coping with the conflict than by engendering it. In this case, the conflict is not inherently valuable so that the only live question is whether the conflict is tolerably valuable. The key to *identifying* interpersonal conflicts as tolerable is given by the distinction between valuable pursuits and their adverse side effects. Driving is (or can be) conducive to the

[6] SLAPP stands for Strategic Lawsuits Against Public Participation.

[7] *See generally* Stewart J. Schwab, *Regulating Noncompetes Beyond the Common Law: The Uniform Restrictive Employment Agreement Act*, 98 IND. L.J. 275 (2022).

[8] *See* Dagan & Dorfman, *Public Nuisance, supra* note 4, at 217.

self-determination of those who engage in this activity as well as to others (say, the driver's family); the risk of accidents and their attendant injuries are the side effects. Notice that these effects do not include the social costs of accidents but rather the setback to the interests of the parties caught in a conflict. The structural distinction between valuable activity and its adverse by-product can be applied to many torts, including to those concerning accidental wrongdoing. Various forms of negligence, including professional malpractice, would fit this description but other traditional torts such as private nuisance, products liability, strict liability for ultrahazardous activities, nonflagrant trespass to land, and mistaken publication of defamatory content could also count. Tort law begins to engage with value in the right way when it identifies the conflict—in terms of the adverse side effects—against the backdrop of the valuable activities that give rise to it. It follows that when the underlying activities are value*less*, the conflict to which they give rise should not be identified as tolerable in the first place. Instead, it should be prevented (by tort law and, at times, by other means).

The next stage on the tort-law analysis is *determination*, which is one of giving effect to the rights and the duties of those involved in conflicts identified as tolerably valuable. As with inherently valuable conflicts, tort law must determine—viz., recognize the very existence and/or fill out the content of—these rights and duties. What needs to be further explored is the distinctive sense in which tort law engages with tolerable conflicts, as opposed to inherently valuable ones. I argue that tort law's task is that of containment, namely, keeping the negative side effects of valuable pursuits under control. It does that by invoking both the *restrictive* and the *enabling* aspects of tort duties. Unlike inherently valuable conflict, the enabling (and restricting) that goes into governing tolerable conflicts is ultimately contingent. In particular, tort law should enable (and at times restrict) certain behaviors for lack of better alternatives of eliminating or reducing the negative side effects of the underlying activities. Let's unpack these claims.

Begin with restriction as a means of containing tolerable conflicts. This aspect is familiar enough. For instance, a duty of care requires some moderation in order to protect the safety of others. In that, it restricts certain excessively dangerous behavior, such as speeding next to an elementary school or playing darts over others' heads. That said, sometimes a discharge of due care fails to contain a conflict because it cannot prevent excessively dangerous activities. As explained in more detail in Chapter 14, when a person is engaging in an activity whose (abnormal) risk to others *cannot* be systematically reduced to reasonable levels, then containment requires imposing a stricter standard of care and ultimately liability, with the doctrine of ultrahazardous activities. I argue that the doctrine fits this characterization. This is an illustration of what it means for tort law to respond to a conflict in the right way by restricting the side effects of desirable activities from undermining the very reason for which these activities are deemed desirable.

However, the task of containing tolerable conflicts by restriction must also be supplemented by an enabling aspect—after all, these are side effects of otherwise *desirable* activities. Here, tort law is not merely engaging with the negative value of addressing human failings by requiring motorists to be properly considerate of pedestrians. Rather than just requiring forbearance, a tort duty gives the risk-creator a facility for pursuing the planned action *even when* it is risky for nearby risk-bearers. Indeed, a duty of reasonable care relieves the risk-creator of taking more than reasonable care and, so, enables advancing the risk-creator's ends *despite* the (reasonable) risks these ends might entail for others. And as demonstrated in Chapter 4, sometimes tort duties facilitate risky behavior that goes way beyond the ordinary baseline of reasonableness. The enabling role of tort law, an instance of engaging with positive value, is part of the containment efforts. It ensures that restricting the negative side effects of interpersonal conflicts does not undermine the valuable aspects of the conflicts in question. As I will argue below, the connection between the enabling aspect of tort duties and the self-determination and equal standing of the duty-ower plays an important role in fixing the standard of reasonableness in a variety of torts, including the torts of negligence and nuisance.

Thus responding to tolerable conflicts by way of enabling is not limited to one-off conflicts, say, between a particular motorist and a particular pedestrian. Rather, tort law often responds to tolerable conflicts at the class-wide level. A paradigm case is the problem of workload that some physicians often face and that their duty of care must accommodate (another concern, which only reinforces this problem, is that of high level of background risk).[9] This duty is meant to contain—to render tolerable—the adverse consequences of an otherwise valuable treatment given by a doctor to a patient. In this case, a duty of due care has a restrictive aspect, to be sure, aiming to reduce physicians' failings, a.k.a. medical malpractice. However, the duty also fulfills an enabling function. The demand for enabling arises because the physician must allocate bounded attention and resources in ways that secure professional care not merely to one patient but rather to all of them. The problem of workload is not about helping a failing professional. Instead, even a nonfailing physician would still need a facility for extending expertise to each patient, and fairly at that. Accordingly, a duty of utmost care might undermine, rather than sustain, professional treatment.[10] For tort law to respond to the conflict at issue in the right way, the enabling is better provided by a duty of due care that bakes into

[9] High background risk can have two adverse effects. First, it may turn health care providers into de facto insurers, prompting them to pass costs on to patients. Second, some providers might refuse to treat individuals with significant background risks.

[10] *Compare* Robert Stevens, Torts and Rights 13 (2007). Stevens analyzes tort liability on the basis of the distinction between common callings and other professions (or services). My explanation of doctors' liability, by contrast, focuses on whether strict liability would undermine the ability to extend care and help to a *class* of patients. Common carriers typically do not face a similar difficulty—discharging one "unit" of care applies simultaneously to all of the carrier's passengers.

the duty a physician owes one patient the care owed to all of the doctor's other patients, taken severally. This would mean that part of what it takes for tort law to engage with a tolerable conflict that arises in this specific context is to conceive of the challenge of containing adverse circumstances, by restricting and enabling in *class-wide* terms.

III. Responding to Valueless Conflicts: Prevention

Identifying valueless conflicts is often straightforward: A punch in the face of an innocent person, locking your co-tenant in the attic, or maliciously fabricating facts about a person's criminal record are easily identifiable as valueless conflicts. Other instances may prove more challenging in terms of identifying the valuelessness of the conflict. Sometimes the difficulty lies in contextual considerations. Thus, whether or not a nuisance must be entirely eliminated or only reasonably abated is, at bottom, a question of whether the case is one of valueless or inherently valuable conflict, respectively. And the answer is heavily influenced by contextual factors as will be discussed in Chapter 8.

At other times, identifying a conflict as valueless raises a different challenge, one of characterization. As discussed in Chapter 6, a failure to provide easy rescue manifests a valueless conflict between the imminent threat to a drowning person's life and the right of a bystander to be free from *any* other-regarding responsibility. The challenge for tort law is one of characterizing in a sufficiently clear way what counts as an easy rescue and precisely whose responsibility it is (assuming that there may be more than one bystander, and that their proximity to the site and abilities to help may vary). That is, the difficulty lies in formulating a judgment about a particular case in terms of a rule or a standard that possesses a recursive structure. This rule-of-law challenge does not change the characterization of a conflict as valueless, but rather suggests that giving effect to it might pose these second-order questions. It further means, as I have argued before, that the traditional reluctance of courts to impose nonfeasance liability for breaches of duties to perform easy rescues is best explained by reference to rule-of-law considerations, rather than by substantive arguments (often made by the Toronto School of corrective justice and Kantian legal theory) that independence is, or should be, an exceptionless and absolute right.[11]

The task of responding to valueless conflicts in the right way does not end with identification. The next stage concerns the determination of rights and duties designed to prevent the conflict in advance or ameliorate it ex post. Tort law adopts its most aggressive stance when dealing with paradigmatic instances

[11] *See* Chapter 6.

of valueless conflicts—deliberately assaulting another comes first to mind, but so too are cases of recklessly inflicting severe injury on others. There are a number of manifestations for this distinctively tough attitude (when compared with tort law's response to inherently valuable and tolerably valuable conflicts). I shall briefly mention five of them.

First, as I elaborate in more detail in Chapter 12, tort law allows awarding super-compensatory damages often inaccurately described as punitive damages when and only when a tortfeasor displays some measure of conscious disregard of the rights of others. Second, tort law often softens the applicable rules in favor of victims of deliberate wrongdoing. For instance, the doctrine of transferred intent allows the victim to recover from a vicious attack *even when* he or she has not been its designated target.[12] Nothing of this sort appears in cases that fall in the category of tolerably valuable conflicts.[13] Third, the traditional common-law rule is that "agreement to fight" is no defense for liability in battery.[14] Accordingly, a consensual act involving the use of illegal (because potentially) deadly violence against the victim could still count as tortious, which is not surprising given the characterization of the underlying conflict as valueless.[15] As one court explains the rule, "an agreement by which one man may have assented to be beaten [should be treated like] an agreement to part with his liberty, and become the slave of another."[16] Fourth, preventing and properly responding to deliberate wrongdoing makes it *in*appropriate to apportion liability between the perpetrator and the victim even when the latter could have been held comparatively negligent for the outcome.[17] Fifth and finally, tort law often views an act of deliberate wrongdoing as a superseding cause, thereby preempting the liability of another wrongdoer whose mere carelessness is likewise causally connected to the victim's injury.[18]

[12] *See* Talmage v. Smith, 59 N.W. 656 (Mich. 1894); Scott v. Shepherd, 96 Eng. Rep. 525 (K.B. 1773).

[13] Hence, the doctrine of transferred negligence (which is an extension of transferred intent in torts such as battery) is generally denied. *See* Palsgraf v. Long Island R.R. Co., 162 N.E. 99, 101 (N.Y. 1928).

[14] *See* Barholt v. Wright, 45 Ohio St. 177, 179, 12 N.E. 185, 188 (1887). The doctrine has been criticized as paternalist. *See* Francis C. Bohlen, *Consent as Affecting Civil Liability for Breaches of the Peace*, 24 COLUM. L. REV. 819 (1924). The Second Restatement calls for abrogating or limiting the doctrine. *See* RESTATEMENT (SECOND) OF TORTS §892C (1979).

[15] This is not the rule, however, when it comes to an adequately regulated practice such as boxing, *presumably* because of its subjection to regulation and the form that it takes—an organized sport among professional or semi-professionals—*might* turn it to a tolerably valuable conflict. *See* Teeters v. Frost, 292 P. 356 (Okl. 1930); Hudson v. Craft, 204 P.2d 1 (Cal. 1949).

[16] Barholt v. Wright, 45 Ohio St. 177, 179, 12 N.E. 185, 186 (1887).

[17] RESTATEMENT (SECOND) OF TORTS §481 (1965).

[18] The traditional doctrine of superseding cause is framed as a per se rule, meaning that a deliberate wrongdoer who is an intervening cause necessarily puts the careless wrongdoer off the liability hook. The emerging trend, however, rejects the per se rule, acknowledging instead the doctrine's role as one of the factors to be considered in the proximate cause analysis.

IV. *Legal* Engagement with Value: Doctrinal, Not Free-Floating

In claiming that the first virtue of tort law lies in responding to conflicts in the right way, one may worry how much ad hoc discretion judges, regulators, and legislators must have in order to discharge this responsibility. In particular, am I suggesting that for any particular case, the judge (et alia) is invited to engage in free-floating, moral reasoning in order to decide whether the dispute is inherently valuable, tolerably valuable, or valueless, followed by a further process of tailoring the resolution of the particular dispute to the kind of value it underlies? Moreover, does talk of determining rights and duties imply a process of ad hoc tailoring of entitlements in each case? The general question here is not new. Nor does it single out the conflict theory in particular while it concerns the connection between value—be it equality, freedom, welfare, and so on—and legality. There is a range of possible ways for judges and public officials to make and apply law that is informed by values. One extreme method that should be rejected outright is the style of free-floating legal reasoning, turning tort law into a domain of idiosyncratic inquiry of value. This way of deploying moral intuitions in the service of putting off (legal) fires is impermissible. Indeed, it amounts to a dereliction of legal officials' ethical duty because it fails the two most basic thresholds of the rule of law as famously articulated by John Locke, namely, that "both the People may know their Duty, and be safe and secure within the limits of the Law, and the Rulers too kept within their due bounds."[19]

The other extreme way for tort law to meet its first virtue of responding to conflicts in the right way is to work out a finite set of crystal-clear rules. Everyone would then know everything there is to know about every possible question in the law of tort (as in the example of speed limit laws). Not only is this state of mechanical law infeasible but the hollowing out of any discretion would turn law into dogma that is undesirable. Hence, the live question is how tort law can manage the complexity of making law both sufficiently reflective of value and sufficiently determined.

The answer is *legal doctrine*, properly conceived. I do not claim that it is necessary and sufficient, but rather that it is necessary, indeed crucial, to make tort law the *law* of conflicts, as opposed to either the applied ethics of or the mechanical manual for handling conflicts. Doctrine provides analytical frameworks that structure how we (judges, regulators, lawyers, scholars, students, etc.) think about the world, identify what are the right questions to ask, and what are the problems that call for our response. For all of these to be possible, doctrine must resist resort to conclusory forms of reasoning and instead, adopt rules and standards that feature robust correspondence to their underlying reasons. An illustration will be apt.

[19] John Locke, The Second Treatise of Government 378 (Peter Laslett ed. 1988).

The doctrine of ultrahazardous activities in tort law governs the question of when and why liability for certain activities deemed ultrahazardous or abnormal should be strict, rather than fault-based.[20] For many years, this doctrine has been informed by a multifactor test marshaled by the Second Restatement of Torts.[21] The test includes six, equally important factors, including factors that do not add up into a coherent whole.[22] As a result, that multifactor test allows conclusory cherry-picking that hides intuitions behind a smoke screen of rigorous legal reasoning. This is precisely when tort law disintegrates into a practice of free-floating considerations of value.

But legal doctrine can, indeed must, know better. Thus courts, legislatures, or regulators can reshape the content of standards to eliminate problematic ad hockery without necessarily saddling standards with dogmatic manual-like rules. Indeed, there is a way out of the free-floating approach triggered by the multifactor test just mentioned. The doctrine of ultrahazardous activities is rendered intelligible when the question of what makes an activity ultrahazardous receives a principled answer, namely, when exercising reasonable care, or, for that matter, utmost care, will *systematically* fail to reduce the activity's risk to the level of reasonable safety.[23] On this approach to the role of doctrine, legal rules and standards should be made to possess *recursive* structures that would enable courts and their addressees to identify more or less definitive answers to particular questions.

Going back to the conflict theory of tort law, there is no special reason to worry about the "translation" of this theory into the actual workings of tort law if the latter is constituted by a set of doctrines, serving as stable analytical frameworks with which to engage in legal reasoning that is sufficiently responsive to value. Much of the discussion in subsequent chapters shows how legal doctrine, properly conceived, could meet this challenge.

[20] *See further* Chapter 14.

[21] RESTATEMENT (SECOND) OF TORTS §520 (1977).

[22] For instance, factors b ("likelihood that the harm that results from it will be great") and d (the "extent to which the activity is not a matter of common usage") do not fit neatly together. They might even pull in opposite directions.

[23] *See* RESTATEMENT (THIRD) OF TORTS: LIABILITY FOR PHYSICAL & EMOTIONAL HARM § 20(b)(1) & cmt. *h* (2010); *see further* Chapter 14.

8

The Propriety of Proprietary Conflicts

Nuisance Law

Introduction

This and the next chapter demonstrate the credentials of the conflict theory as a legal theory whose ambition is to provide a framework for thinking about and determining rights, duties, and remedies in the law of torts. To make this demonstration meaningful, this chapter focuses on nuisance and the next on trespass to land. The advantage of focusing attention on these torts, as opposed to products liability for example, is that they encompass all kinds of conflict—inherently valuable, tolerably valuable, and valueless conflicts. In that, exploring the doctrinal terrain of nuisance (and of trespass) poses an important challenge to the conflict theory, which is to prove its practical bite on a comprehensive scale. Rather than intervening on a limited, and necessarily selective, basis, nuisance law (and trespass) requires legal theory to provide ways to address conflicts with radically diverse underlying values. Hence, theories that see nuisance (and trespass) law through the prism of wrongs—as corrective justice and civil recourse theories typically do—or negative externalities—as welfare economics and the economic analysis of tort law do—will likely miss the important sense in which this law is not reducible to tackling human failings.

Before I begin, it will be apt to preempt the following objection. A somewhat conventional picture of tort law suggests that proprietary torts are governed by property law, not tort law, as they represent straightforward implementation of the *preexisting* rules of property.[1] In fact, however, when courts, legislatures, or tort scholars, for that matter, address conflicts analyzed in terms of nuisance and trespass, they engage in deciding what property rights we have, as they should. They do so by determining their nature, filling out their content, or defining their scope of application. Either way, tort law—as may be found in appellate opinions, regulation, legislation, and other sources of law—is not a mere transmission belt for implementing the fixed rules of property law in concrete cases. The argument in this chapter and the next one, therefore, conceives of the torts of private and public nuisance and trespass to land as key legal frameworks for thinking about and

[1] *See, e.g.*, PETER CANE, ANATOMY OF TORT LAW 139 (1997), viewing property torts as carrying the function of "making the boundary between what is mine and what is yours."

Conflict between Equals. Avihay Dorfman, Oxford University Press. © Oxford University Press 2026.
DOI: 10.1093/9780198979869.003.0011

determining entitlements to use and control real property, respectively.[2] Consider nuisance first.

I. Responding to Land-Use Conflicts in the Right Way: Nuisance Law

The tort of nuisance—private as well as public nuisance—is a powerful proving ground for two basic propositions that lie at the center of my overall argument. First, as a matter of *characterization*, I defend a conception of tort law as the law of involuntary, directed duties, rather than merely the law of wrongs, harms, redress, or cost-internalization. And second, as a matter of *normativity*, I argue that the responsibility of tort law is to respond to conflicts in the right way, namely, by engaging with the kinds of value underlying the variety of interpersonal conflicts. Nuisance law renders vivid both of these propositions as the conflicts falling within its purview span the entire range of conflicts picked out by the conflict theory.

II. Inherently Valuable "Nuisance"

Public nuisance in some US jurisdictions is increasingly deployed by regulators and other public officials as a doctrinal hook for recovery in what is essentially a claim for restitution (or, more precisely, subrogation) of the costs of ameliorating wrongs done to third parties.[3] The essence of such a restitutionary claim concerns the substantial burden imposed by manufacturers (e.g., of opioids) on governmental resources, such as emergency room services, law enforcement agencies, and so on. Often, this burden is the result of weak regulatory schemes and underperforming law-enforcement agencies.

Thus, it is important *not* to confuse the label "public nuisance" as just described with the tort-law notion of public nuisance. Moreover, there is indeed another understanding of public nuisance as a spatial extension of the tort of private nuisance: Whereas private nuisance protects the right to use and enjoy one's own land, public nuisance protects one's right to use and enjoy *public* (real and virtual)

[2] Defining the trespass/nuisance distinction in terms of a distinction between owners' interests in controlling and using land is a definition that contrasts with viewing nuisance as mini-trespass whose role is to tackle small-scale invasions of land. It also does not overlap with the view, most prominently defended by Henry Smith, that the distinction at issue tracks low versus high delineation costs (i.e., costs of singling out particular uses for particular treatment). *See* Henry E. Smith, *Exclusion and Property Rules in the Law of Nuisance*, 90 VA. L. REV. 965, 975–80 (2004). Nor does the trespass/nuisance distinction align neatly with the Calabresi and Melamed distinction between property and liability rules. In fact, and contrary to the argument in Daniel Markovits & Alan Schwartz, Remedies, Revisited (unpublished manuscript, May 2025), the latter distinction cuts across the former.

[3] *See* Hanoch Dagan & Avihay Dorfman, *Public Nuisance for Private Persons*, 74 U. TORONTO L.J. 198, 206–08 (2024).

spaces.[4] On this picture, public nuisance protects our rights as *private* persons in connection with using and enjoying public spaces. An inherently valuable land-use conflict arises, to give an example discussed below, when artistic freedom unleashes harsh backlash on the streets. The value concerns the creation of the conditions necessary for the good of liberal culture discussed in Chapter 2 to arise. Such value, moreover, is an implication of the conflict at issue and its systematic realization cannot be possible in the absence of the conflict, such as by creating nonconflictual mechanisms to bring it about. Consider the following case.

Star Opera v. Hylan featured an NYC opera house staging a series of operas in German a year after the conclusion of World War I. It was found that the person running this production, "a German citizen who has been charged with having stated that he has no intention of becoming an American citizen[,] has also been charged with being the author of a song sung by himself celebrating the sinking of the *Lusitania* [an English liner sunk by a German vessel, foreshadowing the US declaration of war on Germany]."[5] The court reported that on the "evening of the first performance, a riotous crowd of 6,000 or 7,000 people filled the streets surrounding the opera house and resisting large bodies of the police." The "riotous demonstrations" renewed on the night of the second performance; in fact, they were "more pronounced," resulting in three policemen "seriously injured."[6] Mayor Hylan decided to abate the public nuisance by enjoining the performances until animosity toward Germany subsided.[7]

The question for the court was whether performing German operas during that delicate time constituted, or more precisely proximately triggered, a public nuisance by knowingly encouraging public protest resulting in "important thoroughfares blocked with crowds of angry men."[8] The court answered in the affirmative and, so, approved the Mayor's decision. The court reasoned that because the plaintiff did not have a right, not to mention a basic right, to perform operas, the license granted by the City could be suspended up until a treaty of peace (the then forthcoming Treaty of Versailles) was ratified.

However, this analysis is deeply mistaken. The mistake reflects the conventional understanding of nuisance law as tackling unfortunate accidents and interferences that, ideally, should not have happened. On this understanding, nuisance conflicts are about the "right thing in the wrong place"[9] whereby the "place" is often made

[4] *Id.*, at 209–13.

[5] Star Opera Co. v. Hylan, 109 Misc. 132, 133; 178 N.Y.S. 179, 179 (1919).

[6] *Id.*, at 135.

[7] The court intimated that because "the wounds of the war have not yet healed nor lost their tenderness," the injunction should remain in force for the time-being. *Id.*, at 137.

[8] The court mentioned other considerations that may partially overlap with a public-nuisance consideration such as "serious personal injuries." *Id.*

[9] Village of Euclid v. Amber Realty Co., 272 U.S. 365, 388 (1926); *see also* Dan B. Dobbs, The Law of Torts 1326 (2000); Robert C. Ellickson, *Alternatives to Zoning: Covenants, Nuisance Rules, and Fines as Land Use Controls*, 40 U. Chi. L. Rev. 681, 748 (1973); Gregory C. Keating, *Nuisance as a Strict Liability Wrong*, 4(3) J. Tort L. 1, 25, Article 2 (2012) ("Nuisances often are 'pig in the parlor' problems, and as long as we keep farms and residences separate, no one will be seriously harmed.").

wrong by either zoning ordinances' failure to keep conflicting activities apart or technological inability to tame the excesses of human activity.[10] This way of viewing the basics of the nuisance-based conflict naturally leads to the view that the tort law of private and public nuisance is in the business of elaborating rules of "live and let live,"[11] which is often supplemented by the maxim *sic utere tuo ut alienum non laedas* (meaning "use your property so as not to injure another's"). It may explain the outcome of the *Star Opera* decision, but it cannot justify it. That is because the value underlying the conflict at issue is entirely different.

Indeed, the court failed to respond to the conflict between the opera house and the rioting crowd, on the one hand, and the rest of the public, on the other, in the right way by overlooking the conflict's inherently valuable quality. To paraphrase the observation just quoted, the conflict features the right thing in the *right* place. A liberal society ought to embrace a conflict arising from artistic expressions that challenge deep political sentiments, including in particular nationalistic ones. And it should simultaneously embrace, in some measure, the right of engaged citizens to take their grievances to the streets even when doing so denies all other people their right to orderly and reasonably use of public highways. Embracing, you would recall, is no mere disposition. Rather, it depicts a principle of action: The controversial artistic performances at issue and the corresponding angry demonstrations should not be repressed or otherwise sanitized. Rather, tort law's task is a constructive one. More concretely, it creates the conditions necessary for the conflict to exist. Hence, a basic mistake of the court in *Star Opera* is one of identification, namely, failing to identify the conflict in question an inherently valuable one.

Misidentification arises in connection with another failure as well: That of misdetermining the primary and the remedial rights of the parties involved. Indeed, the court makes *no* place in its analysis for the rights of the opera house and its performing artists,[12] nor does it recognize the rights of the "riotous crowd" to denounce publicly the opera house's provocation. Instead, it focuses on the right to pass on public streets along with other law-and-order considerations.[13] Thus determining the primary right at hand results in protecting the live-and-let-live way of the City at the expense of the opera house's entitlement to exercise unrestrained artistic freedom and the public's right to protest their disapproval in public.

This is not to say that the former right (to pass on nearby highways) should be completely negated; as argued in Chapter 3, the priority of one right over the other is a relative, rather than lexical one. Engaging with the inherently valuable

[10] J. E. Penner, *Nuisance and the Character of the Neighbourhood*, 5 J. Envtl. L. 1, 11 (1993). *Cf.* Smith, *supra* note 2, 1047 (discussing the interaction between zoning and other regulatory schemes, on the one hand, and nuisance law, on the other).

[11] A classical statement is *Bamford v. Turnley*, 122 Eng. Rep. 27, 32–33 (Ex. 1862) *per* Bramwell B; *see further* John C. P. Goldberg, *On Being a Nuisance*, 99 N.Y.U. L. Rev. 864, 887 (2024).

[12] Star Opera Co. v. Hylan, 109 Misc. 132, at 136; 178 N.Y.S. 179, 181 (1919) (noting that "This case does not deal with a constitutional right, or, in fact, any right at all.").

[13] *Id.*, at 136.

conflict at issue makes the interest in using public spaces a matter of *secondary* importance.[14] Indeed, although fundamental, setting this interest to one side in light of this conflict is an outcome we should embrace, rather than lament. As such, the court should have allowed the opera and the protest to resume *because*, rather than in spite, of its obstructionist consequences. Moving the Opera and the crowd protesting or rioting against it to an isolated place or even delaying the performance for as long as it takes may sanitize the conflictual settings, but it will also severely undermine the realization of what I called in Chapter 3 the good of liberal culture at the heart of the conflict in question.

Private Nuisance and Two Locality Rules: Normative and Empirical. Can the argument that some conflicts of public nuisance are and should be treated by the law as inherently valuable be replicated to the case of *private* nuisance, too? I answer in the affirmative, as both types of nuisance can bring into existence valuable land-use conflicts. That is, public and private nuisance differ with respect to the venue—public sphere or private land—on which a conflict occurs, but not necessarily in respect of the value underlying the conflict.[15] Further, I argue that there are two distinct legal standards, not one, for determining what constitutes a private nuisance. At times this standard—the locality rule—reflects an empirical test of permissible use, based on actual practices in the particular locality. This approach must still be constrained by basic demands of relational justice to prevent the incorporation of oppressive or regressive social conventions into the law. At other times, however, the locality rule should adopt a fully normative stance, evaluating permissibility based on the underlying value of the uses in conflict. The conflict theory explains why, and when, this normative or empirical standard is appropriate.

Two familiar cases render this observation vivid; they are often discussed in connection with the Fair Housing Act[16] and zoning laws[17] but they are equally relevant and litigated in the context of nuisance law. (Recall that private law, including tort law, is not reducible to a single source of law, such as the common law, as it reflects *any* legal source that constructs relational terms of interaction between free and equal private persons.) Note, further, that zoning laws do not override nuisance law so that even when a certain land-use is permissible zoning-wise, it could still count as impermissible if it happens to constitute a nuisance.[18] The first case involves publicly practicing religious faith in and around suburban residential communities—for instance, church bells, or muezzins summoning

[14] *Contra* Jason Neyers, *Reconceptualizing the Tort of Public Nuisance*, 76 CAM. L.J. 87 (2017).

[15] *See further* Dagan & Dorfman, *supra* note 3, at 206–08, 209–10.

[16] 42 U.S.C. §§ 3601–31 (1994).

[17] *See, e.g.*, Martha Minow, *When Difference Has Its Home: Group Homes for the Mentally Retarded, Equal Protection and Legal Treatment of Difference*, 22 HARV. C.R.—C.L. L. REV. 111 (1987).

[18] Indeed, although there is an important continuity between nuisance and zoning law (on which see generally *Village of Euclid v. Amber Realty Co.*, 272 U.S. 365 (1926)), the tort of private nuisance entitles persons to (reasonably) use and enjoy their premises even against interfering land-uses that do not violate zoning ordinances.

Muslims to prayer.[19] The second case features protected homes, halfway housing, and other caring facilities for persons with mental disabilities situated within residential districts.[20] Both cases can give rise to allegations of private nuisance that claim that the exercise of religious faith and the living presence of mentally or cognitively disabled persons in a residential neighborhood unreasonably interfere with neighbors' ability to use and enjoy their dwellings. The complaint combines the gravity of the interference with the availability of an inexpensive conflict sanitizer: Relocating the interfering activity to more suitable locations, namely, nonresidential or mixed districts.

It might be tempting to treat such instances as though they are materially identical to "right-thing-in-the-wrong-place" kinds of conflicts, by which I mean unfortunate accidents brought about by disorganized urban development, ill-conceived zoning, or failing technologies of insulation. In other words, it is tempting to approach such instances as additional case studies for the Coase Theorem and the rich and sophisticated economic analysis to which it has given rise—to wit, nuisance law as a mechanism for creating secondary markets for addressing negative externalities. However, doing so is a mistake. Integrating religious ways of life, and welcoming the living presence of mentally disabled people into everyday society, calls for a very different reaction, normatively speaking, than a conflict whereby your neighbor decides to house her pig in the parlor instead of the barnyard.[21] All things considered, the latter conflict may or may not be tolerably valuable; zoning ordinances, nuisance litigation, and technological innovation could defuse them by working out a systematic *separation* between the clashing interests. By contrast, creating the conditions for toleration in the case of religious liberty and the inclusion of "others" in the case of mentally disabled persons render inherently valuable the conflict between religious worship and protected homes for the mentally disabled, on the one hand, and living in a peaceful residential neighborhood, on the other. Within limits, therefore, they ought to be embraced, rather than defused or sanitized. They feature activities for which the proverbial "right thing in the wrong place" should be replaced with "right thing in the right place."

Note that talk of "right place" refers not only to the physical location of the conflict but rather also to the normative significance of an inherently valuable conflict, namely, that we have a *reason* to construct the conditions necessary for this conflict to arise. Such a reason purports to make a difference—viz., justify the construction of a conflictual space—in the lived-experience of liberal societies even as they exhibit entirely different attitudes toward conflict.[22]

[19] For more on the latter, see https://www.nytimes.com/2016/11/17/world/middleeast/lod-israel-muslim-prayer.html?searchResultPosition=2.

[20] *See, e.g.*, Smith v. Gill, 310 So.2d 214 (Ala. 1975).

[21] *See Village of Euclid*, 272 U.S. at 388.

[22] It is possible to imagine these attitudes existing along a spectrum, from a typically Canadian neighborhood to a mixed Jewish-Palestinian one. The *reason* to construct a conflictual space applies across this entire range.

Private nuisance law should, and in some measure already does, respond to these conflicts in the right way, namely, by identifying the conflicts at issue for what they are and by deciding the competing rights by reference to the importance of *practicing* both religious toleration and social inclusion.[23]

This way of proceeding plays out, most specifically, in determining private nuisance's standard of impermissible interference with the reasonable use and enjoyment of residential dwellings. Similar noise levels produced by a muezzin and a karaoke club may cause similar material disturbance, say, to the ability of neighbors to enjoy porch reading on sunny afternoons. Or so a mechanical comparison of the decibel levels of the activities in question suggests.

However, courts should not treat these cases alike. In particular, they should employ qualitatively different versions of the locality rule, according to which activities that are ordinary for the relevant area do not constitute nuisance.[24] In the karaoke club (or opera house) example, the locality rule is predominantly an *empirical* one: It amounts to unreasonable interference because operating a karaoke club (or opera house) is not ordinary, in terms of its decibel levels, for a residential district. There is no special reason to insist that those living in a residential district accommodate entertainment and other loud leisurely activities in their daily lives.[25] Indeed, nothing of value is lost when nuisance law (and, by extension, zoning law) is deployed as a conflict sanitizer.[26] Importantly, applying the locality rule in this way can—and should—take into account mitigation measures that are conventional and expected within that locality. For example, in a residential district of a metropolitan area in a developed country, the walls of single-family homes are typically expected to be thicker than those of a camping tent. If a neighbor chooses to live in a tent-like structure, the locality rule should prevent them from successfully complaining about the "loud" noise of a nearby truck parking—even if it happens late at night.[27]

[23] Do courts comply with this prescription? The answer is quite complicated. In matters of religious toleration, courts seem to appreciate the difference between mere interference and interference arising from the exercise of religion (which is further discussed below). By contrast, when it comes to mentally disabled persons, early cases and the Second Restatement take the indefensible view that the interference caused by protected homes should be treated like any other interference (say, a loud factory). *See, e.g.*, Shepard v. City of Seattle 109 P. 1067 (Wash. 1910); Smith v. Gill, 310 So.2d 214 (Ala. 1975); Restatement (Second) of Torts § 828 cmt. *g* (1979).

[24] Osthaus v. Robinson, 12 Pa. D. 25, 26 (Pa. Com. Pl. 1902) ("In business localities, devices and machinery are permitted which, if erected in a residential community, would be nuisances").

[25] On the empirical version of the locality rule, see further Allan Beever, The Law of Private Nuisance 31–33 (2014). *See also* Sandy Steel, *The Locality Principle in Private Nuisance*, 76 Camb. L.J. 145 (2017).

[26] Drawing on the (empirical) locality rule does not mean that nuisance law should not make space for exceptions, especially when it carries regressive outcomes.

[27] The discussion in the main text above helps explain why, according to the conflict theory's interpretation of the locality rule, the recent decision in *Fearn v. Board of Trustees of the Tate Gallery* [2023] UKSC 4 was wrongly decided. As Donal Nolan rightly observes, "in assessing what it is reasonable to expect a claimant to put up with—and, therefore, what is wrongful in the first place—the court should take into account, as one factor amongst many, the measures which an occupier could reasonably be expected to take to minimise the effect of the interference on their use of their property … [I]t is precisely

By contrast, the muezzin case invites into the locality rule a *normative* twist. The question is whether in a liberal society such an expression of faith should, rather than would, be deemed ordinary activity in a residential district, to which the principled answer—grounded in the liberal ideal of religious toleration—is "yes." Contrary to entertaining activities, practicing religious faith presents a *way of life* in the basic sense that it encompasses, and at times even defines a person.

The critical distinction is twofold. The first is between having a taste or a preference—including an intense one—to karaoke and pursuing a ground project.[28] The former is something we consume whereas the latter functions as a constitutive choice. We often express this view when we distinguish between saying that "X is a great karaoke or opera fan" and "X is a religious person."[29] As such, pursuing a religious way of life commands no less respect and recognition than a neighbor's interest in a quiet residential community whose conception of the good life points inward, that is, toward a more seclusive form of everyday existence as exemplified by peaceful porch reading.

The second distinction is between partial and comprehensive pursuits. Often, though not always, religious way of life reflects a comprehensive value system purporting to inform and guide many aspects of a person's life. It provides one with a way to understand and assess one's condition, challenges, and ends. A karaoke way of life, by contrast, typically exerts a rather limited influence on other facets of a person's life. As a result, the good of liberal toleration is greatly implicated in the conflict between the former (religious) way of life and the suburbanite conception of dwelling; it does not manifest itself when the conflicting pursuit, such as karaoke, cannot sustain a genuinely alternative way of life, let alone pose a challenge to the conceptions of the good life that typically figure in residential districts. This is not to say that the muezzin enjoys unrestrained liberty, say, to call to prayer late at night or to use extremely loud speakers—as argued in Chapter 3, the priority of one interest over the other is relative, rather than lexical or categorical. Instead, it means that muzzling the muezzin by enjoining its activity and, hence, forcing it to relocate is off the table of nuisance law.

The proposed distinction between empirical and normative locality rules tracks the distinction between tolerably and inherently valuable conflicts. Further, it illuminates the doctrine. Indeed, the leading case of *Terhune v. Trustees of Methodist Episcopal Church of Matawan* concerns the "very loud, harsh tone"

by means of self-help measures such as drawing curtains or lowering blinds, building walls or fences, and planting hedges or trees, that occupiers generally protect themselves from prying eyes." Donal Nolan, *Nuisance and Privacy*, 137 L.Q.R. 1, 3–4 (2021).

[28] *See further* Hanoch Dagan & Avihay Dorfman, Relational Justice: A Theory of Private Law ch. 3 (2024).

[29] When we say that "X is a karaoke person" or "an opera person," we usually mean that X prefers, including having an intense preference for, doing karaoke or going to the opera.

of ringing church bells.[30] The court finds that if viewed from a purely empirical standard of the locality rule, the interference is "clearly a nuisance."[31] That said, and here is the important point, the court drives a wedge between the interference caused by church bells' announcing the hour, for which an enjoinable nuisance lies, and announcing church service, for which nuisance does *not* lie at all.[32] The latter conclusion reflects the normative variation on the locality rule: Certain religious practices should be deemed ordinary not so much on account of their decibel levels but rather because accommodating them creates the conditions necessary for a valuable, liberal practice of toleration.

Finally, one might protest that church bells and muezzins are of instrumental significance only. They represent traditional, archaic really, ways of summoning people to prayer and, more generally, communicate information to the relevant religious community. Surely, there are better communication technologies than these; text messages and other messaging apps readily suggest themselves. Don't they provide perfect conflict sanitizers? My response is that although they are certainly more effective and far less conflictual than church bells and muezzins, they cannot replace them. The reason is that church bells and muezzins are not just loud notification systems. Church bells function "not simply as a marker of time, but as an auditory enactment of the Christian faith."[33] Likewise, muezzins' call to prayer "is in itself a proclamation of the faith."[34] It is one thing to inform the devout that it is time to attend a prayer meeting, quite another to do so by turning this event into common knowledge.[35] Indeed, they have an irreducibly public dimension: They call on all of us, the nondevout included, to recognize the legitimacy of the religious way of life. Pursuant to the good of liberal toleration, the religious way of life must not only be allowed but also be seen to be—and, in our case, heard by us all as—allowed.

III. Tolerable and Valueless Nuisance

Artistic expression, on-street demonstrations, expression of religious faith, and the social inclusion of mentally or cognitively disabled persons in residential districts

[30] 100 A. 342, 343 (N.J. Ch. 1917).

[31] *Id.*

[32] *Id.* The court identifies two grounds for its decision. First, there is no "necessity" in striking the hour (implying that ringing the bell for religious purposes does have noninstrumental value). Second, the defense of "coming to the nuisance" applies with respect to ringing the bell for religious purposes. *Id.* The emphasis on religious purposes (as opposed to nonreligious ones) is well established in private nuisance jurisprudence, to be sure. *See, e.g.*, Rogers v. Elliot, 15 N.E. 768, 772 (Mass. 1888).

[33] John H. Arnold & Caroline Goodson, *Resounding Community: The History and Meaning of Medieval Church Bells*, 43 VIATOR 99, 115 (2012).

[34] *Id.*

[35] By common knowledge I mean the creation of a genuinely public point of view, namely, that each one of us knows that all of us, taken severally, know that each of us knows, and so on. *See* DAVID LEWIS, CONVENTION: A PHILOSOPHICAL STUDY 52 (1969).

exemplify conflicts between "right things" occurring at the "right places." That said, other land-use conflicts falling into the framework of nuisance law may feature a contrastive structure—right things in the wrong place. They are famously associated with the familiar maxim "live and let live."[36] They are not inherently valuable conflicts. Flawed land-use regulation and inadequate technology explain why they have come into being in the first place. Against this backdrop, tort law's task is one of engaging with them as either tolerably valuable or valueless conflicts. In other words, nuisance law serves as their conflict sanitizer, at times containing their adverse side effects and at other times abating them.

To illustrate, the conflict addressed in *Boomer v. Atlantic Cement Co.*,[37] involving a cement plant causing substantial dust and noise to nearby neighbors, is the upshot of poor zoning law, allowing a large cement plant to be placed close to residential dwellings. The incident also features deficient technologies of pollution prevention and vibration-canceling. Fix either one and the conflict immediately evaporates. In the absence of a feasible solution, the choice of remedy should respond to the court's judgment concerning the kind of value underlying this conflict—is it a tolerable or a valueless conflict? As I argue elsewhere,[38] awarding the neighbors in *Boomer* damages in lieu of injunctive relief properly reflects a demand of relational justice, namely, of taking a "second look" at the extreme disparity in the consequences of enjoining the plant vis-à-vis the relatively mild harm to the neighbors: Whereas the total property damage to the seven neighbors amounts to $185,000 (which at a later stage ended up being $710,000), the loss on the plant's side comes down to 300 employees and an investment in excess of $45,000,000.[39]

At other times, however, the conflict does not concern the unfortunate proximity of residential and industrial areas but rather arises within a single, residential area. The famous English private-nuisance case of *Sturges v. Bridgman* is

[36] Bamford v. Turnley, 122 Eng. Rep. 27, 32–33 (Ex. 1862). In the landmark case of *Fearn v. Board of Trustees of the Tate Gallery* [2023] UKSC 4, the UK Supreme Court repeatedly referred to the live and let live phrase. As noted above, a better way to approach this case—as either a tolerably valuable or valueless conflict—is to consider, with Nolan, "self-help measures." Nolan, *supra* note 27, at 4. It certainly fares better, normatively speaking, than the court's attempt to ground its decision in the sanctity of "the basic right of a person . . . to occupy and build on their land as they choose[,]" further intimating that "[t]he very nature of property rights requires . . . they be respected by all others." *Fearn*, *supra*, at paras. 69, 121, respectively. The conflict theory resists the first point—essentially, the plaintiffs' indefeasible right to construct the walls of their houses, located in a mix commercial and residential district, of glass—as well as the other one—that there is some nature to property rights and that it necessarily commands respect, come what may.

[37] 257 N.E.2d 870 (N.Y. 1970). To be sure, I do not think *Boomer* represents a radical departure from long-standing practice, in which the trial court would issue an injunction but delay its enforcement, effectively prompting the parties to negotiate a settlement, which the trial court would then review for fairness. This observation reinforces my broader point about how tolerably valuable land-use conflicts are addressed in practice.

[38] Hanoch Dagan & Avihay Dorfman, *Substantive Remedies*, 96 Notre Dame L. Rev. 513 (2020).

[39] *Boomer*, 257 N.E.2d at 873; for more details, see Daniel A. Farber, *The Story of* Boomer: *Pollution and the Common Law*, 32 Ecology L.Q. 113, 130 (2005).

a case in point.[40] There, a physician sought to enjoin a confectioner from using large mortars, the noise and vibration of which passed through a wall common to the physician's newly constructed consulting room. Some scholarly discussions of this case proceed by resorting to foundational methods of determining the rights of the parties. For instance, Ronald Coase proposes efficient allocation of social costs as the only nonarbitrary method of deciding who should hold the initial entitlement—the physician or the confectioner. But this method cannot be right in a *liberal* legal order, as the entitlement to use one's own land does not turn solely on its contribution to the greater good. Indeed, a liberal legal order entitles private persons to decide, within limits, how to use their lands even when so doing falls short of the socially optimal use.[41] A competing argument invokes independence, instead of social welfare, as a basis for claiming that the physician is entitled to determine how to use *his* land, in which case the confectioner's setback amounts to no more than *damnum absque iniuria*.[42] But this approach merely begs the question concerning the proper *scope* of the claim to use one's land. After all, both the physician and the confectioner are using their respective lands. The independence of both is at stake; none can be singled out as *the* doer or *the* sufferer simply on account of independence.[43]

By contrast, I argue that the determination of the rights and duties in this case hinges on correctly identifying the conflict for what it is. As there is nothing inherently valuable in it, the live question for nuisance law is whether it is a tolerably valuable conflict—that is, is it containable, or can it be made so? Traditional nuisance law measures containability by reference to the empirical version of the locality rule: Uses that are ordinary for the relevant area need not constitute nuisance, and vice versa. (Ordinariness, recall, should not incorporate oppressive or regressive social conventions; however, it does involve considerations of self-help measures, structurally similar to the concept of comparative negligence). Thus, tort law invokes the locality rule to fix the cut-off point for both enabling some and restricting other land-uses.[44] Forms of interference that violate the locality rule invite tort law's *restraining* measures, including, in particular, by way of enjoining

[40] 11 Ch. D. 852 (C.A. 1879). The case has received ample economic, historic, and philosophical discussions. *See, e.g.*, R. H. Coase, *The Problem of Social Cost*, 3 J.L. & ECON. 1, 8–10 (1960); A. W. Brian Simpson, *Coase v. Pigou Reexamined*, 25 J. LEGAL STUD. 53, 54–58 (1996); ARTHUR RIPSTEIN, PRIVATE WRONGS 73–75 (2016).

[41] For intra-economic criticisms of the Coasean approach to property disputes, including in connection with *Sturges*, see Smith, *supra* note 2, at 1001–02; Thomas W. Merrill & Henry E. Smith, *Making Coasean Property More Coasean*, 54 J.L. & ECON. S77 (2011).

[42] RIPSTEIN, *supra* note 40, at 64, 74.

[43] For an equality-based articulation of a different corrective-justice argument, see ERNEST J. WEINRIB, THE IDEA OF PRIVATE LAW 191–92 (1995). Weinrib begins with a distinction—which I find to be circular—between the plaintiff and the defendant in terms of a distinction between sufferer and doer. He then argues for an empirical version of the locality rule—that the defendant's liability turns in part on whether her interfering land-use is "extraordinary." *Id.*, at 192.

[44] Campbell v. Seaman, 63 N.Y. 568, 577 (1876).

activities running afoul of the locality rule. This was the outcome of *Sturges*, as the court prevented the use of large mortars in a residential area.[45]

By contrast, conflicts that arise as a result of engaging in ordinary activities—viz., without violating the locality rule—may be left to stand. In that, nuisance law's reliance on the locality rule provides a *facility* for liberating land users from having to adjust their conflicting activities in response to each other's sensibilities; for instance, a misophonic person should not be entitled to prevent her neighbor from playing the piano at the evening.[46] Against this backdrop, the (empirical) locality rule provides courts with a nonarbitrary baseline against which to determine whether a particular conflict is, or can be made, tolerable.[47]

Finally, a private nuisance cannot be tolerable if it is relatively easy either to abate or to relocate its source. If so, the conflict is deemed valueless, so that the only right way of responding to it is by enjoining the nuisance. Indeed, courts routinely do just that, for instance, when it is clear that the hardship of relocating an interfering activity, mostly manufacturing as opposed to dwelling, is relatively low.[48] This can include cases in which it is reasonable to believe that enjoining nuisance-generating activities could spur the technological development necessary to abate the interference to others.[49]

[45] *Sturges* also gave rise to a different question concerning the coming of the physician to the nuisance. The court refused to consider this as a freestanding defense.

[46] *See, e.g.*, Amphitheaters, Inc. v. Portland Meadows, 198 P.2d 847 (Or. 1948). *See also* Southwark LBC v. Tanner [2001] 1 AC 1.

[47] The resort to the empirical locality rule should not prevent courts from adopting a critical stance toward instances that merit careful examination of the justice of enforcing the prevailing norm of ordinary use.

[48] *See, e.g.*, Penland v. Redwood Sanitary Sewer Serv. Dist., 965 P.2d 433 (Or. Ct. App. 1998).

[49] Smoke nuisance provides a historical illustration of this point. *See* Kate Markey, *Air Pollution as Public Nuisance: Comparing Modern-Day Greenhouse Gas Abatement with Nineteenth-Century Smoke Abatement*, 120 MICH. L. REV. 1535, 1556, 1558 (2022).

9
The Propriety of Proprietary Conflicts
Trespass Law

Introduction

Trespass to land is tort law's framework for dealing with conflicts concerning control of land often described as possession. It answers the question of when a person's entrance to the property of another is illegal.[1] But as I have been arguing throughout these pages, it is a mistake to think that this is all that the trespass framework is designed to achieve. Tort law is not merely the law of wrongs, harms, or costs. Indeed, anyone who reads appellate and Supreme Court decisions dealing with legal questions knows that it is about determining rights—their form, content, and scope—as much as it is about recognizing and redressing their violations by imposing tort liability. That is, trespass to land governs conflicts concerning land control, rather than merely the wrongdoings and the remedies to which these conflicts may (or may not) give rise. It means that part of what the trespass-law framework offers is a way to think about, and determine, what rights of possession people have.

I. Exclusive versus Inclusive Possession

I argue that there can be rights to *exclusive* possession, in which case it is up to possessors of land to decide whether entering their premises is permissible. By contrast, possessory rights can also amount to *inclusive* possession. Inclusive possession deprives right-holders of full control over who can come (or remain) on the land at issue. It means that it is *not*, or not entirely, up to them to decide who can enter (or remain on) their premises—for instance, places of public accommodation feature such possessory rights. By implication, a right to inclusive possession does not trigger a general tort duty against committing trespass. Hence, the most basic question for anyone who engages with the trespass-law framework is

[1] Unlike private nuisance's focus on the interest in being able to reasonably enjoy and use one's land, the property interest protected by the trespass tort is possession that is a special case of being in control of land. A trespasser setting back the latter interest does not necessarily threaten the possessor in being able to use and enjoy the invaded land.

Conflict between Equals. Avihay Dorfman, Oxford University Press. © Oxford University Press 2026.
DOI: 10.1093/9780198979869.003.0012

the question of whether, that is, why and when, possessory rights are exclusive or inclusive.[2]

What standard should be used to determine this question? My ambition is to show that it is the value underlying the conflict that counts. In particular, the trespass framework responds to land-control conflicts in the right way by engaging with the kind of value underlying the conflict at issue. Contrary to other areas in tort law in which the conflict theory both approves of some aspects of existing doctrine and criticizes others, I argue that a basic assumption underlying the current trespass doctrine as a whole crumbles under scrutiny.

Indeed, with some important exceptions (to be discussed shortly), common-law courts have identified possessory land rights with *exclusive* possession, as if inclusive possession is never, or almost never, an option. The source of this difficulty lies in overlooking the distinction between inherently valuable, tolerably valuable, and valueless conflict over the control of land. It is one thing to recognize possessors' exclusive control of land, such as with respect to valueless conflicts with thieves, and quite another to extend rights of exclusive possession to preclude certain intrinsically valuable conflicts whose occurrence should be embraced rather than prevented. Save for a few historical exceptions, the doctrine of trespass-to-land tends to run together the different kinds of conflict, yielding a near-complete identification of possession with exclusive possession. This is inconsistent with the prescriptions of the conflict theory. Tort law, therefore, should not let it stand.

II. Inherently Valuable Land-Control Conflicts

Entering another person's land can sometimes be valuable *due to*, rather than despite, its being nonconsensual. Being entitled to do so can change the balance of power between the proprietor and the entrant in an important way, namely, it makes possible a social practice predicated on a liberal ideal of relating as equals. There can be a number of instantiations of such a practice. I will discuss two cases with a particular focus on an especially consequential one: employment. This practice could give rise to an inherently valuable land-control conflict, and tort law's task is to construct the conditions for its very possibility. In terms of trespass doctrine, I argue that intrinsically valuable conflicts between land possessors and certain entrants call for inclusive, rather than exclusive, possession so that these entrants should enjoy some, nontrivial measure of nonconsensual access to, and so, some control of, the land in question as a matter of right. In defining the scope of inclusive possession, trespass doctrine also necessarily determines the point at which possessory rights become exclusive ones. Notice that talk of conflict and

[2] It is also possible to recharacterize the exclusive/inclusive distinction in terms of a continuum, asking whether possessory rights are more or less exclusive (or inclusive).

trespass law's task of constructing its conditions is not the same as an argument for *militancy*. My argument does not call for the latter.

The analysis going forward extends the case for nonconsensual access rights to the employer's workplace beyond its usual understanding in the literature in three important ways. First, on the conflict theory, these rights should no longer be viewed as *external* limitations on the common law, for instance, in the form of Section 7 rights of the National Labor Relations Act or state constitutions' free speech clause.[3] Instead, they are part and parcel of what it means for the law of torts to respond to conflicts of land control in the right way. For instance, I argue that rights of access to an employer's premises for organizing and other labor-related purposes find their doctrinal home in a basic trespass-to-land inquiry, namely, what kind of possessory rights employers have *to begin with*. To this extent, my torts-based analysis pulls the rug out from under the constitutional objection to statutory and regulatory attempts to allow union organizers onto the employer's workplace.[4] This objection presupposes, rather than argues for, the existence of exclusive possession rights on the part of employers. However, I argue that this presupposition is neither entailed nor warranted by tort law when viewed from the perspective of the conflict theory (and, as I argue elsewhere, a similar conclusion can be derived from the liberal case for the nature and value of the firm[5]). Second, nonconsensual access rights should no longer be cast in terms of an exception narrowly defined to apply if, and only if, employees and union organizers are unable effectively to engage in labor activities off the relevant workplace.[6] On my account, these access rights should form the rule, rather than the exception, because they are grounded in the inherently valuable conflict between labor and capital over the *character of the workplace*, which is a substantial aspect of employment relationships. That is, the conflict should be engendered, rather than sanitized, by constructing the conditions necessary for employees regularly to relate to their employer as equals by giving these employees nonnegligible control and agency over the employment relationship. Third, although the rights in question may (arguably) remedy political inequality and so reinforce the civic footing of the working-class people in a democracy, their most fundamental moral basis concerns relational equality in the employment relationship *itself*.[7] Hence, these rights matter, irrespective of whether political equality has been achieved or can be achieved in other, extra-employment fora.

[3] NLRA's Section 7 is codified as 29 U.S.C. §157. A leading discussion of constitutional law limitations on employers' private property rights is Cynthia L. Estlund, *Labor, Property, and Sovereignty after* Lechmere, 46 STAN. L. REV. 305, 338 (1994).

[4] *See* Cedar Point Nursery v. Hassid, 594 U.S. 139, 174–78 (2021) (Breyer, J., dissenting).

[5] Hanoch Dagan, Avihay Dorfman, & Katharina Pistor, The Liberal Firm (unpublished manuscript)

[6] *Contra* Lechmere, Inc. v. NLRB, 502 U.S. 527, 539–40 (1992).

[7] Compare with the political-equality grounding offered in Kate Andrias & Benjamin I. Sachs, *Constructing Countervailing Power: Law and Organizing in an Era of Political Inequality*, 130 YALE L.J. 546 (2021).

Although my argument applies most directly to nonconsensual access by employees, I shall focus on the more challenging case, which is that of organizers' right to the same.[8] Consider non-employee union organizers seeking to discuss union organizing with workers in a factory. If all that matters is the ability to convey useful information, then the precise location where the discussion takes place is only contingently important. The question becomes one of securing effective communication between union organizers and employees.

However, the case for providing organizers access to the workplace does not turn on the question of effective communication. I argue that the issue is not about *knowing*, but rather about *being*; the conflict theory makes the case for the proverbial (work) boots on the ground. Indeed, an entitlement to be nonconsensually in the employer's space in order to enhance workers' agency is appealing because of its role in advancing an ideal modus vivendi in which an employer and its employees could relate as equals on an ongoing basis.

The move from nonconsensual access rights to relational equality has a negative and a positive dimension. Negatively, entitling nonemployee union organizers to enter the workplace without leave of the employer changes the balance of power between an employer and its employees.[9] It does that by limiting the employer's control over the activities, conversations, and will-formation processes that take place in the workplace, on the one hand, and increasing the control of employees over the workplace and ultimately the terms of the employment relationship, on the other.

Why should we care about changing the balance of control over the workplace? This is where the positive dimension suggests itself. I argue that weakening the employer's control strengthens the unionized and nonunionized employees' control, and that doing so sustains an inherently valuable conflict between labor and capital. In particular, it creates the conditions necessary for the construction of egalitarian work relations.[10] Ultimately, I argue that securing nonconsensual access entitlements reflects the right way to respond to the inherently valuable conflict between the respective interests of the people on the side of capital and on labor's side.

[8] The case for organizers' nonconsensual access also supervenes on another, more general challenge, which is the principal-agent problem (as when the interests of the union and the interests of workers diverge). I take this problem to be orthogonal to my argument. I will therefore proceed under the assumption that unions could and, in fact, would advance the interests of workers. More generally, I assume that the conflict that matters—normatively speaking—is between labor and capital only.

[9] *See also* Benjamin I. Sachs, *Law, Organizing, and Status Quo Vulnerability*, 96 TEX. L. REV. 351, 375 (2017).

[10] Another condition might be codetermination, by which I mean granting employees' equal voice in the supervisory boards of the corporation. The discussion of codetermination typically emphasizes workers' agency in connection with the *business management* of a corporation. By contrast, I argue for another aspect of agency on the part of workers, that is, having a substantial measure of control over the terms of the employment relationship and, in particular, the allocation of the surplus (on which more below). It is about the employee qua employee, rather than the employee qua director.

To begin with, the value of union organizers engaging an entire class of workers, taken together, is not reducible to the content of what they could have said to each employee, taken severally. Rather, meeting with them all in the workplace itself can facilitate both *class* and *rights* consciousness on the part of the workers. Let's begin with class consciousness. By addressing an entire cohort of workers, the advice and support provided by union organizers become common knowledge among them all so that each worker knows that his or her fellow workers know that he or she knows that they know, and so on.[11] Being out in the open and, so, publicly shared by an entire body of a firm's workers, knowledge concerning their condition and ways to address it is no longer limited to separate individual workers. Nor is it limited to a plurality of workers, taken severally. Instead, it sustains all-inclusive forms of processing information and contemplating collective action. So understood, nonconsensual access rights are key to shaping the consciousness of workers as a class—viz., *labor class*—that stands apart from capital, and indeed contrasts with it.[12]

Next, class consciousness gives rise to *rights* consciousness, which is a moral framework for articulating claims that take the form of rights. Notice that such claims are not limited to the rights that workers currently have as a matter of positive law—that is, union organizers do not merely enter the workplace to inform workers what the posited law happens to say and how it bears on their working conditions (although they do that as well). Rather, the claims at issue articulate demands that reflect what should be the workers' as a matter of right—that is, union organizers help workers engage in reimagining, challenging, and ultimately altering the legal status quo in ways that better reflect the workers' convictions regarding justice in the workplace and, indeed, in employment relations.[13] It contrasts with the quietist assumption that only employers get to decide "the ultimate direction, philosophy, and managerial policies" of their workplaces.[14]

It is important to note that nonconsensual access rights are required on an ongoing, rather than one-off, basis. This is because the facilitation of workers' rights consciousness cannot be fully satisfied at the get-go stage, nor once and for all. Two reinforcing reasons support this observation: That workers' claims should reflect the bargain between employer and employees over the allocation of the surplus,

[11] *See* David Lewis, Convention: A Philosophical Study 52 (1969).

[12] The scope of the class may, but need not, extend beyond a particular workplace to capture an entire sector or even economy. However, the argument in the main text focuses on the narrower case of constructing a labor class in one workplace at a time.

[13] On the reformative potential of rights-consciousness, see E. P. Thompson, Whigs and Hunters: The Origin of the Black Act (1975). On the normalizing effect built into the arrangement of work, including in liberal legal orders, see Jürgen Habermas, Between Facts and Norms: Contributions to a Discourse Theory of Law and Democracy 413 (William Rehg trans., 1996).

[14] Good Samaritan Hosp., 265 N.L.R.B. 618, 626 (1982).

and that the underlying conflict between labor and capital out of which workers' claims arise is structural, rather than transitory.

Let's begin with the first reason. It concerns the object of workers' claims. Such claims surely involve what every employee is entitled to as a matter of law, which is to say a mandatory floor of rules, such as concerning the provision of minimum wage, adequate workplace safety, and nondiscriminatory hiring and promotion policies. The claims may also involve rights that arise from their employment contracts and the above-the-floor provisions those contracts may include. Ideally, a decent employer would anyway want to respect both kinds of right—legal and contractual; accordingly, nonconsensual access rights may have no role to play when it comes to any law-abiding and promise-keeping employer. However, rights-consciousness can, and should, give rise to claims that go *beyond* the legal floor and the existing contract to reflect the bargain between the parties over the allocation of the surplus, namely, benefits to which the employees are not already entitled.

Talk of surplus allocation is not restricted to sharing in the employer's profit by raising wages beyond both the statutory minimum and the contractually agreed upon remuneration. Rather, it also covers any claim to having more control over the design and the agenda of the workplace. It ranges, to give a very partial list, from above-the-floor standards of workplace health and safety, to a more generous accommodation of familial obligations, including at the expense of work hours, to enhanced policies of diversity and inclusion in the workplace, to climate-friendly initiatives, and to on-site childcare. Hence, nonconsensual access rights and their role in facilitating rights-consciousness are required *even when* employers are willing to respect their outstanding, legal and contractual obligations.

Relatedly, the second reason takes up the character of the conflict between labor and capital. It suggests that the claims just mentioned are the surface manifestations of a structural conflict, rather than a transitory one. As a result, pursuing them is an ongoing effort. Indeed, raising rights-consciousness on the part of workers and acting on it is fundamentally dynamic: It is constantly evolving in response to changing circumstances as well as changing perceptions of the workplace and of work itself. The practice of articulating claims may therefore defy any attempt to settle such claims once and for all, at the get-go stage. Instead, it embraces the need to adjust and readjust the employment relationship, by way of better allocating the surplus of production, so as to render it more egalitarian and indeed relationally just.

The argument has so far shown that nonconsensual access rights of union organizers help to construct workers' class- and rights-consciousness. I now wish to argue that the conflict between labor and capital to which such rights give effect is inherently valuable in the sense explained in Chapter 3: The good of relating as equals is a distinctive implication of the conflict. Accordingly, a conflictual control over the workplace should be embraced, rather than either resolved or sanitized.

To render this point more vivid, consider two other familiar approaches to the potential tension between labor and capital. The first approach is famously associated with a laissez-faire vision of free markets and private property which, in turn, tends to support (as in the *Lochner* era) capital's domination[15]; by contrast, the second reflects the Marxist end of labor's domination and, more generally, the public control of the means of production. Despite their contrasting visions, the two approaches are of a piece insofar as they aim at resolving, or at least substantially reducing, the conflict between labor and capital. In either case, control of the workplace should (ideally) be vested in one particular party, rather than in some combination of them. Accordingly, the question of how to allocate the (broadly defined) surplus of productive activities does not turn on the bargain between equally situated employers and employees.

Contrary to both of these approaches, I argue that some measure of private ownership over the means of production, on the one hand, and a genuine freedom to make work-related choices, on the other, are key pillars of a liberal society.[16] The question for the liberal-egalitarian approach, then, is whether the conflict between labor and capital will arise on equal or subordinating terms. Conflictual control of the workplace is required precisely because it facilitates the egalitarian alternative by creating the conditions for its development. Louis Brandeis, a champion of egalitarian employment relationships, made this point very eloquently more than a century ago.[17] He begins by observing that inadequate floors and even the unequal division of profits are mere symptoms of the basic concern arising out of employment relationships, namely, "a condition of inequality between the two contending forces."[18] Hence, an adequate solution involves the creation of conditions under which employer and employees could engage in "contending," more or less, on an equal footing. The key is one of building conflict into the employment relationship so that "the problems" that arise in connection with running productive activities are "not any longer, or to be any longer, the problems of the employer ... [as] they are the problems of the employer and the employee."[19]

[15] *See* Richard A. Epstein, *A Common Law for Labor Relations: A Critique of the New Deal Labor Legislation*, 92 YALE L.J. 1357, 1389 (1983).

[16] It does not mean that ownership over the means of production could not be made more available to workers (perhaps via generous state subsidies, worker-friendly credit markets, or cooperatives). Rather, it means that private ownership (by capitalists) can be one among others, rather than the only, legitimate arrangement for a liberal legal order.

[17] Brandeis used "democracy" as the basic ideal informing his claims, but it seems that what he really had in mind was relational equality in the workplace. The latter may help to promote the former, but on my account the employment relationship is a source of concern and of value in and of itself, that is, quite apart from its impact on democracy. To this extent, the value of an egalitarian workplace does not turn on the national or civic affiliation of the participants, as it can, and should, capture interactions between *persons* simply as such.

[18] Testimony of Louis D. Brandeis quoted in Final Report of the United States Commission on Industrial Relations. S. Doc. no. 415, 64th Cong. 1st sess., at 63 (1916).

[19] *Id.*, at 63–64.

One necessary condition for securing egalitarian employment relationships returns the argument to conflictual control of the workplace. I argued above that union organizers and employees should have nonconsensual access rights to an employer's premises for the purpose of increasing the control and agency of employees over the workplace and, ultimately, the employment relationship itself. Such rights institutionalize a conflictual modus vivendi for the workplace. According to the conflict theory, embracing this much is not extrinsic to the torts analysis of what rights we have to the control of land but rather integral to it. This is, in other words, not just a *mere* modus vivendi but rather an *ideal* one. It is not something that we would aspire to settle, if we could, once and for all. Rather, a conflictual reconstruction of the workplace reflects a desirable continuous state of affairs.

The preceding analysis demonstrates how the distinction between exclusive and inclusive possession should play out in determining rights and duties within the tort-law framework of trespass to land.[20] Responding in the right way to the land-control conflict between labor and capital begins with identifying it for what it is, namely, an inherently valuable one. It then proceeds with recognizing an employer's entitlement to inclusive possession and the corresponding circumscribed entitlement of employees and union organizers to access the employer's premises. Doing so would also require a further delineation of the scope of inclusive possession and the corresponding scope of employees' and organizers' land-control rights: Precisely what areas of the workplace should be subject to labor-related activities, by whom, and under what circumstances (such as during lunchbreak, after hours, etc.). These latter questions depend heavily on contextual analysis—concerning the nature of the work at issue, the number of workers, and so on—that lies beyond the scope of the current stage of the argument. More important at this stage are the broader implications of the conflict theory of tort law for trespass to land. Indeed, because tort law cannot remain indifferent to the values underlying the conflicts falling within its purview, the trespass framework must identify and determine land-control rights accordingly. Contrary to the traditional, near-automatic identification of possession with exclusive possession, the existence of inherently valuable conflicts should guide the trespass-to-land analysis to define possessory rights of employers in terms of inclusive possession.

Note that there could be, and indeed are, other spheres in which a conflictual control of real property is inherently valuable (arguably, recent student activism on some US campuses in response to the war in Gaza may be a case in point). Engaging with them in the right way calls for identifying possessory rights with

[20] *State v. Shack*, 277 A.2d 369 (N.J. 1971) concerns a trespass case in a context of labor/capital conflict. Note, however, that it deals with the protection of workers' mandatory floor of rights. My current discussion, by contrast, focuses on the labor/capital conflict in connection with the allocation of the surplus (broadly conceived).

inclusive, rather than exclusive, possession. The discussion going forward seeks to demonstrate this possibility by reference to consumption markets. Note that my ambition is to show that the preceding analysis of the labor/capital conflict of land control belongs in a larger category of inclusive possession.

Can a pub owner throw out a small group of people the moment the purpose of their gathering—celebrating the same-sex wedding of their friends—is discovered? Ending their celebration, let's assume, is no mere bigotry as it is grounded in a sincere belief that same-sex marriage is sinful and that hosting the celebrating couple and friends might implicate the owner in a religious charge of complicity.[21] Further suppose that the incident occurs at a thriving cosmopolitan metropolis offering a ridiculously vast amount of fine pubs for customers to choose from. In order not to prejudge the matter, imagine there is no antidiscrimination law addressing this case so that much of the legal analysis falls to the common law's trespass-to-land framework.[22]

In rejecting as conclusory the view that possession entails exclusive possession, the conflict theory of tort law determines the rights of the owner vis-à-vis the couple and their friends by assessing the value underlying the land-control conflict at issue. I argue that this conflict is inherently valuable, in which case the owner's right should be one of inclusive possession. As a result, this owner may not exclude customers on account of their choice to celebrate same-sex marriage. Granting these customers a rightful claim to some measure of control over the pub forms the conditions for a conflictual market interaction between the two parties.

To see the connection between inclusive possession and the inherently valuable conflict in this case, it will be apt to compare between a separatist and a conflictual design of the marketplace in pluralists societies. These designs correspond to a libertarian and a liberal approach to the legal construction of the market, respectively. On the libertarian approach, it is not up to law—and government power, more generally—to control market actors' decisions concerning exclusion from one's property. There can be exceptions to this conviction such as the provision of essential goods and services in undercompetitive market settings, but the basic libertarian commitment views competitive markets as a decentralized site of voluntary interactions.[23] Exclusive possession figures prominently in this scheme as it guards against coercion and other forms of legal imposition.[24] As a result, our pub owner should be entitled to throw out customers on account of his or her sectarian objection to their permissive attitudes toward sexual variation.

[21] The basic difference between the bigot and the religious owner concerns the larger conception of the good life that motivates the exclusion. The latter embeds his or her decision to exclude in a religious conception which, unlike the former's conception, is not or need not be sheer hatred, homophobia, racism, and the like.

[22] This could be the case if governed by Mississippi law. Miss. Code Ann. § 97-23-17 (2016).

[23] Robert Bork, *Civil Rights—A Challenge*, New Republic 22 (Aug. 31, 1963).

[24] *See* Richard A. Epstein, *Public Accommodations Under the Human Rights Act of 1964: Why Freedom of Association Counts as a Human Right*, 66 Stan. L. Rev. 1241 (2014).

On a macrolevel, the libertarian approach responds to the competing conceptions of the good life of pub owners and pub goers by pursuing a strategy of *separation*. Everyone should be entitled to satisfy his or her preference and doing so can only be had by engaging in purely *voluntary* transactions. The market conflict between the pub owner and the same-sex couple is, therefore, put to rest by channeling the competing claims in different directions. The couple and their friends will choose from the many *other* available pubs, thus sustaining the pub owner's liberty to decide whom to invite on his or her premises. The libertarian arrangement is, effectively, a conflict sanitizer: It sanctions a principle of separate but equal.

By contrast, the liberal approach responds to the conflict between the two parties by pursuing the opposite strategy of creating the conditions for a conflictual marketplace. The point of structuring the market so as to allow for—and, to some extent, encourage—conflicts concerning the good life is *not* that of ultimately bringing about social cohesion, nor is it even about peaceful coexistence.[25] Rather, it is one of constructing an egalitarian framework in which any participant, simply in virtue of being a free and equal person, has a standing before other participants.[26]

On this view, the marketplace should be radically inclusive in the sense that each and every participant is deemed *interactable*, no matter what conception of the good life he or she affirms. Such an all-inclusive marketplace denies the likes of the pub owner the power to say, or to act on the view of, "not for you." Indeed, an egalitarian market framework gives effect to a certain version of the priority of the right over the good by placing the eligibility to engage in market transactions beyond ethical or sectarian reproach. Inclusive possession manifests this priority by denying the pub owner the right to exclude the couple and their friends. The right of the couple and their friends to remain and, indeed, celebrate a certain conception of the good life is not conditioned on securing conformity with the owner's own conception.

The land-control conflict at issue is indeed valuable because it creates a condition necessary for a liberal-egalitarian practice in which market participants assert themselves as capable of interaction, that is, as being eligible to engage with each

[25] Social cohesion is, at best, a positive by-product of all-inclusive markets. That said, and contrary to the argument most recently made in Daniel Markovits, Market Solidarity (unpublished manuscript), the connection between a conflictual design of the market and social cohesion is rather tenuous to begin with. Both the separatist and the conflictual designs may be more, or less, successful in bringing about social cohesion. It depends on many contingent and context-laden factors of political economy, culture, and other background conditions (such as the demographic composition of society and the geographic distribution of conflicting cultures and religions). Accordingly, all-inclusive markets may sometimes (as a side effect) promote social cohesion and sometimes fail to do so (including even by causing the opposite effect of social instability, segregated markets, and divisive practices of ethical consumerism).

[26] Elizabeth Anderson, *Ethical Assumptions in Economic Theory: Some Lessons from the History of Credit and Bankruptcy*, 7 Ethical Theory and Moral Practice 347, 348 (2004).

other in market interactions. This valuable practice should be contrasted with the separatist design of the marketplace mentioned above: Instead of isolating people in their sectarian corners, the liberal-egalitarian response to pluralism empowers participants to seek one another's recognition as interactable not merely in spite, but rather *because*, of enduring ethical disagreements concerning the good life.

An all-inclusive marketplace is valuable, as I have just argued. I now wish to explain that it is inherently so. The key to this explanation lies in showing that enduring ethical disagreements concerning the good life are not something to be lamented but rather should be embraced. At some level we may find it disappointing and even frustrating that our ethical commitments are not widely shared, but at a deeper level we have a *reason* to want to live in such a world. Thus, it is better (morally speaking) to feel good about experiencing such frustration than to feel good about living together in perfect (ethical) harmony. Enduring ethical disagreements, as Rawls has observed, are the "normal result" of using "human reason within the framework of the free institutions of a constitutional democratic regime."[27] By "normal result" Rawls does not merely provide a causal description of how things have happened but rather makes a moral claim. A state of enduring ethical disagreements, he argues, cannot count as a "disaster"[28] because it is made up of two valuable elements—human reason and a certain human condition, that is, a liberal-democratic rule. On my account, the "normal result" should aim higher than a standard of a negative virtue such as not being a disaster. The possibility that the exercise of human reason yields divergent conceptions of the good life presents a normatively superior alternative to any other, including, in particular, a homogenous society of free and equal persons adopting more or less the same conception of the good life.

There is an additional reason (on top of the Rawlsian one) for this: A lived-experience of ethical divergence is a source of both self- and other-challenge for self-determining persons. It makes for a challenge simply by constructing a reality in which different people face different sets of commitment that move them in deep and profound ways. Such a challenge can push one open-mindedly to reflect on one's conception of the good life and, consequently, lead to either reforming or reaffirming this conception. Exercising self-authorship against *this* backdrop provides an appealing practical expression of the autonomous life.

Against this backdrop, the traditional identification of possessory rights with exclusive possession overlooks the analysis leading to the conclusion that the conflicting pursuit of conceptions of the good life in and around the marketplace is inherently valuable. Simply put, it fails to respond to the conflict at issue in the right way. Inclusive possession, by contrast, constructs a conflictual marketplace in which customers (et alia) can assert their ways of life as a matter of right, that

[27] John Rawls, Political Liberalism xvi (1993).
[28] *Id.*, at xxiv.

is, without finding themselves liable to possessors' sectarian scrutiny. To this extent, the conflict theory suggests that the statutory rights against discrimination, including those enacted by the Civil Rights Acts, should have been recognized by the tort of trespass to land *all along*.

As mentioned several times before, inherently valuable conflicts do not underwrite absolute or lexical priority of one interest—here, patrons' interest in manifesting themselves as self-determining, equal agents—over the other—here, a pub owner's interest in practicing religious faith. Instead, the priority is relative as it reflects two commitments that are integral to the conflict theory. First, the "losing" interest is, or is a subset of, a fundamental interest so that completely negating it is impermissible. Second, the priority at issue loses momentum when the conflict is no longer inherently valuable, as when the reason for denying entrance to the pub is grounded in legitimate concerns (such as illegal conduct, safety concerns, and housekeeping constraints on running a business).[29]

To conclude, there are other contexts in which conflicts of land control are inherently valuable (cases falling under the heading "media trespass" might be an example). My ambition is not only to demonstrate that some measure of inclusive possession in the contexts of labor and consumption markets might be the right response to the particular land-control conflict that each exhibits, but also, and more importantly, to provide the *normative framework* with which to understand in theory, and determine in practice, what rights to exclude, and duties to include, land-possessors have. Instead of invoking the conclusory trespassory framework of exclusive possession, the conflict theory of tort law provides the normative resources suitable to respond to land-control conflicts in the right way, namely, by engaging with the kinds of value underlying these conflicts.

III. Tolerably Valuable Land-Control Conflicts

When it comes to inherently valuable conflicts, entering and, further, partially controlling another person's land is valuable precisely *because* it is nonconsensual. Now I wish to argue that, at other times, entry and control might be valuable *in spite of* its being nonconsensual: Although not valuable in and of itself, tolerably valuable conflict is valuable because of the way it relates to other valuable matters. I argue that tolerably valuable land-control conflicts address the adverse side effects of pursuing valuable activities. In principle, we would want these effects to be eliminated altogether. But until it could be done, trespass to land is tasked with governing the terms of the conflicts at issue. The conflict theory provides the normative resources with which to respond to these conflicts in the right way.

[29] I elaborate on these concerns in Avihay Dorfman, *When, and How, Does Property Matter?*, 72 U. Toronto L.J. 81, 99–109 (2022).

I demonstrate this point by drawing on a category of cases featuring nonconsensual though privileged entry to the property of another.

Seizing control over the premises of another person may sometimes be required to fend off an imminent obstacle to the seizer's pursuit of valuable ends—for instance, using adjoining private land to bypass an impassable highway. If the seizing can be adequately contained, the seizer should have the right unilaterally to assume some measure of control of the possessor's premises. To give effect to this entitlement, the right of the land possessor should be capped at *inclusive* possession. In terms of tort liability, therefore, it means that under the right circumstances a mere entry need not amount to trespass.

Why does containment hold the key to turning the seizer's brute necessity into a right to some control of another's land? The answer goes back to the characterization of the conflict at issue in terms of a tolerably valuable one—the preliminary stage of identifying the nature of the conflict. On the one hand, the control interest of the possessor captures a basic moral principle of the legal institution of private property in a liberal legal order.[30] On the other, the seizer's freedom of movement requires adequate use of, and access to, highways.[31] Having and employing these two sets of interest *could* be frictionless. For instance, advanced roadways construction technology may eliminate the chance that severe weather conditions would block the highway; paving wide highway margins might remove the need to use adjoining private lands; and more sophisticated cars may literally fly over earthly obstacles.

Meanwhile, however, these valuable interests exert tension toward conflict, as when severe weather turns adjoining private lands into the only alternative to an impassable highway. Defusing the conflict entirely by forcing highway users to go back home would amount to "pushing individual rights of property to an unreasonable extent."[32] By contrast, containing the conflict allows both parties to have their respective interests secured, at least in some measure. It does so first by positing a rule of *inclusive* possession according to which forcing the possessor to share some measure of control of his or her premises with highway users under stress of severe weather and, second, by requiring these users to minimize the interference they impose on the possessor, including by paying compensatory damages if needed. The former condition *enables* the freedom of movement of highway users in the face of an imminent obstacle—the right unilaterally to seize control over the land adjacent to the highway sustains this interest and, consequently, highway travelling. The latter condition *restricts* the negative side effects of freeing highway users from the duty of not committing trespass. Hence, the right to enter adjoining

[30] *See further* Hanoch Dagan & Avihay Dorfman, *The Human Right to Private Property*, 18 THEORETICAL INQ. L. 391 (2017).

[31] *Cf.* ARTHUR RIPSTEIN, FORCE AND FREEDOM: KANT'S LEGAL AND POLITICAL PHILOSOPHY ch. 8 (2009).

[32] Campbell v. Race, 61 Mass. 408, 412 (1851).

private land must be strictly circumscribed to cases of necessity, and it would have to render the right-holder liable to by-product destruction that he or she inflicts on the possessor.

This restricting/enabling structure of containment has several doctrinal manifestations. Obstruction of highways is one; retrieval of chattel is another[33]; and private necessity is perhaps the most familiar of all.[34] What unites these (and other) cases is that nonowners are entitled to assert a measure of temporary control over land to which they would otherwise have no right.[35] Their entitlement or privilege, as it is often called, is incomplete in the sense that they could be held liable for the damage they may cause the possessor's premises.[36]

My characterization of the conflicts in question as tolerably valuable provides a more appealing way to explain the *grounds* of the entitlement to nonconsensual control of the property of another than some of the more familiar explanations. One familiar strategy—the Coasean strategy—takes a contractarian approach, suggesting that an entitlement to some control would have been granted by the owner had transaction costs not been prohibitive. However, this strategy fails because it misidentifies what is at stake, normatively speaking.

Suppose that transaction costs are fairly small and the owner is adamant that no one could buy such an entitlement from him or her. Can the owner's refusal—including a nonarbitrary refusal—justify denying the nonowner the control needed under circumstances covered by the doctrines of highway obstruction, retrieval of chattel, and private necessity? The conflict theory answers in the negative.[37] Contrary to the Coasean strategy, the entitlement of the owner should amount to inclusive, not exclusive, possession, and so lie beyond his or her unilateral control. The right to seize control of another's property does not turn on the actual or hypothetical consent of the owner. It is grounded, instead, in the value of securing non-owners' freedom of movement (in highway obstruction cases) when certain conditions obtain.

[33] *See* Wippert v. Burlington Northern Inc., 397 F. Supp. 73, 74, 77 (D. Mont. 1975).

[34] The leading cases are *Ploof v. Putnam*, 71 A. 188 (Vt. 1908) and *Vincent v. Lake Erie Transp. Co.*, 124 N.W. 221 (Minn. 1910).

[35] Mark Geistfeld argues that the doctrine of private necessity turns nonowners into property right-holders (say, the boat owner becomes the dock's right-holder as well as the boat's). As such, they face a trade-off between saving their original property and damaging the property to which they now hold a privilege. *See* MARK A. GEISTFELD, TORT LAW: THE ESSENTIALS 148 (2008). My account shares his emphasis on nonowners' control. That said, I do not accept his view that private necessity really vests nonowners with ownership of some sort. Having control—an ad hoc right-claim to the possession of another's resource—falls far short of ownership, which is the standing to fix the normative situation of others with respect to a resource.

[36] Francis H. Bohlen, *Incomplete Privilege to Inflict Intentional Invasions of Interest of Property and Personality*, 39 HARV. L. REV. 307 (1925–26).

[37] More generally, the question is what should come first, our fundamental interests or contractual arrangements. The equality theory I develop in subsequent chapters defends the former alternative. In the case under discussion it means that, within limits, a basic freedom of movement should figure as a constraint on contractual choice, rather than as its product.

The second strategy resorts to particularistic explanations of closely related doctrines. Instead of providing a general account of the entitlement's grounds across these doctrines (i.e., highway obstruction, retrieval of chattel, and private necessity), friends of this second strategy take one doctrine at a time. As a result, the tailor-made explanation of the entitlement underlying the doctrine of private necessity has nothing to do with the tailor-made explanation of the entitlement to retrieve one's chattel; further, neither illuminates the case for entitling impassable highway users to assert temporal control over adjoining private lands. To illustrate, John Goldberg, Anthony Sebok, and Benjamin Zipursky explain away private necessity's darling, *Vincent v. Lake Erie*,[38] arguing that it can be read as a straightforward case of trespass to land. Indeed, they argue that talk of emergency and necessity in *Vincent* is not merely superficial but rather an upshot of a scrivener's error.[39] This explanation, if true, carries no implications for the neighboring and seemingly similar doctrines of highway obstruction and retrieval of chattel.

Now consider the particularistic strategy applied to retrieval of chattels. In such a case, a sophisticated explanation of one's entitlement to enter the land of another to retrieve one's chattel comes down to the natural distinction between movable and immovable things. Movables, owing to their movability, can find their way onto the land of another. A doctrinal way out of this logjam comes in the form of a circumscribed entitlement unilaterally to retrieve them.[40] Once again, this explanation has no recursive structure, and so cannot illuminate the entitlements associated with such doctrines as obstructed highways and private necessity. The affinity between the three is readily apparent without the benefit of a theory. Explaining it away, therefore, should give way to a more holistic approach. The conflict theory purports to take this path, defending the normative unity to these doctrines. Indeed, a circumscribed entitlement to seize control over another's land is a way of responding to tolerably valuable land-control conflicts in the right way. Simply put, containing these conflicts so as to keep them tolerably valuable requires some such entitlement.

IV. Valueless Land-Control Conflicts

Some nonconsensual entries on another person's land are inherently valuable, whereas others are tolerably valuable. In either case, the traditional identification of possessory rights with exclusive possession runs afoul of engaging with these conflicts in the right way. I now wish to make the case for another category

[38] 124 N.W. 221 (Minn. 1910).

[39] John Goldberg et al., Tort Law: Responsibilities and Redress 836 (4th ed. 2016); *see also* John C. P. Goldberg & Benjamin C. Zipursky, Recognizing Wrongs 190 n.10 (2020).

[40] Arthur Ripstein, Private Wrongs 151 (2016).

of land-control conflicts in which possessory rights should entail inclusive, rather than exclusive, possession. More specifically, the argument is that certain nonconsensual entries may be allowed, and at times even enabled, *precisely because* the conflicts to which they give rise are valueless.

A straightforward case concerns uncultivated private property. Absolutely harmless, nonconsensual entry, such as for purposes of hiking, may undermine a landowner's control of the far edges of the property. That said, the interference posed by the hiker is, or at least could be, purely formal. After all, the land lies uncultivated. Therefore, it appears that the right way to address the conflict between the hiker and the owner seeking the former's exclusion must begin with identifying this conflict as a valueless one. As a result, instead of extending rights of exclusive possession, the conflicting demands for land control should be resolved one-sidedly, namely, in the hiker's favor. Possession should be inclusive. (This does not mean, to be sure, that hikers may not be duty-bound to conduct themselves in appropriate ways such as not to damage the land.)

Traditionally, nonowners used to hold a customary right to nonconsensual engagement in some recreational and commercial activities (such as fishing) on uncultivated private lands.[41] That said, this doctrine has since taken two contrasting paths. Some common law jurisdictions, especially some US ones, have eroded nonowners' nonconsensual entry rights by vesting possessors with the power to decide the question of entry, by way of posting "no trespass" signs.[42] Thus reinstating exclusive possession represents a wrong turn: Owners' full control of their uncultivated lands is the source of the problem. It reinforces the valuelessness of the conflict between the hiker and the owner.

By contrast, other jurisdictions have placed nonowners' customary entry rights on firmer grounds.[43] Chief among them is Scotland.[44] Scotland's Land Reform Act of 2003 grants broad rights of access to uncultivated lands for recreational, educational, and certain commercial activities.[45] It further extends these rights to certain areas of cultivated land on the grounds that accessing them can be kept harmless. In securing this arrangement of inclusive possession against abuse, the

[41] *See* M'Conico v. Singleton, 9 S.C.L. (2 Mill) 244, 244 (1818) ("[t]he hunting of wild animals in the forests, and unenclosed lands of this country, is as ancient as its settlement... [and] the owner of the soil, while his lands are unenclosed, cannot prohibit the exercise of it to others."). *See also* McKee v. Gratz, 260 U.S. 127, 136 (1922) (*per* Holmes J.) (trespass to land would not lie for hunters and fishermen entering the "large expanses of unenclosed and uncultivated land" of another).

[42] Mark R. Sigmon, *Hunting and Posting on Private Land in America*, 54 Duke L.J. 549, 558–64 (2004).

[43] *See, e.g.*, State Ex Rel. Thornton v. Hay, 462 P.2d 671 (Or. 1969).

[44] For thorough analyses, see Gregory S. Alexander, *The Sporting Life: Democratic Culture and the Historical Origins of the Scottish Right to Roam*, 2016 U. Ill. L. Rev. 321 (2016); John A. Lovett, *Progressive Property in Action: The Land Reform (Scotland) Act 2003*, 89 Neb. L. Rev. 739, 775–77, 778–88 (2011).

[45] Land Reform (Scotland) Act, 2003 (A.S.P. 2) §1.1 (defining "access rights" broadly). For a comparison between Scottish law doctrine and the New Jersey doctrine of beach access, see Timothy Mulvaney, *Walling Out: Rules and Standards in the Beach Access Context*, 94 S. Cal. L. Rev. 1 (2020).

Scottish Act imposes on nonowners the burden of exercising their rights "responsibly."[46] For instance, nonowners' rights of access can be exercised "at any time, day or night," as long as doing so does not cause unreasonable interference to owners.[47] Thus, traversing a cultivated tract of land is not allowed, but crossing on its margin is deemed permissible.[48]

Moving beyond the simple case of uncultivated private lands, the conflict theory of tort law can identify and illuminate other cases of valueless land-control conflicts. In that, it provides the normative resources with which to identify possession with inclusive possession in less straightforward circumstances. Indeed, I argue that one of the most familiar trespass cases in property and tort law, *Jacque v. Steenberg Homes*,[49] engages with the conflict at issue in the wrong way. Indeed, its failure begins with misidentifying it for what it is, namely, a valueless conflict. It results in an indefensible response to the conflict between the parties that takes the form of ill-determining their competing rights.

The Jacque couple, retired from farming their 170 acres of land, refused to grant the defendant permission to shortcut through the edges of their premises so as to deliver a mobile home to a neighbor. The crossing was absolutely *harmless* and Steenberg Homes, who preferred not to use the alternative road because it contained a sharp curve and was covered with snow,[50] was willing to pay the fee the landowners would want.[51] But the Jacques were not willing to listen or to even consider the possibility. That is, the refusal was not merely the result of failed negotiation but rather the outright dismissal of the possibility that Steenberg Homes would be allowed to go over the Jacques' land.[52]

A key factual point is that the site of the crossing was so far away from the Jacques' home that they could not even have noticed its occurrence, which meant that *any attempt* to justify their right to exclude Steenberg Homes on the grounds of privacy, well-being, and autonomy (not to mention impairment or dispossession of the land itself) was bound to fail.[53] This was not, in other words, a case of

[46] Land Reform (Scotland) Act, 2003 (A.S.P. 2) §1.2.1 (conditioning access rights on the responsible exercise thereof).

[47] Scottish Outdoor Access Code (2005) §2.2 available at https://www.outdooraccess-scotland.scot/sites/default/files/2018-05/Publication%202005%20-%20Scottish%20Outdoor%20Access%20Code.pdf.

The Code, approved by the Ministers and the Scottish Parliament, lacks authoritative force. Its purpose is to provide guidance to owners and nonowners with respect to the rights and duties that follow from the Land Reform (Scotland) Act 2003. *Id.*, at §§1.4–1.5.

[48] *Id.*, (access rights may also be exercised on "the margins of the fields where crops are growing or have been sown").

[49] 563 N.W.2d 154 (Wis. 1997).

[50] *Id.*, at 157.

[51] *Id.*

[52] *Id.* ("the assistant manager [of the defendant] asked Mr. Jacque how much money it would take to get permission. Mr. Jacque responded that it was not a question of money").

[53] *Jacque*, 201 Wis.2d at 26 (noting that "[o]nce the movers had proceeded far enough down the road to be out of the Jacques' sight, they used their 'cat' to cut a path through the snow-covered field and left the mobile home at the site").

domestic trespass.[54] It is also important to note that it was *not* a case of privileged highway deviation as mentioned above: Arguably, the public road nearby was not impassible, in which case cutting through Jacques' property might have been consequential but not essential to the success of the mobile home delivery.[55]

Was the *Jacque* court right to find for the Jacques and award them a dollar in nominal damages and $100,000 in punitive damages for Steenberg Homes' trespass to land? I argue that it was not and that the court's failure can be traced to its indefensible identification of possession with exclusive possession. Furthermore, if the conflict is valueless, as the facts of the case demonstrate, possession should be made inclusive of the likes of the defendant. Hence, the basic difficulty with *Jacque* comes to liability, rather than remedy. It is not that of awarding punitive damages, but rather the presupposition that the plaintiffs' possessory interests entail exclusive possession in the first place.

It will be apt to elaborate this claim by way of criticizing exclusion-based theorists who defend the *Jacque* decision.[56] Thomas Merrill and Henry Smith have suggested that *Jacque* can find support in our common-sense morality.[57] They observe that common-sense morality condemns violating property rights of others, and that this condemnation cannot be reduced to a simple cost-benefit analysis, certainly not at the micro level of a particular dispute.[58] They also find that this moral condemnation goes beyond property rights violations that setback human interests (such as in privacy and bodily security); indeed, they suggest that the "protection of property is viewed as a moral good in itself."[59]

A major difficulty with this view is that it does not explain what "the moral good in itself" might amount to. Such a difficulty is a surface manifestation of a deeper problem—why must a nonconsensual entry on Jacques' land count as a violation of property rights in the first place? It is one thing to extend exclusive possession rights to the various actual and potential ways in which the possessor could use

[54] Furthermore, it seems that this is not even a case of interfering with what modern Kantians would call the very capacity of owners to set and pursue ends by using their land. *See* Arthur Ripstein, *Beyond the Harm Thesis*, 34 PHIL. & PUB. AFF. 215 (2006). The nature of the "interference" by the defendant—its short duration and sheer harmlessness—and the absence of any affirmative plan on the part of the Jacques to use their land, fit uncomfortably with justifying the right to exclude on grounds of independence. Indeed, *Jacque* is a case of trespass without interference, rather than merely harmless trespass. *See further* Avihay Dorfman, *Private Ownership and the Standing to Say So*, 64 U. TORONTO L.J. 402, 426–35 (2014).

[55] *Contra* John Makdisi, *Uncaring Justice: Why Jacque v. Steenberg Homes Was Wrongly Decided*, 55 J. CATH. LEGAL STUD. 111, 125–26 (2012).

[56] I have criticized the *Jacque* decision on other grounds as well. *See* Dorfman, *supra* note 29, at 114–17.

[57] Thomas W. Merrill & Henry E. Smith, *The Morality of Property*, 48 WM. & MARY L. REV. 1849, 1850 (2007) (defining morality as "simple and accessible to all members of the community"). Smith has also offered an information-cost rationale for the *Jacque* decision. Henry E. Smith, *Exclusion and Property Rules in the Law of Nuisance*, 90 VA. L. REV. 965, 983–84 (2004).

[58] Merrill & Smith, *supra*, at 1870.

[59] *Id.*

his or her land, quite another to disregard the usability question altogether.[60] Furthermore, not only does shortcutting through the far edges the Jacques' land appear literally completely harmless. In addition, it makes easier the delivery of a mobile home to a neighbor, and so carries autonomy-enhancing implications for the recipients as well as, indirectly, the defendants' employees.

How can tort-law reform itself so as to address valueless conflicts such as *Jacque*? As I explain elsewhere, one answer points toward adopting the American modality of trespass to chattels in lieu of trespass to land.[61] The key difference between the two concerns a requirement of material interference.[62] Whereas liability for trespass to land does not depend on its occurrence, trespass to chattels does.[63] With the phrase material interference, tort law implies adverse consequences associated with impairment.[64] It concerns diminishing the thing's value, for instance, by damaging it.[65] On this modality, instead of deeming every nonconsensual entry actionable per se, courts should employ a standard of material interference—in terms of impairment—in order to deny land owners the right to engage in exclusive possession under circumstances of valueless land-control conflicts.[66]

V. Moving Forward: From Conflict to Equality

The ambition of the argument in the previous chapters has been to defend the conflict theory of tort law. The traditional conception of tort law is nicely captured by the idea of tort law as the law of (private) wrongs or harms; it is sometimes supplemented by the law of redress or of cost-internalization. On these conceptions, tort law is tasked with tackling certain forms of human failing (such as by allocating resources back, rectifying wrongs, empowering victims to obtain satisfaction, or internalizing social costs). Its value is negative or preventative.

[60] On the centrality of usability to property, see Ernest J. Weinrib, *Ownership, Use, and Exclusivity: The Kantian Approach*, 31 Ratio Juris 123, 131–32 (2018).

[61] A second, more advanced and systematic solution, recall, is Scotland's Land Reform (Scotland) Act, 2003. A third one would be to keep the current regime of trespass to land, but introduce carveouts that remove protection where conflict theory supports it.

[62] By contrast, the English approach to trespass to chattels makes "minor" interference a sufficient basis for actionability. *See* Simon Douglas, Liability for Wrongful Interference with Chattels 114 (2011).

[63] Restatement (Second) of Torts § 218 (1965).

[64] *See further id.*, at §219. To be sure, interference with chattels is not limited to impairing. At times, a wrongdoer may also execute a plan to convert the thing to their say-so authority. Such instances of *dethroning* are traditionally addressed by the tort of conversion.

[65] Dispossession harms the owner's effective rather than theoretical control, whenever using their thing is blocked by the dispossessor's act. The blocking constitutes dispossession of the thing but it need not involve impairing it. The interpretive task of determining what counts as dispossessing the owner of their effective control over a thing can sometimes be complicated by the nature of the thing and the use to which it is put by the owner. *Cf.* Maureen E. Brady, *Property and Projection*, 133 Harv. L. Rev. 1143, 1166 (2020).

[66] *See further* Dorfman, *supra* note 29, at 112–14.

However, reducing tort law to the law of wrongs (et alia) misses a significant way in which tort law engages with value. Rather than merely preventing, tort law plays an important role in constructing and facilitating conflicts. Unlike the law of wrongs (et alia), tort law responds to conflicts that are anything but instances of human failing. Constructing the conditions necessary for these conflicts—that is, inherently valuable conflicts—to arise partially answers the question of why we have to have (the right kind of) tort law. (I say *partially* because the equality theory, the subject matter of the next Part of this book, is a necessary part of the answer, too.)

Tort law remains loyal to its enabling, positive value even when conflicts are not inherently valuable. This is in the case of tolerably valuable conflicts. I have argued that tort law engages in the realization of any number of fundamental interests, or subsets thereof, across divergent spheres of action. There, tort law is not reducible to the prevention of wrongs, harms, or costs, but rather renders possible, or more available, valuable human interactions and practices.

These conclusions follow from a better appreciation of the moral significance of human conflict and, more specifically, the *variety* of such conflict. My analysis suggests that engaging with the value (and disvalue) of human conflict is the *first virtue* of the legal institution called tort law. It marks the first step in vindicating tort law. Indeed, it is necessary but, as just mentioned, not sufficient for the purpose of addressing the vindication challenge I presented at the outset.

Hence, Part III moves from moral function to form. It takes up the peculiar form of tort law—that of responding to conflicts in the form of imposing one-to-one, directed legal rights and duties. I argue that a necessary element in the vindication of tort law is a certain account of relational equality I shall call substantive equality. This would provide the second necessary step in vindicating tort law, as it seeks to defend the necessary place of *equality* between those whose safety, liberty, sociability, and other fundamental interests come into conflict. The argument going forward, therefore, seeks to defend what I shall call the equality theory of tort law.

One might wonder how the conflict and equality theories of tort law interact. What comes first, the function—conflict theory—or the form—equality theory? I discuss these questions in more detail in Part III. To provide a rough sense of the answer, which has already been outlined in the Introduction, I argue that function comes first in the order of grounds in the sense that the theory of conflict determines what human interactions should typically be governed by tort law, and so what torts we should have in the first place. The conflict theory also guides how we ought to think about and engage with the conflicting interests, namely, as warranting construction (and facilitation), containment, or prevention.

The demand for the equality theory comes to life at this point: conflict theory's regulative principles—construction (and facilitation), containment, and prevention—must lead to the determination of legal rights and duties (along with other legal rules). For instance, recognizing a conflict between an individual's interest in artistic expression and another's reputational interest as inherently valuable implies that the conditions for such a conflict must be constructed. To fulfill this constructivist mandate, tort law must define legal rights and duties that address this conflict in the right way. As mentioned in the Introduction and further demonstrated in Chapters 2, 3, and 8–10, conflict theory already provides the normative resources required to determine the rights and duties in cases involving inherently valuable conflicts. The same holds true for valueless conflicts, as shown in Chapters 5, 6, and 8–9.

Tolerably valuable conflicts are different. In these cases, equality theory complements conflict theory. The task of containing tolerably valuable conflicts requires an assessment of the relative importance of the competing claims. Equality theory offers an egalitarian calculus—considering both interests and conditions—to guide this containment analysis. In this way, it complements the conflict theory by articulating the normative standard necessary to address tolerably valuable conflicts in the right way. Chapters 13–15 further elaborate on and illustrate this complementary relationship.

Finally, the equality theory is necessary for vindicating tort law for a more fundamental reason. As I argue in Chapter 12, equality theory is necessary to defending the very existence of the pairwise structure of tort duties. More specifically, it establishes, first, why have duties at all and, second, why these duties must be *tort* duties. Before turning to that argument, however, Chapter 11 sets the stage for the equality theory of tort law by defending the conflict theory case for a tort of discrimination.

10
The Tort of Discrimination

Introduction

In this chapter, I defend the case for a novel tort of discrimination by addressing two fundamental questions: First, why such a tort is necessary and, second, how its proper scope should be determined. My answer to the first question draws on the discussion of trespass to land in Chapter 9 as well as my earlier philosophical and legal analyses of discrimination.[1] The answer to the second question invokes the conflict theory, which helps to tell legally impermissible from legally permissible discrimination. This distinction has so far proven challenging as not all instances of discrimination are wrongful, some may even be valuable, and even instances of otherwise wrongful discrimination need not give rise to a legal duty of nondiscrimination. I argue that conflict theory's emphasis on the three different types of value underlying conflicts of fundamental interests offers an appealing normative framework for addressing this complexity.

Tort duties, and their corresponding rights, protect our fundamental interests from the conflicting interests of other private persons. However, two interests have not received sufficient recognition. Chapter 17 addresses one of these—free speech and the corresponding tort of private censorship—while this chapter focuses on the other, namely, that of *being treated as an equal* to the other party to an interaction as well as to all the others interacting with this party.[2] A legal right to be treated as an equal entitles one to engage with another private individual on terms that respect both of them as substantively free and equal persons. As a claim-right held against other private persons, this right implies that all else being equal, our traits and choices must not be held against us across a wide range of voluntary interactions, including (though not limited to) market transactions. This right seeks to dismantle transactional barriers set up by other private persons when applying their (genuine or purported) normative powers, such as those

[1] Hanoch Dagan & Avihay Dorfman, The Powers of Discrimination (unpublished manuscript); Hanoch Dagan & Avihay Dorfman, Relational Justice: A Theory of Private Law ch. 13 (2024); Hanoch Dagan & Avihay Dorfman, *The Tort of Discrimination*, 16 J. Tort L. 393 (2023).

[2] The reference here to third parties must not be interpreted as a way of smuggling in the public concerns that dominate existing antidiscrimination scholarship. It is often a necessary means for determining what counts as just terms of interaction between the pertinent parties (say, a seller and a buyer). Eliminating wrongful discrimination of the buyer by the seller implies a comparison to the way this seller treats that buyer to the way this seller treats other (existing and potential) buyers.

Conflict between Equals. Avihay Dorfman, Oxford University Press. © Oxford University Press 2026.
DOI: 10.1093/9780198979869.003.0013

embedded in contractual and property rights. It entails a corresponding duty to avoid wrongful discrimination and warrants a tort of discrimination that further entrenches this duty and provides recourse for its breach. Note that I use "discrimination" not only in the narrow sense of reluctance to employ, sell, lease, or include but also in the broader sense of failure to accommodate the needs—including those related to socioeconomic condition such as poverty—and interests of another. Moreover, the necessary role of (genuine or purported) normative powers in the analysis of discrimination further suggests that wrongful discrimination is not merely a case of bad apples but rather also a feature of the (un)just design of these normative powers—thus, it is not solely a feature of the blameworthiness, irrationality, or harmful effects of a particular discriminator but also a feature of structural injustice.

This way of presenting the matter raises the two questions mentioned a moment ago. The first concerns the need for a *tort* of discrimination—why have a general tort of discrimination (similar to the tort of negligence) when statutory prohibitions against discrimination already exist in specific contexts such as employment, housing, consumer transactions, education, and credit markets? My answer is twofold. First, tackling discrimination through context-specific prohibitions suffers from a structural deficiency: Discrimination is an *evolving* phenomenon and is therefore unlikely to conform neatly to fixed contextual categories. Second, a judge-made tort of discrimination transforms the right to be treated as an equal into a choice-independent entitlement. Unlike statutory rights, which are typically grounded in the choices of the political majority, a common-law tort conveys that this right does not depend—for its validity and cogency—on majoritarian support.

The second question concerns the boundaries of a general tort of discrimination. As already noted, there is an important distinction between discrimination and wrongful discrimination. A general tort, therefore, must rely on a normative framework—a theory capable of distinguishing legally permissible from impermissible discrimination. This is where the conflict theory suggests itself, providing a framework to identify the pertinent considerations and to determine legal rights and duties in response to them.

The case for a tort of discrimination seeks to vindicate the law of torts as the law of conflicts in another way as well. It moves beyond the wrongs, harms, recourse, or cost-internalization conceptions of tort law. Saddling tort law with these conceptions obscures what truly matters. After all, questions about wrongdoing, harming, recourse, or cost-internalization do not themselves provide a *theory* of what substantive rights and duties we have but rather presuppose their existence. In the absence of an account of substantive rights, common-law courts may struggle to address what is, essentially, private discrimination. Moreover, as I argue below, even a rights-based tort theory such as the Toronto School of corrective justice may lack the normative resources not only to determine when private discrimination is wrongful but also, more fundamentally, to explain why it might be wrongful *in the first place*. Tort law as the law of conflicts provides an appealing answer.

I. Private Discrimination Law: From Denial to Partial Acceptance

The right to be treated as an equal is not simply an instance of a legal entitlement gone missing. Indeed, it is not a story of neglect or of an otherwise respectable right having to, perhaps tragically, give way to other more important rights. Instead, the traditional approach to trespass to land, and to private law more generally, *denies* this right's very existence claiming that a right to be treated as an equal undermines the normative order to which this body of law belongs.[3] Recognizing this right, therefore, can change rather than merely revise that order in fundamental ways. I explain these claims by reference to two sets of distinctions—private versus public and formal versus substantive freedom and equality. Other explanations, including historical ones, could be adduced for the absence of a right to be treated as an equal. My goal is to identify and criticize a *conceptual* explanation—I do not ask why this right has failed to attain recognition but what conception of tort law, and private law more generally, might have justified its exclusion.

A. The Permissibility of Private Discrimination: The Traditional Starting Point

Consider a restaurant that refuses to serve green-eyed customers. Should this practice be legally permissible? Traditional private law answers this question in the affirmative. Normatively, this answer rests on a sharp distinction between public and private in terms of a distinction between inclusion and exclusion. In this account, the public space that includes institutions, entities, and goods governed by public-law norms is structurally egalitarian. Discrimination against green-eyed persons, say, when recruiting new government employees or when entering a public park, for example, is not merely unethical but also illegal. The all-inclusive character of the public space contrasts with the private one: Voluntary transactions between private persons should not be governed by public-law norms and, consequently, should not be subject to prohibitions on discrimination.

[3] *See, e.g.*, Robert Bork, *Civil Rights—A Challenge*, NEW REPUBLIC 22 (Aug. 31, 1963); Richard A. Epstein, *Public Accommodations Under the Human Rights Act of 1964: Why Freedom of Association Counts as a Human Right*, 66 STAN. L. REV. 1241, 1260–61 (2014). As will become clear, this is also evident in the modern Kantian (Toronto) account of private law.

The key to this picture is the idea that the justness of an interaction between private persons should be assessed by reference to independence and formal equality.[4] Private persons are thus absolutely free to choose partners for voluntary transactions as they see fit, and it is up to restaurant owners to decide whom to serve. Precluding this prerogative undermines the independence of the owners, who are now subject to other persons' choices regardless of whether green-eyed customers have visited the restaurant. It is the very existence of a right not to be discriminated against due to one's eye color that makes the owner subject to others. At the same time, the absence of a duty of nondiscrimination does not impinge on the independence of green-eyed diners because it only affects the *context* wherein they could still set and pursue ends.[5] For instance, they can eat elsewhere or cook for themselves. A duty of nondiscrimination violates the duty-ower's independence because it entitles customers to demand service from the owner.

This analysis can escape the discrimination-friendly prescriptions just noted in two ways. One is to preclude discrimination indirectly, attributing to the restaurant owner a different wrongdoing, such as misrepresentation or even deceit. The argument is that the restaurant, like many other "public accommodations," extends "a general invitation to the public to come in and do business" without being able to "choose which customers to serve."[6] It thereby implicitly undertakes to be open to the public and, therefore, presents itself as fully committed to serving people irrespective of eye color. Excluding green-eyed customers is certainly wrong, but not because it discriminates against green-eyed diners. Rather, the wrong lies in deceiving green-eyed customers who had relied on the owner's representation.

The second escape route takes the form of publicization.[7] Instead of analyzing this as a horizontal transaction between two private persons, it emphasizes its public aspects, highlighting the function on offer. In this argument, specific private entities cannot discriminate against green-eyed customers because they fulfill inherently public functions. Common carriers are a familiar case in point.[8] Shopping malls and, more recently, major social media platforms share, for free speech purposes, several public characteristics with the traditional town square.[9] Another public aspect concerns monopolistic market power in the provision of

[4] The Toronto School of corrective justice provides the most comprehensive and sophisticated defense of this idea. *See, e.g.*, Christopher Essert, Property in the Society of Equals (2024); Arthur Ripstein, Force and Freedom: Kant's Legal and Political Philosophy (2009).

[5] Ripstein, *supra*, at 49.

[6] Essert, *supra* note 4, at 214–15; Joseph William Singer, *Property and Sovereignty Imbricated: Why Religion Is Not an Excuse to Discriminate in Public Accommodations*, 18 Theoretical Inq. L. 519, 542 (2017). *See also* Creative LLC v. Elenis, 600 U.S. 570, 604–05 (2023) (Sotomayor J., dissenting).

[7] *Cf* Jody Freeman, *Extending Public Law Norms Through Privatization*, 116 Harv. L. Rev. 1285 (2003).

[8] The Civil Rights Cases, 109 U.S. 3, 37–39 (1883).

[9] Packingham v. North Carolina, 137 S. Ct. 1730, 1737 (2017); Robins v. PruneYard Shopping Ctr., 592 P.2d 341 (1979) *aff'd.* 447 U.S. 74 (1980).

basic goods—for instance, being the sole grocery or pharmacy in a small, isolated town can elevate this business to a position of dominance.[10]

Neither of these escape routes, however, explains why our restaurant owner should not be legally entitled to deny service to green-eyed customers. The owner can avoid liability for misrepresentation simply by explicitly announcing their discriminatory policy. In turn, redescribing the owner as a quasi-public official and the restaurant as fulfilling an inherently public or government function is highly artificial. In any event, resorting to a logic of misrepresentation or publicization merely explains away what is truly wrong about the discriminatory policy in question—to wit, that when applying their normative powers, restaurant owners must not treat would-be customers as unequal to them and other customers simply because of the color of their eyes. This failure is inherent in the uncompromising commitment to independence and formal equality.[11] I argue, by contrast, that green-eyed customers have a basic right to be treated as equals and that this right, like any other basic right in the law of torts, is necessary and sufficient to impose a prima facie duty of nondiscrimination on their discriminator.

B. The Civil Rights Acts: Revolution Incomplete

The civil rights revolution of the 1960s in the United States—and especially the creation of statutory duties of nondiscrimination in connection with public accommodations, employment, housing, and education—set out to change the traditional identification of voluntary interactions between private persons with independence and formal equality.[12] Other liberal jurisdictions have followed suit.[13] And yet, what to make of this change—and, specifically, what its nature and scope are—is less clear, at least on the conventional reading.

On this reading, prohibitions on discrimination in public accommodations, housing, education, and employment markets are meant to extend the reach of constitutionalism to some areas in the private sphere[14] by enlisting rights-holders in the service of meeting the demands of public justice.

[10] *See* Richard A. Epstein, *Takings, Exclusivity, and Speech: The Legacy of* PruneYard v. Robins, 64 U. Chi. L. Rev. 21, 39 (1997); Aravind Ganesh, *Wirtbarkeit: Cosmopolitan Right and Innkeeping*, 24 Legal Theory 159, 166–69 (2018).

[11] This relationship of entailment can be resisted by adopting a nonabsolutist conception of independence. *See generally* Anna Stilz, Territorial Sovereignty: Philosophical Exploration 112, 116 (2019).

[12] *See* 3 Bruce Ackerman, We the People: The Civil Rights Revolution 154, 211, 215 (2014).

[13] *See, e.g.*, Ontario Human Rights Code, R.S.O. 1990, ch.19.

[14] *See* Tarunabh Khaitan, A Theory of Discrimination Law 201 (2015); Johan van der Walt, The Horizontal Effect Revolution and the Question of Sovereignty 22 (2014).

Concretely, the state commandeers the support of certain private persons—commercial providers, landlords, and employers—to realize collective goals associated with democracy and distributive justice. The animating concern, therefore, is the justness of society as a whole rather than the justness of interactions between persons. The underlying rationale is that some private institutions, although perhaps less powerful and coercive than state institutions, profoundly influence society's democratic credentials. The citizens' ability to claim they have an equal say in politics and other dimensions of public life is largely contingent on the inclusiveness of markets for goods and services, employment, education, and housing.[15] In this approach, the Civil Rights Acts are primarily intended to remedy political inequality, thereby reinforcing the equal footing of citizens in a democracy.[16]

However, this interpretation is troublesome: Its civic foundation renders its prescriptions contingent on the need to remedy political inequality in our society. The case for these Acts loses momentum when political inequality recedes or even sufficiently narrows. Barring people from a restaurant due to the color of their eyes would then be unethical but entirely legal as long as the number and gravity of such instances remain relatively low. What makes discrimination legally wrong is only the *cumulative* effect of discrete instances of discrimination rather than each one of them severally.

Furthermore, thus perceived, these Acts are mere means to the ends of political equality and a thriving democracy. They can, therefore, be replaced by other means—either legal or extralegal—that may prove capable of attaining these ends in more effective and less costly ways.[17] Thus, generous programs of public housing and robust social practices of ethical consumerism could provide effective substitutes for existing statutory prohibitions of, respectively, private discrimination in housing, places of public accommodation, and employment. Indeed, under certain circumstances, these alternatives may emerge as plausible strategies for promoting political equality. Yet, though plausible from the perspective of the justice of the political community as a whole, they unacceptably relieve employers, lessors, sellers, and other holders of property or contractual power from the *duty* to refrain from discriminating against other private persons.[18]

[15] *See, e.g.*, ELIZABETH ANDERSON, THE IMPERATIVE OF INTEGRATION chs. 6–7 (2010); JUDITH N. SHKLAR, AMERICAN CITIZENSHIP: THE QUEST FOR INCLUSION 79–88 (1991).

[16] *See further* Anthony Sangiuliano, *Against Moralism in Antidiscrimination Law*, 73 U. TORONTO L.J. 467 (2024).

[17] *See* Tarunabh Khaitan & Sandy Steel, *Wrongs, Group Disadvantage and the Legitimacy of Indirect Discrimination Law*, *in* FOUNDATIONS OF INDIRECT DISCRIMINATION LAW 197, 199 (Hugh Collins & Tarunabh Khaitan eds. 2018).

[18] For an account of the value (in terms of relational equality) of being duty-bound to respect others as opposed to voluntarily respecting them, see Chapter 12.

II. The Case for a General Tort of Discrimination

A. Reinterpreting the Civil Rights Acts

The tort of discrimination I propose in this chapter builds on a reinterpretation of the Civil Rights Acts and their corollaries in other jurisdictions. By reinterpreting the Acts, I do *not* mean to imply that the public law of antidiscrimination sketched above should be set aside. Rather, I claim that, besides their important public role, the Acts can and should be viewed as also instantiating an internal reform of the traditional tort-law approach. The private duties of nondiscrimination and the private rights of action against discriminators stand for a transformation of the balance of legal power enshrined in the traditional private-law rules of trespass to land, as well as private ownership, and freedom of contract aimed at securing the status of the interacting parties as substantively free and equal persons.

The interacting parties, it is important to note, are not necessarily members of the same political community. The prescriptions at hand, therefore, focus on how things stand between them rather than only on the collective effects on the political community.[19] This reading of the Acts further implies that their closed list of prohibited grounds and relatively narrow scope need not mean that other types of discrimination are permissible.

On the proposed reinterpretation, the Acts' statutory duties are not exhaustive of the responsibility of private individuals to refrain from wrongful discrimination. This point is important because the Acts' context-based strategy of tackling discrimination leaves significant gaps.[20] For instance, gender and sexual orientation are not listed among the grounds prohibited in the context-based Title II (concerning discrimination in places of public accommodation), but that is no reason to render discrimination on these bases legally permissible. Moreover, many courts interpret Title II as mandating equal access to places of public accommodation but do not extend this norm to prohibiting inferior treatment or service.[21] Their exclusion from the purview of Title II, however, does not entail that they are legally permissible.[22] Finally, existing statutes (Title II and the Fair Housing Act, for instance) may not be suited to deal with a range of discriminatory practices, including discrimination in the enforcement of contracts of adhesion as well as in the platform

[19] *Contra* Erik Encarnacion, *Discrimination, Mandatory Arbitration, and Courts*, 108 Geo. L.J. 855, 865 (2020).

[20] *See* Joseph William Singer, *No Right to Exclude: Public Accommodations and Private Property*, 90 Nw. U. L. Rev. 1283, 1288–93 (1996).

[21] *See* Suja A. Thomas, *The Consumer Caste: Lawful Discrimination by Public Businesses*, 109 Cal. L. Rev. 141, 206 (2021). For the prevalence of such "consumer redlining," see Andrea Cann Chandrasekher, The "Good" Starbucks: Consumer Redlining in Large American Chain Stores (unpublished manuscript, October 2023) available at https://papers.ssrn.com/sol3/papers.cfm?abstract_id=4594953.

[22] *See* Singer, *supra* note 20, at 1290–91.

and gig economies.[23] Allowing discrimination, for example, in ride-sharing and short-term rental platforms cannot be justified on the grounds that statutory duties of nondiscrimination may fail to capture their business models.

B. Beyond the Context-Based Strategy of Contemporary Antidiscrimination Law

A *general* tort of discrimination is called for not merely because current context-based prohibitions on discrimination fail to provide adequate protection. Its absence gives rise to a structural, rather than contingent, deficiency. Thus, discrimination, like negligence, is an *evolving* phenomenon. Just like the failure to discharge a duty of care is bound to take new forms as society changes, attempts to use normative powers in defiance of others' right to be treated as equals can (and likely will) also be manifest in different, including unanticipated, ways. Technological progress only reinforces this difficulty by improving the ability to implement discriminatory practices far beyond the reach of the most comprehensive menu of context-based duties of nondiscrimination.

The evolving nature of discrimination poses unique challenges in the realm of systemic discrimination. This discrimination can persist because context-based duties of nondiscrimination outlaw *some* discriminatory practices while leaving all others in place and, thus, overlooking the intersectionality dimension of some discriminatory practices. Given that discrimination is sometimes structural or systemic, the absence of a general duty amounts to passive authorization of discriminatory practices that fall beyond the reach of existing context-based duties.

Recognizing a general duty of nondiscrimination addresses this significant lacuna. Since a general duty is, by definition, inclusive of wrongful discrimination of any sort, it can breed dynamism into the law of discrimination and its specific context-based duties. A general duty can thus perfect the ability of discrimination law to tackle wrongful discrimination by propelling context-based duties to make desirable changes. A stream of claims against the violation of the general duty can, for example, expose a vulnerability in the existing law and direct the adaptation of context-based duties. For instance, employment discrimination law should add political views and affiliations to the list of prohibited grounds.[24]

A wholesale duty can also help identify the need for and lead to the creation of *new* context-based duties of nondiscrimination. One case in point emerges when, out of a motley collection of discrimination claims, a substantial number

[23] *See respectively* Manisha Padi, *Contractual Inequality*, 120 MICH. L. REV. 825 (2022); Nancy Leong & Aaron Belzer, *The New Public Accommodations: Race Discrimination in the Platform Economy*, 105 GEO. L.J. 1271, 1276, 1297–98 (2017).

[24] Political views are absent from major employment discrimination laws such as United States's Title VII and United Kingdom's Equality Act 2010. *See further* Chapter 17.

of lawsuits happens to form a coherent category. A cluster of discrimination claims raised by gig economy workers (or contractors), for example, can move the legislature or courts to create a new duty of nondiscrimination appropriately attuned to the realities of this economy.[25]

Against this backdrop, a general duty is not merely a rule of conduct but also a potentially powerful engine of legal change. It also imply that, as discussed below, a general discrimination duty does not anticipate a legal path of ad hoc decision-making. Rather, such a duty is fully compatible with the dictates of the rule of law (recall Chapter 7), meaning that tort law's daily operations will mostly be governed by a list of established categories with relatively well-defined context-based duties, to be adapted and refined incrementally.[26]

Indeed, I do not argue against distinguishing between instances of discrimination based on context (such as employment, commerce, housing, education, etc.). Neither do I claim that legal standards for unlawful discrimination should ignore suspicious classifications and grounds for discrimination. Nor, finally, do I object to distinctions between types of discrimination, dividing instances of discrimination into disparate treatment, disparate impact, or failure of accommodation (as in instances of disability). Rather, I argue that the success of a context-based strategy hinges on the *prior recognition of a general tort of discrimination* that protects our basic right to be treated as an equal by other private persons whenever they hold (or purport to be holding) normative powers like those associated with property and contract.

Moreover, a wholesale duty changes the nature of law's commitment to the elimination of wrongful discrimination. A multiplicity of retail duties of nondiscrimination implies that private persons can be effectively protected against discrimination in specific spheres of action taken severally. Missing from this picture is a more holistic commitment against wrongful discrimination in the application of normative powers. To this end, freeing the right to be treated as an equal from its various contextual manifestations springs from its moral significance as a basic right, on par with the right to bodily and emotional integrity, privacy, good name, and so forth.

Indeed, wrongful discrimination should be a tort because, like a breach of the duty of due care at the core of the tort of negligence, it can be instance of grave relational injustice. All else being equal, the *interest* in being treated as an equal by other private persons should not be affected by a person's constitutive choices and traits. The significance of this (fundamental) interest derives from the freestanding role that our voluntary interpersonal interactions play in our ability to lead a life, let alone a successful one, as free and equal agents. Discrimination is analogous to

[25] *See, e.g.*, Naomi Chan et al., *Discrimination by Design?*, 51 Ariz. St. L Rev. 1, 54–55 (2019).

[26] *Cf.* George Rutherglen, *Concrete or Abstract Conceptions of Discrimination?*, *in* Philosophical Foundations of Discrimination Law 115 (Deborah Hellman & Sophia Moreau eds. 2013).

the erection of a transactional barrier and is thus wrongful if this barrier prevents the discriminatee from interacting with the discriminator in terms that reflect the status of both parties as substantively free and equal persons. Wrongful discrimination thus violates a legal right designed to protect this interest (and as I argue below, the conflict theory informs the transition from this interest to a corresponding legal right).

There is another, reinforcing reason to create a general tort of discrimination, assuming, as I do, that it would be judge-made. Currently, the legal response to private discrimination is not only context-dependent but also takes the form of statutory (and regulatory) prohibitions. A tort of discrimination would encourage judges to address a major gap in contemporary tort law: the normative starting point of the legality of private discrimination. It would shift the starting point and give judges (and juries) greater control and agency in shaping, applying, and enforcing duties of nondiscrimination.

There are instrumental considerations, concerning institutional competency, that support adding the judiciary to the governmental effort to combat wrongful discrimination.[27] However, a judge-made duty of nondiscrimination is also valuable in a noninstrumentally sense. Drawing on my work with Alon Harel, the choice of law-making institution can itself implicate the value of the good at stake—in this case, a discrimination-free society.[28] A statutory duty of nondiscrimination stands for the proposition that a majority of the electorate deems certain forms of discrimination impermissible. This duty reflects—and ultimately depends for its legitimacy on—the majority's choice (or judgment). What may be lacking here is not necessarily the concern that the majority could one day withdraw its commitment to opposing wrongful discrimination. After all, it might be that the polity is, and will remain, decent. Rather than identifying the lack of robust entrenchment as the core issue, I argue that the problem with a statutory duty of nondiscrimination lies in its grounding: Its significance derives from what we—the majority, here and now—choose to value, rather than what we are *duty*-bound to value.

By contrast, a judge-made duty of nondiscrimination is not, and should not be, grounded in the will or choice of the majority. Instead, it rests on a universal obligation that exists, and ought to remain, independently of what the people choose or desire. Indeed, the legitimacy of such a court-enacted duty depends not on the preferences of the judges who recognize it but on the force of reason that justifies it. The duty should be understood not only as a prohibition against

[27] For different elaborations of this proposition, see SEANA VALENTINE SHIFFRIN, DEMOCRATIC LAW 81–88 (2021); HANOCH DAGAN, RECONSTRUCTING AMERICAN LEGAL REALISM AND RETHINKING PRIVATE LAW THEORY 50–59 (2013); ALAN BRUDNER WITH JENNIFER M. NADLER, THE UNITY OF THE COMMON LAW ch. 7 (2d ed. 2013).

[28] Avihay Dorfman & Alon Harel, *The Necessity of Institutional Pluralism*, 43 OXFORD J. LEGAL STUD. 753 (2023); AVIHAY DORFMAN & ALON HAREL, RECLAIMING THE PUBLIC ch. 3 (2024). *See also* Avihay Dorfman & Alon Harel, Constitutionalism and Majoritarianism Reconciled (unpublished manuscript).

wrongful discrimination (which could, after all, be enacted through statute) but as an expression of a deeper principle: that such a prohibition does not—and should not—depend on the preferences or judgments of citizens. It binds the political community regardless of its collective will, and its value lies, in part, in the independence of its normative force from our contingent choices.

* * *

In the remainder of this chapter, I elaborate these propositions by addressing three key issues. The first concerns the relational justice foundations of a general tort of discrimination; the second, the critical contribution of conflict theory in delineating the proper scope of this tort; and the third, the doctrinal building blocks of the proposed tort. Concerning the first issue, I argue that wrongful discrimination is not contingent on the discriminator's deliberation or mental state, nor on any specific harm inflicted on the discriminatee, on a particular social group, or on society as a whole. Concerning the second issue, I contend that a general duty of nondiscrimination, like the general duty of care in negligence, is not without limits, and that the conflict theory provides the normative framework necessary to define its proper scope. Concerning the third, I draw on existing doctrines in and around tort law to identify the legal tools required to articulate the essential elements of the tort of discrimination—duty, breach, injury, causation, and remedy.

III. Wrongful Discrimination as a Tort

A. Discrimination's Relational Dimension

Drawing on my work with Hanoch Dagan, relational justice provides the normative basis for a general tort of discrimination.[29] Contrary to accounts of wrongful discrimination that view the discriminatee as a member of a certain social group,[30] relational justice theory makes no such essential reference: the discriminatee figures as a person *even when* not a member of one or another social group. Moreover, unlike the perception of wrongful discrimination as a failure to treat the discriminatee as equal to others in society,[31] my account suggests, as I presently explain, that this failure is ultimately relational—the failure of the discriminator is not treating the discriminatee as equal to the *discriminator*.

This relational failure is measured against the normative baseline that views persons as substantively, rather than formally, free and equal agents, thus rejecting

[29] *See supra* note 1.
[30] *See, e.g.*, Sophia Moreau, Faces of Inequality: A Theory of Wrongful Discrimination 50–51, 59, 62 (2020).
[31] *See id.*, at 191, 227.

the reductive view of persons as possessors of a capacity for choice (recall the Toronto School of corrective justice) or as preference maximizers (according to lawyer economists). It thus relies on the core distinction between the features that make us who we are and our sheer preferences. Hence, while discrimination based on a person's sheer preferences may be frustrating, discrimination based on their ground projects is prima facie wrongful because it is an instance of failing to relate to people as who they really are.[32] Besides such projects, unchosen conditions also partially define who we are in our own perception, which is partially shaped by how others see us. These conditions consist of personal and socially constructed traits and may include a person's height, race, disability, and socioeconomic condition. Many of these traits are socially salient because they immediately link individuals to a social group, subjecting them to the expectations, assumptions, and biases held regarding that group. Other traits, however, lack social salience and may be purely personal—eye color, for instance, is a trait that may cut across social groups. But even these personal traits may become socially salient (including negative stereotypes) or serve as a proxy for other socially salient traits.

That said, a personal trait is literally part of who people are, and holding it against them is, therefore, prima facie wrongful.[33] For instance, barring a person from a restaurant or rejecting someone's job candidacy on this basis is inconsistent with treating them as who they really are, and the fact that this trait (currently or even potentially) carries no badge of social inferiority does not launder the wrong.

Private discrimination is wrongful when it violates a person's right to be treated as an equal. This right, which places the constitutive choices and traits of the right-holder at its moral center, implies that people are prima facie entitled not to have their constitutive choices or traits held against them when others exercise their normative power (qua employers, owners, landlords, providers of goods or services, et alia). Using these powers in defiance of this principle constitutes wrongful discrimination. Three distinctions help to clarify this view: motive versus conduct, harm versus injustice, and process versus outcome.

B. Motive versus Conduct

The motives of wrongful discrimination vary. Discriminators are often moved by attitudes associated with bigotry or animus toward their discriminatees. At times,

[32] There is some overlap between this account and Frankfurt's account of the wrong of disrespect as "deal[ing] with [a person] as though he is not what he actually is." Harry Frankfurt, *Equality and Respect*, 64 Soc. Research 3, 12 (1997). That said, I do not share his narrow understanding (and critique) of what is egalitarianism. Moreover, unlike Frankfurt, I deny that wrongful discrimination (disrespect in his case) hinges on the discriminator's intention. *Id.*, at 8.

[33] *Contra* Kasper Lippert-Rasmussen, *The Badness of Discrimination*, 9 Ethical Theory & Moral Practice 167, 169 (2006).

discriminators act out of rational concerns, such as the economic prospects of their business, as when a business owner realizes that she will lose many White customers if she does not discriminate against Black ones. Another motive for discrimination is ethical or religious beliefs that oppose serving, hiring, or simply interacting with another person in a particular context or in general.

Should motives matter, then, for deeming a discriminatory act wrongful? I say no.[34] Discrimination can be wrongful even when it is *un*motivated. Discrimination should count as wrongful not because it is driven by a specific motive (or attitude) but because it is an act of a certain kind—it denies the discriminatees' ability to interact with the discriminator in terms that reflect their status as substantively free and equal persons. I certainly do *not* argue that motive never matters. It does matter, for instance, for the purpose of determining the fitting response—in terms of a proper remedy—to an instance of wrongful discrimination, as shown below. But ill motive should not be necessary for determining what counts as wrongful discrimination.

To see why discrimination can be unmotivated and, at the same time, wrongful, consider a straightforward instance of indirect discrimination (a.k.a. disparate impact). It features a rigorous audition process for a professional orchestra that, year after year, ends up admitting mostly (or even only) white male players.[35] The auditors could be motivated solely by a desire to recruit the best-qualified candidates and, therefore, the failure to select musicians who are neither white nor male is unrelated to any discriminatory motivations. In tort-law parlance, this procedure reflects inadvertence on the part of unconsciously biased auditors.

Inadvertently failing to include nontrivial numbers of female and nonwhite musicians is, prima facie, an instance of wrongful discrimination. The wrongness lies in the holding of certain traits—race and sex—against musicians who, although as good as those selected, were not chosen. Rather than the motives, the "holding" represents the terms of the interaction that seem to govern the job selection process, implying that certain musicians are less likely to be considered solely on the basis of their professional qualifications because of who they are. Adopting these terms is akin to erecting a transaction barrier preventing candidates from interacting with their auditors (or would-be employers) as substantively free and equal persons.

I do not argue that this barrier reflects a conscious, let alone deliberate, decision to exclude female and nonwhite musicians. Instead, using their normative powers in a way that denies certain candidates their right to be treated as equals reflects

[34] *Contra* John Gardner, *Discrimination: The Good, the Bad, and the Wrongful*, 118 Proc. Aristotelian Soc'y 55, 57–58 (2018); Benjamin Eidelson, Discrimination and Disrespect 17 (2015).

[35] Based, in part, on a true story. *See* Claudia Goldin & Cecilia Rouse, *Orchestrating Impartiality: The Impact of "Blind" Auditions on Female Musicians*, 90 Am. Econ. Rev. 715 (2000).

inadvertence on the part of the auditors, who *could* have adopted a more impartial selection process. Neglecting the right of female and nonwhite musicians to be treated as equals—like similar neglects pertaining to other fundamental rights that we hold against other private persons—is what turns this process into wrongful discrimination.

C. Harm versus Injustice

Influential accounts of discrimination often identify its wrongfulness with one or another harmful consequence.[36] One such approach states that discrimination is wrongful because it is demeaning or subordinating.[37] Other accounts locate discrimination's wrongfulness in the cost it imposes on certain freedom interests of the discriminatees. For instance, discrimination can undermine the discriminatees' ability to deliberate freely about where to work, live, or dine.[38] It can also undermine another aspect of freedom when it limits or reduces the range of available options to choose from.[39] Without denying that wrongful discrimination can often lead to these (or other) adverse consequences, discrimination can count as wrongful even when none of these consequences do or are likely to follow.[40]

Consider a hypothetical case featuring a "harmless" instance of discrimination involving a baker who refuses to bake a wedding cake for a same-sex couple.[41] A discriminatory act of this sort could generate any number of harms to the couple, perpetuating (by themselves or by others) the social and political subordination of the social group they are associated with. Yet, if the market for wedding cakes faces robust competition *and* the society where the parties live is overwhelmingly liberal and inclusive, these effects could be avoided.[42] The refusal at issue, then, does not reflect the baker's "social power" to subordinate the couple.[43] He does not intend to relate to the couple as unworthy or in any way inferior, nor is his message interpreted by most members of the society as an attempt to do so.

[36] I define harm capaciously to include both material harms—such as eliminating options from which to choose or making people worse off in some other ways—and expressive harms—such as conveying the demeaning or subordinate status of the discriminatee.

[37] DEBORAH HELLMAN, WHEN IS DISCRIMINATION WRONG? (2008).

[38] Sophia Moreau, *What Is Discrimination?*, 38 PHIL. & PUB. AFF. 143, 147–53 (2010).

[39] John Gardner, *Liberals and Unlawful Discrimination*, 9 OXFORD J. L. STUD. 1, 18–19, 21 (1989).

[40] *Contra* KASPER LIPPERT-RASMUSSEN, BORN FREE AND EQUAL: A PHILOSOPHICAL INQUIRY INTO THE NATURE OF DISCRIMINATION 157, 161, 173–74 (2014).

[41] As will become clear, I do *not* discuss the true case of *Masterpiece Cakeshop v. Colorado Civil Rights Commission*, 584 U.S. 617 (2018), but a substantively modified one.

[42] For a different discussion of the idea of harmless discrimination, see Adam Slavny & Tom Parr, *Harmless Discrimination*, 21 LEGAL THEORY 100 (2015).

[43] Deborah Hellman, *Discrimination and Social Meaning*, *in* THE ROUTLEDGE HANDBOOK OF THE ETHICS OF DISCRIMINATION 97, 102 (Lippert-Rasmussen ed. 2018).

The same holds when we switch from accounts that emphasize the demeaning impact of subordination to those that take discrimination to be wrongful because it might mark the social group the discriminatees belong to as inferior while perpetuating the superiority of the discriminator's social group.[44] The hypothetical case under consideration does not generate any concern about group subordination since the social and political power imbalance works in precisely the opposite direction. Indeed, it is the baker who may be part of a small and vulnerable religious community. His refusal reflects—and is widely understood to reflect—his attempt to preserve a traditional way of life in the face of strong cosmopolitan pressures.[45] If wrongful discrimination is identified with its demeaning connotations or with its contribution to group subordination, the baker is not necessarily guilty as charged.

Moreover, making the demeaning aspects of this hypothetical case the root cause of what makes the discrimination wrongful is troublesome not only because it is unnecessary, as just intimated. It is also problematic because appealing to indignities and emotional setbacks immediately opens the door to the discriminator's own complaint.[46] His complaint, recall, is grounded in a sincere religious or ethical commitment, and coercing him to serve the couple could be experienced by him and his fellow adherents as demeaning and even humiliating, especially given the existence of many other equally competent bakers out there.

Does this baker harm the freedom of the couple by inviting, or even forcing them, to "factor into their deliberations" their conception of marriage and family life "*as costs*"?[47] That is, is the couple indeed wronged by being forced to "always have before their eyes, as they deliberate" their traits or conceptions of the good?[48] Alternatively, does he harm their freedom by limiting the range of available options to advance their autonomous life or by undermining a public culture of autonomy?[49]

The answer to both these questions is no. Given that the alternatives available to the couple are nearly unlimited, discrimination at the hands of *only* one baker does not threaten their freedom to deliberate without having to internalize the cost of their conception of the good. A similar conclusion applies when the consequential harm is cast in terms of a diminished range of options and a weakened public culture of autonomy: One less option will not destabilize the range itself and the

[44] *See* MOREAU, *supra* note 30, at 50–51, 59, 62.

[45] *Cf.* CHRISTOPHER L. EISGRUBER & LAWRENCE G. SAGER, RELIGIOUS FREEDOM AND THE CONSTITUTION 52, 59 (2007).

[46] *See further* Ontario Human Rights Commission v. Brockie, 222 DLR (4th) 174 (Ont. Div. Ct., 2002) at para. 20, in which a Canadian Court defined the matter in terms of a "conflict of dignities."

[47] Moreau, *supra* note 38, at 149.

[48] MOREAU, *supra* note 30, at 191. *See also id.*, at 83, 84, 85, 91, 94, 105, 109. Moreau argues that being forced to take one's conception of marriage and family life should be seen "as costs." In that light, it is reasonable to claim that these costs (like costs generally) are relative. The cost of being discriminated by one out of two available service providers is entirely different from a case featuring one discriminator out of one hundred providers—to wit, the latter is virtually costless and, accordingly, nearly harmless.

[49] Gardner, *supra* note 39, at 21.

multitude of attractive possibilities. The baker's refusal will not derail the public culture of autonomy since the impact of his discriminatory practice is more than offset by the inclusive commitment of all other service providers in this and all other market contexts.

That said, this discrimination may be harmless and still *wrongful* due to the baker's use of his normative powers in a way that is incompatible with the couple's right to be treated as equals. This instance is strikingly analogous to deeming a physician's interference with their patient's bodily integrity wrong without their consent (when it could have been secured), even if otherwise harmless.[50] Validating the use of normative powers in defiance of the couple's right to be treated as equals would imply *entitling* the baker to turn a constitutive choice of the couple (concerning marriage, family, and love) into a transactional barrier. An entitlement to erect such a barrier is incompatible with interacting with the persons making up this couple as the persons they are. It is also incompatible with the demands of the conflict theory as the conflict between the couple and the baker, recall Chapter 9, is inherently value: Instead of isolating people in their sectarian corners, the liberal-egalitarian response to pluralism empowers market participants to seek one another's recognition as interactable not merely in spite, but rather *because*, of enduring ethical disagreements concerning the good life.

The baker's wrongful conduct reflects a normative shortfall in how things stand between the parties, irrespective of its harmful consequences. Another way to vindicate this point is by replacing same-sex marriage with miscegenation and supposing that the law on the books does not specifically prohibit discrimination based on race. Can a baker wield his normative power to deny service to a mixed-race couple because baking a cake for them contrasts with his sincere religious belief in racial purity? An affirmative answer implies that the practice of contract could legitimately confer such a power. However, this presupposition necessarily flies in the face of liberalism's basic commitment to freedom and equality and, in particular, the right of the marrying couple to be treated as equals.

Therefore, private discrimination is wrongful regardless of whether it carries overtones of contempt or diminishes opportunities. The only way out of this relational injustice is to take back the entitlement in question and hold commercial bakers independently responsible for making their services sufficiently inclusive. The baker should owe the couple a duty to refrain from holding their constitutive choice against them. Their terms of voluntary interaction in applying their normative powers must meet the basic threshold of treating the couple as self-determining and substantively equal persons.

[50] *See* Mohr v. Williams, 104 N.W. 12 (Minn. 1905). Note that battery is an intentional tort. As I argue below, the tort of discrimination should go beyond intentional wrongdoing to capture unintentional acts of discrimination.

D. Process versus Outcome

The question of what renders discrimination in the exercise of legal powers wrongful typically focuses on outcomes rather than processes. It considers the permissibility of final decisions concerning exclusion and inclusion, or favorable and unfavorable treatment. Left outside is the *process* leading up to such decisions. By placing the exercise of normative powers at the center of my account, a tort of discrimination should also address the question of how these powers are exercised.

A key process-based concern arises in connection with discrimination based on statistical inferences. Power-holders often resort to statistical knowledge about persons when making hiring, renting, selling, and other similar decisions.[51] For instance, resorting to reliable data showing a high correlation, say, between eye color and work productivity, or between age and ability to complete difficult manual tasks, represents one way of making informed hiring decisions.

I argue that a power-holder can set aside statistically reliable data or deploy it in ways that are consistent with the demands of relational justice. Opting for the latter, power-holders assume the substantive burden of shifting from generalizations to a person's particular situation. For instance, when a moving company seeks to hire movers, it may be rational, economically speaking, to prefer younger to older candidates given the probability of a statistically significant correlation between old age and poor performance in the moving industry. But the pertinent hiring officer must also be open to consider senior candidates based on their actual physical condition. Thus, while statistical data can establish a default decision-making rule, a real option for rebutting it must be available so that the ultimate hiring decision is based on the candidate's specific data.[52]

As long as this process does not overreach—as long as it does not undermine duty-owers' pursuit of their own self-determination—it should apply to everyone and not only to members of a disenfranchised or otherwise socially marginalized group. Thus, our hiring officer cannot use reliable statistical data—say, that people with a graduate degree in the humanities are highly likely to be physically weak—to refrain from considering a candidate with a Ph.D. in history.

Yet, this accommodation burden could grow more demanding in categories of cases featuring heightened vulnerabilities. (The same is true, I argue in Chapter 15, in the case of disability in the negligence doctrine of the reasonable person.) The relevant concern here is the dignity of the candidates considered. The basic intuition suggests that resorting to statistical data with respect to humanities graduates is quite different from doing so with respect to a member of a disenfranchised

[51] *See generally* Kenneth Arrow, *The Theory of Discrimination* (Princeton Univ. Indus. Rel. Working Paper, No. 30A, 1971); Michelle J. Budig & Paula England, *The Wage Penalty for Motherhood*, 66 Am. Socio. Rev. 204, 208–10 (2001).

[52] A decision is made "on the basis" of specific data if, in the case of refusing to hire the person, such data is a but-for cause for disqualifying the candidate.

social group. Generally speaking, resorting to damaging generalizations reflects a failure to deal with them as the persons they really are. But failing to do so with respect to a member of a marginalized group aggravates the relational injustice by attaching to this person a label of social inferiority.

Thus, the substantive burden of shifting from generalizations to a person's particular situation is not unitary. It should reflect, in some measure, the expected vulnerability of individuals to inferences about who they really are drawn on the basis of their (actual or perceived) membership in disenfranchised groups. *Those* inferences are unacceptable even in contexts where reliance on statistical data is generally justified.[53]

* * *

What makes discrimination wrongful is that it represents a failure to interact with discriminatees as the persons they are, including the constitutive choices and traits that shape them. It is for this reason, as noted, that discrimination's wrongfulness dispenses with the discussion of the discriminator's mental state and deliberative process, disentangling wrongful discrimination from the consequential harms it often inflicts on discriminatees, on certain social groups, or on society as a whole. Releasing the tort of discrimination from the shackles of intentionality and harmful consequences is necessary for it to contend with the basic wrong of discrimination: overreaching the normative power that can be legitimately granted in a liberal society.

IV. General yet Limited Duty: Discrimination Meets Conflict Theory

The distinction between discrimination and wrongful discrimination, which is prima facie impermissible, implies that even a general duty of nondiscrimination must have a clearly defined scope. The idea of a general yet limited duty is familiar from the tort of negligence, which imposes a general duty of due care but does not extend without limits. For instance, this duty excludes certain areas of human behavior (recall Chapter 4's discussion of the business judgment rule and contact sports) where legal oversight is deemed inappropriate. I argue that the structure of the discrimination tort is analogous: A general duty that deliberately avoids encroaching on human interaction that should not fall under its purview. This is precisely where the conflict theory can help in demarcating the duty's proper boundaries by identifying when, and why, it is (im)permissible to hold individuals' constitutive choices and traits against them. In this way, the conflict theory provides

[53] Artificial intelligence and related methods of algorithmic decision-making raise further challenges, which I leave to another occasion.

the standard for determining whether cases that might otherwise be considered wrongful discrimination should *not* give rise to a duty of nondiscrimination.

Section A focuses on inherently valuable conflicts whereas Section B considers tolerably valuable ones. Together, these sections address the "why" and "when" questions posed earlier, demonstrating that the scope of a general duty of nondiscrimination can, and should, be determined on substantive rather than institutional grounds.

A. Discrimination and Inherently Valuable Conflicts

In what follows, I examine two paradigm cases of discrimination based on constitutive choices or traits that, I argue, should not be subject to a duty of nondiscrimination. Either case features fundamental interests whose conflict is inherently valuable, such that relieving the discriminator of a duty of nondiscrimination constructs the conditions necessary for realizing that value. This approach highlights two independently important aspects of the conflict theory of tort law. The first one is structural: The discussion illustrates the conflict theory's capacity as a normative framework to identify relevant considerations and determine their influence on the issue at hand. The second is substantive: The discussion clarifies our moral intuitions about the principled limits of tort duties (particularly, the duty of nondiscrimination).

1. The Good of Liberal Friendship and Intimate Relationships

As noted in Chapter 2, our fundamental interest in voluntary human interaction encompasses a range of activities through which we experience the society of others. Genuine friendship and intimate, loving relationships are subsets of this interest.[54] However, it is important to distinguish between freely chosen and arranged friendships and intimate relationships. I argue, first, that these two forms offer qualitatively different goods; second, that the former (free choice of friends and loved ones) conflicts with the interest in being treated as an equal; and third, that this conflict is inherently valuable. Against this backdrop, I contend that the general duty of nondiscrimination should not apply to relationships of friendship and intimacy *precisely because* these relationships should be based on constitutive choices and traits. On the conflict theory, therefore, the interest in being treated as an equal should not give rise to a corresponding legal right in the context of choosing friends and intimates.

To begin with, friendship and intimate relationships can hold significant value for the individuals involved *even when* they are arranged. Realizing such

[54] I say *genuine friendship* in recognition of other forms of "friendship," such as acquaintance friendship.

value depends on the abilities of the matchmaker, whether an experienced, well-informed human or a sophisticated artificial intelligence program. That said, the shift from arranged to self-chosen friendships or intimate relationships transforms both the nature and the value of these interactions and, ultimately, the broader social good of *liberal* friendship and intimacy. The source of this transformation does not lie in the epistemic and psychological advantages often associated with self-chosen relationships, namely, that individuals are generally best positioned to identify their ideal partners. While self-chosen relationships may be more or less successful than arranged ones, their distinctive value in a liberal society lies precisely in the fact that they are, well, self-chosen. They empower individuals to shape the character of their relationship, particularly by forming the attitudes and setting the expectations that define its role and meaning for them.[55]

Choosing friends and loved ones is deeply influenced by people's constitutive choices and traits. We are often drawn to individuals who possess certain characteristics or lead particular ways of life, as opposed to those who do not. This attraction is sometimes instinctual, shaped by forces that we cannot easily or rationally explain—Bizet's Carman famously captures this point by contrasting love with law.[56] At other times, by contrast, such choices may involve rational deliberation and introspection. In any case, the decision is inescapably tied to an (instinctual or reflective) assessment of the other person's constitutive choices and traits. It, therefore, necessarily comes at the expense of the interest in treating others as equals. To illustrate, inviting only one's male friends to a dinner—whether at a restaurant or at home—inevitably undermines the interest of those excluded on the basis of gender.

The right way to address the tension between the interest in self-chosen friendships and the interest in being treated as equals is to construct the conditions necessary for the good of liberal friendship to arise. The relational egalitarian ideal I defend in Part III of this book—the equality theory of tort law—must yield to the liberal conception of self-chosen friendship. To see why, consider the normative loss that arises when one is required to make decisions about whom to invite to a dinner gathering of friends without regard to gender or, alternatively, with the aim of creating a gender-balanced group of invitees. Filtering decisions about whom to invite, date, or marry through an egalitarian lens alters the nature and value of friendship and intimate relationships. While such requirements may promote a more egalitarian way of social life, subjecting how we practice friendship (or intimacy) to the demands of nondiscrimination ultimately undermines the good of liberal friendship.

[55] *See further* Joseph Raz, The Morality of Freedom 392–93 (1986).
[56] In the famous Habanera aria, Carmen sings (in French) love "has never, never known a law." Georges Bizet, Carmen (1875).

To conclude, the tort of discrimination responds in the right way to the conflict between friendship and equality interests by not extending the general duty of nondiscrimination to relationships of friendship and intimacy. A no-duty rule establishes a necessary condition for the good of liberal friendship to arise even as other forms of human relationships remain, as they should, subject to such a duty.

Finally, two clarifications are in order. First, in defending the priority of liberal friendship over equality, I am not claiming that all—or even most—decisions concerning friendship and intimate relationships are necessarily inegalitarian. At times, people may voluntarily and authentically align their social choices with egalitarian commitments. The case for a no-duty rule does not exclude such instances. Rather, it insists that the good of liberal friendship does not depend on the happenstance of such alignment. Accordingly, individuals should be entitled to choose their friends and loved ones as they see fit, including on the basis of constitutive choices and traits.

The second clarification is that the no-duty rule does not preclude moral criticism of individuals who make unacceptable decisions (e.g., racist) or adopt repugnant policies in selecting friends and intimates. As I argued in Chapters 2 and 3, the interest at stake here—the interest in being treated as an equal—is a fundamental one. Its normative significance does not disappear simply because there is no corresponding legal right; rather, it grounds legitimate moral criticism. Thus, although a person whose interest in being treated as an equal has been undermined by exclusion from a social gathering may not have a legal right to be included, they nonetheless have valid grounds to feel offended, to seek vindication of their equal standing, and to resent the host for the harm caused.

2. The Good of Excellence

The pursuit of our fundamental interest in self-determination often conflicts with other people's interest in being treated as equals. Frequently, the latter imposes constraints on the realization of the former. As previously discussed, and as I have further argued in earlier studies, legal duties of nondiscrimination imposed on providers of goods and services in the housing, consumer, credit, and labor markets reflect the moral necessity of such constraints. In these contexts, providers are entitled to pursue their own ends, but only in ways that remain consistent with the equality interests of their prospective parties (e.g., purchasers and employees).

However, the conflict between self-determination and equality should sometimes be approached differently. The value inherent in the cultivation and transmission of excellence may warrant a different approach, one that, within limits, prioritizes the pursuit of self-determination over the requirement to treat others as equals. To fix ideas, consider practices oriented toward excellence, such as ballet or basketball. It is possible to require that all ballet companies respect everyone's right to be treated as an equal. As a result, these companies would then comprise dancers of varying levels of performance, including dancers that, for objective reasons (say, not being flexible enough), cannot fully realize the aesthetic value that accompanies the skill, discipline, and self-expression of superb ballet dancers. Basketball, likewise, can be a highly competitive practice involving, among other things, the pursuit of athletic achievement, mastery of ball handling and shooting, and fine teamwork. On this view, making use of natural advantages is integral to the practice's value. Alternatively, basketball may also be conceived as an egalitarian activity whose value lies in fostering inclusion and sociability among team members and across teams. Having the right natural advantages, in this view, is neither the sole nor the primary criterion for participation. Instead, basketball becomes a celebration of the liberal commitment to recognize individuals as free and equal, entitled to shape their own lives and relate to others as equals. In what follows, I do not argue that egalitarian versions of basketball (or ballet) should be unsupported by the liberal state. Rather, I focus on their competitive counterparts, arguing for the priority of self-determining over equality in these contexts. The good of excellence in human actions and human beings justifies this ordering and, by extension, renders a general duty of nondiscrimination inapplicable when it comes to decisions about inclusion to or exclusion from such practices.

The conflict between egalitarian and excellence-driven practices such as ballet and basketball vividly illustrates what is at stake: whether the value of professional ballet or professional basketball merits its inescapably discriminatory character.[57] These examples highlight what *might* count as a reason for not recognizing a legal right to being treated as an equal: Prioritizing self-determination over equality in pursuits like ballet and basketball is warranted because, and insofar as, it involves the cultivation and transmission of excellence.

Two questions aptly arise. What is excellence and which practices should be considered excellence-striving for the purposes of the tort of discrimination? I address each in turn.

Excellence, following Anthony Kronman, is essentially "the rule of the best"[58] assessed by objective standards that transcend purely subjective forms of valuation. It stands in contrast to both the rule of the many (as in majoritarianism) and the rule of the wealthy and powerful.[59]

Now consider the scope of the case for exempting excellence-based practices from a general duty of nondiscrimination. Two major considerations figure prominently in this inquiry. The first concerns a critical liberal stance toward elevating excellence above the egalitarian commitment to eradicating status and hierarchy.

[57] Two caveats are in order. The excellence quality of a particular practice should be defined narrowly to include its core aspects only. Thus, professional ballet dancers may be required (by the internal demands of the practice) to a certain dress code while on stage; however, they may not be subject to discrimination for their dress-related choices elsewhere. Moreover, some excellence-striving practices may be (and perhaps have always been) corrupt or seriously deficient from a *liberal* perspective, in which case my argument for a no-duty rule does not apply.

[58] Anthony Kronman, The Assault on American Excellence 22 (2019).

[59] *Id.*

On this view, excellence can be justified in a liberal society only if it confined to "a few islands" within a broader sea of egalitarian social and political practices.

The second consideration involves determining which practices warrant their insulation from egalitarian commitments. The good of cultivating and transmitting excellence lacks the normative resources to answer the question: Excellence in what? That is, it cannot by itself determine which domains of knowledge production and human performance deserve special treatment. Some cases may be clear-cut, while others raise more difficult questions. Consistent with my argument in Chapter 2, the conflict theory does not displace social and political institutions and their commitments to a society's particular aspirations, traditions, and constraints.[60] As a result, identifying which aspects of excellence merit exemption may be partially informed by such "local" considerations, in addition to a more universal theory of what makes people's lives go well.[61] Against this backdrop, excellence-based exemptions from a general duty of nondiscrimination should be granted with close attention to these considerations.

B. Discrimination and Tolerably Valuable Conflicts

The conflict theory identifies another category of cases that should be exempt from the general duty of nondiscrimination: tolerably valuable conflicts. Two important legal doctrines fall into this category—affirmative action and *numerus clausus* (or closed list of suspect categories). I take each in turn.

1. Affirmative Action and the Just Society

The justificatory foundation of contemporary affirmative action programs may be overdetermined. In particular, some of these programs may be justified in terms of removing structural barriers to *relationally* just terms of interactions, say, between employers and employees. However, there are cases where relational justice does not require affirmative action. That said, considerations of distributive justice can also justify affirmative action, though this justification is transitory in nature.

Thus, increasing the participation of systemically marginalized persons and communities in major private and public institutions often requires employers, universities, and other entities to reject competent candidates simply because they belong to nonmarginalized social groups. Such rejections involve holding

[60] One important commitment can, and should, be to fair equality of opportunity. The fact that some forms of excellence are valuable implies that the liberal polity has a duty to provide the goods (such as quality education) that enable individuals to pursue and achieve excellence.

[61] Liberalism, including nonperfectionist liberalism, presupposes what Rawls has called a "thin theory of the good" life. The theory of the good referenced in the main text above need not be distinctively liberal but for the purpose of vindicating tort law within a liberal society, it must not undermine liberalism's fundamental humanistic commitment for self-determination and substantive equality.

individuals' constitutive choices or traits against them that may amount to wrongful discrimination. To this extent, affirmative action can undermine the interest of those rejected in being treated as equals. The only live question is whether the conflict between this interest and that of the beneficiaries of affirmative action is valuable. I argue that, under the right circumstances, it is, and that this conflict is tolerably, rather than inherently, valuable.

The case for regarding this conflict as tolerably valuable begins with the current state of distributive injustice in the major spheres of our social, economic, and political life.[62] Because, and insofar as, the unjust distribution of opportunities in many societies is so pervasive, affirmative action programs may serve as an appropriate corrective. Although such programs can undermine the interest in being treated as equals for some individuals (i.e., members of nonmarginalized social groups), their potential to promote fair equality of opportunity on a society-wide scale may provide a strong justification for exempting participants from the duty of nondiscrimination.

Against this backdrop, giving some measure of priority to the equality interest of members of marginalized members of society over the nonmarginalized can be valuable. More precisely, it is *tolerably* valuable. This is because the justificatory force behind this approach to managing the conflict between the respective equality interests is transitory in nature. Its expiration date, so to speak, is the day society finally fulfills the promise of fair equality of opportunity.

2. *Numerus Clausus* and Antidiscrimination Law

The idea of a general yet limited duty of nondiscrimination should incorporate a commitment to protecting individuals from discrimination based on a *closed list* of choices and traits. Discrimination based on choices and traits outside this list should, therefore, be considered permissible. According to the conflict theory, allowing such instances to stand reflects rule of law principles and other substantive considerations that make this form of discrimination *tolerably* valuable. Notice that the argument going forward does not seek to determine which choices and traits should be included in the closed list—that answer, as I have given above and in earlier work, is constitutive choices and traits. Instead, the argument takes a formal shape: It defends the idea of a closed list, rather than its specific contents.

The necessity of a closed list of choices and traits reflects a special case of a broader challenge: Can a general duty of nondiscrimination be consistent with the fundamental interests of discriminators (holders of normative powers), including their interests in equality and self-determination? The consistency requirement implies that there must be a ceiling to the legal demands imposed by the duty of nondiscrimination. Compelling owners, employers, and other market actors to

[62] *Contra* Students for Fair Admission, Inc. v. President and Fellows of Harvard College, 600 U.S. 181 (2023).

abide by a duty of nondiscrimination beyond this ceiling could ultimately undermine their own freedom and equality. As I explain in Chapter 14, tort duties governing tolerably valuable conflicts may legitimately *constrain*, but not *crush*, the pursuit of ends by duty-owers.

When the cost of refraining from wrongful discrimination is relatively low, the need for a ceiling on nondiscrimination duties remains latent. However, when such duties become excessively burdensome, the necessity of a ceiling claims center stage. For example, it would be impossible for a restaurant owner to tailor the height of the restaurant's tables to the precise height of every potential customer, to render the restaurant accessible to every possible condition of physical disability, or to create a menu that meets all existing dietary restrictions. Performing all these tasks is (arguably) technically feasible, but still normatively undesirable. Imposing terms of interaction that incorporate a requirement of utmost accommodation, or a standard of zero discrimination, would be incompatible with treating restaurant owners as substantively free and equal persons. Hence, the duty of nondiscrimination must not require more than a reasonable measure of accommodation.[63] Consequently, however, were the costs of accommodation to drop substantially (say, due to technological advances), duty-owers might be required to extend reasonable accommodations for constitutive choices and traits *beyond* the current status *quo*. This follows from the view that the conflict between the interests of discriminators and discriminatees is tolerably, rather than inherently, valuable.

Limiting the duty of nondiscrimination to a requirement of reasonable rather than utmost accommodation, however, does not apply across the board. At times—when an act of discrimination constitutes a *categorical* rejection of the discriminatee's standing to relate to the discriminator as a substantively equal, namely, as the person they are—nothing short of utmost accommodation will suffice. The baker case discussed above fits this description: Although the baker may not refuse to sell the couple a generic cake, his refusal to bake them a wedding cake is, nonetheless, categorical in that it rejects the couple for who they truly are. Another instance is that of a racist restaurant owner who singles out people of color for inferior treatment or outright exclusion. Indeed, unlike discrimination against unusually tall restaurant patrons in the design of tables, chairs, and bathroom fixtures, a categorical refusal to serve someone based on their constitutive choices or traits should get no solace from the law. The former reflects the need to consider the freedom and equal standing of *both* parties; the latter, by contrast, repudiates outright the equality interest of the discriminatee.[64]

[63] The defense of undue hardship provides an instantiation of the standard of reasonable accommodation. For more on this instantiation, in the context of employers' Title VII duty of reasonable accommodation, see Groff v. DeJoy, 600 U.S. 447, 468–71 (2023).

[64] *See* Avihay Dorfman, *When, and How, Does Property Matter?*, 72 U. Toronto L.J. 81, 103–04 (2022).

The doctrine of *numerus clausus* (or closed list) represents a special case of this approach to limiting the general duty of nondiscrimination.[65] I argue that in order to respect the equality and self-determination interests of duty-owers, this duty should be governed by a set of established and clearly defined categories. This limitation—recall Chapters 2 and 7—reflects the conflict theory's nature as a legal theory and, by extension, its commitment to the rule of law. The values of stability and predictability in the rule of law require respect for duty-owers' ability to form expectations based on stable legal frameworks. The conflict theory cannot disregard the rule of law and, therefore, must avoid overly particularistic ad hoc judgments.

To illustrate this point, consider a chef who implements a dress code prohibiting barefoot patrons. Further assume that the reason behind this code is not indirectly to target members of socially marginalized groups but to create a specific restaurant atmosphere—formal and grand—in line with a particular aesthetic style. A general duty of nondiscrimination without a closed list of prohibited choices and traits leaves this law-abiding chef in the dark, as it were. By contrast, a clearly defined list provides the chef with the necessary certainty about the permissibility of such a plan.

V. Toward a Doctrinal Framework

Contemporary legal doctrine tends to classify context-based duties of nondiscrimination into two forms—direct and indirect discrimination, often referred to, respectively, as disparate treatment and disparate impact.[66] The distinction is considered qualitative since it reflects the difference between approaches to the responsibility for discrimination—motive-based and outcome-based responsibility—echoing the distinction between deliberate and strict liability torts.[67] Many philosophers and legal theorists view this distinction as fundamental to the normative analysis of discrimination.[68] Accordingly, large sections of the

[65] Elsewhere I defended the doctrine of *numerus clausus* in the context of property rights. Avihay Dorfman, *Property and Collective Undertaking: The Principle of* Numerus Clausus, 61 U. TORONTO L.J. 467 (2011). There, I contended that this doctrine is a principle of constraint on right-holders' normative powers, rather than as a principle of limiting the overall number of incidents in the list. My current argument (in the context of antidiscrimination law) endorses the latter principle. There is no inconsistency between advocating for the former approach in property law and the latter in the context of the discrimination tort. The former focuses on the legitimacy of granting right-holders the normative powers to legislate (i.e., establish new forms of property rights) for other private persons, whereas the latter concerns the legitimacy of imposing unlimited duty of nondiscrimination on duty-owers.

[66] *See, e.g.*, International Brotherhood of Teamsters v. United States, 431 U.S. 324, 335 n.15 (1977); KHAITAN, *supra* note 14, at 151–52.

[67] *See* David Benjamin Oppenheimer, *Negligent Discrimination*, 141 U. PENN. L. REV. 899, 919 (1993).

[68] *See, e.g.*, Deborah Hellman, *Indirect Discrimination and the Duty to Avoid Compound Injustice*, *in* PHILOSOPHICAL FOUNDATIONS, *supra* note 26, at 105; EIDELSON, *supra* note 34, at 19; MATT CAVANAGH, AGAINST EQUALITY OF OPPORTUNITY 199 (2002); IRIS YOUNG, JUSTICE AND THE POLITICS OF DIFFERENCE 196 (1990).

practical and theoretical debates about what renders discrimination wrongful are organized around it.

However, as I have argued above, discriminatory motivations should be neither necessary nor sufficient to characterize discrimination as wrongful. Rather than strict or absolute liability, the basis for rendering discriminatory outcomes prima facie wrongful is negligence. In my account, the general tort duty of nondiscrimination is akin to—though crucially, not coterminous with—negligence law's duty of care.[69]

The duty at hand requires holders of legal powers (e.g., in their capacity as providers of goods and services, employers, and educators) to take reasonable measures to make their voluntary interactions inclusive of the constitutive choices and traits of others. Failure to meet this requirement can be deliberate or inadvertent.[70] I do not argue that the difference between the two is negligible but rather that it should not matter at *this stage* of the legal analysis and will only become crucial at later stages, notably for the purpose of shifting the burden of proving causation and imposing punitive damages for incidents of flagrant discrimination. Moreover, my objection to limiting the tort of discrimination to instances of deliberate wrongfulness does not mean that liability can be assigned when discriminatory outcomes are not reasonably foreseeable.

Driving a (partial) wedge between wrongful discrimination and motivation is reinforced by the psychology of discrimination. Empirical studies suggest that unconscious or implicit bias—viz., when "people act on the basis of internalised schemas of which they are unaware and thus can, and often do, engage in discriminatory behaviours without conscious intent"[71]—figures prominently in our lives.[72] Tackling such implicit discrimination challenges the approach that identifies wrongful discrimination with antisocial or immoral motivations but not the account of wrongful discrimination defended in this chapter. Structurally, implicit bias can prima facie be deemed as wrongful discrimination, just as a motorist may be deemed prima facie negligent (i.e., in breach of a duty of care) for inadvertently speeding in a pedestrian's vicinity. Although the tort of discrimination is not a debiasing mechanism, it does give potential discriminators a mandatory reason—a legal duty—to be vigilant about the impact of their decisions on the fundamental interests of others to be treated as equals.

[69] The connection between wrongful discrimination and negligence is not new. *See* Oppenheimer, *supra* note 67, at 933; Richard Thompson Ford, *Rethinking Rights After the Second Reconstruction*, 123 YALE L.J. 2942, 2945 (2014); MOREAU, *supra* note 30, at 205. As the main text mentions and the discussion of the injury element clarifies, however, my account also draws an important distinction between the (proposed) tort of discrimination and that of negligence.

[70] Note, moreover, that this characterization also captures discrimination based on proxies—for instance, denying service or charging higher prices relying on zip code addresses is often an indirect way to segregate people according to race or socioeconomic condition.

[71] Cheryl Pritlove et al., *The Good, the Bad, and the Ugly of Implicit Bias*, 393 LANCET 502, 502 (2019).

[72] *See* Anthony G. Greenwald & Linda Hamilton Krieger, *Implicit Bias: Scientific Foundations*, 94 CAL. L. REV. 945 (2006).

To prepare the ground for this new tort of discrimination, I address the elements of duty, breach, injury, and causation. I also address some remedial aspects underlying this tort. I take each in turn, raising key questions and identifying ways of addressing them.

A. Duty

This element determines the identity of duty-owers. Two important aspects guide this inquiry. The first is that discrimination presupposes some (legitimate or ostensible) normative power held by the discriminator vis-à-vis the discriminatee.[73] This power manifests itself in the entitlement to allocate goods and services, broadly defined to include opportunities, and operates by fixing the normative situation of those with whom they engage.

As a first approximation, therefore, the duty of nondiscrimination is incumbent on holders of normative powers but not on all such holders; hence, the second aspect of the duty inquiry. The paradigmatic instance of duty-owers is the for-profit and nonprofit provider of goods and services. By contrast, some normative powers may fall outside the purview of any liberal legal order insofar as they are personal choices in intimate relationships, such as those of friendship and romantic love, or in the pursuit of human excellence. Other instances of exercising normative powers may be exempt from legal oversight due to substantive or institutional considerations.

Substantive considerations have to do with free agency.[74] A consumer deciding not to purchase certain goods because the seller is Jewish may reach the exact same decision for other and perfectly legitimate reasons, such as the price of the goods. Thus, there is a space between motives and actions, that is, between why they refuse to do X and doing X. It means that free agents *could*—rather than merely would—change their minds before consummating the act. To respect free agency, therefore, a liberal legal order must furnish consumers with an arena of revisability in the domain of motives or attitudes, allowing them an opportunity to act more appropriately after revising their current attitude. They can, then, decide to do X or to refrain from doing X for perfectly good reasons (such as to remain reluctant to purchase the thing at issue for the legitimate reason that it is too costly for them). A liberal legal order cannot hold them legally responsible on the *sole* basis of forming and acting on repugnant motives. Notice that the same free agency-based analysis does not apply to the buyer's seller: A seller who is not willing to interact

[73] *See further* Dagan & Dorfman, The Powers of Discrimination, *supra* note 1.
[74] *See* Avihay Dorfman, *The Limited Case for Discrimination's Legality*, 83 L. & CONTEMP. PROB. 175 (2020), on which this paragraph draws.

with the buyer typically faces only two options, namely, refrain from doing so or close down the business.

However, the free agency case for relieving consumers from nondiscrimination duties is limited. It focuses on the case of a consumer deciding whether to buy a particular product from a particular seller at a particular time. It does not extend to the very different case of a buyer who sets up a procedure (say, an auction) to be regularly used in its purchasing activity. Unlike the former case, there is no principled basis to relieve buyers engaging in the latter market activity from antidiscrimination duties.

Institutional considerations that might support exempting consumers from legal oversight derive largely from the epistemic difficulty of verifying discriminatory decisions on the part of consumers.[75] This class of considerations, by its very nature, is contingent.

These substantive or institutional considerations (arguably) explain why existing duties of nondiscrimination do not apply to how consumers, employees, lessees, and students exercise their normative, contractual powers vis-à-vis their respective providers. In *these* cases—but not, as noted, in more regularized purchasing activities—discriminating in the choice of provider can be ethically wrongful, though not necessarily legally impermissible.

Subject to these exceptions, providers of goods and services are duty-bound, no matter how big the provider or how essential the provided goods are. It applies to common carriers as well as to small businesses held by sole proprietors, irrespective of the availability of equivalent options furnished by other market providers or by the state.

B. Breach

The breach element fills out the content of the duty. It tells us what duty-owers owe in terms of measures they have to implement and decisions they have to refrain from to lower and, at times, even eradicate transactional barriers. Doing so, as noted, requires a reasonable accommodation standard of conduct. This standard is made up of epistemic, substantive, and legality conditions.

The Epistemic Condition. The first, epistemic condition, is known in tort law as reasonable foreseeability.[76] To refrain from wrongful discrimination, duty-owers

[75] *See* Ian Ayres, Private Prejudice? Unconventional Evidence on Race and Gender Discrimination 127–36 (2001). *See also* Lee Anne Fennel, *Searching for Fair Housing*, 97 B.U.L. Rev. 349 (2017); Saul Levmore, *Title VII to Tinder: Law's Antidiscrimination Asymmetry and Occasional Market Superiority*, 68 Ala. L. Rev. 877 (2017); Katherine T. Bartlett & Mitu Gulati, *Discrimination by Customers*, 102 Iowa L. Rev. 223 (2016).

[76] Foreseeability is most famously associated with the duty and proximate cause elements of the prima facie case of negligence but can also inform the analysis of the breach element. The *locus classicus* is *Adams v. Bullock*, 128 N.E. 93 (N.Y. 1919).

must be able to know what they are required to do or abstain from doing so that the terms of their interactions with others are not discriminatory, that is, that they do not hold the others' constitutive choices or traits against them.

At times, knowing is relatively simple—for instance, when an ice cream parlor refuses to serve foreigners, the owner is fully aware that such an interaction is discriminatory. At other times, foreseeability may be less straightforward—for instance, if auditions to professional orchestras are governed by terms of interaction that, though not by intentional design, turn out to be discriminatory. Reasonable foreseeability, then, becomes the only relevant question. If duty-owers cannot reasonably be cognizant of the pertinent fact, holding them strictly liable in discrimination necessarily undermines their status as free and equal agents since there is nothing they can do in terms of accommodation to avoid liability for the discriminatory outcome. If, by contrast, they might be aware of a nontrivial possibility that the audition process treats women and nonwhites much less favorably than white men musicians, duty-owers can be required to take some measure to rule out that possibility.

Although possible in theory, voluntary interactions resulting in unforeseeable indirect discrimination will rarely exist in practice. We could imagine that, at some historical moment, no reasonable auditor had realized the discriminatory character of the audition process. When complaints and studies begin to pile up, however, appeals to ignorance will not do, and this statement applies not only to auditions for orchestras but almost everywhere. The reason is that today, people are (or can reasonably be assumed to be) acutely aware of the ever-present risk of potentially discriminatory implications, even in generally applicable terms of interactions. The threshold set by the epistemic condition of foreseeability is thus low, which implies that a tort of discrimination would be especially receptive to claims by members of liminal groups.[77]

The Substantive Condition. The second, substantive condition, is more demanding and is meant to insulate the standard of reasonable accommodation from the exacting demand of utmost accommodation. As discussed above, utmost accommodation threatens to destroy the duty-ower's equality and self-determination interests. For this reason, the duty-owers' awareness of discriminatory overtones in their interactions with others will not suffice. Defusing these overtones, however, must be made commensurate with the resources available to duty-holders (including in the form of state subsidies).

Again, the burden of conforming to a duty of nondiscrimination is often negligible, such as simply refraining from excluding green-eyed people from one's restaurant, and thus can, and indeed should, be demanded from duty-owers. Yet, some cases are more challenging and may involve costly accommodations,

[77] *Cf.* Lihi Yona, *Identity at Work*, 43 Berkeley J. Emp. & Lab. L. 139 (2022) (discussing claims raised by asexuals, poor whites, and fat people).

such as structural changes to the built environment or substantial adjustments of production processes and modes of operation in the workplace. A key role of the standard of reasonable accommodation in these instances is to set a ceiling beyond which no additional accommodation is required. A ceiling can be set directly by the standard of accommodation or indirectly by introducing state subsidies that lower the (economic) burden that the duty of nondiscrimination imposes on duty-owers.[78]

The Legality Condition. The substantive condition immediately invites a third one—the legality condition, which concerns the rule of law implications of a reasonable accommodation standard. Attempts to meet the standard of reasonable accommodation might collapse into the ad hoc tailoring of dos and don'ts. But taking this path is, as noted, unacceptable, and to avert this, the presence of recursive structures should be built into the standard of reasonable accommodation, enabling courts and duty-owers to identify clear answers to particular questions.

C. Injury

Infringing a person's right to be treated as an equal can give rise to any number of consequential harms. Some of them are pecuniary, such as lower earnings. Others are nonpecuniary and concern emotional distress as well as other forms of nonmonetizable suffering, including stigmatization and feelings of inferiority. But the right in question is not reducible to any of these consequences, all of them being surface manifestations of a deeper setback to victims of wrongful discrimination: denying them the possibility of relating to others—employers, providers, educators, lessors, and so forth—as substantively free and equal persons.

This characterization of the injury element puts this aspect of the tort of discrimination closer to torts like assault and battery rather than negligence. Thus, breaching the duty of reasonable accommodation is per se a violation of the discriminatee's right to be treated as an equal, as when the victims are denied bakery services based on their sexual orientation.

Two clarifications are in order. The per se quality of the tort of discrimination does not deny the victim's entitlement to recover the legally cognizable consequential harms that may result from the discriminator's failure. Moreover, my account is consistent with a practice of awarding super-compensatory damages (often called punitive damages) under the right circumstances, as will be discussed in Chapter 12.

[78] *See* Eyal Zamir & Barak Medina, Law, Economics, and Morality 255 (2010).

D. Causation

Failure to conform to the standard of reasonable accommodation and the injury the discriminatee complains of must be causally connected. Neither the act nor the injury can, alone, satisfy a prima facie case of wrongful discrimination, and the injury must result, in the right sense, from a (deliberate or careless) failure of reasonable accommodation on the discriminator's part. Failure to render the workplace reasonably accommodative of job candidates with physical disability does not mean that turning down one of them necessarily amounts to wrongful discrimination since the reasons behind the rejection may be irrelevant to this person's disability.

The causation doctrine, as practiced in the common law of torts and as further developed in the context of contemporary antidiscrimination law,[79] is up to this task.[80] The epistemic difficulties that may arise in proving causation here are not qualitatively different from those addressed in contemporary antidiscrimination law.

E. Remedies

The discussion so far seemingly implies that the tort of discrimination entitles victims to the familiar types of remedy available in other familiar torts, ranging from compensatory, super-compensatory, and nominal damages to injunctive relief. It also implies that victims of wrongful discrimination might face familiar hurdles to bringing claims against their wrongdoers. One such hurdle concerns the costs of litigating a case of unintentional discrimination (where super-compensatory damages are not available) with relatively small pecuniary loss. Tort law, civil procedure, and antidiscrimination law may provide different ways of tackling this (and other familiar hurdles).[81]

In addition to private law's ordinary remedial toolkit, wrongful discrimination can also be tackled more effectively using a private-law version of what Owen Fiss

[79] Causation in antidiscrimination law has developed its own standards of proof and, most significantly, rules on burden allocation with respect to causation (i.e., shifting the burden of persuasion in "mix-motive" cases of employment discrimination). *See* Price Waterhouse v. Hopkins, 490 U.S. 228 (1989).

[80] I do not argue that this or the other doctrine does not require some revisions, and I certainly do not agree with the Supreme Court's restrictive understanding of the common-law doctrine of causation in tort law. *See further* Sandra F. Sperino, *The Causation Canon*, 108 Iowa L. Rev. 703 (2023); Sandra F. Sperino, *Discrimination Law: The New Franken-Tort*, 65 DePaul L. Rev. 721 (2016). Rather, I argue that this doctrine, properly conceived, offers a sensible starting platform. *See* Chapter 16.

[81] Consider nominal damages, class action, and fee-shifting provisions, respectively. To be sure, my account can also call for substantially reforming remedies law in response to hurdles, familiar or otherwise, to the implementation of the tort of discrimination. *Cf.* Hanoch Dagan & Avihay Dorfman, *Substantive Remedies*, 96 Notre Dame L. Rev. 513 (2020).

has called structural injunction. This court-centric remedy can, in appropriate cases, supplement the regulators' authority to establish a rigorous ex ante enforcement regime.

Injunctions, according to Fiss, are structural when they vest a judge with the power to order the reorganization of an "ongoing bureaucratic organization," typically a government entity, to bring it into conformity with the commands of the constitution.[82] A familiar instance is the structural injunctions granted by the US Supreme Court to implement the right to nonsegregated education in public schools.[83] Rather than awarding damages to each plaintiff-victim or enjoining public schools from not enrolling Black students, the structural injunction purports to transform an ongoing entity to systematically prevent deprivations of constitutional rights in the future.

An analogous remedy could, and should, be implemented in and around the tort of discrimination. The proposed structural injunction targeting private entities can make a difference, especially when administrative agencies, and regulators more generally, run out of authority or simply fail to provide the needed correction.[84] It is initiated by discriminatees, personally or via some sort of aggregation mechanism, or on their behalf rather than by citizens or the public officials representing them,[85] and its point is not to bring about conformity with constitutional rights but with the private-law right to be treated as an equal. This remedy, which can be consequential when confronting systemic discrimination, can also be most effective against major private entities—employers holding many different places of employment, major chain stores, and a sector-wide class of similar entities such as universities. In these and other instances, several discrete violations of the reasonable accommodation standard can serve as prima facie evidence of a systemic violation of the right to be treated as an equal. If this evidence is substantiated, the structural injunction can be used to challenge the systemic aspects of the discrimination in question.

Conclusion

When a general, privity-independent duty of care was first pronounced in *MacPherson v. Buick* (or, for English tort law, in *Donoghue v. Stevenson*), it added a general tort to the context-based duties of care prescribed in preexisting law. This

[82] *See* Owen M. Fiss, *The History of an Idea*, 78 FORDHAM L. REV. 1273, 1247 (2009); Owen M. Fiss, *The Forms of Justice*, 93 HARV. L. REV. 1, 2, 5 (1979).

[83] Brown v. Bd. of Edu. (Brown II), 349 U.S. 294 (1955).

[84] A particularly promising trajectory for the use of structural injunctions may be their gradual replacement by a robust specialized regulatory apparatus, as in the course followed by the unconscionability doctrine. *See* Anne Fleming, *The Rise and Fall of Unconscionability as the "Law of the Poor,"* 102 GEO. L.J. 1383 (2014).

[85] OWEN M. FISS, THE CIVIL RIGHTS INJUNCTION 18–22 (1978).

decision is now rightly viewed as both a paradigm shift in the history of tort law and as an indispensable feature of private law in a liberal legal order.[86] The private law of discrimination, I claim, is in its pre-*MacPherson* moment. The gaps between its existing context-based duties are indefensible, and its contextual structure fails to vindicate people's fundamental interest in being treated as equals by those exercising their normative powers over them. As in the tort of negligence, a general duty does not call for an all-encompassing scope, given the many spheres of action and human relations that should remain beyond the purview of legal oversight. Yet, again, as in the case of negligence, nothing short of a general tort of discrimination can suffice if the revolution instigated by the Civil Rights Acts is to be completed.

[86] *See further* John C. P. Goldberg & Benjamin C. Zipursky, *The Moral of* MacPherson, 146 U. Pa. L. Rev. 1733 (1998).

PART III

THE EQUALITY THEORY OF TORT LAW

11
Equality First

Introduction

This chapter marks the beginning of the equality theory of tort law, which is an account of the special way in which tort law does things: The pairwise structure of its duty and, further downstream, liability. My ambition is to build the foundations of a conception of equality—a substantive conception of transactional equality—that both explains and vindicates the law of tort as the law of interpersonal conflicts. Put abstractly, there can be different legal and extralegal ways to determine the terms of inherently valuable, tolerable, and valueless conflicts. Tort law's distinctive contribution is in writing an egalitarian commitment into these terms, ensuring that they reflect an ideal of a relation of equals.

The present chapter sets the stage by doing two things. The first task is to explain how the two basic commitments of liberalism—equality and freedom—interact in the law of torts. I argue that a certain idea of relational equality occupies the more foundational level. Freedom is crucial but it is only a part of the indicia that help to determine whether parties in a conflict relate as equals.

The second task is to differentiate the equality theory of tort law from the influential account of relational equality developed by Elizabeth Anderson and other relational egalitarians. The former shares the core intuition of relational egalitarians such as that of Anderson, namely, that what matters for human relations to count as just is not, or not only, equalizing the stuff that the interacting parties independently have, but rather that these persons could genuinely relate as equals. However, I disagree with how this intuition has been developed into a theory, that is, in the political philosophy of relational egalitarianism. In particular, I shall criticize its narrow fixation on three fronts: That relating as equals comes down to the eradication of hierarchy and authority relations; that relational equality concerns social relations; and that relating as equals is a distinctively democratic ideal. By contrast, the equality theory of tort law offers a more general basis for understanding the relational egalitarian's core intuition, which goes deeper than and extends beyond hierarchy and authority, social relations, and democracy.

Conflict between Equals. Avihay Dorfman, Oxford University Press. © Oxford University Press 2026.
DOI: 10.1093/9780198979869.003.0015

I. Equality and Freedom Distinguished: The Independence of Tort Law

Contemporary private law theory is divided between (at least) two conceptions of freedom: Freedom as self-determination and freedom as independence. I have argued for the former and against the latter.[1] The conflict theory, moreover, highlights the importance of our interest in self-determination along with other autonomy-related interests such as free expression and reputation. However, the purpose of the present discussion is to explore the gap between freedom and equality, that is, between either self-determination or independence, on one hand, and equality, on the other.

I argue, first, that tort law cannot be solely vindicated on the basis of self-determination (meaning self-determination is necessary but not sufficient); and second, independence cannot serve as the foundational principle of freedom in tort law (meaning independence is neither necessary not sufficient). It is equality, *not* freedom as independence, that captures tort law's structural core. The claim I pursue in this chapter is that, as between equality and freedom, only equality can explain why what I have called in Chapter 1 "the tort law way of doing things" matters. That is, only equality can vindicate tort law's insistence on establishing a *legal link* between the interest in the safety of one and the conflicting interest in liberty of action of the other. I argue that both the legality and the linking are not entailed by freedom. This is because there can be any number of ways other than the tort-law way of securing freedom. Friends of freedom as self-determination (myself included) have no principled reason to resist this *conceptual* observation.[2] The observation can also include Gregory Keating's theory of tort law, according to which tort law's moral mission is to protect essential conditions of effective agency (such as physical integrity).[3] To be sure, I do not deny that both self-determination and agency may *sometimes* include a relational element: To be autonomous, or to secure effective agency, individuals may have to stand in certain relationships of equal concern, respect, and recognition with others. However, such an element does not entail a single, necessary way of protecting our freedom from risk-creators. The tort-law way of forging a link between persons pursuing conflicting interests, therefore, represents one technology among others for sustaining self-determination and effective agency.

By contrast, friends of seeing freedom as independence might find the disconnect between freedom and the tort-law way of doing things impossible,

[1] Hanoch Dagan & Avihay Dorfman, Relational Justice: A Theory of Private Law (2024).

[2] *Cf.* Charlie Webb, *Three Concepts of Rights, Two of Property*, 38 Oxford J. Legal Stud. 246, 261 (2018).

[3] Gregory C. Keating, *Is Tort Law "Private"?*, *in* Civil Wrongs and Justice in Private Law 351 (Paul B. Miller & John Oberdiek eds., 2020); Gregory C. Keating, Reasonableness and Risk: Right and Responsibility in the Law of Torts 303 (2022).

conceptually, normatively, and doctrinally speaking. Hence, I wish to focus solely on freedom as independence in an effort to show that the nature of the connection between independence and equality is far more tenuous than typically believed. I cannot make this showing with respect to any theory of independence. Instead, I will assume that if my argument is true with respect to a Kantian theory defended by Arthur Ripstein, the champion of independence in contemporary tort theory, it may plausibly hold sway over some other articulations of independence. Notice, moreover, that I do not claim that this theory is the most appealing interpretation of Kant's political and legal philosophy.

A. Independence

There is one definition and two metaphors that render most vivid what independence is, according to Ripstein. I want to suggest that these are *choice*-based definitions and metaphors and that, crucially, choice is conceptually, normatively, and doctrinally irrelevant to the doctrines of negligence and nonfeasance liability.

According to Kant, freedom requires "independence from being constrained by another's choice,"[4] which is framed by Ripstein as the freedom of "not being subordinated to the choice of any *other* particular person"[5] and more recently by Weinrib as "the opposite of the subordination that consists in being subject to or dependent on another's will."[6] The first metaphor is one of despotism, and it tracks the ambition of proponents of this conception of freedom to contrast it with negative liberty (roughly, the absence of constraints or obstacles). Despotism portrays freedom as independence in the sense of, in some respect, an extension of republican freedom: "[E]verything that is wrong with being subject to the choice of a powerful ruler is also wrong with being subject to the choice of another person's choice."[7] The second metaphor illuminates independence by characterizing it in terms of "in charge relations," saying that "[n]obody else is in charge of your body or property."[8]

Thus conceived, independence is negatively connected to the exercise of choice—to wit, others cannot choose, determine, judge (et alia) for me what to do with my person or property and, ultimately, what ends to pursue. According to Ripstein, this way of articulating a conception of independence makes freedom and equality two sides of one and the same coin. Independence is relational in its

[4] IMMANUEL KANT, THE METAPHYSICS OF MORALS 63, [6:237] (Mary Gregor trans., 1991).

[5] ARTHUR RIPSTEIN, FORCE AND FREEDOM: KANT'S LEGAL AND POLITICAL PHILOSOPHY 4 (2009).

[6] ERNEST J. WEINRIB, RECIPROCAL FREEDOM: PRIVATE LAW AND PUBLIC RIGHTS 100 (2022). *See also* ANNA STILZ, TERRITORIAL SOVEREIGNTY: A PHILOSOPHICAL EXPLORATION 95 (2019) who defines independence as "being free from the will of other."

[7] RIPSTEIN, *supra* note 5, at 43. On republican freedom, see PHILIP PETTIT, REPUBLICANISM: A THEORY OF FREEDOM AND GOVERNMENT (1999).

[8] ARTHUR RIPSTEIN, PRIVATE WRONGS 32 (2016).

structure and, so, cannot exist apart from a relation between equally independent persons.[9]

Against this brief presentation, I argue that independence cannot even begin to make sense of two core doctrines of tort law: negligence and nonfeasance liability. This is because it identifies the violation of independence with what can be called choice-based subjection. The two doctrines in question, however, make no essential reference to this notion of subjection. To the contrary, part of the appeal of negligence liability and part of why courts are gradually extending duties of easy rescue[10] lie in conceptions of individual responsibility that do not turn on choosing, but rather on doing. It concerns—as it should—what we do, or fail to do, to others, rather than what we choose for them or they for us to do.

I do not dispute the pairwise structure of independence. In fact, the equality theory I defend in subsequent chapters is a defense of the value—in terms of a certain egalitarian ideal—of this structure. However, I argue that independence cannot even begin to make sense of tort law. As a result, something *else* must account for the pairwise structure or what I call the tort-law way of doing things (my answer, recall, will be a certain idea of quality). Note that this critique is not limited to the explanatory credentials of independence but rather also identifies a normative shortcoming on the part of independence-based accounts of tort law: Tort law in part concerns what we *do* or fail to *do* to others, rather than what we *choose* for them or they for us to do.[11]

Focusing solely on choice-based subordination as the tort law's basic wrong misses out, on two fronts. First, it deflects attention from what really matters. As just mentioned, negligent infliction of bodily harm counts as wrongful not because the harm is in some sense the upshot of the injurer's choice to engage in unjustifiably risky conduct, but rather because this harm is caused by substandard behavior. Second, it fails to provide the normative resources to evaluate some core tort

[9] Ripstein, *supra* note 5, at 17.

[10] An important case in point is *Tarasoff v. The Regents of the Univ. of Cal.*, 551 P.2d 334 (Cal. 1976). Moreover, that the very few US jurisdictions that refused to follow *Tarasoff* grounded their reluctance in institutional rather than substantive terms. *See, e.g.*, Boynton v. Burglass, 590 So.2d 446, 449 (Fla. Dist. Ct. App. 1991); Thapar v Zezulka, 994 S.W.2d 635, 638 (Tex. 1999).

[11] Ripstein emphasizes a rather different distinction between "doing something *to* someone and failing to do something *for* that person." Ripstein, *supra* note 8, at 10. If by "doing something *to*" he means any substandard conduct or omission resulting in rights violation, then he is right in saying that tort law takes up instances of doing-something-to-you rather than not-doing-for-you. However, adopting this characterization means abandoning the principle of independence. This is because doing-something-to-you does not require "in charge of" relations between the doer and the sufferer. As I argue in the main text below, a risk-creator can expose another person to unjustified risk even when the "exposing" is done inadvertently, that is, without ever making a choice concerning what rights or means the risk-bearer has. Perhaps it is better to understand Ripstein's talk of "doing something to someone" within the broader context of independence and, so, choice. On this view, "doing something to someone" *must* involve the doer as being in charge of the sufferer in the sense of subjecting the latter to the determining choice of the former. Taking this interpretive path returns the argument to the structural gap between independence and two central torts doctrines, nonfeasance and negligence liability. I explore this gap in the main text below.

doctrines, including the doctrine of nonfeasance liability and the objective assessment of reasonable care. As I seek to show, although the argument from independence has been deployed by proponents of independence to justify the absence of duties of easy rescue, negligence liability, and the objective standard of reasonable care, independence does not bear on these doctrines. I take each doctrine in turn.

B. Nonfeasance Liability

As explained in Chapter 6, the nonfeasance/misfeasance distinction is used in tort law to characterize the nature of the connection between a defendant and the risk that has materialized into the plaintiff's injury. Misfeasance covers all instances in which the defendant created or contributed to the creation of this risk. By contrast, nonfeasance takes up all instances in which the risk at issue exists entirely apart from any action (or inaction) by the defendant.[12]

Proponents of freedom of independence believe that the best explanation of the no-liability rule lies in substantive considerations, as opposed to some institutional limitations on the implementation of morality to the private law.[13] Further, they claim that this rule lies at the moral center of tort law and private law, meaning we cannot even begin to plausibly understand and justify tort law, and ultimately private law, without accounting for the special moral commitment underlying the no-liability rule.[14]

The independence-based argument against duties of easy rescue begins with the general claim that the "distinction between misfeasance and nonfeasance reflects the irreducibility of the 'in charge of' relation."[15] More importantly, it suggests that duties of nonfeasance, including duties of easy rescue, undermine the independence of duty-owers by subjecting them to the choice of the duty's beneficiary. In Ripstein's words, a duty of easy rescue "would entitle [its beneficiary] to *determine* the purposes for which [duty-owers] use [their] means."[16] Typically, criticism of the independence-based argument against a duty of easy rescue assumes that independence rules out such a duty.[17] For instance, Victor Tadros criticizes the

[12] Restatement (Third) of Torts: Phys & Emot. Harm §37 (2012) (nonfeasance concerns "[a]n actor whose conduct has not created a risk of physical or emotional harm to another.").

[13] Ripstein, *supra* note 8, at 64 ("The distinction between misfeasance and nonfeasance structures the rights of private persons to their bodies and property."). *See also* Peter Benson, *Misfeasance as an Organizing Normative Idea in Private Law*, 60 U. Toronto L.J. 731 (2010); Ernest J. Weinrib, The Idea of Private Law 10 (1995).

[14] *See* the sources cited in *id. See also* Ripstein, *supra* note 8, at 73–79.

[15] *Id.*, at 61. More generally, Ripstein notes that "the moral idea that no person is in charge of another" can "illuminate the familiar categories of private wrongdoing," including "the fundamental distinction between misfeasance and nonfeasance." *Id.*, at 295.

[16] *Id.*, at 25.

[17] My earlier critique of the no-liability rule also makes this assumption (for the sake of argument). *See* Chapter 6; Dagan & Dorfman, *supra* note 1, at ch. 6.

Kantian position against enforcing duties of easy rescue by arguing that independence cannot be the sole consideration on which to decide the duty question and, further, that under the right circumstances the interest of a stranded person can, and should, outweigh the independence of the rescuer.[18] It can also be argued that independence "admit[s] of degree" and therefore can yield to the urgent condition of a stranded person.[19]

Contrary to the line of criticism emanating from interest-based political morality, I wish to argue that an affirmative duty of easy rescue is *fully compatible* with the independence of the duty-ower. My claim is that the argument from independence has *no* bearing on the paradigm case of easy rescue. Therefore, it cannot support the no-liability rule for nonfeasance in its simplest form of easy rescue. It will be apt to mention that the Kantian characterization of the distinction between nonfeasance and misfeasance does not track the characterization I presented above (which represents the law's actual position on the matter).[20] That said, nothing turns on this debate, for both characterizations are in full agreement that the case of easy rescue, including the hypothetical case to be discussed below, is a paradigm case of nonfeasance.

Consider the following hypo. A person is robbed while taking a walk on the shoreline. The robber also throws her into a nearby pothole. The pothole is rather shallow, which means that as you walk past it you can clearly see this poor person lying there. Suppose that you notice her lying there unconscious (you haven't seen the incident itself as it happened some time before you arrived at the scene). Our moral intuitions suggest that you have a compelling reason to help her out either yourself or by calling for help in case it is too complicated or difficult to do it yourself.

Tort law, recall, enforces a rule (subject to exceptions) of no duty of easy rescue. The argument from independence goes deeper than that. It seeks to show why tort law should not impose a duty of easy rescue. That is, compelling us to attend to the predicament of the person lying in the pothole violates our independence. The

[18] Victor Tadros, *Independence Without Interests?*, 31 Oxford J. Legal Stud. 193, 200 (2011).

[19] Joseph Raz, The Morality of Freedom 373 (1986). *See also* Stilz, *supra* note 6, at 112, 116.

[20] The Kantian characterization (also shared by Benson, *supra* note 13) seeks to show that the rule against liability for nonfeasance extends beyond the context of easy rescue cases to capture areas of nuisance law, pure economic loss, and instances of *damnum absque injuria*, more generally. The key to this characterization is a revised definition of nonfeasance as describing all cases where the defendant would be called upon to confer a *benefit* on the plaintiff. Misfeasance, in turn, describes all cases where the defendant actually injures the person or property of the plaintiff through a breach of *duty*. *See* Ripstein, *supra* note 8, at 54.

This approach, however, is wholly conclusory and merely restates the crucial questions: *What* rights do we have, and, ultimately, *why* do we have them? Put differently, the claim that the misfeasance/nonfeasance distinction merely reflects an antecedent system of rights implies that the distinction between the two depends entirely on the applicable system of rights. But then the concept of nonfeasance adds nothing to the analysis: It all comes down to the question of whether the plaintiff holds a right against the defendant. If so, then by definition, this is a case of misfeasance. If not, then by definition, the case becomes one of nonfeasance.

violation is not a feature of how burdensome it is to lift her out; in fact, it might be very easy and it can be even much easier simply to call an ambulance. Instead, the violation of the rescuer's freedom lies in being duty-bound to rescue her. Owing her a duty, that is, undermines the rescuer's freedom because it denies him his independence. Hence, an independence-preserving tort law does not have the legitimate authority to impose such a duty.

This argument fails, however. It is one thing to say that the duty subjects one to the interest of the duty's beneficiary, quite another to say that it subjects the former to the latter's choice. Freedom as independence, as explained above, picks out choice-based subjection only. Thus, the duty does not create the relevant relationship of subjection between the bystander and the person lying in the pothole because the former is not constrained by the *choice* of the latter. In fact, her choice plays no role in this situation. The only reason the bystander must act is the person's life rather than her choosing that he, or someone like him, would (effortlessly) act to rescue her. Rescuing her, therefore, is fully compatible with the bystander's independence, contrastively defined as not "being constrained by another's choice."[21]

Indeed, for this person to be in charge of someone, we need to impute to her certain choices or even intentions regarding the class of persons subject to her charge. I am in charge of you if my choice, plan, or intention gives you either a de facto or de jure reason to act accordingly. A boss is in charge of their staff precisely because their choices can be (de jure) reason-giving for them when it comes to determining what to do at work.[22] Likewise, a parent, an army commander, and a robber are in charge of other persons because they occupy (or seize, in the robber's case) a position of making choices for others.

No element of this de facto or de jure "in charge of" relationship is present in the rescue case just sketched. The person in the pothole is even momentarily incapable of making choices touching on other people as she is lying there unconscious. The irresistible necessity of rescuing her does not turn at all on her choosing, let alone constraining or subjecting the rescuer's person to her choice. If anything, rescuing her is a form of subjecting the rescuer to her fundamental interest in—rather than her choice of—staying alive. It can further be said that the duty puts in place an "in charge of" relation of a very different quality than what Ripstein's Kant offers. The former makes the *interest* of the duty's beneficiary in charge of what the duty-ower must do, whereas the latter places his or her choice in an "in charge of" position with respect to the duty-ower. Interest is, of course, incapable of making choices or determinations for other people; instead, these people are expected to see the existence of the interest as something there is reason to address. Normatively,

[21] KANT, *supra* note 4, at 63.

[22] To be sure, the case of the boss is invoked here to give a sense of what "in charge of" relations look like. A consensual employment arrangement renders this in charge of relation legitimate (i.e., fully consistent with employees' independence).

therefore, it is entirely coherent to claim that tort law should be fully committed to preserving our (Kantian) independence while also insisting that tort law should impose duties of easy rescue.

Can proponents of independence find a way to reintroduce choice into the analysis so as to vindicate their argument against imposing tort duties of easy rescue? They might offer the following argument, though to no avail. The robbery's victim did make a choice, namely, to stroll along the shoreline. But this is surely not the choice that could count for the purpose of establishing a robust connection between her choice and the bystander's duty to rescue her. Another articulation would be to focus on making a choice that anticipates the risk of being mugged and perhaps even of being knocked down unconscious. Implicit in this choice is the victim's expectation that bystanders will not turn their back on her so that she can count on them in a case of emergency (which expectation can be further reinforced by the imposition of a tort duty of easy rescue). She thereby chooses to take the walk on the basis of this expectation.

Can this choice elevate her to a position of "in charge of" with respect to her rescuer? I think not. To see this it will be apt to make a distinction between two senses in which a person's choice bears on the reasons for action that apply to others. At times, choice can be causally relevant to another person's reasons for action. At other times, by contrast, choice is constitutive of such reasons, by which I mean choice that purports to *give* others reasons for action.[23] When one chooses to go for a walk, her choice is only causally related to the bystander's duty to rescue one from the pothole. It is, in other words, a but-for-cause of having a mandatory reason to engage in rescuing this person. With one exception, the causal connection between the rescuee's choice and the rescuer's reasons for action is too tenuous to construct a relationship of dependency or subjection according to the Kantian understanding of independence. The exception is one of making a choice to do X with knowledge to a substantial certainty that doing X will place one in a life and death situation (for instance, a civilian who knowingly traverses a minefield will almost certainly end up needing some help to get out safely). Other than that, however, a mere causal connection between choice and reasons for action cannot sustain the case for independence as a fundamental pillar of morality (including law's special morality).

To render this vivid, consider one implication of invoking a standard of causal relevance, namely, the redundancy of independence. Many activities we regularly choose to engage in—driving, working, skiing, and so forth—are potentially risky to others and to ourselves. When some such risks materialize we could find ourselves desperate for others, including bystanders, coming to our aid. And, indeed, others will often have compelling reasons to lend us their hand. Does it mean that

[23] I say *purports* in recognition of instances of either illicit or illegitimate exercise of choice. A robber exemplifies the former and a boss overreaching her work-related powers illustrates the latter.

we are in charge of them because the many choices we make put everyone in our vicinity in a state of dependency on, or subjection to, us? Does it also mean that by occupying the world we are constantly constrained by the many everyday choices made by others? The causal connection between choice and reasons for action lends support for these absurd suggestions. As a result, the moral significance of independence and the consequent wrong of subordination are substantially diluted and, ultimately, become redundant.[24]

Ripstein need not dispute the redundancy charge. He notes that Kantian independence "does not aspire to isolate people from the effects of other people's choices." Accordingly, he says, "I remain independent if your choices have effects on me," for otherwise a standard of "independence from all effects of the actions of others . . . would subordinate everyone else to that person's choice."[25]

In conclusion, it turns out that considerations of independence are orthogonal to the question of whether tort law should impose a duty of easy rescue. Perhaps surprisingly, the core of the freedom-as-independence case against such a duty must find other grounds, as independence is not implicated by the imposition of a duty of easy rescue. (Negative liberty might suggest itself, though proponents of Kantian freedom as independence explicitly distance themselves from this principle.)[26]

C. Negligence Liability

The tort of negligence is (and should be) essentially about holding people responsible for failing to exercise their various practical capacities such as the capacities for choice, watchfulness, and responsiveness. It is not necessarily about being responsible for making a choice of *any* sort, including a choice that makes reference to other people, such as choosing what rights or means others have on their disposal. Indeed, liability for negligence requires no more, but no less, than conduct that fails to meet the standard of reasonable care. Independence and its

[24] It is important to distinguish the independence-based objection to imposing a duty of easy rescue from another objection, namely, that such a duty might lead to choice-based subjection during the *remedial stage* by granting victims the right to sue those who fail to rescue them. This type of subjection applies to all personal rights of action as they allow plaintiffs to compel defendants to face the choice of being sued. That said, rights of action are grounded in the existence of lexically prior rights, particularly substantive rights and secondary rights of repair. If, as argued in Chapter 6, our substantive right to life and limb justifies a duty of easy rescue—and recall that I argue the argument from independence cannot rule out this justification—then it can also justify the derivative right of action for violating that right.

[25] RIPSTEIN, *supra* note 5, at 38–39. For a different interpretation of this part of the Kantian argument, see Yizhak Benbaji, *Welfare and Freedom: Towards a Semi-Kantian Theory of Private Law*, 39 L. & PHIL. 473, 478 (2020).

[26] Richard Epstein defended the no-liability rule on the grounds of negative liberty in Richard A. Epstein, *A Theory of Strict Liability*, 2 J. LEGAL STUD. 151, 190–95, 198 (1973).

opposite—subordination to another's choice—can neither explain nor justify this major doctrine of tort law. Or so I wish to show.[27]

Begin with a distinction between different characterizations of the relationship between risk-creators and the unjustifiable risk of harm their actions generate.[28] Risk-creators can create unjustifiable risk in many different ways, but it will be apt to mention three of them: deliberate, reckless, and negligent creation of such risk.[29] Deliberate creation means that risk-creators seek to bring about both the risk and its probable consequences.[30] Recklessness involves awareness of the risk accompanied with conscious indifference to the risk's adverse consequences. Finally, negligence connotes the failure to either appreciate the risk calling for mitigation or respond to this risk in the right way. The former picks out inadvertence whereas the latter advertence. Inadvertence means that the risk-creator is unaware of a risk he or she should have been aware of. Consequently, this person should have taken the necessary precautions to reduce the risk at issue.[31] By contrast, a case of advertence features risk-creators appreciating the risk but failing to discharge proper care.[32] I wish to focus on inadvertence for two reasons: First, negligence liability requires no more than inadvertence; and second, responsibility for the adverse consequences of inadvertence can neither be explained by nor grounded in the argument from freedom as independence.

Consider the following case of a driver who abruptly swerves into the adjacent lane, injuring a motorcyclist. Depending on the details of this incident, the driver can sometimes be held morally responsible for undermining the motorcyclist's independence by subjecting the latter to the driver's choice. Thus, conduct that

[27] I am not the only one to make such a claim. Gregory Keating has argued that "Negligence is not a matter of wrongly taking charge of someone else; it is failing to act in a way that shows sufficient respect for the security of someone else's person and property." KEATING, *supra* note 3, at 95. Although I substantively agree with his conclusion, it is not clear that his characterization of negligence can break free of the independence-based characterization of negligence in terms of "in charge of" relations. Thus, Keating identifies the wrong of negligence with "disregard," which might be compatible with the notion, integral to independence, of consciously preferring one's interests over another's. *Id.* Keating further doubts whether Ripstein's conception of reasonable care can account for such failings as "driv[ing] while blindfolded, set[ting] off explosives without taking any precautions, and discharge[ing]weapons in public." *Id.*, at 98. It seems that these instances can be assimilated into an independence-based conception of wrongdoing.

[28] By unjustifiable risk I mean risk that exceeds the level of permissible risk.

[29] The three-part distinction at issue is widely, though not universally, accepted in the law and theory of both torts and criminal law. *See, e.g.*, RESTATEMENT (THIRD) OF TORTS: PHYS & EMOT HARM §§ 1–3 (2010); Douglas Husak, *Negligence, Belief, Blame and Criminal Liability: The Special Case of Forgetting*, 5 CRIM. L. & PHIL. 199, 207 (2011).

[30] Deliberate creation can sometimes be replaced by knowledge to a substantial certainty that the risk at issue will result in adverse consequences (of the requisite kind).

[31] This characterization of negligence as inadvertence contrasts with Shiffrin's motive-sensitive account of negligence. On Shiffrin's account, negligence is a moral failure in the domain of motives. Seana Valentine Shiffrin, *The Moral Neglect of Negligence*, *in* OXFORD STUDIES IN POLITICAL PHILOSOPHY 197 (David Sobel et al. eds., 2017).

[32] This way of characterizing advertence suggests that the boundary between recklessness and negligence (of the advertence type) may need further elaboration. I set this task to one side as my argument does not turn on the nature of the difference between these two categories.

amounts to reckless disregard of the motorcyclist can subject the latter to the choice of the driver. For instance, a case of drunk-driving arising out of voluntary intoxication makes it plausible to say that the driver wrongs his victim by knowingly creating unreasonably risky conditions for other drivers, while demonstrating sheer indifference to such risk.

However, many instances of accidental wrongdoing have nothing to do with subjecting the victim to the driver's choice. A case of negligent inadvertence fits this description. Suppose that instead of drunk-driving, the driver becomes completely engrossed in thoughts about the heartbreaking deterioration of his beloved brother's health. As a result, he swerves into the motorcyclist lane only to deal the latter a similar blow. The swerving is a single and momentary lapse of attention on the driver's part; he has never been involved in similar incidents. Moreover, the driver did not summon the depressing thoughts: Having them and being engrossed in them were not his choosing as they simply popped into his mind (hence, this is not engrossment as a parallel case to voluntary intoxication).[33]

Can this incident be redescribed in terms of an "in charge" relation pursuant to which the motorcyclist is being constrained by the driver's choice? Two related difficulties stand in the way of such redescription. First, the driver does not subject the motorcyclist, and her right to bodily integrity, to his charge by choosing to set out on a drive. Such a choice is only causally related to the accident, and the discussion of nonfeasance liability explained why a standard of causal relevance cannot sustain an "in charge of" relation. Further, the driver does not engage in making choices with reference to the rights or means of the motorcyclist (or, for that matter, other motorists nearby). He does not choose to prioritize his interest at the expense of the motorcyclist's.[34] In fact, the lapse of attention from which he suffers is best understood as a failure to exercise his capacity for vigilance.[35] His failure comes to breaching a duty of reasonable care. According to this duty, a reasonable driver must constantly be on the lookout given the imminent danger that driving poses to the life of others (the motorcyclist included). Saying the driver breached this duty amounts to saying that he must have been more attentive.

To conclude the first point, the problem is not merely that the connection between paradigm cases of impermissible subjection to another's choice—for example, despots, robbers, overreaching bosses, abusive parents, and so forth—and

[33] Gardner may have been right to observe in this respect that "All of us are vulnerable to being lured by thoughts, feelings and wants that we had ample reason to harbour into doing things that we had far too little, or even no, reason to do." John Gardner, *The Negligence Standard: Political not Metaphysical*, 80 MOD. L. REV. 1, 23 (2017).

[34] Using Holly Smith's language, there is no "benighting act," namely, an initial act (including mental occurrence) that has given rise to the lack of present awareness. Holly Smith, *Culpable Ignorance*, 92 PHIL. REV. 543, 547 (1983).

[35] For more on responsibility for negligence (in criminal law) for failing to exercise physical and mental capacities, see H. L. A. HART, PUNISHMENT AND RESPONSIBILITY: ESSAYS IN THE PHILOSOPHY OF LAW ch. 6 (1968).

the case of the inadvertently negligent driver is too weak. Rather, there is no such connection in the first place: The wrong associated with subjecting the means of others to one's choice and the wrong of negligent infliction of physical harm represent distinct forms of wrongdoing.

Second, artificially stretching the normative category of independence to negligence's basic case of inadvertence deflects attention from what really matters. Negligent infliction of bodily harm counts as wrongful but not because the harm is in some sense the upshot of the injurer's choice to engage in unjustifiably risky conduct but rather because this harm is caused by substandard behavior. And the value that calls for protection by the tort of negligence is not the independence of the victim from others' choice but rather her fundamental interest in bodily integrity.

D. Objective Standard of Reasonable Care

The inability of the argument from independence to illuminate, and justify, core areas of tort law does not end with the question of what renders negligent infliction of bodily harm wrongful. It also spans a neighboring doctrine, namely, the assessment of reasonable care. The question of reasonableness figures most prominently in connection with the tort of negligence, but it has doctrinal manifestations in other areas of tort law as well (such as in private nuisance's assessment of interference to reasonable use and enjoyment of one's premises). I shall focus on the standard of reasonable care in the tort of negligence.

Assessment of reasonable or ordinary care can be made subjectively or objectively. Subjective assessment means that the standard of care can make allowance for the peculiar condition of the person whose conduct is being assessed. For instance, accommodating the physical or cognitive disability of the risk-creator could de facto lower the demands of reasonable care. Contrary to a subjective assessment of reasonable care, it is also logically possible to disregard a person's peculiar condition entirely, subjecting him or her to the same demands of reasonable care that persons who do not have this condition would face. The tort of negligence sometimes, though by no means always or even primarily, employs the latter, objective approach.[36]

Can the argument from independence justify tort law's (rather circumscribed) preference for objective assessment of reasonable care?[37] Proponents of independence answer in the affirmative. Subjective assessment of reasonable care focuses on what precautions the risk-creator is capable of taking, rather than what

[36] *See* Chapter 15.

[37] I use this qualified language, concerning circumscribed rather than general preference, because the corrective justice characterization of the standard of reasonable care is inaccurate. Tort law employs both objective and subjective standards of assessing reasonable care. Contrary to corrective justice theory, the former standard is neither the default nor the more fundamental one. *See* Chapter 15.

precautions should be taken. The independence-based rejoinder is that an objective standard is the only way to ensure against entitling one party unilaterally to fix the terms of this party's interaction with another. The issue on which I wish to focus is what, if anything, is the nature of the connection between the duty to exercise reasonable care and the duty-ower's choice. Proponents of independence seem to argue for a rather robust connection. I argue, by contrast, that no connection, not even a tenuous one, exists.

Weinrib suggests that "[u]nder the subjective standard ... the defendant subordinates the plaintiff to the operation of the defendant's moral abilities."[38] It is not entirely clear what subordination is meant here. Does it mean, as Weinrib has said more recently, the opposite of independence?[39] Alternatively, it could mean a causal connection between subjective assessment and the level of care expected from the risk-creator.[40] The connection between independence and the case for objective assessment of reasonable care is cast into sharp relief in Ripstein's work. Thus, he warns that "a subjective standard would entitle one person to unilaterally determine the limits of another person's rights."[41] To avert this difficulty he argues for "objective standards of conduct."[42]

Notice the way Ripstein characterizes what is wrong with subjective assessment of reasonable care—the fact of placing one in a position of making *determinations* (arguably, *choices*) with respect to the safety of others. This characterization speaks the language of independence as described above. Subjective assessment, that is, brings into being "in charge of" relations, according to which the life and limb of the risk-bearer is made subject to the choice (or determination) of the risk-creator.

However, there is no subjection (or subordination) to the *choice* of the person whose conduct is assessed by the standard of reasonable care. The absence of subjection or "in charge of" relations cuts across the subjective versus objective assessment of reasonable care. To see this, consider a physically disabled driver owing a duty of reasonable care to pedestrians. Subjective assessment of reasonable care might effectively lower the precautions the driver is required to adopt whereas objective assessment asks her to meet a higher standard, namely, the same standard of care that nondisabled drivers would be facing.

Is it true to say that subjective assessment violates the independence of risk-bearers by subjecting the rights or means of pedestrians to the choice of the driver, putting the latter in an "in charge of" relation with the former? It is not. A disabled driver does not set the term of interactions, including the quality and amount of care. Instead, her disability is a condition she is simply faced with and, therefore,

[38] WEINRIB, *supra* note 13, at 183.

[39] WEINRIB, *supra* note 6, at 100 noting that "independence is the opposite of the subordination that consists in being subject to or dependent on another's will."

[40] *Id.*, at 9.

[41] RIPSTEIN, *supra* note 5, at 171.

[42] *Id.*

a circumstance that pedestrians have to take into account as they come near her. And when tort law employs objective assessment of reasonable care instead, her disability is a condition of hers and at the same time a circumstance that she has to address by exercising additional care. We may say that her disability is *causally* related to how much care is required of her. But it is not the case that the physically disabled driver *sets* the terms of her interaction with risk-bearers. Her choice, as opposed to her condition, plays no role in determining the level of care that is also the level of risk of harm to which pedestrians are exposed by her driving.

The choice between objective and subjective standards of care cannot be predicated upon independence and its violation, namely, subordination. Instead, I shall argue in Chapter 15 that equality and, in particular, a substantive conception of relational equality delivers on both explanatory and normative fronts. The reason why negligence law makes no allowances for the risk-creators' disabilities when assessing their conformity with the standard of reasonable care lies in the asymmetry between the respective interests of the risk-bearer and the risk-creator. Such asymmetry manifests itself when the interest of the risk-bearer claims some priority over that of the risk-creator. Familiar examples are the driver's interest in liberty of action versus the pedestrian's interest in life and limb, the product manufacturer's economic interest versus the user's safety, as well as the cardiologist's interest in self-realization and the patient's deteriorating heart condition. An objective, unaccommodating assessment of the risk-creator's conduct could then be viewed as tort law's response to such asymmetry. No allowances are made because, and insofar as, the interest of the risk-bearer places a relatively stronger demand for protection than the risk-creator's. Or so I argue in Chapter 15.

* * *

The argument so far has demonstrated that independence is underinclusive: It lacks the explanatory and justificatory resources to account for major doctrinal rules in the law of torts. I now wish to note that some of the arguments I made in the course of developing the conflict theory suggest that it is also overinclusive. Thus, with respect to battery law, Ripstein argues that freedom as independence implies that "[a]nother person is not entitled to so much as touch your body ... without your authorization."[43] But as I have argued in Chapters 3 and 4, certain forms of sociable touching are permissible not just *in spite of*, but rather also *because of* the absence of consent. Moreover, the torts of defamation and intentional infliction of emotional distress, especially in the United States but increasingly also in other liberal democracies, entitle private persons intentionally to inflict reputational and/or emotional harms on other persons, including *private* persons in matters of public concern.[44] On the conflict theory, this trend is grounded in the value of

[43] Ripstein, *supra* note 8, at 30.

[44] Ripstein acknowledges that the US version of defamation law (especially since *New York Times v. Sullivan*, 376 U.S. 254 (1964)) is inconsistent with his account of defamation. His critique

liberal culture that, recall, depends on the conflict between free speech and good name or emotional well-being.

To conclude, my discussion of cases of under- and overinclusiveness implies that freedom as independence is neither here nor there. Tort law does the pairwise linking *even when* independence is not at stake. Tort law does not deem certain injurious interactions wrongful *even when* independence is at stake. One can say, therefore, that corrective justice Kantians are right to insist that independence has a relational structure.[45] However, it is not the relational structure that characterizes tort law's relational structure. A partial overlap between the two is simply not enough. Independence and relating as equals can, and I argue should, come apart.

Note that the identification of tort law's relational structure with equality does not mean that freedom as self-determination has no role to play in the vindication of tort law. To the contrary, equality theory draws on the freedom interests of parties in a tort interaction so as to determine what and how much care is owed by one party to the other. Freedom interests, such as the livelihood, freedom of movement, or expressive agency of persons, are not the only possible considerations that could figure in determining what counts as relating as equals. That said, even interests such as bodily and emotional integrity are strongly related to self-determination as the former are necessary prerequisites for the latter.

II. Relational Equality: Its Appeal and Its Pitfalls

So what *could*, and *should*, account for the tort-law way of doing things? My answer is: equality. And the rest of this book seeks to develop a more precise understanding of the conception of equality that underlies the relational dimension of tort law as the law of interpersonal conflicts. I construct such an account that is specifically focused on the goal of vindicating tort law and, in particular, its pairwise structure or

of the U.S. approach is that it treats the reputation of the victim as the cost of "protecting public debate." RIPSTEIN, *supra* note 8, at 225. On my account of inherently valuable conflicts, by contrast, the protected interest is individualist in its core, which is the speaker's (and the listener's and/or thinker's) right to free speech. With respect to English law of defamation, the rise of the defense of responsible journalism seems to count against the absolutist protection of reputation. Ripstein's response to this defense is to redescribe journalists as public officials. RIPSTEIN, *supra* note 8, at 228. Although I fully agree with his observation that a journalist is, among other things, "a guardian of the public nature of a democratic society," I do not see why it follows that they are also *public* officials (after all, university professors are, among other things, guardians of knowledge and truth but it does not make them public officials). On my view, the reason they should be afforded special protection has to do with the *context* in which journalists exercise their *private* right of free speech, rather than with their *identity* as public officials. The Canadian decision in *Grant v. Torstar Corp.* [2009] 3 SCR 640 further extends this point by characterizing the defense as responsible communication, meaning that it is not even about being a journalist. Our identity as private persons is fully compatible with having an interest in contributing to public matters (broadly defined to include social and economic matters, rather than only political ones).

45 *See* WEINRIB, *supra* note 6, at 100.

what I have called the tort-law-way of addressing conflicts. This section discusses the broader philosophical context of relational egalitarianism. It seeks to provide the philosophical motivation for the equality theory of tort law.

Liberal egalitarians share the basic view that all people's lives are equally important. They part ways in articulating what theoretical and practical implications follow therefrom. Distributive egalitarians suggest that equality should be assessed by reference to the things that people, taken severally, have. These things may be resources, opportunities, capabilities, and so on. An egalitarian society should, therefore, aspire to promote equality in the overall distribution of things among all its members (and, cosmopolitans will argue, even beyond). Relational egalitarians, by contrast, suggest that the good of equality lies not in the things that people have, but rather in the terms of their interactions. This good grounds a commitment to an egalitarian arrangement of our practical lives subject to justifiable exceptions.[46] I argue that the relational view is appealing precisely because it resonates with an important fact about our human condition, namely, the fact of *interdependence*.[47]

Indeed, our practical affairs are either formed or shaped by the interactions we have with other private persons. This is the case not only with respect to the thicker relationships we have as spouses, partners, colleagues, and workers (et alia), but rather also with respect to thinner interactions between mere strangers who happen to pursue conflicting plans at the same time and place, plans that seriously implicate the life and limb and other fundamental interests of the participants. Moreover, the prevalence of interdependence, it is important to note, is not limited to hierarchy and authority relations but also to episodic and hierarchy-free interactions between risk-creators and risk-bearers, at least with respect to substantial risks to serious setback to fundamental interests, such as in bodily and emotional integrity. Things matter for relational egalitarianism but only because, and only insofar as, they might have an undesirable (and at times desirable) impact on these interactions. On this picture, having equal things, or even enough things, is not equality's end. Nor is it an ideal about having an equal starting point (a.k.a. equal opportunity) or equal outcome. Rather, egalitarianism with respect to things, broadly defined, can only serve as a means to sustaining egalitarian terms of interactions between people.[48]

[46] Thus, although the commitment at issue implies that our different spheres of life (e.g., work) should meet the demands of relational equality, there could be some justifiable exceptions. For instance, the provision of national security may depend on robustly inegalitarian arrangements (say, between army officers and their soldiers). Some aspects of education (as in teacher-student in-class interactions) may also fit this category. The parents-children structure of family life, especially when children are in their early stages of moral development, is another case in point. Tort-law interactions do not fall into one sphere of life in particular. At any rate, it is hard to see what might categorically exempt such interactions from the demands of relational equality.

[47] *See* Hanoch Dagan & Avihay Dorfman, *Just Relationships*, 116 COLUM. L. REV. 1395, 1415–16 (2016).

[48] Samuel Scheffler, *What Is Egalitarianism?*, 31 PHIL. & PUB. AFF. 5, 23 (2003).

So what is the relational equality ideal? My answer consists of three elements. First, it is an ideal about human, rather than social or political, relations. Second, these human relations are governed by terms of interactions that reflect the parties' status as agents, rather than patients. And third, contrary to the teachings of the formal conception of relational equality, these terms also reflect—by which I mean incorporate—differences in the underlying interests and conditions of these parties. In its most abstract form, the standard underlying this theory suggests that terms of pairwise interaction count as substantively equal if, and only if, they properly account for differences in interests and conditions. I now proceed to defend the first element by contrasting my understanding of relational egalitarianism with the one associated with the work of Elizabeth Anderson (along with other relational egalitarians). I defend the latter two in Chapters 12–15.

Anderson has famously argued that, on the liberal tradition, egalitarianism is "fundamentally concerned with equality of social relationships."[49] Social relationships of equality are defined contrastively by terms of interaction that are not marred by unjustified hierarchy.[50] Anderson divides hierarchical relations into three types.[51] There are hierarchies of power, according to which one person can exercise some normative power, including in particular authority, over another. There are hierarchies of esteem, according to which a party in an interaction enjoys some special honor and admiration at the expense of the other party who is, accordingly, held in contempt. And there are hierarchies of standing, according to which one party enjoys certain privileges while the other is saddled with an inferior status.

There is much to be said about this classification, as well as on what might justify hierarchical relations.[52] However, doing so is unnecessary for my argument. Instead, I wish to make two critical points about Anderson's relational equality, each of which could then both motivate and inform my reconstruction of the equality theory of tort law.

[49] Elizabeth Anderson, *How Should Egalitarians Cope with Market Risks*, 9 THEORETICAL INQ. L. 237, 263 (2007) [Anderson, *How Should Egalitarians*]; *see also* Elizabeth S. Anderson, *What Is the Point of Equality?*, 109 ETHICS 287 (1999) [Anderson, *What Is the Point*]. Other leading contributions to this theme are Jonathan Wolff, *Fairness, Respect, and the Egalitarian Ethos*, 27 PHIL. & PUB. AFF. 97 (1998); Scheffler, *supra* note 48; Samuel Scheffler, *The Practice of Equality*, *in* SOCIAL EQUALITY: ON WHAT IT MEANS TO BE EQUALS 21 (Carina Fourie et al. eds., 2015). There are some important differences between these, and other, accounts of relational equality. It is beyond the scope of my argument to discuss them. For an illuminating analysis of this point, see KASPER LIPPERT-RASMUSSEN, RELATIONAL EGALITARIANISM: LIVING AS EQUALS 57–59 (2018).

[50] This characterization is shared by another champion of relational equality. *See* Scheffler, *supra* note 48, at 22.

[51] ELIZABETH ANDERSON, PRIVATE GOVERNMENT: HOW EMPLOYERS RULE OUR LIVES (AND WHY WE DON'T TALK ABOUT IT) 127–30 (2017); Anderson, *How Should Egalitarians*, *supra* note 49, at 263.

[52] To say a bit more, I worry that Anderson's answer to the latter question (of what might justify hierarchy) draws too heavily on a certain ideal of democracy. As I argue in the main text below, the basic appeal of relational equality comes not from a political ideal of democracy but rather from a more fundamental concern with human relationship, rather than with relations between members of a political community.

Human versus social relations. Anderson identifies the relational dimension of equality with a certain form of relations, namely, *social* relations.[53] I argue that the "social" deflects attention from the broader category of relations on which relational egalitarianism lays claims, namely, *human* relations. The cases on which Anderson draws involve employment relationships,[54] participants in democratic decision-making processes (such as a round table),[55] contractual parties in a credit transaction,[56] and so on. They typically concern voluntary interactions, by which I mean encounters that are meant by the participants to occur or (if they happen accidently) persist for some span of time. These encounters are of a value, at least in the eyes of the participants, and in entering them they can no longer remain strangers or unknown to one another. They are, therefore, also (or just) *social* relations. Other relational egalitarians have moved beyond the "social" to reclaim the value of economic relations[57] as well as political ones.[58]

I do not dispute the existence of social relations (or, for that matter, economic or political relations) and the importance of subjecting them to the demands of relational equality. My concern is that the case of social relations will serve as a threshold to the kind of relations that should be susceptible to such demands. In particular, the worry is that fleeting interactions between strangers that figure so prominently in our everyday life, and in many tort cases, fall short of being social relations, and so lie beyond the proper reach of relational egalitarianism. After all, tort-law interactions could be purely involuntary and at times lacking intrinsic value. Those who participate in them may even not be aware of the identity of each other (simply consider an encounter between a driver and a nearby pedestrian or a product manufacturer and an end user). Such interactions, in John Gardner's words, are only loosely relational.[59] They concern encounters in the absence of either a prior or a forthcoming relationship.

One might even wonder why care about relating as equals in the context of tort interactions. I argue, in response, that any attempt to address the conflicts

[53] Kolodny emphasizes the ongoing character of inegalitarian relations, to the exclusion of what he calls "episodic interactions." Niko Kolodny, *An Objection to Social Hierarchy Itself?*, *in* Working as Equals 32, 37 (Julian Jonker & Grant Z. Rozeboom eds., 2023); Niko Kolodny, The Pecking Order: Social Hierarchy as a Philosophical Problem 98 (2023). Lippert-Rasmussen notes that "The relational and distributive ideals of justice ascribe different loci of justice—social relations and distributions." Lippert-Rasmussen, *supra* note 49, at 5. Scheffler, by contrast, emphasizes both social and *human* relations as the egalitarian units of analysis. *See* Scheffler, *supra* note 48, at 31.

[54] Anderson, *supra* note 51.

[55] Anderson, *What Is the Point*, *supra* note 49, at 313; Elizabeth Anderson, *The Democratic University: The Role of Justice in the Production of Knowledge*, 12 Soc. Phil. & Pol'y 186 (1995).

[56] Elizabeth Anderson, *Ethical Assumptions in Economic Theory: Some Lessons from the History of Credit and Bankruptcy*, 7 Econ. Theory & Moral Practice 347, 357, 359 (2004).

[57] *See* Daniel Markovits, *Promise as an Arm's Length Relation*, *in* Promises and Agreements: Philosophical Essays 295 (Hanoch Sheinman ed., 2011); Daniel Markovits, *Contract and Collaboration*, 113 Yale L.J. 1417 (2004).

[58] Daniel Viehoff, *Democratic Equality and Political Authority*, 42 Phil. & Pub. Aff. 337 (2014).

[59] *See* John Gardner, *Dagan and Dorfman on the Value of Private Law*, 117 Colum. L. Rev. Online 179, 191–93 (2017).

of interests that animate the law of torts—including even by allowing them to stand—necessarily reflects an egalitarian judgment. That is, determining what either party is entitled to do or refrain from doing necessarily determines how this party—viewed as a free and equal agent—fares vis-à-vis the other. Let me unpack this claim.

Thus, I argue that *human* relations are morally important, too, and that their importance does not necessarily turn on their social or societal credentials. The reason why they matter for egalitarianism is that fundamental interests of the participants come into conflict so that *any* attempt to address this conflict necessarily determines how they relate to *each other*. For instance, any resolution of a conflict between a pedestrian's life and limb and a driver's liberty of action reflects a relational-egalitarian judgment—to wit, determining what either one is entitled to do necessarily fixes the terms of interaction for *both*. It necessarily reflects tort law's judgment as to the relative importance of either party's interest which, ultimately, represents tort law's commitment not merely to take their lives (taken severally) seriously but also to regard them as equally important.

Hence, what matters is not the societal underpinning or the ongoing relationship between a risk-creator and risk-bearer; rather, it is about whether the conflict between their respective interests is governed by terms that regard their holders as (substantively, as opposed to formally) equals. These terms necessarily reflect judgments about the relative significance of their respective interests, the value of the conflict between them, and, ultimately, what taking their respective lives as equally important requires. As these judgments represent the demands of reason, tort law does not have the legitimate authority to sidestep them. The equality theory of tort law provides the normative framework of tort law's response to these judgments.

Addressing vulnerability versus inferiority. What counts as relating as equals? What, to put it differently, is the evil of relational inequality? Philosophers often suggest that it is a society with pervasive status inequalities in which members of certain social groups experience inferiority across many social and economic spheres.[60] Anderson's answer singles out relational inferiority, in particular. Relations of hierarchy of power, esteem, and standing are bad because they subject one party in the relation to an "inferior position."[61] Inferiority is then divided into various instances of domination, subjection, oppression, and being "objects of ridicule, loathing, or disgust."[62]

[60] *See, e.g.*, KOLODNY, *supra* note 53, at chs. 5–6. Strictly speaking, Kolodny's theory of relational equality focuses on claims of inferiority. It is an account against social inequality, and specifically inferiority. Anderson's, by contrast, is best viewed as an account for social equality.

[61] ANDERSON, *supra* note 51, at 127. *See also* Niko Kolodny, *Rule over None II: Social Equality and the Justification of Democracy*, 42 PHIL. & PUB. AFF. 287, 300 (2014);

[62] Anderson, *What Is the Point*, *supra* note 49, at 315, 316, 331; Anderson, *How Should Egalitarians*, *supra* note 49, at 263.

Thus, to relate as equals, the terms of interaction between persons must do away with any and all unjustified inferiorities (or, looked at from the opposite side, hierarchies). It seems straightforward that Anderson's focus on voluntary, social relations will lead her to identify the ills of such encounters with domination and related experiences of being "unwelcome in social settings."[63] Once again, I do not deny that inferiority is a source of relational inequality. My critical observation is that inferiority should be viewed as a private case of a broader category of relational inequalities. More specifically, I argue that it is *vulnerability to certain actions by others*, rather than inferiority, that is the ultimate source of relational inequality.

Being vulnerable to the actions and inactions of another person can sometimes amount to a human relation of inequality. Consider a truck driver that, due to some inattention on his part, swerves into the pedestrian path, severely injuring a pedestrian. The driver's failure need not be the result of a deliberate or reckless disregard of the pedestrian. It can simply be an unfortunate, careless mistake on the driver's part. There is no *social* relation between the two people, but they are caught up in a human relation created by their conflicting pursuits of ends. Their "relating" commences not merely at the moment of the accident and onwards, but rather at the earlier stage of paying attention and taking precautions so as to avoid or moderate the conflict created by engaging in their respective activities of driving and walking. Talk of hierarchical relations of power, standing, or esteem seems unwarranted, but there still is an important sense in which their conflict gives rise to an egalitarian concern. We often criticize such a driver, saying that he failed to treat the interest of the pedestrian as *equally* important as driving; and we can criticize a negligent pedestrian for failing to treat the interest of the driver as equally important as walking, too. Such an encounter cannot but give rise to questions of relational equality: Who is vulnerable to whom? What terms of interaction—for example, the amount of care—should govern their respective pursuits of ends? These are questions of relational equality precisely because they concern how they stand to each other. These things—viz., the pedestrian's life and limb and the driver's freedom of action—are no less important than the things on which Anderson focuses, namely, inferiority resulting from being dominated, subjected, or held in contempt (et alia). This is why the equality theory casts the predicament of risk-bearers in terms of vulnerability, rather than inferiority.

Transactional versus democratic equality. What is the conception of the person that stands at the center of the relational equality approach? Anderson calls her theory "democratic equality." Hers seeks "the construction of a community of equals," in part by imposing the necessary "obligations of citizens in a democratic state."[64] The equality theory of torts I will defend below makes no essential

[63] Anderson, *What Is the Point*, *supra* note 49, at 335.
[64] Anderson, *What Is the Point*, *supra* note 49, at 289.

reference to the political identity of the parties in a conflict governed by tort law. It is an ideal about treating *persons* as equals, rather than seeing to it that their standing vis-à-vis one another would reflect their status as equal citizens or turn on considerations of membership in a political community. The equality theory of tort law, therefore, concerns transactional equality in the simple sense that being parties to a transaction is all that matters.

Now consider the nature of the connection between transactional and democratic equality. Must there be an intimate link between, on the one hand, how you and I stand in relation to each other and, on the other, the fact that both of us are also part of a larger, democratic political community? If the answer is that the former serves the latter, then there exists a fundamental difference between transactional and democratic equality. Transactional equality takes the terms of fleeting interactions, such as between a driver and a pedestrian, as a source of egalitarian concern in and of itself. By contrast, democratic equality can treat such interactions as components of the overall effort to construct "a community of equals" among all members of a democracy. As components, it may be possible to look past this or that interaction by assessing how important it is to the realization of a community of equals. I assume that not all pairwise interactions are necessarily equally important for the democratic ideal of relating as equals. Plausibly, a one-off, fleeting interaction should figure less prominently than recurring interactions between the same parties, for instance, in the context of service provision, work relations, neighbors, and so on. It seems that only the latter could pose an existential threat to a society in which "citizens make claims on one another in virtue of their equality, not inferiority, to others."[65] None of this "looking past" an interaction is allowed if transactional equality is a source of concern in and of itself. Another way to put this point is to say that transactional equality takes a deontological stance whereas democratic equality displays a rather consequentialist approach. The former insists that even one-off encounters count as a source of concern for an egalitarian tort law whereas the latter evaluates the necessity of subjecting these encounters to the demands of relational equality by reference to their cumulative effects and, ultimately, their overall consequences for the relevant political community.

In sum, although the equality theory of tort law is a member in the philosophical family of relational egalitarianism, it does not subscribe to three of its core pillars. The character of the relationship subject to egalitarian assessment is human, rather than social relations; the basic threat to relating as equals is human vulnerability, rather than inferiority; and the ultimate concern of the equality theory of tort law is with how parties in an interaction stand in relation to each other, rather than the overall level of relational equality in a democratic society.

[65] *Id.*

III. The Structure of the Equality Theory of Torts: On What Lies Ahead

Against this backdrop, the argument can now move to the next stage, which is that of constructing and defending the equality theory of tort law. I do that in three principal phases. The first phase, Chapter 12, introduces the most basic layer of that theory, namely, the idea of relating as agents. I argue that tort duties make possible a certain form of an egalitarian interaction between agents. The second and most challenging phase, Chapters 13–15, moves from relating as agents to relating as equals, which is to say from the very existence to the content of tort duties. It explores what aspects of a person's interest and condition should count for the purpose of determining whether parties to an interaction relate as substantive equals. The third phase, Chapters 16–17, extends the equality theory of tort law in two ways: One to the civil procedure aspects of tort law and, in particular, the allocation of the burden of persuasion between parties in a tort dispute; and the second to the terms of interactions that so far have not been recognized as worthy of the attention of tort law. I defend the case for a tort of private censorship in part by drawing on the equality theory of torts. Along the way, I also show that the equality and the conflict theories of tort law are not only mutually reinforcing but also form a normative unity: The equality theory serves the conflict theory by making it possible for the conflict theory to address tolerably valuable conflicts.

12
Why *Tort* Duties? Why Tort *Law*? Relating as Agents

Introduction

Why have tort duties at all? Why must they take the form of law? I argue that it is not necessarily that an individual member receives more safety or freedom (as independence or self-determination) when a fully functioning system of tort law exists; nor is it that the receipt of more accountability for, rectification, or redress of wrongdoings; nor, finally, is it optimal deterrence and the reduction of negative externalities. All of these ends can be adequately provided for by other legal and extralegal means. Rather, tort duties bring into existence a certain relation of equality between people whose fundamental interests are in conflict. This chapter establishes the basic layer of this relation—what I call relating as *agents*—and the next chapters take up the second layer—what I shall call relating as *equals*. Together, they establish the basic pillars of the equality theory of tort law.

More specifically, the good provided by tort duties is that of creating egalitarian frameworks of interaction between private persons. These frameworks are valuable because they make possible a certain form of human interaction that I call relating as agents.[1] I argue that doing so depends on having two formal requirements: Tort duties have to be *publicly* mandated and fixed, on the one hand, and *privately* owed and owned, on the other. Simply put, these duties must be imposed, and their content determined, by operation of law, rather than choice. Moreover, the responsibility for discharging them must fall to private persons, rather than public officials.

Viewing tort duties in this way poses a challenge to another widely held view of the distinction between private and public ordering and, in particular, between contract and tort. On this conception, endorsed by economists as well as some liberal egalitarians, the former holds normative priority over the latter so that the involuntary duties of tort law function as second-best approximations of chosen obligations or, as Dworkin at one point called them, "market-simulating" duties.[2] Fair and costless processes of bargaining—as in perfectly competitive markets with

[1] By agency I draw on the traditional conception of human agency: Very roughly, the ability of one to exercise substantial control over one's thoughts and actions, which is to say self-directed action that reflects the actor's judgments.

[2] Ronald Dworkin, Law's Empire 295 (1986).

Conflict between Equals. Avihay Dorfman, Oxford University Press. © Oxford University Press 2026.
DOI: 10.1093/9780198979869.003.0016

no externalities—represent a superior method of creating or trading in existing, horizontal rights and obligations. Tort law is a nonmarket solution to certain market failures, kicking in only because, and only insofar as, contracting might or does fail.

By contrast, I argue that tort duties—and here I mean tort duties that protect our fundamental interests—are prerequisites to voluntary transactions. The argument is that a tort-law duty—a publicly created and privately executed duty—is constitutive of the ability of parties to engage in market and nonmarket transactions as agents. Tort duties that protect our fundamental interests are not the residue or leftovers of voluntary interactions but rather their foundation; without tort duties, there can be no liberal practices of voluntary transactions (because no agency without baselines that define and defend agency). The argument, therefore, is that a tort-law duty is constitutive of the ability of parties in a conflict to interact with each other as agents.

I. The Tort-Law Way of Doing Things: Setting the Scene

Tort duties represent a special kind of mandatory reasons for action. I begin with presupposing what they are and defend this presupposition in subsequent parts of this chapter. By tort duties I mean primary duties, as opposed to secondary duties of repair. These duties provide their bearers with a mandatory reason to conduct themselves in certain ways, namely, to refrain from committing battery, invading privacy, or creating an unreasonable risk of harm to another (et alia). I do not argue that all the existing primary tort duties, in this or that jurisdiction, matter or that they matter equally. My focus is on primary tort duties that protect our fundamental interests (to bodily and emotional integrity, privacy, good name, and so forth). I further take it that these primary duties are directed duties in the sense that they are *owed* to and *owned* by potential victims. For instance, the duty against defaming another is owed to this other person. It may be owed to others as well, but only insofar as these others are taken severally, rather than together. Hence, when a journalist publishes a piece containing false assertions on five different people, the number of tort duties she might have breached is five, rather than one. Further, these duties are *owned* by these five, taken severally. What is meant by ownership in this context is that they each possess a certain standing in relation to the journalist. As I argue below, owning a duty gives the potential victim some (nontrivial) measure of *control* over some aspects of the duty—more specifically, its existence, performance, or (typically) enforcement.

To set the scene for this chapter's question—why have tort duties in the first place—I begin with presenting two, increasingly abstract, hypothetical cases to render more vivid why this question matters. Begin with the concrete case, which is modeled after a leading case in the canon of modern tort law, *MacPherson v. Buick*

Motor.[3] The question at its center was whether a car manufacturer owes a duty of care to the driver, which is a duty to exercise reasonable care in inspecting the safety of the car before it enters the market. The driver was injured when his Buick collapsed as a result of a defective wheel. While a proper inspection could have discovered the defect, the manufacturer had failed to do so. There was no contractual privity between the parties as the driver bought the car from a car dealership. Up until this case, and save for some narrow exceptions, there could be no duty of care running from the manufacturer to the product user, not to mention to a nonuser victim (e.g., a pedestrian). The only (nonexceptional) way to trigger such a duty was to form a contractual relationship between the manufacturer and the user of its product.[4]

It is, no doubt, an important achievement for the *MacPherson* court to reform the law by making manufacturers duty-bound to users and certain nonusers, that is, independently of contractual agreements. But the crucial question is this: Why? In particular, must we have such a duty? Perhaps its desirability is contingent. One way to defend *MacPherson* is to reason from the imperfections of markets to a contract-independent duty of care. That duty finds its grounds in the inability of actual markets to take into sufficient account all the persons involved. That said, this style of reasoning does not tell us whether correcting for market imperfections is *all* there is to a tort duty of care; further, as I shall argue, it could be epiphenomenal.

To explore this question further, imagine a fully competitive market for automobiles and for accident insurance. On this picture, manufacturers do not need a tort-law duty of care to conduct themselves in the best way, not merely for them but for society as a whole. Rigorous market competition alone gives them ample reason to care about the safety of their consumers, users, and even pedestrians. Manufacturers will then live up to their ambition to provide safe and high-quality cars in full satisfaction of the preferences of drivers and pedestrians. Manufacturers will also compensate victims for mishaps, as doing so becomes a direct implication of the market in which they compete. Furthermore, and again out of market forces alone, manufacturers will each open up fair avenues of recourse for addressing and redressing grievances by injured users and nonusers. In these ways, market competition could perfectly mimic whatever it is that tort law is designed to achieve from *MacPherson* onwards. Proponents of tort law as the law of wrongs (or harms) and of civil recourse will find ample recognition of their accounts of why tort law matters in such a world. So will lawyer-economists. What, if anything, is missing in this private, market ordering? And why might it matter?

[3] 111 N.E. 1050 (N.Y. 1916).

[4] This rule was at the center of a leading English authority, Winterbottom v. Wright 152 Eng. Rep. 402 (1842). *See further* Robert Stevens, Torts and Rights 173 (2007).

Explaining away these questions, for instance, by pointing to the awesome gap between the Pollyannish assumptions I am making and real-world markets, will not do. This is because the point of my hypothetical is to get at the *normative root* of the voluntary/involuntary distinction. It is also so because, ultimately, my aim is to show why a certain way of distinguishing involuntary from voluntary obligations might challenge the conventional understanding of the torts/contract divide.[5]

Now I wish to generalize this case to show that the "why have tort duties" question is not peculiar to negligence or products liability law but rather extends to accidental or other conflicts between private persons. Consider a society in which everything is very much like ours except for the complete absence of tort law. This means that inherently valuable, tolerable, and valueless conflicts are as familiar to its members as they are to us. Speakers, drivers, physicians, potential assailants, would-be trespassers, and more are sufficiently motivated to behave reasonably well both before and after an injurious incident. Perhaps the reason is a successful combination of ethos, reputational pressures, good moral upbringing, and/or a legal scheme of incentives put by the state (such as in the form of tax credits, welfare benefits, etc.). Alternatively, perhaps the reason is the resort to limitless markets in which all practical affairs are governed by contractual allocations of existing entitlement, such as to walk freely at a certain place and time, to speak out in certain ways and at certain places, to have a defined sphere of privacy, and so forth.

Whatever the commitment mechanism is, it takes a private form. Each member of this society *chooses* to moderate his or her conduct appropriately and, when failing to do so, makes good on his or her misdeeds.[6] As a result, there is no observable difference between this society and a society with a fully functioning body of tort law both in terms of the level of risk, violence, and substandard behavior to which people are being regularly exposed, on the one hand, and the adequacy of compensation or satisfaction that deserving victims receive, on the other. After all,

[5] By saying *a conventional understanding*, I do not claim that it is the only understanding. My approach is compatible with the account of contracting defended in Hanoch Dagan & Michael Heller, Liberal Contract Theory (unpublished manuscript). Leading tort theorists have also criticized the priority of contract over tort. *See, e.g.*, Arthur Ripstein, Private Wrongs 73–79 (2016); John Gardner, Torts and Other Wrongs 341, 343 (2019). An importantly different approach has been defended by Mark Geistfeld, namely, dividing tort law according to three different types of social interactions. Aggressive interactions are primarily governed by criminal law, and the tort law that deals with these interactions is in some way an add-on (my term, not his) to criminal law's purposes. Other interactions to which tort law responds are cooperative in nature, in which case tort law maps onto contract law's purposes. Lastly, tort law stands on its own normative foot when it comes to "accidental injuries caused by noncriminal conduct outside of contractual settings." *See* Mark A. Geistfeld, Torts, Contracts, and Categorical Reasoning in the Common Law (unpublished manuscript) at 6. *See also* Mark A. Geistfeld, *Hidden in Plain Sight: The Normative Source of Modern Tort Law*, 91 N.Y.U. L. Rev. 1517, 1544–45, 1566–69 (2016). Note, however, that even the latter category is not necessarily inconsistent with the Coasean superiority of contract over torts.

[6] Morality can be viewed (from a functional perspective) as a commitment mechanism. However, it is not a "system" of private ordering. There is not enough space to develop this point, but I take it that the demands of morality are involuntary, rather than chosen. A stand-alone "system" of morality would have to incorporate tort law—that is, both *tort* law and tort *law*—as its practical embodiment.

wrongdoers may have good reasons not to misbehave, and similarly good reasons to compensate including by providing avenues of redress to their victims, apart from being legally forced to do so. Hence, there is no *empirical* need, so to speak, for tort law in that society. That said, something is missing, normatively speaking.

I proceed by making two main claims. Negatively, I discuss and criticize two prominent answers to the "why have tort duties" question. Both place some notion of freedom at the center of the respective answers. I argue, drawing on the discussion in Chapter 11, that resort to freedom as independence and as effective agency cannot but fail to answer the question. Affirmatively, I argue that tort-law duties matter because they make possible a certain egalitarian ideal I call relating as agents. More specifically, I argue that what is missing in the hypothetical cases mentioned above is the tort-law duty (without yet getting into the other question of what its content should be[7]). In particular, there are three missing elements that jointly make up this duty. First, the otherwise perfectly reasonable behavior of all members of this society ex ante and ex post is not *legally mandated*. Second, the legal mandate must take the form of an obligation *owed to* the potential victims. And third, it must also take the form of an obligation *owned by* these victims. The basis for criticizing that society and, so, making another step toward the vindication of tort law, is equality. In this hypothetical society, risk-creators and risk-bearers do not *relate* to each other as agents. This society must have tort duties and, further, these duties must take the form of law.

II. Why Have a Tort-Law Duty in the First Place?

In a Coasean world of zero transaction costs, it is extremely easy to contract for all the rights that figure in tort law, including in particular the basic rights to life and limb, the liberty to use the outdoors, free speech, reputation, privacy, and more. For purposes of exposition, I will focus on the tort of battery and its contractual cognates. I argue that the absence of a tort-law duty against committing battery denies promisees (would-be victims) their ability to relate as equals to their promisors. The reason is that having to contract for a right not to be intentionally harmed undermines the status of the promisee as an agent not merely in general, but rather also, and especially, in his or her relation to the promisor. To count as an agent, the promisee must be entitled to this right *independently* of the promisor's choice to enter, and carry out, the contract. Having such a right to bodily integrity reflects the status of the right-holder as an independent constraint on another person akin to what Rawls might have meant by asserting that persons are "self-originating sources of valid claims."[8]

[7] *See* Chapters 13–15.

[8] John Rawls, *Justice as Fairness: Political Not Metaphysical*, 14 Phil. & Pub. Aff. 223, 242 (1985).

To forestall misunderstandings, I do not equate the choice of the promisor with whims or brute preferences, an equation that republican theories of freedom often make when characterizing subordination in terms of being put "at the mercy" of another person.[9] It may well be the case that the participants in a Coasean bargaining are motivated by the demands of right reason and, moreover, correctly apply these demands. Let's assume that they are decent people. The problem is that of making the right to bodily integrity the product of choice, rather than an external constraint on choice.

Moreover, as I explain more fully below, the trouble with choice is not limited to the choice of the promisor alone, as the contract also manifests (at least ideally) the choice of the promisee. Instead, the trouble is that to relate as agents, there are certain fundamental interests that should not be up for grabs, that is, as commodities whose fate is determined at the bargaining table (including when shaped by default rules designed to facilitate an appropriate contractual agreement). These fundamental interests (already discussed in Chapter 2) must figure as constraints on, rather than the upshots of, choice because they are necessary *pre*conditions for being free and equal agents.[10] Although bodily integrity is a paradigm case of a fundamental interest, tort law deals with other such interests, such as reputation, free speech, privacy, and the liberty to use the outdoors. They make human agency possible and, so, may not be left to the contractual parties' choosing, at least not in the same way we treat market commodities.

Thus, in order for persons to relate as agents, respecting bodily integrity (et alia) must not merely be binding in the same way that a contractual bargain is. Rather, it has to be binding in the right way, namely, by taking the form of an *in*voluntary duty. The existence of a duty against committing battery is necessary precisely because it is imposed by operation of law. It might be possible to assume that under some conditions a contract can guarantee more protection to the contracting parties' bodily integrity. However, that is not what lies at the heart of my argument. It is one thing to be protected against being violently attacked by another person; quite another to be treated as a person whose bodily integrity imposes a *freestanding* constraint on voluntary arrangements. Hence, contrary to the Coasean view that it is either an add-on to or a replacement for contracting, tort law takes the constitutive role of seeing to it that people relate to each other as agents. Accordingly, their status as agents must be secured prior to, and independently of, bargaining (including bargaining in the shadow of autonomy-sustaining default rules).

[9] PHILIP PETTIT, REPUBLICANISM: A THEORY OF FREEDOM AND GOVERNMENT 4–5 (1999).

[10] Debra Satz has argued that some goods—such as physical security—"function as prerequisites for full inclusion in society, for counting as an equal member." By contrast, my argument focuses more narrowly on whether the risk-creator and a risk-bearer relate as equals, regarding them as private persons, rather than members in a larger, political community. DEBRA SATZ, WHY SOME THINGS SHOULD NOT BE FOR SALE 102 (2010).

Relating as agents depends not only on the existence of involuntary duties—that is, publicly mandated obligations. Rather, it also requires that their content be partially fixed by operation of law, as opposed to choice. The reason for this is to deny the interacting parties' controlling influence over what counts as a minimally adequate level of respect, such as for bodily integrity. After all, leaving it to the parties to fix the mandatory floor of respect opens a backdoor through which to reinstate the supremacy of private ordering (Coasean and otherwise). As I explain below, the content of the duty is only partially fixed by operation of law in the sense that parties can contract for either *more* exacting levels of respect or, under narrowly defined circumstances, less.

It is important to emphasize that the problem at issue is that of subjecting fundamental interests to choice, rather than the different problem of subjection to *unilateral* choice. For even the bilateral choice of both parties in a contract might undermine the possibility of relating as agents. To see this, consider how leading corrective justice theorists characterize the problem of unilateral choice.[11] Their argument is that unilateral choice violates a basic precept of transactional equality because it gives one party control over the question of what respect is due, and how much. They argue that the generic wrong to which tort law as a whole responds is that of subjection to unilateral choice (according to which one attempts to be "in charge" of another person). Chapter 11 has shown that this view can only capture some tort duties, falling short of explaining and justifying others. However, for the sake of my current argument, this shortcoming can be set to one side.

Thus, the argument against unilateral choice does not explain what might be the problem with a shared choice, which is to say an agreed upon determination of the content of the duty. In fact, except for the extreme case of contracting for slavery, contracting for tort duties is not inconsistent with the criticism of unilateral choice as an instance of inequality and subordination.[12] That said, it is inconsistent with the ideal of relating as agents, as just explained.

My argument that respect for a person's bodily integrity (et alia) must be mandated through an involuntary duty whose content is fixed by operation of law remains incomplete, however. Why must this duty be a *tort-law* duty in particular? Surely, there could be other possible legal obligations that take the form of a mandated, involuntary duty. (Certain criminal and administrative law norms come to mind.[13]) My answer returns to the pairwise structure of the tort-law duty.

[11] *See, e.g.*, Jules Coleman, *Tort Law and Tort Theory: Preliminary Reflections on Method*, *in* Philosophy and the Law of Torts 183, 205 (Gerald J. Postema ed., 2001).

[12] According to Ripstein, contract slavery contradicts the very possibility of legal personality and, with it, the possibility of a would-be slave to be under an obligation to abide by his or her contractual promise. Arthur Ripstein, Force and Freedom: Kant's Legal and Political Philosophy 136 (2009). It seems to me that this line of argument reflects the extreme case of slavery, but it is not clear whether it can be extended to capture the two hypothetical cases I discussed in the main text above.

[13] Some criminal law and regulatory norms may best be viewed as add-on to, or extension of, tort duties. However, not all norms of criminal law and regulation are tort-like. My question in the main text above concerns the latter type.

This peculiar structure is necessary in order for the parties not only to sustain their status as agents, taken severally, but rather to *relate* to each other as agents. In other words, the tort duty's distinctive contribution is that of turning agency into a relational construct by putting in place an obligation (to act in certain ways) owed to, and owned by, the right-holder. These two elements (of owing to and being owned by) turn an involuntary duty into a *requirement to relate as agents*. Or so I now seek to argue.

Before I take up these two requirements, I want to address the following objection. While my argument shows why tort duties stand, as they are, apart from choice, it remains unclear why these duties must take the form of *legal* duties. Surely, there can be extralegal obligations that are understood or experienced by their addressees as mandatory ones. For instance, some may regard their religious obligations as binding, irrespective of personal choice. In response, I argue that such obligations are not only unnecessary but also insufficient. A legal duty offers something that religion or other comprehensive doctrines lack: a public recognition of the duty's universal and obligatory nature. Public recognition is not simply a state of mind that we all happen to share, even if this mindset is widely known and accepted across society. Instead, it is something we all share—and publicly recognize as shared by us—in virtue of being members of the society. It requires an unambiguous manifestation: a conventionally entrenched obligation that expresses a collective commitment to a particular principle or value. It is the law (of torts) that gives effect to this acknowledgment.[14]

III. Relating as Agents: What Is It to Owe a Tort Duty *to* Another?

A distinctive contribution of a tort duty is to give the risk-bearer a special standing in relation to the risk-creator. The latter owes a duty to the former, and the former owns this duty. But precisely what does it mean to owe a duty *to* the risk-bearer? How does this notion of *owing-to* bear on the status of the risk-bearer as an agent? And what is the connection between "owing a duty to another" and "relating with him or her"? Two independently necessary conditions make the tort duty a matter of relating to the risk-bearer as an agent: one concerns knowledge and the other action. To relate to another person as an agent, you have to be able to (1) know about this person's presence and (2) make your action responsive to this knowledge. Together, a certain idea of knowledge and action turns the duty from a mere constraint on one's conduct to an obligation *to treat another person* as a constraint on one's conduct. Put differently, these two turn the general directive "be cautious" into the relational precept of "be cautious for this person (or this person's class)."

[14] *Cf.* Avihay Dorfman & Alon Harel, Constitutionalism and Majoritarianism Reconciled (unpublished manuscript).

I call the knowledge component the foreseeability condition and the action component the directedness condition. I elaborate these conditions in connection with the tort of negligence's duty of care as some of the complexities I will be exploring remain latent in the case of many other tort duties (including intentional torts duties and strict liability torts duties).

Relating by Knowing: The Reasonable Foreseeability Condition. I submit that it is not enough that the risk-creator would have sufficient information about the world in order to conduct herself reasonably. Rather, the reasonable foreseeability requirement demands that she take cognizance of the risk-bearer, or the risk-bearer class.[15] Hence, *the requirement is not meant to satisfy an epistemic concern about what the risk-creator knows or could reasonably know, but rather a substantive one concerning her ability to make the risk-bearer her object of the exercise of vigilance.*[16] Accordingly, the reason why you cannot owe a duty to an unforeseeable person is not because you do not have sufficient knowledge to guide your conduct in a careful and responsible way. Instead, it is because the vulnerability of this person cannot be *your* object of careful and responsible conduct.

To see this, consider the following sequence. I am heading to an isolated spot in the desert to try my new boomerang. After spending plenty of time making sure nobody is in my vicinity, I begin practicing. Suddenly, while the boomerang is circling in the air, a person pops up from a nearby sand dune to take a direct hit. I do not owe him a duty of care because I could not have reasonably anticipated his presence and, therefore, cannot take him as a practical constraint on my conduct.[17] There is no meaningful way to relate to another person as an agent if awareness of his or her presence is lacking.

But now suppose that soon after our sandman recovers, and while sitting at a distance to watch me throwing the boomerang, he takes another hit from me. But this time the boomerang bounces off the sandman, picks up intense speed and travels some distance, injuring yet another person. Let's assume that, as a matter of fact, no known boomerang has ever reached that distance—it is a freak accident that no reasonable person could have imagined. The famous case of *Palsgraf v. Long Island Railroad* suggests that while I owe a duty of care to the immediate, foreseeable victim, no such duty is owed to a second, *un*foreseeable victim.[18] The puzzle is this: If foreseeability is an epistemic check on my own agency, then why

[15] I further elaborate on the doctrinal and theoretical aspects of this requirement in Avihay Dorfman, *Foreseeability as Re-Cognition*, 59 AM. J. JURIS. 163 (2015).

[16] I say *ability to make*, rather than *actually making*, because the foreseeability requirement is not limited to subjective (or actual) knowledge. Instead, it concerns what could be reasonably known.

[17] Palsgraf v. Long Island R. Co., 162 N.E. 99 (N.Y. 1928). Even the dissenting judge, Justice Andrews, conceded that "In an empty world negligence would not exist." *Id.*, at 102.

[18] There are other interpretations of *Palsgraf*'s basic ruling, such as that it is about the breach element or that it concerns the proximate cause element. I reject them elsewhere (*see* Dorfman, *supra* note 15, at 174–85). At any rate, my discussion does not turn on the question of whose reading of *Palsgraf* is the most accurate or interesting. Instead, I take up the normative question of why foreseeability with respect to the victim (or victim's class), in particular, matters.

does awareness of the existence of the *second* victim matter at all? After all, the input I needed to make the right—that is, nonnegligent—decision about how to conduct myself with the boomerang has been *exhaustively* controlled by the presence of the (foreseeable) sandman. All I had to do in order to protect the unforeseeable victim is to conform to the duty I already owe to the foreseeable sandman.

Notice that my discussion does not concern the question of liability for the unforeseeable victim. Perhaps the fortuity in which the injury occurred should relieve me of liability (viz., lack of proximate cause). My question is different: Why shouldn't I owe the second victim a duty of care if *all* I need to know in order to act carefully and responsibly is that the *first* victim is around? This question implies that foreseeability is not merely an epistemic check. It requires cognizance of the second victim's presence within the zone of danger. It forges a most basic connection between the risk-creator and the risk-bearer. For how can they stand in even the thinnest "relation" possible, not to mention a relation of *agents*, if the former *cannot* be cognizant of the latter?

Thus understood, the foreseeability requirement demands that the risk-bearer could—though not necessarily would—figure in the deliberation of the risk-creator toward action *even when* thus figuring has zero epistemic value. Again, it is sufficient to base my decision regarding precaution-taking on the foreseeable presence of the first victim. In short, if the significance of the tort duty is in giving the risk-bearer a special standing in relation to the risk-creator, the foreseeability requirement sees to it that talk of "in relation to" is practical, rather than fictitious.[19] The egalitarian ideal of relating as agents, therefore, requires foreseeability *with respect to* the risk-bearer.[20]

Relating by Acting: The Directedness Condition. Suppose that a truck driver inadvertently fails to heed the applicable height limit in the highway in which she drives, accidently crashing into a highway overpass.[21] As a result, the exit intersection will be closed for all traffic for the next several weeks until it is fully repaired. The closure blocks the only route leading to a nearby motel, which is the only business establishment on this highway's exit. It is not implausible to suppose that a reasonable driver could foresee the economic loss—lost business—that will be caused to this motel by the driver's failing to pay attention to the height limit. To make this point trivial, suppose the driver is a frequent guest at this motel and so she literally knows where it is located and what might be the implications of colliding into the overpass. Is it possible to say that the duty of care she owes as a driver puts her in a position of *relating* to the motel owner?

[19] *Cf.* Adam Slavny, Wrongs, Harms, and Compensation: Paying for Our Mistakes 95 (2024).

[20] My account provides a reason to believe that an unforeseeable victim should not be considered as being *wronged*—morally and legally—by the breach of the tort duty owed to the foreseeable victim. *Contra* Nicolas Cornell, *Wrongs, Rights, and Third Parties*, 43 Phil. & Pub. Aff. 109, 123–25 (2015).

[21] I draw, *very loosely*, on the facts of Aikens v. Debow, 541 S.E.2d 576 (W. Va. 2000).

The answer is no. I argue that what is missing is a certain condition of directedness. This condition is essential in order for the duty to mandate the driver into a mode of adjusting her actual conduct to the actual existence of nearby persons and properties that might be harmed by her driving activity. I argue that the driver can only do the adjustments with respect to the people on the overpass and/or its owner, and that any concern she might have about the well-being of the motel owner calls for making adjustments *with respect to the former*, not the latter. That is, the adjustments that are logically required in this case make essential and *exhaustive* reference to the people walking on the overpass. These "adjustments" shape what I mean by the directedness condition. Note that directedness is a matter of practical necessity. The question is not should I make this or that adjustment in response to this or that person but rather can I. Directedness reflects a practical necessity: My adjustments must be made in response to a specific person or a particular class of persons, even when I genuinely care, or ought to care, about the well-being of others. The issue is not whether the risk-creator can be expected to have a wide range of adverse consequences *in mind*; rather, it concerns what must be *done*—through adjustments and precaution-taking—and for *whose* benefit.

Thus, whereas there is no question about the existence of a duty owed to the people walking on the overpass and to its owner, tort law does not, and should not, recognize a duty of care *owed to* the motel owner, irrespective of how foreseeable his presence might be.[22] Some explain that in terms of a distinction between damaging property (the bridge) and interfering with economic expectations (to generate revenue from running a hotel).[23] But this distinction, when applied to commercial entities, might amount to empty formalism: Negligently causing the intersection to close can be a form of violating the motel owner's *property* right. It is like building a hermetic wall around the motel, depriving the owner any meaningful ability to use it. After all, the motel is a *commercial* property, rather than a dwelling house or a private club. Its only use-value lies in generating profit. Hence, the distinction between damage-to-property and pure economic loss cannot provide a nonconclusory starting point to the analysis of negligent infliction of pure economic loss on purely commercial entities.[24]

A better way to approach the matter is to draw on the idea of relating as agents and, specifically, on what it is to "relate to." The driver can owe a duty to a person P only if P's vulnerability *could* figure, in the right sense, in what the duty requires the driver to do. Practical attitudes associated with paying attention, thoughtfulness,

[22] There are exceptions, however. *See, e.g.*, People Express Airlines, Inc. v. Consolidated Rail Corp., 495 A.2d 107 (N.J. 1985).

[23] RIPSTEIN, *supra* note 5, at 53–54; Peter Benson, *Misfeasance as an Organizing Normative Idea in Private Law*, 60 U. TORONTO L.J. 731, 739 (2010).

[24] One way out of this difficulty would be to argue that the motel owner could still use this place for other, noncommercial purposes (for instance, he may live there, turn it into his private gym, and so forth).

awareness, and the like are part of what the duty calls for. Although these attitudes are not, and should not be, legally enforced in a liberal legal order, their outward manifestation certainly is. Indeed, a certain cautious *behavior* is, and should be, mandated by the duty. This behavior can be viewed as a series of adjustments incorporated into a person's plan of action. For instance, the truck driver is required to either check for overpasses prior to driving, take an alternate route, or halt and turn around the truck right before reaching the overpass (in case she had failed to look for the overpass' clearance height prior to her departure). The point is that all of these attitudes and their resulting behavior can only be directed *at the bridge and at the people* that might be using it while the truck passes through. This is what the directedness condition is all about.

Suppose that the driver is motivated to perform her duty out of her sheer concern for the business success of her friend, the motel owner. She does not fail to heed the height limitation, drives carefully solely out of concern for him, and so on. Could that satisfy the directedness condition? The answer is "no." There is a crucial difference between what *motivates* her attitudes and actions, on the one hand, and what these *attitudes and actions* require her to think and do, on the other. What she really has to do in this case is to acquire the relevant practical attitudes (attentiveness, awareness, etc.) and perform cautious driving *with respect to* the bridge and its users—she can adjust her actions according to that input, *and only that*. Hence, irrespective of her motivation, it is only the presence of the bridge's users and owner that could figure in her practical deliberations about what to do, by which I mean what adjustments to make as she approaches the overpass. This is the sense in which the duty she owes is a *duty to* certain people—the bridge's owner and users—and not to all those who motivated her performance of the duty, such as all the people who depend on the bridge other than the bridge users.[25]

To further see the importance of distinguishing between what motivates one's practical adjustments and the practical adjustments themselves (i.e., practical attitudes and conduct), substitute concern for the hotel owner with love of god, nation, community, setting an example for one's children, or any other grand concern that moves people in profound ways. Nothing should change in the description of the situation and in how we should think about proper driving and what it is to relate to pedestrians as agents. I argue that it is a mistake to say that the driver owes her tort-law duty of care to [god, the nation, local community, et alia]. All she can do in order to make good on her religious or other motivation is to take seriously—viz.,

[25] It is not surprising, when taking seriously the notion of "relating to," that tort law does impose a duty toward the economic interest of another when the risk-creator *undertakes* to invite the reliance of this other person on his or her exercise of due care. For instance, an accountant hired by a client may owe a duty of care to nonclients if she "intends to supply the information" for the benefit and guidance of the latter. It is her undertaking, we may say, that creates the possibility of "relating to" these nonclients by adjusting her deliberations and behavior in response to the nonclients' interests. RESTATEMENT (SECOND) OF TORTS §552 (1977).

acquire practical attitudes of attentiveness of and make adjustments in response to—the possible presence of people on the bridge.

Hence, the *directedness* of the tort duty is no mere insincere way to limit a duty-ower's liability for pragmatic reasons[26]; nor is it an implication of the distinction between property damage and economic loss. Rather, it is a reflection of a deeper point about what it means for a tort duty to establish a human relation in which the risk-bearer gets a certain standing in relation to the risk-creator. The motel owner has no such standing in relation to the risk-creator's duty when there is nothing in his condition or circumstances that could affect the practical deliberations, practical attitudes, and actual (conduct-based) adjustments the risk-creator is rationally required to make in order to discharge the duty. To put it in the terms mentioned above, the motel owner cannot figure as a freestanding constraint on her deliberation and actions in connection with discharging the duty of care. The deliberation and actions that go into her actual performance of the duty of careful driving would, and should, remain the same, *irrespective* of the motel owner or any other motivating factor. It is, therefore, not about his being unforeseeable but rather about lack of directedness. Everything the driver must do in terms of discharging the duty is exhaustively given by the vulnerability of those (potentially) using the bridge.

IV. Relating as Agents: What Is to *Own* a Duty?

Having special standing in relation to the risk-creator is not exhausted by imposing on the risk-creator an involuntary duty owed to the risk-bearer. In addition, a duty must be owned by the latter: Her standing in relation to the risk-creator necessitates some (nontrivial) measure of *control*. Otherwise, the risk-bearer would be reduced to no more than the beneficiary of practical attitudes and conduct called for by the duty of care. Ownership and standing in this context share some similar characteristics with ownership and standing in the context of property law, but they are not the same.[27] I begin by outlining a general characterization of "owning" a duty in tort law to provide the sense in which the duty of care is a source of standing in relation to a risk-creator. I argue that it is the case if, and only if, the duty is

[26] This is not to say that there are no other reasons for excluding liability for pure economic losses. As I argue elsewhere, a concern with crushing liability can provide another such reason. Hanoch Dagan & Avihay Dorfman, *Substantive Remedies*, 96 NOTRE DAME L. REV. 513, 547–50 (2020). Note, however, that the case under discussion does not fit the crushing liability doctrine as the expected liability of the truck driver (who is also, very likely, fully insured) is rather manageable. Thus, in the *Aikens* case, the pure economic loss, characterized as lost income, amounted to $9000 and the number of neighboring businesses that could raise similar complaints was not infinite. Aikens v. Debow, 541 S.E.2d 576, 579 (W. Va. 2000).

[27] I elaborate on the nature of the connection between ownership and standing (in the property-law context) in Avihay Dorfman, *Private Ownership and the Standing to Say So*, 64 U. TORONTO L. J. 402 (2014).

subject to the risk-bearer's control—to wit, if and only if the beneficiary of the duty is regarded by tort law as an agent, rather than a mere patient.

To begin with, the tort-law duty establishes a relation of agency between parties to an interpersonal conflict by entitling the risk-bearer to enjoy some measure of control over the duty-holder's fulfillment of the duty and, if necessary, the rectification of its violation. This is the (informal) sense in which the former *owns* that duty. This control is manifested not only in the standing to vindicate (or enforce) the right after it has been violated but also in the standing to set the duty in motion.

Talk of setting the primary duty in motion seeks to capture the legal authorization possessed by risk-bearers to impact the practical affairs of risk-creators qua duty-holders. In some cases, the former can have this impact by way of changing the normative situation of the duty-holder. Indeed, the tort of trespass to land (as well as offensive battery) does precisely this by defining the wrong in terms of entry or use *without the authorization* of the right-holder. In other cases, however, impacting the duty-holder by setting a duty in motion could come down to no more than having the standing to trigger an *existing* primary duty (and hence without assuming a Darwallian relationship of authority).[28] By demanding the employer to furnish a reasonably safe working environment, the employee insists that the relevant duty-holder respect her by *conforming* to what the duty has dictated all along—namely, due regard for the safety of one's employees. On the basis of this, the employee can exercise her agency with respect to her employer—claim her standing in relation to him—not merely by demanding that he discharge the duty of care he owes her but also by seeking injunctive relief to force him to do so.[29] While this instance of setting the duty in motion does not involve changing the normative situation of the duty-holder (and so does not presuppose the conceptual framework of the will theory of rights), it nonetheless entitles the right-holder to compel the duty-holder to treat his or her duty not merely as an outstanding commitment but rather as a real one. In the employment case, the employee (but

[28] I do not share Stephen Darwall's observation that we *normally* or even *typically* possess the special standing to engage others from a second-person point of view by giving moral reasons that emanate, in the right sense, from the interaction between the aggressor and his or her particular victim. *See* Stephen Darwall, The Second-Person Standpoint: Morality, Respect, and Accountability (2006).

[29] *See* Smith v. Western Elec. Co., 643 S.W.2d 10 (Mo. Ct. App. 1982). Note that workers' compensation schemes generally prescribe that injured workers are not entitled to sue their employers for work-related, accidentally inflicted injuries. *See, e.g.*, Iowa Code § 85.20 (2009). However, the nonapplication of the tort-law cause of action does *not* eliminate the employer's duty of care owed to and owned by the employee; this is crucial for the parties in an employment relationship to relate as agents. Indeed, workers' compensation schemes do not strip employees the standing to compel their employers to ensure a reasonably safe work environment. *See Smith*, 643 S.W.2d. Moreover, workers' compensation schemes do not release employers from their tort liability—including the employee's right to resort to a tort-law cause of action—for *non*accidental misconduct resulting in physical injuries (i.e., intentional or even merely reckless wrongdoing). *See* Chapter 5. Hence, my analysis of the moral necessity of tort duties is compatible with regulatory provisions of social insurance such as the typical workers' compensation scheme.

no other person who might come to benefit from the suit) can sue for an injunctive relief in order to enjoin her employer from violating the duty of care.[30]

In these and other ways (such as by calling on the police or issuing cease and desist letters), right-holders get to exercise a measure of control over the course of executing the duty. By possessing the standing to see to it that the duty-holder does not shirk responsibility, right-holders assume agential control that persists in earnest into the remedial stage of a tort dispute, including in the form of awards of supra-compensatory damages.[31] To be sure, this is not a means to counter domination and its resulting dependence (in the Kantian sense described above) as the risk-bearer's control over the performance of the risk-creator's duty applies even when the latter *inadvertently*—and so without subjecting others to his choice—fails to live up to the demands of the duty.

Being the owner of the duty gives rise to another form of control over the duty—the standing to waive it. In negligence law, the doctrinal hook for this is the principle of assumption of risk, according to which risk-bearers are entitled—subject to an important qualification to be discussed below—to waive existing duties by choosing to encounter a known risk. The broader point, however, is that a qualified right to waive a duty follows from characterizing the duty in terms of being owned by the risk-bearer. And this characterization goes back to my earlier observation that the significance of the tort duty is in giving the risk-bearer a certain standing in relation to the risk-creator. Standing in such a relation, in turn, is necessary for the two to engage each other as agents.[32]

V. Treating the Duty-Holder as an Agent

The egalitarian ideal of relating as agents underlies the pairwise structure of torts duties, which I have called the tort-law way of doing things. My argument that tort duties constitute terms of interactions between agents has focused on what relating to the risk-bearer as an agent requires. I now shift attention to the agency of the risk-creator to consider what relating to this person as an agent requires.

[30] The direct strategy does not exhaust additional forms of legal regulation of workplace safety, for instance, the standards of safety fixed by regulatory agencies (such as the United States' Occupational Safety and Health Administration) in order primarily to ensure employers' responsibility to protect employees' workplace safety.

[31] *See further* Section VI below.

[32] As I mentioned in passing in the main text above, the standing at issue need not amount to a normative power to change the normative situation of the risk-creator. The duty of due care arising from the tort of negligence features such a weak sense of having standing in relation to the duty ower. For this reason, my account of tort duties in terms of actualizing a certain ideal of relating as agents does not turn on the will theory of rights. For an intriguing proposal to move beyond the will versus interest theories of right, see Leif Wenar, *The Nature of Rights*, 33 PHIL. & PUB. AFF. 224, 247–49 (2005).

For starters, being a duty-holder is in and of itself a status reserved exclusively to agents. There is no sense in holding a stone, tree, or an animal to a duty. Even human beings may not always exhibit the effective agency necessary in order to *owe* a duty.[33] This is why tort law should, and already does to some extent, adopt a forgiving stance toward instances of ineffective agency. Such instances include cases of unknown disability (such as heart attack and seizure).[34] But the category of ineffective agency is much broader as it includes (or at least should include) all cases featuring the inability to avoid the adverse consequences of one's actions and inactions. *Force majeure* is a case in point,[35] as are some forms of *outright* physical and mental disability.[36]

Most importantly for our purposes, however, is the foreseeability requirement discussed above. It carries agency-based implications not only with respect to the ability of the duty-ower to relate to the duty-owner as an agent but rather also to the former's own agency. This is (and should be) true not only for negligence and fault liability in general but also with respect to strict liability torts.[37] Indeed, being able to know or anticipate the existence and vulnerability of another as a condition to owing this other a duty reflects tort law's concern for the agency of the duty-ower, too. The trouble with ineffective agency is not merely that the act of the risk-creator should not be deemed wrongful, but rather that there is no "act" for which we can say that it is their doing.

Terms of interaction that respect the duty-ower as an agent must not only specify threshold conditions of effective agency. In addition, they must place a cap on how much care and respect is expected from him or her. The underlying worry is that an onerous duty might quash the agency of its holder, literally treating this person as a mere means in the service of protecting the rights of the duty-owner at all costs. I elaborate on this worry in Chapter 14.

[33] I do not argue that it is impossible for law to pronounce that animals (et alia) are duty-bound. Rather, I argue that doing so does not amount to treating these duty-owers as agents. *Cf.* ESTHER COHEN, THE CROSSROADS OF JUSTICE: LAW AND CULTURE IN LATE MEDIEVAL FRANCE ch. 7 (1993).

[34] Ford v. Carew & English, 200 P.2d 828, 833 (Cal. Ct. App. 1948) ("if the jury believed that the accident was without any negligence of defendants and due to an *unanticipated* heart attack of the defendants' agent, it would be an *unavoidable* accident") (emphasis added); Caroll v. Bouley, 156 N.E.2d 687 (Mass. 1959) (an unforeseeable seizure rendering a defendant-motorist unable to control his motor vehicle is not negligence). *See also* SLAVNY, *supra* note 19, at 78.

[35] For instance, in *Vincent v. Lake Erie Transp. Co.*, 124 N.W. 221, 221–22 (Minn. 1910), the court notes (in a dictum) that a defendant cannot be held liable had the injury it inflicted on the plaintiff would have been considered "the act of god."

[36] For instance, in *Wagner v. State*, 122 P.3d 599, 610 (Utah 2005), the court intimates that "involuntary muscular movement or spasm" would have exonerated the defendant from a charge of battery.

[37] *See* W. PAGE KEETON ET AL., PROSSER AND KEETON ON THE LAW OF TORTS §79, at 559 (5th ed. 1984); Gary T. Schwartz, *Rylands v. Fletcher, Negligence, and Strict Liability*, *in* THE LAW OF OBLIGATIONS: ESSAYS IN CELEBRATION OF JOHN FLEMING 209, 218 (Peter Cane and Jane Stapleton eds., 1998).

VI. Duty Maintenance: Preventing Backsliding on Agency

A tort-law duty elevates the interest of the risk-bearer to a nondiscretionary constraint on the choice of the risk-creator. It does so by placing a legally mandated constraint on the conduct of risk-creators, which is owed to, and owned by, the risk-bearer. It constructs terms of interactions under which the parties relate as agents. I now wish to argue that the egalitarian ideal underlying this duty is susceptible to two existential threats. Addressing them, therefore, is necessary. The first threat arises when the duty-ower converts the duty-owner from an agent to a commodity. The former can engage in commodifying the latter by turning the duty from a freestanding constraint into the cost of doing business.[38] The second threat comes from the duty-owner's side. It concerns the power to alienate the duty. As the rights that figure in tort law (for instance, to bodily integrity) are not inalienable, and should not be deemed as such, an overly permissive approach to waiving and selling one's primary rights might erode the significance of the tort duty and its normative priority over contract and, hence undermine agency and relating as agents.[39] Modern tort law is acutely aware of these two threats, at least to some extent. I consider each threat in turn. As I show, an adequate set of remedies (especially injunctive relief and punitive damages) and an appropriate understanding of tort defenses (especially consent and assumption of risk) can address them. Together they perform the duty maintenance needed for sustaining the egalitarian ideal that lies beneath the equality theory of torts.

Non-Punitive, Punitive Damages: Injunctive Relief Granted Ex Post. Cashin v. Northern Pac. Ry. Co.[40] involves construction workers engaging in the removal of 20-ton boulders from a mountain's slope by using explosives. They decided to exercise far less care than legally required by the duty of care they owed to occupants of nearby houses. In particular, the untaken precaution was that of "mud-capping" or "plastering" the boulders to prevent damage to nearby people and property.[41] The important point is that their violation of the duty was not merely one of inadvertence or lack of professionalism but rather rationally calculated. The workers "knowingly employed the method which ... might cause injury or death ... , in order to speedily and economically dispose of the threatening boulder, believing that it was to the advantage of the defendant [employer] to do so and pay for the damage done."[42] Their negligent blasting caused some property damage—two

[38] *See* Marc Galanter & David Luban, *Poetic Justice: Punitive Damages and Legal Pluralism*, 42 Am. U. L. Rev. 1393, 1430 (1993); Arthur Ripstein, Equality, Responsibility, and the Law 153 (1999).

[39] My discussion concerns waving or selling primary rights. I do not believe that selling secondary rights of repair and especially tertiary rights of action should be held to a similar standard. That is, selling one's right to sue should not per se be impermissible; rather, worries of exploitation and related forms of unfair bargaining conditions could cut against permissibility.

[40] *See* Cashin v. Northern Pac. Ry. Co., 28 P.2d 862 (Mont. 1934).

[41] *Id.*, at 867.

[42] *Id.*, at 870.

broken windows—and brought the plaintiff, an occupant of a nearby dwelling house, into a momentary state of fright, unaccompanied by physical injury. Soon thereafter the defendant employer of the workers offered to pay the plaintiff for the broken glass.[43]

A pay-as-you-go liability regime, as leading lawyer-economists would suggest,[44] may certainly be beneficial for defendants, economically speaking. It may well also be beneficial to society as a whole as the costly removal of boulders in *Cashin* was necessary to ensure the safety of the many people using the defendant's trains.[45] Moreover, fully compensating the plaintiff for setting back her emotional well-being and her windows could provide her with an opportunity to leave the incident behind her and to go on with her life. Such an outcome need not diverge substantively from the one the parties would have agreed upon in a Coasean world of zero transaction costs. However, what is necessarily missing from such an arrangement is the defendant's recognition of the *agency* of the plaintiff. More specifically, the defendant's conscious disregard of the plaintiff as an agent is the source of the problem. This is precisely why the terms of the interaction between them, even in a Coasean world, must be governed in part by a legally mandated duty owed to and owned by the plaintiff. In the actual (non-Coasean) world, the defendant's strategic decision to convert the duty into a cost of doing business amounts to a decision to commodify the plaintiff.

Thus, the egalitarian ideal underlying the tort duty might face an existential threat from risk-creators who strategically repudiate the existence of the relational duty as a freestanding, other-regard constraint on their choice. On the equality theory of torts, tort law must preclude the commodification at issue. Two doctrinal tools can do that. The first is injunctive relief—if feasible, a risk-bearer is entitled to ask the court (and, sometimes, law enforcement agents) to enjoin or restrain the risk-creator. However, that is often impossible, pragmatically speaking, as instances of backsliding on the duty may not be anticipated in advance. The second, more feasible doctrinal tool is punitive damages. Viewed from the perspective of the equality theory of torts, this remedy is not strictly speaking punitive but rather remedial through and through (which is why "vindicatory damages" might be a better fit).[46]

43 *Id.*, at 865.

44 *See, e.g.*, Ariel Porat, *Private Production of Public Goods: Liability for Unrequested Benefits*, 108 Mich. L. Rev. 189, 199–200 (2009).

45 *Cashin*, 28 P.2d at 865.

46 According to Hershovitz, punitive damages, like heads of damages such as pain and suffering, are not compensatory. Instead, punitive damages are designed to "mark the gravity of the wrong." While the view I seek to defend shares his compelling, dignitarian defense of punitive damages (and especially the point that the victim's dignity is not "available for purchase"), my account emphasizes punitive damages' wholly *compensatory* basis. Scott Hershovitz, *Tort as a Substitute for Revenge*, *in* Philosophical Foundations of the Law of Torts 86, 97 (John Oberdiek ed. 2014).

The *Cashin* court approved an award of $750 in punitive damages on top of $1,250 in compensatory damages on the basis of the findings just mentioned.[47] One way to make sense of the former remedy is to cast it in terms of punishment, akin to a criminal punishment that takes the form of a fine. That said, the court expressly denies this, saying that the "jury was not called upon to determine the criminal liability of the defendant or what punishment could be inflicted upon it in a criminal action."[48] A better way to make sense of the decision to award damages "as punishment"[49] is to conceive of this award as the functional equivalent of injunctive relief—more precisely, an injunctive relief granted *ex post*.[50]

It is clear that had the plaintiff known that her safety is subject to the defendant's cost-benefit analysis, she would have been able to ask a local court to either enjoin the blasting operation or instruct the defendant to implement the necessary precautions.[51] The underlying rationale for issuing such an injunction—viz., precluding the conversion of the duty into price—cannot simply fade away after the fact, once the risk has materialized into injury. Indeed, just as it commands ex ante intervention in the form of injunctive relief, so too this rationale requires ex post intervention to *reinstate* the commitment to relating as agents. A stand-alone remedy of compensatory damages cannot do the work since it would merely reinforce the defendant's plan of commodifying the plaintiff to "a mere cost of doing business."[52]

As just mentioned, punitive damages can and should be wholly, rather than supra, *compensatory*. They do not, nor should they, punish in the criminal-punishment sense of conveying public condemnation.[53] Moreover, they are *compensatory*, rather than restitutionary in their nature; they concern the injury of the victim, rather than disgorging the gains of the tortfeasor. Indeed, they redress a nonpecuniary injury, namely, setting back the plaintiff's *agency* by treating her as a commodity. An injunctive relief could have preempted this setback, whereas punitive damages—properly computed to frustrate the economic rationality behind the defendant's behavior—vindicate the plaintiff's agency by compelling the defendant to compensate her for consciously regarding her as a commodity. So understood,

[47] *Cashin*, 28 P.2d at 870–71.

[48] *Id.*, at 871.

[49] *Id.*

[50] For an earlier development of this theme, see Avihay Dorfman, *What Is the Point of the Tort Remedy?*, 55 AM. J. JURIS. 105, 153–62 (2010). *See also* Dagan & Dorfman, *supra* note 26, at 537–38; Mark Geistfeld, *The Tort Entitlement to Physical Security as the Distributive Basis for Environmental, Health, and Safety Regulations*, 15 THEORETICAL INQ. L. 387, 400 (2014).

[51] Note that the fact that blasting may have counted as abnormally dangerous activity does not relieve the defendant of exercising due (or even utmost) care. *Cf.* Gregory C. Keating, *Strict Liability Wrongs*, *in* PHILOSOPHICAL FOUNDATIONS OF THE LAW OF TORTS 292 (John Oberdiek ed. 2014).

[52] Galanter & Luban, *supra* note 38, at 1430. *See also* Mark A. Geistfeld, *Tort Law and the Inherent Limitations of Monetary Exchange: Property Rules, Liability Rules, and the Negligence Rule*, 4 J. TORT L., Issue 1, Art. 4, at 8 (2011).

[53] Avihay Dorfman & Alon Harel, *The Case Against Privatization*, 41 PHI. & PUB. AFF. 67, 92–96 (2013).

punitive damages force the defendant to come to terms with the correct meaning of the duty of care it owed the plaintiff all along, namely, a freestanding constraint on its choice of running a business. As with injunctive relief, doing so restores the mandatory bite of the tort-law duty and in this way reaffirms a basic element of the equality theory of tort law: that of relating as *agents*.

Assumption of Risk for Agents. I have argued that contrary to the Coasean picture, tort law takes the constitutive role of seeing to it that people relate to each other as agents whose basic rights figure as constraints on, rather than the product of, contractual bargaining. But I have also argued that because they are agents, risk-bearers are not only owed duties of care but also own them. As such, risk-bearers may waive or "sell" these duties so as to relieve risk-creators of their responsibilities. Can these two arguments be reconciled? In particular, how can the basic rights protected by tort duties be alienable, on the one hand, and function as freestanding constraints on contractual bargaining, on the other?

Tort law adopts what can be called a principle of qualified alienability of tort duties.[54] Waiving or selling the duties one owns is permissible only insofar as doing so is made under the appropriate conditions, namely, conditions under which waiving or selling is an *expression* of one's agency.

A qualified alienability emerges out of a contrast between a certain form of choosing to waive/sell and having to do the same. This contrast is best exemplified by reference to workplace safety. Consider a person facing unreasonably dangerous working conditions. This person decides to stay and assume the risk. There is a normatively important difference between putting oneself in this dangerous state *for the sake* of the risk as opposed to doing so *in spite* of the risk—I argue that the former is a form of permissible alienability whereas the latter is not. Arguably, a rank and file, blue-color employee who assumes the risk of an unreasonably

[54] Qualified alienability is structurally similar to the principle of incomplete commodification developed in Margaret Jane Radin, Contested Commodities 104–07 (1996). Radin locates the latter principle on a continuum between universal or complete commodification and complete noncommodification. Regulated markets give effect to this strategy (e.g., minimum wage laws could prevent labor markets from completely commodifying work). However, Radin's account differs from tort law's qualified alienability in three important ways. First, incomplete commodification does not require a tort-law response, as it could draw on any number of legal (and arguably also extralegal) means of regulation. Furthermore, a perfectly competitive market *could* incorporate participants' preferences against the adverse implications of complete commodification. Second, Radin grounds incomplete commodification in a certain ideal of retaining a "personal aspect" or "the uniqueness of the self" in the subject matter of the market exchange (for instance, by retaining a personal aspect in the labor sold by the employee to his or her employer). *Id.*, at 107 & 127. My account of relating as agents, by contrast, associates qualified alienability with sustaining the preconditions for free and equal agency. To be sure, Radin does discuss agency concerns (for instance, regarding the adverse effects of market inalienability on "poor and oppressed people" in terms of denying them the possibility of having "more money with which to buy adequate food, shelter, and health care in the market" (*id.*, at 125)), but it seems that personhood plays the more prominent role in her argument. And third, tort law's principle of qualified alienability imposes a stricter standard for permissible alienability than Radin's incomplete commodification. The former bars commodification unless the right-holder *genuinely* chooses (in a sense to be explained in the main text below) to waive his or her right. Incomplete commodification, by contrast, is compatible with waiving a right out of economic necessity.

dangerous work environment *undermines* his or her agency by being forced to make this choice. By "forced" I do not mean forced necessarily by the employer but rather by the circumstances surrounding his or her choice (for instance, making ends meet).

By contrast, a person who knowingly and voluntarily assumes this same risk, at least in part, *for the sake of the risk* does not undermine his or her agency. There may be any number of reasons why a person might wholeheartedly want to choose an unreasonably dangerous work environment. For instance, it could be an implication of his or her conception of the good, one which requires a living-on-the-edge way of life. Alternatively, it could arise out of a desire to test one's karma (or god's providence) or simply out of sheer curiosity to get a sense of what it is like to face imminent danger. These and other reasons share the notion that the circumstances surrounding the risk-bearer's choice to assume the risk do not undermine his or her ability to be the author of his or her life. To the contrary, assuming the risk under these circumstances is better viewed as an instance of actively directing, rather than merely participating in, one's life; it is an expression of agency.

The distinction between choosing and having to waive or sell tort duties that stands at the center of the principle of qualified alienability stakes a middle—and liberal—ground between the implausible position that all the choices made by market participants are essentially coerced[55] and the equally implausible laissez-faire position that a voluntary exchange implies consent to all foreseeable consequences.[56]

Moreover, it finds some support in modern tort law. During the nineteenth and early twentieth centuries, the existence of a conscious choice to enter an employment contract in the first place, or to carry on with the work in the face of a known risk, were reason enough to bar the employee from suing the employer in negligence.[57] Courts conceived of the matter in terms of a trade-off between physical safety and wage-based compensation and, moreover, that it ought to be settled according to the preferences of the parties involved.[58] The doctrinal hook on which to hang the immunity of the employer from violations of his or her duty of care was

[55] *See* Robert L. Hale, *Coercion and Distribution in a Supposedly Non-Coercive State*, 38 POL. SCI. Q. 470 (1923).

[56] *See infra* notes 57–62.

[57] A characteristic case of that era is Justice Holmes's *Lamson v. Am. Axe & Tool Co.*, 177 Mass. 144, 58 N.E. 585, 585–86 (1900). For a historical analysis, see JOHN FABIAN WITT, THE ACCIDENTAL REPUBLIC (2004).

[58] This is most eloquently expressed in Lord Bramwell's dissent in Smith v. Baker & Sons, [1891] A.C. 325, 344 (H.L.). The general (laissez-faire) ideology underlying this line of thinking has been succinctly described in *Adkins v. Children's Hospital*, 261 U.S. 525, 545 (1923) where Sutherland J., speaking for the majority of the court in a matter involving the constitutionality of legally mandated minimum wage for female employees, asserts that "the parties have an equal right to obtain from each other the best terms they can as the result of private bargaining." *See further* West Coast Hotel v. Parrish, 300 U.S. 379 (1937) (overturning *Adkins* and upholding the constitutionality of the minimum wage legislation in the State of Washington).

often that of assumption of risk.[59] The fact that all of these employees entered dangerous workplaces in spite of, rather than for the sake of, the risk made no doctrinal difference. That said, the doctrine of assumption of risk has since been substantially modified so as to end the subordination of the employer's duty of care to contractual choice about workplace risks.[60] It has since become almost impossible in the context of workplace safety, and other nonrecreational contexts,[61] to persuade courts that the mere conscious decision to expose oneself to an unreasonably dangerous environment is sufficient to absolve the injurer of liability for negligent infliction of harm.[62]

The preceding discussion has focused on doctrinal mechanisms to prevent duty-backsliding in the context of the tort of negligence and especially in connection with negligent infliction of serious physical injury. They are used as particular illustrations of a broader point: That the egalitarian ideal of relating as agents requires that tort duties retain their normative bite as binding mandates imposed and fixed by operation of law in the face of attempts to transform them into choices, costs, or commodities. Indeed, awards of punitive damages are not limited to (advertently triggered) negligence; and the defense of assumption of risk is a subset of the broader family of defenses associated with consent (or *volenti* as English tort lawyers call it). The basic point, once again, is that duty maintenance, in the form of qualified alienability, is a direct implication of the equality theory of tort law.

VII. The Tort/Contract Interface: The Economic Loss Rule in Products Liability

I now wish to take up the economic loss rule in the context of products liability to explore another dimension of relating as agents, namely, the *scope* of the claim. In the course of arguing that tort duties are necessary for the parties to relate as agents, I have emphasized that these duties purport to guard against setbacks to fundamental interests. This is so because the conflict theory places clashes between fundamental interests at the moral center of tort law. The equality theory adds another angle on this explanation, as it requires risk-creators to deal with risk-bearers as agents, and doing so depends, in part, on elevating the fundamental interests of the latter into a nondiscretionary constraint on the conduct of the former.

[59] *See further* Avihay Dorfman, *Assumption of Risk, After All*, 15 THEORETICAL INQ. L. 293 (2014).
[60] *Id.*, at 297–98.
[61] On assuming risk in part for the sake of the risk in the recreational context, see *Coomer v. City Royals Baseball Corp.*, 437 S.W.3d 184, 194–99 (Mo. 2014).
[62] *See* Tunkl v. Regents of Univ. of California, 383 P.2d 441 (Cal. 1963); RESTATEMENT (THIRD) OF TORTS: APPORTIONMENT LIAB. §2 cmt. *e* (2000).

Thus, tort duties protect fundamental interests and these interests, recall, are prerequisites to a liberal practice of contracting. To fulfill this moral task, tort duties must meet two requirements. The first is a floor-like requirement: Tort duties must cast a sufficiently broad protective net in order to capture our fundamental interests, such as bodily and emotional integrity, privacy, good name, self-expression, and others. Otherwise, the protection of these interests will depend on contractual arrangements, and hence in part on the choice of others. The ideal of relating as agents is all about this requirement—that is, the construction of egalitarian relations that stands at the center of this chapter concerns the interests that sustain human agency, namely, fundamental interests.

The second requirement takes the form of a ceiling: Tort duties must *not* overreach their task of protecting fundamental interests to the point of swallowing contract. This requirement is integral to the conflict theory's commitment to take fundamental interests seriously. Indeed, our interests in self-determination and in voluntary human interaction suggest that tort duties must make ample space for freedom of contract. At times, conformity with the requirement at issue does not raise intricate questions as when contracting is fully compatible with our fundamental interests. At other times, however, drawing the line between tort duties and contractual (and other voluntary) arrangements proves more intricate. Legal doctrine is, therefore, called for to do the heavy lifting. The economic loss rule is one such doctrinal rule. I wish to deploy the equality theory of tort law to outline a reconstruction of this rule in the context of products liability. I then contrast my reconstruction with the opposing view, which conceptualizes tort duties as contract's second-best mechanism of determining rights and responsibilities.

The economic loss rule in products liability operates within the confines of the privity of contract—to wit, it focuses on the contractual interaction between the manufacturer (or distributor) and the buyer-user of a product.[63] The rule establishes a division of responsibility between tort and contract: Manufacturers are subject to tort duties, owed to and owned by buyers, with respect to risk of physical injury or damage to property other than the product itself; by contrast, they have no tort duties with respect to economic losses unaccompanied by physical harm or property damage (a.k.a. pure economic loss). The no-duty rule is of course a rule, which means that it is subject to exceptions (on which more below). Owing no tort duty with respect to economic losses caused by some defect in the product does not mean that the manufacturer is not responsible for them. Instead, it suggests that such responsibility should be determined at the bargaining table (including when shaped by default rules designed to facilitate an appropriate contractual agreement).

[63] This rule differs substantively from the economic loss rule that governs negligence law with respect to the infliction of pure economic loss on strangers (i.e., beyond the privity of contract or any other voluntary undertaking on the part of the injurer).

The equality theory defends a version of this rule. On the one hand, a division of responsibility between bodily integrity and economic loss nicely comports with the distinction between protecting fundamental and nonfundamental interests. It also leaves nontrivial space for the product buyer to contract for warranties and other provisions, including those implicating the economic value of the product. On the other hand, the equality theory does not embrace the seemingly equal status given by the economic loss rule to physical harm and property damage. Instead, risk of property damage should give rise to a tort duty only insofar as the ex ante risks to physical harm and to property damage associated with using a defective product are inextricable. For instance, a defectively designed chemical drain cleaner certainly poses grave dangers to the life and limb of its user, as when the content of the product splashes back in the user's face, blinding and burning him.[64] This very same risk is perfectly capable of causing freestanding property damage, for instance, to some crucial parts of the drainage system. Hence, although property damage can manifest itself as a stand-alone injury, what matters for the purpose of fixing egalitarian terms of interaction is the ex ante risk that is, inextricably, also to the very person of the user.

To unpack the equality theory's reconstruction of the economic loss rule, consider the seminal case of *East River Steamship Corp. v. Transamerica Delaval Inc.*[65] There, defectively manufactured turbines malfunctioned, significantly reducing the capacity and speed of the supertankers in which they were installed. The injury is economic in nature as it involves lost profits and repair costs. Further, it is purely economic in the sense that no person or property other than the ship suffered (or stood to suffer) injuries as a result of the malfunctioning. The question in this case is whether the charterers of the ships could sue the turbines' manufacturer in tort (and, in particular, in a products liability cause of action). Doing so depends, first and foremost, on answering a prior question, namely, does the manufacturer owe the charterers a *tort* duty to avoid causing purely economic loss. The Supreme Court answers in the negative, noting that as between commercial parties no such duty exists.[66] By implication, the question of who is responsible for the economic loss of the charterers is decided by reference to the terms of the bargain between the manufacturer and the users-charterers. In that, the court affirms the division of responsibility between tort duties and contractual bargain, restricting the former to risks of physical harm and property damage (and, perhaps, also pure economic loss arising under circumstances of "large disparities in bargaining power"[67]). Subsequent case law has, with some important variations, adopted some such division.[68]

[64] *See* Chow v. Reckitt & Coleman, Inc., 950 N.E.2d 113 (N.Y. 2011).
[65] 476 U.S. 858 (1986).
[66] *Id.*, at 873.
[67] *Id.*; *see further* Utah Int'l, Inc. v. Caterpillar Tractor Co., 775 P.2d 741, 744 (N.M. Ct. App. 1989).
[68] For a careful discussion of variations and nuances, see Restatement (Third) of Torts: Products Liability §21 (2023).

Now consider how an influential approach to products liability justifies this division of labor.[69] It begins, implicitly if not explicitly, with the Coasean premise that, ideally, contractual bargaining is the best technology of responsibility allocation, not only with respect to the buyer's risk of economic loss but rather also with respect to their potential physical harm. However, in our nonideal world, bargaining over the allocation of responsibility for the latter might suffer from certain defects that, in turn, warrant tort duties as second-best to contract's duties.[70] The defects of contracting for physical safety can be spelled out in different ways. Whereas courts often invoke the obscure consideration of public policy, the approach in question appeals to considerations such as information asymmetries and the cheapest cost avoider to pin down precisely why risk of physical harm and property damage should be governed by tort duties and why, by contrast, pure economic loss (resulting from the defective product) should be governed by contracting for warranties and first-party insurance.[71]

It is beyond the scope of my argument to consider these arguments in detail.[72] Instead, my aim has been to contrast respective, normative starting points. The equality theory insists on the priority of tort over contract not only in our nonideal world of undercompetitive and ill-regulated markets. As I argued in this chapter, tort duties in respect of the bodily integrity of product users construct egalitarian frameworks of interpersonal interactions, wherein the duty-ower and -owner relate as agents. Key to relating as agents is the nature of the tort duty, namely, a publicly mandated and fixed—and, at the same time, privately owed and owned—duty to deal with the fundamental interest of another as a freestanding constraint on one's own choice.[73] Physical safety, on the equality theory, is not itself a product or a commodity; instead, it is a fundamental interest and, so, the ground for a basic human right.

[69] A leading theory within this approach is Mark A. Geistfeld, Principles of Products Liability (2d ed., 2011).

[70] Mark A. Geistfeld, *The Contractually Based Economic Loss Rule in Tort Law: Endangered Consumers and the Error of* East River Steamship, 65 DePaul L. Rev. 393, 396 (2016).

[71] *Id.* The cheapest cost avoider's rationale for the economic loss rule in products liability and service contract by professionals is powerfully developed in Catherine M. Sharkey, *In Search of the Cheapest Cost Avoider: Another View on the Economic Loss Rule*, 85 U. Cin. L. Rev. 1017, 1045–46 (2018).

[72] Very briefly, it is not clear to me why considerations of information asymmetries and the cheapest cost avoider cannot be offset by competitive markets and additionally, if necessary, by adequate regulation. On the equality theory, tort duties are necessary even when markets are perfectly competitive. Moreover, note that in enforcing the economic loss rule courts do not really pay attention to market conditions, which is to say they do not even try to distinguish between manufacturers of "widely sold products" and all other manufacturers. *See* A. Mitchell Polinsky & Steven Shavell, *The Uneasy Case for Product Liability*, 123 Harv. L. Rev. 1437, 1472 (2010).

[73] Keating also emphasizes this private dimension of tort duties. His characterization of the public dimension, however, is that tort duties do "justice, and justice is a matter that affects all of us." Gregory C. Keating, Reasonableness and Risk: Right and Responsibility in the Law of Torts 303 (2022). Although he is certainly right, my characterization, recall, is that tort duties are public in the different sense that they are determined and imposed by operation of law, rather than by either uni- or bilateral choice.

Conclusion

This chapter has returned to two banal ideas, namely, that markets are creatures of private and public orderings and that contract and torts are in some sense complementary to each other. I have argued that tort-law duties are fundamentally public in that their existence and content must, rather than may, be provided by operation of law. These duties are at the same time fundamentally private in that the responsibility to discharge them must, rather than may, fall to private persons. Only thus can the egalitarian ideal of relating as agents be actualized.

Viewing tort duties in this way also shows what the distinction between involuntary and voluntary duties in private law is about. The positive law account of the basic connection between tort and contract has seen many twists and turns, reflecting changing theories, perceptions, and ideologies. One widely held theory underlying this idea supposes that contract (and voluntary duties more generally) comes first in the order of explanation and justification, whereas tort law occupies the role of a supporting cast, safeguarding contractual agreements when transaction costs are relatively low and mimicking the results of hypothetical ones when transaction costs are excessive. However, on the account I defended in these pages, prohibitive transaction costs do not explain, and certainly cannot justify, why tort duties matter. Tort duties, especially those that protect our fundamental interests, are necessary but not because contracting is sometimes difficult or even infeasible, but rather because in their absence parties in voluntary interactions cannot relate as agents, including even when transaction costs pose no threat to contracting. Tort duties are not merely a limitation on contracting and on the market, but rather a prerequisite for voluntary interactions whose participants count as equal agents. The argument going forward will move from the basic layer of relating as agents to that of relating as substantive equals, that is, from the existence to the content of tort duties.

13

Tort Duties for Egalitarians

Relating as Substantive Equals

Introduction

The argument now moves to explain the progression from relating as agents to relating as *equals*. In terms of legal doctrine, the next stage on the equality theory of tort law is that of moving from the very existence of tort duties to their content. The existence of tort duties—recall, legally mandated obligations owed to and owned by risk-bearers—is necessary for persons to relate as agents. The content of these duties—how much and what kind of other-regarding conduct they require—is necessary for persons to relate as equals. My contention is that the terms that address inherently valuable, tolerable, and valueless conflicts matter because the lives of the agents whose rights and duties are fixed by these terms are *equally* important. I argue that a certain moral principle of *substantive* equality sees to it that these terms treat the parties not merely as agents but as equal agents.

The argument going forward, therefore, considers what relating as equals in the tort context might require. My ambition is to outline a conception of relational equality that begins with the basic notion of substantive equality as a commitment to take difference seriously, rather than set it to one side (as proponents of formal equality suggest). Its main challenge is to develop a *theory* with which to identify what differences should be taken seriously and in what ways. This theory, therefore, develops an egalitarian calculus for the purpose of determining tort-law terms of interaction. I seek to show that the legal doctrines that determine the content of tort duties are (ideally) practical instantiations of what substantive equality means in a particular context.

I. Two Conceptions of Relational Equality: Formal and Substantive

Begin with what can be called the generic tort-law duty. Although there are as many primary duties as there are torts, they can all be reducible to a generic form: a mandatory reason for conducting oneself with some vigilance toward certain others. To be sure, tort duties can differ with regard to what interests of these other people warrant vigilance—say, their person, privacy, property, reputation, and so on. They can also differ with respect to the scope of the class of duty-owners. Finally, they can differ

Conflict between Equals. Avihay Dorfman, Oxford University Press. © Oxford University Press 2026.
DOI: 10.1093/9780198979869.003.0017

along the dimension of demandingness, that is, what vigilance requires. That said, it will be apt to begin with the generic tort duty in order, first, to distinguish between relational egalitarianism and all other ways of explaining the normativity of tort-law duties and, second, develop a critical distinction between two conceptions of relational equality.

A characterization of the generic tort-law duty bordering on a platitude is that it demands some measure of other-regard (in the domain of action, rather than motive). The normative question that then arises is what grounds this demand. Before I get to the relational egalitarian grounding, it is important to note that there are other grounds as well. Most of these accounts have focused on the demands of the duty of due care in the tort of negligence, but I believe they can be generalized, with some modifications, so as to capture the generic tort-law duty as well. Indeed, these grounds can range from maximizing social welfare,[1] to sustaining a fair system of social cooperation in a society of free and equal citizens,[2] delineating fair division of responsibility between individuals and their state,[3] recognizing social mores and mutuality,[4] upholding responsible agency,[5] or inculcating virtuous behavior.[6] Whereas some of these grounds are consistent with relational egalitarian commitments, others may not. As I argued above, however, the challenge of vindicating tort law suggests that relational egalitarianism is the most plausible candidate. The challenge, recall, is not merely to explain current practices or even to justify (or criticize) them. Rather, it is to show why it has to be the tort-law-way-of-doing-things in the first place rather than, and indeed given that we could employ, other legal or extralegal ways of achieving whatever it is that we want to achieve (such as more safety, civility, welfare, distributive justice, etc.).

To ground the generic duty's demands of other-regard in relational egalitarianism is to defend a certain conception of equality between the duty-ower and -owner. With such a conception at hand we can then get a better sense of what other-regard requires. That, along with the account of relating as agents in Chapter 12, will bring the equality theory of tort law into a mature shape.

A first step in this direction begins with a distinction between two conceptions of relating as equals: formal and substantive equality. Although both share the egalitarian ideal of relating as equals, they are sharply divided on a basic matter: What

[1] Ariel Porat, *Misalignments in Tort Law*, 121 YALE L.J. 82 (2011); Richard A. Posner, *A Theory of Negligence*, 1 J. LEGAL STUD. 29 (1972).

[2] Gregory C. Keating, *Reasonableness and Rationality in Negligence Theory*, 48 STAN. L. REV. 311 (1996).

[3] ARTHUR RIPSTEIN, EQUALITY, RESPONSIBILITY, AND THE LAW (1999).

[4] Benjamin C. Zipursky, *Reasonableness In and Out of Negligence Law*, 163 U. PENN. L. REV. 2131, 2153–54, 2156, 2161, 2163, 2165, 2168 (2015).

[5] Joseph Raz, *Responsibility and Negligence Standard*, 30 OXFORD J. LEGAL STUD. 1, 17 (2010). *See also* Seana Valentine Shiffrin, *The Moral Neglect of Negligence*, *in* 3 OXFORD STUD. POL. PHIL. 197 (David Sobel et al. eds., 2017).

[6] Heidi Li Feldman, *Prudence, Benevolence, and Negligence: Virtue Ethics and Tort Law*, 74 CHI.-KENT L. REV. 1431 (2000).

to make of differences between the interacting parties. On the formal conception of equality, parties relate as equals if, and only if, differences have no bearing on the terms of their interaction. One may say, borrowing from Ronald Dworkin, that the terms of their interaction must reflect a standard of equal treatment.[7] The champion of relational egalitarianism in tort law and in private law, more generally, is Ernest Weinrib.[8] He defends a version of the formal conception of equality, according to which parties relate as equals when their tort-law terms of interaction make no reference to any differentiating conditions, including powers, vulnerabilities, needs, interests, and virtues.[9] To relate formally as equals means, among other things, to interact on terms that treat them as equally constituting their respective capacities for choice, by which Weinrib means the "abstract equality of free purposive beings."[10] Hence, having a capacity for choice is necessary and sufficient in order for the interacting persons to count as equals. By implication, terms of interactions that incorporate a concern, say, for power imbalance, the priority of bodily integrity over property, or dire need and poverty violate formal equality.[11] This is because they side with one party necessarily at the expense of the other, letting the condition of the former impact the terms of his or her interaction with the latter.

I have criticized this conception of formal equality on conceptual, normative, and doctrinal grounds. Conceptually, I have argued that the dichotomy underlying Weinrib's celebrated distinction between corrective and distributive justice—viz., a dichotomy between formal and distributional equality—is a false one.[12] Normatively, I have argued that setting aside important differences between the interacting parties runs counter to our basic intuitions (and powerful rejoinders by Marx, Rawls, and Dworkin, among others) about equality.[13] Doctrinally, I have

[7] Ronald Dworkin, Taking Rights Seriously 227 (1977) (distinguishing between equal treatment, which is a variation on formal equality, and treating persons as equals, which is a basic pillar of substantive equality).

[8] Although both Weinrib and Ripstein self-define their respective theories as Kantian, I believe there is (or at least was) an important difference between the ways they develop them. Weinrib begins with equality, resorting to independence as a way to answer the question of "equality of what?" By contrast, Ripstein begins with independence as the foundational ideal and finds equality to be a conceptual entailment of this ideal. Ripstein observes another difference—whereas Weinrib begins from the fact of liability and then climbs all the way up to primary rights, Ripstein takes the opposite direction. Arthur Ripstein, Private Wrongs 6 (2016). In his most recent book on private law theory, however, Weinrib suggests that independence is the foundational ideal. Ernest J. Weinrib, Reciprocal Freedom: Private Law and Public Rights 100 (2022).

[9] Ernest J. Weinrib, The Idea of Private Law 77–83 (1995); *see also* Arthur Ripstein, *Civil Recourse and Separation of Wrongs and Remedies*, 39 Fla. St. U. L. Rev. 163, 181 (2011).

[10] Weinrib, *supra*, at 58.

[11] On need and poverty, see Hanoch Dagan & Avihay Dorfman, *Substantive Remedies*, 96 Notre Dame L. Rev. 513 (2020); Hanoch Dagan & Avihay Dorfman, *Poverty and Private Law: Beyond Distributive Justice*, 68 Am. J. Juris. 229 (2023), respectively.

[12] Avihay Dorfman, *Private Law Exceptionalism? Part II: A Basic Difficulty with the Argument from Formal Equality*, 31 Can. J.L. & Juris. 5 (2018).

[13] *Id.*; Avihay Dorfman, *Negligence and Accommodation*, 22 Legal Theory 77 (2016); Hanoch Dagan & Avihay Dorfman, Relational Justice: A Theory of Private Law 28–29 (2024).

shown that major doctrines in modern tort law, and private law more generally, defy the teachings of formal equality.[14] Instead of belaboring these points, I wish to proceed by presenting a competing conception of relational equality, namely, substantive equality.

II. The Two Dimensions of Substantive Equality: Interest and Condition

Substantive equality's basic commitment is to take difference seriously. Hence the challenge it immediately faces is the question of "different how?" The answer is that the content of tort-law duties must reflect interpersonal differences that might distinguish one party from another along two basic dimensions: their respective *interests* and *conditions*. I take each in turn and then explain the relative importance of interest over condition. In doing so, the argument going forward defends the equality theory's egalitarian calculus.

The interest dimension. The interest differential captures a purely normative dimension. It concerns the respective interests implicated by the conflict between the interacting parties. A formal conception of equality takes the interacting parties to be equal simply by virtue of constituting a capacity for choice. By contrast, the substantive conception insists that their relative vulnerability matters, and that they cannot relate as equals, for instance, if their terms of interaction do not reflect (in the right way) the difference between one party's life and limb and the other party's interest in enjoying more time with friends and family.

Indeed, tort doctrines embody a normative hierarchy of interests. It is most apparent when one interest—such as in owning a thing—shades off into a shadow of itself in the face of another, more important interest—such as life and limb. Some of the inherently valuable conflicts discussed in the first part of this book suggest that the conflicting interests should *not* be treated similarly; instead, they should be ordered in a manner that reflects the relative superiority of one over the other. More broadly, there is an important connection between the conflict theory and the equality theory. Both begin with the fundamental interests of private persons and, moreover, take difference among them seriously. The conflict theory focuses on interest differentials for the purpose of addressing conflicts of interests by engaging with the value of these conflicts. The equality theory, on the other hand, draws on interest differential for the purpose of addressing a different concern, namely, the determination of egalitarian terms of interactions between persons caught up in the pursuit of conflicting interests. I now wish to further demonstrate equality theory's treatment of interest differential by presenting two cases.

14 *See, e.g.*, Dorfman, *supra*, at 88–92; Dorfman, *supra* note 12, at 28–31.

Consider the following valueless conflict. In an attempt to ward off thieves, an owner of a farm house installed a spring shotgun—rigged with wire from the doorknob to the gun's trigger—capable of killing or seriously maiming trespassers.[15] And indeed, one thief opened the door and got shot, in which case much of his leg was "blown away."[16] The tort doctrine that governs this incident is called the defense of property. It answers the question: Can the owner escape liability for battery on account of defending his property? In the course of deciding this question, the court essentially determines the content of the duty against committing battery, including its outer limits. To do so, the court must not only recognize that the conflict between the property owner and the thief is valueless, but rather also that the terms of the interaction of the two must reflect the different interests at hand.

And, indeed, this is precisely what it did. The court draws a distinction between life and limb, on the one hand, and property, on the other. It then creates an intraproperty distinction, saying that it is one thing to defend one's dwelling house, quite another to do the same with respect to one's unoccupied farm house.[17] Hence, not only does property shade off in the face of the primacy of life and limb. In addition, the court determines duties and liabilities based in part on the inferiority of our proprietary interest in a mere thing—an unoccupied farm house—relative to a formally similar interest in our dwelling house. On the basis of this, the court decides that the duty against committing battery does not relieve an owner of an unoccupied house of his or her obligation to respect the bodily integrity of others, including trespassers and, indeed, thieves. Essentially, this approach conforms to the egalitarian ideal of relating as equals because the duty at issue reflects a commitment to bake the interest differential into the terms of the parties' interaction.

Now consider an egalitarian reconstruction of the standard of extraordinary care expected from common carriers. The traditional rule is that a common carrier—viz., a professional service of transporting members of the public—must exercise "the utmost care, so far as human skill and foresight can go" which therefore amounts to a more demanding standard than the default rule of ordinary care.[18] This rule has come under pressure by courts and scholars arguing that it lacks a compelling justification.[19] Some of this pressure concerns institutional rather substantive reasons concerning the division of responsibility between judge and jury. The pushback is not so much against introducing stratification of degrees of care, but rather that a sufficiently vague standard of "reasonable care" allows the jury broad leeway to apply an exacting standard of care from common carriers.[20]

[15] Katko v. Briney, 183 N.W.2d 657 (Iowa 1971).

[16] *Id.*, at 658.

[17] *Id.*, at 657–58.

[18] Kelley v. Manhattan Ry. Co., 20 N.E. 383, 450 (N.Y. 1889). For reasons I explain in the main text below, New York tort law does not follow this rule.

[19] According to Fredrick Green, the traditional rule mischaracterizes the English common law pertaining to common carriers. Fredrick Green, *High Care and Gross Negligence*, 23 ILL. L. REV. 4, 5 (1928).

[20] Bethel v. New York Transit Auth., 703 N.E.2d 1214, 1217 (N.Y. 1998).

However, this is not a principled objection to the desirability of extraordinary care in the case of common carriers, but rather an argument that this standard should be determined as a matter of fact (namely, by the jury), rather than of law (namely, by a judge).

By contrast, the substantive critique of the traditional rule is that it has lost its justifying purpose and, so, should be replaced with the usual standard of ordinary care. The purpose of this rule, the critique goes, was to offset the "primitive safety" technology of steam railroads and other vehicles of mass transportation that had made public transportation highly dangerous, in an era of lax safety regulation and poor road conditions.[21] Nowadays, however, carriers have become "at least as safe as private modes of travel."[22] Add to this the charge, made by Lord Chief Justice Cockburn, that imposing a standard of extraordinary care is tantamount to forcing common carriers to be "insurers of their passengers' lives."[23]

That said, the comparison between private modes of travel and common carriers reaffirms, rather than repudiates, the merits of the traditional rule. The key distinction is between travelers and passengers. If travelers' safety is to govern the choice of standard of care, then ordinary care might be good enough. However, being a passenger represents a relational dimension not captured by a concern for travelers' safety simply as such. What also matters, as I demonstrate below, is that the common carrier and its passengers relate as equals, and to do so their terms of interaction must reflect the distinctive way in which the common carrier's pursuit of its interest—in turning a profit—implicates the interest of the passenger in his or her life and limb.

What is distinctive in this interaction when compared to the risk posed by common carriers to other pedestrians and motorists whose lives are just as important is the *absolutist* terms of the vulnerability of the passenger. A common carrier's passenger is not merely vulnerable to all the risks to which other travelers are equally vulnerable but rather also vulnerable to the carrier itself, which can be described as the "total dependency upon the [carrier] for safety precautions."[24] This sense of complete surrender of control over the operation of the vehicle and, hence, over one's safety is very familiar to anyone seated in an airplane high above the ocean or simply taking an express train. It is no less familiar and true when we ride a city bus. What this way of approaching the situation captures is an important aspect in the life-and-limb vulnerability of the passenger and, moreover, that this special aspect is literally *handed over* to the carrier. Thus, for the latter to relate to the former as an equal, this additional aspect of vulnerability—viz., the total

[21] *See, e.g.*, Michael D. Green, *Negligence = Economic Efficiency: Doubts* >, 75 Tex. L. Rev. 1605, 1622 (1997).

[22] *Bethel*, 703 N.E.2d at 1216 (quoting *Adams v. New York City Tr. Auth.*, 666 N.E.2d 216, 219 (N.Y. 1996)).

[23] Pym v. Great Northern R. Co., (1861) 2 Foster & Finlason 619.

[24] *Bethel*, 703 N.E.2d at 1217.

surrender of control over one's life and limb—must be reflected in their terms of interaction that may therefore explain, on egalitarian grounds, why tort law ought to impose on common carriers a duty of extraordinary care to their passengers.

It is beyond the scope of this illustration to provide a comprehensive account of the common carrier doctrine. Before moving to the next stage of the argument, however, I wish to preempt two objections concerning the scope of the argument from substantive equality in the common carrier context. To begin with, must the egalitarian grounds apply to individual taxi drivers, pedicabs operators, and other petty carriers who offer themselves to the public? My answer is that it can, but need not, and under some circumstances even should not, apply. There can be compelling considerations, which I discuss elsewhere and in Chapter 14, to restrict the duty of extraordinary care to large-size entities, private and public ones.

The second objection is that the aspect of life-and-limb vulnerability associated with being a common carrier's passenger is not unfamiliar in other contexts. In particular, we sometimes surrender control over our body to a physician (such as when undergoing a surgery). Why don't we impose a duty of extraordinary care on these professionals as well?[25]

The analogy is not completely right, but at any rate there is an important difference between transporting passengers and treating patients: the characteristic manner in which each task is being performed. Exacting more precautions from a physician on the latter occasion will most likely come at the expense of doing the same with respect to the next patient (put differently, the alternative cost of extraordinary care for one patient is under-ordinary care for another patient). Such a trade-off in the allocation of care among one's patients stems from the one-to-one character of medical treatment. It does not manifest itself, at least not as pervasively, in a typical case, such as that of bus driving. Hence, class-wide considerations counsel against extending the duty of extraordinary care of common carriers to the case of physicians and any other practice that is susceptible to workload effects.

The condition dimension. Now consider the second dimension of substantive equality, namely, condition. It takes up the circumstances adversely impacting a person's ability to deliberate, choose, or act (including by refraining from acting). Dearth of information and its resulting epistemic asymmetry, inadequate experience in general or in particular areas, insufficient physical, mental, or cognitive abilities, imminently dangerous situations, and unavailability of affordable insurance are paradigm cases of condition that often stand in the way of relating as substantively equals.[26] The thought is straightforward: Facing either might adversely affect the possibility of one party to interact with the other on equal footing. Rather

[25] *See* Robert Stevens, Torts and Rights 12–13 (2007).

[26] With respect to insurance, the idea is that the availability of affordable and effective coverage—and thus the ability to shift the financial cost of taking precautions or bearing risks through insurance—can also affect a person's condition. *See further* Dagan & Dorfman, *Substantive Remedies*, *supra* note 11, 542–43.

than setting it aside, as the formal conception of equality commands, the equality theory of tort law structures rights, duties, liabilities, and remedies in ways that accommodate it, at least in some measure. Two illustrations will be apt, taken from the torts of false imprisonment and products liability (which can also be extended to the tort of negligence). Chapter 15 provides detailed, theoretical and doctrinal, analysis of this dimension.

The first illustration concerns the tort of false imprisonment, and the important role that inadequate real-life experience might play in filling out the content of the duty. The duty-ower is required to avoid depriving the freedom of movement of the duty-owner by way of confining them. Much turns, therefore, on the question of what counts as confinement. Confinement is very easy to tell in some cases (such as locking someone in a room), but can get more intricate when the confinement is the product of implicit or explicit threats and costs (such as calling the police if one dares leave an unlocked room). Inadequate experience on the part of the detainee may certainly affect this question in the latter category of cases. Some persons, due to a condition of inadequate real-life experience and sophistication, may not bring themselves to challenge the confiner's threat, or may not even understand that it is up to them to decide what to make of this threat.

On a formal equality inquiry, this condition must not only take the back seat but rather be ignored completely. After all, lacking experience may lead one to make bad choices, but it does not reflect on their very capacity for making (good or bad) choices. On the substantive conception, by contrast, inadequate experience matters—it is an important consideration that tort law must take for the purpose of determining the standard of depriving freedom of movement. Indeed, modern tort law pays substantial attention to inadequate experience. For instance, a recurring question in false imprisonment law is whether a rehabilitation center can threaten a person that he be forcibly committed if he does not voluntarily submit himself to an inpatient treatment. A similar question arises in other contexts as well—whether an employer can resort to threats in order to detain an employee to interrogate them on theft accusations.

Precisely as the equality theory of tort law would require, courts focus their inquiry on the "plaintiff's vulnerability and oppressive circumstances" in order to decide whether a threat amounts to confinement or, alternatively, is better seen as a mere request. To do so they consider the experience, or lack thereof, of the plaintiff. On one occasion, the factual condition of being a female employee of "an eighteen year old ... with a tenth grade education" led one court to find her employer's threat to be capable of depriving her the ability to resist the detention.[27] On another occasion, by contrast, the court was impressed by the "experience" of the plaintiff, so as to find that a threat to forcibly commit him to a rehab facility did not amount

[27] The case is *Black v. Kroger*, 527 S.W.2d 794 (Tex. App.—Houston [1st Dist.] 1975). The quote is from *Fojtik v. Charter Med. Corp.*, 985 S.W.2d 625, 630 (Tex. Ct. App. 1999).

to false imprisonment: This plaintiff was "a forty-five-year-old man who had run several businesses.[28] He was not a young, inexperienced [person], like the plaintiff [in the case previously mentioned]."[29] Hence, condition matters—it is partially invoked to determine what a duty-ower owes, in terms of actions and inactions, to the duty-owner.

The second illustration of the condition dimension concerns lack of information resulting in epistemic asymmetry. A buyer of a product is vulnerable to a manufacturing defect that he or she may not be able to inspect. For instance, bodily integrity may be on the line by consuming a piece of coffee cake inadvertently baked with dangerously defective ingredients. The baker-seller and the buyer-consumer are, in many respects, pretty much alike in their respective conditions. This is not the familiar case of David versus Goliath that we often see in the law of products liability. In fact, it could be that the baker owns a small boutique bakery, barely making ends meet, whereas the buyer is a well-to-do person.

Thus, the only relevant difference in their respective conditions is access to information. Whereas the baker could know what's inside the cake, the buyer may not (as even tasting it may not necessarily reveal the defect). And if one believes that this is not a tort-law case, but rather a contractual arrangement that enlists tort law's products liability as a supplemental legal technology, consider a slightly different set of facts: Immediately after the wealthy buyer throws one half of the cake to the trash (as he is on a diet), a homeless person snatches the piece just before it sinks into the bin and happily consumes it. As I argued in Chapter 12, the Coasean idea of subordinating torts to contracts fails to come to terms with the freestanding foundation of the tort duty; the homeless person is, and should be, owed a duty of care and respect *even when* she is neither a party to the contractual transaction between the baker and the buyer nor an intended beneficiary of it. Indeed, the buyer does not account for the interest of this homeless person (or any other stranger) when contracting over the cake. Here, too, the relevant difference that should bear on the content of the baker's duty to the homeless person is the latter's epistemic inferiority relative to the duty-ower.[30]

One of the most important developments in modern tort law, along with warranties law, has been the (gradual) appreciation of precisely this difficulty. This appreciation is typically identified with the pathbreaking decisions of Judge Cardozo in *MacPherson*[31] (and England's Lord Atkin in *Donoghue*[32]) and Judge

[28] *Fojtik*, 985 S.W.2d at 631.
[29] *Id.*
[30] My analysis contrasts with the contract-based approach to products liability defended in Mark A. Geistfeld, *The Contractually Based Economic Loss Rule in Tort Law: Endangered Consumers and the Error of East River Steamship*, 65 DePaul L. Rev. 393, 403 (2016). This contrast is a surface manifestation of the deeper contrast between the equality theory and the contractual theory of tort law with respect to the relationship between tort and contract. *See* Chapter 12.
[31] MacPherson v. Buick Motor Co., 111 N.E. 1050 (N.Y. 1916).
[32] Donoghue v. Stevenson [1932] A.C. 562 (H.L.) (appeal taken from Scotland).

Traynor in *Escola*[33] and *Greenman*,[34] all the way to its adoption of §402A(2) of the Second Restatement of Torts[35] and its approval (despite the substantial revision of other parts of products liability) in the Third one.[36]

But it actually begins much earlier, with the common law's grasp of the problem. For instance, the court in *Parks v. G. C. Yost Pie Co.* imposes a duty of strict liability on food producers, noting that the producer "must know it is fit or take the consequences, if it proves destructive."[37] The first third of this quote emphasizes the epistemic consideration that leads to the quoted conclusion, namely, strict liability. The *Parks* court further intimates that "[a] manufacturer . . . who puts human food upon the market for sale or for immediate consumption does so upon an implied representation that it is wholesome for human consumption."[38] Accordingly, the cake eater in our example (be it the well-to-do buyer or the homeless person) suffers from the systemic epistemic deficit of not being able to tell in advance whether the cake is dangerously defective. This may explain the rise of a duty of *extra*ordinary care and its corresponding regime of strict tort liability not only in connection with physical injuries caused by food impurities but rather in most other cases of manufacturing defects of hard-to-inspect products (food-related or otherwise). A duty to go beyond ordinary care, or else to "take the consequences," is therefore supported by substantive equality's concern for the respective conditions of the parties and their impact on the ability of the risk-bearer to deliberate, choose, or act properly in connection with using the product.

III. Putting the Dimensions Together: Interest, Then Condition

The equality theory of tort law is doubly substantive in its egalitarian aspirations—to wit, it takes difference in both interest and condition seriously in the course of determining tort-law terms of interactions. I now wish to explain how these two dimensions relate.

To begin with, there are many cases in which integrating the respective interests and conditions of parties to a conflict is seamless. Indeed, sometimes a duty of extraordinary care fits both the relative priority of the interest of the risk-bearer and

33 Escola v. Coca Cola Bottling Co. of Fresno, 150 P.2d 436 (Cal. 1944) (Traynor J., concurring in outcome, dissenting in judgment).

34 Greenman v. Yuba Power Prods., Inc., 377 P.2d 897 (Cal. 1963).

35 RESTATEMENT (SECOND) OF TORTS §402A(2) (1965).

36 RESTATEMENT (THIRD) OF TORTS: PRODUCTS LIABILITY § 2(a) (1998). My focus is on manufacturing defects. The revisionary aspects of the Third Restatement primarily concerns *design* defects.

37 Parks v. G. C. Yost Pie Co., 144 P. 202, 203 (Kan. 1914). This case is also cited, with approval, by Traynor in *Escola*.

38 *Id.*

the vulnerable condition he or she encounters. The discussion of food impurities is a case in point and as I argue in Chapter 15 this is, as should be, negligence law's approach to the duty of due care owed to, and owned by, a person with a disability in connection with risk to this person's bodily integrity. Other cases of seamless integration of the two dimensions arise when only one of them—either interest or condition—makes a difference in the determination of the duty's content. The *Katko* decision concerning the defense of an unoccupied farmhouse is a case in point as only the interest dimension—the difference between the trespasser's life and the owner's property—figures in determining the terms of the interaction between the owner-turned-shooter and the trespasser-turned-victim.

That said, other cases might pit one dimension against the other. For instance, a driver with a disability who generates serious risk of physical injury to an abled-body pedestrian is a case in point. Whereas the interest of the pedestrian—life and limb—pulls in favor of demanding a higher degree of care from the driver, the condition of the driver—for instance, physical or cognitive disability—may impact his or her ability to exercise due care. How does the equality theory of tort law address the tension? More generally, is there a principled way to do the "addressing?"

I argue for the *lexical* priority of interest over condition. The argument stems from the conflict theory of tort law. As I already explained above, this theory captures tort law's distinctive moral point. The equality theory of tort law, in turn, provides the structuring mechanism with which tort law not only engages with conflicts' value in the right way but also does so in a certain way, namely, by treating the parties as substantive equals. Accordingly, interests are the source of concern out of which tort law arises; further, interests are also the source of value (and dis-value) to which tort law responds by constructing, containing, or preventing the different kinds of conflict between these interests.

Interests, therefore, come first in the order of vindication. After all, putting condition before interest would have placed the vindication of tort law beyond reach as it undermines what makes tort law valuable in the first place. For instance, suppose that considerations of condition favor a stringent duty against defaming members of historically disenfranchised communities (say, because of some genuine vulnerability on their parts).[39] Imposing such an exacting duty is inconsistent with the understanding that the conflict between free speech and good name or emotional well-being is inherently valuable and that, therefore, the moral responsibility of tort law is to embrace it rather than soothe it. Condition, therefore, comes second in the order of vindication.

I return to the priority of interest over condition in Chapter 15, where I argue that the priority in question illuminates important areas in contemporary tort law. But before I do so, I seek to complete the more preliminary elements of the

[39] *Cf.* Jeremy Waldron, *Dignity and Defamation: The Visibility of Hate*, 123 Harv. L. Rev. 1597 (2010).

argument from substantive equality. Chapter 14 does precisely that—it takes a major area in tort law, the standard of due care, and demonstrates how the equality theory of tort law determines the standard at issue.

To conclude this chapter, I wish to address skepticism about the possibility of clearly distinguishing between interest and condition. If a person faces conditions that significantly impair their ability to perform certain actions, then they have an interest in these actions not being demanded of them, as well as in not facing legal (and other) consequences when they fail to meet this demand. Isn't it an important interest rather than merely a condition?[40]

In response, there is no doubt that we have an interest in removing obstacles that stand in the way of realizing our projects and other things we care about. That said, I use "interest" in a narrower sense to distinguish between having an interest in *x* and facing a condition that might affect the ability to realize *x*. This distinction implies that we first assess what interests we have (such as leading an autonomous life, having friendships, maintaining a good reputation, etc.). We then identify the conditions that stand in the way of fulfilling these interests. This way of distinguishing between interest and condition highlights a crucial point: While conditions may change (for better or for worse), our fundamental interests remain, and should remain, constant. Furthermore, this distinction helps clarify why we should prioritize interests over conditions. Conditions become a source of concern only because, and only insofar as, they undermine our pursuit of fundamental interests. Put differently, the interest/condition distinction captures the difference between value and concern: Interests are the source of value, while conditions are the source of concern.

This is not to say that there are no borderline cases where the concepts of interest and condition overlap. Bodily integrity is a case in point: We have an interest in the integrity and functioning of our body, and at the same time, certain disabilities can be seen as conditions that impact the realization of our interests (both in bodily integrity and in most other interests). My response is twofold. First, as just mentioned, this overlap suggests that sometimes an interest can also figure as a condition. However, having this dual role does not undermine the importance of distinguishing between treating bodily integrity as an interest and treating it as a condition. What matters is that we are mindful of how we use the concept of bodily integrity (or any other concept), namely, as an interest or as a condition. Second, I concede that there could be cases, arguably very few, where the distinction between interest and condition becomes overly blurred, but this is hardly a reason to doubt its overall value.

[40] I thank an anonymous reviewer for pressing this objection.

14

Due Care and Substantive Equality

Hand Formula Redux

Introduction

In Chapter 13, I began to sketch what the equality theory of tort law consists in. The present chapter provides a more detailed study of both the duty of due care in the law of negligence and its longtime competitor, a regime of strict tort liability for accidental infliction of physical injury. It explains how tort-law duties can fix egalitarian terms of interactions for conflicts whose occurrence is accidental rather than intentional. The argument going forward, therefore, explicates the equality theory of tort law in the context of a major site of tort law. As I explain below, this context primarily features tolerably valuable conflicts that makes it relatively simpler, methodologically speaking, to focus attention on the equality theory without letting the conflict theory get in the way.

I. Mandating Due Care to Contain Tolerably Valuable Conflicts

I begin with an explanation of the precise place of the doctrine of due care in the grand scheme of tort law. This way forward will further demonstrate how the conflict and the equality theories of tort law are enmeshed in legal doctrine. I argue that tolerably valuable conflicts are, and should be, the primary concern of the standard that makes up the content of the duty of care, namely, the standard of due care. To see that, I wish to show why the two other kinds of conflict—inherently valuable and valueless conflicts—take the back seat when it comes to the duty of due care.

Begin with inherently valuable conflicts. All the cases falling in this category call for constructing the conditions necessary for conflicts to arise rather than containing them. They do not merely allow risk-creators to engage in risky activities, as long as the risks do not exceed reasonable, ordinary, usual, or some other "middle-of-the-road" level of care. Rather, they introduce some forms of relaxation, and at times even abrogation, of the requirement to exercise that level of care. The cases of inherently valuable conflicts discussed in previous chapters take this path, including cases involving accidentally manufactured conflicts. Consider in this regard the discussion of inherently valuable land-use conflicts (in private and

Conflict between Equals. Avihay Dorfman, Oxford University Press. © Oxford University Press 2026.
DOI: 10.1093/9780198979869.003.0018

public nuisance law). There is a sense in which these cases can be redescribed as requiring some measure of due care or due abating. After all, "some" measure of "due" care encompasses even a requirement to exercise minimal care. That said, this form of reductionism should be rejected because it elides the important distinction between wanting to *strike a balance* between the competing interests of the parties and wanting to *encourage* their conflict.

To avoid this problem, I limit my analysis of the duty of due care to the former case, which is typically a case of tolerably valuable conflicts. This is not to say that all tolerably valuable conflicts meet this analysis. Thus, the discussion of uncompromising journalism, the business judgment rule, and vigorous sports competitions demonstrated that addressing tolerably valuable conflicts may sometimes go beyond striking a balance or ordinary containment. In these and other cases, engaging with the value of these conflicts in the right way requires robust relaxation of the duty of due care. Hence, the equality theory takes the back seat and, for this reason, I set to one side such cases.

Now consider valueless conflicts and their tenuous connection to the standard of due care. Although most valueless conflicts involve deliberate acts of violence or other criminal behavior, there can be valueless conflicts that are essentially accidental. For instance, some valueless conflicts feature negligent infliction of physical harm arising out of a clearly illicit behavior on the part of the risk-creator. It can be an explosion at an illegal drug lab located in the basement of a house that, due to carelessness on the part of the drug maker, damages nearby houses, or a shooting accident that takes place in the vicinity of an area designated for hiking. Because these are valueless conflicts, the duty of "due care" does not really require reasonable or ordinary moderation in the performance of the risky activity at issue but rather insists on severely reducing the risk and even refraining from it altogether. At times, these types of valueless conflicts may give rise to a regime of strict tort liability; at other times, they may escalate into forms of reckless disregard of the interests of others, in which case there is no point in analyzing them in terms of a failure to display *due* care.

Against this background, tolerably valuable conflicts should take center stage in the discussion of what the standard of due care requires. As the conflict theory of torts suggests, you would recall, tort law ordinarily engages with tolerably valuable conflicts in the right way when it contains its adverse side effects. Due care is a doctrinal manifestation of the more abstract notion of containment. Indeed, I argue that the duty of due care, properly conceived, provides an appealing interpretation of what "containing" requires. Rather than merely addressing conflicts' side effects, the standard of due care adds an egalitarian twist, namely, by seeing to it that the risk-creator and -bearer interact on terms that reflect their substantive equality along its two dimensions, interest and condition. As such, this standard instantiates the equality theory of tort law.

II. Due Care as a Basic Commitment to (Some Principle of) Equality

I argue that due care is a form of balancing and that balancing presupposes some conception of equality (note that although balancing is often associated with ad hoc, ex post facto analysis, it also can be employed in a principled way, as I seek to show in this chapter). I defend the substantive conception of relational equality as an appealing account of the balancing that governs the standard of due care in tort law. But precisely how should one assess the appeal of one over another account of due care? Is it a matter of rejecting efficiency, on the one hand, and defending substantive equality, on the other? Is it a metaphysical question about pluralism, and how to adjudicate the clash between irreconcilable values? I think not. There is an important sense in which competing accounts of due care are, at bottom, different versions of a deeper commitment to equality. They cannot even begin to show appeal in a *liberal* society if they aim to justify legal rules that undermine the notion that all people's lives are equally important (for instance, a duty of under-ordinary care must be resisted even when, as Ariel Porat demonstrates, it would increase overall social welfare in some situations[1]). To this extent, disagreements about the standard of due care cannot be separated from the more abstract question of what equality requires. Against this egalitarian backdrop, I argue that the substantive conception of relational equality represents a more appealing interpretation of the demands of equality than the competing ones.

According to the Second Restatement of Torts, a duty-ower complies[2] with the duty of due care by giving "impartial consideration to the harm likely to be done to the interests of the other as compared to the advantages likely to accrue to [that actor's] own interests."[3] The question of due care becomes what impartiality requires. And this latter question presupposes some conception of equality—crassly put, a reasonable person must take into account, or act in ways consistent with, the fact that the interests of other persons need not be of less importance than theirs.

To "take into account" the interests of others can invite any number of interpretations. The one most famously associated with leading versions of corrective justice insists on self-abnegation—that is, any nontrivial risk of harm to other

[1] Ariel Porat, *Misalignments in Tort Law*, 121 YALE L.J. 82, 97–105 (2011).

[2] Compliance differs from conformity in that the former involves acting on or for the reasons given by the duty, whereas the latter requires no more than doing what the duty requires. A person complies with a duty when she drives carefully because there is a duty to do so; another person acts in conformity with the duty when he drives carefully regardless of whether a duty directs him to do so. For more on the compliance/conformity distinction, see JOSEPH RAZ, PRACTICAL REASON AND NORMS 178–82 (1999). As will become clear, my analysis does not turn on this distinction.

[3] RESTATEMENT (SECOND) OF TORTS §283 cmt. *e* (1965).

persons must be eliminated, irrespective of costs or burdens, more generally.[4] That interpretation is certainly on point when the conflict is valueless, but it is hard for egalitarians to defend it in connection with tolerably valuable conflicts as the interests of risk-creators are *also* important.

Moreover, it seems that self-abnegation is surprisingly inconsistent with the formal conception of equality. I say surprising because leading corrective justice theorists are the champions of formal equality in tort theory. On the formal conception, to "take into account" the interests of others is to accord equal weight to the competing liberties, which is why the Third Restatement of Torts suggests, on behalf of corrective justice, that a person who "impermissibly ranks personal interests ahead of others" violates "an ethical norm of equal consideration."[5] Equal consideration (or equal treatment, as Dworkin would say[6]) implies that the risk-creator's and -bearer's interests should place a similar demand on the deliberation and actions of the risk-creator. To give an example, the life and limb of the risk-bearer and the liberty of action of the risk-creator are formally equal in the sense that they should be getting the same measure of respect and concern. At any rate, however, I reject both the self-abnegation and the formal equality interpretations of what "taking into account" the interests of others might require. As argued above, there is no good reason to ignore the difference between life-and-limb and proprietary interests (and even with respect to the latter, there are important differences between having an interest in a dwelling house and in an unoccupied house). Indeed, the substantive conception of equality rejects both self-abnegation and equal treatment and defends, instead, an ideal of relating as equals by taking seriously differences of interest and of condition.

Now consider the welfarist (law and economics) account of due care and its underlying conception of equality. On the economic rendition of the standard of due care, a particular variation on the famous Learned Hand Formula,[7] the failure to act as a reasonably careful person amounts to "the failure to take precautions that would generate greater benefits in avoiding accidents than the precautions would cost."[8] It is crucial to note that the "benefits" and the "cost" just mentioned are social ones, rather than personal ones, as they pertain to answer the question of whether taking additional precautions are worth our—read, society's—while.[9]

[4] Ernest J. Weinrib, The Idea of Private Law 148, 152 (1995); Jules Coleman, *Tort Law and Tort Theory*, *in* Philosophy and the Law of Torts 183, 205 (Gerald J. Postema ed., 2001); Arthur Ripstein, Force and Freedom: Kant's Legal and Political Philosophy 59 (2009).

[5] Restatement (Third) of Torts: Liab. for Physical Harm §6 cmt. *d* (2010).

[6] Ronald Dworkin, Taking Rights Seriously 227 (1977).

[7] United States v. Carroll Towing Co., 159 F.2d 169, 173 (2d Cir. 1947).

[8] McCarty v. Pheasant Run, Inc., 788 F.2d 1554, 1557 (7th Cir. 1987) (*per* Posner J.).

[9] It can be worth our while if the size of the social pie is the biggest possible, or if the average slice of a pie is the greatest possible. Nothing in my argument turns on choosing between these (or other social welfare) alternatives.

This is rightly viewed as a point about identifying due care with optimal allocation of scarce resources in society, but it also *necessarily* presupposes a conception of equality.

Requiring the risk-creator to sacrifice his or her resources, including his or her time and energy, whenever it maximizes society's total resources is a form of equal treatment in the sense that it insists that *no one's resources count for more or less than any other person's*. But this welfarist interpretation of equality is inadequate, normatively speaking, because (among other things) it disregards our status as distinct autonomous beings and, instead, conscripts us all into the collectivist enterprise of maximizing aggregate welfare. Such an idea of equality ends up with the troubling effect of effacing the individual clashes with a fundamental liberal-egalitarian commitment to treat persons as free and equal agents.[10]

Finally, consider Benjamin Zipursky's theory of due care as an idea about civil competency.[11] On this theory, a duty of due care is best understood as a subset of our broader network of "social practices, norms, and social mores"[12] regarding a basic human quality of being "well-socialized."[13] In particular, to be well-socialized means to take "others' well-being seriously in conducting oneself."[14] And to take them seriously in the context of negligence law, a reasonable person owes "an obligation to [these] others to temper one's conduct so as not to injure them."[15] It is, therefore, a matter of other-regard.[16] Zipursky is careful not to turn other-regard into self-abnegation, as ordinary care is neither utmost nor optimal care.[17] Indeed, he observes that "[r]easonable prudence ... involves being other-regarding to a certain extent."[18] The qualifier "to a certain extent" suggests that other-regard can be made compatible with equality, though it remains to be seen precisely what conception of equality underwrites the civil-competency account of due care.

III. Due Care and Substantive Equality

On the equality theory of tort law, the standard of due care determines terms of interaction according to which the risk-creator and the risk-bearer can relate as

[10] The famous charge against utilitarianism, that it does not take seriously "the distinction between persons," is right on point. JOHN RAWLS, A THEORY OF JUSTICE 27 (1971).

[11] Zipursky presents his theory as a synthesis of three different ideas concerning the duty of due care: that it concerns prudence, meshes with social mores, and protects rights.

[12] Benjamin C. Zipursky, *Sleight of Hand*, 48 WM. & MARY L. REV. 1999, 2040 (2007) [Zipursky, *Sleight*]. *See also* Benjamin C. Zipursky, *Reasonableness In and Out of Negligence Law*, 163 U. PENN. L. REV. 2131 (2015).

[13] Zipursky, *Sleight, supra*, at 2034.

[14] *Id.*, at 2035.

[15] *Id.*, at 2037.

[16] *Id.*, at 2036–38.

[17] *Id.*, at 2034.

[18] *Id.*, at 2036.

substantive equals. These terms may sometimes undermine the maximization of aggregate welfare, the promotion of distributive justice, or the realization of democratic ideals of equal citizenship. This is because they are designed to construct forms of one-to-one interaction that treat their participants as substantive equals, as opposed to these or other goals. I argue that an egalitarian interpretation of the Hand Formula provides an adequate method to determine what counts as relating as equals. By "determining," I do not mean that this Formula is akin to an algorithm. Rather, it serves as an analytical framework with which to identity the considerations that make up the standard of due care, which is to say the content of the duty. Further, such a framework can be employed in a more and less robust way—it can either guide the resolution of a particular instance or merely constrain the range of legitimate resolutions of a particular instance. Nothing in my argument turns on choosing between these procedural arrangements, so that my argument does not make any essential reference to a jury system, judge-centric system, regulator-based supervision, or otherwise.[19]

The Learned Hand Formula reads:

> [I]f the probability be called P; the injury, L; and the burden [of taking adequate precautions], B; liability depends upon whether B is less than L multiplied by P: i.e., whether $B < PL$.[20]

My interest in this formulation is instrumental rather than exegetical. I wish to reconstruct this form of analysis in a way that brings out the connection between the standard of due care and the ideal of relating as equals. To do so, I take "injury" to mean none other than injury, rather than loss or "L." That is, the interest on the part of the potential victim is not his or her personal loss, nor is it society's loss. Instead, it is impairing their interest, for instance in bodily integrity, property, and so on. Likewise, talk of burden or "B" should refer to the predicament of the risk-creator in terms of setting back their interests, for instance in liberty of action, free speech, and so on. The burden is normative, not economic—the very same amount of investment toward precaution-taking may have trivial, substantial, or overwhelming consequences for the self-determination of risk-creators, depending on their respective conditions and the circumstances under which they

[19] I say *otherwise* because the properly conceived value of a standard of due care is not limited to the remedial aspect of tort law. Instead, its significance lies in creating egalitarian terms of interaction even when these terms are set and enforced by another public legal institution.

[20] United States v. Carroll Towing Co., 159 F.2d 169, 173 (2d Cir. 1947). Strictly speaking, the case is one of admiralty law and the question of due care at its center is, to some extent, the defense of comparative negligence. (I say to some extent because the substandard conduct of the negligent actor, the bargee, can also be viewed as an instance of imposing risk on others, that is, the property of the plaintiff.) As I show in Chapter 15, the difference between the defendant and the plaintiff's fault is often highly important, morally and doctrinally speaking. However, it is of less importance to the present exposition of the (risk-creator's) standard of due care in egalitarian terms.

are called to act (on which more below). Lastly, the variable "P," or probability, is a mediating factor—it traces both the *nature* and the *intensity* of the connection between the predicament of the risk-creator and the vulnerability of the risk-bearer by informing us whether, and if so to what extent, curtailing the interest of the former can help sustain the interest of the latter.

Against this backdrop, an egalitarian Hand Formula is not a device of cost-benefit analysis geared toward maximizing welfare, and not even of maximizing the protection of interests. Rather than maximizing anything, its role is to *contain* tolerably valuable conflicts by reference to the relative importance of the conflicting interests.

To see this, consider a case featuring a clear imbalance between the conflicting interests, according to which the interest of the risk-bearer ranks higher than the risk-creator's. The paradigm case is a conflict between the life and limb of the former and the liberty of action of the latter. Further, it concerns an involuntary interaction in the sense that the risk at issue is nonreciprocal. Under these circumstances, the standard of due care calls for taking precautions so as to eliminate, within limits, the risk to the risk-bearer's interest. By "eliminating," I mean the total reduction of the risk down to the "background" risk levels to which the risk-bearer is ordinarily exposed. By saying elimination "within limits," I mean limits on the amount of care expected from the risk-creator. I will take up the question of limits in Sections IV and V below. Before doing so, I wish to explain what is meant by saying that the standard of due care sets egalitarian terms of interactions.

An illustration will be apt.[21] Consider a truck driver pulling his vehicle into a designated rest area to go to the restroom and get some coffee. Upon his return to the cabin he records the stop in a logbook (which takes him about two minutes) and reverses the track to get back on the highway. While doing so he strikes a person standing in a blind spot right behind the truck. This is a tolerably valuable conflict as it concerns the adverse side of effects—viz., the (nonreciprocal) risk of harm—generated by the close proximity between a person engaging in driving and a pedestrian enjoining his free time. The duty of due care contains these effects in a certain way, namely, by fixing terms of interaction according to which the parties relate as equals.[22] The relative importance of the victim's life and limb over the liberty of the driver must therefore set the basis for deciding precisely what precautions are due under the circumstances.

Suppose that, given the poor technology of road safety at the time the event took place (for instance, the mid-twentieth century), a helpful way to contain the conflict is to have the driver run an outside-the-vehicle check right before backing

[21] The illustration draws very loosely on the factual situation in *Martin v. Evans*, 711 A.2d 458 (Pa. 1998).

[22] In fact, the duty of due care does not exhaust the matter as other requirements may also be necessary, including in particular the ones encapsulated in the doctrine of comparative negligence.

up.[23] If doing so can eliminate the risk of striking the victim, then there is no doubt that failing to do so is tantamount to a breach of the duty of due care. The reason for this does not lie in efficiency considerations. Taking this additional precaution may well be cost-justified but only contingently so. In fact, it could even be the case that the cheapest avoider of this conflict is the victim whose choice idly to stand behind a long, tall truck puts him in an unnecessary grave danger.[24] And from a macroeconomic analysis of law, if not from its microeconomic counterpart, there is no good reason to suppose that efficiency supports a rule that demands truck drivers to walk the extra mile, as it were.[25]

But even if there are good (economic) reasons to treat the victim's behavior as a matter of comparative negligence, rather than as a reason to exonerate the driver from owing the victim a duty in the first place, efficient care does not require taking the additional precaution at issue if the *social* cost of doing so exceeds the expected *social* costs of the injury to the victim. Certainly, under some circumstances, reconnoitering while circling the truck could be exceedingly costly in just this way (perhaps due to stormy weather or seemingly violent people lurking all over the parking area). At other times, it may only bring about slight, rather than substantial, reduction in the risk of harm to nearby pedestrians as other pedestrians may approach the rear of the truck by the time the driver is ready to resume driving.[26] In other words, circling around the truck may not beef up the mediating factor on the Hand Formula, viz., the probability or "P." (Suppose the burden of taking the additional precaution is high (e.g., 5), but it is likely to yield only a small reduction in the victim's expected injury (e.g., 4). A simple cost-benefit analysis would suggest that the driver should not be compelled to take this precaution.)

By contrast, the equality theory of tort law provides a noncontingent way to explain why the driver's duty of due care requires him to take this other-regarding measure of looking behind the truck for potential victims. Such a requirement is entailed by the priority of life and limb over liberty of action, not by the benefits that might accrue to society from doing so. For the driver to treat the pedestrian as substantively equal, the priority at issue must bear on what due care amounts to under the circumstances, namely, the elimination of the risk generated by backing up a long, tall truck. This approach holds even when taking the precaution

[23] *See further* Heidi M. Hurd & Michael S. Moore, *Negligence in the Air*, 3 Theoretical Inq. L. 333, 362–63 (2002).

[24] The cheapest cost avoider, as introduced by Guido Calabresi, is a basic principle in economic analysis of tort law.

[25] The macroeconomic analysis of law does not analyze the efficiency of tort-law rules on a retail level but rather asks the wholesale question of how these rules, properly construed, contribute to the fiscal and monetary policies of the particular country. *See generally* Yair Listokin, Law and Macroeconomics: Legal Remedies to Recessions 196–97 (2019).

[26] The rule known as outside-the-vehicle check has been subject to debate in the context of railroad crossings. Compare its subsequent rejection by Justice Cardozo in *Pokora v. Wabash Ry. Co.*, 292 U.S. 98 (1934) with its initial approval by Justice Holmes in *Baltimore & O. R. Co. v. Goodman*, 275 U.S. 66 (1927).

at stake does not make for a dramatic reduction of the risk of harm to potential pedestrians.[27] Further, this holds true even in circumstances where precautions are taken at an *un*justified cost, such as when the burden of taking precautions exceeds the reduction of expected injury (say, it costs 5 to reduce the probable loss by only 4).

To further reinforce this point, and also demonstrate the practical difference between the equality theory of tort law and both efficient care and corrective justice's idea of due care, replace the injured person with personal property. The latter could be an expensive laptop computer, violin, or any other item a backing truck could effortlessly crash. Further assume that the circumstances under which this item escaped its owner's control preclude the viability of holding the owner fully liable for the breakage—to wit, there is no assumption of risk on his part as this owner neither chose to let it stand behind the truck nor displayed conscious indifference about the whereabouts of his item. Instead, it could be the upshot of comparative negligence on his part, for instance, by driving his car while inadvertently leaving the trunk slightly open. But it could also be the upshot of no fault on his part, such as when the item was stolen from his apartment and then ditched behind the truck by the fleeing thief. To this extent, the question of what due care the truck driver owes the item's owner is not easily preempted under these circumstances. One last assumption to be made here is that the truck's circling is not necessary in order to avert an injury to a person who may be standing behind the rear of the truck: Making loud noises, either by shouting or using the truck's horn, provides adequate warning to anyone (without hearing disability) who might stand there. Hence, I assume that the truck driver has met this requirement. The only live question is whether he also owes it to the item's owner to take the additional precaution of reconnoitering around the truck.

Consider efficient care, self-abnegation, and formal equality. A standard of efficient care must answer in the affirmative if the expected benefit of saving the expensive item exceeds the cost of taking the precaution in question. As mentioned above, such an approach defies a principled answer as it is wholly contingent on the costs and the benefits at stake. A self-abnegation standard of due care requires that the truck driver take the precaution in question as, save for exceptional cases,[28] the burden of doing so must *not* figure in determining the standard of due care.[29]

On the formal equality alternative, due care should reflect the formally equal status of the parties as bearers of the capacity for choice. The fact that the owner's

[27] By arguing that "P" or probability in the Hand Formula should not figure prominently in fixing the standard of due care under these circumstances, I do not make a universal claim about this variable. Rather, my claim focuses on nonreciprocal risk to life and limb. Thus, when the risk is to a person's financial interest, P should have a central role in fixing the standard. *See* Zipursky, *Sleight*, *supra* note 12, at 2025 (discussing the overlap between the economic interpretation of the Hand Formula and the legal idea of ordinary care in cases involving primarily financial interests).

[28] *See* Bolton v. Stone [1951] AC 850 (HL).

[29] Weinrib, *supra* note 4, at 148.

vulnerability is restricted to their property, rather than their person, should not figure in the determination of the standard of due care—their life and their property should extract the same level of care from the truck driver. Admittedly, it is not clear to me what the bottom-line answer of the formal equality conception should be to our hypothetical case.[30] What is clear, however, is that that answer should not discriminate between the real case, in which the victim's person is at grave risk, and the hypothetical one, in which a piece of property is on the line.

An ideal of relating as substantive equals, by contrast, *need not* require taking the precaution in question if its sole purpose is to eliminate the risk of destroying another person's property. The care that is due in order to eliminate risk of serious harm to a person's own body should not be dispositive of protecting this person's tangibles. If under the circumstances, the burden—as measured in terms of diminished liberty of action—borne by the truck driver is substantial enough, vocal warning and resort to four-way flashers, may satisfy what the standard of due care requires of them. Hence, a substantive conception of equality puts forward a liberal principle of other-regard that is not only limited in its demands of recognition of the risk-creator's own autonomy but rather also susceptible to the differing importance of the conflicting interests. As mentioned above, rather than serving as an algorithm, its basic value lies in identifying the relevant considerations and articulating the right questions in order to guide ex ante deliberations of risk-creators and ex post decision-making on the part of the entity, be it a judge, jury, or otherwise, tasked with resolving the dispute.

IV. The Upper limit of Egalitarian Due Care: Against Over-Demandingness

The argument has so far focused on the standard of due care as a doctrine of balancing conflicting interests based on a metric of substantive equality. I now wish to extend the discussion outwards by exploring a major limitation on the duty to exercise due care. As I argued above, the standard of due care calls for taking precautions so as to eliminate, *within limits*, the risk to the risk-bearer's interest. Indeed, eliminating risk must not amount to annihilating the self-determination of the risk-creator by imposing on him or her a de-facto requirement of self-abnegation. This is because the ideal of relating as equals takes seriously the interests of *both* parties, including the self-determination of the risk-creator.

[30] The reason it is not clear does not stem from insufficient discussion of such questions by corrective justice theorists but rather because the normative resources that corrective justice provides to address them are self-consciously underdeterminate. *See* Arthur Ripstein, Private Wrongs 102–16 (2016). Ripstein summarizes his account of due care by saying "If you want to know what it is to be careful—given that, at the most abstract level, being careful is just a matter of limiting the foreseeable side effects of your conduct on others—you ask what ordinary careful people do." *Id.*, at 108.

Inequality, therefore, can go either way. The purpose of this section is to take up one such way, namely, when the standard of due care sets terms of interaction that fail to treat the *risk-creator* as substantively equal.

Contrary to the commodifying language in which lawyer economists tend to describe the predicament of the risk-creator, the morally important burden (the "B" in the Hand Formula) involved in exercising due care is not material but rather normative. Moreover, contrary to the thought that negligence law should promote distributive justice, democratic equality, or any other societal goal, the "normative" burden is not reducible to the value that society as a whole derives from the activity of the risk-creator: Some risk-creators may do more, or less, service to us all by engaging in their risk-creating activities. Instead, it concerns the ability of the risk-creator to lead an autonomous life by making and executing his or her choices simply as such. The self-abnegation concern that arises in connection with the standard of due care is, therefore, one of substantially undermining the ability to engage in *chosen* activities.[31] It seems that this point resonates with Judge Hand's assertion in *U.S. v. Carroll Towing* that, rather than imposing a self abnegating duty of due care on the barge's guard, "the barge must not be the bargee's prison."[32] The burden involved in experiencing a prison-like condition represents, first and foremost, a normative setback to one's autonomy. Even a genuinely happy and well-to-do inmate is fundamentally and entirely unfree.

The crucial question, then, is what counts as too much care? Is there a way to draw a principled distinction between permissible and impermissible imposition of precaution-taking? I answer in the affirmative and show traces of this distinction in the case law. Two sets of distinction, followed by illustrations, will help to show that negligence should, and in fact already does, place an upper limit on the standard of due care so as to sustain the standard's commitment to an interpersonal ideal of relating as substantive equals.

The first distinction, really a preliminary distinction, goes back to the conflict theory's distinction between valueless and tolerably valuable conflicts. It concerns the difference between illegitimate and legitimate activities pursued by the risk-creator. The egalitarian case for placing an upper limit on the duty of due care takes up the latter category (i.e., legitimate activities) *only*. The reason, to repeat, stems from the conflict theory's insistence on addressing conflicts by engaging with their underlying values—in particular, valueless conflicts warrant prevention rather than containment. Hence, the problem of over-demandingness does not apply to those engaging in valueless conflicts by pursuing illegitimate activities; these should be prevented. To be sure, preventing illegitimate activities may have its own

[31] The ability to engage in chosen activities is not the same as the very capacity for choice, as the latter is almost never implicated by imposing a duty of due care on the risk-creator.

[32] United States v. Carroll Towing Co., 159 F.2d 169, 173 (2d Cir. 1947).

challenges, but they are very different from the standard of due care's concern with legitimate activities and the tolerably valuable conflicts to which they give rise.[33]

The second distinction goes to the heart of the equality theory of tort law. It drives a wedge between two ways in which precaution-taking can adversely affect the self-determination interest of the risk-creator, namely, by crushing and by constraining it (note that these two qualitatively different ways of undermining a person's interest must inform the egalitarian calculus underlying the equality theory of tort law). Sometimes, taking additional precautions may shut down one's livelihood, ground project, or calling (including even vocation).[34] At other times, however, it may constrain, but not preclude, the pursuit of this or that valuable end. On the basis of this distinction, I argue that imposing a duty of due care is impermissible if two conditions are met: First, the underlying conflict is a tolerably valuable one, consisting of legitimate activities; and second, taking additional precautions may likely annihilate the risk-creator's pursuit of his or her livelihood, ground project, or calling.

To illustrate, consider the contrast between two landmark cases: *Adams v. Bullock*[35] and *Bolton v. Stone*.[36] Start with *Adams*. There, a twelve-year-old boy walking on a bridge below which a trolley runs held an eight foot (2.4 meters) long metal wire that he swung over the bridge's rail. The wire came into contact with the trolley's high voltage overhead wire, which was lying perpendicularly about five feet under the bridge, causing the boy's electrocution and consequent burns. The New York Court of Appeals overruled judgments entered by lower courts in favor of the victim, deciding instead that the defendant-trolley did not deviate from the standard of due care. The court, led by Judge Cardozo, began with an observation that maps onto my distinction between tolerably valuable and valueless conflicts: A system of overhead-wire trolley provides a "lawful" means of urban transportation.[37] Part of what makes this "lawful" activity also a legitimate one is that the risk it poses to passengers and nonpassengers is not terribly high, though it is a *real* risk[38]—that is, it is not "very unlikely to occasion harm,"[39]

[33] I take it that the illegitimacy of an activity, and the valueless conflict in which it participates, is not specific to tort law. For instance, manufacturing (certain) street drugs is illegitimate not merely for the purpose of determining tort liability. So, too, is the case of a layperson conducting a complicated surgery on another person in a non-catastrophic situation.

[34] My emphasis on livelihood (et alia) reflects an underlying distinction between constitutive choices and mere preferences (including intense ones). The distinction informs the egalitarian calculus I propose in the main text. For more on the distinction, see HANOCH DAGAN & AVIHAY DORFMAN, RELATIONAL JUSTICE: A THEORY OF PRIVATE LAW ch. 3 (2024).

[35] 128 N.E. 93 (N.Y. 1919).

[36] [1951] A.C. 850 (H.L.). I will focus on Lord Reid's famous dicta, that "If cricket cannot be played on a ground without creating a substantial risk, then it should not be played there at all," rather than on the facts of the case. *Id.*, at 867.

[37] *Adams*, 128 N.E. at 93.

[38] A risk is "real," according to Weinrib's analysis of the English-law doctrine of due care, if it should not be "brushed aside." WEINRIB, *supra* note 4, at 149, 152. As explained by Lord Reid, the notion of "real risk" contrasts with "a mere possibility which would never influence the mind of a reasonable man."

[39] WEINRIB, *supra* note 4, at 149.

"infinitesimal,"[40] or "fantastic or far-fetched."[41] Thus, such a system had *back then* a valuable role to play in society, in which case the task of the *Adams* court was to employ the law of negligence so as to contain the adverse side effects of the conflict at issue rather than prevent the operation of the trolley system. (Notice that the "conflict at issue" is not reducible to the particular plaintiff and defendant but rather involves constructing terms of interaction between transportation enterprises, on the one hand, and customers and pedestrians, on the other). Engaging in containment, then, calls for fixing terms of interaction—including a standard of due care—that reflect an ideal of relating as substantive equals. This is the point in which the upper limit of egalitarian due care might be crossed.

Indeed, Cardozo is acutely aware of what is at stake, namely, the very enterprise associated with the defendant's trolley system will likely not survive a duty to eliminate the risk of harm posed by its overhead wire. Insulation is technically impossible as operating the trolley turns on using the wire uninsulated. The only other option is for the wire system to go underground that is tantamount to entirely shutting down the trolley enterprise (which is what the self-abnegation conception of due care might require). Indeed, Cardozo holds that abandoning the overhead system and putting the wires underground is not within the defendant's "power," or at least has not been shown by the plaintiff to be within the defendant's "power."[42] Requiring the risk-creator to take this precaution (or an alternative, though a no less expensive one of putting guards virtually everywhere) does not merely constrain the range of options available for the owners and employees of the trolley company to pursue their ground project or livelihood. Rather, it may likely crush their ground project or livelihood and, by extension, undermine the interests of people who rely on the trolley service to pursue their own ground projects or livelihoods.[43]

In the language of the economic analysis of negligence, the difference between a constraining and a crushing burden of precaution-taking is the difference between forcing the trolley company to take cost-*un*justified precautions and forcing it to go out of business. From the economic perspective in question, both options should be avoided. In contrast, the equality theory requires the imposition of any burden of precaution-taking, including economically cost-unjustified burden, as long as it does not crush the livelihood of the risk-creator.

Now, consider *Bolton v. Stone*. The distinction between crushing and constraining the pursuit of valuable ends (especially livelihood, ground projects,

[40] Overseas Tankship (U.K.) Ltd. v The Miller Steamship Co. Pty. (Wagon Mound no. 2) [1967] 1 A.C. 617, 642.

[41] *Id. See also* WEINRIB, *supra* note 4, at 149

[42] *Adams*, 128 N.E. at 93, 94.

[43] The trolley company does not have ground projects, at least not directly. Indirectly, however, the ground projects of its employees, management, and, in some cases, owners may be at stake. *See further* Hanoch Dagan, Avihay Dorfman, & Katharina Pistor, The Liberal Firm (unpublished manuscript).

and callings) can be further reinforced by a comparison to the self-abnegation account of due care, and especially the one developed by Weinrib's interpretation of the English case law. His account presents as its exhibit A the famous cricket case of *Bolton v. Stone*. According to Weinrib, recall, the predicament of the risk-creator (the "B" in the Hand Formula) does not lay a moral claim on the duty of due care: "From a corrective justice standpoint, disregard of B makes sense, because it is the risk, not the cost of eliminating it, that connects the parties to an accident as doer and sufferer."[44] Weinrib is right to say that "the cost of precaution is irrelevant" if all that matters is the social benefit generated by investing in taking additional precautions. I disagree, however, that what I have called the *normative* burden of taking precaution—in terms of the risk-creator's self-determination—is irrelevant for the risk-creator and risk-bearer to relate as substantive equals. Moreover, I believe that my argument is not inconsistent with Lord Reid's account of due care in *Bolton* and elsewhere.

In *Bolton*, a cricket ball hit over the fence and struck a pedestrian standing at a nearby side road. The risk of being so hit was fairly small as the ball had topped the surrounding fence "on the average once in three seasons"[45] and the nearby road on which the ball landed was rarely occupied by a "great number of people."[46] Lord Reid decided that playing cricket under these circumstances does not deviate from the standard of due care. But the more important part of the decision concerns Lord Reid's understanding of what the standard of due care should require in the more usual class of negligence cases, namely, when the risk-creator generates substantial risk rather than a "bare possibility" of harming others.[47] That is, substantial risk of harm calls for its elimination, irrespective of "the difficulty of remedial measures."[48] The memorable conclusion, therefore, is as follows: "If cricket cannot be played on a ground without creating a substantial risk, then it should not be played there at all."[49] One way to read this statement is that it identifies due care with self-abnegation. This is Weinrib's interpretation. But there is another way to approach this statement, which is illuminated by the substantive conception of equality.

What Reid is saying is *not* that the (normative) burden does not matter. He focuses on a narrower question—whether or not cricket should be played "there," namely, in this specific field with its relatively low fence. Forcing players to relocate to another, better-fenced field places a *constraint* on their self-determination, no doubt. Further, it would have been very much warranted had the risk of serious harm to passersby been substantial—in fact, the field was constructed decades

[44] WEINRIB, *supra* note 4, at 148.
[45] *Bolton*, A.C. 850, at 864.
[46] *Id.*
[47] *Id.*, at 865.
[48] *Id.*, at 867.
[49] *Id.*

before the nearby road on which the victim stood had been built, suggesting that *this field* may not fit the changing landscape of a growing city.[50] However, it is a qualitatively different burden than shutting down the defendant's cricket club as such. Indeed, nothing in Reid's conclusion suggests that cricket should not be played full stop. The latter possibility is an instance of crushing the livelihood, ground projects, or calling of those engaging in the game of cricket. Such a self-abnegation amounts to a form of impermissible imposition on the risk-creator precisely because self-determination is integral to the ideal of relating as equal*s* (in the plural). The right way to decide the question of due care in future iterations of this case must assess the requirement to display additional vigilance (including by taking more precautions) along the crushing versus constraining distinction. Thus, assuming as I do that the risk-creating activity in question amounts to livelihood, ground project, or calling, the fact-finder must have sufficient understanding of the real-world implications of additional vigilance on the self-determination of the risk-creator.

V. The Lower Limit of Egalitarian Due Care: Against Under-Demandingness

Sometimes a standard of due care might require too much in just the way discussed above, namely, when taking additional precautions might amount to crushing, rather than constraining, the risk-creator's pursuit of valuable ends. Doing so is inconsistent with the demands of substantive equality. At other times, however, this standard requires too little, which is the subject matter of the present section. Both the "too much" and the "too little" are assessed against the baseline of relating as equals. Focusing on the latter, I identify a category of cases in which the standard of due care *systematically* fails to sustain terms of interactions between substantive equals. The failure is systematic in the sense that the standard is bound to fail in eliminating substantial risk to the life and limb of risk-bearers. Hence, by exercising due care—even utmost care—the risk-creator puts the life and limb of the risk-bearer in a substantial danger. Tort law must, therefore, adopt an alternative method of constructing terms of interactions that treat both parties as equals. I argue that properly conceived, the strict liability doctrine of *ultrahazardous activities* can be viewed along these lines, namely, as an effort to address this egalitarian challenge.

The concept of ultrahazardous or abnormal activities may strike one as itself abnormal. This is so especially if one begins from a neighboring context, namely, products' safety. There, Cardozo introduced in *MacPherson v. Buick* a powerful

[50] The field has been in existence since "about 1864." The nearby road was built in 1910. *Bolton*, A.C. 850, at 851.

deconstruction of the then-prevailing distinction between products, such as a poison, which are *inherently* dangerous and products, such as automobiles, which are *merely* dangerous. The distinction was meant to extend tort liability to the former products, but not to the latter. Cardozo convincingly showed that the inherently/merely distinction is pointless, as what should matter to negligence law is that a manufacturer of a product, who can reasonably foresee that its product could harm users, should owe them due care irrespective of contract. The fact that the product is only merely dangerous does not make the product any less disconcerting if not properly inspected before hitting the market.

Now substitute activities with products and a similar puzzle might arise: Why care about the difference between ultrahazardous and merely hazardous activities? That is, why should *ultra*hazardous activities be treated differently from all other, potentially risky activities? A satisfying answer must also provide a good sense of what counts as ultrahazardous activity in the first place. And, ultimately, this answer will also explain why it is that, for egalitarians, strict tort liability provides a more appealing solution for conflicts arising out of ultrahazardous activities. For a reason I mentioned above, I focus on relating as equals in connection with tolerably valuable conflicts; valueless ones, by contrast, raise no special difficulty from an egalitarian point of view as they should be prevented rather than contained.

Typically, basic concerns with the standard of due care take up a risk-creator's *inability* to meet such a standard. Certain disabilities, as I explain in Chapter 15, might stand in the way of the risk-creator's responsibility to relate to risk-bearers as equals—in the grand scheme of the equality theory, disabilities pertain to the condition, rather than the interest, dimension. The case for strict liability takes up the opposite concern, namely, that the very requirement to make an effort to discharge due care, rather than the ability to make such an effort, is the source of the problem. This is because, and insofar as, making such an effort leaves unaddressed a substantial part of the danger generated by the activity. The concept of ultrahazardous activity is meant to capture precisely this *functional deficiency* on the part of the duty of due care: Exercising ordinary care, or, for that matter, extraordinary care, will systematically fail to reduce the activity's risk to sufficiently satisfactory levels of safety. I argue that the imposition of strict tort liability for injuries caused by those who engage in ultrahazardous activities is a familiar common law response to *this* deficiency. Note that this deficiency and its strict liability solution is nothing new in tort theory and practice. My ambition, instead, is to defend the normative connection between this deficiency, strict tort liability, and the equality theory.

To see this, consider a nineteenth-century case of a defendant whose business is transporting the explosives of the day—nitroglycerine—for construction purposes. There is no doubt, let's assume, that using the explosives is key to building the infrastructure (roads, tunnels, etc.) for the modern society. (Notice the valuable purpose in question; there would be no difficulties for egalitarians if, instead, these explosives were used solely for the purpose of criminal activities.)

Further suppose, and this is a *natural* fact about nitroglycerine, that handling this material simply defies human control. Thus, there is no non-ad hoc way to make sure it will not explode prematurely. The very choice of engaging in this business places potential victims in a special state of vulnerability. It is special in the sense that mitigating the danger is beyond the systemic control of any risk-creator, and irrespective of their resources and abilities.

From the point of view of the duty of due care, I argue that the source of the concern in such a case is one of under-demandingness. To begin with, it is not the self-determination of the risk-creator that concerns us here. That is, the worry is *not* necessarily about the standard of due care being too demanding, including to the point of crushing the self-determination of the risk-creator. Rather, the worry is that the standard necessarily demands *too little* and, indeed, that the standard itself is hopelessly deficient when it comes to addressing ultrahazardous activities. The risk-creator can take all the precautions at his or her disposal, which may well be self-constraining though not necessarily self-crushing, without yielding substantial decrease in the risk of harm to others. By implication, a *mere* duty to exercise due care cannot establish terms of interaction that display appropriate concern for the difference between the self-determination of the risk-creator in pursuing an activity and the life and limb of the risk-bearer.

Against this backdrop, society could implement several different measures to contain the tolerably valuable conflicts that arise in connection with pursuing ultrahazardous activities. *The tort-law way of doing things* takes the question of containment to be a matter of equality—fixing terms of interaction according to which the risk-creator and risk-bearer could relate as equals. Thus, the first step is to impose a relational legal mandate, which is a duty owed to, and owned by, the risk-bearer. The next step takes up the content of the duty—its details and legal implications. A regime of strict tort liability belongs in this secondary stage, seeking to make good on the functional deficiency of the standard of due care. It implies that, in a context of tolerably valuable conflicts, an ultrahazardous activity can be allowed only insofar as it can be made accountable for the mishaps that even a reasonable exercise of care could, rather than merely would, not eliminate. Otherwise, falling back to a regime of negligence liability would, in effect, relieve a risk-creator of responsibility for their *decision* to embark on an activity whose dangerousness—in terms of risking the physical safety of others—cannot be systematically mitigated by the exercise of reasonable care. In egalitarian terms, it means that the parties could not relate as equals if the terms of their interaction are fixed according to the standard of due care, which is why a regime of strict liability is called for in its stead.

The argument has so far identified the basic difficulty out of which a regime of strict liability arises. It has further justified its rise by reference to the equality theory of torts. Finally, this argument contains a definitive answer to the question of what counts as ultrahazardous activity. Contrary to the Second Restatement's "grocery list" of factors that are indicative of the ultrahazardous nature of a particular activity,[51] my approach sides with the Third Restatement's focus on "the most important factor,"[52] namely, whether a particular activity "creates a foreseeable and highly significant risk of physical harm even when reasonable care is exercised."[53] This is another way to restate the functional deficiency that stands at the center of my argument in this section.

At the close of this section, it is important to note that my discussion assumes that the concept of ultrahazardous activities is not vacuous. For instance, courts disagree on whether the activity of storing water in a reservoir[54] or launching fireworks[55] is properly called ultrahazardous. A disagreement of this kind would be pointless if it turns out that the concept of ultrahazardous activities is empty.

This is not to deny that we should all want the category of ultrahazardous activities to die out entirely. Such a happy ending will transpire if owing to technological advances all risk-creating activities become subject to effective, perhaps even total, human control. After all, the horrors of nitroglycerine no longer occupy us. This is precisely where the equality theory returns the normative keys, as it were, to the conflict theory of tort law. Need we worry, or might we even wish, that the doctrine of strict tort liability for ultrahazardous activities ceases to be? The answer is, of course, that we wish to leave this doctrine behind us, as there is nothing inherently valuable in the conflicts under discussion.

VI. From Status to Interest: Premises' Liability and Substantive Equality

Premises' liability is the doctrinal area governing what land possessors owe entrants on their land. It is a subset of the tort of negligence, and it is doubly interesting from the vantage point of the equality theory. First, it provides another demonstration of the larger question, explored in Chapter 12, of the tort/contract relation—I argue that land possessors owe a duty of reasonable care toward the physical safety of entrants and that this duty is a genuine tort duty, namely, it is not the residue or some extension of voluntarily- or contractually assumed responsibility by the land possessor. Second, and closer to the ambition of the current chapter, premises liability demonstrates the resolving power of the equality theory when it comes to the

[51] The six factors are listed in RESTATEMENT (SECOND) OF TORTS §520 (1977).

[52] RESTATEMENT (THIRD) OF TORTS: PHYSICAL & EMOTIONAL HARM §20 cmt. *h* (2010).

[53] *See* RESTATEMENT (THIRD) OF TORTS: PHYSICAL & EMOTIONAL HARM §20(b)(1) (2010).

[54] *Compare* Dye v. Burdick, 553 S.W.2d 833 (Ark. 1977) (denying strict liability) *with* Forrest v. Imperial Distrib. Serv., Inc., 712 P.2d 488 (Colo. Ct. App. 1985) (upholding strict liability). *Cf.* Jed Handelsman Shugerman, *The Floodgates of Strict Liability: Bursting Reservoirs and the Adoption of Fletcher v. Rylands in the Gilded Age*, 110 YALE L.J. 333 (2000).

[55] Klein v. Pyrodyne Corp., 810 P.2d 917 (Wash. 1991) (imposing strict liability on a pyrotechnic company in charge of a public fireworks display).

content of the duty of reasonable care, namely, what and how much care is owed by land possessors to entrants on their land. While the preceding discussion in this chapter focused on the upper and lower bounds of reasonable care, the case of premises liability deals with filling out the content of the duty by choosing the right measure of due care from a range of options within the permissible bounds. Hence, premises liability showcases the granularity of the equality theory of tort law: Rather than merely ruling out over- and under-demandingness, the equality theory also can help to determine what should be the right level of demandingness in a specific context, namely, premises liability.

Premises liability takes up risks arising out of dangerous conditions on land. It concerns the responsibility of people qua land possessors (rather than as parties in a contract). Unlike risks that flow either from their activities or personal property under their control, the duty of land possessors arising out of dangerous conditions on land has traditionally been determined by reference to the *status* of the entrant.

Thus, entrants on land are traditionally divided into three statuses: invitee, licensee, and trespasser.[56] Save for some exceptions, status controls both the existence and content of the duty. An invitee, who is typically a business visitor, is protected by the full-blooded duty to take reasonable care that the premises are safe.[57] A licensee, who is typically a social guest or anyone who holds the occupier's bare permission to enter the land, is owed a limited duty of care: that of protecting the licensee against concealed danger known, or which can reasonably be known, to the possessor.[58] Finally, a trespasser is typically owed no protection except for being protected from wilful or wanton harm.[59]

Many jurisdictions still follow the traditional approach, but a growing number of others has introduced modest to substantial changes.[60] In some cases, moreover, jurisdictions have even adopted the opposite approach by enforcing a general duty of reasonable care toward all entrants of the land.[61] The normative question, then, becomes what land possessors owe entrants on their land.

I begin with a brief sketch of the case for the traditional, identity-based approach, followed by discussion of the reasons that animate the trend toward a general, status-free approach. As will become clear, the traditional approach is best explained by reference to contractual logic. I then argue that the basic reason to abolish the traditional approach and to impose, instead, a general duty of reasonable care goes back to equality theory's commitment to take seriously interest

[56] *See* Robert Addie & Sons (Collieries), Ltd. v Dumbreck, [1929] A.C. 358, 364 H.L. (Scot.).
[57] *Id.*, at 364–65.
[58] *Id.*
[59] *Id.*
[60] *See, e.g.*, Restatement (Third) of Torts: Phys. & Emot. Harm §51 (2012) (providing a Table containing data on the state of premises liability law in all US jurisdictions); Occupiers' Liability Act, 1984, c. 3 (Eng.).
[61] *See, e.g.*, Rowland v. Christian, 443 P.2d 561, 568 (Cal. 1968); Pickard v. City & Cnty. of Honolulu, 452 P.2d 445 (Haw. 1969); Basso v. Miller, 532 N.E.2d 868 (N.Y. 1976).

differential. Hence, it is both the prominence of bodily integrity and its relative priority over land possessors' freedom that make the case for a duty of *no less* than reasonable care.

On the traditional approach, the stringency of land possessors' duty of care turns on who the entrant is, rather than what interest the entrant has. There are different rationales for an identitarian conception of the duty. The more influential of them turns to analyzing the interaction between land possessors and entrants on their land in terms of voluntary undertaking including, most importantly, a contractual one. Thus, the leading torts treatise of its time observes that "a large number of the courts" support the view that invitees are owed a full-blooded duty of care because of a certain representation of safety made by land possessors.[62] Hence, the duty is triggered by conveying an implied assurance that the safety of the premises at issue has been subject to the exercise of reasonable care. Licensees, by contrast, receive an implicit or explicit permission to enter the land without also being encouraged to rely on the exercise of reasonable care. Voluntary undertaking can also explain why trespassers enter the land on their own peril: Land possessors do not convey representation of safety toward trespassers, in which case no duty of care (other than to refrain from wanton or wilful injury) arises with respect to them.[63]

A similar set of prescriptions can be established without making essential reference to the fact of representation by land possessors. As Keith Hylton argues, the typical invitee (for instance, a repairperson entering to fix a malfunctioning faucet handle) has no knowledge of the premises and, so, cannot assess the expected cost of injury from dangerous conditions on the premises.[64] As a result, invitees may not be able to charge the economically correct price of his or her service. By contrast, the typical licensee, such as a friend of the land possessor, may be in a better position to know about the condition of the premises. His or her decision to enter the premises is therefore better informed, safety-wise.[65] Against this backdrop, the different duties of care reflect information asymmetries that stand in the way of invitees making informed decisions concerning entry on another person's land. Like many other duties, duties of premises liability constrain but simultaneously also enhance the prospects of entering consensual interactions with far less informational distortions.

The growing trend to abolish parts or even the entirety of the traditional approach has emphasized institutional considerations. Two of them stand out. The

[62] W. Page Keeton et al., Prosser and Keeton on Torts §61, at 422 (5th ed., 1984).

[63] Another theory resorts to fairness considerations, suggesting that invitees, as opposed to licensees and trespassers, warrant reasonable safety because they benefit the land possessor who invites them in. That said, this argument suffers from a serious incoherence. It presupposes that only economic benefit matters, to the exclusion of the important noneconomic benefit, such as social benefits, that is associated with a paradigm class of licensees, namely, social guests.

[64] Keith N. Hylton, *Tort Duties of Landowners: A Positive Theory*, 44 Wake Forest L. Rev. 1049, 1055 (2009).

[65] *Id.*, at 1061.

first is the "semantic morass" critique, pointing to the increasingly unstable, and deeply ambiguous, boundaries between the three categories.[66] The multiplicity of exceptions to the rule further blurs the differences between the duties owed to entrants falling in either category. The second concerns the implication of the traditional approach for the division of labor between judge and jury. The worry is that the three-part framework for duty in premises liability cases empowers judges to decide both the existence and content of the duty as a matter of law necessarily at the expense of the responsibility of the jury—the fact-finder—to determine whether the land possessor has failed to exercise due care.

More importantly, there is a substantive consideration against the traditional approach. It nicely reflects the demands of the equality theory of tort law. To begin with, contrary to the contractarian underpinnings of the traditional approach, the responsibility of land possessors to the safety of entrants should not turn on whether the former draw either business or social (or any other) benefits from the latter. More generally, it should not turn on their choice of welcoming the presence of others on their land—by implication, dangerous conditions threaten the safety of trespassers, too. For this reason, a genuine tort duty of care in premises liability cases arises independently of choice as it reflects a concern with entrants' fundamental interest in bodily integrity. This concern may be further reinforced by condition-based disparities between the parties, such as asymmetrical knowledge of the risk.[67]

The case for the existence of a tort duty irrespective of choice can then move to the content dimension of the duty. On this dimension, what matters is not the legal status of the entrant—namely, his or her being an invitee, licensee, or trespasser. As the California Supreme Court noted in the landmark case of *Rowland v. Christian*: "A man's life and limb does not become less worthy of protection by the law nor a loss less worthy of compensation under the law because he has come upon the land of another without permission or with permission but without a business purpose."[68] Thus, due care grounded in the equality theory must integrate, rather than disregard, interest differentials. The interest of entrants, as already noted, is one of bodily integrity, whereas the interest on the part of the land possessor is often cast in terms of freedom or liberty of action in the context of one's premises.[69] The former interest is far more important than the latter, once again demonstrating why the stringency of the duty of care should disregard the differences between invitees, licensees, and trespassers. On the equality theory, the priority of bodily integrity over the freedom of land possessors warrants a full-blooded duty to exercise reasonable care toward the safety of all entrants. Imposing

[66] Kermarec v. Compagnie Generale Transatlantique, 358 U.S. 625, 631 (1959).
[67] The increasing availability of homeowners' liability insurance is another reinforcing, condition-based reason.
[68] 443 P.2d 561, 568 (Cal. 1968).
[69] *See further* O'Leary v Coenen, 251 N.W.2d 746, 749, 752 (N.D. 1977).

a less demanding duty, such as a duty of common humanity,[70] amounts to failing to address the interest differential at issue.

This is not to say that there should not be exceptions to this general, full-blooded duty rule. Assumption of risk can extinguish the duty if, as seen in Chapter 12, the entrant seeks to encounter a known and unreasonably dangerous condition on land for the sake of the danger. This could be the case if an adult entrant wishes to test his ability to sprint through a frozen pond on another person's backyard. Another sense in which the general, full-blooded duty can allow for limited circumscription is the case of *ex turpi causa non oritur actio*, which means that no cause of action can arise from an illicit cause.[71] This would be the case of the flagrant, rather than the ordinary, trespasser who enters the land of another for the purpose of committing a crime (on top of trespassing on land, such as assaulting people on the land possessor's premises).[72]

In conclusion, deciding what land possessors owe entrants on the land turns on identifying the pertinent considerations and their relative weight. The equality theory of tort law provides a normative framework to do just that. Contrary to the contractarian analysis, the equality theory calls for determining terms of interaction on the basis of the relative importance of the conflicting interests of the parties. It shows that the kind of status that should figure in deciding land possessors' duty in premises liability cases is not given by the choice of the land possessor concerning inviting, permitting, or excluding others. Instead, it is the status of both parties as substantively equal agents. This latter status, I argued, warrants an *in*voluntary tort duty of care and, further, its content must reflect the relative priority of entrants' bodily integrity over land possessors' freedom.

Conclusion

Two interpretations in particular have dominated the normative theory of negligence law: First, the economic interpretation of due care in terms of a cost-benefit analysis; and second, the self-abnegation conception of due care (alternatively, formal equality may suggest another, less demanding interpretation of what due care requires of risk-creators). The former looks outward to the overall consequences to society of taking more, or less, precaution, whereas the latter (the self-abnegation conception) focuses almost exhaustively on the vulnerability of the risk-bearer to the conduct of the risk-creator. The equality theory of tort law does neither. Instead, it suggests that the standard of due care determines terms

[70] On the duty of common humanity, see *British Railroad Board v. Herrington* [1972] AC 877, 909, 922–23 (HL).

[71] *See further* ROBERT STEVENS, TORTS AND RIGHTS 211–12 (2007).

[72] For more on the notion of flagrant trespassing, see RESTATEMENT (THIRD) OF TORTS: PHYS. & EMOT. HARM §52 (2012).

of interaction according to which the risk-creator and the risk-bearer can relate as substantive equals. These terms may sometimes undermine the maximization of aggregate welfare; further, they reject self-abnegation and formal equality as inconsistent with taking seriously the fundamental interests of *both* parties. In these pages I defended an egalitarian interpretation of the Hand Formula, arguing that it provides an adequate (though not an exhaustive) approach to determining what due care requires.

More broadly, the equality theory presents a top-down sequence of reasoning about the content of the duty of due care. It begins by setting out a normative framework for thinking about the demands of equality that, in turn, helps to identify doctrinal rules (such as that of fixing the upper limit of due care by reference to the crushing/constraining distinction). These rules, in turn, guide the factual inquiry into their existence (such as what evidence must be gathered in order to prove or disprove the real-world implications for the risk-creator's self-determination of shutting down a particular cricket stadium). As already mentioned, the equality theory, along with the conflict theory, is a *legal* theory. Its bite is, thereby, practical and doctrinal and also, no less importantly, political, rather than only theoretical.

Finally, the analysis focused on *interest* differentials, showing that they can yield important insights into the content of the duty, including its upper and lower limits as well as what lies in between (as in the example of premises' liability). Chapter 15 further elaborates the equality theory's approach to the content of the duty of due care by adding the second dimension of substantive equality—condition differential—to the equation. It also returns the argument to the priority of interest over condition as an organizing principle of the equality theory of tort law.

15
Egalitarian Accommodation

Introduction

Accommodating the condition of another person may lead to flatly inegalitarian, including even oppressive, terms of interaction. It can give either too much or too little allowance for the respective conditions of the parties. The equality theory of tort law, by contrast, seeks to render accommodation compatible with equality. More precisely, it aims at showing how a commitment to accommodation can be an *implication of* the substantive conception of equality underlying the equality theory of tort law. A key doctrinal manifestation of this ambition is the standard of due care. I argue that by determining what condition of a person should be accommodated and precisely when, the standard of due care can, and should, fix egalitarian terms of interactions that take seriously not only difference of interest but rather also condition.

Thus, whereas Chapter 14 has focused on how interest differentials bear on the determination of the standard of due care, the present chapter takes up the conditions of the respective parties in order to explain their place in fixing the standard of due care. Doing so does not mean that interest can be set to one side or held constant. To the contrary, as I argued above, the lexical priority of interest over condition makes resorting to the former necessary to addressing the questions of what condition merits accommodation and precisely when. I argue that tort theory's fixation on the objective—read, unaccommodating—standard of due care runs afoul of understanding and vindicating the doctrine of due care *as a whole*. Thus, an objective standard is not, and should not be viewed as, negligence law's signature feature. In fact, I argue, the doctrine is much richer than that and, further, it is better viewed as sustaining, albeit rather imperfectly, the ideal of relating as substantive equals.

The structure of the argument can be summed up in terms of the following questions: Must condition bear on the determination of the standard of due care and, if so, whose and what condition? I ask the "must" question because my basic ambition is to employ the equality theory of tort law to the vindication of this law. That said, I will also discuss contemporary tort law, showing that in some respects it is already getting closer to the prescriptions of the equality theory. Moreover, current law rejects basic pillars of the teachings of both corrective justice and economic analysis of tort law, the most comprehensive theoretical accounts there are on this subject matter.

Conflict between Equals. Avihay Dorfman, Oxford University Press. © Oxford University Press 2026.
DOI: 10.1093/9780198979869.003.0019

I. Holmes and the Myth of Tort Law Not Taking "Personal Equation into Account"

In a memorable passage from *The Common Law*, Holmes asserts that

> The law [of torts] takes no account of the infinite varieties of temperament, intellect, and education which make the internal character of a given act so different in different men. It does not attempt to see men as God sees them.[1]

The reason to begin with Holmes's assertion lies in its enormous influence on contemporary tort theory. His understanding of the normative challenge of enforcing an *unaccommodating* approach toward the condition of the interacting persons has shaped normative tort theory ever since. The challenge, it is often said, is that such an approach divorces legal fault from the moral meaning of fault.[2] The worry is not merely that the law employs moral concepts in ways that deviate from their intuitive, moral understanding (a theme Holmes pursued elsewhere[3]), but rather that tort law suffers a justificatory deficit by creating a noncontingent—viz., structural—gap between morality and legality, that is, between the reasons for action we have and what the law tells us we have reason to do. Against this backdrop, it is possible to view the two most comprehensive attempts to explain why tort law should *not* take one's "personal equation into account" as responding to Holmes's challenge. The two are corrective justice and economic analysis of negligence law.

That said, I argue that Holmes's assertion is right only if construed *very narrowly* to address the case of the under-skilled risk-creator, but that it must be rejected if extended to capture the *general* question concerning the accommodation of condition in determining the standard of due care.[4] In particular, it is and should be false with respect to determining the standard of due care in connection with both the over-skilled risk-creator and the under-skilled risk-bearer. Not only does it mean that Holmes, and with him corrective justice and economic analysis, missed important aspects of the question of accommodating condition in the context of due care. In addition, he has failed to identify the ultimate reason for taking, or for refusing to take, "personal equation into account." The equality theory of tort law, I argue, produces this reason.

Lawyer economists respond to Holmes's challenge by explaining that an unaccommodating approach to the standard of due care is warranted as a second-best

[1] Oliver Wendell Holmes, Jr., The Common Law 108 (1991) [1881].

[2] *See, e.g.*, Heidi M. Hurd, *Finding No Fault with Negligence*, *in* Philosophical Foundations of the Law of Torts 387, 405 (John Oberdiek ed., 2014); Larry Alexander & Kimberly Kessler Ferzan, *Confused Culpability, Contrived Causation, and The Collapse of Tort Theory*, in *id.*, at 407, 409.

[3] Oliver Wendell Holmes, *The Path of the Law*, 110 Harv. L. Rev. 991 (1997) [1897].

[4] I use *skill* to capture both innate and acquired human faculties that bear on how well persons can cope with the risks flowing from their own activities or from those of others.

strategy to assess human capabilities in the face of prohibitive information and search costs.[5] The argument can concede Holmes's point that a personalized assessment of due care may be more compatible with the demands of raw morality but that the true reason behind the unaccommodating approach is institutional, not moral. As long as the economic costs of personalizing the standard of due care remain high,[6] it is all-things-considered better for courts to adopt plan B, which is the adoption of a standardized assessment of due care. Its unaccommodating property, therefore, is not designed to drive a wedge between legality and morality. Rather, it reflects the limited competency of tort law to make an individualized assessment of the skills pertinent to the exercise of reasonable care in a particular case.

Contrary to lawyer economists, corrective justice theories emphasize the intimate connection between an unaccommodating approach and the demands of formal equality and independence. In particular, the unaccommodating approach is no mere second-best strategy to cope with excessive costs of one sort or another but rather an *entailment* of corrective justice's commitment to formal equality and independence.[7] This is because anything short of an unaccommodating assessment of care will let the condition of one party in the interaction unilaterally fix how much care is owed.[8] A position of unilateral influence, the corrective justice argument goes, must be avoided save for some exceptions.[9] Doing so requires an unaccommodating standard of care, which is to say a standard objectively determined by abstracting away from the abilities of either party to the interaction.

One further interesting point worth mentioning is that lawyer economists and corrective justice theorists suppose that the unaccommodating standard of care applies, and should apply, *across the defendant/plaintiff distinction*. This symmetry is required because both the argument from efficiency and the argument from formal equality apply indiscriminately to the risk-creator and the risk-bearer.[10]

None of this, however, reflects what negligence law is actually doing and what it should be doing.

[5] William M. Landes & Richard A. Posner, The Economic Structure of Tort Law 123 (1987).

[6] Were personalization to become feasible, subjective assessment of due care would be the most efficient strategy for welfare-enhancing negligence law. *See* Omri Ben-Shahar & Ariel Porat, *Personalizing Negligence Law*, 91 N.Y.U. L. Rev. 627 (2016).

[7] As you might recall, going back to Chapter 11, independence does not really yield this conclusion.

[8] Ernest J. Weinrib, The Idea of Private Law 148, 177–178 (1995); Arthur Ripstein, Force and Freedom: Kant's Legal and Political Philosophy 171 (2009); Jules Coleman, *Tort Law and Tort Theory: Preliminary Reflections on Method*, *in* Philosophy and the Law of Torts 183, 205 (Gerald J. Postema ed., 2001) ("[f]airness requires that no person be permitted to set the terms of cooperative interaction between individuals unilaterally"); *see also* Alan Brudner with Jennifer M. Nadler, The Unity of the Common Law: Studies in Hegelian Jurisprudence 296 (2d ed., 2013).

[9] *See* Weinrib, *supra*, at 183 n.22.

[10] I explain this in more detail in Avihay Dorfman, *Negligence and Accommodation*, 22 Legal Theory 77, 93–109 (2016).

II. *Not* Taking the "Personal Equation" of Under-Skill Defendants into Account

In a previous study I have shown that Holmes, lawyer economists, and corrective justice theorists (along with the *Restatement* and leading tort treatises) are wrong on the doctrinal front.[11] In particular, a thorough examination of the case law suggests that, in fact, negligence law entertains an unmistaken *a*symmetry between the under-skilled defendant and under-skilled plaintiff. Although these two may experience an identical disability, negligence law applies contrasting standards of assessing the reasonableness of their respective conduct: The under-skilled defendant faces an unaccommodating standard of due care whereas the under-skilled plaintiff receives favorable treatment in that their condition warrants some—not necessarily full—accommodation in assessing their comparative negligence. Further, I have preempted (and will resort to it again in Section IV) a familiar attempt to justify this asymmetry—that a negligent plaintiff is merely failing to exercise *self*-care and, therefore, need not be held to the same, unaccommodating standard to which the defendant is held. What I wish to do at present is to extend the argument in two, increasingly abstract ways. The first is to explain another case of asymmetry, namely, between the under-skilled and the over-skilled defendant. The second is to provide a general account, grounded in the equality theory of torts, of how condition and interest interact in determining terms of interaction that treat the defendant risk-creator and plaintiff risk-bearer as substantive equals.

How can the determination of the standard of due care be indifferent to the condition of the under-skilled defendant and, at the same, sensitive to the condition of the over-skilled defendant? By skill I mean any innate or acquired human faculty that bears on how defendants cope with the risks flowing from their own activities or, in the case of plaintiffs, from those of others. It often involves physical, mental, and cognitive capacities, though it can also include knowledge, talent, or expertise.

An instance of an under-skilled defendant may be the defendant in the famous case of *Vaughan v. Menlove*.[12] This defendant appears to experience some mental or cognitive disability and as a result may not be in a position to assess and respond to the adverse consequences of his actions. Hence, placing a stack of hay at the far end of his premises on a hot summer day may put his neighbor in grave risk to his person or property in case the hay catches fire. The reason why negligence law should not accommodate the defendant's (Menlove's) condition is not the prohibitive costs of verifying his true condition: Courts insist, as they should, on an unaccommodating assessment even when these costs are minimal, as when the defendant experiences an easily verifiable physical disability (such as blindness). Nor does the reason arise from a concern to sustaining formal equality between the

[11] *Id.*, at 88–92.
[12] 132 Eng. Rep. 490 (Ct. Com. Pl. 1837).

neighbors: Contrary to the teachings of law and economics, courts regularly allow, as they should, the condition of the *plaintiff* to fix the amount of care he or she is owed by the defendant, in clear violation of formal equality's maxim that no one party can unilaterally affect the standard of due care.

Instead, I argue that the reason underlying the unaccommodating approach goes back to the lexical priority of interest over condition discussed in Chapter 13. As I argued there, putting condition before interest would have upset the vindication of tort law by undermining what, according to the conflict theory, makes tort law valuable in the first place. Indeed, *Vaughan* features a clear interest differential: The liberty of action of the defendant renders vulnerable the life and limb (and the property) of the plaintiff.

It is true that in the end this risk materialized to property damage as the fire destroyed some cottages of the plaintiff. However, what matters for purpose of fixing egalitarian terms of interaction is the ex ante risk which is, again, to the very person of the plaintiff (or any other person on his premises). Now, lowering the standard of care so as to accommodate Menlove's condition would have necessarily run afoul of the interest differential just mentioned. It would effectively let Menlove's liberty of action figure more prominently than Vaughan's life and limb in the determination of their terms of interaction. On the equality theory of torts, this is precisely why the court was right to insist on an unaccommodating assessment of Menlove's conduct.[13] And this is precisely why courts are right to relax this standard when assessing the behavior of the under-skilled *plaintiff*—letting her condition require more precaution-taking on the part of the defendant risk-creator is fully consistent with the lexical priority of interest over condition. After all, it is her interest in life and limb that calls for constraining the plaintiff's liberty of action in the first place.

One clarification will be apt before I shift attention to the case of the over-skilled defendant. In Chapter 14, I argued that the equality theory places an upper limit on what might count as due care. To repeat, the animating concern has been that of crushing the risk-creator's self-determination by effectively requiring her to forgo her livelihood, ground project, or calling. The question, then, considers the compatibility of this limitation with an unaccommodating assessment of the conduct of the under-skilled risk-creator. If the latter amounts to an "undue burden,"[14] how can it meet the egalitarian upper limit?

My answer is that they are compatible. Cases featuring unaccommodating assessment of a defendant's conduct certainly impose an extra burden on the under-skilled. However, an additional burden need not amount to a crushing imposition. Moreover, this boundary between additional and crushing imposition typically

[13] I do not argue, however, that this is also how the court explains the decision to apply an uncompromising standard.

[14] Adam Slavny, Wrongs, Harms, and Compensation: Paying for Our Mistakes 91 (2024). *See also id.*, at 96.

remains firm. Many of the cases dealing with unaccommodating assessment of conduct of under-skilled risk-creators are those of road accidents.[15] They assess the conduct of a disabled motorist as if this person does not experience the disability he or she actually has. In that, the duty of due care effectively requires some extra care in comparison with what a non-disabled motorist would have been required to exercise under similar circumstances. An additional burden may compel the risk-creator to reduce speed, refrain from nighttime driving, or even shun driving altogether. These are all autonomy-constraining measures, to be sure. They are not—at least not typically and certainly not necessarily—autonomy-crushing. Indeed, there are, and the liberal state should see to it that there are, alternative options of public and private transportation.[16] Thus, although imposing an extra burden can effectively eliminate a certain course of action (such as driving), it does not foreclose alternative courses (such as bus riding).

The only category of cases of unaccommodating assessment of a defendant's conduct that is (potentially) autonomy-crushing concerns courses of action that are themselves ground projects or callings, as when the risk-creator seeks to pursue a career as a surgeon but frequently experiences tremors in both hands. In this category of cases, the autonomy-crushing implication of employing an unaccommodating assessment of conduct is straightforwardly justified by the equality theory of tort law. In particular, the justification lies in the lexical priority of interest (of the surgeon's patients) over condition (of the surgeon). Note, finally, that the autonomy-crushing implication at issue is fundamentally contingent rather than fundamental. The duty of care could turn into a mere constraint on the risk-creator's autonomy with the introduction of adequate medication or assisting technology so as to defuse the disability in question.

III. Taking the "Personal Equation" of the Over-Skilled Defendant into Account

Over-skilled defendants are expected to make their precaution-taking commensurate with their above-average skill, knowledge, or expertise. Essentially, they are required to adjust their care level upward, not because of some external circumstances (e.g., road conditions or stormy weather) but rather because of *their* unusual traits or *their* special knowledge. Doing so reflects their ability to reduce the risk to which they subject the plaintiff more effectively than most other defendants occupying their professions or engaging in their activities. Thus, a

[15] Dorfman, *supra* note 10, at 91–92.

[16] Avihay Dorfman, *Reasonable Care: Equality as Objectivity*, 31 L. & PHIL. 369, 404–05 (2012); Dorfman, *supra* note 10, at 115–16.

top-notched physician, or a "specialist," may be required to exercise care that a mere physician, or a "general practitioner," need not.[17]

To forestall misunderstandings, some courts would say that the special skills and knowledge of the over-skilled defendant set the background circumstances against which to apply the same old general standard of the reasonable person.[18] Another variation on this theme would be to say that over-skillness affects the "amount" of care rather than the "standard" of care.[19] On this or that presentation, the standard of due care to which the over-skilled risk-creator is subject is the same legal standard faced by the average or ordinary person. Nothing in my analysis turns on the choice between these two ways of presenting the matter. There may be reasons to present the case of the over-skilled in this, one-standard-fits-all way rather than the way I present it.[20] That said, I insist that there is a genuine difference between the standard of care owed by the over-skilled risk-creator and the one owed by the ordinary risk-creator. The former is adjusted upward in the sense that it demands a higher level of precaution-taking than the latter. And this heightened requirement is based on the unusual traits, skills, and knowledge of the particular risk-creator. To this extent, it allows the condition of the actual defendant to influence the terms of her interaction with the plaintiff. This approach is rejected, explicitly or implicitly, when it comes to assessing the conduct of an ordinary-skilled risk-creator. More dramatically, it stands in sharp contrast to the case of the under-skilled risk-creator as just discussed.

Here, too, the traditional debate between lawyer economists and corrective justice theorists is not particularly helpful because it pursues the wrong target. Both begin with the flawed Holmesian picture, according to which the standard of care is predominantly objective in the sense that the particular skill of the risk-creator should not bear on determining his or her duty of due care. Lawyer economists ground this "should" in information costs and corrective justice in formal equality's proscription of letting one party's particularities determine the terms of the interaction. Contrary to both, the case of the standard of care of the over-skilled risk-creator finds its grounding in the equality theory of torts.

So why *not* ignore the skills of the highly competent defendant? The reason is that, contrary to the case of the under-skilled risk-creator, the two dimensions of substantive equality—interest and condition differentials—are mutually reinforcing when it comes to the over-skilled risk-creator. The combination of the latter's advantageous condition and inferior interest vis-à-vis that of the risk-bearer

[17] *See* Toth v. Cmty. Hosp. at Glen Cove, 239 N.E.2d 368, 372–73 (1968). English tort law adopts a similar approach. *See* James Goudkamp & Donal Nolan, Winfield & Jolowicz on Tort §6-008 (20th ed., 2020).

[18] *See, e.g.*, Dakter v. Cavallino, 866 N.W.2d 656 (Wis. 2015). *See generally* Restatement (Third) of Torts §12 (2010).

[19] Sinai v. Polinger Co., 498 A.2d 520, 529 (D.C 1985).

[20] For instance, generating simple instruction to the jury may (arguably) support a single formulation across the entire domain of defendant's due care.

supports the imposition of higher, rather than lower, due care. Thus, the risk-creator exercises his or her liberty of action in pursuing an end that happens to place the life and limb of the risk-bearer in danger. This interest differential calls for demanding the former to draw on, rather than overlook, his or her unusual skills so as to reduce the latter's vulnerability. The alternative of setting aside his or her condition amounts to disrespecting the difference between the risk-bearer's interest and that of the risk-creator: It would expose the risk-bearer to risk even when the risk-creator can, in virtue of their special skills, reduce it. Here, too, demanding extra care does not mean, and should not amount to, crushing the risk-creator's autonomy. Instead, it means that the constraints on their liberty of action reflect the risk-creator's ability to pursue their ends in the face of another person's vulnerability.

To see this, consider *LaVine v. Clear Creek Skiing Corp.*[21] There, an over-skilled skier, described as a ski instructor with twenty years of experience who also had his own ski school and served on the National Ski Patrol in the Midwest as well, failed to change his direction, slow down, or yell at LaVine, an amateur skier who was traversing at a very slow angle and was down slope from the ski instructor. The collision resulted in LaVine's physical injury. It was a purely accidental collision in the sense that there was no preexisting relation, beneficial or otherwise, between the two.

The question that arises in a case of this sort concerns the content of the duty of care. In particular, should the unusual expertise of the risk-creator bear on the level of care expected from him, in which case he would be held to an effectively higher standard than the average skier? From a substantive equality perspective, the answer is in the affirmative. His risk-creating activity imposes nontrivial risk of serious bodily harm to others that, therefore, calls for constraining, though not crushing, his liberty of action. A condition of having extraordinary skiing abilities reinforces this point as it suggests that the risk-creator can in fact make it safer for others to pursue their ends despite the risk involved. The *LaVine* court reinforced this point, saying that "in order to satisfy the standard of care, a person having special knowledge must exercise a quantum of care which is commensurate with . . . his or her special skill and training."[22]

The Third Restatement of Torts supports this approach but somewhat reluctantly.[23] It contrasts this case with two other cases for which upward adjustment of the duty of due care is "easily justified."[24] The first concerns monopolistic or quasi-monopolistic actors engaging in activities that involve "distinctive and significant dangers," such as electric-power companies.[25] The Restatement argues (correctly)

[21] LaVine v. Clear Creek Skiing Corp., 557 F.2d 730 (10th Cir. 1977) (Colo. Law).
[22] *Id.*, at 734.
[23] Restatement (Third) of Torts §12 (2010).
[24] *Id.*, at cmt. *a*.
[25] *Id.*

that such actors owe risk-bearers a duty to acquire "special knowledge and special skills."[26] But notice that this is a completely different issue: The case of the utility company raises the question of whether it should do more in terms of skills acquisition. By contrast, the case I discuss (which the *LaVine* decision exemplifies) does not concern itself with a duty to acquire skills, but rather whether the already-skilled risk-creator must draw on their special skill for purposes of determining how much care they owe others. No doubt, in some cases the latter question might adversely affect the incentives of risk-creators to acquire special skills in the first place. However, it is far from being clear whether the defendant in *LaVine* would have refrained from becoming an expert skier in order not to meet tort law's standard of extra care. Furthermore, many cases of super-skilled risk-creators do not allow for such adverse effects to take place as they feature gifted risk-creators—to wit, people whose special abilities are innate, rather than acquired.

The second case mentioned by the Third Restatement involves a preexisting relationship between the over-skilled risk-creator and the risk-bearer, in which the latter relies on the former's representation of special skill. Here the case for a more exacting duty of care is clear. It is used by the Third Restatement to show why the argument for such a duty in cases of mere collision between strangers, as in *LaVine*, is "less compelling."[27] According to the Restatement, the special skill of the risk-creator "is a fortuity" as far as the risk-bearer is concerned.[28] That is, it could have been another, less qualified risk-creator skiing in the vicinity of LaVine. The presence of the super-skilled is a coincidence and, so, places a less pressing claim for a duty of extra care than does the case of preexisting relationships.

That said, negligence law features at its (noncontractual) core conflicts that give rise to injuries that are fundamentally *accidental*. The fact that it is LaVine's good fortune that her injurer was an over-skilled, rather than an average-skilled, skier does not really bear on why not require extra care from the one who can meet such a standard. The pervasiveness of fortuity in negligence law can even be extended to the claim that it is the victim's good fortune to have been injured by a negligent person rather than by some natural cause (for instance, by an earthquake for which, let's assume, there is no insurance coverage). The equality theory of torts as just explained provides a framework with which to determine the terms of the completely accidental interactions between risk-creator and risk-bearer, which emphasizes the interest and condition differentials. The "personal equation" of the super-skilled risk-creator must be taken into account so as to reflect not only the relative priority of physical safety over liberty of action but also the superb ability of the risk-creator to further reinforce this priority by way of exercising (more) care.

[26] *Id.*
[27] *Id.*
[28] *Id.*

IV. Taking the "Personal Equation" of the Under-Skilled Plaintiff into Account

The most familiar argument for accommodating the condition of the under-skilled risk-bearer in negligence law suggests that his or her failure to exercise due care is prudential rather than moral.[29] More specifically, the due care expected from the risk-creator and that expected from the risk-bearer reflect opposing philosophies: Whereas the defendant's breach of the duty of care is a moral failure of disrespecting *others*, the plaintiff's failure to respond reasonably to the defendant's negligent conduct is, at best, a prudential failure to protect *oneself*.[30]

The legitimate authority of the liberal state, the argument goes, might run out if pressed too hard against instances of plaintiffs' want of self-prudence. Those who hold this view do not ignore the implications of choosing between an accommodating and unaccommodating method of assessing plaintiff's conduct as it impacts the extent of the defendant's liability.[31] They insist, however, that this causal effect does not make it legitimate for the state to compel plaintiffs to discharge as much care as it demands from the defendants.

I disagree. The method of assessing plaintiff's comparative negligence is partially *constitutive* of what counts as primary negligence on the part of the defendant. It is certainly true to hold that comparative fault reflects a failure on the part of the plaintiff to protect himself from danger posed by another. However, this self-referential failure is *not* irrelevant for the purpose of determining egalitarian terms of interaction. To begin with, to say that only the defendant's negligence expresses wrongful conduct, and that therefore the doctrine of comparative negligence does not play a role in analyzing the method of assessing primary negligence, is to beg the question. In particular, it begs the question because the method of assessing comparative negligence may sometimes determine the *character* of the defendant's

[29] *See* Robert Stevens, *Should Contributory Fault Be Analogue or Digital?*, *in* DEFENSES IN TORT 247, 253 (Andrew Dyson et al. eds., 2015); Benjamin C. Zipursky, *Reasonableness In and Out of Negligence Law*, 163 U. PENN. L. REV. 2131, 2162 n.81 (2015); Gregory C. Keating, *Reasonableness and Rationality in Negligence Theory*, 48 STAN. L. REV. 311, 371 (1996); Kenneth W. Simons, *Contributory Negligence: Conceptual and Normative Issues*, *in* PHILOSOPHICAL FOUNDATIONS OF TORT LAW 461, 476–477, 480 (David G. Owen ed., 1995); Dale A. Nance, *Civility and the Burden of Proof*, 17 HARV. J. L. & PUB. POL'Y 647, 660 n.37 (1994); Gary T. Schwartz, *Contributory and Comparative Negligence: A Reappraisal*, 87 YALE L.J. 697, 722–23 (1978). Professor Richard Wright also argues that "no issue of Right immediately arises" in connection with contributory negligence. However, he does acknowledge that considerations of fairness (or, as he prefers, Kantian Right) "arise[] indirectly and appl[y] in a much more limited manner." Richard W. Wright, *The Standards of Care in Negligence Law*, *in* PHILOSOPHICAL FOUNDATIONS OF TORT LAW (David G. Owen ed., 1995), at 249, 259. I argue, by contrast, that they arise directly and, more precisely, that primary and contributory negligence are interdependent.

[30] *See* the sources cited in *id*. For support in the case law for the proposition that a plaintiff's fault marks a prudential, rather than a moral, failure, see *Welsh v. Jordan*, 194 A.2d 841, 844 (Me. 1963); *Cowan v. Doering*, 545 A.2d 159, 163 (N.J. 1988); *Hofflander v. St. Catherine's Hospital*, 664 N.W.2d 545, 566 (Wis. 2003).

[31] *See, e.g.*, Simons, *supra* note 29, at 475 (acknowledging that the defendant incurs the cost of the precaution taken by the plaintiff "in the form of legal liability to the plaintiff for that injury").

conduct—viz., is the conduct negligent *at all*?—and at other times determine the *scope* of the negligence that can be attributed to the defendant's risky conduct.

To see this, consider a society consisting of three classes of foreseeable tort victim. Pedestrians in the first class—the class of Olympic athletes—can easily escape the danger of an approaching car traveling at a maximum speed of 60 mph. The second class—the pedestrian pedestrians, as it were—can do the same when the car's speed is no more than 40 mph. Finally, the third class—consisting of persons with physical disabilities—can successfully respond safely insofar as the approaching car's speed does not exceed 20 mph.

Any nonarbitrary attempt at identifying the "reasonable" speed limit presupposes a *prior* judgment concerning what counts as reasonable conduct on the part of foreseeable plaintiffs responding to an approaching car. That is, the method of assessing the conduct of the responding plaintiff partially constitutes the standard of due care expected from the defendant. It will be unreasonable to drive at 39 mph under the relevant circumstances if, and only if, the law accommodates the reaction of the physically disabled plaintiff to thus driving. But when the method of assessing plaintiff's reasonable conduct turns unaccommodating, the law disregards the vulnerability of that (physically disabled) potential victim.

Thus, the method of assessing the plaintiff's negligence is not merely causally connected to the determination of the defendant's negligence; rather, it in part determines the *wrongful character* of the defendant's conduct. All else being equal, the difference between an unaccommodating and accommodating assessment of comparative negligence makes the difference between characterizing a 39-mph drive as wrongful and deeming it to be risky but, nonetheless, reasonable driving.

Now consider another, more familiar, instance of interdependence between plaintiff's and defendant's negligence, namely, the determination of the *scope* of defendant's liability. Suppose the defendant's activity is certainly wrongful; suppose that the defendant drives at the speed of 61 mph. The different methods of assessing comparative negligence will not bear on the question of whether the defendant's driving is wrongful at all. It certainly is. Rather, the choice between accommodating and unaccommodating assessment of comparative negligence in effect determines the *scope* of the defendant's negligence. The former assessment implies that the driver's breach of the duty of care expresses disrespect for the victim but only because, and only insofar as, the latter reacts to the former's negligence as a reasonable person would react under the circumstances. In effect, upon determining what precautions to take the driver is not required to take into consideration the peculiar degree of skill of the potential victim. His decision is deemed negligent for failing to respect the victim qua reasonable person, defined as possessing ordinary skills and capabilities. His liability will be apportioned accordingly. It is only when the method of assessment turns accommodative that the scope of the negligent act comes to reflect disrespect for the victim herself, including, in particular, her actual makeup (such as a certain disability). The scope of his liability will follow suit.

Determining the character of the defendant's act and delineating the scope of the negligence are two ways in which the method of assessing the plaintiff's negligence can be said to be partially constitutive of deciding the question of defendant's negligence. Each of these ways shows that the objection that considerations of comparative negligence do not bear on primary negligence is misplaced. Accommodating the condition of the under-skilled risk-bearer gives this person's condition a controlling impact on the terms of the tort interaction. An account of due care that denies the interdependence between primary and comparative negligence must be rejected in favor of accounts that take a more holistic approach.

The equality theory of torts argues for taking the condition of the risk-bearer into account by making the standard of plaintiff care commensurate with the plaintiff's vulnerable condition. This suggestion follows naturally from the preceding discussions of the under- and over-skilled risk-creator.

In contemporary tort law, the conduct of plaintiffs experiencing certain disabilities is typically assessed subjectively.[32] By "subjectively" I mean that courts would make some—although not necessarily complete—allowance for certain forms of plaintiffs' disability. In that, tort law sets a lower standard of plaintiff care based *in part* on the particular traits and disabilities of the person in question. It turns out that the debate between lawyer-economists and corrective justice theorists misses the actual working of the law—recall that they, along with the Restatement and leading commentators, suppose that the standard of care is either unaccommodating (objective) or accommodating (subjective) *for both* defendants and plaintiffs and, so, frame the inquiry in terms of what standard should prevail.[33] However, to repeat, tort law works out qualitatively different standards with which to assess the conduct of the disabled defendant and that of the disabled plaintiff.

Why is the accommodating assessment of under-skilled risk-bearers warranted? The answer draws on substantive equality's commitment to take difference—in both interest and condition—seriously. An accommodating assessment reflects the thought that the bodily integrity of under-skilled risk-bearers must *not* be exposed to greater levels of risk as a result of their disabilities. By contrast, applying an unaccommodating standard of care (as in the case of a defendant with disabilities) would increase the risk to which the under-skilled risk-bearer is put when compared to the average-skilled risk-bearer. To avoid this difficulty, accommodating the risk-bearer's condition—read, allowing his or her condition unilaterally to influence the terms of the interaction with the risk-creator—is necessary.[34]

32 Dorfman, *supra* note 10, at 90–91.
33 *Id.*, at 88–90.
34 *See further id.*, at 113–14.

V. Taking the "Personal Equation" of the Over-Skilled Plaintiff into Account

Accommodating the condition of the over-skilled risk-bearer might decrease both the level of care owed to him or her by the risk-creator and the scope of the risk-creator's liability. The former instance of standard-decreasing means that the special knowledge or expertise of the risk-bearer should count in favor of demanding less precaution-taking from the defendant than is usually required. This idea is captured by the "sophisticated user" defense in products liability law. On this rule, a product manufacturer does not owe its user a duty to warn about potential hazards if this user possesses "advance knowledge of the product's inherent hazards."[35]

The latter instance of standard-decreasing goes to the apportionment of liability between a negligent risk-creator and a negligent risk-bearer. Accommodating the over-skillness of the risk-bearer means that they may not be able to recover from the negligent risk-creator the same amount of damages that an average-skilled victim would be entitled to under similar circumstances. To see this consider *Jackson v. Axelrad*.[36] There, a patient who was himself a physician sued his doctor for failing to diagnose his medical condition and prescribe the right treatment. On top of his failure, the treating doctor argued that the patient was also to blame by neglecting to report a critical symptom that would have made the diagnosis far more straightforward.[37]

Should the patient's condition—his professional expertise—be factored in the legal terms of his interaction with the treating doctor? The answer is, and should be, yes. As the court observed, "the plaintiff here was not a layman, and jurors judging his actions could consider his expertise."[38] On the equality theory of torts, taking the risk-bearer's personal equation into account is not inconsistent with the interest differential at issue (i.e., the patient's health and the doctor's freedom and responsibility to this and other patients). Imposing on him the onus of disclosing information regarding his specific symptoms does not undermine the priority of his interest over the treating doctor's. Nor does it substantially dilute the care the treating doctor owes him. Instead, it puts a near cost*less* burden on such an expert patient that can only improve the treating doctor's ability to meet their duty of due

[35] Johnson v. American Standard, Inc., 179 P.3d 905, 907 (Cal. 2008). Formally speaking, this rule can be extended to capture not just strictly speaking professionals and experts, but rather any lay person who is sufficiently aware of a product's potential danger (such as knowing that a utility knife is dangerous and precisely in which ways). *See* Restatement (Third) of Torts: Products Liability §2 cmt. *j* (1998).

[36] Jackson v. Axelrad, 221 S.W.3d 650 (Tex. 2007).

[37] The plaintiff's comparative negligence concerned a failure to report precisely where his abdominal pain began. It seems that the neglected report is highly indicative of the true source of the illness from which the plaintiff suffered. *Id.*, at 652–53.

[38] *Id.*, at 652.

care. It reflects the antiformalist idea underlying substantive equality, namely, that of taking difference (of interest and of condition) seriously.

Conclusion

The equality theory of tort law generates the conclusion that there is no one way to assess due care. The distinction between being under- and over-skilled and the difference between being a risk-creator and a risk-bearer both matter. Treating the parties as substantive equals, by which I mean taking seriously the differences in their respective interests and conditions, gives rise to the following approaches: An unaccommodating assessment of the conduct of the under-skilled risk-creator, on the one hand, and an accommodating assessment of conduct when it comes to the other three categories, namely, the over-skilled risk-creator, the over-skilled risk-bearer, and the under-skilled risk-bearer. These approaches are, in some measure, in line with the contemporary law of negligence. In fact, it is the Holmesian conviction that for the most part negligence law takes an unaccommodating stance toward the assessment of due care that appears grossly out of sync with the law. At any rate, it is the normative point that stands at the center of the case for the equality theory of torts—the construction of a robust connection between accommodation and substantive equality. As mentioned above, accommodation may have different normative groundings, including illiberal and inegalitarian ones. The equality theory articulates a basis for accommodating condition (which includes under- and over-skillness) in a manner consistent with the ideal of relating as equals.

16

Equality and Uncertainty

The Burden of Proof in Tort Lawsuits

Introduction

The boundaries between substantive bodies of law, such as torts and contract law, are delineated on account of both moral and institutional considerations. My discussion of the torts/contract interface in Chapter 12 has emphasized a principled division between the two. Likewise the boundaries between substantive and procedural bodies of law have emerged as a result of both principled and pragmatic considerations. In this chapter, I seek to encroach on the imaginary fence erected (at times for good reasons) between the substantive and the procedural aspects of tort law. Doing so is not unheard of in the realm of tort theory. For instance, a basic idea in the civil recourse theory concerning victim's special standing to sue is inseparable from core elements of the laws governing the procedural aspects of tort law (such as civil procedure[1]); the influential presentation of corrective justice in terms of the juridical relation between a *plaintiff* and a *defendant*, as opposed to the more general one between right-holder and duty-ower, is another.[2] The link between substantive and procedural aspects of tort law goes deeper when Arthur Ripstein asserts that "The most basic [structural idea of private law] is the idea that any allegation of wrongdoing must be established."[3]

The argument going forward also celebrates the important connection between substantive and procedural law, more generally. Indeed, I take it that procedural law is, and should be, subservient to substantive law. Further, by "substantive law" I do not mean any conception of tort law, but rather tort law as governed by the conflict and equality theories of tort law. However, contrary to the accounts of substantive tort law mentioned above, I employ the equality theory of torts in order to *challenge* the procedural aspects of tort law. Negatively, I argue that the contemporary doctrine of allocating the burden of proof (especially, the persuasion burden) is inconsistent with the egalitarian ideal of relations between equals. Affirmatively,

[1] Benjamin C. Zipursky, *Rights, Wrongs, and Recourse in the Law of Torts*, 51 Vand. L. Rev. 1 (1998); John C. P. Goldberg & Benjamin C. Zipursky, Recognizing Wrongs (2020).

[2] Ernest J. Weinrib, Corrective Justice 12–13 (2012). *See also* Jules L. Coleman, Risks and Wrongs 213, 215 (1992).

[3] Arthur Ripstein, Private Wrongs 191 (2016).

Conflict between Equals. Avihay Dorfman, Oxford University Press. © Oxford University Press 2026.
DOI: 10.1093/9780198979869.003.0020

I argue that the equality theory provides a normative framework with which to determine how the burden in question should be allocated.[4] The reformist spirit of this argument is clear but, at the same time, I also show that tort law already, implicitly and *very* imperfectly, moves in the direction dictated by the equality theory.

I. The Object of Allocation: Burden of Persuasion

In taking up the allocation of the burden of proof, I wish to set to one side the different question concerning the level of proof (be it the preponderance of the evidence, clear and convincing evidence, or any other standard). Within the doctrinal box of burden of proof, I focus on one particular kind of burden, namely, the burden of persuasion. This section sets the stage by explaining what this kind of burden is and why it deserves special attention.

The burden of proof consists of two different burdens at the trial stage (preceded by the pretrial stage burden of pleading). There is the burden of producing the evidence and there is the burden of persuasion.[5] Although both set out to determine who bears the onus of proving facts pertinent to satisfying the elements of the case, they have different functions. The burden of production decides, as between the plaintiff and defendant, who should suffer the consequences of failing to produce evidence of a fact. This burden ordinarily shifts during trial if the initially burdened party produces evidence that would justify the belief of a reasonable fact-finder that a certain fact obtains or fails to obtain.[6] The burden of persuasion, by contrast, does not decide the question of evidence production. Instead, it determines, as between the plaintiff and defendant, who loses if the fact-finder is in equipoise—such as where the evidential state is evenly balanced.[7] To be sure, contrary to a familiar but unduly parsimonious view,[8] a state of equipoise is "more of a zone, or range of probabilities, than a line," in which case the burden of persuasion is likely to "affect many more cases that those few in which all the conflicting and

[4] Another intriguing attempt to establish principled grounds for rethinking the allocation of the burden of persuasion in tort law is Andrew S. Gold, *The Relevance of Wrongs*, *in* CIVIL WRONGS AND JUSTICE IN PRIVATE LAW 41, 47–50 (Paul B. Miller & John Oberdiek eds., 2020).

[5] The distinction has been treated as such at least since JAMES BRADLEY THAYER, A PRELIMINARY TREATISE ON EVIDENCE AT THE COMMON LAW 335–64 (1898).

[6] *See generally* H. L. A. HART & TONY HONORÉ, CAUSATION IN THE LAW 421–22 (2d ed. 1985); Kevin M. Clermont, *Death of Paradox: The Killer Logic Beneath the Standards of Proof*, 88 NOTRE DAME L. REV. 1061, 1118 (2013).

[7] *See, e.g.*, Hendricks v. Stalnaker, 380 S.E.2d 198, 203 (W.Va 1989). *See also* Clermont, *supra*, at 1124–25.

[8] That view has recently reappeared, at least implicitly, in *Goldman Sachs Grp., Inc. v. Ark. Teacher Ret. Sys.*, 594 U.S. 113, 127 (2021) in which the court asserted that the "burden of persuasion will have bite only when the court finds the evidence in equipoise—a situation that should rarely arise." The better view, I believe, is that a state of equipoise arises more frequently than the Golden Sachs court supposes. *See, e.g.*, Philadelphia Newspapers, Inc. v. Hepps, 475 U.S. 767, 776 (1986). Moreover, if a state of equipoise is a range property, then it is certainly anything but a rarity.

contradictory evidence results precisely in a dead heat."[9] This burden is far less dynamic than the burden of production in the sense that it typically rests on the same party throughout the trial stage,[10] a point I seek to challenge presently.

Why is the allocation of the burden of persuasion far more important for the vindication of substantive tort law? There are two, increasingly abstract, reasons. First, although the burdens of production and of persuasion are functionally distinct, the former can to an important extent be seen as subservient to the latter.[11] This is not to say that the initial burden of production is inevitably allocated between the parties in the same way as the burden of persuasion. To give an example from the area of defendant's insanity in criminal law, in some jurisdictions the defendant must initially produce some evidence of insanity, but the prosecution is ultimately responsible to persuade the fact-finder that the defendant was sane. That said, it is typically the case that the allocation of the burden of persuasion also dictates the allocation of the initial burden of production. Second, and more importantly, the burden of persuasion has a noncontingent role to play in any system of litigation. The same does not hold with respect to the burden of production. The distinction between adversarial and inquisitorial styles of adjudication reveals this point. An adversary system relieves the court of the responsibility to make facts appear as the judge is neither a case manager nor an independent investigator.[12] It is therefore in virtue of *this* way of structuring the litigation that the burden of production has an important role to play. By contrast, the need for the burden of persuasion, and hence for deciding on its proper allocation, cuts across the adversarial/inquisitorial divide. Indeed, the necessity of deciding "what follows?" if the evidential state is evenly balanced (including hopelessly unknown) is not a feature of any particular system of litigation—it is a preinstitutional problem concerning our (i.e., humans') imperfect access to information.

II. The Question-Begging Appeal of the Status Quo

Using a distinction between rule and exception, it will be apt to describe the allocation of the burden of persuasion in contemporary civil procedure's tort law along the following lines: The default rule is that the plaintiff-victim bears the burden of

[9] Kevin M. Clermont, A General Theory of Evidence and Proof: Forming Beliefs in Truth 255–57 (2024). *See also* Kevin M. Clermont, Standards of Decision in Law: Psychological and Logical Bases for the Standard of Proof, Here and Abroad 18–23 (2013).

[10] *See* Hood v. Webster, 2 N.E.2d 43, 44 (N.Y. 1936); Fleming James, Jr., *Burdens of Proof*, 47 Va. L. Rev. 51, 62–63 (1961).

[11] John T. McNaughton, *Burden of Production of Evidence: A Function of a Burden of Persuasion*, 68 Harv. L. Rev. 1382 (1955).

[12] *See* Edmund E. Morgan, *Some Observations Concerning Presumptions*, 44 Harv. L. Rev. 906, 910 (1931); Walter H. Rechberger, *Standard of Proof: The Austrian Approach*, in The Standard of Proof in Europe 123, 131–32 (Luboš Tichý ed., 2019).

persuasion with some exceptions in which the defendant takes the lead instead. Hence an evidential state of equipoise regularly, though not categorically, favors the defendant (in adversarial and inquisitorial systems alike).[13]

Why so? To further motivate this normative question, it will be interesting to make a sociologically revealing observation. It is anecdotal but illuminating nonetheless. The observation is that there seems to be a critical divide between torts and civil procedure (and evidence law) scholars concerning the right way to approach the question of how to allocate the burden of persuasion between the plaintiff and defendant. Tort scholars tend to be more strict or principled in the sense that there is a near perfect overlap between the prima facie case of every particular tort and the allocation question—to wit, the plaintiff almost always bears the burden of persuasion.[14]

By contrast, civil procedure (and evidence law) scholars may be the first to identify that contemporary law is, indeed, reluctant to impose the burden of persuasion on the defendant save for asserting affirmative defenses and privileges.[15] However—and here is where the divide suggests itself—they are also the first to note that the allocation question is governed by a hodgepodge of mainly instrumental considerations.[16] Thus, unlike criminal-law's darling, that is, the presumption of innocence, there is nothing fundamentally, not to mention necessarily, true about the current allocation of the burden of persuasion between plaintiff and defendant. They would explain that this stance resonates with the law of burden allocation and with its underlying rationales. On the law point, civil procedure scholars provide examples, in and outside tort law, to the effect that the burden of persuasion was, and sometimes still is, less defendant-friendly than it might appear at first glance (for instance to a torts scholar).[17] On the rationales point, the ambivalence to which these counterexamples gives

[13] *See* KENNETH S. BROUN ET AL., MCCORMICK ON EVIDENCE 696 (7th ed., 2013). This approach is not uniquely American or even akin to common law. *See*, in the case of German law, Mark Schweizer, *Standard of Proof as Decision Threshold*, *in* THE STANDARD OF PROOF IN EUROPE, *supra* note 12, at 19, 41–42.

[14] COLEMAN, *supra* note 2, at 213, 215. This point is so clear in the 1L study of torts in US law schools that it is only when the typical casebook gets to exceptional doctrines in causation (such as alternative liability and loss of a chance) and to the subject matter of defenses that the allocation of the burden becomes a live question. *See, e.g.*, JOHN C. P. GOLDBERG ET AL., TORT LAW: RESPONSIBILITIES AND REDRESS 493 (5th ed. 2021).

[15] BROUN, *supra* note 13, §337, at 695.

[16] *Id.*, §337, at 697–701; Morgan, *supra* note 12, at 911, 931; James, *supra* note 10, at 58–61. Civil procedure in civil law may stand on similar footing. *See, e.g.*, Mark Schweizer, *Standard of Proof as Decision Threshold*, *in* THE STANDARD OF PROOF IN EUROPE, *supra* note 12, at 19, 42 (German law); Magne Strandberg, *Standards of Evidence in Scandinavia*, *in id.*, at 135, 155 (Danish law). *See generally* Issachar Rosen-Zvi & Talia Fisher, *Overcoming Procedural Boundaries*, 94 VA. L. REV. 79, 93 (2008) ("procedural advantages and safeguards to one party at the expense of the other would constitute a serious breach of the equality principle and thus undermine due [civil] process").

[17] *E.g.*, Morgan, *supra* note 12, at 920–21; James, *supra* note 10, at 59. This is also true in partnership law in instances of breach of loyalty. *See* Meehan v. Shaughnessy, 535 N.E.2d 1255, 1267 (Mass. 1989).

rise is further reinforced by the oft-cited considerations employed by judges to address the allocation question: For instance, who has better access to evidence, what is the pretrial likelihood of the plaintiff (or defendant) being correct on the matter, what is the relative cost of erroneous decision against the plaintiff (or the defendant), and so on.[18] More recently, moreover, psychological analysis of law has suggested that the allocation of the burden might have distortive effects on fact-finders, often in the form of bias against the burdened party.[19] These considerations, because they are inextricably contextual and policy oriented, cannot generate a principled, noninstrumental approach to the allocation question. Thus, as a leading treatise observes, not only that "there is no key principle governing the apportionment of the burdens of proof,"[20] it seems that "[t]here is no satisfactory test for allocating the burden of proof."[21] Perhaps this state of affairs is an upshot of a deeper ambivalence concerning the purposes of civil procedure, including the nature of the connection between these purposes and the purposes underlying the substantive law of torts.[22]

And yet, contemporary tort law does seem to adopt a principled approach, namely, that the plaintiff bears the burden of persuasion with respect to any and all elements of a tort's prima facie case. Hence the question raised a moment ago returns: Why so? Further, why should not tort law adopt a different approach? After all, antidiscrimination law has replaced the one-sided approach of tort law to a doctrine of burden shifting: If the plaintiff proves that their protected class (such as race) has played a substantial factor in the defendant-employer's adverse action, the defendant will then bear the burden of showing that the same adverse action would have been taken irrespective of this factor.[23] And even beyond the realm of private-law litigation, courts have employed nuanced approaches to the allocation question, for instance, in connection with exaction cases in Takings' law,[24] as well

[18] BROUN, *supra* note 13, §337, at 697–701; Morgan, *supra* note 12, at 911, 931; James, *supra* note 10, at 58–61; Bruce L. Hay, *Allocating the Burden of Proof*, 72 INDIANA L.J. 651 (1997); Bruce L. Hay & Kathryn E. Spier, *Burdens of Proof in Civil Litigation: An Economic Perspective*, 26 J. LEGAL STUD. 413 (1997).

[19] *See, e.g.*, Mark Schweizer, *Loss Aversion, Omission Bias and the Civil Standard of Proof*, *in* EUROPEAN PERSPECTIVES ON BEHAVIORAL LAW AND ECONOMICS 125, 134–38 (2015); Eyal Zamir & Ilana Ritov, *Loss Aversion, Omission Bias, and the Burden of Proof in Civil Litigation*, 41 J. LEGAL STUD. 165, 197 n.23 (2012).

[20] BROUN, *supra* note 13, §337, at 700.

[21] James, *supra* note 10, at 58.

[22] I do not deny that civil procedure has its own purposes (such as doing epistemic justice, generating legitimacy and resolving disputes, and promoting distributive justice). However, as I have asserted at the outset, civil procedure is essentially subservient to substantive law and so should proceed with giving effect to the values of the latter.

[23] *See* Price Waterhouse v. Hopkins, 490 U.S. 228, 258 (1989) (plurality opinion). *See also*, to a somewhat similar effect, United Kingdom's Equality Act 2020 sec. 136(2).

[24] *See* Dolan v. City of Tigard, 512 U.S. 374, 385 n.8 (1994); Nollan v. California Coastal Comm'n, 483 U.S. 825, 836 (1987).

as in other jurisdictions, such as in Canadian constitutional law and in international human rights law.[25]

A prevalent answer resorts to different versions of the moral significance of the status quo. It defends a defendant-friendly allocation of the burden of persuasion. The basic thought is that one who seeks to upset an existing situation—and to do so by suing the defendant in a court of law—has the responsibility to make the case to this effect. More concretely, the responsibility should be understood in maximalist terms: One is required to assume *full* responsibility for making the case in support of upsetting the status quo. It is full, as opposed to partial, responsibility because the target of this argument is the burden of persuasion, rather than the much lighter burden of pleading, alleging, or complaining.[26] No one should deny that, all else equal, the one who complains by way of filing a lawsuit must give *some* sense of what one is complaining about.[27] Thus, asserting that "you did it," or calling me "to come forward," may not be enough in order to let me understand what the "it" is at issue or what the occasion is for which "coming forward" is required.[28] It might also unduly encourage baseless lawsuits as there is no epistemic barrier, not even a minimal one, to preempt their submission.[29] Thus, the argument from the status quo takes the maximalist version, which calls for imposing the burden of *persuasion* on the person seeking to upset it, rather than merely the burden of pleading, alleging, or complaining.

To fix ideas, consider the following case. A suspects she was a victim of a tort of negligence committed by B. Apart from having the burden of pleading or complaining, why must A bear the entire burden of persuasion with respect to all of the elements of the prima facie case (i.e., duty, breach, injury, and a causal connection between the last two). Suppose that A does not have access to the facts that could establish her case for B's breach of duty and/or for a causal connection between that breach and the injury from which she suffers. The argument from status

[25] Concerning Canada, the Supreme Court, in *R. v. Oakes* [1986] 1 S.C.R. 103, para. 66, has noted that

> The onus of proving that a limitation on any Charter right is reasonable and demonstrably justified in a free and democratic society rests upon the party seeking to uphold the limitation. Limits on constitutionally guaranteed rights are clearly exceptions to the general guarantee. The presumption is that Charter rights are guaranteed unless the party invoking s. 1 can bring itself within the exceptional criteria justifying their being limited.

Concerning international human rights law, see *Velasquez-Rodriguez v. Honduras*, Inter-Am. C. H. R. (July 29, 1988) (merits), paras. 122–39.

[26] By saying *lighter burden*, I do not mean to say that it is trivial or otherwise completely insignificant. *See*, on this point, *Bell Atlantic Corp. v. Twombly*, 550 U.S. 544, 570 (2007) (introducing a plausibility test for the pleading stage). Rather, my point is a comparative one—the burden of pleading is less demanding than the burden of persuasion.

[27] I say *all else equal* because at times it would be highly unlikely to expect victims to assert claims against their perpetrators.

[28] No doubt, in some cases the perpetrator knows perfectly well what the complaint is all about even without being informed by the victim.

[29] Mike Redmayne, *Standards of Proof in Civil Litigation*, 62 M.L.R. 167, 173 (1999); Richard A. Epstein, *Pleadings and Presumptions*, 40 U. Chic. L. Rev. 556, 572 (1973). *See also* Goldberg & Zipursky, *supra* note 1, at 207–08.

quo suggests that she ought to bear the burden precisely because she is the one who seeks to upset the status quo. By status quo I mean the normative situation in which A and B relate as mere strangers, as opposed to a tortfeasor and his tort victim.

A number of reasons have been offered in support of this argument. Some identify an asymmetry between the plaintiff and the defendant in terms of the harshness of "taking" from the defendant in comparison to "not giving" the same to the plaintiff.[30] Accordingly, it is better to decide erroneously in favor of the defendant rather than the plaintiff. Another reason to the same effect lies in the ethics of civility: It is argued that a presumption of innocence should apply to defendants in civil cases, not only in criminal cases, because a commitment to civility demands that we presume that any given person has acted lawfully until proven (by the plaintiff) otherwise.[31] Finally, and most recently, Arthur Ripstein has argued that a basic commitment to freedom as independence puts certain demands on the common law system of tort law litigation, chief among them a sibling of criminal law's presumption of innocence, namely, the principle of "being beyond reproach." On Ripstein's account, being beyond reproach is not merely the organizing idea of the tort of defamation but rather a broader structural idea about "the burden of proof in legal proceedings."[32] Therefore, it grounds "your right to be presumed by others not to be a wrongdoer."[33] The plaintiff, rather than the defendant, bears the burden of disturbing the status quo because the defendant has a right (grounded in independence) that no one is in charge of his or her good name.[34]

However, appealing to the status quo is question-begging. In particular, it obscures a crucial difference between two different accounts of "the status quo." Recall A's suspicion that she suffered an injury negligently inflicted by B. Although her suspicion may be plausible, she cannot substantiate it (according to whatever level required by the prevailing standard of proof). Against this backdrop of uncertainty, there are two different accounts of what the status quo consists. The difference comes down to the power of the "if." *If* it turns out that B did not commit a tort against A, the correct description of the status quo is that B is not a wrongdoer and A is not his victim. But *if* B committed the tort, then the correct description of the status quo is that B is, in fact, the wrongdoer and A is, in fact, his victim. The problem is an epistemic one, as it turns on the choice between the two *if*-statements. The argument from the status quo (grounded in civility, independence, or otherwise) is conclusory because it assumes away this epistemic

[30] This is Alex Stein's explanation of the Jewish Law's tradition of assigning the burden of proof to the claimant. *See* Alex Stein, *The Refoundation of Evidence Law*, 9 Can. J. L. & Juris. 279, 335, 335 n.226 (1996). In my view, however, that tradition may be read as aiming at the lower threshold represented nowadays by the burden of pleading or complaining. For a refined account of the act/omission rationale, see Sandy Steel, Proof of Causation in Tort Law 122–23 (2015).

[31] *See* Dale A. Nance, *Civility and the Burden of Proof*, 17 Harv. J. L. & Pub. Pol'y 647, 648, 659–62, 689 (1994).

[32] Ripstein, *supra* note 3, at 202. *See also id.*, at 205.

[33] *Id.*, at 227 n.77.

[34] *Id.*, at 192, 232. For another, freedom-based justification of the traditional allocation of the burden of persuasion, see Steel, *supra* note 30, at 125.

problem.[35] It singles out one description of the status quo to the exclusion of the other. But, and unlike the case of criminal law, there is no good reason to make the "innocence" of B lexically prior to the injury of A, at least not with respect to all torts and under all circumstances. This means that a successful articulation of the basis for allocating the burden of persuasion cannot appeal to the status quo *ante*. Instead, it should draw on normative, rather than epistemic, claims about who should bear the burden, why, and when.

III. The Mismatch Thesis: Substantive Transformation Meets Procedural Stagnation

If appeal to the status quo *ante* fails to explain the defendant-friendly approach to allocating the burden of persuasion, what might the explanation be? I believe the reason lies in history. Although the ambition of my argument is the vindication, rather than the explanation, of tort law, it will be apt to begin with identifying the root cause of tort law's seemingly defendant-friendly approach to allocating the burden of persuasion. Doing so could provide an understanding of the historical shackles into which modern tort law litigation is placed. It can, therefore, expose to the bright light of reason an awesome gap between the substantive and the procedural aspects of tort law.

The *mismatch thesis* suggests that the defendant-friendly approach to the allocation question might have been appropriate with respect to the premodern tort law. But this approach remains stuck even as substantive tort law has transformed itself in deep and profound ways. Hence, there exists a mismatch between the procedural law that warrants the defendant-friendly approach to the question of burden allocation and the substantive law we recognize today as tort law. The latter law does not support the former law's approach, at least not in the same way and to the same extent as did its old counterpart.

The conventional wisdom among tort students and scholars is that contemporary tort law is a *modernized* version of the *ancien régime*. In particular, although there are important continuities between the new and the old, tort law has undergone fundamental changes, one of which lies at the center of the argument: a shift from a unidimensional idea of responsibility—that is, for outcomes—to a bidimensional notion of responsibility—that is, for outcome and conduct, combined.[36] On the "ancient forms of liability," as Cardozo put it, "conduct is held

[35] *See also* Redmayne, *supra* note 29, at 174.

[36] Contemporary tort theorists (including, in particular, Tony Honoré, Stephen Perry, Jules Coleman, John Gardner, and Stephen Smith) have made illuminating contributions to the study of the distinction between these two conceptions of responsibility. *See, e.g.*, Stephen A. Smith, *Duties to Try and Duties to Succeed*, *in* DEFENCES IN TORT 65 (Andrew Dyson et al. eds., 2015). An early statement (about law in general) is James Barr Ames, *Law and Morals*, 22 HARV. L. REV. 97, 99 (1908), saying that "the old law has been radically transformed" so that the "ethical standard of reasonable conduct has replaced the unmoral standard of acting at one's peril."

to be at the peril of the actor."[37] Modern tort law, by contrast, takes conduct more seriously. More specifically, it has developed sophisticated doctrinal pathways to putting together outcome and action. The causal inquiry in negligence law is perhaps the most vivid illustration of this trend as it sets out to assess whether the connection between the defendant's substandard conduct and the plaintiff's injury is sufficiently robust. The movement from outcome-based to outcome- and conduct-based notions of responsibility stands at the center of the mismatch thesis I wish to develop presently.

But before I can do so, a caveat is in order. I introduce it to preempt possible objections and to further clarify the *ahistorical* ambition of my historical gloss. As with Henry Maine's famous case for a shift from status to contract, the transformation of tort law is a helpful generalization of a murkier trend of underlying commitments and ideas. For instance, in his famous lectures on the common law, Holmes offered a sympathetic reconstruction of tort law to show that core areas of the common law of tort law repudiated the notion of "absolute responsibility"[38] by which he meant the maxim that a person unqualifiedly acts at their own peril.[39] Holmes argued that the repudiation at issue went beyond accidental wrongdoing (trespass on the case and, ultimately, negligence) to capture strict tort liability as well. His argument was that considerations of foreseeability and avoidability constrain the imposition of strict liability, including in the case of trespass to land.[40] Holmes may well be right, but there is no necessary tension between his reconstruction of tort law and the transformation of tort law from being concerned *primarily* with responsibility to outcome to becoming *far more* concerned with responsibility to outcome and conduct, taken together. This weaker version of the historical transformation of tort law seems plausible, historically speaking, even to those who are more skeptical of the conventional wisdom.[41] Further, it is sufficiently attentive to the manner in which tort law has grown—that is, through a process of piecemeal change over increasingly vast areas of life. Hence, there are areas in tort law—for example, trespass to land—that have undergone moderate changes,[42] and there are areas—for example, defamation—that have been reformed in profound ways, including in moving from no-fault liability to liability based on fault (and at times even deliberate wrongdoing).[43]

Now the mismatch thesis. When the idea of responsibility in the typical cause of action is outcome-based, it seems only natural to believe that the plaintiff should

[37] Palsgraf v. Long Island R. Co., 162 N.E. 99, 99 (1928).

[38] Oliver Wendell Holmes, Jr., The Common Law 89 (1991) [1881].

[39] *Id.*, at 112.

[40] *Id.*, at 95 (avoidability) & 96 (foreseeability).

[41] *See, e.g.*, David Kretzmer, *Transformation of Tort Liability in the Nineteenth Century: The Visible Hand*, 4 Oxford J. L. Stud. 46 (1984).

[42] For more details, see Avihay Dorfman & Assaf Jacob, *The Fault of Trespass*, 65 U. Toronto L. J. 48 (2015).

[43] Recall the discussion in Chapter 4, Section III above.

bear not only the burden of pleading or complaining but also of persuasion. The reason is that merely alleging that B did X to A *does not change how they relate to each other, morally speaking*. To elaborate and illustrate, suppose that the relevant tort is trespass to land, and further suppose that *all* there is to show in order to satisfy the prima facie case of this cause of action is that B entered or used A's premises. B may have made a truly innocent mistake, for instance, believing that the last apple tree in his century-old orchard stands on his premises. His mistake can be traced to A's and B's ancestors who failed to identify the accurate boundary or to a mistake made by the county's registrar of real estate records. Such a mistake would not have been discovered, by either B or A, until a recently conducted land survey found that the area in question is in fact A's.[44] Upon realizing the mistake, A sues B in trespass to land. She pleads the relevant facts so that B can get a sense of what allegations he is facing. How, then, should the burden of persuasion be allocated between the parties? In particular, who will lose if the evidential state concerning who owns the land on which B's tree lies is evenly balanced?

The legal wrong complained about by A *cannot* impute, implicitly or explicitly, any moral failing to B. The cause of action, the assumption goes, is one of no-fault liability. Accordingly, there is no consideration of relational equality, that is, no reason originating from how they stand in relation to each other as A and B, that dictates in a non-question-begging way who should bear the burden of persuasion. I further take it that this example illustrates a typical—that is, outcome-based—cause of action for the *ancien régime* of tort law.

Hence, the only reasonable way to address this question is by resorting to a range of considerations that, according to civil procedure theories, decide the matter. Note that this is not meant as a tailor-made, ad hoc resolution of the particular case of this A and that B. Rather, these considerations can guide courts to identify categories of cases that pull in one party's direction and other categories that point in the opposite direction. In a trespass to land category of cases, for instance, it is important to take into account the existing technology of publicity of the particular legal system: The difference between a registry, a system of recordation, a method of metes and bounds, or some other technology becomes a relevant consideration. In assigning the burden of persuasion to A, tort law must have identified a vector of such considerations pointing in her direction.

Even early Twentieth century defamation law may fit this description. In a leading English case,[45] a Paris Correspondent of a Manchester-based newspaper published a description of a motor festival in France to which a Londoner church warden attended with his lover. In order not to identify the true name of

[44] This is not a wholly fantastic story even by today's standards. *See* Burns Philp Food, Inc. v. Cavalea Cont'l Freight, Inc., 135 F.3d 526 (7th Cir. 1998) (Ill. Law).

[45] E. Hulton & Co. v. Jones [1909] A.C. 20. The factual details of the case are further analyzed in Jeremiah Smith, *Jones v. Hulton: Three Conflicting Judicial Views as to a Question of Defamation*, 60 U. Penn. L. Rev. 365, 373–75 (1912).

this warden, the correspondent described him as Artemus Jones (he preferred to use a fictitious name to avoid resorting to initials). It turned out that there was a real person who bears this name (actually, he was Thomas Artemus Jones). But the latter was a barrister, not a church warden. He lived and practiced law in Wales, not in London. And he did not set foot in France at the relevant time (and perhaps even never). There was no complaint that the story caused any actual harm to the plaintiff's reputation as no such argument was necessary to sustain a case in libel, which is actionable per se. Nor did the court find, or even contemplate the possibility, that the newspaper was careless for using a fictitious name under these circumstances. It was, nevertheless, held that the newspaper is liable in defamation. Bluntly put, it was a *strict* case of strict tort liability. The outcome of publishing this story may have constituted the legal wrong of defamation but it does not, as such, imply that the defendant truly, that is morally, wronged the plaintiff in *conducting itself* the way it did. To be sure, *Hulton*'s commitment to strict liability is not an outlier.[46]

Finally, the disconnect between legal responsibility for an outcome and moral failure on the part of the defendant is discernable even in contemporary tort law, albeit to a very limited extent. The tort of conversion is considered an intentional tort, which means that an act of conversion requires forming an intention to treat a certain good as one's own. That said, tort law employs a watered-down notion of intention. Conversion does not require a deliberate plan to take another person's thing, but rather merely an intention to treat that thing as one's own even if there is no good reason to believe otherwise. Thus, to take one of the memorable illustrations of the Second Restatement, suppose C takes from a restaurant rack the hat of D and does so by mistake, as both patrons' hats are very much alike. As she reaches the sidewalk, a sudden gust of wind blows it from her head and as a result the hat is lost.[47] C could be liable for conversion.

It is a freak accident but it conveys an important point about conversion—that its underlying conception of responsibility is outcome-based. Thus, to give a less fantastic example, a truly innocent purchaser of a good could be liable for conversion if it turns out that the seller does not have a right to the good.[48] Indeed, if C buys silverware from a thief, believing he is the true owner, or if C negotiates a sale of a good on behalf of her principal but that good turns out not to be the principal's, she is either way liable for conversion.[49] However, her legal wrongdoing need not reflect a moral failure on her part.

[46] Leading illustrations are *Burton v. Crowell Pub., Co.*, 82 F.2d 154, 155 (2d Cir. 1936); *Peck v. Tribune Co.*, 214 U.S. 185, 189 (1909).

[47] Restatement (Second) of Torts § 222A, ill. 3 (1965).

[48] The Uniform Commercial Code provides one important exception: If an owner entrusts a thing to a merchant who deals in such things, then the unauthorized sale of that thing to a good faith purchaser does not expose the purchaser to liability in conversion. U.C.C. §2-403 (2).

[49] *See* Kahn v. Quintana, 811 P.2d 458 (Colo. App. 1991); Dan B. Dobbs et al., The Law of Torts § 62 (2nd ed., 2021), respectively.

It is important to note that none of these examples seek to suggest that it is a mistake to impose tort liability for these forms of legal wrongdoing. This is a separate question. Instead, I explore these cases to make a different point, namely, that there can be, and there surely were, torts whose underlying conception of responsibility makes no essential reference to substandard behavior on the part of the (legal) wrongdoer. Accordingly, the question of who should bear the burden of persuasion can be decided (in a non-question-begging way) on account of the variety of instrumental considerations that civil procedure theories have accurately identified (such as who has better access to the pertinent evidence).

Enter, modern tort law.

As just mentioned, contemporary tort law does not completely eschew the *ancien régime*. It has even developed new forms of outcome-based responsibility, including most prominently strict liability for the defective manufacturing of products. That said, it puts specific emphasis on torts whose underlying conception of responsibility is either conduct-based or an integration of conduct- and outcome-based. Offensive battery and assault fit the former whereas the torts of negligence, some forms of private and public nuisance, fraud, and intentional infliction of emotional distress exemplify the latter. They all make essential reference to substandard behavior on the part of the defendant. Further, the failure associated with substandard behavior is not some bad behavior in the abstract but rather concerns specifically the interests of the plaintiff or the plaintiff class.[50] For this reason, it is apt to say that disrespecting the plaintiff can change the parties' normative situation, that is, how they relate to each other.

To see what is meant by substandard behavior and why it connotes a certain disrespect for the plaintiff (or plaintiff class), consider the proposition that a simple breach of the duty of care is an instance of mistreating the risk-bearer by failing to pay attention to their vulnerability. While driving, E's attention is occasionally drawn to the marvelous scenery of fall foliage adjacent to the road. As a result, E fails to heed the signs alerting drivers of a nearby crosswalk yet, luckily, inflicts no harm on F, a crossing pedestrian, by swerving out of the person's way. Although she breached the duty of care, E did not commit a tort as the breach did not harm F. There is no legal wrong for which F is entitled to complain.

That said, E morally owes F some form of acknowledgment of E's risky driving. An acknowledgment may come down to just that, namely, acknowledging that she drove inappropriately in the face of F's crossing. It could also be the case, depending on the particular circumstances, that mere acknowledgment may not be sufficient. E's substandard behavior can give her reason to apologize to F for putting him in imminent risk of serious harm, in which case an expression of regret and a feeling

[50] *See further* John Oberdiek, *It's Something Personal: On the Relationality of Duty and Civil Wrongs*, *in* Civil Wrongs and Justice in Private Law 301, 306 (Paul B. Miller & John Oberdiek eds., 2020).

of remorse would be warranted.[51] Mere acknowledgment and apology are both attitudinal manifestations of a certain change in how E and F stand to one another. In particular, E's lapse in due care undermines the sense in which they relate as equals precisely because it reflects the failure to pay sufficient attention to the existence and, therefore, vulnerability of F (and the class of Fs, more generally). As equals, the life and limb of F deserves better than this, whereas "better" is defined in terms of a standard of due care expected from E. Note that the failure I have identified with a simple instance of inadvertently breaching a duty of due care need not amount to more than a moral failure to respect another human being as an equal. More specifically, I do not argue that this failure necessarily harms an interest of his, let alone undermines his autonomy by foreclosing some options or rendering them too dangerous.[52] Nor do I argue that this failure should count as a *legal* wrongdoing.[53] Disrespecting or mistreating the risk-taker is all that the argument going forward needs in order to establish the mismatch thesis.

The case of negligence illustrates a broader phenomenon, namely, the assimilation of substandard behavior into tort law's idea of wrongdoing. Thus, to give some familiar examples, private nuisance is predicated upon unreasonable interference with the plaintiff's right to use their land and its public counterpart taking up unreasonable interference with rights to use the public sphere. Offensive battery takes up physical contacts that are wrongful because "offensive and insulting ... to an ordinary person not unduly sensitive to personal dignity"[54]; intentional infliction of emotional distress requires, in addition to proof of severe emotional injury, deliberate or reckless disregard on the part of the defendant; and even an area that was, at one point, perceived as the latest reincarnation of strict tort liability—that is, products liability—has come to incorporate some notion of faulty behavior on the part of the manufacturer, including a failure to provide reasonable warning and a failure to design a product whose safety meets either users' expectation or some risk-utility test. In short, the ascendance of conduct-based responsibility, either as a stand-alone principle of responsibility or in conjunction with outcome-based responsibility, marks a central achievement of *substantive* modern tort law.

The mismatch presents itself when the substantive change at issue renders tort law's procedural aspects out of sync. In particular, rather than recalibrating it

[51] Kathleen Gill, *The Moral Functions of an Apology*, 31 PHIL. FORUM 11, 12 (2000); ERVING GOFFMAN, RELATIONS IN PUBLIC: MICROSTUDIES OF THE PUBLIC ORDER 113 (1971).

[52] On the possibility of characterizing (some instances of) risk imposition as a freestanding setback to a nonmaterial dimension of the risk-taker's autonomy, see JOHN OBERDIEK, IMPOSING RISK: A NORMATIVE FRAMEWORK 85, 88, 97 (2017).

[53] The law cannot, and should not, compel acknowledgments, let alone apologies. The ethical aspects of owing care and respect for others are beyond the legitimate authority of tort law, or any law in a liberal legal order. This is because the value of making an acknowledgment or apologizing turns on its being sincere, rather than coerced. For a helpful discussion of the ethics of reconciliation and the limits of tort litigation as a system of reconciliation, see Linda Radzik, *Tort Processes and Relational Repair*, *in* PHILOSOPHICAL FOUNDATIONS OF THE LAW OF TORTS 231, 246, 248 (John Oberdiek ed., 2014).

[54] Paul v. Holbrook, 696 So.2d 1311, 1312 (Fla. App. 1997).

in light of tort law's changing conception of responsibility, the allocation of the burden of persuasion has remained stuck in the older, outcome-based conception. The problem that such a mismatch creates—indeed, the reason why it deserves the pejorative term "mismatch"—is that of giving *no* effect to the substandard behavior of the defendant when deciding how to allocate the burden at issue. I argue that this mismatch undermines tort law's egalitarian ideal of relating as equals.

IV. Egalitarian Allocation of the Burden of Persuasion

Tort law's egalitarian aspirations govern the terms of the parties' interaction throughout all of the stages of their conflict: from its get-go stage as risk-creator and -bearer, to its trial stage as defendant and plaintiff, and to its ultimate resolution in liability imposition or exoneration. Indeed, the procedural law that governs the trial stage cannot be insulated from the demands of value that originate in the substantive law that is the subject matter of the trial. I do not argue that *all* that civil procedure is, and should be, doing comes down to instantiating the values underlying substantive law. For instance, some rules of civil procedure are in the nature of housekeeping rules and others concern procedure-related values such as information-inducing, truth-seeking, and legitimacy-generating.[55] That said, because civil procedure is subservient to substantive law, these extra-tort values cannot repudiate the values underlying tort law. Treating the parties to a tort suit as unequal, such as by requiring the plaintiff to prove her case beyond reasonable doubt, violates the equality theory of tort law. So, too, the allocation of the burden of persuasion must not systematically undermine the equal standing of parties in torts litigation.[56] To this extent, the allocation of the burden of persuasion should inform their terms of interaction in connection with one—potentially consequential—stage of the interaction: the stage of litigating their conflict. Therefore, the equality theory's insistence on the principle of relating as substantive equals should implicate the question of burden allocation, too.

This is precisely why a similar concern does *not*, and should *not*, implicate criminal law and procedure. Indeed, an animating theme of criminal law is the inequality between the defendant and the prosecution—indeed, the asymmetry between these parties lies at the *structure* of the criminal justice system. The presumption of innocence and the high-water-mark standard of proving guilt beyond reasonable doubt are the procedural manifestations of the *inegalitarian* foundations of

[55] On truth and information-seeking, see ALEXANDRA LAHAV, IN PRAISE OF LITIGATION (2017); Elizabeth Chamblee Burch & Alexandra D. Lahav, *Information for the Common Good in Mass Torts*, 70 DEPAUL L. REV. 345 (2021). On legitimacy as the first virtue of legal process (in adversarial civil procedure and even beyond), see DANIEL MARKOVITS, A MODERN LEGAL ETHICS: ADVERSARY ADVOCACY IN A DEMOCRATIC AGE (2008).

[56] I say systematically because some exceptions to the rule of equality could be justified.

this area of law.[57] It is further manifested in the typical consequences of finding against a criminal defendant: incarceration, exclusion from certain positions and entitlements, and everlasting social stigma. (This is why [as was famously the case in the O. J. Simpson trials] a tort defendant can be held liable in battery and not guilty in a criminal trial in relation to the same misdeed.) By contrast, tort law reflects the diametrically opposite structural idea.[58] It is time, therefore, to extend its egalitarian commitments to its procedural aspects.

Relating as equals, I have argued in Chapters 12--15, begins with the existence of the duty and then takes up its content. The very existence of the duty matters, I argued in Chapter 12, because it makes possible a certain form of an egalitarian interaction between agents—that is, a duty owed to and owned by the risk-bearer gives him or her special standing in relation to the risk-creator: *The duty elevates the interests of the former to a nondiscretionary constraint on the choice of the latter.* I argue that part of what it means for the risk-bearer to have special standing in relation to the risk-creator can, and should, affect how courts allocate the burden of persuasion between the parties.

Thus, the moral significance of a tort duty—viz., a way of establishing a relation of equal agency between risk-creator and -bearer—can make a difference in how we should approach the allocation of the burden of persuasion. In a tort-law world full of outcome-based responsibility, no such difference is called for. But when conduct—which is governed by a tort duty—occupies tort law's center stage, the allocation question cannot remain indifferent to the inegalitarian consequences of substandard or improper conduct. This conclusion defies the prescriptions of the main positions on the allocation question mentioned at the outset. Contrary to adherents to the status quo, the equality theory of torts takes the burden of persuasion to be far less static and certainly far less defendant-friendly. And contrary to those who view the allocation question as wholly contingent, the equality theory adds a noncontingent consideration to the determination of who should bear the burden in question.

The underlying thought is straightforward. The burden of persuasion must be responsive, at least in some measure, to the fact that the duty-owner has this standing in relation to the duty-ower. That is, if you breach a duty of due care you owed me, I can demand that you bear (at least some of) the epistemic burden of illuminating what really happened in our encounter, such as whether or not your

[57] The distinction between the egalitarian structure of tort law and the inegalitarian structure of the criminal law does not imply that the identity of the parties in a tort dispute—such as the differences between natural persons and corporations, big and small—may not matter. To the contrary, substantive equality requires that difference, insofar as it is relevant, should not be overlooked when determining terms of interactions. On party differentials in the context of civil procedure law, see Rosen-Zvi & Fisher, *supra* note 16, at 101–08.

[58] A tort defendant's interest is not recognized by the trial court as the tortfeasor does not override, at least not in principle, the plaintiff's interest in being recognized as a victim of the defendant's wrongdoing.

breach of duty was a but-for cause of my injury. This is so, I argue, because we are equals.

Indeed, a breach of a duty, while not a complete tort, changes the normative situation between the risk-creator and risk-bearer. In particular, the former has placed the latter in an unduly dangerous situation and, in this respect, failed to treat her interest in bodily safety as *equally important* as his interest in pursuing his ends. In that, he fails to relate to her as an equal. This form of mistreatment discredits the views discussed above, that the risk-creator is entitled to the status quo ante the breach because he is beyond reproach, or because civility requires us to presume his innocence, until proven otherwise. Clearly, breaching the duty upsets the status quo. More specifically, it contrasts with the moral significance of having a tort duty to begin with, namely, that of having the risk-creator and the risk-bearer interact as equals by vesting the latter with a certain standing in relation to the former. The ability to breach the duty with impunity—that is, when the breach luckily caused no harm—renders superficial the risk-bearer's standing. The parties, therefore, relate unequally.

Consider by analogy, once again, the ethics of apology. If you subject me to unreasonable risk of bodily harm that, fortunately, does not materialize into injury, you *owe me* an apology or some such acknowledgment as a fitting response for mistreating me. This sense of "owing me" is a surface manifestation of the deeper point made above—that our normative situation has changed and, further, that I am entitled to reassert my equal standing with respect to you by demanding your fitting response. Thus, mistreating me represents not only substandard behavior but also a violation of a responsibility to treat me as you should, namely, as an equal.

Now, the law's imposition of the burden of persuasion on the breaching party provides a fitting response. It reflects the risk-bearer's standing in relation to the *substandard behavior* of the risk-creator. More specifically, it responds to the consequences of the risk-creator's failure—the breach of the duty—by asserting the risk-bearer's claim to be regarded by the risk-creator as an equal. Hence, to return to a previous example, if a pedestrian proves that a motorist violated the duty of due care by driving excessively fast while she was lawfully crossing the street, the motorist would no longer be entitled to recuse himself from bearing at least some of the epistemic burden of proving or disproving other elements of the tort at issue (including causation, as I argue presently).

Although the argument has so far traveled at a highly abstract level, it can be further elaborated by reference to particular torts. The shift from the abstract to the concrete will, therefore, help in answering not only the question of who should bear the burden of persuasion but also, and no less importantly, *when*. I discuss three cases in furtherance of this end: proving causation in negligence, proving consent or lack thereof in the somewhat related torts of battery and trespass to land, and proving truth or falsity in defamation. All three raise important, and seemingly hard-to-settle, questions concerning the allocation of the burden of persuasion; the equality theory provides the answers.

V. Elaboration and Illustration: Egalitarian Burden of Persuasion Redux

To set the scene for the three cases to be discussed, two points must be made at the outset. Both return the argument to observations I made at the start of this chapter. First, the burden under discussion is persuasion. It already assumes that the plaintiff has met the burden of pleading or filing a complaint. It is only when the complaint is made out in a sufficiently coherent fashion that the next couple of questions can be triggered, that is, who should bear the burden of production and—that which stands at the center of this chapter—the burden of persuasion. Second, the contingent considerations that are widely recognized by courts and civil procedure scholars, such as who has better access to evidence, remain valid and important. The principled consideration I introduce in this chapter supplements, rather than supplants, them. To this extent I assume, with the leading studies on this point,[59] that it is often warranted, at least *presumptively*, to place the burden of persuasion on the plaintiff.[60] The equality theory would then intervene by determining at which point in the process of making out the prima facie case this burden should be assigned to the defendant. As mentioned above, rather than understanding the burden of persuasion as typically static, the equality theory insists that it should be dynamic so as to reflect the ways in which substandard or improper behavior affects how the plaintiff and the defendant stand in relation to each other. Thus, the shift in substantive tort law from the outcome-oriented *ancien régime* to the conduct- and outcome-oriented modern tort law commands a proceduralist shift, namely, from static to dynamic burden shifting. Consider the following cases.

A. Negligence: Why and When Should Defendants Prove Causation

To state a cause of action in negligence, the plaintiff-victim currently bears the burden of persuasion with respect to all the elements of the prima facie case. This means that she must show that the defendant owed her a duty, that he breached it, and that the injury from which she suffered was caused (in the right sense) by that

[59] *See* sources cited in *supra* note 18. And see also, to the contrary, sources cited in *supra* note 19.

[60] Thus, I go along with the leading studies on the (contingent) considerations at hand, but in a limited way: they can only establish the initial allocation of the burden of persuasion. As I show in Section V.A (negligence), this concession is typically not detrimental to an equality-respecting trial.

breach. (In the early days of this tort, the plaintiff also bore the burden of proving that she was not contributorily negligent, but this is no longer the case.) There are three explanations for this way of allocating the burden; two of them are indefensible. The first exemplifies the mismatch thesis—the allocation in question is the upshot of the everlasting inertia of the *ancien régime*. The second resorts to the question-begging appeal to the status quo, according to which the defendant is entitled to a presumption of innocence. The third and the only plausible explanation draws on considerations of access to information and other contingent, but commonsensical conceptions about how the world works supporting the imposition of the burden of persuasion on the plaintiff, save for some exceptions (on which more below).

As I have argued above, the equality theory of torts treats the breach of the duty of care as capable of changing the way the plaintiff and the defendant stand in relation to one another quite apart from whether that breach actually caused the plaintiff's injury (or from whether she was injured at all). It means that by showing that the defendant breached the duty he had owed her, the plaintiff *need not* assume the burden to persuade the court that that breach caused her injury. I say need not, rather than should not, because, recall, there are those instrumental considerations that ordinarily (so I assume) pull in favor of imposing the burden on the plaintiff. Thus, *if* usually the plaintiff has, or can have, better access to the information needed to prove a causal connection between breach and injury, there is no (nonsymbolic) reason to insist on assigning the burden of persuasion to the defendant.

However, and here comes the important break from the *ancien régime*, the fact of breach should make a difference to the allocation of the burden especially when the contingent considerations that ordinarily favor burdening the plaintiff lose momentum. Then, an egalitarian allocation of the burden calls for shifting the burden onto the defendant with respect to the causation element, namely, the burden of disproving its existence.

At first glance, this prescription seems to advocate a revolutionary turn in procedural tort law. This may be the case. (After all, if it is valuable, why shouldn't we embrace it?) But on a deeper level, I take this prescription to carry evolutionary, rather than revolutionary, undertones. In particular, there are established doctrines and leading cases that move in this direction. There, judges seem to be moved by underarticulated sentiments about the just way to allocate the burden of persuasion with respect to causation (and sometimes also breach) under conditions of uncertainty.[61] The equality theory of torts provides the framework—the language

[61] I set to one side the case of proving breach, including in particular the doctrine of *res ipsa loquitor*, according to which the existence of breach is, effectively, proved by resort to statistical evidence and the burden to disprove its existence is the defendant's.

and the normative resources—with which to explain these sentiments and, ultimately, turn them into a working legal doctrine of the civil procedure of negligence law.

Relaxing proof of causation short of burden shifting. Anyone who reads appellate court decisions on factual causation may notice an informal practice of leniency toward the plaintiff's burden of proving causation under a certain set of circumstances. That is, when the plaintiff has managed to prove, thoroughly and convincingly, that the defendant breached a duty of care and that this breach is sufficiently correlated to the sort of injury from which the defendant has actually suffered, courts may not insist that the plaintiff exclude other possible causes. As one court has observed (quoting a leading study on this point), when the case for breach is robust, "courts have shown very little patience with the efforts of defendant to question the sufficiency of the [plaintiff's] proof on cause."[62] And vice versa: the less robust the plaintiff's proof of the breach element, the more stringent courts become with respect to proving causation. Thus, contrary to a case featuring "positive evidence of negligence," courts employ a stringent approach when faced with "a mere transitory risk."[63]

To fix ideas, a plaintiff suing on a theory of premises liability may complain that the landowner breached a duty in having the stairs on his premises inadequately lit. There is no specific evidence—neither direct nor circumstantial—to prove that that breach actually caused the plaintiff's fall, which is to say, it is not sufficiently clear whether the substandard behavior of the defendant was a but-for cause of the plaintiff's injury given that there could be alternative explanations for the fall. Courts' response to this uncertainty may vary according to the strength of the case for the defendant's *breach* of his duty of care. If the plaintiff puts forward a particularly clear case of defendant's breach, not to mention proving egregious breach, courts may often adopt a relaxed stance toward the former's burden of proving a causal connection between the breach of duty and the resulting injury. A relaxed stance does not mean lowering the official standard of proof, such as from the preponderance of the evidence to the substantial factor test, but rather taking a more lenient, plaintiff-friendly approach to the question of whether the trier of fact could infer a causal connection between breach and injury in the face of the inevitably speculative nature of the evidence submitted by the plaintiff. However, if the case for breach is merely plausible, which is to say short of proving breach with flying colors, courts may be much less permissive in assessing the existence of a causal connection between breach and injury.[64]

[62] Brown v. Tesack, 566 So. 2d 955, 957 (La. 1990) (*quoting* Wex S. Malone, *Ruminations on Cause-in-Fact*, 9 Stan. L. Rev. 60, 73 (1956)).

[63] *See* Brooks v. Kinsley Iron & Machine Co., 88 N.E. 771, 772 (Mass. 1909).

[64] For instance, *compare* Muckler v. Buchl, 150 N.W.2d 689 (Minn. 1967), in which the court adopted a relaxed stance toward proving factual causation, *with* Butts v. Weisz, 2010 WL 703238 (W.D.Pa.), aff'd 410 Fed. Appx. 470 (3d Cir. 2010), where the court took the opposite approach.

The real thing: Burden shifting. The clearest cases manifesting the judicial sentiments underlying the equality theory of torts are those that break with the *ancien régime* and, instead, adjust the allocation of the burden of persuasion to the fact of the breach of the duty. On these lines of cases, the breach of the duty together with genuine epistemic uncertainty concerning the casual connection between this breach and the plaintiff's injury are jointly sufficient to assign the burden in question to the defendant.[65] Three such cases stand out: *Haft v. Lone Palm Hotel*, featuring breach of an affirmative duty to protect and warn,[66] *Summers v. Tice*'s resort to alternative liability to overcome the problem of tortfeasor identification,[67] and the doctrine of market share liability as developed in *Sindell v. Abbott Laboratories*.[68] I take each in turn.

Haft and his child died from drowning in a pool without a lifeguard in the hotel in which they had stayed. The hotel breached an affirmative, statutory duty it owed the Hafts to either provide a lifeguard service or clearly indicate the absence of such service. No one actually witnessed the drowning and, so, the causal connection between the breach and the fatal injuries is deeply uncertain. The California Supreme Court, appealing to the "unfairness of this burden situation"[69] and to considerations of "policy and justice,"[70] shifted the burden to disprove causation onto the hotel.

Summers v. Tice is an earlier Californian decision, featuring two hunters simultaneously, and negligently, shooting in the direction of a third hunter, Summers. Although only one of the former two hit him, Summers could not adduce evidence to prove whose negligence caused his injury. Citing considerations of fairness[71] as well as of "policy and justice,"[72] the court imposed on the hunters-defendants the burden to absolve themselves on the question of causation.

And in *Sindell*, the same court extended the alternative liability of *Summers* to impose liability on several potential injurers based on the market share of each of them. There, approximately two hundred manufacturers within the pharmaceutical industry produced a generic drug, the consumption of which subsequently resulted in cancerous growths in the daughters of the pregnant women who had ingested it. The basic obstacle in the case was the same as in *Summers*—that is, tortfeasor identification. The plaintiff may not have been able to prove a causal connection between breach of the duty and her injury because she could not identify *whose* breach was responsible for her injury. The solution, however, was different,

[65] I say *genuine* epistemic uncertainty, to exclude cases in which the plaintiff is responsible (in the right sense) for the uncertainty.

[66] Haft v. Lone Palm Hotel, 478 P.2d 465 (Cal. 1970).

[67] Summers v. Tice, 199 P.2d 1 (Cal. 1948).

[68] Sindell v. Abbott Laboratories, 607 P.2d 924 (Cal. 1980).

[69] *Haft*, 478 P.2d at 475.

[70] *Id.*, at 476 (quoting *Summers v. Tice*, 199 P.2d 1 (Cal. 1948)).

[71] *Summers*, 199 P.2d at 3, 4.

[72] *Id.*, at 5.

at least to some extent.[73] In addition to imposing proportional liability on the basis of manufacturers' respective share in the drug market, the court effectively shifted the burden of disproving causation to the manufacturers-defendants, such as by showing that they did not manufacture the drug until after the victim-plaintiff was borne.[74]

There have been attempts to account for each of these three landmark decisions on its own, that is, irrespective of the continuities between them (and the fact that the judges in these cases proceeded under the assumption that they do contain some overlap). A better strategy, therefore, should view them as surface manifestations of a single normative principle. The only question is, then, what principle is this? I wish to cast doubts over one influential answer and in its stead offer the one I developed above, that is, the equality theory of torts.

Before I begin, it is important to note that contingent considerations, such as who has better access to the relevant evidence, may not do. The causal uncertainties in these cases plague both parties, and, often, equally at that.[75] The most sophisticated unifying explanation is the argument from evidential harm. This has been suggested by Canada's Justice Rand[76] and further elaborated to its most mature and sophisticated form in the writings of Ariel Porat and Alex Stein.[77] The basic point on this view is that the source of the causal uncertainty in cases such as *Haft*, *Summers*, and *Sindell* can be traced back to the conduct of the defendant(s). While in ordinary cases governed by negligence law, the substandard conduct of the defendant causes an injury, the unusual cases at issue involve conduct that causes causal uncertainty. The argument from evidential harm is that tort law should conceive of such uncertainty as a freestanding injury. Hence, instead of suing the defendant (such as in *Haft*) for causing the material injury, the plaintiff should have a claim against the defendant for causing the causal uncertainty that prevents this plaintiff from proving causation between breach and the material injury. One way to give effect to the evidential harm, short of allowing an independent cause of

[73] Ernest Weinrib argues that that *Sindell* departs from *Summers* in that the former defines the at-fault pool broadly to include the entire, national market for the drug. By implication, market share liability may allow the imposition of liability on a drug manufacturer whose products were sold in the East Coast only for the injury suffered by those who bought the drug in the West Coast. *Summers*, by contrast, defined the at-fault pool narrowly to include only wrongdoers whose wrongdoing imposed risk to the plaintiff. I am not convinced by this line of thinking. As I explain in the main text below, *Sindell* allows manufacturers-defendants to disprove causation (such as by showing that they did not sell their products in the West Coast). *See* Ernest J. Weinrib, *Causal Uncertainty*, 36 Oxford J. Legal Stud. 135, 149–50 (2016).

[74] Sindell v. Abbott Laboratories, 607 P.2d 924, 927 n.4, 930 (Cal. 1980).

[75] Moreover, relying on the peculiar situation of no more than two shooters may not be helpful, at least when the number of potential wrongdoers is higher. *Contra* Arthur Ripstein & Benjamin C. Zipursky, *Corrective Justice in an Age of Mass Torts*, *in* Philosophy and the Law of Torts 214, 241 (Gerald Postema ed., 2001).

[76] Cook v. Lewis [1952] 1 DLR 1, 4. According to Rand, in a case like *Summers*, one of the shooters "by confusing his act with environmental conditions ... has in effect destroyed the victim's power of proof." *Id.*

[77] Ariel Porat & Alex Stein, Tort Liability Under Uncertainty chs. 6–7 (2001).

action for the spoliation of evidence, is that of shifting the burden of persuasion with respect to the causation element to the defendant.

For instance, the hotel in *Haft* breached the duty of care by failing to either provide a lifeguard or warn of its absence. Not only does this failure create substantial risk of harm to pool-goers. In addition, it deprives drowning pool-goers the ability to prove a causal connection between having a lifeguard on duty and avoiding drowning (or the connection between giving a warning that no lifeguard is on duty and the decision of a potential victim to shun the pool). As the *Haft* court observed, "the absence of definite evidence on causation is a direct and foreseeable result of defendants' negligent failure to provide a lifeguard."[78] *Summers*, too, is often explained in terms of two hunter-wrongdoers, one of which caused the plaintiff's material harm and the other the evidential harm of depriving the plaintiff the ability to ascertain whose shot caused the former harm.

Porat and Stein extend the argument from evidential harm to the case of *Sindell* and to market share liability, more generally. They argue that the manufacturers of the drug "deprived the plaintiffs of information critical to the tortfeasors' identification."[79] They conclude that "the defendants should be held liable [for] the evidential damage" that, according to *Sindell*, manifests itself in market share liability.[80]

However, the argument from evidential harm is weak, at least with respect to the *Summers* and the *Haft* types of cases, as it rests on indefensible artificiality. The difficulty is not that defendants in any one of the cases just discussed may not have foreseen that their breach of duty might result in the spoliation of evidence.[81] Rather, the argument from evidential harm bakes unrealistic assumptions into the content of the duty of care, namely, that in addition to owing a regular duty of care, defendants also owe a duty not to spoil the evidence necessary to prove a causal connection between the breach of the regular duty and the material injury of the plaintiff.

To get a sense of its artificiality, consider the duty of care in the cases just discussed. Thus, in *Haft*, the argument from evidential harm suggests that the hotel is duty-bound not only to protect its guests from pool-related risks but also to help them understand what is the nature of the connection between providing a lifeguard (or a warning of its absence) and drowning in the pool. This understanding, the argument goes, will allow them to consider whether, in case they have drowned, they should sue the hotel and, moreover, be in a position to prove the causal connection between breach and their material injury. The hotel is to be blamed not merely for failing to provide proper warning. Rather, it also failed by depriving the victims the ability to understand what would be the case—viz.,

[78] Haft v. Lone Palm Hotel, 478 P.2d 465, 476 (Cal. 1970).

[79] Ariel Porat & Alex Stein, *Liability for Uncertainty: Making Evidential Damage Actionable*, 18 Cardozo L. Rev. 1891, 1916 (1997).

[80] *Id.*

[81] *See* Weinrib, *supra* note 73, at 143. *See also* Porat & Stein, *supra* note 79, at 1916.

whether or not they would have entered the pool—had the proper warning been given to them. In practical terms, one possible way to discharge the duty is to place a sign next to the pool detailing the expected contribution of the failure to post "no lifeguard on duty" signs for drowning.

As for *Summers*, both hunters owed the victim a duty to exercise due care not to injure him. However, the hunter whose shot luckily missed the victim also, and highly artificially in my view, owed a duty not to open fire simultaneously with the other hunter. That is, he wronged the victim by not waiting a couple of moments before pulling the trigger.

Finally, the argument from evidential harm becomes less absurd in the *Sindell* case. The DES (which is a synthetic estrogen) drug manufacturers in *Sindell* breached a duty not to deprive its users the ability to identify the specific manufacturer whose drug caused the plaintiff's injury. Their fault was not merely the production and distribution of a dangerously defective drug. Rather, it also lay in *simultaneously* selling the same drug to the same pharmacies and, in doing so, obscuring the ability to establish a causal connection between the particular manufacturer of a particular defective drug and the material injury of the plaintiff. Contrary to both *Summers* and *Haft*, the possibility that sophisticated manufacturers of a similar drug would, separately, design their products in ways that conceal the specific identity of the manufacturer is not entirely without merit, although it is not clear that this is true of *Sindell*.[82]

By contrast, the equality theory of torts provides a principled and, with respect to cases such as *Haft* and *Summers*, nonartificial way to approach the question of burden shifting in these cases. That is, it offers a way out of the mismatch between tort law's procedural and substantive aspects. The starting point is that typically, contingent considerations pertaining to access to evidence (et alia) support the imposition of the burden of persuasion on the plaintiff, including with respect to the causation element. However, the fact that the defendant has breached a duty owed to and owned by the plaintiff can function as a tiebreaker when those considerations (such as access to evidence) do not obtain. The tiebreaker is principled in the sense that it stems from the basic egalitarian ideal of the tort duty. As mentioned above, the duty is tort law's way of establishing a relation of equal agency between parties to a tort interaction: It turns the interest of the risk-bearer into a nondiscretionary constraint on the risk-creator's choice. By breaching the duty, the risk-creator no longer relates to the risk-bearer as an equal. Indeed, the breach represents a certain form of disregard for the risk-bearer that can justify allocating the burden of proving causation to the defendant (the risk-creator). Talk

[82] For more on the connection between opportunistic behavior and burden shifting in the context of fiduciary law, see Henry E. Smith, *Why Fiduciary Law Is Equitable?*, *in* PHILOSOPHICAL FOUNDATIONS OF FIDUCIARY LAW 261, 274–75 (Andrew S. Gold & Paul B. Miller eds., 2014).

of wronging the plaintiff by causing her evidential harm becomes redundant, as it should.

The judicial sentiments that move courts in the direction of shifting the burden of persuasion and relaxing the burden of proving causation can now draw on the normative resources of the equality theory to transform these sensibilities into a legal doctrine. On this doctrine, proving breach under circumstances of causal uncertainty, as in *Haft*, *Summers*, or *Sindell*, should support assigning the (persuasion) burden of disproving causation to the defendants. The underlying reason will not turn on the artificial argument from evidential harm but rather on letting the ideal of relating as equals determine not only the terms of the ex ante interaction between the parties qua risk-creator and risk-bearer but also their terms of interactions as litigants, and specifically, as a duty-breaching defendant and a mistreated plaintiff.

B. Who Should Prove Consent: The Battery/Trespass Divide

The torts of battery and trespass to land are not just historically related but also structurally similar. Battery is, at bottom, trespass to person and, so, while the object of the trespassory interference is entirely different—the person versus the property of the plaintiff—the nature of the interference looks alike. That is, both involve the commission of an intentional contact with the (person or property) of another person. Both, moreover, may impose liability even when the contact in question is an upshot of a good-faith mistake on the part of the defendant. Finally, lack of consent is typically the reason why intentional contact with the person or property of another counts as wrong in the first place.

A recurring question in the study of battery and trespass is whether consent should be treated as an affirmative defense or, alternatively, as an element of the prima facie case of each of these torts. The civil procedure aspect of this question is who should bear the burden of proving consent or lack of consent, the plaintiff or the defendant. This question is often crucial not merely for expressive or symbolic reasons but rather also materially: Failing to meet the burden of persuasion on this point is often tantamount to losing the entire case. Solving disputes that take the form of "he-said-she-said" or "it's your word against mine" often turns not on who is right but rather on who bears the burden of persuasion concerning consent.

Despite its significance, however, the question of who bears this burden is "muddled in the case law," with different courts taking different positions with respect to both the general question of the burden of proving consent in intentional torts and the particular questions of consent in battery and in trespass to land.[83]

[83] *See, e.g.*, Dobbs, *supra* note 49, at §105. *See further* Restatement (Third) of Torts: Inten. Torts to Persons § 12 cmt. *e*, Tentative Draft No. 4 (2019). The Tentative Draft supports, for reasons

This jurisprudential muddle is quite staggering given the extremely long history of these two torts. One would expect that disagreements and inconsistencies over the very basic question of who bears the burden have already been resolved (at least) decades ago; after all, we do not have to believe that the law works itself pure to expect a more definitive and consistent approach to the allocation of the burden at issue.

Is there a principled way out of the "muddled" state of consent in battery and trespass? Is there a *right* way to determine who should bear the burden of proving consent (or lack of consent)? The equality theory of torts suggests itself. The key point, once again, is to reconcile the demands of *substantive* tort law with tort law's *procedural* aspects. Avoiding procedural mismatching requires a proper understanding of how parties in a battery or in a trespass dispute stand to each other: for instance whether or not plaintiff's proof of offensive touching by the defendant commands shifting the burden to prove consensual touching to the defendant; and with respect to trespass, whether or not plaintiff's proof of defendant's entry on her land supports assigning the burden of proving consensual entry to the defendant. In particular, I argue that in battery the defendant should bear the burden of proving consent, whereas in trespass to land the plaintiff is typically the one who should bear the burden to prove lack of consent. Hence, their historical and structural affinities to the contrary notwithstanding, the equality-theory case for allocating the burden sets the two torts apart. This divide is anything but surprising, as the ideal of relating as *substantive* equals begins with a commitment to taking difference—here, between bodily integrity and control of land—seriously.[84]

Begin with trespass to land. The tort consists in unauthorized entry, and the "entry" has to be intentional, rather than accidental. Intentionality, however, is devoid of moral content. It makes no essential reference to substandard behavior on the part of the entrant. Rather, it concerns an intentional *act*, such as traversing a particular piece of land without necessarily intending to enter or use another's land. It thus renders immaterial the existence (or inexistence) of intent to commit an unlawful or immoral act.[85] Moreover, the same is true with respect to prosocial behavior, as when a person enters another's land for the purpose of making a friendly gesture.[86] Bluntly put, neither ill-will nor good-will on the part of the

of fairness and efficiency, the imposition of the burden of persuasion in the tort of battery on the plaintiff. *Id.* The equality theory supports the opposite conclusion.

[84] Substantive equality—and especially taking certain differences seriously—rejects the forthcoming Restatement's concession that although the "greater procedural protection of property rights" vis-à-vis bodily integrity "might seem anomalous," "the difference has historical roots and is embedded in some of the case law." RESTATEMENT (THIRD) OF TORTS: INTEN. TORTS TO PERSONS § 12, cmt. *e*, TD No. 4 (2019). The Restatement's proposition is, indeed, anomalous. In a liberal society, the difference between bodily integrity and property supports the superiority of the former over the latter.

[85] *See, e.g.*, Meyer v. Pacific Employers Inc., Co., 43 Cal. Rptr. 542 (App. Ct. 1965).

[86] The rule dates back at least to the *Case of the Tithes* (1507), YB Trin. 21 Hen. VII pl 5, fol. 27.

potential trespasser has any bearing on whether the entry counts as intentional. Accordingly, placing a foot on Blackacre may be sufficient to ground liability for trespass if so "placing" is made intentionally, rather than accidentally.[87] As the *Restatement (Second) of Torts* points out, liability for unauthorized intentional entry would lie irrespective of whether the trespasser "honestly and reasonably believes that he has the consent of the lawful possessor to enter, or, indeed, that he himself is its possessor."[88]

Against this backdrop, because it does *not* turn on substandard or improper behavior on the part of the defendant, proof of intentional entry need not implicate how the plaintiff and the defendant stand in relation to each other. Hence, upon proving an intentional entry, the plaintiff should also be deemed responsible to prove that the entry was unauthorized, perhaps because it was nonconsensual. This is a case where the allocation of the burden of persuasion reflects the miscellaneous, contingent considerations emphasized in the civil-procedure perspective.[89]

Battery is different. It, too, requires intentional, rather than accidental, interference with the person of another. And its conception of intentionality likewise concerns itself with forming an intention to touch another person, though not necessarily an intention to wrong him or her by so touching. But unlike intentional entry in the context of trespass to land, and save for limited exceptions, the intentional touching that figures in battery does amount to *substandard* behavior.[90]

To see that, it is important to note that battery concerns two different types of intentional touching—an offensive one and a harmful one. A touching can count as offensive without necessarily being harmful, and vice versa. A paradigm case of the former is that of a passenger on the bus caressing a stranger sitting next to him, whereas a paradigm case of the latter would be punching this other passenger in the face. What makes the former wrongful is the indignity associated with using another person's body as an instrument of pleasure or for domination-seeking. By contrast, harmful battery is wrongful because it causes brute bodily harm (such as a broken nose). At any rate, a plaintiff who proves that she was subject to either offensive or harmful contact (or both) can thereby do more than merely satisfying one element in the prima facie case of battery. She also shows that her position in relation to the defendant has changed in a certain way as the defendant seems to

[87] The sufficiency of being upon Blackacre refers to committing the tort. It may not suffice, however, for other purposes such as that of awarding compensatory and punitive damages.

[88] RESTATEMENT (SECOND) OF TORTS § 164 (1965).

[89] I assume (as I should, given that tort law is and should be part of private law) that the trespasser is a private person rather than law enforcement officer. The latter case is in substance an aspect of the vertical relationship between political authority and its subjects. It would then be better, perhaps necessary, to place the burden of proving authorization on the government. I leave this aspect of tort law to another occasion.

[90] Two exceptions are worth noting. The first, discussed in Chapter 3, concerns social touchings while the other involves medical-related touchings.

avail himself of her body.[91] Accordingly, as between the two, it is the defendant who should bear the burden of proving consent, which is to say proving consensual touching. Such shifting the burden of persuasion responds, in the right way, to the substandard behavior integral to engaging in intentionally touching another person in a harmful or offensive fashion.

C. Defamation and the Burden of Proving Falsehood

A case for defamation, either libel or slander, turns on proving that the defendant's publication or statement is defamatory and, moreover, false. There are other considerations, such as that the defamatory material is of and concerning the plaintiff, but they can be safely set to one side. The prima facie case of the traditional tort of defamation (be it libel or slander) entertained a division of labor between proving defamatory content and proving its true or false nature. Traditionally, the plaintiff bears the burden to prove defamatory content whereas the defendant can avoid liability by proving this content is true.[92] On this division, a defamatory statement is presumed wrongful unless (the defendant proves that) it is true. And for content to count as defamatory, it has to be in the nature of exposing the plaintiff to hatred, contempt, or certain other forms of lowering others' perceptions of this person. Familiar examples are imputing to the plaintiff the commission of a crime, serious incompetency (such as that P is a terrible lawyer), flagrant immoral behavior (such as that P is a liar), or some other form of heterodoxy that might undermine others' sense of her good name or reputation.

Some courts keep with the traditional division of labor between plaintiff and defendant so that the former must prove defamatory content and the latter its truth.[93] Other courts, mainly in the United States and partially—though *not* exclusively—as a result of the constitutional impact of the First Amendment on the tort of defamation, place the burden of proving both elements on the plaintiff.[94] On this approach, the plaintiff bears the burden of proving that the defendant's statement was both defamatory and false. And yet other courts take a middle ground. For instance, Colorado law of defamation burdens plaintiffs with the responsibility

[91] For an extensive discussion of the seemingness or appearingness of wrongdoing in the law of torts, see Rebecca Stone, *Private Liability Without Wrongdoing*, 73 U. Toronto L.J. 53 (2023).

[92] *See, e.g.*, Bird v. Hudson, 18 N.E. 209, 210 (N.C. 1893).

[93] English defamation law adheres to this approach as well as South Africa's law (see *Khumalo v. Holomisa* [2002] 5 SA 401).

[94] I stress the point that the fundamental changes in the tort of defamation are not reducible to the constitutionality of free speech. The importance of free speech to private law and, so, tort law in particular reaches beyond public law and the First Amendment. *See, e.g.*, Crump v. Beckley Newspapers Inc., 320 S.E.2d 70, 77 (W.Va. 1984); Simpson v. Mars Inc., 929 P.2d 966, 967 (Nev. 1997). *See* the discussion of uncompromising journalism in Chapter 4, Section III and especially the discussion of private censorship in Chapter 17.

to prove, by clear and convincing evidence, "material falsity," whereas defendants bear the burden of proving "substantial truth" to defend themselves from liability.[95]

Since the common law of defamation is, to this extent, "all over the place," it is especially important to go normative—to wit, what is the right way to determine who should bear the burden of proving falsity (or truth). The equality theory takes a principled approach to argue that it should be the plaintiff.[96] I shall argue that the traditional approach should be rejected as it unjustifiably sustains a mismatch between the procedural and the substantive aspects of the tort of defamation. One way to introduce the argument going forward is by criticizing traditional defamation law: Why should truthful imputations by the defendant ever be considered wrongful?

I argue that the mere communication of defamatory content need not count as substandard behavior on the part of the defendant. It is the falsehood contained in that content, rather than its defamatory connotation, that renders her conduct substandard. Hence, the plaintiff should bear the burden of proving falsity, and only then can we say that the defendant's standing in relation to her has changed in a way that warrants imposing the burden of persuasion (such as to assert affirmative defenses and privileges) to exonerate themself from liability.[97]

There has been a point in the early history of the tort of defamation in which uttering a defamatory statement—such as imputing a serious crime or incompetency to the plaintiff—was considered morally wrongful in and of itself. Indeed, this tort was once mainly litigated in, and so shaped by, English ecclesiastical courts. On these courts' religious conception of right and wrong, "defamation was a sin."[98] This view has (surprisingly) survived the shift to secular, common-law courts for some centuries. In fact, it lasted well into the early twentieth century when courts imposed on defendants an unusually exacting burden of proving truth. Even minor factual inaccuracies would transform an otherwise true statement of the defendant into a false one.[99] Furthermore, a publication was presumed false, as a matter of law, simply because it was shown to be defamatory.[100]

[95] *See, e.g.*, Brokers' Choice of America, Inc. v. NBC Universal, Inc., 861 F.3d 1081 (10th Cir. 2017) (Colo. law).

[96] A contingent approach can further support my principled argument if it is assumed that "there are good reasons to question the common law allocation of the burden of proof [as the] plaintiff has better access to information concerning her own conduct and therefore is in an excellent position to rebut the charges against her." RICHARD A. EPSTEIN & CATHERINE M. SHARKEY, CASES AND MATERIALS IN TORTS 1128 (10th ed. 2012).

[97] To be sure, the plaintiff may also have to prove additional elements (such as that the statement is of and concerning himself, that he suffered reputational harms, that the defendant acted with some degree of fault, and so on).

[98] Smith, *Supra* note 45, at 370. *See also* Van Vechten Veeder, *The History and Theory of the Law of Defamation*, 4 COLUM. L. REV. 33, 35 (1904).

[99] On the "artificial reasoning" in defamation law of the day, see James C. Courtney, *Absurdities of the Law of Slander and Libel*, 36 AM. L. REV. 552, 562 (1902) and its discussion of *Sharpe v. Stevenson*, 34 N.C. 348 (1851).

[100] *See, e.g.*, Post Pub. Co. v. Moloney, 33 N.E. 921 (Ohio 1893).

Modern defamation law, by contrast, does not subscribe to this view about the morality of the interaction between persons.[101] On this conception of morality, imputing a serious crime or incompetency to a criminal or to an incompetent professional is just that, namely, pointing a finger to the truth of the matter. "Pointing" can take any number of forms, ranging from calling attention to what some of us already know, to assiduously investigating a person's record to reveal the so far unbeknownst truth about them. Rendering the truth about a person's criminality or incompetency more accessible to the world is not the same as turning this person into a criminal or making them incompetent. The truth of the matter concerning this person exists *independently* of what the defendant has said or published of and concerning this person. The defendant simply exposes the truth about who the plaintiff is.[102] In a liberal society, of which free speech is constitutive, informing others about the truth cannot, in and of itself, count as substandard behavior *even when* the truth lowers the plaintiff in the opinion of others. If anything, it is the falsity of the defamatory statement, rather than its defamatory content, that could turn the statement into an instance of substandard conduct, which is to say a way of mistreating the plaintiff.

Accordingly, the traditional rule features a mismatch between the procedural and the substantive aspects of defamation law. To fix it, the plaintiff should be the one who bears the burden of proving that a statement is both defamatory and false (among other elements). Only then can the behavior of the defendant toward the plaintiff count as substandard. Only then, that is, can the defendant be said to engage in mistreating the plaintiff. To this extent, in a nonmismatched law of torts, proving a statement's falsity by the plaintiff is a prerequisite for shifting the burden of negating it to the defendant (among other possible affirmative defenses and privileges).

VI. Allocating the Burden of Persuasion: Moving Forward

The three cases just discussed were meant to exemplify the implications of the equality theory of torts for the procedural question of burden allocation. More generally, they offered a way to bridge the gap between the substantive and the procedural aspects of tort law. I leave other cases (such as the burden of showing malice, or lack of justification, in the tort of inducement of breach of

[101] Hence, courts nowadays mostly focus on substantial rather than literal truth.

[102] So doing may occasionally interfere with plaintiff's reasonable expectations of privacy, but this is a different matter altogether. Moreover, at times the *manner* in which the statement is made, rather than its content, may be unusually offensive. The ethical (and legal) implications of engaging in this form of wrongdoing, however, do not strictly speaking concern defamation.

contract[103]) to another occasion. Two general points will be apt by way of concluding this chapter. Both concern the extension of the discussion to the entire domain of torts.

The first point concerns method. How should the burden of persuasion be allocated in torts other than negligence, battery, trespass, and defamation? Are there general prescriptions coming out of the equality theory of torts on the burden allocation question? The answer begins with understanding the role of the equality theory in fixing the mismatch between the *ancien régime* and modern tort law. Substandard behavior on the part of the defendant is a form of mistreating the plaintiff. It, therefore, adversely reflects on how the parties stand in relation to one another; in particular; it undermines the possibility of relating as equals. The procedural question of who should bear the burden of proving what element of the prima facie case must be responsive (in the right way) to this fact. More specifically, proof of substandard behavior supports shifting the burden of proving the remaining element(s) of the prima facie case to the defendant.

Identifying substandard behavior is not an exercise of free floating moral assessment of defendants. Rather, substandardness is embedded in the elements that make up the tort at issue. For instance, breach of a duty of due care in the case of negligence can support shifting the burden to negate factual causation to the defendant; intentional misrepresentation of facts in the tort of fraud can support shifting the burden to negate the element of inducing plaintiff's reliance of these facts to the defendant; or in the tort of inducement of breach of contract, drawing on unlawful means to induce the breach of the plaintiff's contract with a third party can support shifting the burden of proving the element of justification (i.e., that the inducement was justified) to the defendant. This concern naturally moves the argument to the second point.

The second point concerns the rule of law. Here I insist that the case for overcoming the mismatch is not an invitation to judicial ad hockery. Indeed, identifying substandard behavior, once again, is not a form of open-ended moral assessment of conduct. Instead, it is structured by the various elements of the particular tort at issue, as just illustrated. On top of that, the allocation of the burden should be made in a principled, rather than piecemeal, fashion. Thus, rather than deciding the allocation of the burden for each dispute at a time, the civil procedure aspect of tort law should be determined on a category-wide basis. Hence, courts (or lawmakers) will have to decide, in advance, for a *category* of cases falling into a particular tort cause of action, how the allocation of the burden of persuasion between the plaintiff and the defendant should go. For instance, it can be sensible to make a category-wide exception to placing the burden of proving falsity in a defamation cause of action on the plaintiff in cases involving perishable agricultural

[103] *See, e.g.*, Alyeska Pipeline Service Comp. v. Aurora Air Service, 604 P.2d 1090, 1096 (Ala. 1979).

products. On this exception, only the defendant will face the burden of proving truth (as a defense). The underlying rationale is the imminent losses resulting from (suspiciously) false statements by food critiques concerning such goods.[104] This way of proceeding, by the category rather than the specific case, could sustain certainty and constrain judicial discretion and, at the same time, form a better alignment between the procedural aspects of tort law and its substantive ones.

[104] For more on agricultural disparagement state laws, see Eileen Gay Jones, *Forbidden Fruit: Talking About Pesticides and Food Safety in the Era of Agricultural Product Disparagement Laws*, 66 Brook. L. Rev. 823, 824 n.4, 839 n.82 (2000).

17
The Tort of Private Censorship

Introduction

In this chapter, I propose a novel tort of private censorship—one that calls for a fundamental shift both in the societal ethos surrounding free speech and in the legal framework that sustains it.

The case for this tort begins with the prescription that the inherently valuable conflict between free speech and competing interests should be engendered. Currently, the modern tort of defamation (partially) responds to this prescription by severely limiting liability for certain reputational harms. However, the ambit of the facilitation that this tort does is narrowly confined to instances of reputation-undermining publications. The construction of the conditions for inherently valuable conflicts involving free speech should capture expressive acts that come into conflict with other interests far beyond reputation. Indeed, speech is often subject to censorship for a number of reasons unrelated to defamation, such as because it is too divisive, upsetting and discomforting, emotionally harmful, politically incorrect, and so on. Hence, the conflict theory of tort law articulates the basis for a new tort-law framework with which to determine free speech rights and corresponding duties of respect. This theory, however, does not explain the *form* that these rights and duties must take, namely, whether they are relational and if so, do they extend to interactions between private entities or focus more narrowly on the vertical interactions between the state and its citizens. Nor does the conflict theory have all the resources to fix the content of these rights and duties. This is precisely why the equality theory assumes an equally consequential role in making the case for the tort of private censorship. Or so I shall argue.

Moreover, the argument going forward has a constructive moral ambition.[1] Such an ambition goes beyond re-constructing, re-forming, and re-fining the existing building blocks of the law of tort—that is, the various existing torts that make up the law of torts. It seeks to provide the normative resources to identify and pursue what is truly missing, namely, the tort law that addresses conflicts involving fundamental interests that have so far fallen off the radar of the theory and the practice of tort law. In Chapter 10, I have argued that a novel tort of discrimination

[1] For a defense of normative jurisprudence in legal theory more generally, see Robin West, Normative Jurisprudence: An Introduction (2011).

Conflict between Equals. Avihay Dorfman, Oxford University Press. © Oxford University Press 2026.
DOI: 10.1093/9780198979869.003.0021

should be integrated into the law of tort.[2] The missing piece I wish to focus on in this chapter concerns *horizontal* free speech, which is to say the conflict between the fundamental interest of private persons in free speech and the contrastive set of interests that move other private persons to engage in censorship—that is, private censorship.

Our interest in being free to express views and judgments, communicate information, and engage in creative acts receives substantial protection against public—that is, state or vertical—censorship. For instance, the conflict between a person's political or artistic speech and the state's interest in sustaining public order is a feature, rather than as a bug, of the constitutional legal order. This is why constitutions in liberal legal orders typically protect such speech precisely when it undermines a state's interests and, moreover, inflicts nontrivial emotional, dignitary, or reputational harms on individuals and groups.

This constitutional-law regime of free speech falls short in two important ways, however. First, it mainly governs *vertical* interactions between the state and its citizens—it deals with state-imposed censorship on citizens' speech. Second, it is often grounded in *democracy* and, in particular, a certain ideal of collective self-governance. The reason why these two properties of the free-speech regime (as we know it) count as shortcomings is that they fail to recognize that the significance of free speech extends beyond, and so is not reducible to, vertical interactions and democratic self-governance. I argue that our interest in free speech is no less compelling when it comes to (some of) our horizontal interactions with other private persons or entities. Further, it is compelling because it is (sometimes) constitutive of our ability to relate to these others as free and equal persons. Tort law as the law of interpersonal conflicts between equals provides the normative framework with which to understand the problem of non-freedom and relational inequality caused by private censorship, and construct the solution, namely, the tort of private censorship.

The case for a tort of private censorship is meant to vindicate the law of torts in another way as well: It moves beyond the wrongs, harms, recourse, or costs conceptions of tort law. Saddling tort law with these conceptions obscures what really matters. After all, questions about wrongdoing, harming, recourse, and cost-internalization do not come, as it were, with a *theory* of what substantive rights and duties we have, but rather presuppose their existence. For instance, a tenant is not allowed by her landlord to post a political sign at the front door of her dwelling house. How can freedom as independence determine whose position of being "in charge" count as wrongful? Or how can we determine whether this or that instance of private censorship counts as improper behavior on the part of the censor—need it be subject to some Coasean bargaining over speech-cum-commodity? In the

[2] *See also* Hanoch Dagan & Avihay Dorfman, Relational Justice: A Theory of Private Law ch. 13 (2024); Hanoch Dagan & Avihay Dorfman, *The Tort of Discrimination*, 16 J. Tort L. 393 (2023).

absence of some such theory of substantive rights, common-law courts may not be able to address what is, essentially, *private* censorship.

The conflict and equality theories of tort law aspire to provide such a theoretical framework. First, they provide a theory of what substantive rights and duties we have and hence overcome the theoretical impasse of reducing tort law to the law of wrongs, harms, recourse, or cost-internalization. Second, they move the legal analysis from constitutional law—and the extension of constitutional law to certain private entities (common carrier, shopping malls, etc.)—to where it should be, namely, the horizontal dimension of private individuals interacting with others, typically under circumstances of a power imbalance. I take up both the generic case of private censorship and more concrete cases of censorship inflicted by employers, landlords, and online social-media platforms.

I. The Public/Private Censorship Gap

Free speech is valuable, in part, because of its intimate, positive relation to individual autonomy and relational equality. Our autonomy depends on our ability to *think* freely and deliberate in the absence of "distortive influences" of various sorts.[3] Our autonomy also depends on our ability to *speak* out, that is, to express our views, perceptions, and creativity.[4] Finally, it depends on our ability, as *listeners*, to be informed by views, information, and creative expressions of others.[5] In terms of relational equality, relating as equals may depend on having an entitlement to think, deliberate, speak out, and listen to others' speech. Indeed, standing as an equal to another may sometimes turn on being able freely to express one's beliefs to this other, including to "talk back."[6] For instance, prohibiting wives from talking back to their husbands is partially constitutive of the inegalitarian structure of the patriarchal family relationship. For these two reasons, curtailing free speech is not only inimical to democratic self-governance but rather also to the autonomy and equality of persons in pairwise interactions.[7] From a liberal point of view, the

[3] Seana Valentine Shiffrin, *A Thinker-Based Approach to Freedom of Speech*, 27 Con. Commen. 283, 290 (2010); Thomas Scanlon, *A Theory of Freedom of Expression*, 1 Phil. & Pub. Aff. 204, 215–16 (1972).

[4] *See, e.g.*, Thomas Nagel, *Personal Rights and Public Space*, 24 Phil. & Pub. Aff. 83, 96 (1995).

[5] *See, e.g.*, David Strauss, *Persuasion, Autonomy, and Freedom of Expression*, 91 Colum. L. Rev. 334, 357 (1991); Joseph Raz, Free Expression and Personal Identification, in Ethics in the Public Domain: Essays in the Morality of Law and Politics 146 (1995). *See also* Morris Lipson, *Autonomy and Democracy*, 104 Yale L.J. 2249, 2265 (1995).

[6] Bell Hooks, *Talking Back*, 8 Discourse 123, 123 (1986–87). *Cf.* Gayatri Chakravorty Spivak, *Can the Subaltern Speak?*, *in* Marxism and the Interpretation of Culture 271 (Cary Nelson & Lawrence Grossberg eds., 1988).

[7] As Robert Post, who defends the First Amendment on democratic grounds of collective self-determination (See Robert C. Post, Democracy, Expertise, Academic Freedom 10–15 (2012)) suggests, "to attribute to the First Amendment the purpose of facilitating collective self-determination is not necessarily to deny that the First Amendment can also serve other, distinct purposes." Robert Post, *Equality and Autonomy in First Amendment Jurisprudence*, 95 Mich. L. Rev. 1517, 1521 (1997).

connection between democracy, on the one hand, and individual autonomy and relational equality, on the other, runs even deeper: Democracy's value ultimately depends on its success in sustaining the free and equal status of the individual members of a political community, *taken severally*.[8] The liberal case for protecting free speech in a democracy is, therefore, also a case for reinforcing autonomy and equality at the private individual's level.[9]

This conviction permeates the constitutional-law fabric of liberal democracies and, ultimately, results in a robust liberal ethos of free speech; indeed, it accounts for the distinction between "democracy" and *liberal* democracy. It can certainly justify extending the constitutional protection of free speech to private entities on account of their contribution to sustaining democratic self-governance as well as to public[10] and semipublic spaces, such as shopping malls and company towns.[11]

That said, it receives insufficient recognition in the private law of the liberal legal order. Let me be clear: Constitutional rights to free speech are not and should not be absolute. Moreover, they do not protect every kind of speech, let alone expression.[12] However, they do afford generous protection—indeed, public censorship is, to an important extent, legally impermissible. Tort law, by contrast, does not single out the right to free speech for special protection. The right to free speech only gets limited recognition on certain, narrowly circumscribed occasions.[13] As already mentioned, modern defamation law extends free speech protection to defendants in private-law contexts when it conditions liability on proving some degree of fault on their part[14] and when it applies Anti-SLAPP statutes to protect defendants against meritless, retaliatory lawsuits.[15] Similarly, liability for other torts, such as intentional infliction of emotional distress, may be restrained to sustain the free speech of the tortfeasor.[16] To give another example, liability for trespass to chattels can be narrowed so as to protect an employee's right to criticize a former employer by way of sending bulk emails to current employees.[17]

[8] *See further* Avihay Dorfman & Alon Harel, Reclaiming the Public ch. 1 (2024). *See also* Robert Post, Constitutional Domains: Democracy, Community, Management 7 (1995).

[9] This view contrasts with Fiss's argument that collective self-determination is not reducible to, and perhaps even not grounded in, individual freedom, see Owen Fiss, Liberalism Divided: Freedom of Speech and the Many Uses of State Power 5, 13, 21 (1996).

[10] Snyder v. Phelps, 562 U.S. 443 (2011).

[11] *See infra* text accompanying notes 22–23 & 60. *See* Matthew H. Kramer, Freedom of Expression as Self-Restraint 53 (2021); Johan van der Walt, The Horizontal Effect Revolution and the Question of Sovereignty 92 (2014).

[12] *See* Frederick Schauer, *The Boundaries of the First Amendment: A Preliminary Exploration of Constitutional Salience*, 117 Harv. L. Rev. 1765 (2004).

[13] *See further* Genevieve Lakier, *The Non-First Amendment Law of Freedom of Speech*, 134 Harv. L. Rev. 2299, 2363–65 (2021).

[14] *See* Chapter 4, Section III.

[15] Anti-SLAPP (Strategic Lawsuits Against Public Participation) statutes mostly provide procedural protections against meritless claims.

[16] Snyder v. Phelps, 562 U.S. 443 (2011). For a critique of the decision (from a tort-theory perspective), see Benjamin C. Zipursky, Snyder v. Phelps, *Outrageousness, and the Open Texture of Tort Law*, 60 DePaul L. Rev. 473 (2011).

[17] Intel Corp. v. Hamidi, 71 P.3d 296 (Cal. 2003).

Another example is that trespass-based protection to free speech can be found in the emerging doctrine often called media trespassing. And some US states protect, in some measure, employees' speech against employer retaliation (which is discussed further, below).[18] These, however, are exceptions that prove the rule of *no* general recognition that private abridgment of speech is prima facie impermissible. Furthermore, a multiplicity of narrowly tailored protections against private censorship may not achieve what a general commitment to horizontal free speech could sustain, namely, the good of liberal culture (recall Chapter 3) and its consequent widespread liberal ethos of free speech for the horizontal dimension of our life as private persons.[19]

The incongruity of public and private rights of free speech may have historical explanations. Most significantly, the rise of online platforms has turned virtually anyone from a mere passive consumer of views, information, and artistic creations into a potential agent of speech.[20] Relatedly, online platforms seem to pose a substantial threat to people's freedom of speech (as well as other freedoms) in ways that have not been experienced before except for the threat traditionally posed by the state. However, the case for horizontal free speech, and thus the argument for a tort of private censorship, is not limited to content moderation and user-blocking by online platforms nor exhausted by the unusual market power held by some of these platforms. For instance, it extends to both landlord/tenant and employment contexts, in which case the incongruity of public and private free speech far preceded the rise of social media networks. It even preexists the legal powers—property and contract—that bring the categories of landlord/tenant and employment relations into existence. Censorship in the context of spousal and other familial relationships featuring social, economic, or physical power imbalance, is infamously pervasive in many past and present societies (recall Mr. Murdstone's harsh censorial control over his spouse Clara, David's mother, in Charles Dickens's *David Copperfield*). More fundamentally, historical reasons for the incongruity in question do not exhaust the normative question of why it *should* have existed. There are, no doubt, differences in how free speech should be protected against public censorship, on the one hand, and private censorship, on the other hand.[21]

[18] For extensive discussion of this point, see Eugene Volokh, *Private Employees' Speech and Political Activity: Statutory Protection Against Employer Retaliation*, 16 Texas Rev. L. & Pol. 295 (2012).

[19] Talk of ethos of free speech does not mean that tort law requires would-be censors to acquire a certain set of *attitudes* in favor of tolerating other people's freedom of speech. The conflict and equality theories are legal theories and in particular theories for a liberal legal order, and so can only give us reasons to act in certain ways, rather than purport to determine what attitudes or motivations we ought to acquire.

[20] *See generally* Kate Klonick, *The New Governors: The People, Rules, and Processes Governing Online Speech*, 131 Harv. L. Rev. 1598 (2018).

[21] According to the High Court of South African, the prohibition on public censorship has an affirmative dimension that goes beyond the duty (also applicable in case of private censorship) of noninterference. *See* Boycott, Divestment and Sanctions v. Continental Outdoor Media [2014] 4 All SA 347, para. 80. *See also* Jack M. Balkin, *Free Speech Is a Triangle*, 118 Colum. L. Rev. 2011 (2018).

However, such differences can hardly justify full-blown protection of the former and the near exclusion of the latter. In what follows I wish to explain both *why* horizontal free speech matters and *when*.

II. Why Horizontal Free Speech?

It may be tempting to take a statist approach to grounding horizontal free speech rights. A statist approach is traditionally employed against threats posed by the state, state actors (including broadly conceived[22]), and quasi state entities.[23] Can this approach be extended to capture purely private censors? I discuss both theoretical accounts and doctrinal mechanisms that take this path, arguing that they fail; horizontal free speech is not merely an extension of the free speech rights that we hold against the state or political authorities, more generally. My critique of these accounts consists in two different claims: First, extending constitutional rights can only go so far; and second, and more fundamentally, the extension of constitutional rights seems to presuppose, implicitly if not explicitly, that private law cannot, and should not, give rise to a right to free speech. The two claims mutually reinforce the conclusion that the private-law solution—a tort of private censorship—is indispensable.

Begin with theory. Theoretical accounts associated with the concept of "constitutional horizontality" attempt to remedy the absence of free speech rights in the private law by extending the constitutional right to free speech to (some or all) interactions between private persons. In the course of doing so, these accounts implicitly or explicitly invoke a two-system picture according to which private law—system one—is the problem for which constitutional law—system two—is the solution.[24]

[22] In retrospect, the Supreme Court of California has suggested that even its celebrated shopping mall case, *Robins v. Pruneyard Shopping Ctr.*, 592 P.2d 341 (1979) *aff'd.* 447 U.S. 74 (1980), is consistent with the state action doctrine, meaning that a shopping mall's restriction on the speech of mallgoers is an instance of governmental encroachment on their constitutional right to free speech. Golden Gate v. Tenants Association, 29 P.3d 797, 806–07 (Cal. 2001).

[23] *See* Kramer, *supra* note 11, at 53, 57–60; *see generally* Biden v. Knight First Amendment Institute at Columbia University, 141 S.Ct. 1220, 1222–25 (2021) (Thomas J., concurring).

[24] *See*, most recently, Ernest J. Weinrib, Reciprocal Freedom: Private Law and Public Right chs. 7–8 (2022). *See also* Aharon Barak, *Constitutional Human Rights and Private Law*, *in* Human Rights in Private Law 13 (Daniel Friedmann & Daphne Barak-Erez eds., 2001); Stephen Gardbaum, *The "Horizontal Effect" of Constitutional Rights*, 102 Mich. L. Rev. 307 (2003); Walt, *supra* note 11, at 92.

Mathew Kramer argues that the principle of free expression grounds an obligation of self-restraint on the part of the state. Kramer argues that a restaurant owner (his example of private party) may not be allowed to suppress the speech of a waiter-employee (at least on some occasions). The wrong of private censorship, in his view, is not that one private person engages in censorship of another, but rather that the government "assign[s] viewpoint-suppressing legal authority to the restaurant." That is, the basic wrong lies in state action (or inaction), rather than in private action. Kramer, *supra* note 11, at 61.

This picture is problematic. It runs together historical and normative claims. To be sure, free speech has not received its due recognition by the positive laws that make up the private law (at least in most jurisdictions). But this unfortunate—and unjustified—historical fact does not imply that private law in modern, liberal societies is doomed; certainly, it does not imply that private law is necessarily the culprit. Further, its basic commitment to autonomy and substantive equality suggests that private law does possess the normative materials to introduce free speech to its own system of basic rights. Neither a variation on nor a watered-down version of the constitutional right to free speech would work in this way: This right—as all other private law's basic rights—is integral to what private law in a liberal society is about, which is the construction of terms of interactions between free and equal private persons.[25]

Now consider doctrinal mechanisms invoked in the service of the statist approach to free speech. Courts sometimes make this extension when they say that court enforcement of private censorship is itself a form of state action and, so, must meet the constitutional rules governing public censorship.[26] At other times, the extension takes the form of analogizing certain private entities, such as shopping malls, to a quasi state entity or to a public space.[27] Finally, some courts, moved by the theory of constitutional horizontality, have sought direct and indirect application of constitutional rights to some private disputes.[28] The problem with all of these mechanisms is that they implicitly dismiss the freestanding significance of free speech to how we—private persons—relate to each other. Its significance is freestanding in the simple sense that it does not make essential reference to the state (broadly conceived) or to our status as members of a particular constitutional order. Thus, I argue that only by taking individuals' autonomy and equal standing

[25] I defend this claim in DAGAN & DORFMAN, *supra* note 2. For an early exposition, see Hanoch Dagan & Avihay Dorfman, *Just Relationships*, 116 COLUM. L. REV. 1395 (2016).

[26] *See* New York Times Co. v. Sullivan, 376 U.S. 254, 265 (1964). Resort to this particular instantiation of the state action doctrine (an offspring of *Shelley v. Kraemer*, 334 U.S. 1 (1947)) is on the wane, though still remains good law. *See, e.g.*, Gerber v. Longboat Harbour N. Condo., Inc., 757 F. Supp. 1339, 1341 (M.D. Fla. 1991).

[27] *See* State v. Schmid, 423 A.2d 615 (N.J. 1980) (noting that the New Jersey constitutional right to free speech extends, strictly speaking, beyond state action to capture some private entities such as a private university campus (in this case: Princeton University)). *See also* Packingham v. North Carolina, 137 S. Ct. 1730, 1737 (2017).

[28] Indirect application is by far the more common method among liberal democracies (a leading case is Lüth, 7BVerfGE 198 (1958)). *See* Gavin Phillipson & Alexander Williams, *Horizontal Effect and the Constitutional Constraint*, 74 M.L.R. 878 (2011). South Africa (and, at some point, Ireland in *Meskell v. C.I.E.* [1973] I.R. 121) has adopted the exceptional method of direct application. It is telling, in my view, that in the famous case of *Khumalo v. Holomisa* [2002] 5 SA 401, the direct application of the constitutional right to freedom of expression shaded off into preserving the traditional common law of defamation law, effectively siding with the interest of a leader of a political party in protecting his reputation at the expense of a newspaper's interest in free speech. For a defense of direct application of constitutional rights, see Erwin Chemerinsky, *Rethinking State Action*, 80 NW. U. L. REV. 503, 509, 510, 516 (1986).

in relation to other private persons seriously, the case for free speech can finally throw off its statist shackles.

Begin with a straightforward case. Being entitled freely to express our values and judgments when interacting with other private persons can influence at every turn our ability to manifest our free and equal agency in the world. Most obviously, private persons whose livelihood, profession, or calling literally depends on expressive activity render this point vivid. Journalists fall into this category of expressive pursuits, including those whose journalism does *not* take issue with governments, public officials, and politics, more generally. Artists, ranging from sculptors to showbiz performers, also depend not only on being able to express themselves but also on having control—and, thus, agency—over what to express and precisely how. So do authors, poets, essayists, and so on. Free speech of journalists and artists (et alia) constitutes agency not merely in their affairs with the government but rather also vis-à-vis other private persons, such as their audiences, employers, and most importantly their objects of critique, namely, those who might be harmed as a result.

Are journalists (et alia) truly idiosyncratic or rather private cases of the more general category of horizontal free speech? The former construal suggests that the case against private censorship is strictly limited to certain civil-society functions or to some special positions, to the exclusion of all other private persons; by contrast, the latter implies that horizontal free speech can take the form of a general entitlement. (Notice that a general entitlement does not mean that it is scopeless; instead, it is general in the sense that it does not turn on the special identity or role of the speaker or listener.)

I defend the latter. The argument proceeds in two principal stages. The first stage sets out the relational argument against private censorship. It draws on the equality theory to argue why private censorship might be wrongful. The second stage explains when what *might* be wrongful becomes that which *is* wrongful. The conflict theory leads this move from "what might be" to "what is," showing that the conflict between free speech and conflicting interests should be engendered rather than mitigated. This stage is necessary because free speech rights are, in one sense, importantly different from other basic rights protected in the private law, such as the right against wrongful discrimination in employment, commerce, or housing settings. I take each stage in turn.

The first stage. Why might private censorship be wrongful? I argue that holding rights of free speech against other private persons enables us—private persons—to relate to these persons as free and equal agents. Indeed, like physical mobility, religious belief, and certain other aspects that define who we are, the ability freely to think, express ourselves, and get informed bears on how we relate to others. Free speech is a way in which private persons can manifest their agency in the world and, specifically, relate to others as equals. In that, free speech belongs in the category of properties that make those who possess and act on them free and equal agents in their interactions with other private persons. By agency I mean the ability to exercise substantial control over one's thoughts and actions, which is to say self-directed action that reflects one's judgments.

It is important to note that the argument is not limited to the connection between agency and the brute ability to express one's views, and engage in expressive activity more generally, when relating to another person. Rather, what matters is a certain *entitlement* to do so. Furthermore, such an entitlement means that the other party to the interaction *owes a duty* to the right-holder to act in conformity with this entitlement, namely, refraining from bowdlerizing or stifling the speaker. Indeed, relating as an equal to another private person may often turn on being entitled to express one's beliefs and judgments to this other. For instance, a person cannot relate to her spouse as an equal if the latter denies her the standing to express her views on family planning issues or on politics. So too an employee cannot relate to his employer as an equal if the employee lacks the retaliation-free ability to express his deep concern about the employer's plan to buy materials from a sweatshop-run manufacturer.[29] More generally, having one's expressive acts subject to the legal or de facto, control of another suggests that one may not be in a position to relate to this other as a free and equal agent.

For this reason, the tort of private censorship provides the legal framework with which to address horizontal interactions, especially those that feature asymmetric power, by which I mean the power of one party to determine what expressive acts the other party may, or may not, engage in. Notice that the power in question is often a normative one, namely, the legal standing to change the normative situation of others. However, the power associated with private censorship can also be de facto power, which is to say raw, prepolitical power to control the expressive agency of another person. The latter can be exercised on an ad hoc, even one-off basis, including by parties who momentarily hold a superior position relative to the other party (for instance, having one's finger at a striking distance from the power switch at a large concert hall during a talk by an otherwise powerful public figure).[30] Most typically, however, it occurs in the course of ongoing relations,

[29] For more on free speech and equality in employment law, see Sabine Tsuruda, *Working as Equal Moral Agents*, 26 Legal Theory 305, 311, 313–16 (2020); Cynthia Estlund, *Freedom of Expression in the Workplace*, *in* Oxford Handbook of Freedom of Speech 110 (Adrienne Stone & Frederick Schauer eds., 2021). *See also* Herbai v. Hungary, App. No. 11608/15, para. 37 (05/11/2019) https://hudoc.echr.coe.int/eng?i=001-197216.

[30] The fleetingness of power imbalance in and around free speech resembles, in broad terms, the radical vulnerability of *all to all* in the Hobbesian state of nature. Further, it aligns with the evolving concept of toleration, more generally. In the pre- and early-modern discussions of toleration (consider John Milton or John Locke), the world was viewed as a conflict between a dominate orthodoxy and a few heterodox sects. Against this backdrop, toleration was a theory meant to justify why unorthodox speech or belief did not harm members of the orthodoxy (and, further, why suppressing it could even be counterproductive). Our lived-experienced, by contrast, may be fundamentally different in at least one key respect: the erosion of a single, unified orthodoxy. As a result, unorthodox speech may now be seen as harmful by many reasonable members of society. This sociological shift further reinforces my earlier observation about the fleeting nature of (normative or brute) power imbalance.

such as inegalitarian relations between spouses where one spouse (recall David Copperfield's Mr. Murdstone) gets to decide for the other what can and cannot be said, when, and to whom. And although couples are perhaps a paradigm case of de facto power, there can be other instances—such as among friends or members in a voluntary association—of private censorship that are neither constituted nor mediated by legal powers. Instances of de facto power further show that private censorship should be classified as a tort, and that this classification is *not* merely one doctrinal hook among others to tackle what is essentially a case of acting beyond one's legal power (akin to corporation law's proscription on ultra vires).

The second stage. Although private censorship might amount to a relational wrong, relying on the equality theory may not be sufficient. I argue that a combination of two facts can render private censorship less objectionable and, at times, even unobjectionable. Hence, it is also required to show that there is value in putting the interest in self-expression into conflict with the interests underlying the censor's decision to engage in censorship. I take each stage in turn.

The first fact is that private censorship need *not* deny the person subject to censorship the good or the service offered by the person engaging in censorship. For instance, in the case of employment, a prohibition on employee speech does not prevent the employee from working for the censoring employer; and a tenant whose right to fly a flag is denied by her landlord is not thereby denied housing at this landlord's place. More generally, insofar as expressive acts are incidental, rather than integral, to the primary purpose of an interaction, acts of censorship need not frustrate the purpose in question. To this extent, private censorship is different from other instances of discrimination or nonaccommodation. There, unlike private censorship, discrimination in the provision of goods or services often amounts to denying the victim of discrimination the very ability to transact with the discriminator for these goods or services.

The second fact about private censorship is that it can be, and often is, fully and costlessly mitigated.[31] Generally speaking, the mitigation principle imposes on victims the burden of minimizing their injuries. Typically for tort law, mitigation cannot undo the harm. On many occasions, mitigating a serious bodily injury involves avoiding further aggravation of the harm. At other times, mitigation requires taking some steps to alleviate rather than prevent the adverse consequences, such as of suffering grave emotional harm. By contrast, mitigation in connection with private censorship is different. On many occasions, a person subject to censorship by another can take his or her expressive act elsewhere by resorting to other, including even more effective, outlets (such as available platforms, public squares, etc.). Hence, mitigating censorship's adverse consequences can sometimes bring about the elimination, rather than merely the

[31] *See also* J. P. Messina, Private Censorship 17 (2023).

reduction, of censorship. To be sure, there are exceptions. One such exception is when the medium is the message, in which case private censorship is not mitigable. This has been the case of the San Francisco 49ers' quarterback Colin Kaepernick who "took a knee" during the national anthem at the start of National Football League (NFL) games. His kneeling was a statement against racial injustice in the United States. Arguably, the medium is (at least in part) his message. Arguably, censoring him cannot be mitigated by taking his protest off the field.[32]

Another exception is when alternative outlets are far too costly and far less effective. Consider censorship in the housing context. For most house dwellers, residential signs (on political, religious, or ethical issues) are not just one way, among many equally available others, to engage in self-expression. Such signs "are an unusually cheap and convenient form of communication."[33] For many people, it is the most effective way *publicly* to express their views.

But apart from the two exceptions just mentioned—regarding where the medium is the message and effectiveness—and save for the special case of journalists (et alia) mentioned above, people can easily and readily separate their expressive acts from the other aspects of contracting for goods and services with other private persons. This observation is also familiar in the case of public censorship; a strict prohibition on visitors' free speech in a courtroom does not make the censorship wrongful. This is in part because there are other public outlets at which people can freely (within limits) engage in expressive acts as a matter of right.

Against the backdrop of the two facts just discussed, the case for deeming private censorship wrongful cannot rest solely on the equality theory. What is further required is to show that there is value in putting the interest in self-expression into conflict with the interests underlying the censor's decision to engage in censorship. Put differently, what is missing is an argument to the effect that mitigating private censorship by *sanitizing* the conflict at issue is in general *not* harmless. The conflict theory, I argue, provides this missing piece.

The basic elements of the argument have already been discussed in some detail in Chapter 3. There I argued that putting the interest in free speech in conflict with the interests in good name and emotional well-being is valuable and, moreover, that the value in question can be realized only if the former interest gets some measure of priority over the latter. I now wish to elaborate this argument in two opposing levels of abstraction. Most abstractly, good name and emotional well-being are private cases of the more general category of interests and considerations that exert pressure toward valuable conflict with free speech. Most concretely, the

[32] It appears that his team and the NFL retaliated against him, engaging in ex post censorship that took the opaque form of blackballing him. The facts of the matter, however, remain contested. Kaepernick filed grievance for collusion against the NFL. The parties reached a confidential settlement. *See* Kevin Draper & Ken Belson, *Colin Kaepernick and the N.F.L. Settle Collusion Case*, N.Y. TIMES (Feb. 15, 2019) available at https://www.nytimes.com/2019/02/15/sports/nfl-colin-kaepernick.html.

[33] City of Ladue v. Gilleo, 512 U.S. 43, 57 (1994).

interests underlying acts of private censorship fall in this category. I defend the latter claim in Section III below by discussing three cases of private censorship, exercised by social platforms, landlords, and employers. In what follows I take up the former, abstract claim.

Begin with why the conflict between free speech and good name or emotional well-being does not exhaust the range of inherently valuable conflicts between free speech and countervailing considerations. The good of liberal culture can also be realized by putting free speech into conflict with interests other than good name and emotional well-being. In all these cases, the conflict between free speech and countervailing interests is necessary to construct the condition for the liberal culture to arise. This is because free speech possesses the normative—really, critical—force of both challenging existing forms of unfreedom and inequality and informing the construction of new terms of interactions. This force goes well beyond free speech's conflict with good name and emotional well-being, as already demonstrated in connection with Chapter 8's discussion of the conflict between free speech and public safety in *Star Opera*.[34]

Moreover, sometimes the conflict between free speech and countervailing interests is valuable for reasons other than the good of liberal culture. As I argue below, based in part on the discussion of nonconsensual entry to the workplace in Chapter 9, the conflict between an employee's free speech and an employer's welfare can be inherently valuable for reasons concerning the construction of egalitarian employment relationships rather than the good of liberal culture. Similarly, the conflict between the free speech of tenants and the economic interest of landlords (which topic is discussed further below) can count as valuable on account of its relation to the good of liberal toleration discussed in Chapters 8 and 9 above.

I wish to move from the abstract to the concrete by pressing this claim in connection with three major types of relationship—employment, housing, and social media. They typically feature fundamentally inegalitarian tendencies. Moreover, employee, resident, and platform-user speech can often breed substantial disruption and, in most cases, private censorship can be readily mitigated by allowing speakers to pursue their expressive acts elsewhere (e.g., using another social media platform or, in the case of employee speech, invoking extra-workplace venues). Can the case for a tort of private censorship explain why—built-in hierarchy, potential disruption, and mitigability to the contrary notwithstanding—employees, residents, and platform users should hold horizontal free speech rights against their respective censors? I answer in the affirmative. The conflict theory of tort law

[34] Recall *Star Opera*'s concern with whether performing German operas during a delicate period and thereby knowingly encouraging public protest and the blocking of highways amounted to public nuisance. This case, discussed in Chapter 8, features a conflict between the free speech of artists and protestors, on the one hand, and human safety, freedom of movement, and public order, on the other. It has nothing to do with good name. Arguably, a concern with emotional well-being is not the animating countervailing consideration in this case.

suggests that because the conflicts at issue are (or can be made) inherently valuable, these speakers should be entitled, within limits, to express themselves as tenants, employees, and platform users. Moreover, the equality theory of torts suggests that the entitlement at issue places landlords, employers, and online platforms in particular under a correlative duty.

III. Elaboration: Employee, Tenant, and Platform-User Speech

The generic case of private censorship presupposes de facto or de jure power imbalance between the two persons involved. At times, the imbalance can arise in connection with an ad hoc interaction between persons (such as on the occasion of an informal social gathering). At other times, however, the imbalance at issue arises out of established or categorical relationships, such as employment or spousal relations. On these occasions, the generic case can be made more concrete and, more importantly, more responsive to the intricacies of the relevant category of interaction. I discuss briefly three such categories: housing, employment, and online platforms. The discussion also uncovers the substantial gap between "what is" and "what should be" the tort law of private censorship in concrete and rather immensely important social settings.

A. Resident (including tenant) Speech

A dwelling house is more than a place that insulates us from society. It is also a major locus of self-expression. This is clearly evident in its internal decoration and whatever else we choose to make of it. But the intimate connection between a dwelling and self-expression can go beyond taste and style. We use our homes publicly to express our religious and cultural traditions, not merely inwards but rather also—and sometimes even mostly—outwards. Christmas decorations and the placing of the menorah at the front door or on a window facing the street during Hanukah exemplify the robust connection between dwelling houses and (religious) self-expression. Another way in which self-expression in and around dwelling houses goes beyond taste and style is political speech, broadly conceived to include matters of public concern, rather than merely elections—to wit, it covers posting signs such as "Black Lives Matter" and flying flags (containing political or some other controversial message), rather than only endorsement signs endorsing this or that person for an elected office. The robust connection between self-expression and one's dwelling is further reinforced by the pragmatic consideration mentioned above, that often residential signs are an especially effective way to *publicly* express their views.

To set the scene, residents can hold a variety of property rights to their place of residency, ranging from being tenants, to leaseholders of units in a cooperative apartment building, condominium's unit owners, homeowners living in a common interest community, or independent house owners (such as in a suburban subdivision). The nature of their property right may be relevant to the legal analysis, but it should have a secondary role only. This is because the concern in question arises not simply in connection with one's property rights but rather one's dwelling house and, indeed, home. Therefore, resident speech stands for the interest in self-expression of a private person qua house dweller.

The case for resident free speech proceeds on the basis of the twin principles—self-determination and relational equality—that underlie my generic case against private censorship. It also brings about important society-wide implications. Indeed, resident free speech shapes the character of residential life, turning it into a liberal one wherein the goods of liberal culture, liberal toleration, and all-inclusive markets, as discussed in Chapters 3, 8, and 9, figure prominently. It provides an appealing alternative to a sanitized, deeply apolitical arrangement of living together. I take up autonomy and relational equality first.

I argue that the case for self-determination literally brings home relational equality. First, resident free speech matters to dwellers' interest in expressive agency not only in general but also in the particular context of the dwelling house. As mentioned above, the ability to be at home is not reducible to manifesting our tastes and styles, as it extends to deeper convictions, including religious, ethical, and political ones. Guarding against governmental encroachment on this interest in and around one's home does not—indeed, cannot—eliminate residents' *systemic vulnerability* to censorship. After all, the tenant's landlord or the homeowners' association can occupy the de facto or de jure position of a censor, and very effectively at that.

Second, resident free speech matters to the ability of a tenant (et alia) to relate as an equal to the landlord (et alia) and at times also to their neighbors and passersby. Dwelling in a house without being able to express, in some nontrivial measure, ethical and political convictions (along with religious beliefs), certainly undermines the dweller's self-determination. And when such inability on the part of the resident is the upshot of being subject to the censorial control of the landlord (et alia), the parties cannot relate as equals. Thus, if the landlord (et alia) gets to decide whether a tenant can engage in expressive activities in and around the house in the first place and, if so, what contents are permissible, then it is fair to say that the terms of their interaction fail to treat them as equals.

The current law governing resident speech, along with the lived-experience of house dwellers,[35] is an excellent foil for the broader ambition of this book, namely,

[35] *See* Debra Kamin, *What Kind of Flag Can I Fly Outside My House?*, N.Y. Times Section RE, 8 (Apr. 20, 2021).

vindicating tort law. That is, it motivates a resort to the conflict and equality theories of tort law to both understand and determine the rights, duties, and liabilities that attach to expressive activities in and around the dwelling house. Reducing tort law to the law of wrongs, harms, recourse, or cost-internalization does not even begin to come to terms with the challenge posed by conflicts between private persons involving speech. This shortcoming is not merely theoretical but also political and doctrinal and, so, practical. Once again, current law vividly renders this trend.

To begin with, courts and legislatures do recognize the absence of a legal framework to address private censorship in the housing context given, you will recall, the intimate connection between one's self-expression and one's dwelling house. However, it appears that courts have been struggling to identify doctrinal hooks on which to address the conflict between a resident's expressive activity and the competing interests (such as aesthetic, economic, and neighborliness interests). This struggle reveals that there is no other way out of the challenge but to recognize a freestanding tort of private censorship in the residential housing context in particular, and in horizontal interactions more generally.

Most strategies invoked by courts draw on the constitutional-law hook in one way or another. One such strategy is to deem court enforcement of private agreements state action.[36] For instance, a condominium association may well prohibit the flying of the national flag by units' owners. It does not count as encroaching on resident speech because there is no horizontal right to free speech. However, in seeking court-enforcement of such prohibition, the association might implicate the court itself in infringing the First Amendment rights of the owners.[37] Another strategy is to extend the constitution's vertical prohibition on government censorship to private entities. The extension begins with quasi- or semipublic spaces held by private entities, such as shopping malls. Some courts are willing to extend the reach to housing complexes, including even to enclosed common interest communities that have no public throughways.[38] Note that going beyond shopping malls and their equivalents is often grounded in state constitutions (such as California's and New Jersey's) that afford generous protections to free speech, namely, against interference by certain nongovernmental entities.[39] At other times, courts resort to the catch-all standard of "public policy" to invalidate covenants that unreasonably (or unconscionably) burden constitutional rights (including free speech rights).[40] I have already criticized the constitutional approach for being

[36] The most familiar instance of such strategy arises in the context of restrictive, racial covenants. Shelley v. Kraemer, 334 U.S. 1 (1947).

[37] Gerber v. Longboat Harbor North Condominium, 757 F.Supp. 1339, 1341 (M.D. Fla. 1991). However, this strategy is not widely accepted. *See, e.g.*, Midlake on Big Boulder Lake, Condominium Ass'n v. Cappuccio, 673 A.2d 340 (Pa. Super. Ct. 1996).

[38] Mazdabrook Commons Homeowners' Association v. Khan, 46 A.3d 507 (N.J. 2012).

[39] *See, e.g.*, Robins v. PruneYard Shopping Ctr., 592 P.2d 341 (1979) *aff'd*. 447 U.S. 74 (1980).

[40] *See* RESTATEMENT (THIRD) OF PROPERTY (SERVITUDES) §3.1(2) (2000).

fundamentally statist even though private censorship is, at its core, about how two private persons relate. I shall not belabor this point again.

The structural gap between the problem—viz., private censorship—and the solution—viz., constitutional law—is further exacerbated when we move from courts to legislatures. Legislatures sometimes lend their formal support to tackling private censorship. The most straightforward way they do that is by affording statutory protection to resident speech under some, *very* limited circumstances: Often, these statutes give rise to homeowners' right to fly the national flag.[41] They do not necessarily protect free speech of dwellers as such but rather only that of homeowners against homeowners' or condominium associations.[42] Moreover, they define the object of the protection very peculiarly to include the display of the national flag (or the military's) only.[43] Resident speech is, of course, irreducible to the case of homeowners. Nor can it be identified with flag flying, and certainly not with a certain flag (or flags).

The tort of private censorship provides a better response. To begin with, it gets the basic matter right—to wit, resident speech concerns an interaction between *private* persons that, due to a certain power imbalance, undermines the expressive agency and the equal standing of one party, that is, the house dweller. Further, it focuses on house dwellers, including tenants, rather than homeowners only. And, finally, it sets the contract/tort boundary at the right place (as you will recall from Chapter 12). As with other prerequisites for free agency, such as the nonwaivable warranty of habitability's provision of "adequate heat, light and ventilation, serviceable plumbing facilities, secure windows and doors, proper sanitation, and proper maintenance,"[44] free speech of house dwellers may not be determined at the bargaining table: It is theirs as a matter of right. Thus, although some justifiable limitations on the scope of the right are permissible (on which more is said below), the core of the resident's right to free speech functions as a genuine—that is, noncommodifiable—constraint on the landlord's choice.

Accordingly, vindicating the right of the resident qua resident to free speech is called for by the equality theory of tort law. Once again, a legally mandated obligation to respect resident speech is necessary in order for a tenant (et alia) to relate as an equal to their landlord (et alia). Rather than having one's expressive agency qua house dweller subject to the control of one's landlord (et alia), one stands as an equal to the latter if one is entitled, rather than merely able, to express one's beliefs in and around the dwelling house.

41 *See, e.g.*, Freedom to Display the American Flag Act, 4 U.S.C. §5 (2006) (federal law); 765 Ill. Comp. Stat. 605/18.6 (Illinois state law). *But see* Cal. Civ. Code 1353.6(a) (California law entitles homeowners the "posting or displaying of noncommercial signs, posters, flags, or banners on or in an owner's separate interest, except as required for the protection of public health or safety or if the posting or display would violate a local, state, or federal law.").

42 *See, e.g.*, Freedom to Display the American Flag Act, 4 U.S.C. §5 (2006).

43 *See* Ill. Comp. Stat. 605/18.6 (national and/or military flags).

44 Javins v. First Nat. Realty Corp., 428 F.2d 1071, 1074 (D.C. Cir. 1970).

Yet invoking the equality theory is necessary but not sufficient. As mentioned above, restrictions on the ability to speak out are often readily mitigatable. For this reason, the conflict theory becomes necessary, too. In employing the conflict theory of tort law, it is important to first identify the kind of value that might underlie the conflict between resident's speech and the competing interests, cast perhaps in terms of the aesthetic appearance, economic value of nearby assets, and neighborly civility. Building on Chapter 3, I argue that the conflict at issue is often an inherently valuable one and, for this reason, tort law should construct the conditions for its existence. Thus, even if residents would be able to secure easy access to other, no less effective expressive outlets, such as social media or town hall meetings, the value of putting the clashing interests in conflict calls for protecting residents' free speech as a matter of right vis-à-vis their respective landlords.

Notice that resident speech is not a scopeless right. Although content-based interference is inconsistent with the right way of engaging with inherently valuable conflicts featuring resident speech, some restrictions may be permissible. In particular, restrictions that take the form of time, place, and manner could be used to tackle some of the excesses of resident free speech. As mentioned above, such restrictions are designed to coordinate the pursuit of competing interests. They can outlaw signs made of hazardous materials; they can restrict the posting of signs on a condominium's common elements; they can limit the size of such signs to maintain *some* measure of aesthetic appearance; and they can determine an "expiration date" for signs so as to prevent visual clutter. While the list of permissible time, place, and manner restrictions may vary depending on any number of contextual factors, no such restriction can amount to banning resident speech entirely, as doing so would turn coordination into de facto suppression of resident speech.

B. Employee Speech

Employee speech concerns three different categories of expressive activities: Speech about working conditions, speech about the political, social, and economic agenda of the employer, and political speech in general. The first takes up hours, salaries, unionization, and other typical subjects of bargaining. The second category considers criticism or opposition to the employer's stand on matters of public concern, such as an employer's support of certain politicians, certain public policies, or a certain moral vision. The third and final category involves political speech that is not specifically related to the speaker's employer, although it may, at times, indirectly affect the character of the workplace and the business model adopted by the employer. For instance, tax and immigration policies are matters of broad, political concern. However, they may have profound impact on production and employment decisions made by employers.

Whereas employment and labor laws nowadays protect employee speech of the first category,[45] the protection of speech of the latter two is currently "spotty and sparse"[46] and, in principle, could be either abrogated by the legislature or under-enforced by regulators. To make this point clear, consider the exceptional case of *Novosel v. Nationwide Insurance Co.*[47] The plaintiff was fired by the defendant for refusing to support the defendant's effort to lobby the Pennsylvania House of Representatives to reform parts of its torts system by introducing a no-fault liability regime. In particular, the plaintiff was terminated not only for his refusal to participate in the lobbying effort, but rather also for the fact that he "stated opposition to the company's political stand [concerning the desirability of a no-fault regime]."[48] The court found for the plaintiff, noting that a case for wrongful discharge could lie under these circumstances. The reason given was that terminating his employment amounted to interference with "public policy."[49] The court further intimated that the public policy at issue is grounded in the "political freedoms" of the employee, stating that employers should not be entitled to "dictate the terms of employee political activities."[50]

It is widely recognized, however, that *Novosel* is truly exceptional—to wit, an exception that proves the *rule* of employer's control of employee's political speech.[51] This rule has been criticized mostly on the grounds of political equality among citizens in a democracy.[52] The problem with employer control, on this view, is the perpetuation of political inequality of the working class. Thus, the equality that matters is democratic equality, rather than equality in and around the employment relationship itself. I argue, by contrast, that the latter is the most fundamental moral basis for employee speech. Whereas suppression of employee speech need not hinder the political equality of workers qua citizens, it necessarily undermines their equal standing vis-à-vis their employers.

Thus, according to the conflict theory, the tort of private censorship responds to an employer's suppression of employee political speech by first identifying what kind of value underlies the conflict between employee speech and employer prerogatives. I argue that the conflict at issue is within limits inherently valuable and that, therefore, employers cannot engage in censorial acts on the basis of the content, not to mention viewpoint, of employee speech. The argument is based on an integration of my earlier discussions of free speech in general, labor/capital

[45] *See, e.g.*, 29 USC §157 (2012) (a.k.a. National Labor Relations Act).
[46] Estlund, *supra* note 29, at 429.
[47] 721 F.2d 894 (3d Cir. 1983).
[48] *Id.*, at 896.
[49] *Id.*, at 900.
[50] *Id.*
[51] Estlund, *supra* note 29, at 429; Matthew T. Bodie, *The Best Way Out Is Always Through: Changing the At-Will Default Rule to Protect Personal Autonomy*, 217 U. Ill. L. Rev. 223, 250–52 (2017).
[52] By contrast, Sabine Tsuruda develops a compelling, relational equality case for employee speech. *See* Tsuruda, *supra* note 29.

conflict, and the inegalitarian implications of employers' control of employees' expressive agency. I explain how this integration works below. Having said that, I also argue that there should be limits to the scope of the claim of employee speech.

As I argued in Chapter 3, the conflict between the interest in speaking out and its competing interests (such as emotional and reputational interests) is inherently valuable. In a liberal society, such a conflict should be embraced, rather than pacified or resolved. The fact that such a conflict occurs in the special context of the employment relationship further strengthens this general prescription. Drawing on my argument in Chapter 9, the conflict between labor and capital is inherently valuable insofar as it can tackle power imbalance and facilitate the equal standing of employees vis-à-vis their employers. In that chapter, I argued that employees and union organizers should have some rights to enter the workplace without the leave of the employer. Their holding some measure of control over the workplace, I argued, is necessary for the making of egalitarian work relations.

The case against employer censorship follows this logic. Thus, in order for the employee and the employer to relate as equals, the latter cannot get to control the expressive agency of the former. A right to employees' speech, therefore, doubly matters: First, it sustains the employee's ability to manifest his or her agency in the world, assuming, as I do, that work forms an important part of a person's life; and second, it is a condition necessary for an employee to relate as an equal to his or her employer. On this account, the task of a tort of private censorship is to facilitate the inherently valuable conflict between employers and employees by protecting employees' expressive agency and equal standing in relation to their employer. This tort does that by removing this fundamental aspect of agency from both the bargaining table and the control of the employer. Indeed, as I argued in Chapter 12, tort duties that protect our most fundamental interests are prerequisites to a liberal practice of contracts. They are constitutive of the ability of parties to engage in market (including labor market) transactions as agents. The present argument fits this characterization: The employee's free speech should figure as a constraint on, rather than the product of, the unilateral or contractual choice of the employer to engage in censorial acts.

Now consider the limits on employee free speech. As I observed above, free speech rights are never absolute. Even a constitutional right to criticize the government does not give one the entitlement to engage in this valuable activity during a court session.[53] The case of employee free speech is no exception. The animating concern on this front pertains to the disruptive consequences to productivity and workplace morale.

To begin with, facilitating the inherently valuable conflict between employee speech and employer's competing interests does not imply that the latter interests

[53] As opposed to doing the same in a corridor of the courthouse. *See* Cohen v. California, 403 U.S. 15 (1971).

should be negated. If anything, sustaining a conflictual workplace implies that employers' interests matter even if they do not override employee speech. Furthermore, the ideal of relating as equals requires that the terms of the employment relationship treat *both* parties as substantive equals. For these reasons, the protection of employee speech may be subject to time, place, and manner constraints. For instance, free speech rights should not entitle an employee to turn her workstation at the factory into the Speakers' Corner of Hyde Park (which has been set aside for public speaking by The Royal Parks and Gardens Regulation Act of 1872). Nor should employees be entitled, as they see fit, to congregate for political conversations in the midst of their shift. Prohibiting these and other excessively disruptive practices do not place employers in the censor position, however. Instead, employee speech can still thrive—viz., an employee could engage in substantively the same expressional activity in the workplace—in the face of reasonable time, place, and manner restrictions.

C. Online User's Speech

The speech at the center of this subsection concerns itself with expressive activity on what may be called online platforms, namely, internet intermediaries such as internet service providers, websites, search engines, and most importantly social-media networks.[54] Private censorship of online speech, including content moderation, is not limited to tackling libelous publications, although it also does this. Rather, it extends far beyond protecting reputation to capturing online speech that might interfere with people's interest in safety, emotional well-being, privacy, personal and group dignity, preventing the spread of misinformation, and so on. Such interference also implicates the interests of the platform itself, and therefore its business model, as the willingness of users to use the platform is partially informed by the platform's commitment to user safety.

Online platforms nowadays wield enormous normative powers over the expressive activities of their users. Although they may be bound by their own undertakings, either unilateral or contractual (often called "community standards"),[55] online platforms are in many jurisdictions legally entitled to engage in private censorship. In particular, they are entitled to block or suspend users, suppress contents, and engage in any number of content-moderation practices.[56]

[54] Klonick, *supra* note 20, at 1604.

[55] On Facebook's commitment to the free speech of their users, see the Introduction to the Oversight Board Charter (noting that "Freedom of expression is a fundamental human right"). For discussion, see Kate Klonick, *The Facebook Oversight Board: Creating an Independent Institution to Adjudicate Online Free Expression*, 129 YALE L.J. 2418, 2477–79 (2020).

[56] Moreover, online platforms draw, often heavily, on AI systems to do the work of identifying which users and publications warrant one or another censorial response.

The legal reason for this stems from the identity of the censor, namely, it is a case of *private*, rather than public, censorship. In the United States, current federal statutory law further reinforces this state of affairs by affording these platforms immunity from civil liability insofar as their censorship amounts to a good-faith effort to block and screen offensive material (so as to protect third parties, for instance, against libelous publications made by platform users).[57] Florida and Texas have recently sought to change the current balance of power by granting users (arguably unprecedented and nearly limit*less*) rights against viewpoint discrimination by large social media platforms.[58] The legal situation in the European Union might be changing dramatically, although it is not yet clear in what direction, with the recent enactments of the Digital Services Act and the Digital Markets Act.[59]

I do not deny that online platforms can, and should, make some content moderation decisions (for instance, blocking unlawful behaviors, deliberate spreading of lies, and preventing imminent, catastrophic consequences). It does not follow, however, that platform users must surrender control of their expressive activities to these platforms. In particular and within limits, the ability of users to assert beliefs and make claims should be, and remain, theirs, rather than the platforms'.

Why does this right matter? There are different ways to make the case for users' rights of free speech. As mentioned above, the most influential ones concern democracy and, in particular, the role of free speech rights in sustaining collective self-governance. One animating worry combines size and function. Concerning size, current online platforms are unusually big and powerful. Concerning function, these same platforms are controllers of public forums or facilitators of the modern public square.[60] The two combined pose serious threats to democracies. Thus, when users do not have the right freely to express their views, and further when they may be excluded from the platform, the virtual public square might undermine collective self-governance, especially when there is only one (or very few) such squares available. Furthermore, their for-profit nature only exacerbates this undemocratic predicament as online platforms' "public square" is designed to promote the self-interest of the platforms rather than the general interest of the polity.[61] Hence, granting free speech rights could be a first step toward democratizing the

[57] 47 U.S.C. §230 (a.k.a. Communication Decency Act (1996)). On the relationship between §230 and the First Amendment, see Eric Goldman, *Why Section 230 Is Better than the First Amendment*, 95 Notre Dame L. Rev. Ref. 1 (2019).

[58] *See* NetChoice, LLC v. Paxton, 142 S.Ct. 1715 (2022) (concerning Texas's H.B. 20), NetChoice, LLC v. Attorney General, Florida, 34 F.4th 1196 (11th Cir. 2022) (concerning Florida's S.B. 7072).

[59] *See* the Impact Assessment Report at https://digital-strategy.ec.europa.eu/en/library/impact-assessment-digital-services-act and, in particular, the possible tension between these Acts' objectives (*id.* at (i) and (iii)).

[60] *See* Kramer, *supra* note 11, at 59 and Packingham v. North Carolina, 137 S. Ct. 1730, 1737 (2017), respectively. For a historical perspective, see also Eric Berkowitz, Dangerous Ideas: A Brief History of Censorship in the West, from Ancients to Fake News 6 (2021).

[61] *See generally* Niva Elkin-Koren & Maayan Perel, *Separation of Functions for AI: Restraining Speech Regulation by Online Platforms*, 24 Lewis & Clark L. Rev. 857 (2020).

virtual political sphere by reinstating users as full-blown citizens who can contribute to a genuinely public discourse.

This way of identifying the problem naturally leads critics of platform's censorship to consider one or another "public law" solution. The basic effort is to redescribe these platforms in ways that would justify holding them to the higher standards expected from the state, state actors, or quasi-state entities (such as common carriers and providers of essential goods[62]). The redescription then serves as the doctrinal window through which to incorporate free speech rights that users generally hold, as citizens, against the government.

The democracy-based approach, and with it the constitutional-law solution it offers, is good as far as it goes. However, it does not go far enough. In particular, it identifies one set of problems—bigness and control of public forums—rather than private censorship. Responding to the former does not require, at least not necessarily, resolving the latter. More generally, private censorship by online platforms remains a going concern even when democracy is fully restored. One straightforward way to address the unusual power and functional control of public forums by online platforms is to increase competition. The public square may look entirely different if instead of a small number of all too powerful platforms we would face many, more or less equally effective options. Users could then exercise their economic powers of voice to secure effective online avenues for expression and deliberation without necessarily holding free speech rights against this or that online platform. A competitive market for online platforms can certainly produce echo chambers but, in response to users' demand, it may also furnish pluralist, all-inclusive platforms.

Suppose that the market for online platforms has indeed changed for the best. Does it matter that platforms can—as a matter of right—engage in private censorship? If the size and control of public forums and their adverse effects on democracy are the only major concerns then, as just explained, it may not matter. Further, recall my observation that restrictions on free speech are often readily mitigatable. In the case of a fully competitive market among online platforms, mitigation is especially seamless.

However, I argue that private censorship remains a genuine concern to the user/platform relationship. Two stages transform this concern into a claim of right of users to free speech vis-à-vis the particular online platform: The first concerns the equality and the second the conflict theory of tort law. First, the ability of a user to relate to the owner and other users of an online platform as an equal depends, in part, on being entitled to free speech, which is to say without having the user's viewpoint or the content of his or her speech subject to the approval of

[62] *See* Ganesh Sitaraman & Morgan Ricks, *Tech Platforms and the Common Law of Common Carriers*, 73 DUKE L.J. 1037 (2024); *see also NetChoice*, 49 F.4th at 447–48.

the platform.[63] Thus, expressive agency is undermined not merely if users lack an entitlement to express themselves freely but rather also if the platform is not subject to a legally mandated obligation to respect that right. Only then can the user relate as an equal to the platform and its other users.[64] Securing this much may not be enough if censorship is speedily mitigatable as when users can costlessly choose from a wide menu of competing platforms. This is why the second stage is called for. Indeed, and second, the conflict between the user's interest in speaking out and the platform's (and other users') competing interests is, within limits, inherently valuable. Thus, rather than setting up echo chambers or employing other technologies of conflict sanitation, imposing on these platforms an obligation to respect a robust user right to free speech is designed to create the conditions necessary for the conflict to exist. The good of liberal culture could, therefore, extend beyond the physical world to manifest itself in the virtual domain as well.

Against this backdrop, to conclude this section, I submit approaching the problem of private censorship from the combined perspectives of the conflict and the equality theories to substitute the statist, public-law framework with the tort law approach to online platforms' control of the expressive affairs of their users.

IV. When Private Censorship Might Be Justified: The Hierarchy Exception

Private censorship is not always wrongful. Subjecting free speech to time, place, and manner regulations is a permissible form of restricting speech by both governments and private persons. As I explain below, these content-neutral restrictions are meant to achieve reasonable coordination of competing activities rather than the suppression of speech.[65] Another way private censorship may not count as wrongful is when the restricted speech falls outside the scope of permissible speech.[66] A familiar example is speech that poses imminent danger to life and limb (such as by shouting "fire" in a crowded theater). It should be noted that different jurisdictions sometimes identify different boundaries—for instance, some types of racist speech fall outside the coverage of free speech in some jurisdictions (e.g., Germany) but not in others (e.g., United States and Sweden).

[63] That said, this prescription comes with an important limitation: It applies to online platforms that hold themselves open to the public, as opposed to subject matter or professional platforms (such as a platform dedicated to the love of god, physical therapy, or LinkedIn's no-politics optional setting).

[64] The argument in the text above specifies a necessary, rather than sufficient, condition.

[65] The First Amendment's parallel doctrine dealing with the government's obligation to accommodate citizen speech has been (rightly) criticized for shifting its orientation from coordination to subordination in *Buckley v. Valeo*, 424 U.S. 1 (1976).

[66] For more on the distinction between the coverage and the protection dimensions of free speech, see FREDERICK SCHAUER, FREE SPEECH: A PHILOSOPHICAL ENQUIRY 89–92, 134–35 (1982).

However, the more challenging question concerning justifiable private censorship arises when the ability of a speaker to engage in what in a liberal legal order would be deemed *permissible* speech is subject to the control of another person. Can suppression of permissible speech ever be justified and, if so, why? I argue that it can and that justifying it turns on justifying hierarchical relationships whose value depends on putting one party in control over the expressive agency of the other. Thus, when hierarchical relationships are justified and part of their justification refers specifically to the standing of one party to control the other party's speech, the conflict between free speech and its competing interests is no longer inherently valuable. Accordingly, rather than facilitating free speech, tort law must, in some measure, let suppression stand so as to sustain the hierarchical structure of the relationship at issue.

I begin by saying the obvious, namely, that free speech can be disruptive. This is why the interest in expressive agency often breeds conflict and which is, in many cases, inherently valuable at that. Hence, disruption as such cannot provide a compelling basis for justifying private censorship. What needs to be shown is that subjecting one's expressive agency to the control of another party to the interaction is part of what makes this interaction valuable—that this form of subjection is necessary for the interaction, and its resulting product, to count as valuable.

To fix ideas, consider the traditional teacher/student relationship. Its purpose is the education of students, which is to say (in the context of higher education) to "train them to think for themselves, and to provide them access to those materials which they need if they are to think intelligently."[67] Pursuing this purpose of bringing about independence of mind, I take it, is immensely valuable both intrinsically and instrumentally.

To realize the value of education, the hierarchical relationship between a teacher and her students must not be limited to determining what should go into the curriculum, to assigning homework, and to grading students' final exams. In addition, it involves having some measure of authority over student speech (when in class).[68] Thus, a teacher can decide whether students may share their comments during class. She can further decide who can speak including by compelling students to speak when she calls on them, when can students speak, and what type of "speaking" is deemed relevant to the topic of the class. The latter point renders the teacher's control over the expressive agency of her students strong as it provides her with the power to make decisions about the *content* of students' speech. Indeed, a teacher can prevent a student from elaborating a point he wishes to make if, in her assessment, it does not contribute to class discussion. She can also make

[67] The American Association of University Professors, General Declaration of Principles (1915) available at https://www.aaup-ui.org/Documents/Principles/Gen_Dec_Princ.pdf.

[68] I say "some measure of authority" in recognition of exceptions under which students are entitled to speak out (for instance, when the teacher makes clearly false allegations).

judgments of quality concerning what students say in class, which might implicate her in content (and sometime even viewpoint) discrimination.[69]

This is not to deny that some teachers find it desirable, perhaps even consequential, to foster debate and intellectual disputes in the classroom, including by encouraging students to openly express their views and offer criticism of others' (including the teacher's own) views. However, doing so is (or should be) at the discretion of the teacher. It is fully compatible with the preceding discussion as it is within the teacher's academic freedom to integrate live discussion into class discussions.

Education is a paradigm case of justified private censorship, but it is not the only one. Parental control over the parents' *small* children may be another case in point. So, too, is the case with editorial selection of op-eds and columns written by guest writers, as well as with professional journals, including peer-reviewed publications. Another paradigmatic case concerns the commander/soldier relationship (although this is not a case of private censorship if both parties serve in the national defense force). The four cases at issue hold in common a negative connection between conflict and value. That is, their value depends, in part, on containing or even preventing conflicts between the party in a position of authority and the party whose expressive agency is subject to that authority. Indeed, raising a caring, competent, and self-determining child, on the one hand, and sustaining national security, on the other, are valuable pursuits, but their realization depends on some measure of control over the expressive agency of the child or soldier. Similarly, sustaining excellence in the publication of research studies, journalistic investigations, and mind-opening op-eds depends on having professional authority in charge of accepting papers for publication. To this extent, traditional media and current social media, especially online platforms, represent entirely different substantive visions as the latter has no built-in commitment to—in fact, it rejects—the quality standards to which the former aspires.

V. The Doctrinal Framework of Horizontal Free Speech: The Prima Facie Case

A private person can engage in horizontal censorship in either of the two following ways. First, by *discriminating* against the views of his or her party to an interaction; and second, by failing to *accommodate* this party's interest in expressing his or her views. Discrimination is primarily a content-based form of censorship. It involves denying expressions on the basis of disapproving the particular views they convey. By contrast, refusing to accommodate expressive activities is, or could be,

[69] *See* Robert Post, *The Classic First Amendment Tradition Under Stress: Freedom of Speech and the University*, *In* THE FREE SPEECH CENTURY 106 (Lee Bollinger & Geoffrey Stone eds., 2019).

a content-neutral form of censorship. Disapproving expressive activities as such, that is, irrespective of their content, is a case in point. The tort of private censorship addresses both failings, namely, discrimination and nonaccommodation.

The generic tort-law approach to private censorship begins with the imposition of a duty to refrain from engaging in censorial acts. A prima facie case of private censorship consists in three separately necessary and jointly sufficient elements, concerning certain conduct and its causally related outcome:

> 1. Censorial act; 2. injury to the censored person's expressive agency; and 3. a causal connection between the first two elements. I take each in turn.

The censorial act element gives rise to two basic questions—what counts as *censorship* and what counts as an *act* (of censorship)? Censorship may involve the imposition of prior restraint on another person's expressive activity. This could amount to the full suppression of a person's ability to express herself; that said, suppression may also admit of degree, ranging from total suppression, to being required substantially to moderate one's speech, and to sugar-coating it. In addition to ex ante instances, censorship may also involve undermining free speech ex post by singling out the speaker for negative treatment. Formal and informal punishment are paradigm cases. Creating freezing and chilling effects is another.

More generally, censorship depends on a certain standard of honest exchange of views and information, meaning that one's right to speak out does not include the right to silence another person's speech (irrespective of how powerful the latter may otherwise be). Hence, the conflict theory of tort law views demonstrations and disruptions as fully compatible, indeed highly desirable, liberal practices *insofar as* they do not render the exchange of views and information impossible.

Now consider the required standard of action (as in censorial action). Deliberate suppression of speech or infliction of punishment for speaking out is certainly sufficient. To this extent, establishing a policy or making an ad hoc decision to stifle another person's expressive activity amounts to a deliberate act of censorship.

But must deliberate censorship be necessary? The answer should be in the negative.[70] I argue that carelessness can be sufficient, for example, when an online platform implements a "fake news algorithm" that aims at blocking misinformation but also, and inadvertently so, bowdlerizing legitimate views. The reason why this is so goes back to the conflict theory of torts and, in particular, to the inherently valuable conflict between speaking out and the harmful consequences to which it can give rise (in terms of hurt feelings and discomfort, setback to reputation, social unrest, and more). On the conflict theory, recall, tort law should facilitate

[70] *Contra* Andrew I. Cohen & Andrew J. Cohen, *The Possibility and Defensibility of Nonstate "Censorship,"* New Directions in the Ethics and Politics of Speech 13, 14 (J. P. Messina ed., 2023); *see also* Messina, *supra* note 31, at 5, 7, 8.

inherently valuable conflicts. As a result, the standard for censorial act ought not to be confined to deliberate censorship as it will leave out substandard behavior that might moderate, suppress, or punish speakers. Thus, careless conduct short of deliberate censorship should also satisfy the element of (censorial) act.[71] This further suggests that the duty against engaging in censorship can have affirmative, not merely negative, implications, such as that of taking reasonable precautions to reduce the risk of impermissible censorship.

The next element concerns the consequence of engaging in censorial acts, namely, an injury. The object of the injury has two, related components: First, the expressive agency of the censored person and, second, his or her ability to relate as an equal to the censor. Consider physical agency by analogy. When one is denied reasonable access to a place of commerce, one's ability to manifest her agency in the world is compromised. So too is one's ability to relate as an equal to one's parties to commercial transactions. I argue that suppressing or punishing the speaker might bring about parallel injuries, namely, to the expressive aspects of their agency and to their ability to interact on equal footing with their censor. For instance, suppressing his spouse's desire to support publicly the conservative movement is a way of wronging this spouse by undermining *both* her expressive agency *and* her ability to interact with him as an equal. In tort-law parlance, the damage is classified as nonpecuniary loss as it reflects the interference with a person's interest in the free expression of beliefs and judgments, arguably beliefs and judgments that this person finds, or even feels compelled to find, most fitting under the circumstances.

Finally, there must exist a causal connection between the censorial act of the censor and the injury of the censored person. Neither the act nor the injury can alone satisfy a prima facie case of private censorship. It must be the case that the injury results, in the right sense, from the censor's (deliberate or careless) conduct. The causation doctrine, as practiced in the common law of torts and as further developed in the context of antidiscrimination law,[72] is up to this task.[73] The epistemic difficulties that may arise in proving causation in the present case are not

[71] Why stop at carelessness? Should we impose strict or even absolute liability? The answer is in the negative as doing so may amount to autonomy-crushing standard of care that, as I argue in Chapter 13, is inconsistent with the principle of relating as equals.

[72] Causation in antidiscrimination law has developed its own standards of causation and, most importantly, rules on burden-allocation with respect to causation (i.e., shifting the burden of persuasion in "mixed-motive" cases of employment discrimination). *See* Price Waterhouse v. Hopkins, 490 U.S. 228 (1989). Note, however, that antidiscrimination causes of action in the United States have been confined to acts of deliberate or intentional discrimination (in the context of disparate treatment), to the near exclusion of negligence-based discrimination. The tort of private censorship, by contrast, extends to negligent infliction of censorship.

[73] I do not argue that this doctrine is in perfect shape or that it does not require some (including substantive) revisions. Chapter 16 is a case in point. Rather, I argue that this doctrine provides a sensible basis from which to begin.

qualitatively different from the ones addressed by the causation doctrine, more generally.

VI. The Institutional Question

The case for a tort of private censorship suggests that tort law, rather than constitutional law, provides the more appealing framework for understanding and determining rights and duties in and around expressive interactions between private persons. The discussion proceeded abstractly, leaving much of the doctrinal heavy lifting for another occasion; for instance, difficult questions of line drawing and boundary setting will have to be answered in the course of operationalizing the tort of private censorship. I leave them to another occasion.

I now wish to take up some of the institutional aspects of creating a new tort. Indeed, the discussion so far has focused almost exclusively on the substantive questions concerning private censorship. Most importantly, I have not discussed the question of whose responsibility it is to call that tort into law and fill out its doctrinal details. Does it matter whether courts assume this responsibility, or perhaps it should fall to the legislature or some other public body? I answer that it does matter and, in particular, that it should be made by courts or courts-like lawmaking institutions. The reason is the *normative status* of judge-made law: A right to free speech should be viewed as an entailment of justice and, ultimately, reason, rather than an upshot of the choice of the majority of the electorate. It does not mean that the legislature would have no role in systematizing and perfecting the tort of private censorship, nor does it rule out the role of specialized institutions, such as a university's tribunal handling instances of in-campus censorship. Rather, it means that the legal *source* of the tort, and its underlying right to horizontal freedom of speech, is the court.

Building on an argument I developed elsewhere with Alon Harel,[74] my basic contention is that a judge-made right to freedom of speech is not the same as a legislated right to the same. That is, although the content of these rights might be identical, they are, nonetheless, different rights in virtue of their sources—a court and a legislature, respectively.

The first stage of the argument begins with the literature on institutional competency in private law.[75] On this literature, the judicial process differs from the legislative process along many dimensions, two of which are crucial for my

[74] Avihay Dorfman & Alon Harel, Reclaiming the Public ch. 3 (2024); Avihay Dorfman & Alon Harel, *The Necessity of Institutional Pluralism*, 43 Oxford J. Legal Stud. 753, 765–72 (2023).

[75] This literature is vast. *See, e.g.*, Seana Valentine Shiffrin, Democratic Law 81–88 (2021); Hanoch Dagan, Reconstructing American Legal Realism & Rethinking Private Law Theory 50–59 (2013); Alan Brudner with Jennifer M. Nadler, The Unity of the Common Law ch. 7 (2d ed. 2013).

discussion: discretion and justification. Processes of judicial lawmaking feature limited discretion and rigorous practices of justification; neither fairly characterizes the practice of lawmaking by legislatures. Both dimensions ensure robust connection between reason and judicial lawmaking. On the other hand, legislatures are typically far less constrained by these two dimensions, which is why statutory rights reflect choice rather than reason. To be sure, I do not argue that legislatures are not committed to reason or that their enactments only coincidentally meet the demands of reason. Rather, the argument is that their resort to reason is necessarily and fundamentally mediated by choice. Once again, discretion and justification can render this observation clear.

Begin with discretion. Judges are committed to a certain ideal of self-restraint. Certainly, judicial innovation occurs frequently, but the point is that the innovation does not proceed on the basis of the judge's "own idea of beauty or of goodness."[76] Indeed, whereas statutory lawmaking is thoroughly discretionary *by design*, judicial lawmaking is designed in ways that severely limit the discretion of the judge. Judges may not get to pick and choose what disputes to hear and, indeed, adjudicate; legislatures, by contrast, face no such constraints. As a result, judges must often decide cases that they would otherwise prefer not to hear, a principle aptly characterized by Owen Fiss as "nondiscretionary jurisdiction."[77]

Thus, the questions of whether private persons have rights of free speech against their private censors and what are the implications of having such rights would, to an important extent, be *forced* upon the court. This is so not only in the straightforward sense that it is up to the plaintiff to decide whether to pursue the defendant, but rather also in the parties' ability to frame the precise legal question on which the court is requested to weigh in. Indeed, I say parties because even the defendant's objection to the plaintiff's claim may matter (consider, by analogy, a defendant that decides to object to the plaintiff's suit by raising a factual argument, rather than a legal argument about the inexistence of a duty to respect the plaintiff's freedom of speech).[78] Finally, the judgment of a court is necessarily limited to the facts of the case and to the context out of which it arises: as the distinction between *ratio decidendi* and *obiter dictum* implies, it is not up to a court to use a particular case, including even a blockbuster case, as a springboard to reforming areas of law not directly implicated by the case at issue.

[76] Benjamin N. Cardozo, The Nature of the Judicial Process 141 (1921).

[77] Owen Fiss, Law as It Could Be 163 (2003).

[78] In the pathbreaking decision—really, a genuine instance of judicial lawmaking—of *MacPherson v. Buick Motor Co.*, 111 N.E. 1050 (N.Y. 1916), the defendant-manufacturer decided to object to the plaintiff's negligence suit for a defective car wheel by raising the no duty argument, rather than by arguing that it did not fail to exercise due care. In torts parlance, the defense's strategy was to attack the "duty," rather than "breach," element. The court's innovation—that manufacturers owe a duty of care, irrespective of contract—would likely not have been made in the first place had the defendant not framed its objection in that particular way.

One important implication of this last observation goes back to the claim I made in passing above—that the piecemeal character of judicial innovation may, though not necessarily, call for the legislature to serve as the court's earthly champion. This will be the case if the intricacies of filling out the details of the tort prove too complicated, epistemically speaking, for judges.[79] For instance, in the context of resident speech, the tort of private censorship would inevitably have to specify what size of political signs a tenant may post, precisely where, and for how long. Although courts could work out these details, it seems that a legislature (or even a local legislature) may often be better situated to make these calls. Talk of a cooperative endeavor between courts and legislatures is obviously familiar; that said, what is interesting about this endeavor is that the legislature takes the supporting cast, rather than the other way around. Such a role reversal is not surprising, however, for it reflects the notion that the tort at issue can give rise to a basic right to freedom of speech if it is ultimately judge-made.

Now consider justification. Judges face a substantively different standard of justification than legislators. To begin with, judges must justify their decisions in terms that are independent of either their own choosing or the support they have from the constituents: It is not what new rights they, or the people, choose to establish, but rather what new rights reason, as mediated by legal analysis, dictates. As Robert Burt observed:

> Congress is less burdened by the principled constraints under which courts labor ... Congress can make distinctions among classes that the Court would itself be hard to put to explain on principled grounds ... [partly] because the institutional legitimacy of a legislative act depends not so much on the rational persuasiveness of its decisions as on the simple fact that a majority of "responsible" elected officials were willing to vote for the proposition.[80]

Indeed, a judge does not justify a judgment by reference to having secured a majority of his or her fellow judges to agree with this judgment. Thus, securing a majority among the judges is better seen as a positive side effect of getting it right, rather than the other way around.

I do not suggest that courts can, or should, engage in free-floating assessment of what is right, just, or desirable. Judge-made law by reason is compatible with a constrained process of judicial reasoning. To begin with, judges reason from past, including precedential, decisions to the present case; this is true, to be sure, also in cases of first impression and in cases that break new grounds. They articulate the basis for novel rights by arguing from prior recognition of basic principles,

79 *See generally* Hanoch Dagan & Avihay Dorfman, *Precontractual Justice*, 28 Legal Theory 89, 109–12 (2022).

80 Robert A. Burt, *Miranda and Title II: A Morganatic Marriage*, 1969 Sup. Ct. Rev. 81, 112–14.

canonical cases, and influential dicta. Judicial reasoning is further constrained by the fact that judges assiduously seek coherence across legal domains (such as contracts, property, and torts), so that the creation of new rights must be reconciled with the rights recognized in these other domains. In the case of private censorship, the free speech jurisprudence that has been developed to address vertical censorship could serve as an important repository of constraints on the judicial creation of the private censorship tort. To this extent, determining the coverage of the new private right to freedom of speech may benefit from the legal analysis of previous scope-questions concerning obscenities, fighting words, and racist slurs.

Against this backdrop, I argue that a judge-made right can be qualitatively different from a perfectly identical (in content) statutory right to freedom of speech. The key difference goes to the meaning of *entrenchment* by court, on the one hand, and by legislature, on the other. Having a statutory right implies that its value lies in popular support that is grounded in acceptability among a majority of the constituents. Having such a right reflects the majority's belief that private persons in positions of power over others must, to some extent, respect the latter in connection with their expressive activities.

Accordingly, being duty-bound to allow another person to express his or her beliefs (et alia) is ultimately as variable as the actual support of the polity in horizontal free speech.

By contrast, a judge-made right imposes a duty to respect the freedom of speech of another, one that is grounded not upon the will of the governed but rather on a claim of reason. The decision of the court does not purport to capture the actual preferences, will, or judgments of the people, but rather what should (in terms of justice and reason, more generally) be the right way to engage with the conflict between the free speech of the plaintiff and the competing interests of the defendant-censor. In this way reason stands apart from the choice of the majority. It implies that it is not up to the majority to decide whether would-be private censors are duty-bound to respect the right at issue. Moreover, reason stands apart from communal mores and traditions. It implies that calling this right into law does not aim to articulate, distill, or reflect existing convictions concerning free speech in the horizontal sphere of interaction but rather to change the consistent reluctance among the powerful[81] to accommodate the freedom of speech of those with whom they interact.

A judge made tort of private censorship, I conclude, does for horizontal freedom of speech what constitutional law does for vertical freedom of speech. To this extent, the institutional question turns out to be much more than a question concerning institutional competency. Courts may be more or less competent than legislatures in identifying the right considerations, articulating the new

[81] Recall that I use *powerful* to denote either normative or brute power (or both).

legal norm, and preempting some unintended consequences. However, what they have, and what legislatures typically lack, is the ability to give horizontal freedom of speech its due, namely, its normative status as a genuinely basic—that is, majority-independent—right.

Conclusion

This chapter offers a revisionary view of the role of tort law in protecting people against private abridgment of speech by defending a horizontal right to free speech and a corresponding tort of private censorship. It is revisionary in the straightforward sense that current tort law fails to recognize such a right. But it is not quite revisionary in another sense; tort law already protects some of our most fundamental interests (including bodily and emotional integrity, privacy, reputation, and more). Either way, I have argued that a tort of private censorship is a direct implication of answering the grand question of why tort law matters.

In the course of making this argument, this chapter has sought to demonstrate two central themes. The first theme concerns the connection between conflict and equality. The conflict and equality theories of tort law, I have argued, are independently necessary conditions for vindicating tort law. This chapter has emphasized the important sense in which the two theories are *also* mutually reinforcing. Indeed, the case for the tort of private censorship is a direct implication of these two theories, combined.

The second theme concerns the distinction between public and private law. There are a number of ways to explain this distinction, and it is not the place to unpack them. What is important to note, however, is the freestanding significance of *private* rights and duties. The case of free speech is probably the best proving ground for this claim. Against the near-automatic association of free speech with constitutional law and democratic politics, this chapter has made the case for an independent legal framework addressing free speech in interpersonal or horizontal interactions. Rather than serving as a transmission belt for implementing conclusions reached elsewhere in the (constitutional or other) law, tort law develops its own moral form and function. On this view, tort law is not merely the law of wrongs, harms, recourse, or costs; instead, it matters precisely because it is the law of conflict between equals.

PART IV
CONCLUDING REMARKS

Conclusion

Arriving at the final stage of this intellectual journey, I would like to offer some concluding observations on five general themes that have remained implicit throughout the book. Hence, instead of summarizing the entire argument of *Conflict between Equals*, I wish to pose and reflect on some of its broader lessons. I will then make a final, brief observation on one of tort theory's emerging challenges: the question of its extension beyond the category of persons to (at least some) living organisms.

I. From "What We Owe to Each Other" to "How the Conflict between Our Fundamental Interests Shapes What Rights We Have"

Tort law governs the terms of involuntary interactions in the many settings where private individuals encounter one another. These terms impose duties, define what constitutes a breach of these duties, and specify the consequences of such breaches, among other things. At the moral center of this legal framework lie interests, such as bodily integrity and self-expression, which are fundamental to living as free and equal individuals in the world. These interests must undoubtedly be protected. This book addressed the questions: Why is tort law required for this task and, if it is, what specific form of tort law is called for?

The answer to these questions—viz., tort law as the union of the conflict and equality theories—challenges many past and present studies of tort law. According to these studies, understanding and defending tort law hinges on one or more *dependent concept*—concepts whose quality is largely determined by prior ideas. The concepts of wrong, harm, and social cost have given rise to some of the most influential interpretive and normative accounts of tort law: tort law as the law of wrongs, as the law of (primarily accidental) harms, and as the law of social costs, respectively. There are disagreements between proponents of each concept—for instance, should tort law impose strict liability? There are also intraconcept disagreements—for instance, are the wrongs of tort law moral wrongs, or are the different wrongs that figure in tort law localized expressions of a single, overarching wrong?

Conflict between Equals. Avihay Dorfman, Oxford University Press. © Oxford University Press 2026.
DOI: 10.1093/9780198979869.003.0023

The conflict theory of tort law defended in this book rejects the centrality of dependent concepts in the study of tort law (and this rejection may also have broader implications for moral and political theory[1]). Such concepts cannot be fully specified or comprehensively evaluated without a normative baseline against which to determine whether a certain action or outcome should be considered wrongful, harmful, or costly in the eyes of tort law. This is not to say that some actions and outcomes are not straightforwardly wrongful, harmful, or costly. However, as this book clearly demonstrates, such instances barely scratch the surface of the complex universe of human conflict to which tort law responds. As I argue elsewhere, dependent concepts like wrongdoing also fail to provide sufficiently robust resources to identify and address instances of structural injustice.[2] There is no way around articulating and defending an appealing normative baseline.

A key ambition of *Conflict between Equals* has been to establish such a normative baseline. It does so by adopting a sequence of reasoning that moves from fundamental interests to conflicts between these interests, and finally, to legal rights. According to this sequence, people can interact as free and equal agents only insofar as their fundamental interests are sufficiently protected. For reasons explained in Chapter 2, some of these interests constantly come into conflict, while others should be put into conflict even when preventing the conflict is possible. The value of these conflicts can be reduced to a three-part distinction: These conflicts are inherently valuable, tolerably valuable, or valueless. Tort law determines legal rights and the duties generated from them by engaging with these conflicts according to their respective value. Only then can the law of torts satisfactorily address the questions of wrong, harm, and cost (as well as other dependent concepts, such as repair and redress).

As this study demonstrates, the conflict theory provides the normative framework for understanding and vindicating certain torts that should form the foundation of the law of torts. However, this normative ambition does not stop at the existing rules and building blocks of tort law. It also has the resources to ask what is missing and how tort law should evolve in response. The reformative spirit presented in connection with the tort of trespass to land and the case for the new torts of discrimination and private censorship illustrates this normative commitment. Much more can, and should, be made by drawing on the conflict theory to assess "what is" and address the "what should be" and "what must be."

[1] The Scanlonian standard of reasonable rejectability might be vulnerable to this critique: What rule is, or is not, reasonable for us to reject seems to depend on prior normative questions. *See* T. M. Scanlon, What We Owe to Each Other (1998).

[2] *See further* Hanoch Dagan & Avihay Dorfman, The Powers of Discrimination (unpublished manuscript).

II. Against Trans-Substantivity in the Study of Torts

This book does not engage directly with the instruction of tort law. That said, the normative framework it develops has immediate implications for thinking about—and specifically teaching—this law. A typical method of instruction addresses each tort one at a time, explaining the elements of the prima facie cause of action and then inviting students to read cases that further elaborate and refine their understanding of the tort in question. Virtually nothing is said about the qualitative difference between applying the same tort to address inherently valuable, tolerably valuable, and valueless conflicts. For example, teaching the tort of private nuisance as a cause of action that applies uniformly to protected half-way houses and places of worship, on the one hand, and to a clash between nearby commercial and residential activities, on the other, obscures the important doctrinal implications that follow from acknowledging the normative differences between these cases. To avoid this difficulty, it would be better to teach the three different paths that private nuisance takes in response to the kind of value it addresses—some allegations of nuisance concern inherently valuable conflicts, others tolerably valuable conflicts, and yet others are valueless. Tort law should, and in some measure already does (recall Chapter 8), react to this normative landscape appropriately. Torts students should be encouraged to approach the study of this tort accordingly, asking questions about the underlying theory (or theories) that courts implicitly or explicitly invoke when treating *formally* identical causes of action—private nuisance—in *substantively* different ways.

III. Substantive Relational Equality and the Liberal Society

This book also develops a novel conception of relational equality for the law of torts, which I have called the equality theory of tort law. For a very long time, at least since Holmes's monumental lectures on tort law,[3] the theoretical study of tort law has often reflected a commitment to context-insensitivity. At the center of this commitment lies a certain idea of equality, specifically formal equality. While there are different conceptions of formal equality in and around tort law, they are of a piece insofar as they perceive parties in a tort interaction as no more and no less than A and B. Some such accounts may adopt this view because the "A vs. B" framework is seen as a valuable characteristic of tort law; others, by contrast, may embrace it simply because they lack better alternatives. In any case, the A vs. B picture set to one side the relative importance of the respective interests of A and B and, further, overlooks the vulnerability arising from the differences in the respective

[3] Oliver Wendell Holmes, Jr., The Common Law lec. III (1991).

conditions of these parties. Marginalizing the difference between the interests of A and B, and failing to recognize who these parties really are, threaten to unsettle the reflective equilibrium between theory and conviction (among other difficulties discussed in the Introduction to this book).

The equality theory of tort law, which forms the foundation of a broader account of the equality theory in private law, offers a sustained critique of formal equality. More importantly, it develops a substantive conception of relational equality designed to address two dimensions of interpersonal difference: interest and condition differentials. By identifying which differences matter and specifying how they should be treated, the equality theory generates three key insights. First, it explains why relating as equals necessitates duties—specifically, tort duties—as opposed to voluntarily assumed duties. Second, it demonstrates that moving away from formal equality does not lead to a chaotic collection of intuitions that defies systematic analysis. The second part of this book explores how major areas of tort law (such as negligence) construct egalitarian terms of interaction based on the prescriptions of the equality theory. And third, it argues for the inclusion of tort law within the modern liberal legal order. Instead of defending a division of labor where public law promotes substantive equality and private law preserves the status quo by enforcing formal equality, this book contends that tort law is a crucial pillar in the modern liberal legal order. In essence, tort law rejects the unappealing aspects of formal equality in favor of "real-world justice."[4] It does so by constructing terms of interactions that take (the right kinds of) difference seriously.

IV. Micro and Macro Tort Law: From One-to-One Remediation to the Liberal Society

It is tempting to consider tort law by focusing on its back end, namely, the ex post facto process of adjudicating complaints and administering appropriate remedial responses. From this picture, tort law is primarily a backward-looking enterprise, concerned with restoring, rectifying, or vindicating lives severely affected by the actions of a wrongdoer.

That said, this book demonstrates that tort law cannot be reduced to the ex post task, traditionally carried out by courts—responding to discrete instances of wrongdoing and their aftermath. Instead, it is tasked with an ex ante mission: To construct terms of interactions that, first, engage with the conflicting interests of the parties in the right way and, second, treat these parties as substantive equals. Moreover, as I argued in the first part of the book, this task entails—not merely opens the possibility—that the constructivist ambition of tort law extends beyond

[4] 3 Bruce Ackerman, We the People: The Civil Rights Revolution 211 (2014); *see also id.*, at 154, 215.

establishing appropriate terms for pairwise transactions, one relationship at a time. Indeed, tort law constructs edifices of the normative universe we inhabit in daily life, including, in particular, social goods that constitute liberal society (recall, for example, the good of liberal culture).

V. The Role of Value in Theorizing Tort Law: Thick versus Thin Normativity

Tort law does not shy away from making substantive judgments by appealing to values such as what interests matter, what justice requires, what rights we have, and so on. At times, torts lawmakers—whether judges, legislators, or regulators—do so only implicitly, often in intuitive and unsystematic ways. To this extent, *Conflict between Equals* does not seek to change the practice of tort law by emphasizing the centrality of value-based questions in legal analysis and reform. Instead, it offers a comprehensive normative framework for engaging with legal analysis and reform.

This framework makes two contributions. Formally, it structures the thought process by which we understand and determine rights, along with other downstream rules, by focusing our attention on the threefold distinction between conflicts and the two dimensions of substantive equality (interest and condition). Substantively, it provides a liberal theory of the considerations that should inform how we analyze and reform the law of torts.

The substantive contribution of the normative framework developed in this book is meant, first and foremost, as a defense of tort law and, more specifically, tort law's necessary role in the construction and protection of the liberal society. However, it also serves as a defense of liberalism itself. Indeed, tort theory does not merely occupy the passive role, that of a receiver, in the relationship between political and legal theory. Among other things, the legal theory underlying *Conflict between Equals* refines the normative reasoning process, moving from fundamental interests to conflicts between them, and, ultimately, to legal rights. It advances our understanding of what relating as substantive equals requires in the context of involuntary interactions between private persons. It also explains why duties—specifically legal duties—can sometimes be necessary for people to relate as free and equal agents. Moreover, it establishes the case for recognizing interpersonal rights to be treated as an equal and to free speech from the perspective of relational equality.

As in part a defense of liberalism, tort theory must move beyond the modest ambition of engaging in "thin" normative analysis. Hence, tort theory cannot espouse the quietist commitment to merely restoring the status quo. This also means that the defense of tort law cannot be reduced to appeals to overlapping consensus or any other method akin to a common denominator, where tort law merely serves to enforce public order and safety. Instead, tort theory should defend normative positions that are rooted in substantive commitments to equality, freedom, and other values that lie at the moral center of any legal order that seeks to meet the exacting demands of justice and legitimacy.

* * *

Tort law is, by and large, a humanistic project. *Conflict between Equals* further suggests that a particular humanistic—really, liberal-egalitarian—vision of this law places our fundamental interests at its moral center. However, it does not follow that the emphasis on human beings must exclude concern for other living organisms. Can tort law require private persons to take some measure of concern for some or all living organisms? More importantly, should it?

These questions raise a number of foundational and institutional challenges. For example, insofar as tort duties reflect, as they should, a conception of relating as equals, can they be owed to nonhuman animals and plants? What are we to make of conflicts between our fundamental interests and those of nonhuman animals and plants? This, in turn, raises a prior question concerning the moral status of these organisms. Institutional hurdles may also loom large—for instance, nonhuman animals and plants cannot occupy the position of plaintiff (though, as argued in Chapter 5, this hurdle can, and should, be overcome).

Tort law, like most other areas of law, constantly responds to changing circumstances and convictions. Often, it evolves by introducing incremental modifications to its existing fabric. At other times, however, the appropriate response is more transformative. Whatever course of action tort law may take, if any, in protecting nonhuman living organisms from certain forms of human violence, *Conflict between Equals* suggests that tort theory should assume a leading role in identifying the considerations that should guide the selection of the right course. To Be Continued!

Index

For the benefit of digital users, indexed terms that span two pages (e.g., 52–53) may, on occasion, appear on only one of those pages.